AMERICAN ARISTOCRACY

The Lives and Times of
JAMES RUSSELL, AMY, AND
ROBERT LOWELL

Also by C. David Heymann

THE QUIET HOURS (VERSE)
EZRA POUND: THE LAST ROWER

AMERICAN ARISTOCRACY

The Lives and Times of
JAMES RUSSELL, AMY, AND ROBERT LOWELL

C. David Heymann

DODD, MEAD & COMPANY · NEW YORK

ACKNOWLEDGMENT is made to the following for permission to reproduce the material indicated:

Doubleday & Company, Inc. for excerpt from "In a Dark Time" copyright © 1960 by Beatrice Roethke, Administratrix of the Estate of Theodore Roethke, which appeared in *The Collected Poems of Theodore Roethke*.

Harcourt Brace Jovanovich, Inc. for excerpts from the following poems appearing in *Lord Weary's Castle* by Robert Lowell: "Colloquy in Black Rock," "As a Plane Tree by the Water," "Children of Light," "Mary Winslow," "Where the Rainbow Ends," and "After the Surprising Conversion." For excerpts from "The Quaker Graveyard in Nantucket" from *Lord Weary's Castle,* copyright 1946, 1974 by Robert Lowell.

Houghton Mifflin Company for excerpts from *The Complete Poetical Works of Amy Lowell,* copyright 1955 by Houghton Mifflin Company. For excerpts from *Amy Lowell: A Chronicle* by S. Foster Damon, editor. Copyright © renewed 1963 by S. Foster Damon.

Unless otherwise indicated, the poetry of Robert Lowell is published by Farrar, Straus & Giroux, Inc.

Grateful acknowledgment is made to Allen Ginsberg for his kind permission to quote from his correspondence with Robert Lowell.

1   2   3   4   5   6   7   8   9   10

Library of Congress Cataloging in Publication Data

Heymann, Clemens David, 1945–
American aristocracy.

Includes bibliographical references and index.
1. Lowell family. 2. Poets, American—Biography.
3. Lowell, James Russell, 1819–1891—Biography.
4. Lowell, Amy, 1874–1925—Biography. 5. Lowell,
Robert, 1917–1977—Biography. 6. New England—
Intellectual life. I. Title.
PS129.H44   811'.5'209   [B]   79-9351
ISBN 0-396-07608-4

TO JEANNE
for everything

CONTENTS

CONTENTS

III. AMY LOWELL
Last of the Barons (1874–1925)

IV. ROBERT LOWELL
Noble Savage (1917–1977)

PREFACE

THE familiar scrap of rhyme that unites the Lodges, the Cabots, the Lowells, and the powers-that-be is a ditty well despised by all parties concerned. At the same time it is true that one can fairly hear the woof and tweet of history whistle through the names of the ramified Lowell tribe: Amory, Aspinwall, Cabot, Cotting, Crowninshield, Higginson, Hunsacker, Jackson, Lodge, Russell, Sargent, Winslow, and all the rest. The members of these Boston First Families—with their supposed Puritan virtues of piety, sobriety, frugality, productivity, and diligence—constitute what can best be termed an American Aristocracy.

The term "Aristocracy" derives from the Greek *aristos* (best) and *kratia* (rule). Its original connotation was "government by the best citizens," although Webster extended the meaning to encompass such definitions as "a privileged ruling class or nobility" and "those considered the best in some way." If the word's meaning is thus somewhat vague, its pronunciation is equally confounding, the two preferences being "*ar*-istocracy" and "a-*ris*-tocracy." While it can probably be convincingly argued that there is no such thing as an American aristocracy, it is easier and more convenient to assume that there is, and that what exists is, if not a nobility, at least practically its equivalent.

The Lowells have manifested their regal legacy for some three centuries and through numerous generations. Today's members of the clan include the usual array of debutantes, "preppies," Masons, Junior Leaguers, patrons of the Massachusetts Society of National Colonial Dames —men and women whose names appear regularly in the white-linen pages of that Old Testament of haut monde, the American version of the *Almanach de Gotha:* the *Social Register.* But essentially what makes this the nearest thing to a royal family that has ever appeared on the American scene is its triad of poets, the very subjects of this study: James Russell, Amy, and Robert Lowell.

As individuals they occupied positions of considerable influence and power during their respective lifetimes, especially in the domain of belles lettres. Each was associated with his or her own literary school or movement, either as founder or as dominant figure: James Russell Lowell (1819–1891) was a Fireside Poet and a member of the famous Saturday Club; Amy Lowell (1874–1925) was a leader of the Imagist movement; Robert Lowell (1917–1977) is credited with having inaugurated the Confessional School of Poetry. As a group they were strong-willed, ambitious figures, able to accept with little reservation the responsibilities which were thrust upon them.

They shared other qualities. All three grew up in a secure, if not always affectionate household, were given every possible opportunity to develop themselves both mentally and physically, and were doubtless made clearly to understand that, having been given much, much was expected of them. Each of them came of age in a milieu that preferred plain but solid living to extravagantly ostentatious lives. Their individual houses—Elmwood, Sevenels, 91 Revere Street—reflected this lifestyle. Many of their furnishings were there because they had always been there. Money was also present in considerable abundance, though never as a particularly salient feature.

Part of being an aristocrat in the nineteenth-century worlds of James Russell and Amy Lowell meant spending an entire lifetime in the house of one's birth, even dying there. To sell one's homestead was a sign of moral and fiscal decay. Good people were respectable people, and respectable people owned their houses and all the land they could see. Robert Lowell was the single exception. He was much more the wanderer, the nomad, than his literary ancestors, an Odyssean voyager in search of *Nostos:* home. Yet in his peregrinations even Robert Lowell never completely renounced his Boston ties. At the end of his life he was still writing of Boston, returning to it both in body and mind, beginning the long journey anew.

By way of acknowledgement, this book could not have been completed without the cooperation of many informed conspirators. Among them was Robert Lowell, who was kind enough to answer questions and suggest leads. One lead was his Massachusetts relation Ralph Lowell, whose anecdotes of Lowelldom were profuse with wit. Both Lowells died before my project was complete. Others no longer extant who aided the cause include Jean Stafford, Allen Tate, and Louis Untermeyer.

But there were those that survived the writing of this book. Elizabeth Hardwick endured a lengthy interview. Ideas, commentary, remembrances were furnished by many kind souls, including Adrienne Rich, Allen Ginsberg, Malcolm Cowley, Stanley Kunitz, John J. Gruesen, Mrs. Harriet Ropes Cabot, Patricia Cristol, Glenn Richard Ruihley, Sidney Bernard, Curt Meyer-Clason, Eva Hesse, Ian Hamilton, James Laughlin, Milton and Nettie Lunin, Theodore Weiss, James Atlas, Tom Dublin, Harry Duncan, Peter du Sautoy, John Coolidge, Thomas Greenslade (curator, Chalmers Memorial Library, Kenyon College), John Broderick (chief, reference department, Library of Congress), Louise M. Womack (public relations, McLean's Hospital), Donald Gallup (curator, collection of American literature, Beinecke Rare Book and Manuscript Library, Yale University), Steven Gould Axelrod, Mrs. Theodore H. Best (Amy Lowell's private secretary, 1921–1924), William H. Bossert (Acting Master of Lowell House, Harvard University), and Jacques Barzun.

Among friends and acquaintances I was abetted by Steven Madoff, Katherine Ruby, Wilson R. Gathings, Vincent Alfieri, Leah Shatavsky, and Lois Gilman.

Institutions and libraries that proved invaluable include The Bostonian Society, The Huntington Library, The Morgan Library, The Library of Congress, Lowell (Mass.) Historical Society, The Boston Public Library, The New York Public Library, Beinecke Rare Book and Manuscript Library (Yale University), Butler Library (Columbia University), The Joseph Regenstein Library (University of Chicago), The Lowell Observatory (Flagstaff, Arizona), New England Historic & Genealogical Society, The Dalton School Library, American Antiquarian Society, The Library of the Boston Athenaeum.

I am indebted as well to my literary agent, Peter H. Matson, and his associate, Victoria Pryor. My mother, Renee Heymann, was a font of encouragement. Genia Graves went leagues beyond the call of duty in her efforts to prepare this manuscript for publication. Finally I would like to mention my editor, Allen T. Klots, whose patience rivals that of any saint: without him this book would not be.

C.D.H.

The Boston Lowells

PERCIVAL LOWLE
b. in England, 1571; d. in Newbury, Massachusetts, 1664
Settled in Newbury, Massachusetts, 1639
m. in England, Rebecca —; d. in Newbury, 1645

JOHN LOWELL
b. in England, 1595; d. in Newbury, 1647
m. (1) in England, Margaret — m. (2), 1639, in Newbury, Elizabeth Goodale, b. in Yarmouth, Eng.; d. 1657

JOHN LOWELL
b. in England, 1629; d. in Boston, 1694
m. (1), 1653, Hannah Proctor m. (2), 1658, Elizabeth Sylvester m. (3), 1666, Naomi Sylvester

EBENEZER LOWELL
b. in Boston, 1675; d. in Boston, 1711
m. 1694, Elizabeth Shailer, of Hingham

REV. JOHN LOWELL
b. in Boston, 1704; d. in Newburyport, 1767
m. (1), 1725, Sarah Champney, d. 1756 m. (2), 1758, Elizabeth Cutts Whipple, d. 1805

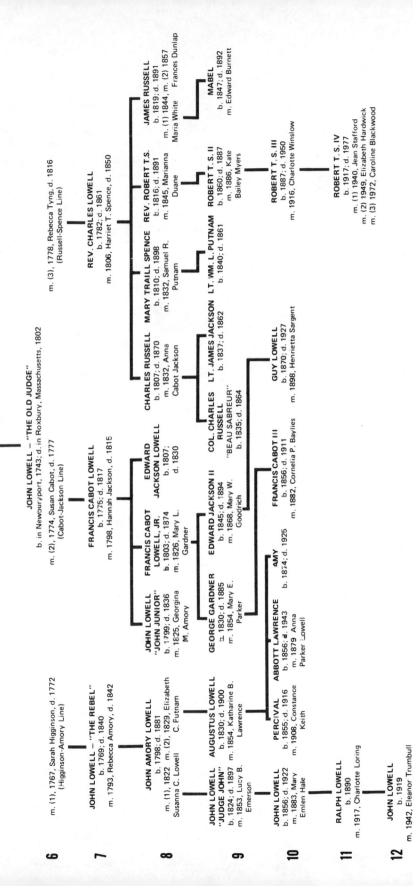

JOHN LOWELL — "THE OLD JUDGE"
b. in Newburyport, 1743; d. in Roxbury, Massachusetts, 1802
m. (2), 1774, Susan Cabot, d. 1777
(Cabot-Jackson Line)

m. (3), 1778, Rebecca Tyng, d. 1816
(Russell-Spence Line)

REV. CHARLES LOWELL
b. 1782; d. 1861
m. 1806, Harriet T. Spence, d. 1850

FRANCIS CABOT LOWELL
b. 1775; d. 1817
m. 1798, Hannah Jackson, d. 1815

JAMES RUSSELL
b. 1819; d. 1891
m. (1) 1844, m. (2) 1857
Maria White   Frances Dunlap

MABEL
b. 1847; d. 1892
m. Edward Burnett

CHARLES RUSSELL
b. 1807; d. 1870
m. 1832, Anna
Cabot Jackson

MARY TRAILL SPENCE
b. 1810; d. 1898
m. 1832, Samuel R.
Putnam

REV. ROBERT T.S.
b. 1816; d. 1891
m. 1845, Marianna
Duane

ROBERT T. S. II
b. 1860; d. 1887
m. 1886, Kate
Bailey Myers

ROBERT T. S. III
b. 1887; d. 1950
m. 1916, Charlotte Winslow

ROBERT T. S. IV
b. 1917; d. 1977
m. (1) 1940, Jean Stafford
m. (2) 1949, Elizabeth Hardwick
m. (3) 1972, Caroline Blackwood

EDWARD
JACKSON LOWELL
b. 1807;
d. 1830

FRANCIS CABOT
LOWELL, JR.
b. 1803; d. 1874
m. 1826, Mary L.
Gardner

EDWARD JACKSON II
b. 1845; d. 1894
m. 1868, Mary W.
Goodrich

COL. CHARLES   LT. JAMES JACKSON
RUSSELL   b. 1837; d. 1862
"BEAU SABREUR"
b. 1835; d. 1864

LT. WM. L. PUTNAM
b. 1840; d. 1861

GUY LOWELL
b. 1870; d. 1927
m. 1898, Henrietta Sargent

JOHN LOWELL
"JOHN JUNIOR"
b. 1799; d. 1836
m. 1825, Georgina
M. Amory

GEORGE GARDNER
b. 1830; d. 1885
m. 1854, Mary E.
Parker

FRANCIS CABOT III
b. 1856; d. 1911
m. 1882, Cornelia P. Baylies

AMY
b. 1874; d. 1925

ABBOTT LAWRENCE
b. 1855; d. 1943
m. 1879 Anna
Parker Lowell

m. (1), 1767, Sarah Higginson, d. 1772
(Higginson-Amory Line)

JOHN LOWELL — "THE REBEL"
b. 1769; d. 1840
m. 1793, Rebecca Amory, d. 1842

JOHN AMORY LOWELL
b. 1798; d. 1881
m. (1), 1822 m. (2), 1829, Elizabeth
Susanna C. Lowell   C. Putnam

AUGUSTUS LOWELL
b. 1830; d. 1900
m. 1854, Katharine B.
Lawrence

PERCIVAL
b. 1855; d. 1916
m. 1908, Constance
Keith

JOHN LOWELL
"JUDGE JOHN"
b. 1824; d. 1897
m. 1853, Lucy B.
Emerson

JOHN LOWELL
b. 1856; d. 1922
m. 1883, Mary
Emlen Hale

RALPH LOWELL
b. 1890
m. 1917, Charlotte Loring

JOHN LOWELL
b. 1919
m. 1942, Eleanor Trumbull

6

7

8

9

10

11

12

BACKGROUNDS
The Lowell Landscape

PART

I

Leadership requires great aristocratic families with long traditions of administration and rule; old ancestral lines that guarantee for many generations the duration of the necessary will and necessary instincts.

—*Friedrich Nietzsche*

And this is good old Boston,
The home of the bean and the cod,
Where the Lowells talk to the Cabots,
And the Cabots talk only to God.

—*John Collins Bossidy*

That hour is blessed when we meet a poet. The poet is brother to the dervish. He has no country nor is he blessed with the things of this world; and while we poor creatures that we are, are worrying about fame, about power, about riches, he stands on a basis of equality with the powerful of the earth and the people bow down before him.

—*Aleksander Sergeyevich Pushkin*

1

HEIRS AND FOREBEARS

IN THE midst of a mid-nineteenth-century visit to England, the poet James Russell Lowell attempted to trace the deeply buried roots of his family tree. His findings were recorded in an unpublished manuscript —"A Brahmin's Self-Laughter"—a mock-solemn chronicle full of the author's inimitable whim and fancy. The first authentic record of his ancestry, he crooned, could be found in the Book of Enoch, thirty-first chapter, which stated that "about this time [300 before Adam] flourished Lowell of the Zarrows—a great king over much people." Adam's Eve, the chronicle went on, would not for a moment have hesitated to marry a Lowell, had the opportunity presented itself. That it hadn't was history's loss.

James Russell Lowell, proud of his heritage, merely intended in this burlesque to "lampoon the absurdities of ancestor-worship" and thereby deride the traditional and typical family history so common during this period—those vast genealogical tomes found today in almost every New England historical and antiquarian society. An easier to verify, although less comical, version of the family's genesis was traced by Ferris Greenslet in *The Lowells and Their Seven Worlds*, published in 1946. Greenslet drew upon another source—*The Historic Genealogy of the Lowells of America from 1639 to 1899*, by the Reverend Delmar Lowell—for much of his information. The genealogy runs to more than eight hundred pages and took its compiler (and his father before him) some twenty-five years to complete. It serves as an example of the kind of ponderous family history James Russell Lowell was so anxious to mock in "A Brahmin's Self-Laughter."

Although the poet in his facetious account traced the clan's origins to an earlier period, both Greenslet's version and the *Historic Genealogy* set the eleventh century as the correct date for the first recorded trace of Lowell family existence. It was in 1066 that a member of the tribe fought on the side of William the Conqueror at the Battle of Abbey Roll during the Norman invasions of England. "After a blank of a century and a half," writes Greenslet, "the name was once again attached, in 1220, to William Lowle of Yardley in Worcestershire." Thence down, the line is clear to Percival (b. 1571), the son of Richard Lowle and Richard's bride, the daughter of a well-landed family, descendants of a cousin of the Conqueror. It was Percival Lowle who later became the first of the family to make the long voyage from England to America.

The Lowells (or Lowles, in the original) were among the few settlers in the New World to arrive bearing the heraldic ensign of knighthood, bestowed upon them in the fifteenth century. In the language of the day their coat of arms was described as follows: "Sable, a dexter hand couped at the wrist grasping three pointless darts, one in pale and two in saltire argent." In modern terminology: a clamped fist clutching three blunted arrows against a black background.

What is known of Percival's background is that he was brought up in North Somerset at Kingston-Seymour on the shore of the Severn Sea. His education was similar to that of Shakespeare, his contemporary; both attained a working knowledge of the Italian dialect known as "Mantuan" and a taste for Ovid in the original. The curriculum, considered rich by prevailing standards, enabled Percival to marry well and be appointed, at age twenty-six, to the office of Assessor of Lands, a position held before him by his father.

Shortly after the death of his father and a sizable inheritance, Percival and his wife and children moved to the thriving seaport of Bristol. It was as a wholesale trader in exports and imports that he was determined to make his mark. His decision to shift careers appeared to be well-timed. For one thing, trade was booming in Bristol. Situated at the confluence of the Avon and Frome rivers, seven miles from the open sea on the western coastline, Bristol quickly emerged as the leading port of England. Fleets of merchant ships left the harbor bound for France, the Baltic, and the Mediterranean, weighted down with shipments of woollen cloth, glassware, salt-cod, and pickled sturgeon; they returned bearing cargos of wine and woad, the brassicaceous plant from which was extracted the deep blue dye that was used to color the sound woollen products that went out on the next voyage.

Percival Lowle & Co. quickly prospered. Percival's sons John and Richard, together with a family friend, William Gerrish, joined the firm. Then, in the course of the firm's continued growth, England underwent a series of drastic upheavals, beginning in 1630 when Charles Stuart, eager to strengthen his position, prorogued and later disbanded Parliament. Conciliar government went into effect. Judges were authorized to collect all impositions and fines and to raise poundage and tonnage rates. Pursuivants and commissioners invaded shops and shipping firms, monitoring private accounts and auditing profit-and-loss statements, examining invoices and supervising inventories. Taxes were levied against private shipping lines and tradesmen and the bulk of them spent on the Royal Navy, with which Charles endeavored to dominate the surrounding waterways.

The tightening of economic controls in Great Britain encroached most heavily upon the interests of the gentry and commercial classes, just when they were being denied the means to influence national policy through the existence of representative parliament. One result was the rapid increase of colonial expansion. The first New England colony, settled by the *Mayflower* Pilgrims in 1620, gave way to a second pilgrimage, which settled mainly in Massachusetts with small groups migrating to what would become Rhode Island, New Hampshire, and Connecticut. Within the first two decades of Britain's colonial expansion, forty thousand persons attempted the strenuous passage.

These facts, coupled with the lore associated with the adventures of exploration, were encouraging factors that helped reinforce Percival's vision, convincing him that he too should consider making the journey. It was a difficult decision for a man sixty-eight years of age who had spent his entire life within the boundaries of a single country and whose family, although pressured by new laws, had no concrete reason to transplant its roots. Eventually the resolution was made.

Lowle took ship on April 12, 1639, boarding the *Jonathan* at London, the crossing itself lasting just over nine weeks. The Lowle party consisted of Percival Lowle; his wife Rebecca; his sons John and Richard, with their wives and four children; his daughter Joan, and her husband John Oliver; his partner, William Gerrish; his clerk, Anthony Somerby, with Somerby's brother Henry; and Richard Dole, company apprentice —sixteen in all. The ship accommodated one hundred, including a ten-man crew. The quarters of the hundred-foot vessel were cramped; food and water rations were low. For a family accustomed to comfort it proved a difficult passage.

The ship's destination was Newbury, forty miles northeast of Boston, a stretch of flat, fertile land between the Merrimack and Quascacunquen rivers, settled four years earlier by the Reverend Thomas Parker, a graduate of Magdalen College at Oxford, and his youthful Congregationalist coadjutor, James Noyes. Because they possessed considerable funds, the Lowles were not granted the usual free lots of land. The record indicates that "Percival Lowle, Gent." contributed fifty pounds to the common stock in exchange for one hundred acres of "marsh and meadow" in a choice section of Newbury. He purchased additional land a few years later.

Two or three houses were subsequently constructed on the property, and the newest residents of Newbury began to work their way into the thick of the community. William Gerrish, who married Joan Lowle after the death of her husband, was made a captain in the local militia and fought in the early Indian wars. Anthony Somerby, the clerk, became Newbury's first schoolmaster. Richard and John Lowle between them fathered eight additional children, a dozen in all. The family of Richard Lowle later moved inland where they led useful but unremarkable lives. It was John's line that attained prominence in its numerous activities, from engagement in the professions to entry into merchandising and manufacturing, as well as in the arts and sciences.

In 1649, having lost his wife and resettled in Newburyport, two miles to the north of Newbury, Percival Lowle memorialized the death of Massachusetts Bay Governor John Winthrop in a hundred-line elegy. It was Winthrop, hero of Bradford's *History of Plymouth Plantation,* who consecrated the Puritan Covenant with God, registering the arrival of the settlers upon the stony soil of New England and announcing their intention to establish a society of saints as a model for all future societies: "We shall be as a city upon a hill. . . . The eyes of all people are upon us." Lowle's elegy for Winthrop, utilizing the conventions of the day's meditations, rises to the occasion, concluding on a fashionably self-denigrating note:

> Here you have Lowle's loyalty
>   Pen'd with his slender Skill,
> And with it no good Poetry
>   But certainly good Will.
> Read these few verses willingly,

And view them not with Momus' eye.
Friendly correct what is amiss.
Accept his Love that did write this.

Lowle's house in Newburyport stood on a picturesque rise of land directly off Main Street. He lived peacefully, reading the writings of Richard Hooker and writing occasional bits of verse. He took long walks along the banks of the Merrimack and worked his garden. Surrounded, as the family biographer puts it, by in-laws and infant grandchildren, he undoubtedly contemplated the phenomenon of old age with a touch of wonderment. Looking back, he must have felt a keen sense of pride and fulfillment; he had come farther and attained more than he had imagined possible in a single lifetime. He died in 1664 at the astonishingly ripe age of ninety-three, and was laid to rest at Newbury in a small graveyard not far from the old town green.

2

REVEREND JOHN

THE Lowells, after adopting the modern spelling of their family name, continued to increase in number and to prosper, gradually spreading out from their verdant country setting. John "the Elder," as he was known, and Joseph, the sons of John Lowell, son of Percival, left home together and moved to Boston, a burgeoning community with a population in 1675 of fifteen thousand. There they engaged in the trade of cooper, making crates and barrels for the exportation of salt fish (mostly cod) and rum. From cooper to cordwainer: from hammering nails and wood they progressed to working cordovan or shoe-sole leather and distributing it to the foot-weary masses. Presently, the business was in the hands of Ebenezer Lowell, son of John the Elder, listed as a "merchant" on King Street (now State Street) and remembered as a "stately, refined, commanding looking person." When Ebenezer died in 1711, at the age of thirty-six, his estate was valued at £900, a tidy sum in those days, suitable testimony to the man's energy and business acumen. But the real significance of this figure is that it enabled Ebenezer's son, the future Reverend John Lowell, third in a long line of Johns, to become the first of the family to attend college.

Harvard, founded in 1636 at Cambridge, Massachusetts, was no ordinary school. Advertising itself as an institution "for gentlemen, educated like gentlemen," this oasis in the desert existed from the beginning to ensure the sons of Boston's gentry a sound training. Books, especially the Scriptures, were the great Puritan weapons in the perpetual search for truth, for liberty. Harvard's emblem—three open books and the word *Veritas*—represented the school's ideal.

Books, however, were only part of it. To earn his diploma, a student was expected to be sufficient "as much in learning as in Manners." To this end his daily schedule was carefully regimented. Public prayer, at the beginning and end of each school day, was strictly enforced. Attendance at lectures, recitations, and disputations was mandatory. Until the end of the seventeenth century, almost every class was conducted in Latin, as were final examinations, which were purported to be inordinately rigorous. Students were as closely supervised outside as they were inside the classroom. They were neither permitted to leave Cambridge without proper authorization nor encouraged to participate in the "company and society of such men as lead ungirt and dissolute lives."

By 1717, the year of John Lowell's admission to Harvard, conditions there had eased. The main reason for the school's newly adopted attitude was presumably the twin leadership provided by William Brattle, long-time tutor and resident fellow, and John Leverett, "the great Leverett," Harvard's first lay president. Inaugurated in 1708, Leverett had helped "shake off the incubus of the fierce orthodoxy of the Mathers"—Increase and Cotton, father and son—whose personalities had so dominated the college in its early years. Students were given more latitude in their choice of curriculum; there was less of that heavy-handed supervision of scholars that had marked the previous administration.

What had not changed was the reprehensible practice of ranking students according to family income and social status, without regard to academic accomplishment. On entering Harvard, John Lowell, to his immediate discomfort, discovered that his name had been placed at the bottom of the class list, far below such names as Sewall, Wolcott, Hancock, and Winslow. A second list, prepared a semester later, placed Lowell sixth from the bottom. At the apex of both lists stood Mr. Foster Hutchinson and Mr. John Davenport, sons of already established and extremely prosperous families. They were still there in 1721, the year of Lowell's graduation.

The patrician families of Boston regarded Harvard as nothing less than a family trust; they considered it a public duty not only to endow and foster the school, but to maintain its standards. One of the best measurements of these standards was the quality of the clergymen it produced. The church was still a logical choice of vocation for the scholarly young man determined to rise in the world and make something of himself. The New England parson was ex officio a gentleman and a member of the ruling class, respected and venerated within the community. It was therefore no accident that John Lowell, following his graduation, decided to remain at Harvard three more years to complete his Master of Arts degree, a prerequisite for the Congregational ministry. Upon receiving the degree, he ventured to Newbury, where the townspeople had constructed and dedicated the Third Parish at the upper end of Market Square. He was appointed pastor of the new parish in 1725, a month after marrying Sarah Champney, the cousin of a Harvard classmate.

Central to Lowell's religious orientation had been the culturally broadening teachings of Edward Wigglesworth, appointed in 1721 to the first endowed chair at Harvard, the Hollis Professorship of Divinity. It was Wigglesworth who first introduced Lowell and others of his generation to the writings of Voltaire, Rousseau, and Plato and thereby helped lay the foundation for the ascent of enlightened Christianity in New England, a move away from the "lush but fearsome jungles of Calvinism, into the thin, clear light of Unitarianism."

Wigglesworth's idea of a sound secular education, while precisely in keeping with the new liberal regime at Harvard, was nevertheless in direct opposition to the established orthodox faith of the surrounding countryside. The college, in fact, was considered dangerously lax and easygoing, especially by those living outside Boston. Surveying the lay of the land, Van Wyck Brooks (in *The Flowering of New England*) wrote that "West of Worcester, and up the Connecticut Valley, the clergy, Calvinist almost to a man, united in condemning the Cambridge collegians, in the very words of George Whitefield, as 'close Pharisees, resting on head knowledge.' " Whitefield's loud and vengeful, but convincing cries of terror had spread, reaching Reverend Lowell's ears around 1740, when mention of Whitefield was first made in the Pastor's correspondence.

Whitefield, an English evangelist preacher and a leader of the Calvinistic Methodists, had first joined the Methodist group led by John and Charles Wesley at Oxford. Breaking with the Wesleys and adopting a number of Calvin's views, especially predestination, Whitefield made several important tours of America, where he drew eager throngs and became instrumental in the Great Awakening, a wave of religious revivals in the Colonies that caused bitter altercations and resulted in certain doctrinal changes in the Church.

Initially, impressed with Whitefield's eloquence and vitality as an orator, Lowell invited him to address the members of his Newbury congregation, a decision he soon came to regret. Hell, fire, and brimstone were neither Harvard's nor his own notion of a forward-looking theology. Unlike Whitefield, Lowell was not a religious doctrinarian. His views were exceedingly moderate even by moderate standards. A freethinker, he denied the Trinity, the divinity of Christ, the personality of the Devil, and the theory of man's total depravity. He believed that the New Testament was meant to be interpreted as a work of logic and reason. If such a thing as a "personal hell" existed, it was one that had to be reckoned with here on earth and not in the hereafter. Lowell began to see Whitefield for what he was, a mortal enemy and threat to human liberty and understanding. The disorderly and unorthodox assemblies inspired by Whitefield's followers represented a danger to the entire community. The Newbury minister sought to curtail Whitefield's local appearances by closing his own pulpit to outside agitators. But the damage had already been done: thirty-eight members of Lowell's congregation, with their families, withdrew, and with the authorization of the General Court, established the First Presbyterian Church of Newburyport.

Adding the term "Godless Harvard" to his previous characterization of the school, Whitefield had little to say directly about Lowell, who is mentioned only in passing in his adversary's daily journal. The Harvard graduate was much admired by his personal followers, however. Sara Emery, an author of early eminence, wrote of Lowell: "He was a lover of all good men, though of different denominations, and given to hospitality in all its forms." By "different denominations" she obviously did not have Whitefield's in mind.

A fuller portrait of the Reverend, at least in physical terms, is to be found on one half of an old diptych, which was later mounted over the mantel in James Russell Lowell's sitting-room at Elmwood. In this painting seven eighteenth-century divines are seated around a velvet-decked, rectangular table. At the head of the table sits the Reverend John Lowell, nursing a long church-warden's pipe, attired in charcoal robe and white bands, an earnest yet self-assured expression on his face. The other ministers, all from Newburyport, are ostensibly of different denominations—Baptist, Presbyterian, Congregationalist. Over the picture, inscribed on a scroll, is the following epigram: *In necessariis unitas; in non necessariis libertas; in utrisque charitas* ("In essentials unity; in nonessentials liberty; in both charity").

The Reverend's temporizing spirit permeated his every deed. In

1755, by now a distinguished, white-haired senior member of the community, he delivered a farewell sermon to a battalion of colonial soldiers about to go off to do battle in the French and Indian War. The sermon, later published under the title "The Advantages of God's Presence with his People in an Expedition against their Enemies," cautioned against the dangers of war and called for as little spilling of blood as was humanly possible. Despite this gentle warning, it was the Reverend who, prior to his death in 1767, added to the family crest the inscription *Occasionem Cognosce,* which translated comes close to meaning "Seize the Opportunity"—a most appropriate family motto.

The Reverend was survived by his second wife, Elizabeth Cutts Whipple, whom he had wed following the death in 1756 of Sarah Champney Lowell. He was survived also by a Champney-born son, John, later called the Old Judge, for all intents and purposes the father of the present-day clan.

ᥬᥩ 3 ᥫᥭ

THE OLD JUDGE

THE stately old houses of Newburyport still stand, a remembrance of days past—spacious houses with landscaped lawns and formal gardens, widow's walks and thatched fences. They are a joy to behold, these mansions, four-square and three stories high, of weather beaten wood and solid red brick. One of them, located well back on the south side of High Street, belonged to John Lowell, the Old Judge. It was graced with large, square rooms, ceilings formed of stalactite wood carvings, a marble staircase, roomy corridors, capacious fireplaces, and ornate overmantels decorated with caryatids and cherubim. John Adams, always wary of another man's success, wrote to his wife Abigail, "John Lowell at Newbury Port, has built him an House like the Palace of a Nobleman, and lives in great Splendor." He appended an afterthought: "Lowell's business is very profitable."

Born in 1743, the same year as Thomas Jefferson, the latest John Lowell, like his father before him, entered Harvard at age thirteen. Unlike his father, whose name appeared thirty-first in a class list of thirty-one, John was placed seventh in a class of twenty-seven, an indication of the family's rising social fortunes. He graduated second scholar in the class of 1760, but turned away from his father's calling, the ministry, to read law in the office of Oxenbridge Thacher, the famed Boston barrister who opposed the growing rift between the colonies and England. Admitted to the bar in 1763, Lowell returned to Newburyport to open his own practice, earning a reputation as a criminal lawyer and three times being elected a selectman.

He was a hearty, ambitious soul, full of patriotic zeal, but like

Thacher, a political moderate who advocated conciliatory and prudent behavior whenever possible. He did not support the pernicious Stamp or Townsend acts, imposed upon the Colonists for the sole purposes of harassing and embarrassing their government; and he agreed with the popular tenet that decreed there must be no taxation without representation—that being the prime reason his ancestors had departed England in the first place. But by the same token, he was sensitive to the practical considerations that lay behind the rhetoric of taxation. To sever the umbilical connection between the motherland (Great Britain) and her cherished infant (America) would be a drastic hardship for all parties, particularly for the citizens of Newburyport, who depended upon British trade for their very lifeblood. The path Lowell favored was that of least resistance, or at least of well-tempered restraint, a road that clearly placed him "out of step with the martial beat of the hour."

On May 24, 1774, Lowell was one of a small group of attorneys-at-law to sign a farewell address to Loyalist Governor Thomas Hutchinson on his recall to London, an action frowned upon by press and public alike. A month later he compounded the gravity of his position by signing an address of welcome to the arriving governor, General Thomas Gage, sent over by the British to replace Hutchinson and restore order. Fellow townsmen took these as signs of Lowell's support of the English and wasted little time in conferring upon him the labels "Tory" and "King Lover."

The year 1776 began with the publication of Thomas Paine's stirring pamphlet *Common Sense*, attacking the British and presenting the Colonists with the first clear and popular statement of their cause. There was excitement in the air, with troops drilling on the village Common, officers on horseback riding through the town, the intoxicating aroma of rebellion everywhere. On July 5 word arrived from Philadelphia that the Declaration of Independence had been signed the previous day. On July 9 a formal copy of the Declaration was read aloud from the steps of Newburyport's Town Hall. The muskets of Lexington and Concord had resounded; war was general and raging when John Lowell, eager to join the campaign and dispel his Tory reputation, donned pistol and uniform and hurried to the front.

He fought briefly but valiantly, convincing his countrymen that he was as trustworthy as the next man; after the war he sold his house in Newburyport and moved to Boston. As a respected leader of the bar, a man who held the confidence of the departed Loyalists and who enjoyed the trust of the patriots, Lowell represented Boston in the General Court, in the Constitutional Convention of 1779, and in the Continental Congress of 1781. The latter was held at Philadelphia, where Lowell shared rooms with his friend James Madison. President Washington appointed him Judge of the District Court; President Adams named him Chief Justice of the First Circuit Court, which is where he was graced with his biblical sobriquet, the Old Judge. It was during the Constitutional Convention of 1779 that he introduced into the Massachusetts Bill of Rights the words "free and equal," as in "All men are created free and equal, and have certain natural, essential, and inalienable rights, among which may be reckoned the right of enjoying and defending their lives and liberties." This phrase became the key clause in the court battle setting free every man, woman, and child then being held as a slave in the Commonwealth.

In the Old Judge can be found family traits that were to reappear in his descendants. Physically he was of middle height, with dark hair, lively blue eyes, strong nose and chin; he possessed the square-cut features and broad brow that are still a family characteristic. He was confident, sensible, persuasive in his courtroom battles. As he approached middle age he turned his attention to maritime law, filing hundreds of claims against vessels captured at sea by American privateers, augmenting his income with his own agency for rich Tory émigrés—families such as the Hutchinsons, Coffins, Lorings, and Lechmeres, who had departed America with the outbreak of war.

With two distant relations, Thomas Russell and Steven Higginson, he founded the First National Bank of Boston. Banking was an untried business in America but quickly proved itself financially rewarding. Imbued with the Puritan need to join and serve, the Old Judge saw ways to put his steadily increasing wealth to good use—in humane societies, agricultural organizations, immigration councils. He was a founder of the American Academy of Arts and Sciences and for eighteen years a fellow of the Harvard Corporation, which early in the school's history was the operating arm of the college, subject to the advice and consent of its sole senior corpus, the Board of Overseers. The Corporation, consisting of the president of the college, the treasurer, and five fellows, set itself up as an autonomous, self-perpetuating body. When a member of the Corporation stepped down or passed on he was replaced by someone whose nomination was secured from within the Corporation's ranks.

Lowell's years of service as a member of the Corporation set a precedent that would not be broken for generations. Over the next century and a half, up to and including Abbott Lawrence Lowell's demise in 1943, there was only one ten-year span in which a member of the Lowell family did not serve in some capacity on behalf of Harvard's ruling coalition. Five fellows, five overseers, two professors, and one president—a total of 210 man-years—have been attributed to this very proper Bostonian clan.

Lowell's later years were spent amid the tranquility of a pastoral setting, in a spacious hilltop house surrounded by acres of tree-studded land in Roxbury, then three miles outside the city limits. Here he devoted himself to botany and to the joys of family life, attempting to instill in his children the same independent and lively streak that he himself demonstrated in abundance. Twice a widower, he was thrice married, first (1767) to Sarah Higginson of Salem, daughter of a shipbuilder, by whom he had two daughters and a son, John, the so-called Rebel. His second wife, Susanna Cabot, a descendant of the well-landed Cabots of Massachusetts, produced two Lowell children, including Francis Cabot Lowell, the inventor in this country of the textile manufacturing industry and the fury behind the founding of Lowell, Massachusetts. After his second wife's death in 1777, Lowell married Rebecca (Russell) Tyng, widow of a Dunstable barrister, who bore him three daughters and a son, Charles, the father of James Russell Lowell. The Old Judge's three sons—John Lowell, the Rebel; Francis Cabot Lowell; and Reverend Charles Lowell—were to become the patriarchs of the three major branches of the family tree.

4

"MILL AND MANSION"

Two decades before his death in 1802, the Old Judge, in a note to Rebecca Tyng evaluating the overall state of his surroundings, summarized life in rapidly expanding Boston:

> I have met with no disgust here either in my Business or Society, but like most other Theatres when you are behind the Scene the Movements appear so little extraordinary that the Eye of Curiosity, once abated, everything appears common. There appears to me to be but few great and not many little People among us—they are generally of the middle size.

Given the attitude of facile superiority conveyed in this brief, it is easy to see how and why the Old Judge was able to identify—socially and economically—with the country's leading conservative element, the Federalists of Massachusetts.

He was considered one of the central figures in the ranks of the wealthy landowners of Essex, that feisty conglomerate known as the Junto. The *Dictionary of American Biography* sums them up in several choice phrases: "Socially, the solidarity of these plain, energetic Essex County families of Lowell, Cabot, Lodge, Lee, Higginson, and Jackson, who moved to Boston after the Revolution, was . . . significant. For over a generation they remained a compact social group, frequently intermarrying, and helping one another in business, to such good purpose that eventually they were regarded as typical Boston aristocracy."

Despite his insistence on the "free and equal" clause in the Massachusetts Constitution, the Old Judge was a rigid supporter of class rights, a backer of commercial, manufacturing, and general business interests, a member of a distinctly pro-British, pro-Adams, aristocratic social cult. He was a good hater of Jefferson, who led the pro-French or Republican party. The Federalists included Washington, Hamilton, and John Jay. The Republican leaders were Madison, Monroe, and Burr. The Republicans were for the most part dominated by Virginians, led by Jefferson and his dreams of an "arcadia from which cities and manufactories and banks were excluded." The Federalist philosophy was perhaps best expressed in 1796 by John Jay:

> As to political reformation in Europe or elsewhere, I confess that . . . I do not amuse myself with dreams about an age of reason. I am content that little men should be as free as big ones and have and enjoy the same rights, but nothing strikes me as more absurd than projects to stretch little men into big ones, or shrink big men into little ones. . . . We must take men and measure them as they are, and act accordingly.

More politically volatile even than the Old Judge was his eldest son, John the Rebel, a Harvard-trained attorney who began to promulgate the Federalist cause in a series of pamphlets of varying effect and on a wide range of topics. Under the pseudonym A Citizen of New England, the Rebel published his first important pamphlet in 1797, at the age of forty-two. Entitled *Anti-Gallican, Or the Lover of his Own Country,* the tract denounced the "false patriotism" of Jefferson, Monroe, and Albert Gallatin, the Swiss-born U.S. Secretary of the Treasury, simultaneously attacking the doctrine of national neutrality toward European conflicts and defending the Federalists against Republican charges of blatant aristocracy and monarchism. That same year he was appointed by his father director of the First National Bank of Boston, serving until 1803, when, his health broken through overwork, he traveled abroad with his wife, Rebecca Amory, and son, John Amory Lowell. Returning to Boston, he was soon again churning out Federalist pamphlets and articles, filling many pages with violent denunciations of Napoleon and Madison, his father's old friend. He accused Jefferson of undermining the country by means of "anarchist" tactics and of sweeping away all form of organized government; he blamed the Embargo Act of 1807 and the Non-Intercourse Act of 1809 on Jefferson and cited both actions, as well as the War of 1812, as the prime causes for

the monetary crisis that subsequently swept through New England. In no uncertain terms, the Rebel believed that only well-educated men who had shown (or whose fathers had shown) competence in *practical*, hard-nosed affairs by amassing fortunes should do the ruling.

While the first-born of the Old Judge's sons invoked Federalist imprecations and maledictions upon his country's government, the next-born was dreaming up ways to improve and streamline the nation's mercantile and industrial complex. Traveling to the British Isles in 1810, Francis Cabot Lowell, his wife, Hannah Jackson, and their four children spent the better part of the next two years visiting the cotton factories of Manchester, Birmingham, and Leeds. Although there were a number of small-scale cotton mills scattered about New England, the material itself was still being processed by hand- or foot-power in a highly wasteful and disorganized manner. No progress along these lines had been made in the States since the invention in 1770 of the spinning jenny, a device by which a single operative turning a crank could whirl forty or more spindles at once. Lowell saw immediately that the mass production of cotton and woollen goods was a necessity, lest the country persist in importing these products at considerable expense and inconvenience from abroad.

One problem was that stringent patent regulations prohibited the importation into America of English machinery or even of drawings and blueprints of English machinery. But there was no law that said a man could not commit to memory the complex processes and inner workings of cloth production and later re-create these methods on his own.

Lowell returned to America in 1812 and with his brother-in-law, Patrick Tracy Jackson, and an initial outlay of $400,000, started a firm he called the Boston Manufacturing Company on land purchased in Waltham. The following months were spent designing and constructing, from memory, the complicated spinning machinery and a working power-loom. With the help of a mathematician, Paul Moody, Lowell was able not only to "reinvent" the British mill system, but to improve on it. As John Coolidge wrote in *Mill and Mansion,* a study of Lowell, Massachusetts, the manufacturer could now use unskilled labor throughout his plant—a breakthrough that not even Samuel Slater's experimental "family mills" in Pawtucket, Rhode Island, in the 1790's, had been able to accomplish. Under Lowell's design, "the small, indi-

vidual concern might be indefinitely extended. Every stage in the transformation of raw fiber into cloth might be performed under one roof, and for the first time in this country the mass production of finished goods was possible." From the spinning wheel to the automatic loom: textile manufacturing in this country was to become the first trade group to develop into a modern mass-production industry. The Industrial Revolution, of which this was a vital stepping-stone, was called America's second Revolution, and Lowell, Jackson, and Moody were dubbed the Washington, Jefferson, and Adams of the struggle to industrialize the nation.

Francis Cabot Lowell died before realizing his final dream. But by 1817, the year of his untimely death at age forty-two, the mill operation in Waltham was in full swing, producing nearly forty miles of cotton cloth daily, paying dividends to investors of over 20 percent. That "rapidly ramifying" clutch of shareholders included a large portion of the Essex Junto: the Lowells, Jacksons, Amorys, Higginsons, Russells, Gorhams, Tyngs, Duttons, and Lees. Those who could afford to invest ready funds had found themselves a veritable gold mine. The money they made in cotton mills and factories—seventy years before the Rockefellers, Vanderbilts, Mellons, and Fords amassed their fortunes—went into other entrepreneurial ventures: shipping lines, railroads, distilleries, mutual funds. One historian astutely observed that first family money was like a tree that somehow never stopped growing.

Lowell's long-range objective of an independent textile manufacturing center, self-run and self-sufficient, began to take shape. In December 1821 a group calling itself the Boston Associates, made up of John and Kirk Boott, Nathan and William Appleton, Warren Dutton, Nathaniel Bowditch, the Abbots, the Jacksons, the Lawrences, and the descendants of Francis Cabot Lowell, invested in a new company, the Merrimack Manufacturing Corporation. Within a brief span this aggregate took over a section of the farming village of East Chelmsford and transformed it into America's first factory town. The name they gave it was Lowell, after Francis Cabot Lowell.

The location of this industrial complex, about twenty-five miles north of Boston, had everything to do with its subsequent growth. The Merrimack River makes a wide turn at this point and drops thirty feet in the space of a mile. The town's main canal, the Pawtucket, was constructed in the 1790's, joining the Merrimack and Concord rivers and providing a transportation link to the Atlantic Coast. The cotton nabobs

purchased the Pawtucket Canal, expanded it, built a dam and a lateral canal to carry the power to the site of the mills. Eventually, a six-mile-long labyrinth of locks and canals connecting various sections of the enlarged mill town was built, water being the sole source of power in those days.

The first cotton cloth was processed at Lowell in 1823. The last major textile mill went up in 1845, by which time the "Manchester of Massachusetts" had mushroomed into the world's leading textile manufacturing center, surpassing even its British competition. The Lowell experiment, a model for later American industrial centers, was conceived as a total enterprise, the entire community given over to the mass manufacture of woollen, linen, cotton, and other saleable fabrics, but without the mass exploitation of family and child labor that was so prevalent in England.

Scarcity of unskilled labor, which was always a problem for industry in the northeastern United States, proved a major obstacle for the mill owners as well. It was alleviated by the employment in the factories and mills of the unmarried young women of the farms—the daughters of proud and resourceful Yankee farmers, the struggling and hard-toiling core of early New England rural society. In order to make day-to-day existence in the factories inviting, the manufacturers sought to guarantee that working in the mills "could neither corrupt the girls, nor debase them socially." To accommodate them, low-cost boardinghouses were built within easy walking distance of their places of employment; shops, a town hall, a mall, a hospital, schools, and churches were also constructed. Each private boardinghouse was administered by a seemly houselady, usually an elderly widow who kept careful watch over her youthful charges, invoking a strict 10:00 P.M. curfew and mandatory church attendance on the Sabbath. At all other times the girls were under the direct supervision of the management of the mills, who saw to it that they were kept gainfully employed.

The industrial complex inadvertently attracted a catch of vociferous detractors. Henry David Thoreau referred to the mostly unlettered farm girls as "wage slaves"; like Ruskin in Britain, he advocated razing the factory system and returning to the handicraft virtues of colonial America. But the system also produced its share of rabid supporters. Davy Crockett, while a Representative from his home state of Tennessee, visited Lowell and paid it high praise, as did the British novelist Anthony Trollope. Another Englishman, Charles Dickens, in *American*

Notes, recounted an 1841 journey he undertook to "The Spindle City." "Lowell," he ventured, "is a large, populous, thriving place. Those indications of its youth which first attract the eye, give it a quaintness and oddity of character which, to a visitor from the old country, is amusing enough."

This comment represented one of the author's few kind remarks about America, and yet it is difficult to imagine just what he found so quaint and appealing about Lowell. Certainly not its immense six-story brick-and-mortar sweatshops crammed full with pulsating machinery and topped by rows of smoke-spewing chimneys. The town's narrow streets, lined with coarse patches of gray rock, were drab and treeless. The odor of grease and grime permeated each brick and stone. Soot filled the air, obliterating the sun's rays, casting the landscape into bleak and permanent shadow. Yet compared to the stockade factories of England, the Victorian hellholes of Sheffield, Leeds, and Birmingham, Lowell was a virtual paradise.

Until 1840 the mill hands, except for the English dyers and calico printers, were predominantly New England girls. Few males worked the mills. The females began as "bobbin girls" and gradually worked their way up to machine operators, paying for board and lodging out of their weekly earnings. The conditions in the mills—the noise, the overcrowding, the poor lighting and ventilation, combined with long hours (80–90 a week) and low wages (an average of ten dollars a month) —left much to be desired. But the gravest problem facing these employees (some of whom started working the mills at age nine) was the oppressive and dehumanizing regimentation of their daily lives, the intolerable tedium and boredom associated with the incessant repetition of trivial and menial tasks. One anonymous operative, unimpressed with the Protestant work ethic that equated toil and virtue, described the systematized labor process in less than glowing terms: "Up before day at the clang of the bell—and out of the mill by the clang of the bell —into the mill, and at work, in obedience to that ding-dong of a bell— just as though we were so many living machines." What limited funds the women were able to accumulate were used to help pay off their fathers' farm mortgages or to educate a brother or even to finance the girl's own future education or dowry.

Aside from these not inconsiderable benefits, the system boasted several additional features that recommended it. Charles Dickens pointed out that each boardinghouse contained not only an upright piano but its own circulating library. The girls themselves organized self-improvement circles as well as music and literary societies. More important, from 1840 to 1845, they edited and distributed *The Lowell Offering,* a periodical that housed the workers' letters, poems, plays, songs, sketches, and essays. Because the tabloid was carefully inspected by the mill owners for evidence of rebellion or insurrection, little was published in the way of outright criticism—and most of what did appear was written in the sentimental and flowery literary style of the day. An exception to both rules was Sarah G. Bagley's ironic "The Pleasures of Factory Life" (December 1840), which began:

> Pleasure, did you say? What! pleasures in *factory* life? From many scenes with which I have become acquainted, I should judge that the pleasures of factory life were like "Angels' visits, few and far between". . . . I could not endure such a clatter of machinery, that I could neither speak to be heard, nor think to be understood, even by myself. And then you have so little leisure . . . Call it by any other name rather than pleasure.

Yet even Bagley, who was to become the first woman labor leader in American history, felt compelled to restrain herself in the pages of the *Offering.* Midway through her "Pleasures" piece she suddenly shifted gears, lavishing praise upon the Lowell experiment, particularly the health-care plan and the abundant means of information available to employees by way of public lecture rooms (John Quincy Adams, Horace Mann, and John Greenleaf Whittier were among those invited to speak). All this, of course, was window dressing, a false front devised by the Boston-based mill owners to convince others, if not themselves, that these medieval labor camps were "a shining example of those ultimate Yankee ideals: profit and virtue, doing good and doing well." Bagley did not, unfortunately, press her attack to conclusion; like others in her position, she was forced to temporize her natural instincts, to allay them until the moment for a counterrevolution was ripe.

For years the Lowell mills continued to operate at a torrid pace. So lucrative was the cotton-manufacturing industry that the economic panics of 1837 and 1857, devastating for other commercial enterprises, barely affected the textile trade. As industrial output rose, the mill town expanded in size; it soon became necessary to search abroad for labor to construct new canals and mills and to produce the expanded supply of cotton textiles and machinery. Lowell emerged as an important locus for foreigners, with Irish, French-Canadian, Greek, and Polish immigrants arriving in significant numbers. Gradually, however, the vicissitudes of change took their inevitable toll. In the end what crushed Francis Cabot Lowell's utopian vision of a one-industry, living-and-working community were not only the demands of enraged and underpaid mill operatives—though that too—but the failings of succeeding generations of labor bosses, men who possessed little, if any, technical knowledge of mass-production procedures or understanding of the complex nature of labor relations. The shortcomings of these avaricious entrepreneurs were first disclosed to a curious public in the 1840's via a convoy of newly founded labor-oriented periodicals, including *The Factory Girl, Factory Girl's Garland,* and *Voice of Industry.* Although none of these publications alone gained quite the fame and wide circulation attained by the *Offering,* as a group they represented a more heroic effort to combat and improve the desperate working conditions in New England's mills. Written, edited, and published by the region's militant factory employees, these periodicals repudiated the vague and often conciliatory editorial policies propounded by the *Offering.*

They offered their contributors and readers the opportunity to "correct the imbalance" by documenting their complaints and grievances, at the same time providing future historians with an absorbing record of early battles for women's rights and liberation in this country. By the turn of the century the system had been uprooted and overturned, battered into submission by a weighty Marxist proviso that insisted on the right of manual workers to the whole product of their labor. The emergence of trade unions, radical and frequently recalcitrant bands of labor, and well-organized feminists played a key role, as did an expanding and economically viable textile manufacturing system located south of the Mason-Dixon line. As of 1900 the town of Lowell showed all the signs of permanent decay, a process of destruction that left it a storm-blown ghost town, a desiccated remembrance of what it once had been, but not before the mill management and investors had reaped their inevitable gain.

~~§ 5 §~~

THE LOWELL INSTITUTE

MANUFACTURING arms and munitions proved itself less of a financial risk than weaving and spinning cloth. The du Ponts of Delaware discovered as much during the conflagration of 1812, when the U.S. government ordered half-a-million pounds of gunpowder from the family works in Wilmington, Delaware. While the du Ponts were accumulating riches, John the Rebel (often praised as the most brilliant of all the Lowells) was disbursing his—building schools (Phillips Academy) and hospitals (Massachusetts General), but also banks (the Provident Institute for Savings) and industries (Boston Shipping Lines). Falling into the proper Lowell groove, he invested his profits in a cornucopia of nonprofit organizations: the Massachusetts Agricultural, Massachusetts Historical, and American Antiquarian societies; he was president and trustee of the Boston Athenaeum, that insuperable, privately funded library that George Ticknor, Andrews Norton, and Samuel Appleton helped launch. From 1810 to 1822, he served as a fellow of the Harvard Corporation and for the next five years sat on its Board of Overseers.

When his father, the Old Judge, died, shortly after the turn of the century, he inherited the thirty-acre Roxbury estate; naming it Bromley Vale, he added three new greenhouses, a windmill, a wading pond, the tower of a medieval castle, and the most lavish European furnishings money could buy. The manor became a center of hospitality for foreign dignitaries and leading American politicians. Entertained there on separate occasions were both Alexander Hamilton and Aaron Burr. The pamphleteer owned another house, a winter residence, in Boston proper, off ritzy Park Street, one block from the Commons, an area where for two generations an entire enclave of Brahmins lived and prospered. "Magnificently *honnête*," Henry James exclaimed of the street, adding that it had been "founded on all the moral, material, social solidities instead of on some of them only—which made all the difference." Park Street had an exclusive air about it, with its proud brownstone and rose-brick structures designed in the grand manner and boasting verandas, heavily and richly draped windows, flowering lawns framed by massive gateways and stone walls. But the street's grandeur held little appeal for the Rebel, whose years of retirement were spent at his Roxbury estate—writing letters, conducting horticultural experiments, penning poems of a light, teasing nature:

> Oft as we glide the seas along
> I try the power of *limping* song
> Kill time, and cheat my *yawning* leisure,
> With verse which boasts nor rhyme, nor measure . . .

If social conviction and passion played a significant role in the Rebel's life, they played an equally vital role in the life of his half-brother, Charles Lowell (1782–1861), the youngest of the Old Judge's three sons, himself the father of six, including James Russell Lowell. After graduating Harvard and briefly attending the Harvard Law School, Charles departed for Edinburgh to study theology under the famed Dugald Stewart—a return to the ministerial profession of his grandfather in Newburyport.

The liberal Whiggery and intuitional philosophizing of Stewart rubbed off on his protégé. Lowell returned to Boston in 1806 to become pastor of the old West Church on Cambridge Street, shortly afterward marrying Harriet Traill Spence of Portsmouth, New Hampshire, whose family was half-Scottish Highlands—on her father's side—and half-Orkney Island—on her mother's. She was the grandniece of the Reverend John Lowell's second wife, which made her practically a cousin. Her immediate ancestors are described by Ferris Greenslet as being "Tories in sympathy and Episcopalians in religion," a combination not wholly compatible with her husband's liberal religious bearings.

Although he reacted against the trinitarian view of God and believed in His single personality (Christ being only His Son and the Holy Ghost nonexistent), the Reverend was by no means a dogmatist. Members of his congregation testified that he was patient and bookish and an eloquent and attractive speaker. He was soft-spoken and rational, a religious leader who preferred the magic of the mind to the psychedelics of the spirit. Emerson thought him "a natural orator." As important as his conception of the ministry was his belief in man's social responsibility to his fellow man. He preached Grace and Good Works; the good works he favored demanded practical results—money collected, laws passed, decisions carried out, the poor fed, the sick cured. It was not unusual for him to be seen wandering down the back alleys of the North End, seeking out the needy of his parish, "carrying to his flock what were to him the indistinguishable comforts of Christianity and human love."

The Reverend's sole self-indulgence was his purchase of the thickly wooded Cambridge estate of Elmwood. The gracious, three-story colonial residence stood opposite Sir Richard's Landing, on what is today Mount Auburn Street, where at the edge of the Charles River the settlers of Watertown led by Sir Richard Saltonstall landed in June 1630. The house was built in 1767 for Thomas Oliver, the lieutenant-governor of the province, appointed by George III. During the Revolution Elmwood was seized by local dissidents and used as a hospital for soldiers; later the Committee of Correspondence was quartered there. It eventually fell into the hands of Elbridge Gerry, Governor of Massachusetts, Vice-President of the United States under James Madison, and the great original of "gerrymandering." Lowell bought Elmwood from the Gerry estate in 1818.

Boston, "the Athens of the New World," had entered a new age. Periclean in its splendor, the epoch was marked by the growth of the city proper and by the rapid expansion of its populace. Harvard, too, had kept pace, mushrooming from a small elitist college into a full-blown elitist university. Edward Everett became Eliot Professor of Greek Literature, and George Ticknor was named Smith Professor of Belles-Lettres and Modern Languages. Francis J. Child, still remembered for his treatise on the language of Chaucer, helped modernize Harvard's English literature program; Jared Sparks did the same for its department of American history. Within two decades Harvard's library had nearly trebled its inventory of books; its treasury of sixty thousand volumes made it the nation's largest, most impressive collection of its kind.

On another front, native American literature was just coming into its own, having apparently taken its cue from Ralph Waldo Emerson's

1837 Phi Beta Kappa delivery of "The American Scholar": "We have listened too long to the courtly muses of Europe. . . . We will walk on our own feet; we will work with our own hands; we will speak our own minds." The ensuing years saw the publication of Hawthorne's *The Scarlet Letter,* Melville's *Moby-Dick,* Whitman's *Leaves of Grass,* and Thoreau's *Walden, or Life in the Woods.*

The Lowells, keeping abreast of the times, had produced their own author of note. James Russell Lowell, born in 1819, was to create, among other works, *A Fable for Critics* and *The Biglow Papers.* By the year of his birth the family oak had sprouted three separate boughs. The poet belonged to what was styled the Russell-Spence line. Named for the distaff members of the clan, the line attained its tag when Reverend Charles Lowell, son of the widow Tyng, nee Russell, married a Spence. Similarly, the descendants of Francis Cabot Lowell and Hannah Jackson called themselves the Cabot-Jacksons; those descended from John the Rebel and Rebecca Amory, the senior branch, were known as the Higginson-Amorys.

A closer examination of the individuals who comprised the tripartite flock reveals a preponderance in each group of powers of mind and spirit that we have come to associate with ambitious, talented, old-money families such as the Cabots, Lodges, and Lowells. Moreover, there existed a distinct, though not absolute, division of traits and talents that separated one branch of the Lowell family from the other. Whereas the Russell-Spence line distinguished itself in the ministry and the arts, the Cabot-Jacksons made their name in textiles and commerce, and the Higginson-Amorys in administrative, judiciary, and educational endeavors. The family as a whole left a trail of laudable achievements —philanthropic, commercial, and cultural—unequaled by their Brahmin brethren.

Among the clan's most robust and ambitious representatives was John Amory Lowell (1798–1881), son of the fiery Rebel. Attending the posh Boston Latin School, he enrolled at Harvard in 1811, at the customary family age of thirteen. Toward the end of his senior year he received a letter from his father which reveals something of their interaction:

> Let me, my son, now advert to a danger at the very thought of which I tremble because I consider it the greatest to which you are exposed. It is the most prolific source of all other failings and even vices. You will

already have anticipated that I allude to the habit of idleness. You have never been idle, and therefore can have no just conception of the degrading, powerful effects of this habit. But though you have not been idle, yet paradoxical as it may seem, you have not been studious. I have never been able to perceive in you till within the last three months, the smallest disposition to study for the sake of acquiring knowledge, or from a principle of duty.

The Rebel need not have fretted. His son, whose commencement thesis dealt with the ponderous subject of "Whether or Not Prosperity and Increase of Wealth Have a Favorable Influence upon the Manners and Morals of the People," combined all the best characteristics of Lowelldom—spirit, vigor, good common sense. In time he proved himself adept at all phases of family leadership. He was an influential businessman and banker, treasurer of four large cotton mills, cofounder of the mill town of Lawrence, Massachusetts, gas company president, officer of the Boston Athenaeum, fellow of the Harvard Corporation, vice-president of MIT, trustee of the Lowell Institute, father, son, brother (to four sisters), and spouse.

He was married twice. In 1822 he was betrothed to his first cousin, Susan Cabot Lowell, the daughter of Francis Cabot Lowell. In their son, John, a future Federal judge, "Lowell, Higginson, Amory, Cabot, and Jackson blood were all commingled to good effect." Two years after his first wife's death, in 1827, he married *her* cousin, Elizabeth Cabot Putnam, a cousin also of the Cabots; in 1830, she gave birth to their only son, Augustus, father in turn of five, Amy Lowell among them.

Another life crowded with activity was that of John Lowell, eldest son of Francis Cabot Lowell; born in 1799, he became involved in local politics and philanthropic causes, devoting himself to a succession of what he called "projects," which included purchases of storehouses of books for the Athenaeum, art collecting, farming ventures, and travel. There were those who accused him of possessing one rather dangerous proclivity: great wealth and an urge to do something useful with his money, accompanied by an unusually short attention span. His opportunity to put his capital to good use occurred in 1835, a year before his death. Attaching a codicil to his last will and testament, he set aside a figure approaching a quarter of a million dollars—eight million in today's currency—toward the establishment of a trust to be known as the Lowell Institute. The terms of this endowment were laid out by its architect in a document notable for its perspicacity:

As the prosperity of my native land, New England, which is sterile and unproductive, must depend hereafter, as it has heretofore depended, first, on the moral qualities, and secondly, on the intelligence and information of its inhabitants, I am desirous of trying to contribute towards this second object . . . and I wish courses of lectures to be established on physics and chemistry, with their application to the arts; also, on botany, zoology, geology, and mineralogy, connected with their particular utility to man.

This series of public lectures and symposiums, eventually supplemented by the establishment of courses of lectures on literature and history, promised to be an invigorating experiment, a way of promoting the advancement and diffusion of knowledge and understanding, and the appreciation of beauty, among the general populace. The success of the project, however, depended on much more than mere funding: an eager, receptive audience was needed and a team of distinguished speakers had to be found. Aware of this, John Lowell formulated certain farsighted stipulations for the program's organization, and these he also included in his will. He declared, first, that the Institute should be administered by a single trustee, preferably a kinsman in direct descent from the Old Judge, "provided there be one competent to hold the office and of the name of Lowell." A second bylaw maintained that each trustee must appoint his own successor within a week of his accession to office. The need for this kind of dogmatic one-man rule, as opposed to the committee-controlled Boston Lyceum—the second of the city's major public-lecture series—was dictated by the trustee's chief responsibility—the investment and supervision of the Institute's funds and the interest derived therefrom. Whatever profits the fund accrued were to be reinvested in the endowment or employed as remuneration for the Institute's lecturers. There was a further stipulation, a safety clause, which provided that in the unlikely event the single Lowell trustee should prove derelict in his duties, the burden of responsibility would be turned over to the trustees of the Boston Athenaeum, who were empowered to displace him and to nominate a three-man directorate in his stead.

John Amory Lowell, the executor of John Lowell's estate, was named the Institute's first administrator. His shrewd investments of endowment funds, coupled with the interest raised from short-term loans to local merchants, enabled the foundation to prosper. The Institute's auditors were treated to a series of courses delivered by the foremost authorities in their respective fields: Benjamin Silliman and Charles Lyell on geology, Thomas Nutthal and Asa Gray on botany, John Palfrey on evidences of Christianity, Jeffries Wyman on comparative anatomy, Jared Sparks on American history, O. M. Mitchell on astronomy, George Willard on Milton. Given the credentials of its lecturers, it is not surprising that the Institute, together with Harvard, soon emerged as the nucleus of Boston's intellectual community, a center whose sole purpose was the generation and communication of ideas.

Over the years speakers of high caliber helped maintain the foundation's image. A list of subsequent, twentieth-century expositors featured a whole new wave of generic "moderns"—McGeorge Bundy, Henry Cabot Lodge, Arthur M. Schlesinger—and "modernists" of a bardic sensibility—Robert Frost, Dylan Thomas, T. S. Eliot, E. E. Cummings, Archibald MacLeish. By the time these speakers stepped to the podium the Institute had expanded in still another direction. It now owned and operated its own public television and radio broadcasting station (WGBH), the first educational communications network in the country.

If the Institute had any serious drawback, it was its extreme conservatism and stodginess, especially in its administration of the public lecture series. Civil rights, women's rights, and the rights of labor were topics that were simply never given a public airing. Although a number of Lowells lectured there, Abbott Lawrence Lowell (who was to become its third trustee) would not permit his sister Amy to address an Institute audience, "because women were even then *streng verboten* as public figures." James Russell Lowell, on the other hand, who was more acceptable in the role of public spokesman, lectured before the Institute on a number of occasions; a speaker of imperturbable self-possession, he was the most popular of orators.

Just as popular a lecturer was Louis Agassiz, Neuchâtel Professor of Zoology and Geology, whose appearance before the Institute in 1846 created a furor among the highbrows of Boston. So advanced were the Swiss scientist's views that to keep him in Cambridge became the responsibility of anyone even remotely concerned with the future of the natural sciences in America.

Designated a member of the Harvard Corporation a year after the school's bicentennial celebration, John Amory Lowell convinced his fellow officers of the importance of this mission. Going a step further, he persuaded his affluent business affiliate and personal friend, the Honorable Abbott Lawrence, cofounder (with John Amory Lowell) of the town of Lawrence, to make an initial donation of $50,000 toward the establishment at Harvard of the Lawrence Scientific School. Agassiz was forthwith named professor of zoology and geology at the new school, and America had its first major boost in this relatively unclaimed domain.

Agassiz was to remain his entire life an opponent and critic of Darwin's controversial theory of evolution. Yet his strict attention to the job at hand and his gracious public demeanor and personality made him a beloved figure about Cambridge. In 1873, the year of the scientist's death, James Russell Lowell composed a tender ode in his honor, a glowing finis to a life of undiminished virtue:

> Nay, let himself stand undiminished by
> With those clear parts of him that will not die.
> Himself from out the recent dark I claim
> To hear and, if I flatter him, to blame;
> To show himself, as still I seem to see,
> A mortal, built upon the antique plan,
> Brimful of lusty blood as ever ran,
> And taking life as simply as a tree!

6

WAR AND PEACE

As EARLY as 1850 the ominous percussions of civil war could be heard rumbling in the not-far-off distance. A tidal wave of rivalries and conflagrations was drawing the country closer to that evidently irrepressible conflict. Chief among the struggles was the issue of chattel slavery and the national and sectional socioeconomic battles that it encapsulated. This was the age of the fanatical fire-eaters and runaway slaves, the abolitionists and the compromisers, the leaders of the ascendant Free-Soilers and the new Republicans, as well as the disintegration of the once-powerful Whig party of New England.

When the war came, as Alexis de Tocqueville and others predicted it must, the Lowells were immediately drawn into it. Their reaction to the crisis varied from brother to brother and cousin to cousin. Between the two male offspring of John Amory Lowell, for instance, there ran a clear line of personality cleavage. John Lowell (1824–1897)—"Judge John"—soft-spoken, gentle, and progressive, had come out in 1857, as editor of the *Law Journal,* with a vicious attack on the Dred Scott decision, the case of a Southern slave who was denied his liberty after having been transported into a free-soil state. Lowell's assault on the spoils of segregation played a decisive role in his appointment in 1865, by President Abraham Lincoln, to the position of federal district judge, a post he held until his death.

Augustus Lowell (1830–1900), a product of John Amory's second marriage, was more "a chip off the old block," sharing his father's libertarian views, and opposing his half-brother's radical outlook. A mercantile monarch who considered himself the last of the Union Whigs, Augustus was of that species easily swayed by big-business and social connections with the great planters of the Old South. He was an advocate of hard money and laissez-faire capitalism and favored the time-tested Federalist principles associated with strong, centralized government. To protect his banking and commercial interests—increased many times by his betrothal to the daughter of his father's prosperous business associate, Abbott Lawrence—he supported a policy of conciliation and appeasement, of trying to win the South over with alms rather than guns. That the dissolution came to pass, that the country descended into civil rebellion, was the result, he claimed, of a mob gone absolutely mad.

More important than either Augustus or Judge John's sentiments concerning the war were the lives of the three young Lowells lost in battle: William Putnam Lowell, James Jackson Lowell, and Charles Russell Lowell (anointed Beau Sabreur). The saga of their heroism became a notable part of the family legend. Of Beau Sabreur, James Russell Lowell remarked, "Charles Russell has long been the pride of the family . . . by far, the best we had."

Graduating first in his class at Harvard in 1854, Beau Sabreur worked for John Murray Forbes on the Michigan Central and Chicago, Burlington & Quincy railroads before enlisting and distinguishing himself in combat. The valor of his death at Cedar Creek, Virginia, in October 1864—leading a cavalry charge while mortally wounded—earned him the posthumous rank of brigadier general. It also earned him a place, together with his fallen kinsmen, in several poems by their poet uncle, notably in James Russell Lowell's dialect-strewn *Biglow Papers,* second series:

> Why, hain't I held 'em on my knee?
>   Did n't I love to see 'em growin',
> Three likely lads ez wal could be,
>   Hahnsome an' brave an' not tu knowin'?
> I set an' look into the blaze
>   Whose natur', jes' like theirn, keeps climbin',
> Ex long 'z it lives, in shinin' ways,
>   An' half despise myself for rhymin'.
>
> Wut's words to them whose faith an' truth
>   On War's red techstone rang true metal,
> Who ventered life an' love an' youth
>   For the gret prize o' death in battle?

To him who, deadly hurt, agen
  Flashed on afore the charge's thunder,
Tippin' with fire the bolt of men
  That rived the Rebel line asunder?

Shortly before his death, Beau Sabreur married Josephine Shaw, the daughter of a wealthy New York City merchant family. Her brother, Robert Gould Shaw, also a Civil War casualty, was killed while leading the 54th Massachusetts Volunteers, a regiment of free Northern blacks, in an attack on Fort Wagner, the outermost defense of the Charleston, South Carolina, harbor. Leaving Boston, marching down Boylston Street, Shaw and his black troops were seen off by William Lloyd Garrison, John Greenleaf Whittier, and Frederick Douglass, two of whose sons marched with the contingent. The actual battle, waged less than two months later, on July 18, 1863, resulted in the obliteration of a large portion of the Union company, approximately fifteen hundred men. By all accounts, Shaw and his troops fought gallantly, proceeding with their charge even when it became apparent that they were severely outnumbered. Because the rank and file of the regiment were black, the Confederate commander refused their chief officer the honorable burial to which his rank entitled him. His corpse was defiled and heaved into a common grave with the bodies of his troops. The massacre and subsequent mass burial of Shaw and his soldiers served the double purpose of reaffirming the selfless idealism of the Union cause, "while demonstrating for the first time in the war that Negroes would fight bravely if given the opportunity." In terms of its propaganda value, the rout became one of the decisive actions of the campaign; in artistic terms, it led to the creation of James Russell Lowell's "Memoriae Positum," a poem of private sorrow penned "to salve a personal wound, that of the versifier's own guilt over the disparities and inhumanities of war." For the dynastic-minded James, the annihilation of Shaw and his own valorous Lowell nephews represented a catastrophe of the first magnitude. A similar spirit permeates Robert Lowell's "For the Union Dead," a commemoration of Shaw's tragic death, written nearly a century later. Both meditations stress the commander's asceticism, self-discipline, and inner serenity.

The embers of war having at last been extinguished, other Lowells gradually emerged to fill the gap left by those of the clan who had perished in action. Fortunately, the war had not depleted the coffers of Lowell family wealth; if anything, the tribe's financial holdings had increased with the passage of time and increased further as industrialization accelerated in the period following the war. This considerable, though unostentatious, accumulation of riches served to illuminate a salient aspect of the family personality. Whereas the Lowells stood apart as true American aristocrats, the individual members of the clan, in keeping with their enduring image, seemed anxious to sink patrimony and excess profits into Boston's cultural and humanitarian treasure-trove. Although they wanted due recognition for their generosity, they were genuinely concerned with the maintenance and underwriting of Boston's fabled heritage.

Gore Vidal has repeatedly insisted that while the Founding Fathers mandated against hereditary titles, a number of families achieved the equivalent of "peers of our realm"; the Lowells, although neither society- nor money-mad, were among those whose names were just as awesome as titles. This was true of the later generations of the clan as well. Edward Jackson Lowell II (1845–1894), the grandson of Francis Cabot Lowell, in keeping with this image, showed barely a flicker of interest in the family business, preferring instead to live the life of landed and well-established gentry. Although he attended Harvard and even opened a law office with his friend, the historian Brooks Adams, he was not in the least disappointed when the office shut its doors. Abbott Lawrence Lowell, in a memoir for the Massachusetts Historical Society, claimed that Edward lacked the *gaudium certaminis* that makes arguing in court so intensely attractive to the born attorney. Eventually, Edward became an accomplished author of literary histories, among them books on the Revolutionary War and the French Revolution, and was for years a contributor of articles to *The New York Times,* having wed the daughter of one of its founders.

Edward's son, Guy Lowell (1870–1927), like his father, steered clear of the everyday family enterprises, studying design and architecture at the École des Beaux-Arts in Paris. Guy Lowell did not possess the innovative talents of a Richardson or Bulfinch, but family connections enabled him to establish a reputable name in his profession. Among his accomplishments was the neo-Georgian presidential mansion at Harvard, built in 1912 at the behest of President Abbott Lawrence Lowell. A codesigner of the Boston Fine Arts Museum, erected mainly on the basis of Lowell family financing, Guy Lowell was later responsible for the massive New York County Court House in downtown Manhattan, a $20 million, fifteen-year project, completed a week after the architect's death.

Another John Lowell (1856–1922), the son of Judge John, early attained a reputation as one of Boston's finest trial lawyers and as such was appointed chairman of the executive committee of the American Bar Association. He was highly respected among various of the clan for his virtuosity and quiet leadership. His home in Chestnut was a mecca for all Lowells, one of the popular meeting places where relatives frequently assembled. "Hospitable, comfortable, always homelike, always full of the children and grandchildren, nieces, nephews, relations, and hosts of others as well," was the way one cousin described it.

These large informal gatherings of the clan became part of the tradition. In general the Lowells were a closely knit family; they gravitated toward one another, conversing with the same zest and vehemence that was characteristic of their dealings with the outside world. From generation to generation, an extraordinary ebullience was apparent, as if self-confidence and freedom from money worry went hand in hand. Just as noticeable was the family's strange mixture of rare freedoms and Victorian stiffness. The combination of such incongruous traits not only separated the Lowells from their fellow Brahmins, but dominated and distinguished the work of the family's emblematic trio of poets.

7

MODERN TIMES

THE NEW directions initiated by men such as Edward Jackson Lowell II and Guy Lowell became the mainstay of the clan's current course. While scions of the Astor, Kellogg, Armour, and Woolworth families continued to make enormous fortunes in fur, grains, meat processing, and retail stores, the Lowells were investing and reinvesting in gilt-edged stocks and bonds, securing their own lives and the lives of their children. It relieved them of a financial burden and left them free to turn their attention to more idealistic affairs. Thus, at a time when many upper-class American dynasties were engaged in the blood and money tactics associated with mindless expansionism and profiteering, the Lowells (and several other Brahmin cliques) were busy becoming the autocrats of the plutocratic cosmos of literary, educational, and philanthropic advancement in New England, a sort of aristocracy within an aristocracy. If the Lowells tended to snub and stiff-arm their fellow rich, it was because they considered themselves to be of a higher and more dignified caste, a caste which looked down upon publicity, showiness, and greed. As opposed to their wealthy adversaries, Lowell family roots were solidly intertwined with those of Harvard, the Massachusetts Institute of Technology, the Museum of Fine Arts, the Boston Symphony Orchestra, the Boston Opera House, the Massachusetts General Hospital, as well as the Perkins Institute for the Blind, the Cotting Association, and the Peabody Society. What started out as a harmless avocation had developed into an important facet of the family philosophy. To be useful to the community, to contribute to the common good: that was what the Lowells knew best.

The idea behind this kind of philanthropy, explained Samuel Eliot Morison in a period history of Boston *(One Boy's Boston: 1887–1901),* was that when a family—that is, a *Boston* family—had accumulated a certain fortune, instead of trying to build it up still further, to become a Rockefeller or Ford or Carnegie or Guggenheim and then perhaps discharge its debt to society by some great endowment or foundation, it would step out of business or finance and try to accomplish something in literature, education, medical research, the arts, or public service. Generally, one or two members of the family continued in business, looking after the family securities, enabling the creative brothers and cousins to carry on the sacrosanct job of culture and public charity. In Boston this practice represented a way of life. "One has only," remarks Morison, "to think of the Prescott, Parkman, Cabot, Lodge, Forbes, Peabody, Eliot, Saltonstall, Sargent, and Lowell families, and what they have accomplished for the beauty and betterment of life, to see what I mean."

If these select, cultured leaders of the community were to set the prevailing standards of behavior and judgment, if they were to accept the responsibility for maintaining serious criteria of appreciation of learning and the arts in what was already a worldly and epicurean city, it was necessary for them to break away from that aristocracy of entrenched capitalists whose sole concern was the augmentation of their own powers and resources. And this, in the case of the Lowells, is precisely what occurred. As the present century dawned, family successors turned away with greater persistence than ever before from the outright accumulation of wealth, into fields more directly related to the attainment of knowledge and the dissemination of funds. The siblings of James Russell and Amy Lowell are a case in point.

Of James Russell Lowell's brothers and sisters, one (Charles Russell Lowell) was an administrator of the Boston Athenaeum; another (Mary Traill Spence Lowell) was a scholar and linguist. In his *Homes of American Authors,* C. F. Briggs writes (hyperbolically, one would hope): "Mary Lowell converses readily in French, German, Italian, Polish, Swedish, and Hungarian, and is familiar with twenty modern dialects, besides Greek, Latin, Hebrew, Persic, and Arabic." Born in 1810 and married in 1832 to Samuel Raymond Putnam, a Boston businessman, Mary is best remembered today for a volume published anonymously under the title *Records of an Obscure Man,* a portrayal of the black man's plight in America and his past achievements in Africa.

Robert Traill Spence Lowell (1816–1891), the poet's next oldest brother, was the first of the Old Judge's line to retreat completely from the Boston scene. As an Episcopal clergyman (the religion of his mother), R.T.S. Lowell served in churches as far away as Bermuda and Newfoundland. When not off in a distant land on some do-gooding adventure or fund-raising escapade, he occupied himself by churning out didactic narrative poetry that attempted to promote among children and adults the virtues of self-discipline and redemptive toil. His best known narrative, "The Relief of Lucknow," was about the defense of Fort Lucknow in India by Scottish soldiers during the Sikh wars. Included in his volume *Fresh Hearts that Failed Three Thousand Years Ago, and Other Poems* (1860), the poem also appeared in the *Atlantic Monthly,* under James Russell Lowell's editorship, earning for its author the present-day distinction of being rated the fourth Lowell "poet," although his work is perhaps best left to the occasional dusty shelves of rare book and manuscript collections. The minister did produce a rash of blandly humorous novels, one of which, *The New Priest at Conception Bay,* the tome's publisher brashly proclaimed "the best book ever written in the United States." Containing scenes of his life in Newfoundland, the volume features one character, Elnathan Bangs, who is "as racy a Yankee" as Hosea Biglow in his younger brother's *Biglow Papers.* After administering a parish in New Jersey, this father of seven (having married Marianna Duane of Duanesburg, New York) renounced the high pulpit to become the first headmaster of the St. Mark's School, Southboro, Massachusetts, before being called to fill the chair of Latin language and literature at Union College, Schenectady, New York. He remained in Schenectady until his death on September 12, 1891, just a month after the decease of James Russell Lowell. It should be noted that still another brother, William Keith Spence Lowell, born in 1813, was "first scholar" in the Boston Latin School when he died at age ten, a victim of consumption.

Amy Lowell's immediate family was of the same respectable stock. Her sisters, Katherine and Elizabeth, both older than she, were inveterate joiners. Condemned to the lifestyle of the idle rich, they found abundant opportunity to express themselves in voluntary work to help the indigent and sickly, serving on the boards of dozens of foundations, associations, and institutions, collecting and dispersing a steady flow of funds, engineering sundry philanthropic drives, in effect raising their own perspective and easing the plight of America's lower classes.

Their brother Percival (1855–1916), named for the first Lowell to set foot in America, early renounced a successful business career and traveled to Japan and Korea to study Oriental rites and rituals. While in the Far East he engaged in occasional diplomatic work as Foreign Secretary and General Counsellor to the Embassy sent from Korea to the United States, a position which enabled him to return periodically to his homeland. During these visits Lowell found time to work on a series of travel books, one of which—*Soul of the Far East* (1888)—inspired the scholar Lafcadio Hearn to visit Japan in 1890.

Repatriating to America after nearly a decade in the Orient, Lowell found himself excited by still another phenomenon. Giovanni Schiaparelli, an Italian astronomer, had recently announced the sighting of faint lines on the surface of the planet Mars, and his reports referred to them as *canali,* or "canals," which implied they were manmade. Lowell, long an astronomy buff, was fascinated by the possibilities suggested by Schiaparelli's findings. With generous funds supplied by his father he undertook the construction of an observatory atop a hill outside Flagstaff, Arizona; this was the beginning of the Lowell Observatory, one of the first in this country to be situated in a remote spot for clear visibility, and still a major astronomical institution today.

Spectrographic observations were begun at Flagstaff in 1894. Continuing the visual, photographic, and telescopic observations of earlier astronomers, with particular attention paid to the planet Mars, the star-gazer filled volumes with carefully calculated notations, which when published became known as the *Annals of the Lowell Observatory.* Included were notes and discussions concerning the existence and appearance of Schiaparelli's *canali.* What Lowell claimed he saw on Mars was, in his own words, "over a geography not unakin to the Earth's . . . a mesh of lines and dots like a lady's veil." This elaborate webbing of canals, "because of their extreme length, precision, and straightness," could only—Lowell surmised—have been created by a "highly advanced civilization" in order to irrigate Mars with melt from its polar caps, which is where the channels seemed to originate.

The argument sounded reasonably convincing and even inspired several authors, including H. G. Wells and Edgar Rice Burroughs, to create fictional Martian worlds mirroring our own. In 1938 a radio adaptation of the Wells classic, *The War of the Worlds,* panicked thousands of listeners who accepted the science-fiction drama of a Martian invasion as a news report. As widely accepted as Lowell's habitation theory became among the general public, it nevertheless met with furious opposition on the part of astronomers and scientists. One knowledgeable opponent was the Englishman Alfred Russell Wallace, the codiscoverer with Darwin of the theory of natural selection. Wallace maintained throughout that there was no evidence whatever to indicate that the channels Lowell claimed to see on the surface of Mars were anything but "non-natural" and that the possibilities of life existing on the "red planet" were at best slim.

Wallace was correct. The flight of Mariner 9 in 1971 showed that Mars is laced with scattered channels that give every indication of being dry riverbeds. They meander in sinuous curves. They often have tributaries. They get wider and deeper in the downslope direction. They have interlacing deposits along their floors, resembling the "braided" sediments in terrestrial dry riverbeds. In short, they have everything riverbeds are supposed to have—except water. Most important, they are not manmade but are the result of natural forces.

Although Lowell's exobiological speculations never materialized, he did make one invaluable extraterrestrial determination—namely, his revelation that our solar system was comprised of nine and not eight planets. This theory was confirmed by radio astrophysicists in 1930, nearly fifteen years after Lowell's death, with the discovery of Planet X, later named Pluto, the first two letters ("p" and "l") chosen for their namesake, Percival Lowell.

Amy's other brother, Abbott Lawrence Lowell (1856–1943)—"The President" to every Harvard-worshiping Brahmin—began his career as a State Street attorney in partnership with his cousin, Francis Cabot Lowell III. Stretching nepotism to the bursting point, he married his cousin-partner's sister, Anna Parker Lowell, before embarking on the text, *Governments and Parties of Continental Europe,* which earned him a part-time lectureship in science and government at Harvard. From the beginning, Lawrence and Anna settled into a comfortable, superficially companionable life together. He was aloof and imperious; she was a veritable slave to manners, morals, status, and class—intangibles which he helped provide her. They were nonetheless far from ideally suited and were forced to face a series of unpleasant confrontations that drove Lawrence more and more out of the house and into the sanctity of Boston's private men's clubs. In predictable Lowell manner, he managed to convey to the outside world a veneer of blissful domesticity.

Marital difficulties did not dampen his ambitions. In 1900, after the death of his father, Lawrence was named sole trustee of the Lowell Institute, bringing to the post the same titanic force of will he would later bring to the presidency of Harvard. Elevated the same year to the position of full professor of government, Lowell embarked on a personal campaign directed against President Charles Eliot and his educationally outmoded elective system. Eliot's resignation was tendered in 1908, after more than four decades of service; it provided Lowell with one of those "opportunities worth seizing." His suitability for the post had been enhanced by the 1907 publication of a second book, *The Government of England,* whose favorable reception in conjunction with his strong ties to the college, became decisive factors in Lowell's election, during January 1909, to Harvard's godliest office.

At once, Lowell set about to modify Eliot's controversial academic system. His belief, as expressed in his inaugural address, was that "the best type of liberal education should aim at producing men who know a little of everything and something well." With the overwhelming support of his faculty, he instituted a program that called for the distribution of credits between major and minor fields of study, with a general exam to be administered to all graduating seniors. Concurrent with these requirements was Lowell's adoption of a tutorial program based on a scheme used at Oxford, and a "House Plan" to replace the outdated convention of eating clubs.

Harvard's eating and living clubs represented a kind of rarified forerunner of the modern-day fraternity system, with prospective members chosen on the basis of wealth, affiliations, and background. The best known of these clubs—Porcellian, A.D., and Fly—were located in a section of Cambridge known as "The Gold Coast." For years these clubs were the backbone of social existence at Harvard. Students who were not members of a club, and preferably of one of the better clubs, were considered outcasts by those who did belong. Porcellian was the most prestigious club; it was very Bostonian, "yet very British and tweedy," modeled after the men's city clubs of London. The loftiest names in Boston's business and social swirl had been members: Owen Wister, T. R. Roosevelt (Teddy's father), John Jay Chapman, Oliver Wendell Holmes, Jr. (the "great dissenter"), along with numberless Cabots, Lodges, Adamses, Saltonstalls, and Lowells.

President Lowell's House Plan promised to expunge the "undemocratic" overtones of such a system and establish instead an ecumenical setting whereby students and tutors might live together in an environment conducive to the exchange of ideas, without anyone caring about the name of one's prep school or where one's family did its banking. With Lowell's encouragement a New York oil magnate, Edward S. Harkness, donated $12 million to Harvard (he later aided Yale with a similar amount) for the establishment of seven Georgian residence centers. Work on them was begun in 1930.

Lowell presided over the construction of these houses with almost maternal concern, hoisting his lordly and portly bulk, elegantly clad in British tailored suits, up into the various scaffoldings to examine the work of the masons. He made his rounds of the campus accompanied by a tiny brown spaniel that he controlled not by a leash but by holding his walking cane by the bottom and looping the crook of it around the unfortunate animal's neck.

Of the seven houses—Lowell, Eliot, Dunster, Adams, Kirkland, Leverett, and Winthrop—the first-named, with its blue-domed bell tower and Russian monastery bells, was the most ornate. Fittingly, a bust of the president was placed inside the courtyard of the complex. In addition to the completion of the House Plan, Lowell succeeded in doubling Harvard's student enrollment from four thousand to eight thousand, while increasing the school's endowment from $23.5 million to five times that figure. Under his administration the Law and Medical schools were expanded and the School of Business Administration was founded.

As an educator of standing, Lowell firmly believed in the ivy mantle of academic excellence that Harvard represented. He further believed that the cornerstone of academic superiority was freedom of thought and expression. So adamant was he in his support of the First Amendment that he was frequently forced to defend those whose convictions did not coincide with his own. During World War I, in spite of bitter opposition, he refused to dismiss from the faculty the German philosopher Dr. Hugo Munsterberg, whose vehement denunciation of the Allies alienated nearly everyone at Harvard. But just as stoutly he defended the rights of the British Socialist Dr. Harold Laski; Laski's radical ideals made him highly unpopular among the university's conservative alumni, who threatened to boycott the university and cut off contributions unless the good professor was dismissed. That he was allowed (and even encouraged) to stay was predominantly Lowell's doing.

Lowell's strong personality frequently embittered his opponents. Disliked in equal proportion by reactionaries as well as radicals, he

had resorted to the old trick of personal abuse of those who do not agree with them." To the charge that the defendants were persecuted for alien political beliefs, Lowell countered: "If they had been Yankees, they would have been executed long ago and would have had no sympathy." In summing up his position, he wrote: "I have long felt that a belief in the innocence of Sacco and Vanzetti would, like the belief that Bacon wrote Shakespeare, continue forever, wholly unaffected by evidence. Our final impression was that Vanzetti was the plotter and Sacco an executioner."

Convinced that the defendants were guilty and that justice had been served, Harvard's president returned to the arduous task of running the university. He had rather enjoyed the diversion; a Lowell dispatch to Judge Grant read: "To tell the truth, I did not find the work over the Sacco-Vanzetti case tiresome, but rather restful, perhaps it was so much of a change of occupation, and the companionship was delightful. We shall get more cuffs than kisses for our work, but it was done by citizens as an important public service, and was very much worth doing." Lowell's sense of duty was unrelieved by any sense of humor or feeling of sympathy for the two victims whose executions he had condoned and even endorsed.

He seemed to live his life by dividing it into pigeonholes, existing intensely in each, but not uniting the separate spaces. Thus, while despotic in the role of university administrator and public prosecutor, he could be a gracious and charming host, entertaining serried ranks of elderly and remote cousins, a substantial number of young Bundies, Cabots, and Ropeses, at the annual clan social each Christmas Eve. Cousin Lawrence was very much head of the clan on these formal and sumptuous occasions, polite, kind, always a bit distant as the party broke into groups by closeness of relation. He was just as much in his element entertaining the pick of the social elite, personages as powerful and portentous as J. P. Morgan, Charles Francis Adams, Governor Leverett Saltonstall, James Bryant Conant—his successor at Harvard—Senators Nelson W. Aldrich (father-in-law of John D. Rockefeller) and Henry Du Pont. Like these men and others of their select status, Lowell believed in and was motivated by an ethic of communal benefaction and social responsibility. There was a humanitarian streak in him that allowed the proud Yankee to respect the Brahmin tradition of philanthropy, if only in a somewhat condescending and jaded manner. Upon vacating his presidential seat in 1933, he made an anonymous donation—later made public—of more than $2 million to Harvard to help establish the Society of Fellows Foundation, which over the years provided free and undirected study for scores of young scholars of merit in a wide selection of fields.

The president's years of retirement were spent in colorful fashion, watching polo matches (both he and Percival had been avid polo players in their youth), joining big-game hunts in Africa, racing up and down the Cape in one of several touring automobiles he kept on hand for just such occasions (he was arrested more than once for speeding and several times had his license revoked). Equally embracing were his activities on behalf of a passel of philanthropic and charitable organizations, predominantly devoted to educational endeavors of one sort or another. During his retirement he remained a trustee of the Lowell Institute but nominated his cousin, Ralph Lowell, as cotrustee, with sole trusteeship devolving upon Ralph when Lawrence died in 1943. Thus the circle is pulled together with perfect tidiness, Ralph being the great-grandson of the first trustee, John Amory Lowell; the father of the present trustee, John Lowell; the senior member of the senior branch of this resilient, enterprising, prominent clan.

Ralph Lowell, whose bushy mustache and rotund, ruddy face called to mind William Howard Taft, proved himself a paterfamilias of robust order. Born in Boston's Chestnut Hill section in 1890, he studied anthropology at Harvard, graduating as a Phi Beta Kappa in 1912. In subsequent years he served the school in a variety of positions, including director of the alumni association, permanent treasurer of his class, and member of Harvard's policy-formulating Board of Overseers.

After college he became involved with State Street and with Boston gray flannel and pinstripe business associates, marrying the resolute but placid Charlotte Loring, a descendant of William Ellery, a signer of the Declaration of Independence. Lowell and his bride complemented one another insofar as both were avid lovers of the outdoors, easily energized by a multitude of activities, from sailing and horse racing to fox hunting and game fishing. They lived active social lives, partying almost exclusively with close friends and family. Before retiring to Sunrise Farm, Westwood, in the mid-1960's, Lowell directed and presided over a network of institutions and organizations, a fortress of supernal conglomerates, more than sixty-five in all, among them the Boston Safe Deposit and Trust Company, the Provident Institution for Savings, the Suffolk Savings Bank, John Hancock Associates, *The Boston Globe*, MIT,

Northeastern University, Massachusetts General Hospital, the Boston Museum of Fine Arts, and King's Chapel (of which he was treasurer for a number of years). Lowell wore the uniforms of many trades and professions: industrialist, financier, banker, sportsman, military officer, racehorse owner, dog breeder, art patron, television pioneer, donor of clinics and pavilions, benefactor of foundations on a gargantuan scale. His friends and business associates described him as a man of complex vision; he was thoughtful, hardworking, charming, and intellectual on the one side, capricious, rude, arbitrary on the other. He was further depicted as tough and wily, a board chairman who understood the inner workings of high finance and power politics. His most glaring feature, in contrast to the three emotionally effusive family poets, was his inability and unwillingness to show private feelings in the public eye, a trait that we have gradually come to associate with all those of his regal rank.

In the touch-and-go 1950's, when Boston's business community found itself on the brink of extinction, Ralph Lowell—envisioning for himself something like the role of the egregious Lord North—convened a board of a dozen leading financiers and hurriedly formed a coordinating committee, otherwise known as "The Vault" because its meetings were held sub rosa in the basement of one of Ralph Lowell's banks. In concordance with the Inventors of the nation, Lowell believed profoundly in the sacredness of property and the necessary dignity of those who owned it. That such hereditary nobility was in many respects undemocratic bothered him not in the least. The Vault, although severely protective of its own interests, devised a downtown renovation program and tax-base renewal plan that helped save Boston.

Ralph Lowell was a paradigm of the traditional and persevering Bostonian, a businessman-scholar whose energies extended everywhere at once. Through the Lowell Institute he formed the Broadcasting Council in the early 1950's, an amalgam of educational and cultural institutions that included Harvard, Boston University, the Boston Symphony Orchestra, and the New England Conservatory. WGBH-FM and WGBH-TV, the nation's first educational networks, eventually grew out of the Broadcasting Council. Since he was not involved in the arts directly, Ralph Lowell played the rewarding role of entrepreneur, ensuring that the arts received ample coverage and promotion on the air. His philosophy regarding such matters, as expressed shortly before his death in 1978, stipulated that "most of us are given a great deal, in one way or another, and I believe it is our duty and privilege to return that bounty to our fellow man in whatever way our talents direct us."

Upon the old man's retirement, the reins of family leadership were dutifully handed down to his eldest son, John. Along with the trust funds and directorships of a vast plot of enterprises, John Lowell inherited his father's baronial desk in the great oak-paneled, high-ceilinged State Street office that served as a central clearinghouse for the clan's multifarious financial and business ventures. A lover of the wheel-and-deal, the mean grandeur and farce of big business, young Lowell soon mastered the ins and outs, the complexities, of modern industry. From the beginning he was at ease with unbridled wealth and power, managing the family fortune with the cool efficiency and skilled assurance of a seasoned veteran, fitting into his surroundings with the equanimity of spirit that one has come to expect of the Lowells. The family seat of power could not have fallen into a more adept pair of hands.

John Lowell constitutes living proof that if the modern-day Brahmins no longer seem quite as staid and proper as they once were, they are still on the whole dedicated to hard work, education, culture, the noble pursuits of truth and happiness. With their venerable and valuable past history, the clan maintains its dispensation for profuse accomplishments and devotion to public, civic, and professional rites. No real key exists that explains their ongoing accumulation of laurels, their continued compulsion to succeed and flourish. Yet for a dynasty living in a shrinking backwater, a country in which high society is gradually diminishing, the present generation somehow manages to persevere. According to *Town & Country,* the Lowells remain the quintessential clubmen and clubwomen of the quintessential club town; they inhabit the Hub's oldest, most elegant combines: the Chilton, the Union, the Somerset, the Tavern, the Myopia Hunt Club, and Harvard's exclusive Institute of 1770. Each summer quantities of Lowells, together with throngs of Putnams and Bundies, flock to Cotuit on Cape Cod or to Nahant on the North Shore. At other times of the year they tend to live in clusters—in Boston, in Concord, in Manchester, in Westwood, where each Thanksgiving for years the various of the clique gathered at an annual turkey roast and codfish broil, in honor of the saltwater scavenger that for so long remained a staple of the early New England diet, a dependable source of income for many of the original colonists, including the Lowells.

Ralph Lowell, Jr., John's younger brother, vice-president of the institutional division of Merrill Lynch, Pierce, Fenner & Smith, describes the Westwood contingent as a "suburban republic": "There are five houses all in a row, plus one around the corner, and they're all *us.* My youngest brother, Jimmy, lives in the Loring house where my mother was brought up. I live in another house that I bought from the Loring estate. My sisters Lucy [Grimm] and Susan [Wales] live in houses they bought from our great-aunt, Mrs. Richmond Fearing. And Cousin Em [Mary Emlen Wheeler] lives just around the corner." The sixth house belongs to the widow of Ralph Lowell.

Emulating their forebears, the current Lowells maintain a low profile; despite their super-wealth and renown, no Lowell heir has found it necessary to hire a public relations firm to keep the family name in or out of the news. Publicity offends the Lowells in the same way that public scandal embarrasses the British. But times have wreaked considerable change, even among a supranational caste linked by intermarriages and common goals. The politics of contemporary finance demand that today's rich invest not only in mutual funds and blue-chip Wall Street portfolios but in the scathing markets associated with expansionism and wildcat real estate: housing projects, shopping centers, skyscrapers, arcades, plazas, malls, athletic complexes, movie theaters, and outdoor parking emporiums. The strange thing about the assorted members of the House of Lowell is that money itself is secondary to them. The family as a whole is worth many millions of dollars, though money itself is hardly a subject of conversation at family reunions. As one powerful tribal dowager recently explained it: "Money has been there so long that it's just there." Conspicuous wealth and leisure may satisfy the material cravings of some families of means, but what energizes the Lowells is the clan's past, its heritage and genealogy—more than three centuries and some thirteen generations of American family roots. It is against this backdrop of tradition and individual talent—the emergence from aristocratic origins, the acquisition of knowledge and rank—that the lives and times of James Russell, Amy, and Robert Lowell have developed and evolved.

JAMES RUSSELL LOWELL

The Natural Aristocrat

1819–1891

PART
II

JAMES RUSSELL LOWELL

8

YOUTH AND POETRY

ONE could approach the Village, as it was called in 1819, by a ride of a few miles, mostly westward from Boston. Founded in 1632 by Governor John Winthrop as a self-governing town, Cambridge was settled now on the banks of the Charles, a stable community of five thousand well-rested souls. Traveling the rising countryside by way of the New Road, one might pause on the brow of Symond's Hill to take in the distant view. In the foreground stretched the town itself, tufted with the foliage of elms, lindens, and horse chestnuts, above which rose the noisy belfry of the landmark college, the square brown tower of the church, the thin yellow spire of the parish meetinghouse. To the left on the Old Road stood some half-dozen dignified houses of colonial vintage, all comfortably fronting southward. On the right, the broad and serpentine river glided through green and purple salt meadows, darkened at intervals with blossoming black grass. Beyond the marshes that surrounded it, low hills defined a gray horizon.

Such was the panoramic landscape James Russell Lowell contemplated as a young boy. An eighth-generation Lowell, he was born on George Washington's birthday, February 22, 1819 (the same year as Whitman, Melville, Queen Victoria, George Eliot, and poet, essayist, and abolitionist Julia Ward Howe), at the family manse of Elmwood, the youngest of a household of six children, three brothers and two sisters. Elmwood, a mile and a half southwest of Harvard, with its lawns, gardens, orchards, pastures, trees—especially the stately English elm—was the last of a series of country estates. The others were southward-facing houses that extended for a mile along the Old Road from Cambridge toward Watertown: the Brattle House, the Vassall House, the Craigie House, the Lechmere House, the Judge Joseph Lee House, the Fayerweather House, and Elmwood. British Tories had modeled each of these dwellings after the square-form English brick manor houses of the Georgian period. Lowell valued the estate not just for what it meant to him while he lived there, but also for its historic associations. Demonstrating his affection for it he once wrote to a friend: "I have but one home in America, and that is the house where I was born, and where, if it shall please God, I hope to die. I shouldn't be happy anywhere else."

As a small child Lowell was brought up in a low-studded room on the third floor of the house, a room he later modestly called "the garret." From this "high quoin of vantage," he could see the Charles, "a stripe of nether sky"—

> I can see one long curve of the Charles, and the wide fields between me and Cambridge, and the flat marshes beyond the river, smooth and silent with glittering snow.

In this room, at night, he was read to sleep, sometimes by his mother but just as often by his sister Mary. His favorites were Spenser's *Faerie Queene* and the novels of Walter Scott, natural choices for the day and age. Of the other children in the family he was closest to his brother Robert, three years his senior, who at age eighteen left Boston to pursue a career in the ministry. Then, and throughout their lives, the two brothers maintained an active correspondence, writing affectionate letters in mock verse.

"Jemmie's" first school, entered when he was four, was owned by a Miss Mary Dana, recalled in the introduction to *The Biglow Papers,* first series, as the "Daughter of Danaüs," a reference to the capricious mythological ruler of Argos. Lowell's distaste for Miss Dana no doubt arose because he was sent to her school "under cover of a broad-brimmed white hat with a gold tassel suspended from it by a blue ribbon." He soundly despised the hat. One day, while returning home from school, he paused by a brook and threw it in.

The next school he attended was kept by another Miss Dana, Miss Sophia Willard Dana, the granddaughter of President Samuel Willard of Harvard and the wife of George Ripley, founder of Brook Farm. All the students here were girls, with the exception of James and one other boy. At age eight both were transferred to the Brattle Street school of Mr. William Wells, an English schoolmaster of strict military manner who taught with a book in one hand and a rattan in the other. In preparation for Harvard, the Wells curriculum consisted of Greek, Latin, and mathematics, with a smattering of religion tossed in for good measure.

Lowell enrolled at Harvard in 1834, at age fifteen, continuing his studies in the three major disciplines but supplementing these with wide and rather casual readings from his father's well-stocked and well-rounded library: Edward Young, William Paley, Samuel Butler, Francis Bacon, Gilbert White, Shakespeare, Landor, Dodsley, Cotton, and Hakluyt. Later he favored authors who exercised a more direct cast over his own literary endeavors: Carlyle, Southey, Coleridge, Shelley, Byron, Bunyan, Pope, Horace, and Tennyson. Even in adolescence Lowell had a passion for words, the more syllables the better, and often astounded his aunts and uncles by talking like a professor of classic philosophy. At Harvard the only course that held his attention was Rhetoric: it required no memorization and little homework, concentrating instead on the preparation and presentation of public speeches, with supplementary work in composition. The course was taught by Edward Channing, younger brother of the abolitionist William Ellery Channing.

Charles Eliot Norton, editor of Lowell's collected correspondence, sketches him at Harvard as a modestly shy youth, of genial disposition, of high spirits, of undeveloped but very definite tastes. Despite his shyness, he was popular among classmates and made friends with several of them, especially with one who afterwards rose to distinction in political circles, George Bailey Loring. It was through Loring that Lowell was elected to the Hasty Pudding Club, the bohemian version of the socially august Porcellian and Fly clubs. By hereditary right, the Lowells had always joined the aristocratic clubs of Harvard. James Russell Lowell, in the true spirit of youthful rebellion, became the first of the family to join Hasty Pudding, known for its all-male theatrical reviews and boisterous drinking parties.

During his senior year he became an editor of *Harvardiana*, the college literary magazine, contributing poems and essays to the semi-annual, enjoying this aspect of his education far more than the deadening routine of classroom studies. He attributed his lack of motivation in school to an overabundance of "animal spirits"—too much curiosity and a "healthy" refusal to confine same. Others attributed his capriciousness to his mother's erratic temperament, a condition related to Harriet Spence Lowell's background—the combination of her "wild Celtic blood" and her milder Orkney Island heritage. The union of two such opposing temperaments, contends Ferris Greenslet, caused "a certain mystical dreaminess that sometimes obscured the need for immediate action in the small, imperative affairs of daily living." In family privacy this seeming defect was graced with a genteel euphemism; it was called "the Spence negligence" and over the years became something of a family joke.

Whatever the real reasons for James Russell Lowell's deportment, it caused concern on his family's part. In May 1837 the boy's father, Reverend Charles Lowell, about to sail with Mrs. Lowell for a stay of several years abroad, decided that he might do something to encourage his son. "You know the necessity for economy," he wrote, informing James of the half-dollar a week he was to receive as an allowance during their absence, "and you know that I shall never deny you, but from necessity, what will afford you pleasure." But, "regardless of necessity," he pledged that the allowance would be raised to seventy-five cents the moment his son became a member of Phi Beta Kappa and to a dollar should he be one of the first eight admitted. To this he appended further stipulations and rewards: "If you graduate one of the first five in your class, I shall give you $100 on your graduation. If one of the first ten, $75. If one of the first twelve, $50. If the first or second scholar, two hundred dollars. If you do not miss any exercises unexcused, you shall have Bryant's *Mythology* or any book of equal value, unless it is one I may specially want."

The student, however, was influenced neither by want of money nor desire for Bryant's *Mythology*. His neglect of academic assignments and his frequent, unexcused absences from recitations and chapel exercises did not abate. He was so indifferent to classes that not even the newest faculty member, Professor Henry Wadsworth Longfellow, could attract him to a course of lectures on classical European literature. The inevitable outcome of all this was that on June 25, 1838, a week before the end of his final semester, the faculty of the college

voted, That Lowell, Senior, on account of continued negligence in college duties be suspended till the Saturday before Commencement, to

pursue his studies with the Revd. Mr. Frost of Concord . . . and not to visit
Cambridge during the period of his suspension.

He was not the first Lowell to be suspended from Harvard. Francis
Cabot Lowell and John Amory Lowell were both rusticated for similar
offenses, although neither had been banished to Concord, considered
by many Bostonians to be nothing short of purgatory. There was an
added hardship. Young Lowell had been elected Class Poet, but the
prohibition against a return to Cambridge would prevent him from
carrying out his duties at the Class Day celebration scheduled for mid-
July. His classmates held a mass rally in protest, but Lowell had already
departed for Concord, "damning everyone" and vowing that "he would
neither smoke nor shave" so long as he remained "in the wilds."

In the end, Lowell's banishment was no more than a mild bore to him.
The Reverend Barzillai Frost, recently graduated from Harvard Divinity School, was only a few years older than his charge. His main shortcoming, according to Lowell, was a sincere and persistent addiction to
Locke, a philosopher quite out of step with the young intellectuals of
the day. Concord was also the home of Ralph Waldo Emerson. Emerson
was not exceedingly popular in those days, especially not with select
members of the older crowd—men such as Andrews Norton, whose
old-fashioned political and literary views left little room for the advanced thinking of Transcendentalism. Emerson's speech that year
before the Harvard Divinity School was considered the height of unor-
thodoxy; Harvard did not invite him to return for the next thirty years.

Emerson, while still a student at Harvard, had been subjected to the
same disciplinary action as Lowell and like Lowell was elected Class
Poet. It seemed reasonable, therefore, that the two should meet. The
older man, with his natural friendliness toward the young, took kindly
to Lowell, recognizing in the student's appearance and conversation
the first seeds of promise. Lowell was more cautious; he felt well disposed toward Emerson personally, but was wary of his philosophy. He
wrote to friends, "Emerson is a good-natured man in spite of his doctrines."

During his enforced exile Lowell also had occasion to meet Henry
Thoreau, whom he liked less. He first mentions Thoreau in one of his
letters: "I met Thoreau last night, and it is exquisitely amusing to see
how he imitates Emerson's tone and manner. With my eyes shut, I

shouldn't know them apart." He sensed Thoreau's bitterness, his distrust of Brahmin civilization and everything that Lowell stood for or came from. Then, too, he was in direct competition with Thoreau, who was only a few years his senior, whereas Emerson represented a father figure to both. Nor did Lowell's negative impression of Thoreau change over the years; if anything, it grew worse.

The *Class Poem,* which he had been selected to write, was begun and completed at Concord. It included the dedication "To the Class of '38. By their Ostracized Poet, (so called) J. R. L." and was printed as a broadside, evidently for distribution to members of the class and their friends, since its creator was not allowed to read it. It was a lengthy poem, thirty pages, full of biting lampoons and burlesques. In one fell swoop the poet tackles an entire regiment, including Kant, Carlyle, Emerson, the abolitionists, the advocates of women's rights, and the fiercely maligned teetotallers. For the most part the Tory-inspired satire strides along glibly in decasyllabic meter, pausing now and again to savor a deliberate, well-turned phrase; but in general it is too obvious, too filled with bathetic barbs and japes, to be as effective as it otherwise might have been. What is perhaps most interesting about it is that it reflects a point of view radically different from Lowell's future leanings. His own poetic commentary on the sequence, years after the fact, appeared in a letter to John W. Field (December 1885):

> Behold the baby arrows of that wit
>   Wherewith I dared assail the woundless Truth!
> Love hath refilled the quiver and with it
>   The man shall win atonement for the youth.

It was with considerable reluctance that Lowell, following his graduation from college in the summer of 1838, entered the Dane School of Law at Harvard. A fondness for preaching was in his blood, yet his father's and brother's profession was closed to him because he lacked the necessary conviction in the formal rituals of the church to devote himself to the pulpit. Lowell had a religious passion then rare among cultivated New Englanders but was convinced, perhaps through the lapsed Unitarianism of Emerson, that Christianity had become a mere social rite. Nor did he possess the right temperament for such a calling. He was too impatiently impetuous and quick-tempered to make a commitment of this sort. And literature, "toward which all his inclinations tended," also presented a number of practical difficulties; among other considerations, he was too aware of the impossibility of earning his livelihood by wont of the written word.

Lowell began the study of law that autumn and in spite of his vacillation over its continuance, graduated from the Harvard Law School in 1840, quite a few years after his father's withdrawal from the same program. His correspondence during this period was dampened by uncertainty and doubt. To his friend George Loring, he wrote (June 4, 1839): ". . . I begin to like the law. And therefore it is quite interesting. I am determined that I *will* like it and therefore I *do.* " Six weeks later he again confided in Loring: ". . . I don't believe I shall ever *(between you and me)* practice law. I intend, however, to study it and prepare myself for practising. But a blind presentiment of becoming independent in some other way is always hovering around me."

Rather than believe any success might lie ahead as a writer, Lowell submitted to the need for an orthodox career and decided to muddle his way through. At times he enjoyed the study of law. Cases were short stories, dramatic presentations. Law was language. Judges, brief writers, the mighty professors could be great authors, after all. The Constitution was perhaps the best book an American (or Americans) had ever devised. Although he toyed with the notion of setting out in another field, the reality of the situation kept him chained to the rock. An unhappy youthful love affair with Hannah Jackson, the younger, very enticing sister of Anna Cabot Jackson (wife of Lowell's brother Charles) contributed to his unsettled state of mind. The schism that occurred when she became engaged to Samuel Cabot left Lowell feeling "like a bruised seed." In 1866 he recalled these dour days: "I remember in '39 putting a cocked pistol to my forehead—and being afraid to pull the trigger." Suicide seemed an unlikely alternative for someone with so healthy a taste for melodrama and such a vibrant sense of humor.

Then, early in December 1839, his future began to take shape. He had made the acquaintance of Maria White, the gifted and pleasantly attractive sister of a Harvard classmate; her family lived in Watertown, immediately adjoining Cambridge. "She knows," he wrote, "more about poetry than anyone I am acquainted with. I mean she is able to repeat more. She is more familiar, however, with modern poets than with the pure well-springs of English poetry." The wooing proceeded at once and for the next eight months ran its exuberant course. The couple became officially engaged in August 1840, just as

Lowell was completing his degree in law. She was nineteen, he twenty-one.

They made a handsome couple. Maria, by witness of the portraits preserved of her, was a girl of charming pale blond beauty, with deep blue eyes, delicate features, and a sensitive, extremely expressive face; James is described at that time as slight of stature, with rosy cheeks and starry eyes, his light brown hair wavy and parted down the middle. Lowell's prospects for self-support were such, however, that they were forced to defer their marriage for nearly five years. In the course of these years he made a halfhearted effort to get his law career underway, entering the law offices of his distant cousin Charles Greely Loring, even taking a room in town to be closer to work. Maria, meanwhile, counting herself among Boston's intellectually curious and eman- cipated women, joined a group chaired by Margaret Fuller, which met weekly at Elizabeth Peabody's rooms on West Street, to discuss the controversial topics of the day—everything from art, politics, and po- etry, to ethics, religion, and philosophy. The circle numbered among its participants Mrs. George Bancroft, Mrs. Lydia Maria Child, Mrs. Ralph Waldo Emerson, Mrs. Horace Mann, Mrs. Theodore Parker, Mrs. Wen- dell Phillips, Mrs. George Ripley, Mrs. Nathaniel Hawthorne, Maria White, and Elizabeth Peabody, who was Hawthorne's sister-in-law and the purported model for Henry James's Miss Birdseye, that untiring clubwoman from *The Bostonians.*

Another group to which Maria belonged, and into which she intro- duced James, called itself The Band, or The Band of Brothers and Sisters. During their senior year at Harvard, four friends had been drawn together by common interests, mainly in the assorted pre-Civil War movements designated to achieve perfection by abolishing, vari- ously: war, private property, slavery, the family, inequality of the sexes, and also strong drink, tobacco, meat, tea, coffee, and spices. The group was full of faith in various prescriptions guaranteed to exorcise all the ills that sociopolitical flesh was heir to—instantly, totally, painlessly. The quartet—William White, John Gallison King, Nathan Hale, Jr., and Wil- liam Wetmore Story (the future sculptor, poet, and playwright, now best remembered as the subject of a Henry James biography)—were fortunate in having sisters their own age, young, enlightened, well-read women who shared their political ideals and liberal standards. At first the members of this group resisted Lowell's presence; they could not forget the Brahmin's infamous *Class Poem,* which had ridiculed all the general reform groups supported by The Band, including the Transcendentalists and abolitionists.

What The Band did not and could not know was that in the years following his graduation from Harvard, Lowell on his own had become increasingly sympathetic toward certain aspects of the humanitarian movement. His daybook for 1838–1839, even before he met Maria White, was crammed with passages on slavery. As early as November 1838 he wrote to George Loring, "I am fast becoming ultra-democratic," and proceeded to discourse on the industrial riots at Manchester: "It almost brings tears to my eyes when I think of this vast multitude starved, trampled upon, meeting to petition the government which oppressed them, and which they supported by taxes wrung out of the very children's life blood." The same brief alludes to the abolitionists: "The abolitionists are the only ones with whom I sympathize of the present extant parties."

Lowell's impending support of the quixotic reform movement was not simply the sudden gesture of an inflamed rebel; it had its base in his past—in the tradition fostered by his grandfather, the Old Judge, a devoted Federalist but at the same time a sincere abolitionist, whose "free and equal" clause in the Massachusetts Bill of Rights helped emancipate Northern blacks. It should also be kept in mind that the Russell-Spences were not the wealthiest branch of the family tree. Elmwood was four or five miles from Boston Common, where the cousins of the clan resided in what can only be described as sinful splendor; life at the Cambridge manor was always somewhat apart from the family center and infinitely less lavish. Nor was his father's church the seat of some cushy pastorate; it was a slum parish populated predominantly by the poor. Like his grandfather in Newburyport, the Reverend was an idealist, a man never very deeply concerned with either church dogma or the politics of religion. An idealist in the old American grain, he believed in social progress and social equality, and used the pulpit to alleviate the injustices he saw about him at every level and at every turn. He preached Grace through Good Works, forming alliances with those who achieved them, regardless of their class or background.

His son was thus a prime candidate for the reformation movement, of which Maria White had been an avid supporter for much of her young life. James and Maria both agreed there was need, as Emerson had once put it, for "a general inquest into abuses" in every aspect of daily experience—church, state, domestic affairs, coined money, religion, the law, commerce, education, even agriculture. Maria paid special attention to two of the major reforms—the temperance crusade and the abolition movement, but was particularly vehement about the second. She accepted and shared the views of the extreme faction of this movement, comprised of the likes of Maria Weston Chapman and Anne Phillips. Lowell at first could not muster quite the enthusiasm of these devotees, but under Maria's influence and The Band's coercion was drawn faster and deeper into the pitch.

Because his law practice was attracting few new clients, he spent more time in the movement and even had time left over to devote to literature. His letters were filled with references to Keats, whom he now considered "one of the old Titan brood." There was mild talk of the possibility of a multivolume biography of Keats. He additionally considered the feasibility of writing an "American tragedy" on the trial of Anne Hutchinson, who was condemned for heresy and in 1637 banished from Boston; later she was tried before the Boston church and formally excommunicated. Neither project, however, materialized until another member of the family, Amy Lowell, produced her two-volume Keats biography in 1925.

Tossing caution to the winds, James began contributing semiautobiographical poems to the *Southern Literary Messenger,* an ambitious but impecunious journal, using as his pen name Hugh Perceval, in honor of his long-deceased ancestor. In 1841, having gained the support of a Boston publisher (Little, Brown), he gathered together these early efforts—including several poems published in the *Knickerbocker Magazine*—into a single volume, titled *A Year's Life.* The volume contained thirty-two longer poems and thirty-five sonnets, besides an envoi headed "Goe, Little Booke," and a dedication addressed, though not formally, to his future bride:

> The gentle Una I have loved,
> The snowy maiden, pure and mild,
> Since ever by her side I roved
> Through ventures strange, a wondering child,
> In fantasy a Red Cross Knight
> Burning for her dear sake to fight.

If there be one who can, like her,
Make sunshine in life's shady places,
One in whose holy bosom stir
As many gentle household graces,
And such I think there needs must be,
Will she accept this book from me?

Only a few hundred copies of the "Little Booke" were sold, the verse mingling vague emotionalism with overt bookishness, resulting in a kind of sentimental fog respresentative of the youthful efforts of Tennyson, Keats, and Shelley. The book, though not a commercial success, showed its author to be a man of literary promise. One poem, "Irene," written for Maria White ("Hers is a spirit deep, and crystal-clear; / Calmly beneath her earnest face it lies") is conspicuous for its felicity of phrase—it shines above the rest. But even Lowell attached little value to the volume's contents or to its reception; on gathering material for his first volume of selected poems in 1849, he retained a mere handful of those printed in *A Year's Life,* silently dropping the rest.

Having discovered a small but active clique of editors and publications sympathetic to his work, Lowell had stepped up his pace. Samples of his prose and poetry appeared at regular intervals in *Graham's Magazine,* the *Democratic Review, Arcturus, The Dial,* and the *Boston Miscellany.* Lowell's prose contributions to the first three were of a light and airy nature, laced with journalistic good humor, dealing primarily with subjects as jocular as songwriting, grooming, popular entertainment, food and spirits. Of greater substance were the scholarly essays he scribed for *The Dial* and *Miscellany* on the Elizabethan dramatists—Chapman, Webster, Ford, and Massinger—a series well received by the critics, even by one so testy and rambunctious as Edgar Allan Poe.

Toward the end of 1842, convinced he could never succeed at the bar, Lowell decided once and for all to abandon the profession. His decision to turn full time to writing was predicated on the theory that no matter how badly he wrote, he would do anything else even worse, and that the only way he would ever be something other than a preacher's son was to do what pleased him most. He announced his intention in a note to a friend: "I cannot write well here in this cramped up lawyer's office, feeling all the time that I am giving the lie to my destiny and wasting time which might be gaining me the love of thousands." Having renounced his private practice and proclaimed his desire to write, he prepared now to fulfill another ambition, the publication of his own little magazine. He took as an operating model *The Dial,* that startling review with the bold lilac covers, the organ of the West Street circle of Miss Peabody's rooms; Margaret Fuller was its editor. Lowell was impressed with the journal's commitment to the movement; it had taken a giant step forward along the road to literary emancipation and rapid political reform.

Besides Fuller and her followers, its chief contributors were Emerson, Thoreau, Bronson Alcott, Theodore Parker, Hawthorne, and the eminent music critic John Sullivan Dwight. It was Lowell's intention to produce a periodical that would prove an artistic as well as a commercial success, as opposed to *The Dial,* whose circulation had always been low.

He named his magazine *The Pioneer* and took as a publishing partner Robert Carter, a native of upstate New York. Carter, with practical newspaper experience, would handle the business end of the publication, with Lowell controlling its editorial policies. The two issued a prospectus outlining *The Pioneer*'s future plans:

> The object . . . is to furnish the intelligent and reflecting portion of the Reading Public with a rational substitute for the enormous quantity of thrice-diluted trash, in the shape of namby-pamby love tales and sketches, which is monthly poured out to them by many of our popular Magazines—and to offer, instead thereof, a healthy and manly Periodical of Literature, whose perusal will not necessarily involve a loss of time and deterioration of every moral and intellectual faculty.

Lowell and Carter labored assiduously to launch their new monthly, soliciting writings from the foremost litterateurs, both American and British. Longfellow and Whittier were asked for poems, Hawthorne for short fiction, John Dwight for musical criticism, and Emerson for "anything." They contacted Elizabeth Barrett Browning in London and invited her to submit all the poems she could spare. They wanted to include work by Tennyson but were unable to locate him; Poe volunteered to become a regular contributor and for the first issue supplied them with his story, "The Tell-Tale Heart"; he eventually sent along his poem, "Lenore," and an essay, "Notes on English Verse."

The Pioneer's first number appeared in January 1843 and contained, along with Poe's tale, contributions from Jones Very, Elizabeth Barrett

Browning, John O'Sullivan, John Dwight, T. W. Parsons, John Neal, and others. The magazine paid its contributors ten dollars for prose and five dollars for poetry and pledged to increase these figures once its circulation rose. Lowell's lead editorial for the inaugural issue set the periodical's tone: "Everything that tends to encourage the sentiment of caste, to widen the boundary between races, and put further off the hope of one great brotherhood, should be steadily resisted by all good men."

Within a week of *The Pioneer*'s maiden appearance, Lowell developed a mysterious ailment of the eyes. How much his impaired vision was the result of psychological duress is hard to say. His withdrawal from the bar and his participation in the abolitionist movement probably added to the strain. Members of the clan, excluding his immediate family, began to think of him as the tribal outcast, the black sheep, an assessment which no doubt disturbed the insecure young rebel. At Elmwood other events were taking place which may also have contributed to his condition. Harriet Lowell, the author's mother, showed signs of mental debilitation, an illness that gradually reduced her to a speechless remnant of her former self and that her son described in the poem "The Darkened Mind": "The wide chasm of reason is between us; / Thou confutest kindness with a moan; / We can speak to thee, and thou canst answer, / Like two prisoners through a wall of stone . . ." The nature of the disorder, besides being psychological, was never fully determined, although its effect was to destroy any semblance of domestic life at Elmwood. In addition to his mother's disorientation, James watched powerlessly as his oldest sister, Rebecca, showed some of the same crippling symptoms. Shades of Spence negligence: a brother, Charles Russell Lowell, later a cataloguer with the Boston Athenaeum, demonstrated his own patterns of eccentric behavior. After a promising beginning as a State Street merchant, he lost the bulk of his assets in the economic panic of 1837, as well as a substantial share of his father's, which had been entrusted to him while the elders were living abroad. Actual misconduct, the result of "moral delinquency" on Charles Russell Lowell's part, seems to have been the cause; it was suggested that Charles had been involved in a plot to defraud his father and that Harriet Lowell's insanity was subsequently brought about by the "disgrace" caused by her son's actions.

Eager for any excuse to leave home, the high-strung young poet placed himself under the care of the eminent physician Dr. Samuel Mackenzie Elliot, whose sanatorium on Staten Island, New York, catered to some of Boston's leading literary and academic celebrities, among them Longfellow, Agassiz, Francis Parkman, and William Emerson (the brother of Ralph Waldo). Elliot's popularity was related to his alleged practice of prescribing opium, cocaine, and other hallucinogens for any and all ailments regardless of their origin. We can safely presume that Lowell underwent the standard cure.

Conceivably Lowell's illness served him conveniently as a means of conveyance to New York, where he surely expected to enjoy himself. While there he became friendly with an assemblage of writers known as Young America, whose primary concern was the advocation of a new national literature, one that rebelled against the romantic slush—the colored fashion plates, sheet music, sentimental swill—that dominated such commercial magazines as *Gleason's Pictorial Fireside Companion* and *Godey's Lady Book*. The leaders of Young America were Evert Duyckinck, Cornelius Mathews, and Parke Godwin; through Duyckinck, Lowell met the editor and critic Charles F. Briggs; he also renewed his acquaintance with the portrait painter William Page, whom he had known briefly in Boston. Lowell saw eye-to-eye with the members and friends of Young America, particularly with regard to the necessity of fomenting a literary upheaval that would rock the Establishment down to its bare roots. Poets, they observed, were the seers of the race, the soothsayers of society; in Shelley's phrase, they were "the unacknowledged legislators of the world." They had a redemptive and social as well as aesthetic function. They possessed insight into the "moral nature" of man and were able to communicate the essence of man's nature to the nonseers.

Surrounded by New York's bohemian art crowd, Lowell shared in their caustic arguments about literature, life, and sex, occasionally partaking of their all-night drinking bouts and morning-after sexual forays. Boston's intellectual crowd was subdued in comparison to New York's. With The Band, Lowell attended elegantly refined dinner parties, conversed in French and Italian, and heard informal concerts of chamber music performed by other members of the local intelligentsia. Lowell's life in New York was a less tame experience sustained by literary readings and cultural gatherings, with a lot of running here and there, suddenly absorbed in big-city culture. Although he preferred aspects of New York's undisciplined lifestyle, he felt out of place amid this unruly sea of bawdiness. As he saw it, there was nothing in the city "to match the New England character, or to compare in general enlightenment" to the ennobling life-force that one found in Boston. In letters home Lowell described New York as a large metropolis with "an accumulation of vice and witchcraft—thousands of loathsome dens where aristocratic charity is afraid to enter lest she should soil the purity of her white raiment." In Boston, religious and charitable organizations cared for the indigent, whereas in New York, the poor went hungry. From Lowell's vantage point, Boston was still the hub of the universe.

In the course of the poet's absence, *The Pioneer* went bankrupt. Robert Carter, Lowell's coeditor, was unable to bear the full burden of the magazine upon his own frail shoulders. Bills went unpaid; the periodical went into debt. March marked the journal's third and final appearance. Later that month Lowell was back in Cambridge, reestablished at Elmwood, preparing for publication a volume of poems that appeared in December 1843.

Of the sequences in the new book, *Poems,* two stood out: "A Legend of Brittany" and "Prometheus." The writing of the latter, as Lowell informed his early companion, George Loring (June 15, 1843), pleased him immensely: "I have been very happy for the last day or two in writing a long poem in blank verse on Prometheus, the Greek archetype of St. Simeon Stylietes, the first reformer and locofoco of the Greek Mythology. . . . It is the longest and best poem I have ever written, and overrunning with true radicalism and anti-slavery." It was indeed the best and longest poem he had written to date, and while infused with ultraradical rhetoric, it was a far cry in terms of language and style from similarly directed poems on Prometheus by Goethe, Byron, and Shelley. "A Legend of Brittany," dedicated to William Page and full of "sighs, pale corpses, heart's travail," was a spirited and vivifying love sequence whose ultimate value resided in the record it contained of Lowell's poetic temperament at this precarious stage, his taste for romantic images, underlined by the hopeful melancholy of youth.

Aside from these efforts the volume's principal reflections consisted of "Ode" and "Rhoecus." The former represented a reaffirmation of Lowell's central belief that literature was the handmaid of reform. In the poem he revealed the contemporary poet to be an "empty rhymer," aestheticism a "misnamed art." The genuine artist, insisted Lowell, must endeavor to right the wrong that hovers like a cloud above his own time.

"Rhoecus," based on a fairy legend of old Greece, combined myth with moral didacticism. In a nutshell, this was the blank-verse tale of a mortal who loses his love (the Dryad) after heedlessly wounding a harmless bee. Reflecting the poet's early humanitarian stance, its message came through in the Dryad's parting words:

> he who scorns the least of Nature's works
> Is thenceforth exiled and shut out from all.

There was a sentimental egalitarianism at work here, a kinship between emotion and nature, both placed on the highest plateau. This prevailing Romantic attitude toward the primacy of feeling over intellect dominated a number of Lowell's early poems. In "An Incident in a Railroad Car" the poet described his faith in the goodness of "the primitive soul" and espoused the view that "all thought begins in feeling." In "The Shepherd of King Admetus" he again discovered that the source of inspiration is nature, not only for himself but for the First Poet: "It seemed the loveliness of things / Did teach him all their use, / For, in mere weeds, and stones, and springs, / He found a healing power profuse." And in his poem for the abolitionist Wendell Phillips, Lowell reiterated the proposition that the man of emotion is the virtuous man, more fortunate than the intellectual and infinitely "nearer to God."

While the critical reception of *Poems* was on the whole gratifying to Lowell, it received a poor notice from Margaret Fuller, Maria's former mentor. Miss Fuller, writing for *The Dial,* found the book "absolutely wanting in the true spirit and tone of poesy." To this she added: "His interest in the moral questions of the day has supplied the want of vitality in himself; his great facility of versification has enabled him to fill the ear with a copious stream of pleasant sound. But his verse is stereotyped; his thoughts sound no depth, and posterity will not remember him." It was a harsh judgment to render against one so young and ambitious as Lowell, who had barely begun to uplift his wings.

9

THE HUMANITARIAN

JAMES RUSSELL LOWELL'S divergent path from "the clan's straight and well-paved highway" was, we have already seen, partially the result of his parents' influence. His father, although not an avid abolitionist, placed the emphasis of his spiritual teaching directly upon the mind-broadening straits of humanitarianism—or in James Russell Lowell's words, upon the need for "a wider and wiser humanity." In place of the Puritans' "vertical" love of man for God, "a stress on perfecting one's higher self," the pleasant, cautious minister directed his congregation toward the "horizontal" division of man's love for man. His influence in such worldly concerns can be traced to the moral philosophizing of his former teacher Dugald Stewart and to the Reverend's reading of the works of Benjamin Franklin, whose Deism as stipulated in writing proclaimed that "the most acceptable service of God was the doing good to man." The Reverend maintained for Franklin the same high degree of admiration that James Russell Lowell reserved for his father. Writing to C. F. Briggs in 1844, the poet said of the Reverend:

> He is Dr. Primrose in the comparative degree, the very simplest and charmingest of sexagenarians, and not without a great deal of the truest magnanimity.

The poet was named after his father's maternal grandfather, Judge James Russell, of Charlestown, but it was from his mother's side of the family that he derived much of his talent and charm. His mother's grandfather, Robert Traill, had traveled at a young age from the Orkney Islands to America, had married there and left a daughter, Mrs. Lowell's mother, when he returned to Great Britain with the outbreak of the Revolutionary War. "My grandmother," Lowell ventured, "was a loyalist to her death, and whenever Independence Day came round, instead of joining in the general rejoicing, she would dress in deep black, fast all day, and loudly lament 'our late unhappy differences with his most gracious Majesty.' " Lowell's mother inherited a touch of her own mother's feeling for "the old country." Full of Orkney Islands imagination and sympathies, she liked to trace her heritage (and in turn her son's) to persons no less portentous than Minna Troil and Sir Patrick Spens, legendary figures in the colorful history of Celtic balladry. Other Traills to descend from the same Orkneys bloodline included Bishop Trayle (author), Alexander Trail (poet), Archbishop Adamson (poet), Henry Duff Traill (author), Dr. Thomas Traill (author), Walter Trail Dennison (author), Thomas Traill (author), David Balfour (poet and essayist), and James Boswell, the celebrated biographer of Samuel Johnson. Family historian Ferris Greenslet notes that Harriet Lowell not only possessed an abundance of the wild beauty of the dwellers of those "windy northern isles," but their irresistible tendency toward poetic occultism. She had revived this propensity by visiting the Orkney Islands in company with her husband early in their married life. Henceforth, until the onset of her mental decrepitude late in 1842, Harriet was "a faerie-seer." Some credited her with an acute sense of "second sight," others merely with the possession of a musical ear for sound lyric verse. From the lips of his mother, Lowell listened with delight to the singing of the old ballads. Her changeable, brooding, fanciful nature—as unrestrained as that of any Gothic heroine's—lived again in the poetic inclinations of her poet son and in his own arrogant, mawkish, humorous, self-contradictory ways.

If his turning to verse was partially the result of his Orkneys background, another important influence was that of the community of his birth. During his adolescence the fashion of Cambridge was predominantly literary. At Harvard, during Lowell's student days, Byron, Shelley, and Keats were much in vogue, with Tennyson fast joining the ranks and Carlyle, that most Teutonic Scot, not far behind. The New England literary tradition, inspired by the dominance of the German universities in the first half of the nineteenth century and filtered through the German Romantic notion of natural self-sufficiency, encountered boundless support. Literary men, among whom Lowell was recognized from the start, were considered Harvard's first citizens. That dowdily intellectual crowd—the Danas, Nortons, and Parkmans, to name a few—was widely read and dedicated in an ardent way to all the humanities. If they lacked anything as a group, it was a firmly developed political conscience, an abiding interest in government as an institution and as an instrument to effect necessary political change.

There were notable exceptions, as for instance the sometime Bostonian John Greenleaf Whittier, who struck the loudest political note of all with his raging pro-abolitionism: "Poetry that won't speak and ring is worse than none. Poetry is the match, the torch of our little field piece, and if it is not fiery, if there is no ignition in it, no explosion, we might as well put an icicle to our priming." In 1843, as a contributor to *The Pioneer,* he encouraged its editor to write the "liberty song" which "shall be to our cause what the song of Rouget de Lisle was to the French Republicans." Of Lowell's early poems, Whittier was partial toward "On Reading Wordsworth's Sonnets in Defence of Capital Punishment," a series of six sonnets directed against Wordworth's old-age philosophy espousing the virtues of capital punishment.

By September 1844 it was decided that Lowell and Maria White would be married on the day after Christmas and depart at once for Philadelphia, where he would accept the position of contributing editor to the *Pennsylvania Freeman,* an abolitionist newspaper. In the hectic weeks and months before their wedding, the author slaved to complete his latest project, *Conversations on the Old Poets,* a selection of essays published previously in the *Miscellany* and *The Pioneer.* Chaucer, George Chapman, John Ford, Edward Taylor, Donne, Marvell, and Keats were among the cast members of Lowell's pantheon. *Conversations* appeared in December 1844, both in Boston and London, with a dedication to Reverend Charles Lowell followed by a note stipulating that the volume contained "many opinions from which he will wholly, yet with the large charity of a Christian heart, dissent." A "literary" preface anticipated the reader's would-be reservations: "If some of the topics introduced seem foreign to the subject, I can only say that they are not so to my mind, and that an author's subject in writing criticism is not only to bring to light the beauties of the works he is considering, but also to express his own opinions upon those and other matters."

Those "other matters" are unfortunately accorded more than their rightful due. The essays in *Conversations* appear to be compiled rather than written, filled with a stream of personal views and impressions with little regard for the works of the authors themselves. The pieces are in fact veritable rewrites of entire sections of Lowell's personal correspondence and portions of his daybook, rambling endlessly, wandering without direction across the page. Moreover, they are laden, as Greenslet has said, with "defects of judgment," such as where we are told that "Ovid is the truest poet among the Latins" or that Alexander Pope was far and away the weakest poet of his generation (other authors are both praised and condemned with equal indiscretion). In mood and style there is too much of the sentimental pap and self-indulgent mawkishness that we find in great globs in Lowell's early verse. What can be said in favor of the book is that the poet's fervent love of literature is manifest on almost every page. The overflow of emotion in no way redeems the manuscript, but it does lend it the authority of literary conviction.

Lowell's arrangement with the *Pennsylvania Freeman* called for a monthly salary of ten dollars, plus an honorarium to help cover moving expenses. In addition, he received a small stipend from home and earned extra income from free-lance literary work. Briggs and Poe were currently editing a small magazine out of New York called *Broadway Journal*, and there Lowell and his bride, who also wrote, found a temporary home for their verse. Briggs took a rather dim view of Lowell's *Conversations* and penned an acerbic attack for the *Journal*, taking issue with his friend's "hot and excited" abolitionism, excoriating him for "a certain impudent egotism." What annoyed Lowell more than the review itself was the editor's refusal to publish an essay the poet had recently written decrying the annexation of Texas; in turning it down Briggs claimed that its tone was overly dramatic and severe. Lowell retained sincere affection for Briggs but for a time suspended his contributions to the magazine.

In Philadelphia the couple boarded with the Parkers, abolitionists and Quakers who were active in local political circles. For eight dollars a week they were fed three meals a day and given a small room, third-floor rear, with white muslin curtains trimmed with evergreen. It was quiet and they spent their free time at home, reading and writing, "happy as two mortals can be." Lowell visited Philadelphia's Whister Club, a weekly gathering of scientific and literary minds, but found the town bereft of educational and cultural attractions. Maria was disappointed with Pennsylvania's abolitionists, agreeing with Lydia Maria

Child that they were all "fussy, ignorant, old women," too prim and proper to benefit the movement.

Lowell, upon joining its staff, condemned the *Freeman* for its timid editorial policy, its refusal to admonish New England's religious sects, including those that had demonstrated little sympathy for the abolitionists and that supported a "non-extension" policy. The non-extenders believed that slavery must not be allowed to spread beyond the boundaries it presently occupied but that it should not be interfered with in those regions where it already existed. The Lowells, however, were convinced that slavery "posed too great a danger for equivocation" and inactivity; it threatened "the very basis on which the nation rested, the very heart of its professed principles, democratic and Christian," and inasmuch "could not be dealt with 'gradually' or in a 'compromising' spirit." William Garrison had put the matter into terms which even the man on the street could understand: "As leave tell a man to 'go slow' on slavery, as tell him *slowly* to put out a fire destroying the house in which his wife and children lay asleep." Lowell, picking up on Garrison's words, transposed them into his own subdued idiom: "There is something better than Expediency and that is Wisdom, something stronger than Compromise and that is Justice."

The termination of his relationship with the *Freeman,* after five months of incompatibility, left little reason for the Lowells to remain in Philadelphia. By the end of May 1845, they had returned to Cambridge, having stopped briefly in New York to call on Poe; the difference in their background and temperament, coupled with Poe's alcoholism, made communication between the two poets difficult, although they had previously enjoyed a long and warm correspondence.

In Cambridge the Lowells were presently living on the top floor of Elmwood. The deteriorating mental condition of Harriet Lowell forced them to transfer her to McLean's, a private hospital located in Belmont, a suburb of Boston. Although all reason spoke against it, the Reverend refused to give up hope for his wife's eventual recovery. In a letter to James, written while his son was living in Philadelphia, he expressed the futile expectation that "the aberration of mind has its origins in the stomach, and is not an affliction of the brain. I desire to trust in God."

Elmwood became a less grim place when, in December 1845, Maria gave birth to her first child, a daughter named Blanche. That summer the family rented a small farmhouse at Stockbridge, in western Massachusetts. When Longfellow came to visit, he found his Cambridge neighbor "hale as a young farmer" and just as occupied. Isolated from the rest of humanity, the Lowells had turned to subsistence farming; surrounded by dogs and cats, goats (they made their own cheese), chickens (which they were breeding), ducks (purely ornamental), and an occasional hog, they were surviving nicely. They had learned to cope with raccoons, porcupines, and deer in the vegetable garden and were coming to terms with the short and unpredictable growing season in this part of the country. Although husband and wife appeared to be in the best of spirits, something was apparently disturbing the poet; a letter to Briggs that he wrote at about this time belied a troubled interior:

> My sorrows are not literary ones, but those of daily life. I pass through the world and meet with scarcely a response to the affectionateness of my nature. I believe Maria only knows how loving I am truly. Brought up in a very reserved and conventional family, I cannot in society appear what I really am. I go out sometimes with my heart so full of yearning toward my fellows that the indifferent look with which even strangers pass me brings tears into my eyes. And then to be looked upon by those who *do* know me (externally) as "Lowell the poet"—it makes me sick. Why not Lowell the man,—the boy rather,—as Jemmy Lowell, as I was at school?

One source of the poet's depression stemmed from his concern with the apparent lack of interest among his contemporaries in the plight of the abolitionists. In order to gain support for the movement he wrote a series of articles on "Anti-Slavery in the United States" for the London *Daily News.* The articles were published anonymously, the author's impression being that they would be better received if not known to be the work of a committed abolitionist. Fully devoted to the cause of humanitarianism, the Brahmin engaged in a furious letter-writing campaign with numerous men of letters, including Oliver Wendell Holmes, whom he tried to swing over to the side of "abolition, temperance, the claims of the poor, pacifism, and reform and reformers in general." But the future Autocrat would have none of it; he countered Lowell's gibe with a thrust of his own: "I must say, with regard to art and a management of my own poems, I think I shall in the main follow my own judgment and taste rather than mould myself upon those of others. . . . Let me try to impress and please my fellow men after my own fashion at present. When I come to your way of thinking (this may happen) I hope I shall be found worthy of a less qualified approbation than you have felt constrained to give me at this time."

Lowell fought on, accepting a position as a regular contributor to the *National Anti-Slavery Standard*, the Garrisonian-controlled, militant newspaper, whose base was New York. Its editors were Maria Weston Chapman, Edmund Quincy, and Sydney Gay, who were all from the wealthiest, best-bred families of New England. Edmund Quincy was the son of Josiah Quincy, one-time mayor of Boston and president of Harvard. Gay's distinguished bloodline could be traced to John Cotton, Increase Mather, and Governor Bradford of Plymouth, while the Chapmans were of equally highborn origin. Despite the wealth and sobriety of its editorial staff, the *Standard* espoused most of Garrison's hard-fought values; it championed women's rights and the plight of the Northern factory worker, supported temperance and abolition. These four issues became the main concerns of the Garrison-backed Liberation Party.

Lowell, in full agreement with the *Standard*'s basic views concerning abolition, did not on the other hand concur with all of the Liberation Party's tactics, finding some of them too rigid for his own peace-loving blood. Although he admired Garrison and identified with him in an intellectual sense, he disdained the majority of the activist's followers. "They treat ideas," he once wrote, "as ignorant persons do cherries. They think them unwholesome unless they are swallowed, stones and all."

The *Standard* paid Lowell an annual salary of five hundred dollars for a weekly contribution of prose or verse. A number of the poems he contributed, starting with the issue of September 1847, were at once widely circulated and attained a high degree of popularity. Here first appeared the compassionate poem for Garrison—comparing him as an effective reformer with Luther—and a poem for John G. Palfrey (a stalwart of the movement), the stirring stanzas to Freedom, and other lines of poetic repute. Besides the poems that spoke out against slavery, there were those that revealed Lowell's feelings for the great outdoors, the green and natural world as sung by Wordsworth and Coleridge, Keats and Shelley. Best known of this group were "Eurydice," "The Parting of the Ways," and "Beaver Brook."

It was in the *Standard* that Lowell published his poem "The First Snow-Fall," a mellow outflow of the grief that overcame the author with the sudden and tragic death of his daughter Blanche in March 1847, and a record of the "tremulous happiness renewed" in the birth of a second daughter, Mabel, in the fall of the same year. "May you never have the key which shall unlock the whole meaning of the poem to you," Lowell wrote to the editors of the antislavery periodical. Writing the poem helped assuage the poet's sorrow:

> I stood and watched by the window
>   The noiseless work of the sky,
> And the sudden flurries of snow-birds,
>   Like brown leaves whirling by.
>
> I thought of a mound in sweet Auburn
>   Where a little headstone stood;
> How the flakes were folding it gently,
>   As did robins the babes in the wood.
>
> Up spoke our own little Mabel,
>   Saying, "Father, who makes it snow?"
> And I told of the good All-father
>   Who cares for us here below.

These fragments point to the poem's final stanza, a quatrain dense with emotion:

> Then, with eyes that saw not, I kissed her,
>   And she, kissing back, could not know
> That *my* kiss was given to her sister,
>   Folded close under deepening snow.

"She Came and Went" and "The Changeling," both written at this time, likewise reflect the sad circumstance of the tiny shoe that for years hung over a picture of Blanche in Lowell's study. As a group the three poems depict the gross and frightening depressions that continued to plague him his entire life. Often these bouts of wallowing and melancholy came upon him without warning and for no apparent reason. They were accompanied by mental torpor, paranoia, unexplainable fears that he was going mad, pangs of guilt. The tumultuous conflicts, guilts, and fears that possessed him seemed to be the result of the incongruities between his personal longings and the actualities of his existence—the eternal conflict in his soul between infantile intensity of passion and profound self-control, between Brahmin conservative roots and romantic impulse. But there was no clinical explanation, only the florid symptoms, the tortured visual signs, the anguished shorthand—talking with his fingers, popping and tapping them, while his nerves constricted and his brain wandered. There was an animal inside his skin, eating away at his mind and marrow. The bouts of depression drove him into seclusion. For weeks he remained bedridden, refusing to see anyone, refusing to eat, unable to work, trapped within the confines of his own skull.

Frequently these episodes of melancholia gave way to their manic counterpart—great gushes of mental activity and physical exertion, as though the melancholy were prerequisite to the flow of energy. After weeks of inactivity he could churn out as many as twelve hundred words of polished prose an hour, or fifty printed pages a day, the equivalent of two medium-length essays, or one-fifth of a finished book. Poems poured out of him at the rate of three or four daily, needing little or no revision. Or else he might take long walks or run or shadowbox, dance, sing, play cards, take sleigh rides, engage in a round of plain buffoonery. He would extemporize long-drawn-out accounts of make-believe figures such as "Mitchell Bonyrooty Angylo," or would compose and execute a full-length opera "entirely unassisted and, à la Beethoven, on a piano without any strings." He could barely contain himself. Words, ideas, and thoughts churned out of him. He became a geyser, spouting theories on literature, quoting endless sections of books that he knew verbatim, imitating brogues and foreign accents, reciting poems, making puns, cracking jokes, insulting friends. His extraordinary mannerisms, his tics and convulsions at these explosive moments were often frightening to behold. On one occasion he hoisted himself up a lamppost, where for hours he perched and crowed like a rooster. Acquaintances recalled Lowell unconcernedly removing and proceeding to eat with knife and fork a bouquet of flowers from the centerpiece at a literary supper in one of Boston's great houses. At an important meeting of poets he astounded everyone by gathering up his coattails and galloping around the room to illustrate the movements of a horse. He was known to accost strangers on the street and swing them about as though they were his closest friends, whom he had not seen in years. Nor was the stone wall built that he could resist mounting and conquering, balancing himself along its edge with the finesse of a tightrope artist. People who knew him took Lowell at these instances for a rowdy showoff or a violent madman, rather than the intellectual hero and cultural ideologue he prided himself on being. Had he been any less accomplished a poet he would surely have been handcuffed and led off, never to be heard from or seen again.

The February 1848 Treaty of Guadalupe Hidalgo marked the end of the bloody, one-sided war between Mexico and the United States. Ratified in October, the treaty enabled the United States to seize Texas and the territory that later became New Mexico, California, Utah, Nevada, Arizona, and parts of Colorado and Wyoming. The Mexican War, as future historians would note, was the major turning point in the country's exploratory trek westward. It was also a watershed event in Lowell's personal campaign for literary recognition; 1848 was his annus mirabilis in terms of creative productivity. During his thirtieth year Lowell produced four major volumes: a new collection of *Poems; A Fable for Critics;* the first series of *The Biglow Papers;* and *The Vision of Sir Launfal.*

In a single year the poet had emerged, overcoming the depressions that were so substantial a part of his nature and that threatened always to lay him low. Included in his latest book of *Poems* were many of the selections originally contributed to the *Standard* and other radical organs, among them many purely artistic creations and some that read substantially like political tracts, prophetic diatribes that might better have been composed as prose. "The Present Crisis," dealing with the controversial annexation of Texas ("Careless seems the great avenger; history's pages but record / One death grapple in the darkness 'twixt old systems and the Word"), and "An Indian-Summer Reverie," commemorating the same village smithy celebrated by Longfellow in his poem by that title, are prime examples of the poet striving valiantly to conjoin the sonorous and the inspirational in his verse. The first is moralistic in design, the poetician here at odds with the preacher in him, the poem rising out of the dialectic with a surge of power and persuasion. The second poem is a spiritual hymn to nature, subject to the same schismatic shortcoming as the first, but full of tenderness and resounding with passion and vulnerability:

> The ash her purple drops forgivingly
> And sadly, breaking out the general hush;
> The maple-swamps glow like a sunset sea,
> Each leaf a ripple with its separate flush;

All round the wood's edge creeps the skirting blaze
Of bushes low, as when, on cloudy days,
Ere the rain fall, the cautious farmer burns his brush.

With a few quick strokes the poet draws us beneath the surface of the poem, fusing objective description with atmosphere and feeling as though tentatively reaching out for more than the lines might otherwise yield. Among other poems that come close to matching these are "Freedom," "On the Capture of Fugitive Slaves Near Washington," "To the Dandelion," "The Pioneer," and "Beaver Brook."

A *Fable for Critics*, subtitled "A Glance at a Few of Our Literary Progenies," appeared anonymously as a pamphlet at the beginning of the year. In a prefatory note attached by Lowell to a subsequent edition of the poem, following his identification as its author, he explained the *Fable*'s origin: "This *jeu d'esprit* was extemporized, I may fairly say, so rapidly was it written, purely for my own amusement and with no thought of publication. I sent daily installments of it to a friend in New York, the late Charles F. Briggs. He urged me to let it be printed, and I at last consented to its anonymous publication. The secret was kept till after several persons had laid claim to its authorship."

The poem created a minor sensation among those whom Lowell singled out for attack; yet the portraits he drew of his contemporaries were sufficiently generalized that even the nonliterary could partake of the fun. In his 1966 biography of the aristocrat, Martin Duberman reflects that Lowell was hardest on those whom posterity also treated unkindly: N. P. Willis, Richard Henry Dana, Sr., John Neal, Cornelius Mathews, and Fitz-Greene Halleck. In their particular poetic form, Lowell's views represented the best spontaneous literary criticism that the nineteenth century would endeavor to produce. The rambling poem featured none of the black hearted satire we find in great abundance in Melville's short fiction or in parts of Swift or Ben Jonson; instead, the poem is an iconography of caricatures, containing the light ticklish humor but not the political immediacy of Byron's "The Mask of Irony"; equally apt might be a comparison between the Lowell poem and Byron's "English Bards and Scotch Reviewers." The Brahmin's portrait of Halleck serves as adequate illustration of the technique; dismissed as a poet, he is subsequently taken up by Lowell as a personality:

> Halleck's better, I doubt not, than all he has written;
> In his verse a clear glimpse you will frequently find,
> If not of a great, of a fortunate mind,
> Which contrives to be true to its natural loves
> In a world of back-offices, ledgers, and stoves.

This judgment is made more brutal (but at the same time more palatable) by Lowell's use of restraint, his desire to hold something in reserve. What is not said, or what is said in jest, is ultimately as damaging as anything the poet may offer by way of outright criticism. His qualification of Halleck's literary faults, his use of the phrase "if not of a great, of a fortunate mind," makes Lowell look a bit like the smiling viper, the friendly, accommodating assassin.

Even those writers the poet outwardly admired—Emerson, Longfellow, Bryant, James Fenimore Cooper—were in for a bluff and earthy drenching. Emerson is a case in point. At first, lauding the Transcendentalist, Lowell compares him favorably with Carlyle and then Plato:

> There are persons, mole-blind to the Soul's make and style,
> Who insist on a likeness 'twixt him and Carlyle;
> To compare him with Plato would be vastly fairer,
> Carlyle's the more burly, but E. is the rarer;
> He sees fewer objects, but clearlier, truelier,
> If C.'s as original, E.'s more peculiar;
> That he's more of a man you might say of the one,
> Of the other he's more of an Emerson.

But just as quickly, reversing his field, he attempts to portray Emerson as a seething and ornery radical:

> All admire, and yet scarcely six converts he's got
> To I don't (nor they either) exactly know what;
> For though he builds glorious temples, 'tis odd
> He leaves never a doorway to get in a god.

Similarly downgrading is the humorist's comment that Cooper, having invented a new and creative character, had then proceeded to plagiarize himself, endlessly repeating it:

> His Indians, with proper respect be it said,
> Are just Natty Bumppo, daubed over with red,

And his very Long Toms are the same useful Nat,
Rigged up in duck pants and a sou'wester hat . . .

By far the author's most vicious attack was reserved for Margaret Fuller, whose negative evaluation of his own early work he had never forgiven. Calling her Miranda in the *Fable,* he unleashes the following invective:

> But there comes Miranda, Zeus! where shall I flee to?
> She has such a penchant for bothering me too . . .
> One would think, though, a sharp-sighted noter she'd be
> Of all that's worth mentioning over the sea,
> For a woman must surely see well, if she try,
> The whole of whose being's a capital I:
> She will take an old notion, and make it her own,
> By saying it o'er in her Sibylline tone,
> Or persuade you 't is something tremendously deep,
> By repeating it so as to put you to sleep;
> And she well may defy any mortal to see through it,
> When once she has mixed up her infinite *me* through it.
> There is one thing she owns in her own single right,
> It is native and genuine—namely, her spite . . .

The *Fable* elicited a full tableau of responses. John Ruskin labeled the poem "in animal spirit and power . . . almost beyond anything I know." Oliver Wendell Holmes found it "capital—crammed full and rammed down hard—with powder (lots of it)—shot—slugs—very little wadding, and that is guncotton—all crowded into a rusty-looking sort of blunderbuss barrel, as it were—capped with a percussion preface—and cocked with a title page as apropos as a wink to a joke." William Wetmore Story, a member of The Band and a close friend of Lowell's, enjoyed the poem but rejected its bitter characterization of Miss Fuller. Edgar Allan Poe, whom the poet summed up in the *Fable* as "three fifths . . . genius and two fifths sheer fudge," resented the whole, blaming Lowell's "distortions" on his misguided and roaring abolitionism. It is probable that Poe was still smarting from his personal meeting with Lowell some years before.

These varied responses gained the *Fable*'s author the kind of notoriety that helps sell books. Three thousand copies of the first edition were sold immediately. Lowell's sudden "drawing room" popularity was felt by the general reading public as well as by the literary elect. On another level the poem illustrates Lowell's early contempt for tradition ("Forget Europe wholly") and his gradual turn from sentimentalism to the critical temper that was to be developed and broadened in his future work. A final and fitting touch to the poem was provided by the scrivener's probing self-examination:

> There is Lowell, who's striving Parnassus to climb
> With a whole bale of *isms* tied together with rhyme,
> He might get on alone, spite of brambles and boulders,
> But he can't with that bundle he has on his shoulders,
> The top of the hill he will ne'er come nigh reaching
> Till he learns the distinction 'twixt singing and preaching;
> His lyre has some chords that would ring pretty well,
> But he'd rather by half make a drum of the shell,
> And rattle away till he's old as Methusalem,
> At the head of a march to the last new Jerusalem.

The Vision of Sir Launfal, published on the heels of the *Fable,* proved equally popular. This was a story-poem, a mini-epic, written in the half-mystic, half-mocking language that characterized the medieval Arthurian lai. Lowell's modest but charming version of this talismanic legend recounts the tale of Sir Launfal's search for the Holy Grail. As the gallant knight-errant begins his search he encounters a leper outside his castle gate. Determined to complete his quest, the knight ignores the stranger and passes on into the night. Time elapses; the knight ages. By the time of his return, unsuccessful in his search, he finds that another lord has inherited his earldom. Amidst memories of summer days breaks the voice of the long-forgotten leper: "For Christ's sweet sake, I beg an alm . . ." No longer scornful of the poor stranger, the knight gladly feeds him bread and water. A transformation ensues, the leper metamorphosing into a holy man; the man speaks:

> Lo, it is I, be not afraid!
> In many climes, without avail,
> Thou hast spent thy life for the Holy Grail;
> Behold, it is here,—this cup which thou
> Didst fill at the streamlet for me but now;
> This crust is my body broken for thee,
> This water his blood that died on the tree;
> The Holy Supper is kept, indeed . . .

Appearing at the same time as *Sir Launfal* was the collected first edition of *The Biglow Papers,* nine poems of varying length, the first five published individually in the Boston *Courier,* the remaining four in the *National Anti-Slavery Standard.* It was in these constructions that Lowell for the first time appeared in his full stature as a humorist of the highest order; satirist, however, may be the preferable term here, for political affairs and social mores underscore the entire sequence.

A dozen years after the volume's appearance, on the eve of the Civil War, Lowell provided the editor of the British edition, Thomas Hughes, with a brief declaration of his political position at the time the *Papers* were originally issued:

> I believed our war with Mexico (though we had as just ground for it as a strong nation ever has against a weak one) to be essentially a war of false pretenses, and that it would result in widening the boundaries and so prolong the life of slavery. . . . I believed and still believe that slavery is the Achilles heel of our polity: that it is a temporary and false supremacy of the white races, sure to destroy that supremacy at last, because an enslaved people always prove themselves of more enduring fibre than their enslavers.

Lowell portrays three principal characters in *The Biglow Papers,* each representative of a different aspect of American life. The first is Parson Wilbur, resident of the invented village of Jaalam, Massachusetts, whose personality is an amalgam of the qualities of at least three people—the pedantry of Reverend Barzillai Frost, Lowell's Concord tutor during his rustication from Harvard; the sweetness and gentleness of Reverend Charles Lowell; and the moral earnestness of the author himself. Writing a good deal of *The Biglow Papers* in dialect, Lowell felt that he "needed on occasion to rise above the level of mere *patois,*" and for this purpose conceived the Reverend Mr. Wilbur, who expressed the more scholarly and erudite element of the New England personality. Second, we have young Hosea Biglow, the unsophisticated, unlettered, independent rustic, who nevertheless represented the "homely common sense" of his region. Scornful of slavery, politicians, and the war with Mexico, it is Hosea who pens the majority of these Papers. Third, we encounter Birdofredum Sawin: "I invented Mr. Sawin for the clown of my little puppet show. I meant to embody in him that half-conscious *un*-morality which I had noticed as the recoil in gross natures from a puritanism that still strove to keep in its creed the intense savor which had long gone out of its faith and life." Sawin as rascal and Southern sympathizer represented the darkly humorous Falstaffian villain, a striking counterpart to the charm and beneficence of the remaining members of the cast. Moreover, Sawin epitomized his country's blind faith in Manifest Destiny, which according to Lowell's standards was unequivocably its archenemy.

The main feature of *The Biglow Papers* was Lowell's use of a cracker-barrel drawl or Yankee dialect, a mode of communication whose propriety he soon began to question. Shortly after the appearance of the poem in book format the poet notified a friend: "As for Hosea, I am sorry that I began by making him such a detestable speller. There is no fun in bad spelling of itself, but only where the misspelling suggests something else which is droll per se. You see I am getting him out of it gradually." This statement notwithstanding, the later Papers of the series showed no marked departure from the general scheme of Yankee spelling and phonetics that graced the earlier ones. The overwhelming popularity attained by the successive numbers of the sequence may have convinced Lowell that he had discovered a gimmick worth developing. While he made a number of minor changes, shaping the body of the work and fleshing out several secondary characters, the basic configuration of the series remained intact.

In choosing to write in dialect, Lowell was convinced that the outstanding vice of American literature was a studied want of simplicity. His contemporaries were in danger of coming to look upon English as an archaic language that one sought in the grammar and dictionary rather than in the heart. The writings of the day were obscure, formal, moralistic, unnatural. Lowell noted in his introduction to the second series of *The Biglow Papers* that "few American writers or speakers wield their native language with the directness, precision, and force that are common as the day in the mother country."

The poet's ambition to get closer to common man and to the experience of common men by way of their diction and language was possibly an unconscious reaction on his part to the overeducated inhabitants and stifling atmosphere of Cambridge. It was quite conceivably a reaction against the Lowell clan itself, which not only disapproved of his role as a poet but also seemed shocked by and opposed to his outspoken political musings. The two in tandem, the poetry coupled with an unorthodox political philosophy, sufficed to single him out as a patrician renegade, an aristocratic exile. *The Biglow Papers* did little to ingratiate him with the wealthier and more conventional members of his family.

The first number of *The Biglow Papers*—in the form of a letter from Ezekiel Biglow to a newspaper editor, enclosing a poem by his son and a note announcing the circumstances under which it was written—sets the sequence's thematic tone. Hosea Biglow, according to his father's letter, had gone down to Boston the week before and there saw a recruiting "Sarjunt" walking about with twenty rooster tails stuck in his cap and enough brass displayed on his shoulders to make a six-pound cannonball. One look at Hosea, and the "Sarjunt" was convinced that this backwoods lad from Jaalam had the makings of a model recruit to help fight the war against Mexico.

That night, highly agitated, Hosea composed a poem about the officer and the army he represented. The poem repeatedly makes the point that warfare is tantamount to cold-blooded murder: "Ef you take a sword an' dror it, / An go stick a feller thru, / Guv'ment aint to answer to it, / God'll send the bill to you."

Other particulars quickly come into play, from militant editors, whom Lowell glibly derides, to the Bay State itself, which had sunk to its knees before the unhallowed altar of servitude. Let Massachusetts speak out, Hosea's poem reads—let the bells in every steeple toll, let them sing to the South a song of rebellion: "I will not help the Devil make man the curse of man: / I am a tyrant hater and the friend of God and Peace. / I prefer separation to a forced and unholy union of them that / God has no ways jined."

The second Paper consists of a note from Mexico, from Private Sawin, who had enlisted with the Massachusetts Regiment; unlike Hosea, he had been taken in by the sergeant's glitter and fanfare, and as we gradually learn, lived to regret it. We find out why in letter eight, the most humorous epistle of the lot, which recounts in verse form Birdofredum Sawin's wanderings in war. Fate has dealt the Army Private a harsh blow. "I spose you wonder ware I be," his letter to the Parson begins: "I can't tell fer the soul o' me, / Exactly ware I be myself,— meanin' by / thet the holl o' me." A serious wound incurred in battle has resulted in the amputation of Sawin's leg. The soldier's sole consolation is that whisky can't get into the wooden stump.

In addition to the leg, Sawin has lost an eye in battle, to say nothing of his left arm and four fingers of his right hand; a half dozen of his ribs were also fractured. Speaking of ribs reminds him of the one he left behind—his wife. Sawin instructs Wilbur to inform her that one day he will be eligible for a military pension, yet at the same time admits that his previous expectations of wealth never materialized; when he enlisted he expected Mexico to be a Garden of Eden, overflowing with milk and honey, rum and gold. "But sech ideas," he writes, "soon melted down an' didn't / leave a grease spot; / I vow my holl sheer o' the spiles would not / come nigh a V spot."

In the same vein Sawin complains that his sole military souvenir, besides battle scars, is a case of shaking fever. He insists that though the enlisted men fought and won the strategic battles, it was the officers who received all the glory: "We get the licks—we're just the grist that's put into War's hoppers; / Leftenants is the lowest grade that helps pick up the coppers." He drones on about meager rations for the troops, accusing the officers of stuffing themselves like pigs on a fare fit for kings. In the middle of his rant he conceives of a plan: When he returns to the States he will run for political office and use his war record and wooden leg as a platform; whenever his opinion on an issue is solicited, he will simply point to his head and yell, "One Eye Put Out!"

Sawin closes his letter by examining his account with the "Bank of Glory," debiting and crediting such items as the loss of a leg against three cheers in Boston's Faneuil Hall, an evening of band music, a uniform, and a homecooked meal. Attached to the document is a note from its recipient, Parson Wilbur, indicting America's system of "indirect taxation" that was used to finance the war: "If we could know that a part of the money we expend for tea and coffee goes to buy powder and balls, and that it is Mexican blood which makes the clothes on our backs more costly, it would set some of us thinking."

The third Paper, "What Mr. Robinson Thinks," depicts a humorous debate between a Whig and a moderate over a forthcoming gubernatorial election, while Letter Five, "The Debate in the Sennit," delivers a sneering, unsparing attack on John C. Calhoun, the Southern congressman who argued unconvincingly for state sovereignty. With unfaltering ribaldry Lowell, as Wilbur, obliterates the villain, asserting that Calhoun represents the worst sort of bigot, the man who believes in the superiority of race.

The Biglow Papers presented the poet with a vehicle for his iconoclastic views and his vision of New England's dual state—its "common sense and canniness, its poetry and pedantry, its idealism, all minted into something as racy and of the soil as a pine-tree shilling." Although the *Papers* effectively transmitted both sides of the New England story, the manuscript was too freighted with Lowell's shrill antiwar rhetoric to serve as an objective account of the events in question. Lowell's "hard sell" campaign was well suited for the political dais but less satisfying as a mode of legitimate literary communication. Lowell had been partially blinded by his eagerness to see the issue of slavery, the annexation of Texas, and the Mexican War in realistic terms. He was convinced that the tragedy of the first two and the catastrophe of the third were intertwined, and he was determined to single out those factions he held responsible for all three.

The poet's use (some claimed "abuse") of dialect became a contentious issue. Proud of his intimacy with the finer shades of the Yankee vernacular—"I reckon myself a good taster of dialects"—Lowell carried to the nth degree of phonetic exactness his reproductions of the peculiarities of New England speech. Not unexpectedly, a major disagreement arose over Lowell's employment of language, with half the world's critics castigating him for catering to popular tastes by creating not a poem but a patchwork document, a quilt of notes and asides, an unwieldy mass of homely satire, moral aphorisms, and Yankee dialect, replete with an index, a glossary, and other secondhand devices. The main objection of the critics was that the verse, for all its spontaneity, was weighted down by the excessive machinery of the accompanying prose. The poet was attacked, too, on the grounds that the New England dialect, while satisfactory for a character like Hosea Biglow, was far too limited and confining to allow the author to give adequate expression to his deeper and more serious responses to life. The joking colloquialisms, it was argued, served the poet's wit but not the flow or fabric of his ideas. The poem tried to be too many things to too many people; it was narrative, chronicle, journal, biography, history, obituary, fable, parable, and myth; it was the public memory, the voice of the New England mind, the conscience of the urbanite, all wrapped into one.

Whatever Lowell may or may not have accomplished with this series, he did help liberate the language, expose it to a broader audience, open it to a new mode of expression, while serving the important radical "causes" of his day. The Transcendental radicalism espoused by such poems as *Prometheus* and "A Glance behind the Curtain" (1843), "Columbus" and "The Present Crisis" (1844), "On the Capture of Fugitive

Slaves near Washington" (1845), and "The Pioneer" (1847), found its purest and most effective outlet in *The Biglow Papers*. With its composition Lowell established himself as a working model for future satirists and dialecticians, not only Mark Twain but men such as William Dean Howells, H. L. Mencken, and Ring Lardner. Although the *Papers* created certain negative responses, the book as a whole made a strong impression, and the political philosophy secreted in its lines became a part of household literature. Sections of the work, more than a hundred years after their composition, still seem compacted of the stuff of lasting verse.

⚜ 10 ⚜

FIRESIDE POET

IN 1861 *The Biglow Papers* was published in England; the volume contained the preface by Thomas Hughes that began, "Greece had her Aristophanes; Rome her Juvenal; Spain has had her Cervantes; France her Rabelais, her Molière, her Voltaire; Germany her Jean Paul, her Heine; England her Swift, her Thackeray; and America has her Lowell." The inclusion of his name on this roster of renowned Tory masters of satire must have pleased Lowell. But his name was now beginning to appear to an increasing degree on still another list of authors, this one consisting of living American poets. This new group had a title; they were called the Fireside Poets.

The term "Fireside Poet," writes Professor William Charvat in his provocative introduction to the section on Henry Wadsworth Longfellow and James Russell Lowell in *Major Writers of America* (1962), "accurately describes a group of writers who were well known in New England in the 1840's, acquired a national audience after 1850, and were of unrivalled popularity in the quarter-century before World War I." Included in this select group were Henry Wadsworth Longfellow, Oliver Wendell Holmes, John Greenleaf Whittier, William Cullen Bryant, and James Russell Lowell. All, Charvat informs us, were native New Englanders; indeed, all with the exception of Bryant lived in eastern Massachusetts, and Longfellow, Holmes, and Lowell resided, for most of their lives, in Cambridge proper or in adjacent Boston.

The word "Fireside" suggests that they enjoyed a family audience— men, women, and children—and that their poetry was read aloud in the family circle. For this reason they were sometimes referred to as household poets. For years the morally uplifting (yet often parochial and bland) work of these versifiers served as a classroom aid or exercise in memory control for students. Hence these authors also came to be known as classroom poets, a designation that did not overly please them, primarily because it had negative connotations.

The fact remains that their work was immediately accessible. Their themes were universal. Their style was rustic, avuncular, and benign. They wrote about home, family, and children; New England, nature, idealized love; religion—Protestant, but usually nondenominational; love of country; faith, peace, prosperity, and sometimes war. A high proportion of their verse had its roots in history, legend, the Bible, the classics. "Their view of life," Charvat observes, "can be described by the term 'sunshine and shadow,' which implies a balance of good and bad in human experience. The emphasis . . . varies somewhat from poet to poet. All had been taught to believe, through their heritage of eighteenth-century rationalism, that in the divine plan apparent evil was part of a total good." The total good, however, was all important; if the Fireside Poets too often hovered between slick didacticism and sheer virtuosic description, they nevertheless had a kind of reverent openness before life and a marked moral intensity that separated them from their literary forebears.

There were additional factors that drew them together. They were all—with the exception of Whittier—members of the social elite. They came from families whose names carried considerable prestige; a college education and membership in a respectable profession was an a priori, a given. Thus Lowell and Longfellow were college professors; William Cullen Bryant was an attorney and a newspaper editor; Whittier was an editor; Oliver Wendell Holmes was a practicing physician, who also wrote pioneering medical pamphlets of considerable importance in such areas as histology and puerile fever. In addition to their professions these poets came from families in which public service of some sort—in the courts, churches, legislatures, and in the military during the Revolutionary War—was part of their heritage. The place of these poets in the social structure of New England and their relation to the sense of an American past was extremely secure.

Stylistically their poems had this in common: their rhythms, though at times interestingly varied, took their strength from conventional meters; their stanzas followed set patterns; they avoided alliteration and other submerged devices such as those commonly found in the work of Whitman or Dickinson; they stayed with elementary forms of blank verse or the more traditional end rhyme. The Fireside Poets were traditionalists as well in their use of language (Lowell's experimentation with various forms of diction and dialect was the exception, not the rule); their images and metaphors were straightforward and familiar; they adhered to the plain style of Anne Bradstreet and Edward Taylor and had not progressed beyond either one in their frequent use of inversions and archaisms. In the end the poetry these men produced functioned primarily as a vehicle for their socioeconomic and political views. It was instructive; it insisted on imparting a comprehensive moral or lesson, a Socratic infusion of rules.

One of the remarkable facts about this group is that they were read alike and with as much enthusiasm by the well educated as by the barely literate. Which is not to say that they were understood on the same level by both. Nor does it mean that the Firesiders were necessarily "mass"-oriented poets. What it does suggest is that the gap between two major sociological bodies was rapidly narrowing. A rather sophisticated middle-class audience was sprouting up in America. To some extent this was the result of the social upheaval that was taking place abroad, a restructuring of class order related directly to the European revolutions of 1789 and 1848. On American soil the corrosion of a previously well-defined class system made itself most felt within the field of education. For the first time students in other than private colleges were being exposed to subjects of meaningful academic merit: philosophy, languages, sciences, rhetoric. This was true at the high-school level and in denominational colleges. Students graduating from high school were familiar with the writings of Shakespeare, Milton, Pope, and Bunyan. Authors could expect a better-educated and better-read, and therefore a more attentive and demanding, audience.

Another consideration that added to the wide reception accorded the Firesiders was the growing belief that it was not beyond reason, in Poe's phrase, "to suit at once the popular and the critical taste." Not only Poe but Emerson, Howells, even early Henry James shared this sentiment; all were convinced of the assumption that in a democracy writers could offer their best with some hope that even the culturally unsophisticated would accept them and support them sufficiently to make the literary life possible. What is more, there was a fair amount of respect among the general populace for the "high-born," especially for those able to earn their keep by achieving some measure of professional or public distinction.

Lowell was the literary statesman of the group—erudite, versatile, intellectual. In literary circles he was considered more influential than the other Fireside Poets and less of a popularizer. Hyatt H. Waggoner, in *American Poets: From the Puritan to the Present* (1968), remarks that "reading Lowell today is likely to awaken a stronger sense of unrealized potential than is the case with any other of the 'schoolroom poets.'" While this assessment does not really say much for Lowell, the fact remains that his contributions to the world of belles-lettres surpassed those of his Fireside contemporaries. Lowell was more diverse as a poet than Bryant, whose reflections on love and death never moved far beyond these themes. Within his given framework Bryant operated admirably, writing public poems of note, creating unparalleled eloquence of tone in all his work, as in these lines from the opening of "Thanatopsis," written before his twentieth birthday:

> To him who in the love of Nature holds
> Communion with her visible forms, she speaks
> A various language; for his gayer hours
> She has a voice of flatness, and a smile
> And eloquence of beauty, and she glides
> Into his darker musings, with a mild
> And healing sympathy, that steals away
> Their sharpness, ere he is aware.

This fragment, although of undeniable quality, lacks the width and breadth in terms of symbol, meter, and rhythm that we find throughout the best parts of Lowell.

Lowell was quite adept at the use of rhythm and meter and extremely conscious of poetic form, whereas Holmes—to name another—restricted himself to conventional tones and effects. By his own admission Holmes was a facile inventor of light and occasional verse, while Lowell went after confections of a major format. Lowell was better informed than Holmes; his learning was broader and deeper in scope and more solidly anchored than any of the other Fireside Poets. Of the men who comprised this quintet none was better read than Lowell; none had cultivated quite his level of taste.

Perhaps he was too well-read. His critics accused him of being over-cultivated, too bookish and derivative for his own good, too conspicuous in his learning—qualities that tended to work against the creative grain, robbing his verse of all sense of poetic freedom and spiritual gain. Longfellow, by far the most popular of the Fireside Poets, in his best work found it easier than Lowell to locate his individual voice. Whittier too, whose power of language did not approach Lowell's, was able to articulate his thoughts in words closer to his own, without hiding behind the dense foliage of ideas.

Lowell's poetry was full of ideas, full of history and philosophy and anthropology. The net effect of this surplus of intellection was frequently a kind of scattered rendering of emotion, a lack of focus, the poet losing control of the fragments he had culled from the writings of his precursors. Or else the threads of his thoughts got so tangled that he stumbled and fell, unable to tie them together, unable to make sense of a thousand loose strands.

The significant facts in the poet's life from 1848 to 1850 ranged markedly in emotional impact. A third daughter, Rose, born in July 1849, contracted a fatal childhood disease and died in March 1850, just three years after the death of her sister Blanche. To Sydney Gay, her father wrote: "She was very beautiful—fair, with large dark-gray eyes and fine features. Her smile was especially charming, and she was full of smiles till her sickness began. Dear little child, she had never spoken, only smiled." There was no funeral; the tiny corpse was simply buried next to her sister's at Mount Auburn Cemetery. Lowell worried over the fate of his remaining child; the air, he said, was "full of deadly, invisible bullets flying in every direction, so that not a step can be taken in safety." Maria White, always of delicate and uncertain health, fell seriously ill from the strain and sorrow of her infant daughter's death and for weeks remained bedridden. During the same month Lowell's mother, by now permanently disabled and institutionalized, suffered a fatal (but merciful) stroke. She had been "so long in the world but not of it," read a letter of condolence from the Longfellows. The last day of her life her youngest son sat beside her bed, watching her labored breathing, until he could stand it no more. Then he went for a long walk on the grounds of the hospital, and when he returned he sat for more hours on a park bench facing her window, until he saw the shade go down, the signal that she had died. December brought the first breath of relief to the stricken family in the birth to Maria of a strapping son,

Walter, "who showed all the uncommon promise that came with being born a Lowell."

The poet, presently much more at ease, embarked upon a revitalizing exercise regimen—hiking, jogging, swimming, lifting weights. As usual he did things to excess: "I strike out three hundred strokes with a pair of twenty-four pound dumb-bells every morning and evening." He rose at dawn and ran five miles before breakfast. Puritan ambition wielded a heavy whip. He jokingly complained that his "whoreson appearance of health and good spirits" gave friends and acquaintances a false impression of his prosperity.

Among the impressions we have of a life under the eaves at Elmwood during this period is Frederika Bremer's record of a visit, which she published in her *Homes of the New World* (1853):

> Her [Maria's] mind has more philosophical depth than his. Singularly enough I did not discern in him that deeply earnest spirit which charmed me in some of his poems. He seemed to me occasionally to be brilliant, witty, gay, especially in the evening, when he has what he calls his "evening fever," when his talk is like an incessant play of fireworks. I find him very agreeable and amiable. He seems to have many friends, mostly young men.

The young men to whom Miss Bremer refers were probably fellow enthusiasts in the abolitionist movement. Although Lowell retained his former political connections, his interest in the movement itself had begun to flag; he had too much of the poet and creator in his blood to give all his time and thought over to political endeavor. "I find that Reform cannot take up the whole of me," he confided to a companion, "and I am quite sure that eyes were given us to look about us sometimes, and not to be always looking forward. . . . I am tired of controversy." The creative impulse of his annus mirabilis carried over into the following year. In 1849 he published a two-volume selected edition of his poems, excising a number of the less-cohesive samples and tightening some of the others. Exhilarated by the commercial success of *The Biglow Papers,* Lowell formulated plans for a second long project, to be called *The Nooning,* consisting of a number of tales in verse, some tragic, some comic, the assemblage based on Chaucer's *Canterbury Tales.* The project, as conceived by Lowell, was more or less carried out by Longfellow a dozen years later as *Tales of a Wayside Inn.* Lowell completed one of his projected tales, "Fitz Adam's Story," a light but wordy sketch told in the same "down-home" Yankee dialect as *The Biglow Papers.*

Because of his wife's fluctuating health, Lowell decided to take his family for an extended stay abroad. Thus, in the summer of 1851, with their two children, Mabel and Walter, along with a nurse and a goat, the Lowells sailed from Boston aboard the three-masted *Sultana* bound for Italy. After spending two months in a small rented villa, Casa Guidi, on the Via Maggio in Florence, the entourage traveled south to Rome. Shortly thereafter word arrived that Lowell's aging father had suffered a paralytic stroke. The poet's first impulse was to return home, but it soon became obvious that Maria's health was too uncertain to weather an arduous cross-Atlantic winter voyage; she had developed a chronic bronchial cough, an affliction doctors only later diagnosed as tuberculosis.

They remained in Rome in a rented two-family house; William Story and his wife Emelyn occupied the floor below. The proximity of the two families afforded both creators excellent companionship. During the initial leg of his stay, Lowell found the Italian capital a gloomy and oppressive place; later, as his Italian improved, he grew to appreciate the city and its people.

As "a son of Puritan New England," it was reasonable to assume that the poet would find in Roman Catholicism themes and subjects of interest. But according to entries in his Italian notebooks, later published as *Leaves from My Journal in Italy and Elsewhere,* he remained unimpressed with Rome's churches, finding them garish and ornate. Even the Basilica of St. Peter's failed to move him; he admitted to its "noble" interior but maintained that it suffered from "architectural elephantiasis." Michelangelo, like Victor Hugo in literature, had mistaken quantity for quality. Moreover, the pomp and ceremony of the Church offended his sensibilities. The Christmas Day spectacle of "the servant of the servants of the Lord in cloth of Gold, borne on men's shoulders" was, he wrote, an altogether tasteless affair.

While in Rome the poet befriended the British expatriate poet Walter Savage Landor, and the Robert Brownings, with whom the Lowells went regularly to the opera. Mrs. Lowell frankly preferred Rome's sights over visits with friends: "Human nature is not greatly different, and educated human nature in the nineteenth century does not amaze one like the Coliseum." They did their socializing weekends; incredibly, there were fourteen Lowells staying concurrently in Rome, underscoring a statement the poet had issued before leaving Boston, that he was going abroad to become better acquainted with his own family.

Late in March 1852 the Lowells left Rome for a two-week sojourn in Naples. Now occurred an extraordinary series of family misfortunes, beginning with the contraction by their young son of cholera infantum. The Lowells returned directly to Rome to secure expert medical care for their son. The boy, who had already begun to learn his a-b-c's, died after a month of intense illness. "How beautiful and full of promise he was nobody but we will ever know," the distraught father (who had very much wanted a son) wrote to his sister Mary Putnam. Of four children Maria had borne her husband, only one survived. "I am tired of broken promises," she wrote, "and dare not think of a future for Mabel. She is well now, today, but I have no certainty for tomorrow."

In October 1852 the Lowells sailed from Liverpool for the United States. Aboard ship they encountered William Thackeray and Matthew Arnold's confrere, Arthur Hugh Clough, who helped distract them from their latest sorrows. It was Thackeray who convinced Lowell to attempt a serial poem, called "Our Own," about life in New England, the first installment of which he published in *Putnam's Magazine*, edited by Charles F. Briggs and George William Curtis. But the work was not to be completed. Maria had suddenly taken ill again. That quiet, intense, and stalwart spirit had been crushed by the last catastrophe, the death of her young son. Lowell tried desperately to revive her but soon began to lose hope. "I cannot bear to write it," he informed Briggs, "but she is very dangerously ill—growing weaker and weaker. . . . It is only within the last week that I have realized the danger. She has been so often ill and rallied from it that I supposed she would soon begin to get better. But there seems no force left now." The decline went on, unfought on her part, and seemingly unregretted. She died on October 23, 1853, at the age of thirty-two.

Her death shattered the poet. For months he lived as if she had never left his side. "I have the most beautiful dreams," he rhapsodized to one correspondent, "and never as if any change had come to us. Once I saw her sitting with Walter on her knee, and she said to me, 'See what a fine strong boy he is grown.' And one night as I was lying awake and straining my eyes through the gloom, and the palpable darkness was surging and gathering and dispersing as it will, I suddenly saw far, far off a crescent of angels standing and shining silently. But oh! it is a million times better to have had her and lost her, than to have had and kept any other woman I ever saw." To Briggs, who had known them both so well, he wrote (November 25):

> I feel now for the first time old, and as if I had a past—something, I mean, quite alien to my present life, and from which I am now exiled. How beautiful that past was and how I cannot see it clearly yet for my tears I need not tell you. I can only hope and pray that the sweet influences of thirteen years spent with one like her may be seen and felt in my daily life henceforth.

Lowell spent the months following Maria's death gathering together her scattered verse into a small volume that he had privately printed in an edition of fifty copies—and these he distributed among friends. The twenty or so poems collected in the volume ring with tenderness and delicacy. Several of the poems reveal a sure and resounding talent. "Africa" is such a poem:

> She sat where the level sands
> Sent back the sky's fierce glare;
> She folded her mighty hands
> While the red sun dropped down the steaming air.
>
> Her throne was broad and low,
> Builded of cinnamon;—
> Huge ivory, row on row,
> Varying its columns dun,
> Barred with the copper of the setting sun.
>
> Up from the river came
> The low and sullen roar
> Of lions, with eyes of flame,
> That haunted its reedy shore,
> And the neigh of the hippopotamus trampling the watery floor.
>
> Her great dusk face no light
> From the sunset-glow could take;
> Dark as the primal night
> Ere over the earth God spake:
> It seemed for her a dawn could never break. . . .

Like Emily Dickinson, Maria White did not live to see in print, except in a smattering of small magazines, the fruits of her artistic labors. Not that it mattered: her poetry was homespun, composed principally for herself and her immediate family. She was too aware of the difficulties of a life in literature to wish to compete with her husband for acclaim on that front. One of her last letters to him, composed while he was on a brief trip to New York, addressed itself in a lighthearted vein to this very point. After explaining why she considered herself a "bad" wife, she wrote: "But still bad as I am, I perhaps make thee happier than some better women. At any rate, I understand and appreciate thy intellect and nature, and do not thwart it very much, do I?"

11

HARVARD REDUX

HIS GRIEF was real, not imagined, not simply the vagary of a romantic Victorian. He had adored Maria, worshiped her. Without her he felt himself drowning. "The waters have gone over me," he told Briggs. Neither family nor friends could console him. The easy assumptions of the Transcendental faith did not mitigate his sorrow. He knew that his despair could be healed only by the slow passage of time. "By and by," he assured himself, "by and by."

Life at Elmwood ticked mechanically forward. In addition to the loss of his wife, Lowell had to face the invalidism of his father and the deteriorating condition of his sister Rebecca, whose mental disorder had grown more severe. Her oscillation of mood suddenly became dangerously pronounced. She turned ever inward, gave herself over increasingly to stretches of brooding and silence. When Rebecca was not fighting the same self-dividing illness that had destroyed Harriet Lowell, she was able to help care for the aged Reverend Charles, and teach Mabel, now six, to read and write. Mabel was her father's sole source of joy at Elmwood, his only comfort during these trying days. It was mainly for her sake that he was determined to persevere.

"I know perfectly well that my nature is naturally joyous and susceptible of all happy impressions," he speculated three months after Maria's funeral, trying to reassure himself that he was on the road to recovery. He was not, and in his mourning he sealed himself off from all flow of life. He remained in seclusion, venturing out of his eyrie only for an infrequent dinner appointment at Longfellow's house or at the home of his gentle friend Charles Eliot Norton ("loving Charles") or at Edmund Quincy's. Convinced that his emotions would be misunderstood, he isolated himself from the world. He suffered insomnia and brooded over the heaviness that kept him from his work. Numbness and enervation swept over him like the sea. He was haunted by his past, dogged by pangs of undefined guilt.

He kept a daily journal, a record of pain and sorrow:

> Jan. 15 [1854]: M. L. anima beata! carissima, ahi de vederti una volta ancora per un momentino solamente!
> Feb. 9: M. L. M. L. M. L. A sad day—piangeva acerbamente . . . Dearest! dearest!
> Feb. 22: 35 years old today & no better.
> March 10: Dark without & within. M. L. M. L. M. L. . . .
> Oct. 17: Itamane ancora piangera. Sancta Maria, ora pro me!

On many days Lowell simply wrote "M. L." in capital letters across the top of the page, too distraught to do more than scratch her initials in ink. Seven months after her death, Longfellow, whom Lowell saw with some frequency now, reported finding his friend "low spirited and weary . . . says he would write no more if he were not forced to do it. He has no heart for the task, and is lonely and desolate."

When he did attempt writing again it was to prose, not poetry that he turned. He began reworking his Italian travel notes, completed his "Moosehead Journal," a charming and humorous account of a fishing and camping expedition he had undertaken into the verdant region surrounding Maine's largest lake, and started a commemorative sketch on "Cambridge Thirty Years Ago." Substantial chunks of these essays appeared as magazine pieces in *Putnam's* and *Graham's* during 1854 and were reissued in book form a decade later; accompanied by additional articles, the 1864 collection was entitled *Fireside Travels.* For the *British Poets* series, published by Little, Brown under the editorial aegis of Francis J. Child, Lowell compiled editions of Dryden, Marvell, and Donne and wrote biographical sketches of Keats and Wordsworth. There was talk of a selected Shakespeare and a life of Swift, but neither of these projects materialized.

As early as the winter of 1853 the Firesider had been invited by John Amory Lowell, the trustee of the Lowell Institute, to deliver a series of lectures on a subject or subjects of his choice; he chose "The English Poets," informing Briggs that he would use the opportunity to revenge himself on dead poets "for the injuries received by one whom the public won't allow among the living." There were rumors afloat that Lowell had been selected for the Institute lectureship predominantly on the basis of family connections and because it was believed by various members of the clan that the preparation of the lectures would jolt him out of his intense depressions.

Determined to dispel any charges of nepotism, Lowell completed the preliminary work on his lectures the summer of 1854, while vacationing with his brother Charles Russell Lowell and his brother's family at "Underhill," an estate at Beverly Farms along the beautiful North Shore coastline of Massachusetts Bay. All the big Boston names—Lowell, Cabot, Lodge, Forbes, Crowninshield—summered in estates along the North Shore, or they went to Newport, Rhode Island, which Lowell found overcrowded and too snooty for his rustic tastes. Although the Boston rich tended to call their summer estates "cottages," they were hardly that. Underhill was small only in comparison to Elmwood. The house, on a rise above the bay, was surrounded by cedar, wild cherry, and barberry; a sand beach at the foot of the hill came with the house and afforded excellent swimming. The salty, pine-scented air, the rocks, the changing lights and colors improved Lowell's disposition immensely. He had lost a good deal of weight since his wife's death, but his sister-in-law's cooking and the cleansing sea air brought back his appetite and Lowell quickly regained the lost weight. He swam, fished, yachted, and relaxed by taking slow strolls along the shore, even trying his hand painting watercolors of North Shore scenery.

Across the bay from Underhill, within easy viewing distance on a clear day, lay a line of islands—some bare rock, some shrubby, some wooded. Lowell called these "the true islands of the Sirens." One of them, formerly named Cat Island (after Robert Catta, its first owner), had recently been purchased by the Salem Steamboat Company and transformed into an offshore resort for the vacationing millworkers of Lowell, Massachusetts. The name was changed to Lowell Island and the Lowell Island House, a hotel with a hundred rooms, dining hall, and bowling alley, was built for the purpose of uplifting the spirits of the faceless textile employees. It apparently did not work because "the rowdies," as the North Shore summer rich called them, soon stopped coming to the island and the hotel was eventually sold. Lowell's sole comment on the situation was that Cat Island had been "disenchanted by a great hotel, to which a steamboat runs innumerably every day with a band—the energetic *boong! boong! boong! boong! boong!* of the bass drum being all we hear."

Another of the islands—Appledore—was to have a completely different effect upon the poet, encouraging him after months of spiritual and creative paralysis to turn again to verse; the result was "Pictures from Appledore":

> But mountains make not all the shore
> The mainland shows to Appledore;
> Eight miles the heaving water spreads
> To a long, low coast with beach and heads
> That run through unimagined mazes,
> As the lights and shades and magical hazes
> Put them away or bring them near,
> Shimmering, sketched out for thirty miles
> Between two capes that waver like threads,
> And sink in the ocean, and reappear,
> Crumbled and melted to little isles,
> With filmy trees, that seem the mere
> Half-fancies of drowsy atmosphere . . .

While not among his better-known folios, "Appledore" is filled with pleasant surprises. It begins with the isle of Appledore as viewed by the poet in the midst of a winter storm—"A heap of bare and splintery crags / Tumbled about by lightning and frost"—followed by an examination of the distant shoal at night and again during the subdued season of spring. Lowell's natural world in this poem is not the dreamy landscape of Wordsworth or Keats but a rather grim and frightening setting, not unlike the caustic, sometimes terrifying contemplations of cosmic emptiness we find in the strongest poems of Robert Frost, or even in several poems by the Firesider's future heir, Robert Lowell. In "Appledore" a relatively untried poetic voice emerges; thought and language, idea and image fold into a new being. The author of this sequence is the well-bred Boston Brahmin free for once of his urban setting, in deep relation with the tangible yet changing universe of the sea. The sea becomes the poet's pathless terrain, an anti-Edenic vision, a body symbolic of Milton's foregone paradise, after the fall but before the apocalypse.

The poet put the finishing touches on his Lowell Institute lectures at Elmwood in the fall of 1854 and delivered the first lecture—on Milton

—January 9, 1855, in an auditorium packed to the hilt; he was forced to repeat his performance the following afternoon to those who could not find standing room the night before. Lowell, who had never lectured in public before, performed as admirably as any pulpit discerner. He was so impressive, for that matter, that when Longfellow resigned from his long-standing position as Smith Professor of Belles-Lettres and Modern Languages at Harvard, Lowell was offered the job.

The Harvard Corporation, encouraged by John Amory Lowell, made the official proffer while the poet's Institute lectures were still in progress. The annual salary attached to the chair was at that time only twelve hundred dollars; however, as Lowell's private income was but half that, and his miscellaneous income from writing not considerable, the additional sum provided him with a much-needed financial ballast. He worried about the possible effects the routine of teaching might have on creative impulse, but consoled himself with the sobering realization that Longfellow had held the post before him and George Ticknor before Longfellow. Besides, he would be required to deliver only two courses per semester; also, Harvard had granted him permission to spend a year abroad preparing himself by boning up on German grammar and literature.

He sailed on June 4, arriving in Le Havre and traveling from there to Paris; while in Paris he journeyed to Chartres, a spot that inspired him fourteen years later to write his poem *The Cathedral.* From Paris he went to London to visit old friends—the Storys, Thackeray, the Brownings—and dropped in on Leigh Hunt and his crowd. But work and study beckoned and within a fortnight he arrived in Dresden. A depressing heaviness hung over the Saxon city. Lowell was plagued by memories of Maria; he plunged to new depths: "I confess frankly that I am good for nothing, and have been for some time, and that there are times almost every day when I wish to die, be out of the world once for all." He had not only lost his wife but was without Mabel, whom he had left behind in Cambridge under the care of a governess, Miss Frances Dunlap, whose sister had been close friends with Maria.

Lowell's German studies, difficult as he found them, kept him temporarily occupied. "The confounding genders!" he railed. "If I die I shall have engraved on my tombstone that I died of *der, die, das,* not because I caught them but because I couldn't." He took German lessons mornings from his landlady; afternoons he read; evenings were reserved for such worldly concerns as theater, opera, or a concert. But he was unable to clear his mind long enough to enjoy himself. His letters were filled with references to his terrible loss, his "open wound." To Maria's sister, Lois White Howe, he wailed: "It is little to say that such a loss is irreparable—it becomes every day a greater loss—and a real sorrow is forever at compound interest. I look sadly at my wedding ring and it is empty, as empty as a magic circle after the Prospero is dead who traced it— the obedient spirits come no more."

By August he was again in Cambridge, living with Mabel and her governess in the house of his brother-in-law, Dr. Estes Howe, on Kirkland Street, then known as Professors' Row. This was to be his residence from the end of 1856 until January 1861; the poor health of his father and the dangerous psychological state of the poet's sister made Elmwood an unsuitable home for a growing girl. Within a month of his return the novice professor met his first class at Harvard. Although accounts of his success as a university lecturer vary markedly, the general consensus has it that he was wholly devoid of academic mannerisms and conventions and that there was a freshness and individuality to his method of teaching—at the beginning, that is. As time wore on, and the anonymous stream of students passed through his classroom, he grew weary and detached and his lectures lost some of their initial glitter. After more than two decades on the job he was down on the entire prospect of the academy. He blamed Harvard and his professorial duties for having indeed drained him of all creative energy and for having taken time away from his "real" work: the writing of poetry.

But the first years came as a welcome change and represented a period of valuable challenge. The elementary language classes in Spanish and Italian and German did not, it is true, hold nearly the excitement for him that he mustered for the literature courses. Yet both, in their own way, offered him a chance to reacquaint himself with material that he found entirely rewarding. His first semester's literature course was based on the lecture series he had presented at the Lowell Institute on the English poets. After that he organized a course in Dante, a seminar he gave for noncredit in the privacy of his home, first at Kirkland Street and afterwards in his library at Elmwood. He offered a course in German literature and delivered at stated intervals public lectures before the college on seventeenth- and eighteenth-century British poets. Later he taught courses in Spanish and Old French literature, dropping the German.

Lowell's methodology of instruction was typically his own. While practically every language teacher of his day utilized literature as a means of teaching grammar and philology, Lowell believed that language should always be taught as a vehicle of beautiful literature. He considered it more important that his students learn to appreciate and love the elegance and grace of literature as a transmitter of sound philosophy and living truth than to become familiar with the etymology of words or the logic of grammar. He wanted them to enjoy the rhythm and flow of poetry rather than belabor and study to death the technique of its meters.

Barrett Wendell, a student in one of his seminars, recalled the "human friendliness" of the gatherings, and Henry Adams praised Lowell's teaching gifts in *The Education of Henry Adams*. William Dean Howells, never an official student but the recipient of an avalanche of avuncular advice from Lowell, remembered his captivating wit and instant charm. Bubbling over with animal spirits, Lowell must have excited the fancy of his auditors. He had a worldly air, antiquarian tastes, a love of literature, a streak of the ridiculous in him—all the qualities of the first-rate teacher. Lowell's classroom loquacity was marked by an open, ardent manner, outraging dignity, an almost comic grandeur. His voice running up and down a sliding scale of sarcasm and wit, he discussed literature with nervous, moving hands, demonstrating an important point by cutting the air with a minatory finger. His voice, with its vibrant tenderness and crispness in the tones, the perfect modulation, clear enunciation, elect diction, was a voice fit for the stage.

Outside the classroom the poet luxuriated in the privacy of his library, preparing his college lectures there and carrying on a constant, voluminous reading campaign. He read biographies, histories, the social and natural sciences, letters, theologians and philosophers, poets and novelists. His reading was extraordinarily wide, learned, alive. Visitors to Elmwood recorded vivid memories of the poet in his lair. When Sir Leslie Stephen, the British biographer and critic, called on him at the beginning of the Civil War, he found at first glance "a singularly complete specimen of the literary recluse." With his pipe and velvet jacket, Lowell was practically domiciled among his books. Howells, a frequent visitor, recalled that "when Lowell quoted anything from a book, he liked to get it and read the passage over, as if he tasted a kind of hoarded sweetness in the words." This penchant for the written word led the poet to his next major feat: the editorship of the newly established *Atlantic Monthly*.

Originally conceived as a literary bond between Old and New England, the *Atlantic* was the brainchild of F. H. Underwood, a native

New Englander who taught school and studied law in the Deep South before arriving in Boston in 1850 to open a private law practice. Always interested in the arts, Underwood recognized that Boston would provide an excellent site for a national magazine devoted to politics and literature. When the publishing firm of Phillips, Sampson agreed to back it, Lowell, who had already agreed to participate, wrote to Arthur Hugh Clough that "a publisher has gone mad and is willing to sink I know not how much out of pure patriotism. If he be not sent to the Lunatic Asylum before the year's end—I think he will be able to make the Magazine go."

A host of Boston's shining literary stars was quickly mobilized. Those who became involved initially were Emerson, Oliver Wendell Holmes (who gave the publication its name), the historian John Lothrop Motley, James Elliot Cabot, Longfellow, and the essayist Edwin Whipple. It was Emerson who suggested that Lowell be appointed editor; Underwood became business manager and assistant to the editor. The first number of the magazine appeared in November 1857 in a format not entirely alien to the one it bears today, combining poetry, articles of current interest, short fiction, and book reviews.

From the beginning Lowell proved himself an editor of shrewd faculty and judgment, lending the monthly the stamp of high literature and bold speech on literary affairs it continued to uphold for years. If the job had a shortcoming, it was the arduousness of trying to combine it with his teaching duties at Harvard. But he was determined to create in the pages of the *Atlantic Monthly* a forum for the leading writers of the period. He wanted it to be "free without being fanatical," a symposium capable of bringing together "all available talent of all shades of opinion." The keynote editorial called for a monthly that would speak its mind openly, at the same time maintaining a "scholarly and gentlemanlike" perspective. Abroad, Charles Norton appealed for contributions to John Ruskin, William Morris, and the Rossettis. On the home front Lowell activated such pens as belonged to Dr. Holmes, Emerson, Whittier, Longfellow, Harriet Beecher Stowe, Thomas Higginson, Charles Norton, Thomas Bailey Aldrich, John Trowbridge, William Howells, and a score of less formidable names. The mélange yielded many admirable manuscripts and several of historical import: Emerson's "Brahma" and "Days," Whittier's "Skipper Ireson's Ride," Holmes's *The Autocrat of the Breakfast-Table* series.

If in many respects the *Atlantic* demonstrated itself worthy of Lowell's devotion, there was nevertheless a good deal of negative reaction from outsiders to his participation in the venture. For one thing, it became apparent to all that the magazine had failed in its pre-announced mission to bring together under one roof British as well as American thought. From the first, Lowell refused to reprint previously published British and European works, choosing instead to look to his homeland for the bulk of the magazine's contents. He was similarly accused of provincialism, of pandering exclusively (or almost exclusively) to New England intellectuals, both in terms of writers and audience.

His defense against this charge was that his main literary and publishing contacts were located in and around the Boston area; as a result he was forced to draw his authors predominantly from this locale. Moreover, he understood and appreciated Boston's wit and charm and the propitious intellectual climate of Back Bay and Cambridge better than he comprehended the traits and traditions of any other region; it stood to reason, therefore, that he would exploit his familiarity with the life and times of this geography and allow his interest in New England's culture to color the layout of the publication as a whole.

More serious was the charge levied against him by critics concerning a policy of editorial discrimination at the *Atlantic,* particularly his failure to represent adequately the work of three of the day's formidable talents: Whitman, Melville, and Thoreau. Lowell did not deny the charge; to the contrary, he openly admitted that Whitman's "barbaric yawp," his stoic and authoritative muscularity, was "solemn humbug" as far as he could tell. *Leaves of Grass,* that earthy anti-Victorian hymn, never appealed to Lowell. It aimed too consciously at extravagance, was too broad and otherworldly. Lowell's antagonism toward Whitman's work was in many respects similar to his dissatisfaction with Thoreau's. Lowell's view of the universe was grounded "in the belief that satisfaction and wisdom come from being in the world, not apart from or above it." Although it wavered from time to time, his basic conception of the ideal poet was less a romantic exordium than Emerson's, Thoreau's, or Whitman's, all of whom characterized the Poet as "the man of Beauty and Spirituality"—not a mere verse-maker or man of letters, not even a leader of society, but a bona fide Seer and Sayer, a mortal imbued with godly powers.

In his role as editor, Lowell probably attempted to judge fairly the work of his contemporaries, a feat not always easily accomplished. A letter from Lowell to Charles Eliot Norton touched on the subject of Whitman: "When a man aims at originality he acknowledges himself consciously unoriginal, a want of self-respect which does not often go along with the capacity for great things. The great fellows have always let the stream of their activity flow quietly—if one splashes in it he may make a sparkle, but he muddies it, too, and the good folks down below (I mean posterity) will have none of it." Lowell eventually agreed to publish one Whitman poem, "Bardic Symbols," a concession he refused to make in the case of Melville, whose work he would not let appear in the magazine at all. So total was his lack of compassion for Melville that he could barely bring himself to talk about the author, whose name appears but once in Lowell's formal writings. The problem with *Moby-Dick*'s creator, from Lowell's point of view, was his morbid fascination with evil and the powers of darkness. Not exactly the perennial optimist, Lowell was still far more positive in his outlook than Melville, whose depressive personal philosophy was anathema to the general attitude of hopefulness propounded by most of the Fireside Poets.

Thoreau was a flag of a slightly different color. Because Emerson had recommended him for the editorial job, Lowell felt obliged to ask Thoreau to contribute something to the magazine. Thoreau complied by sending along "Chesuncook," the first of a proposed series of long essays. Lowell, finding it difficult to resist temptation, promptly bluepenciled a sentence in which Thoreau had waxed anthropomorphic over a pine tree: "It is as immortal as I am, and perchance will go to as high a heaven, there to tower above me still." The deletion of this sentence Thoreau took as a personal attack: "I could excuse a man who was afraid of an uplifted fist, but if one habitually manifest fear at the utterance of a sincere thought, I must think that his life is a kind of nightmare continued into broad daylight." Thoreau did not contribute to the *Atlantic* again.

There were further complaints registered against Lowell's management of the magazine. He was castigated for disorderly and scatterbrained editorial methods, a fault that had become something of a James Russell Lowell trademark—that of the absentminded professor. By his own admission, he was neither organized nor systematic, frequently misplacing manuscripts, occasionally losing them altogether. He was notorious for his delaying tactics in replying to correspondents; when he did respond, his letters were often long-winded and off the point, not the sort usually associated with the publishing trade. Despite these shortcomings he managed to produce, almost singlehandedly, a magazine whose quality rivaled and surpassed that of the other leading periodicals of the era: *Graham's, Putnam's,* and the newly founded *Harper's Magazine.* As time wore on and the danger of civil war increased, the prevailing tone of the *Atlantic* grew more serious, addressing itself to the problems of slavery. It became a mouthpiece for abolitionist thought and theory, clear-visioned in its newfound sense of purpose.

A privacy and an interlude: in the middle of the busiest year of his life, while teaching at Harvard and editing the *Atlantic Monthly,* Lowell made still another commitment that helped restructure his existence. He decided to remarry. His choice of a bride was Frances Dunlap, Mabel's governess. During the period of her employment, Lowell had grown close to "Fanny" and had come to depend on her as much for her solid presence as her patient understanding and care of his daughter. She had a warmth and gentleness, a strength and depth of character, which he greatly admired. The Dunlaps themselves were a large and proud family from Portland, Maine. Economic misfortune had thrown the daughters on their own resources for support. This combination of wealth and poverty was a good breeder of character. Frances Dunlap was refined, quiet, simple, and direct—qualities that Lowell cherished in a mate. There was an added consideration: should anything happen to him in the future, his daughter would be well looked after.

They were married on September 16, 1857, by Lowell's brother the Reverend R. T. S. Lowell. The reaction to Lowell's wedding among those who knew him was mixed. Mrs. Longfellow, upon meeting the new bride, decided that she was "neither pretty nor attractive" and maintained that the overall impression was one of disappointment. Sydney Gay's wife was equally disappointed. Edmund Quincy found the second Mrs. Lowell self-effacing and overly reserved, noting that he never knew her to start a conversation; she merely "smiles and assents to what you say." But there were those who came to appreciate her finer qualities. Henry James, hardly a poor judge of character, found she improved on acquaintance and was a "very sweet and excellent woman." Annie Fields, wife of the Boston publisher James T. Fields, "always felt indignant that so few people appreciated Frances Lowell's unselfish devotion to her husband, her willingness to dedicate herself to his comfort and needs."

Ultimately, of course, the only opinion that meant anything was Lowell's. No one was more aware than he of his wife's shortcomings—her shyness, reticence, lack of worldliness. Yet all the evidence indicates that his life with her was a joyous one. Shortly after their marriage he spoke of feeling "stronger and better, with an equability of mind" he had not enjoyed for years. Marriage was a necessity of his nature, an institution without which he felt incomplete. Frances Lowell's unassuming efficiency, her quiet strength, gave him strength. She was a timid person yet there was an air of unstated elegance about her, a reminder that the family of her birth was of uncommon stock. She was not a Brahmin but she came across as a dignified, disciplined, organized woman who knew what she was and what she wanted. When Annie Fields suggested to her that perhaps she devoted too much energy to housekeeping and that she was overly protective of her new husband, she simply responded that she had "a sensitive and superior being to care for."

The Lowell household was built around the premise that nothing mattered as much as Lowell's freedom to write without interruption. If this arrangement caused strife, or the feeling of resentment on Mrs. Lowell's part, it was nowhere in evidence. The fact is that Frances Lowell had interests of her own. She was a talented watercolorist and a gifted linguist. She spent hours each day sketching and painting the local Cambridge scenery, afterward donating her canvases to charity or giving them away to friends. The poet's only regret in his second marriage was their inability to produce children. Nor did marriage entirely free him from his chronic bouts of manic depression. These periodic waverings were as much part of his constitution as the deep divisions within him between strength and vulnerability, between aggression and guilt, between bohemianism and traditionalism, between moral and literary order and disorder, between cowardice and courage. That he sometimes complained of feeling "out of place and out of sorts," of being unable to get himself "into right relations with men and things" was to be expected. Frances Lowell could not combat these psychogenic disorders; but her presence helped limit the frequency and intensity of his alternating highs and lows. After his marriage Lowell felt the reemergence of a budding life-force, the need to retrain his thoughts on an active world. He had not felt such sobering emotions since before the death of Maria White.

In his enthusiasm to get back into the world, he became a member of the renowned Whist Club and later joined the Adirondack Club, whose annual fall outing and game hunt attracted its fill of predatory intellectuals, including the likes of Emerson, Agassiz, and Longfellow. Those who participated did so primarily in an effort to commune once a year with nature; they enjoyed the spectacular Adirondack scenery, the idyllic unspoiled landscape, the massive acreage of colorful trees and spring-fed waterways. On one memorable camping expedition Lowell was accompanied by Emerson and Robert Louis Stevenson, who described the area as "a kind of insane mixture of Scotland, and a touch of Switzerland, and a dash of America." The distant mountain view brought the naturalist in Lowell to the surface. Everybody should own a tree, he was overheard advising Emerson—or a valley full of trees, or a whole hillside. Not legally, not in the formal sense, but the way that one comes to own a tree by seeing it at the turn of the road, or down the street, or in a field, and watching it day after day, and seeing color come to its leaves. That way it is your tree whenever you choose to pass that way, and neither fence nor title can take it from you. And it will be your tree as long as you want it to be.

In the end, the sight of the myopic and peaceful Reverend Emerson beating the underbrush in search of small game, shotgun in hand, proved more than anyone could bear. The Adirondack Club dissolved, and Lowell inscribed in still another organization, the Saturday Club (sometimes called the Atlantic Club), whose membership was drawn predominantly from the Boston-Cambridge-Concord literary circuit. They met the last Saturday of each month, like the golden spirits of Samuel Johnson's literary salon, usually over a lavishly dressed dinner table: Porterhouse steak at the Porter House, Parkerhouse rolls at the Parker House, guinea fowl and venison on all occasions, and wine— gallons of Chablis, sauterne, and bloodred port.

Emerson, John Dwight, Edwin Whipple, Samuel Ward, Horatio Woodman were the organizers of the group; Lowell was invited to join and was followed by John Lothrop Motley, E. Rockwood Hoar, Oliver Wendell Holmes, Longfellow, Hawthorne, Agassiz, and others. The Saturday Club was not what literary historians have blown it up to be —a hushed gathering of sedate, parochial, pedagogical graybeards. To the contrary, these dinner parties were animated, raucous affairs that began at three in the afternoon and usually ran late into the night. Wit and wine flowed in concert. Science, theology, and literature were discussed and debated from every conceivable angle. The club was a way of crossing what Julia Ward Howe termed "the frozen ocean of Boston intellectual life." Many a book idea was harvested at these congregations. Lifelong friendships were formed. So devoted to these monthly banquets were the literary lions of the area that summers they often gathered at a restaurant in Nahant, where many of them vacationed. When someone tagged them "The Mutual Admiration Society," Oliver Wendell Holmes retorted: "If there was not a certain amount of 'mutual admiration' . . . it was a great pity, and implied a defect in the nature of men who were otherwise largely endowed." The brotherhood of such sage and knowledgeable companions stood them all in excellent stead. Toward the end of his life, after years of hobnobbing with Europe's high-living elite, James Russell Lowell declared he had "never seen society on the whole so good" as he used to meet on those select Boston Saturdays.

12

THE BLUE
AND THE GRAY

AFTER the appearance of Lowell's "Prometheus" in 1843, he wrote to Charles Briggs explaining the poem's political point of reference: "I have made it *radical,* and I believe that no poet in this age can write much that is good unless he give himself up to this tendency. For radicalism has now for the first time taken a distinctive and acknowledged shape of its own. . . . It has never till now been seen to be one of the two great wings that upbear the universe." But by 1850 Lowell had disavowed almost the entire body of what he came to consider the tropes and jitters of youth. Age and experience made the noisy knight-errant style and thought pattern look tarnished and stale. He disowned such apostasies as expressed in a pool of early abolitionist poems and disengaged himself to a large extent from the movement as such.

If his impulses were at base liberal and his heart generous, he was nevertheless not strong enough to resist the inviting temptations of the Brahmin lifestyle. He was becoming more of a Brahmin each day, and every day more himself. Before sailing for Italy with Maria White in 1850, the poet sang a quiet song renouncing his radical beliefs: "The farther I can get from American slavery the better I shall feel. Such enormities as the Slave Law weigh me down without rebound, make me unhappy and too restless to work well in my own special vineyard." The gist of his mid-century political stance was one of uncertainty; Lowell no longer knew what he felt.

The poet's eighteen-month stay in Italy served as a welcome sabbatical from the political fury that was taking hold in the United States. When he returned to his homeland, Lowell brought with him the same indecision, the same mixed emotions, he had carted away. He recognized that the problems of abolition and reform were of greater complexity than he had ever imagined; the "black man's right" was no longer the only or even the "hardest question":

> The trouble is to 'mancipate the white;
> One's chained in body an' can be sot free,
> But t'other's chained in soul to an idee.

This fragment, from *The Biglow Papers,* second series, was written during the Civil War, but it expresses Lowell's feelings about slavery prior to 1861. The poet realized that any permanent solution would have to emerge slowly out of the events of the near and distant past:

> Young folks are smart, but all ain't good that's new:
> I guess the gran'thers they knowed sunthin', tu.

As if awakening from a twenty-year slumber, Lowell began to toy with an entire mint of new ideas, notions he had never seriously considered before. In a letter to Sydney Gay he expressed his dislike for the purely vituperative attacks levied by the abolitionists and asked that the editors of the *Standard* treat the slaveholders with dignity—because even "they are human." In the same breath he confessed that his heart was out of tune with abolition writing: "My own house has too many vitreous points about it to allow me to think of throwing stones." He was a member in good standing of the Executive Committee of the Massachusetts Anti-Slavery Society, but acknowledged "with shame" that for some time he had not attended meetings; he kept up his membership because he did not wish to be excluded—it would make him feel, he told Edmund Quincy, as if he had "lost caste."

While such promulgations do not necessarily indicate a complete shift to conservatism, they seem to point to a radical reinterpretation by Lowell of previously constated liberal asseverations, a refocusing of the poet's entire political orientation. This fresh way of looking at things, a new-fashioned sense of nationalistic fervor, became the controlling concept in Lowell's life from roughly the beginning of his employment at Harvard to about 1870, and was in part brought about by his association with the conservative and intellectual elements that populated the professorial and administrative ranks of the academy. Lowell's association with Harvard rejuvenated the old Brahmin instincts that had first peeped through the lines of his 1838 *Class Poem* and which had since lain quietly dormant. The Elmwood bookman was rapidly becoming the Boston clubman, a member of such elite societies as the Union and Somerset clubs, whose meetings he began auditing on a regular basis. Repudiating his first wife's strict observation of the temperance decree, Lowell gradually developed into what is politely known as "a heavy social drinker." For several years he became a problem drinker, his moods swinging back and forth under the influence of alcohol from euphoria to frenzy. His talk was either slurred or had a frenetic edge to it. He became involved in several ugly disturbances—temper tantrums, drink-induced tirades, even a brawl or two. Most notable on these drinking binges was the tenor of Lowell's talk; invariably the flow took a sharp turn to the right. He clashed with friends and developed an embattled, feverish social style guaranteed to alienate acquaintances and make enemies. Besides other less savory subjects, he is said to have expounded at length on the benefits and delights of the American Constitution. He described the document as "the most remarkable monument of political wisdom known to history," a Magna Carta devised by pioneer Federalists who had "a great respect for authority in all its manifestations; for the law first of all, for age, for propriety, for learning, and for experience." The designers of the document were "led astray by no theories of what *might* be good, but clave closely to what experience had demonstrated to *be* good." In these sentiments the poet seemed increasingly to be following in the footsteps of other members of the Lowell enclave—the various Johns, Jameses, Percivals of former generations, for whom the family motto—*Occasionem cognosce*—meant something.

Whatever writing he managed between 1857 and 1860 he published in the pages of the *Atlantic Monthly*. Among his notable poems during these years were "The Origin of Didactic Poetry," "The Dead House," "Italy, 1859," and "L'Envoi: To the Muse"—the entire lot devoid of political interpretation or allusion. "Ode to Happiness" (1861), moderately analogous thematically to Wordsworth's "Ode to Duty," was one of the few poems of this period to deal, even marginally, with Lowell's revised political platform. The sequence speaks of the inadequacy of the humanitarian movement and of reform measures that are not carefully directed toward a specific end. In it Lowell bids adieu to the short-lived "half-earthly" happiness of boyhood and bids welcome to the tranquility that comes with age to those who match impulse with control.

Lowell's increasing respect for tradition and permanence made him a moderate among that class of old stamp New England aristocrats who supported the abolition movement and who inevitably saw the racial struggle in terms of absolutes. Dislike of Southerners among this crowd reached fanatical proportions. Henry Cabot and John Lodge, to cite representatives of two typically resplendent clans, were filled with a deep-seated anger, an intense hatred for the forces of slavery. Their sense of outrage and humiliation could be righted, they insisted, only by the obliteration of the South by the North and of the Democrats by the Republicans. Lowell, in a dozen papers later collected in a volume entitled *Political Essays* (1888), showed himself to be less concerned with regional affairs and more interested in issues that involved the nation at large. He averred that the antislavery question was presently an issue of secondary concern. In an essay, "E Pluribus Unum," he explained himself: "Slavery is no longer the matter in debate, and we must beware of being led off upon that side-issue. The matter now in hand is the reestablishment of order, the reaffirmation of national unity." This was "not a commonplace war, not a prosaic and peddling quarrel about cotton" and slavery, but "a question of national existence"; "the faith of a nation in its own manhood" was being threatened by "the formless void of anarchy." In 1876, looking back, Lowell wrote: "The war was fought for nationality. . . . Emancipation was a very welcome incident of the war and nothing more."

A further turnabout on Lowell's part was activated by the 1860 election of President Abraham Lincoln. At first, like many another Brahmin, Lowell was suspicious of Lincoln, wary of the "noble bends of concession" that seemed to motivate him during the early stages of the Civil War. He gradually decided that Lincoln had exercised excellent judgment after all "in never moving too far in advance of public opinion." In terms of emancipation, "the President had correctly seen that his chief object had not been 'to proclaim his adhesion to certain doctrines' but 'to achieve their triumph by quietly accomplishing his ends.' "

In January 1861, two months before the outbreak of the North-South conflict, the Reverend Charles Lowell, after a number of years of ill health, suffered a fatal heart attack. After a brief period of mourning, his poet son decided to move his small family back to Elmwood. By the middle of March, Lowell would inform Briggs that he had returned, as it were, to his first home: "You will see by my date that I am back again to the place I love best. I am sitting in my old garret, at my old desk, smoking my old pipe, and loving my old friends. I begin already to feel more like my old self than I have these ten years."

It was shortly after this, in May of that year, that he relinquished his editorship of the *Atlantic Monthly,* the magazine having been sold to the publishing firm of Ticknor and Fields and the editorial duties assumed by James T. Fields. There was no animosity between Lowell and the new owners; the poet continued to be a regular contributor on an intermittent basis for several years thereafter. It was between the covers of the *Atlantic* that he chose to publish the eleven sections that comprised the second series of *The Biglow Papers.*

His decision to add to the first series was reached toward the end of 1860, at which time he announced: "As for the new *Biglow Papers,* God knows how I should like to write them, if they would only *make* me as they did before. But I am so occupied and bothered that I have not time to *brood,* which with me is as needful a preliminary to hatching anything as with a clucking hen." The brooding that Lowell required as impetus was provided by the untimely deaths during the Civil War of the poet's three young nephews: William Putnam Lowell, James Jackson Lowell, and Beau Sabreur.

Fourteen years had elapsed since the publication of the Mexican War *Biglow Papers* and Lowell's affirmation that "war is murder." The Civil War series picked up roughly where the other had left off. His characters were the familiar ones, albeit with slight modifications. Parson Wilbur tended to be a bit more urbane and less radical than before, having recalled something of his Harvard education, or at least Lowell had decided to inject his own persona more directly into the poem's flow. Whatever the case, Hosea was still Hosea—the same self-righteous rustic, whose dislike of the South had simply widened over the years. And Birdofredum Sawin was still Birdofredum Sawin, as unprincipled as ever, yet surely Lowell's most animated and engaging character.

On the whole these seriatim documents retain the former collection's air of smoothness and ease. There is possibly a slight lessening of buoyancy and spontaneity, but there is a compensating gain in the touch of wisdom and total impact of emotion. Horace Scudder, Lowell's first biographer, noted that by this point the poet was so sure of himself, so at ease with the rustic form he was using once again and of the old-fashioned pedantry of Reverend Wilbur, that he was able to draw confidently on those elements which lend a poem depth and give it the true ring of artistry. If there was any falling off between the two series it was not readily apparent, although one could probably fault Lowell for having felt the need to return to a format already used and thoroughly exploited.

For all the good grace of the later sequence, it begins on a disappointingly weak chord, with a verbose introduction justifying the poet's use of the New England colloquial dialect and explaining his "careful tracing of many of the words and phrases to the English usage of the seventeenth century, brought over by the early settlers and then domesticated under conditions which served to preserve them in common speech." Lowell's introduction appears for no apparent reason other than to delay the opening section of this series. But the selfsame function is fulfilled by the existence of still another introduction, this prior one spoken by Parson Wilbur at the immediate outset of the present section's first Paper. The Parson's prefatory remarks, as tedious as Lowell's, neither expand upon the poem's theme nor add to our understanding of the Parson as a multidimensional character.

It is only with the second Paper, "Mason and Slidell: A Yankee Idyll," that the series begins to take shape. In taut, lyrical verse, Lowell elaborates on the tentative and complex relationship that existed between England and the United States during the first years of the Civil War. In the poem two Southern agents, Mason and Slidell, have been taken off the British mailship *Trent* by Captain Wilkes of the Union vessel, *San Jacinto,* for allowing Confederate privateers to be fitted out in British shipyards:

> You wonder why we're hot, John?
>   Your mark wuz on the guns,
> The neutral guns thet shot, John,
>   Our brothers an' our sons . . .
> We own the ocean tu, John:
>   You mus'n' take it hard,

Ef we can't think with you, John,
It's just your own back-yard.

The British government, outraged by this military tactic, responds by issuing an angry protest directed at President Lincoln, contending that the British flag has been violated at sea. Lincoln, aware that war with one government is less objectionable than open conflict with two, relents by releasing the prisoners. This turn of events sets off the citizens of the Union; Lincoln is charged with consorting with an ally of the enemy. Lowell, although in real life opposed to British intervention during the war, shows himself in the poem to be less belligerent than his compatriots; he points out that "England ain't *all* bad, coz she thinks us blind," and he supports Lincoln's decision to release Mason and Slidell as proof that the country had arrived at "years of discretion"— "If courage be the sword, yet is patience the armour of a nation."

The Paper proved as popular as any in the series, with the possible exception of the sixth, "Sunthin' in the Pastoral Line," which was written in the spring of 1862 to coincide with Lincoln's preliminary Proclamation of Emancipation. The poem in question presents a symbolic, politically oriented "pastoral" by Hosea Biglow celebrating the advent of a New England spring and the foreseeable end of slavery:

> Fust, come the blackbirds clatt'rin' in tall trees,
> An' settlin' things in windy Congresses,—
> Queer politicians, though, for I'll be skinned
> Ef all on 'em don't head aginst the wind.
> 'Fore long the trees begin to show belief,—
> The maple crimsons to a coral-reef,
> Then saffern swarms swing off from all the willers
> So plump they look like yaller caterpillars,
> Then gray hossches'nuts leetle hands unfold
> Softer 'n a baby's be at three days old:
> Thet's robin-redbreast's almanick; he knows
> Thet arter this ther' 's only blossom-snows.

This description of the season of rebirth is augmented by Hosea's rambling discussion of his need for solitude, his belief in the present moment, his impatience with those who linger in the past. Contemplating such thoughts, he falls asleep upon the steps of a church and dreams that a distant family relation comes to visit him with queries about the current war. A debate ensues between the dreamer and his querulous visitant over the contrasting and timeless issues of war and peace, thought and action, continuity and disjunction. The question arises whether or not abolition can be solved completely in a brief span of time. The poem's narrator is all for a policy of restraint:

> . . . I want's to hev all we gain stick,
> An' not to start Millennium too quick;
> We hain't to punish only, but to keep,
> An' the cure's gut to go a cent'ry deep.

Hosea's Puritan forebear, on the other hand, is a man of unrestrained action:

> It's Slavery thet's the fangs an' thinkin' head,
> An' ef you want selvation, cresh it dead,—
> An' cresh it suddin, or you'll larn' by waitin'
> Thet Chance wun't stop to listen to debatin'—

And there the issue rests—in the poem and in its maker, totally unresolved. Critics, while generously praising the poetry, attacked Lowell personally for his apparent lack of interest in the cause, his inability to settle his mixed feelings about the slavery bond and its related issues. "It was more than painful," wrote one of his detractors, "to find him limping along at such a momentous emergency." The devoted abolitionist Samuel May, Jr., accused Lowell of trying for years to quit the movement, laying the blame for his vacillation on the Brahmin's association with Harvard: "Having got into the smooth, dignified, self-complacent, and change-hating society of the college and its Boston circles, Lowell has gone over to the world, and to 'respectability.'" Martin Duberman took the opposite stance, contending that Lowell's cautionary approach to emancipation should not be taken simply at face value: "Lowell's concern for the slave had not died, only his evaluation of how that concern could best be implemented." The poet himself was uncomfortable in his current position, marked by his inability to resolve the issue one way or the other. In an article for the *Atlantic Monthly*, he epitomized the dichotomy: "It is a question we have hardly the heart to discuss, where our best wishes, our hopes, almost our faith in God, are on one side, our understanding and experience on the other."

The Civil War and its aftermath were to remain open issues for the poet for years to come. Toward the end of the war he was offered a new forum in which to express himself on this and other conundrums. In 1864 he and Charles Eliot Norton were asked to take over the editorship jointly of the *North American Review,* the country's oldest literary journal of note. Their duties were to be divided, Norton to handle the editorial work proper, and Lowell to lend the periodical his name, rank, and writing acumen.

The poet rejoiced when in April 1865, shortly after Lincoln's reelection to office, Lee surrendered to Grant at Appomattox. "The news, my dear Charles, is from Heaven," he wrote to Norton. "I felt a strange and tender exaltation. I wanted to laugh and I wanted to cry, and ended by holding my peace and feeling devoutly thankful. There is something magnificent in having a country to love. It is almost like what one feels for a woman. Not so tender, perhaps, but to the full as self-forgetful."

The Brahmin gave poetic expression to this strange and tender "exaltation" in the "Ode Recited at Harvard Commemoration," which he delivered at Harvard on July 21, a day of memorial exercises in commemoration of her ninety-three sons lost at war, among them the three tender-aged nephews of the poet. The entire "Ode"—with the exception of the Lincoln strophe which was added after the poem's delivery —was composed in less than forty-eight hours.

No other poem meant as much to Lowell and into none did he pour a greater part of himself. Its delivery on so momentous an occasion could not have failed to be by comparison something of a letdown. To Jane Norton, the sister of Charles Eliot Norton, the poet candidly expressed disappointment over his performance: "I did not make the hit I expected, and am ashamed of having been again tempted into thinking I could write *poetry,* a delusion from which I have been tolerably free these dozen years." The fear of failure that gripped Lowell had gripped him before and would take hold again. He was plagued by moments of self-doubt and a steady, unexplainable need of affection and encouragement.

His apprehensions aside, the Harvard Commemoration "Ode" is, in terms of its grandeur and nobility, in a class with three other mature Lowell poems: "Memoriae Positum," *The Cathedral,* and "Agassiz." If none of these had any significant or lasting effect on the development of American verse, they at least demonstrated that Lowell was capable of producing "public" poetry that was both original and passionate, deploying conventional features of meter and rhyme in such a way that they appeared unconventional but at the same time ceremonial and brave.

Of the three poems, the Harvard "Ode" is most similar in subject matter to "Memoriae Positum," written prior to the "Ode" as a memorial to Robert Gould Shaw, killed while leading his all-Negro regiment against Battery Wagner in Charleston Harbor. There is nothing for such a tragic death, Lowell advised Shaw's mother, "but to bow the head and bear it." "Brooding in the heart," he wrote a modern, low-keyed, quiet, dignified poem for this son of close friends. Full of self-questioning and personal suffering, the poem laments the young man's death as a sign of morality in an otherwise immoral age. The poem is less lofty but more personal and ambiguous than the "Ode," the poet exhorting the reader not to forget Shaw's sacrificial slaughter. Although attempting to affirm the positive values in society, Lowell fears the worst. "Hope's forlorn-hopes that plant the desperate good," he pipes, faith and despair modifying each other. The poet bids memory kindle a candle to the Civil War deaths of three youthful nephews: "I write of one, / While with dim eyes I think of three." In the end the song turns hopeful, the author terminating on a note of renewed faith in the country and the future.

One of the major problems facing Lowell in regard to his Commemoration "Ode" was his long-term ambition, his high hopes for it. The poem was an "attempt to restore the country to unity after the Civil War," to solemnize "the triumph of truth and high ideals and to urge a return to national purpose." If it failed to accomplish all that he had hoped it might, the opus—with its hortatory and figurative echoes of Milton—nevertheless contained several eminently quotable sections, such as its sixth strophe, in praise of Lincoln:

> Here was a type of the true elder race,
> And one of Plutarch's men talked with us face to face
> I praise him not; it was too late;
> And some innative weakness there must be
> In him who condescends to victory
> Such as the Present gives, and cannot wait,
> Safe in himself as in a fate.
> So always firmly he:
> He knew to bide his time,
> And can his fame abide,

Still patient in his simple faith sublime,
Till the wise years decide.

On the heels of that most fratricidal and tragic of struggles, Lowell's energies went not into poetry but into prose—literary criticism, social commentary, and critical reviews—which appeared at regular intervals mainly in the pages of the *North American Review* and *The Nation*, E. L. Godkin's eclectically intellectual weekly whose first list of contributors featured William and Henry James, William Dean Howells, Henry Wadsworth Longfellow, and James Russell Lowell. Assembling the perorations that he wrote over these years, Lowell published them as collections: *Among My Books* (1870); *My Study Windows* (1871); *Among My Books*, second series (1872). Shakespeare, Dryden, Lessing, Rousseau, Dante, Spenser, Wordsworth, Milton, Keats, Carlyle, Thoreau, Swinburne, Chaucer, Emerson, Pope, Gray—these were the principal subjects of his prose, many of them the by-products of Lowell's classroom discernments. The three volumes featured several broader extemporizations as well, excursions into the fields of nature and society such as "My Garden Acquaintance," "A Certain Condescension in Foreigners," and "New England Two Centuries Ago," the last an endorsement of Massachusetts life past and present, an anecdotal exploration of Cambridge as the seat of American seventeenth-, eighteenth-, and nineteenth-century culture.

In examining Lowell's scholarly writings from our present distance, more than a century after their original publication, we find a literary reputation of diminishing visibility. A certain aridness pervades these prolix commentaries; their Augustan bookishness lends them a closed-in, claustrophobic feeling. To use an epithet that Lowell bestowed upon Cotton Mather, the whole seems "book suffocated": there was always some book or author that stood between Lowell and his ideas. This most social and learned of men was a superior public speaker but a plodding, pontificating scrivener of literary essays, vital only in a few isolated passages. What saved him from total ruin in his prose was a healthy ration of sincerity and wit, coupled with occasional bursts of passion and a rare abundance of moral depth. Lowell's ability to amuse was not a mere jest-making faculty but the result of a well-flavored and intelligent sense of humor, the kind we usually associate with a Swift or Dryden. He was a master of the pun, a literary juggler whose favorite ploy consisted of referring to common objects in a poetic diction reminiscent of the eighteenth century; hence whitewash became "candent baptism" and Holland gin became "Batavian elixir"; in the essay on Milton it is aptly said of the facetiousness of an obese man that "he tramples out the last spark of cheerfulness with the broad, damp foot of a hippopotamus." Of Emerson he wrote: "His eye for a fine, telling phrase that will carry true is like that of a backwoodsman for a rifle; and he will dredge you up a choice word from the mud of Cotton Mather himself." And after quoting a stanza from a less than melliferous poem by Dryden, he quipped: "One might fancy this written by the secretary of a board of trade in an unguarded moment."

The English critic and translator Edward FitzGerald thought Lowell the only critic capable of doing for Anglo-American letters what Sainte-Beuve had done for the French. But it was not to be. Although word plays and colorful phraseology range throughout the criticism, there are shortcomings of serious consequence in these essays. He demonstrates sympathetic appreciation of his subjects and a richness of language in his best passages, but Lowell is also guilty of discursiveness, inconsistency, and a tendency to smother his pages with lists of learned citations. This last, what De Quincey termed "the gluttony of books," is overshadowed by the more serious sin "of making a generalization on the basis of an instance." At one point, for him, Milton's "place is fixed as the most classic of our poets"; at another, Goldsmith's "Village" and "Traveller" are "perhaps the most truly classical poems in the language." This obvious contradiction is one of many. Early in his essay on Dante, he writes:

> We read the *Paradise Lost* as a poem, the *Commedia* as a record of fact. It is false aesthetics to confound the grandiose with the imaginative.

Yet a few pages further we read:

> To consider [Dante's] hell a place of physical torture is to take Circe's herd for real swine. . . . His hell is a condition of the soul.

Thus two diametrically opposed generalizations are left standing side by side. Among responsible critics only Coleridge was as impervious to the laws of logic.

Self-contradiction is one thing; lack of literary judgment is something else. Lowell's encomium on Shakespeare—"Shakespeare Once More"

—is a sample worth citing. This selection, ostensibly on *Hamlet*, sheds little interior light on the play; instead it enumerates and applauds the Bard's all too obvious virtues, simultaneously compiling an endless list of epigrams and aphorisms, homilies and analogies. Lowell's treatise becomes simply another document, another bit of lavish testimony to be tossed upon the already overburdened Shakespearian heap. Praise displaces critical insight also in Lowell's flippant piece on Pope, in which the Brahmin writes:

> Pope had *one of the prime qualities of a great poet* in exactly answering the intellectual needs of the age in which he lived. . . .

One need not be a prodigy to appreciate the defectiveness of vision inherent in this generalized exposition. Marking contemporary vogue a prime quality of *great poetry* is not the kind of rationale one expects of a leading professor of languages and letters at Harvard.

Lowell's view of the art of criticism, as expressed more than once, contended that "the higher wisdom of criticism lies in the capacity to admire." He applied this one-sided romantic maxim to those select writers he considered the most illustrious of post-Roman times: Dante, Machiavelli, Montaigne, Bacon, Chaucer, Shakespeare, Cervantes, Pascal, Calderon, Lessing, and Goethe. Neither in art nor in literature did Lowell possess a classical spirit. He preferred painting to sculpture, the medieval cathedral to the Greek temple, Gothic art to classic art, and Shakespeare and Dante to Homer, Sophocles, and Virgil.

For all their shortcomings, Lowell's writings found favor with a number of the critics of the day. Those who revered Lowell the conversationalist, the outstanding personality, "talking down the ages," establishing the literary law and a neoclassical moral code of his own making, overlooked the glaring conflicts and unresolved debates that lurked beneath the surface of his prose. One indication of the poet's popularity and influence is that his unfavorable review in the *Atlantic* of Thoreau's posthumous *Letters* (1865) helped delay the general acceptance of Thoreau for a good twenty-five years. Despite his influence, Lowell's position as a scholar and critic of the first magnitude was never universally established. He was accused by one knot of critics, not unjustly, of repeatedly rejecting or ignoring the literature of his own day, preferring to seek his values and principles "in the literatures of those older European societies whose cultures reflected stable and slowly changing orders in which each individual had his accepted place." Like Dryden, Lowell was ill at ease in the currents of thought that prevailed in his own age. His uneasiness amid the "multiplying confusions" of the nineteenth century was very much in keeping with his central conviction that "literature which celebrates the ego of the individual, at the expense of the social values which civilize him, is unhealthy." This trumpet blast, from the Firesider's essay "Rousseau and the Sentimentalists" (1867), bears no small resemblance to a later statement issued by Lowell concerning the introspection of Romanticism; he called it the "melancholy liver-complaint of our self-exploiting nineteenth century." Perplexed and disturbed by it, he sought his literary inspiration in the immortal masterpieces of men such as Chaucer and Shakespeare.

☙ 13 ❧

THE PLENIPOTENTIARY

FOR James Russell Lowell the span immediately following the Civil War, the period known as Reconstruction, was a duration of slow change and gradual growth. Politically he held out little hope for Andrew Johnson, Lincoln's successor, who combined "all the obstinacy of a weak mind and a strong constitution." Lowell was equally pessimistic about the future of universal suffrage. He had faith in the basic tenets of the movement but was convinced that the long history of degradation and ignorance suffered by the Negro race presented a barrier too difficult to overcome in so brief a passage of time.

The poet's personal dealings with recently emancipated slaves were hardly encouraging. Four women were hired to serve as domestics at Elmwood but only one of them ("as black as the darkness inside Andrew Johnson's head") was "neat and hard-working." The others proved "intractable and unreliable" and were soon dismissed. To Edmund Quincy, Lowell professed grave doubts that "this first generation of ex-slaves" could be employed in any meaningful way. "They are dirty, lazy and lying," he wrote, a sentiment not too far removed from the anthem sung by Southern slaveholders. The learning and civilizing period, he opined, would have to be a piecemeal process, made possible by virtue of federal aid and protection. In time, as the black man's capacities "were first restored and then developed, he could be expected to rise according to his individual abilities."

Whether or not such glib speculations as Lowell was wont to make can in consequence be construed as racism is a question open to debate. Certainly, racist overtones abound in Lowell's statement, issued at a later date, to the effect that Caucasians, through their "intellectual and traditional superiority," would "retain sufficient ascendancy to prevent any serious mischief from the new order of things." Martin Duberman asserts that a belief in racial differences, and thus in racial inequality, was the "hallmark of advanced opinion in Lincoln's age," especially among a generation of Anglophiles convinced that they were of purer stock than the British. But Lowell's prejudices, if that is indeed the correct term for it, transcended the norm.

William Howells, himself frequently accused of flagrant racist views, recalled in several memoirs Lowell's harangues against the Irish and Italian immigrants, coupled with the poet's hostile asseveration that he could remember the days when "almost every dweller in Boston had been born in it." Stating that "the few cannot absorb the many," Lowell claimed that escalating immigration, though perhaps necessary as a source of cheap labor, could not sustain itself and would eventually lead to economic catastrophe. Full of distrust, Lowell insisted that these recent immigrants were ruining the cities by forming their own unruly enclaves, creating frightening pockets of destitution in the midst of fashionable Brahmin society; they engaged in criminal activities, encouraged political corruption by becoming its unwitting dupes, and frequently took jobs away from able-bodied native laborers. Lowell's growing negativism represented a complete reversal from the aristocatic magnanimity he had demonstrated as a youth. So rapidly were his attitudes stiffening that by the mid-1880's the erstwhile humanitarian of the 1840's—"who had espoused the cause of freedom for the Negro slave in as thrilling language as any abolitionist"—had seen himself deteriorate into "an after-dinner monologuist and rampant village-explainer." Further discourses on the subject were not limited to the Irish, Italians, and blacks, but presently took in other minorities, including the Jews. Alarmed by the disappearance of the fixed distinctions in American society, Lowell became a fanatic on the subject of the "ubiquity" and "universal ability" of the alien Hebrew.

Lowell was not the only local citizen to think of the Jew as the natural enemy of democracy or to identify him with the menace of plutocracy. Other patricians of New England extract harbored anti-Semitic feelings that exceeded mere social discrimination. Henry and Brooks Adams, R. H. Dana Jr., and Senator Henry Cabot Lodge were among those aristocratic seaboard intellectuals who associated the Jew with the downfall of Brahminism. But Lowell's mania on the issue, in keeping with his other biases, went a step beyond.

In tracing the history of the Jews to their European roots, he noted that they had gained prominence "everywhere"; this "insidious race" had penetrated to the very bowels of human society. All bankers were Jewish, all brokers, most of the great financiers—but that was to be expected; the majority of barons and baronets were Jewish; the Jews had taken over the foreign press and the military and were forcing their way into high political offices; there were Jewish physicians and barristers and Jewish professors and university administrators; because of their education they had gained access to the cabinets of Europe and had even "slipped" into diplomatic circles. Only a short time before, many had been packed into the ghettos; now they inhabited palaces and were members of the wealthiest clubs. Once they had not been allowed to own land; now they owned most of Europe and would soon rule the world.

This was the materia prima of his talk about the Jewish race. It was particularly unpleasant coming from one so highly respected, an intellectual spokesman for those who believed in an elite of property, breeding, and education as the natural leaders of the republic. Lowell's presence was as impressive as that of Daniel Webster, and like Webster he misread his own times. He was more a spokesman for the past than the present. He had difficulty understanding the broad-based democratic sentiments that had eroded the richness of the Federalist soil. In his best moments, he was considered staunch, monumental, imperturbable, a man much admired, indeed revered. But the other side of this monumentality may have been a hardened core, a callousness that blocked his vision to anything beyond his immediate ken.

His views on the slavery issue and the Jewish question were bewildering, to say the least. The notion of slavery, for example, had been abhorrent to him. He said so time and again. Yet when the time came, when the war was settled and the slaves freed, he spoke about them as an inferior, belligerent race. It was a far cry from the Lowell who had cursed Philadelphia's abolitionists for their timidity and lack of spirit in the battle to further the human cause or from the Lowell of "The Present Crisis" (1844), with its "When a deed is done for Freedom, through / the broad earth's aching breast / Runs a thrill of joy prophetic, trembling / on from east to west." Fortunately, ethnic fervor was not the only thing on this short, stocky, muscular man's mind. In addition to the literary distillations previously mentioned, he completed and collected such prosaic disquisitions as "Witchcraft," "A Good Word for Winter," and "Emerson the Lecturer," in which he acknowledged

Emerson as the stellar mind of the age. At the beginning and end of his career, Lowell demonstrated certain reservations toward Emerson, although for the moment he was overawed by the magic of what he considered Emerson's great and lasting art. As coeditor of the *North American Review,* a position retained through 1872, Lowell produced a steady flow of reviews covering a variety of current literary releases, from Hazlitt's *Library of Old Authors* to Christina Rossetti's *Shadow of Dante.* His distillations were ultimately marred by an unwillingness to indulge in critical inquiry—by his lifelong insistence on boosting art for art's sake—which may have been a consequence of his avoidance of the old Puritan mode of introspection, a trait his family had inherited but somewhere along the line forsaken. Although his output had slowed, he never entirely stopped producing poetry, and some of his most characteristic public verse appeared during this period. In 1870 he published *The Cathedral*; in 1874, "Agassiz"; in 1875, the "Ode Read at the Concord Centennial" and "Under the Old Elm"; and the year following, "An Ode for the Fourth of July, 1876." The last three were published together in 1877 as *Three Memorial Poems.*

Both *The Cathedral* and "Agassiz" attempt to come to terms with the contrasting problems of faith and doubt. In "Agassiz," Lowell attempts to resolve the conflict by focusing on his friend's warmth and humanity, leaving the science and politics for future biographers to untangle. *The Cathedral* is a personal plea "for a return to a monolithic faith to replace the confusion of conflicting Protestant creeds." Engaging the Cathedral of Chartres as his central and unifying image—"Imagination's very self in stone"—Lowell ruminates in a discursive fashion on the difference between the Middle Ages and his own age, "an age that lectures, but does not create." In almost every respect *The Cathedral* is larger and more sustaining than many of the middling gleanings contained in Lowell's 1869 volume, *Under the Willows and Other Poems*, or in his final *Heartsease and Rue*, published in 1888.

Heartsease and Rue served as a repository for the poems Lowell had been publishing all along in small magazines and journals. But for once the poet's voice begins to flag and though there are minor compensations, one senses that his heart was not in this project. This is not the case with *Under the Willows*, which although burdened by a sampling of lesser-quality songs, also boasted jewels of the ilk of "The First Snow-Fall," "The Parting of the Ways," "The Voyage to Vinland," "The Nightingale in the Study"—melodies as mellow as any he had ever sung.

The "willows" of the title, which appeared earlier as a symbol of nature's magnificence in "An Indian-Summer Reverie," was a clump of trees a half mile from Elmwood. Lowell took a strange pleasure in their gnarled and umbrageous forms, their mysterious beauty, and was horrified to learn of their impending destruction at a time when the volume which took its title from them was about to go to print. Waxing as anthropomorphic as Thoreau, Lowell wrote to James T. Fields: "My heart was almost broken yesterday by seeing nailed to *my* willow a board with these words on it: 'These trees for sale.' The wretch is going to peddle them for firewood! If I had the money, I would buy the piece of ground they stand on to save them—the dear friends of a lifetime."

This sentiment quite apart, it was evident that his early radicalism had been only a passing phase—a pose or persona—sustained and encouraged largely by the presence of Maria White and in a minor way by the poet's inexperience and youth. Under his first wife's gentle coaxing, Lowell was indoctrinated in the then-current philosophy of reform politics, induced to speak at abolition meetings and contribute to the abolitionist press. For the moment, the poet's spiritual base lay midway between Park Street café society and the intelligentsia of Harvard Yard. There was throughout Lowell's later years a longing for the republican tradition, the wish to return America to its eighteenth-century condition of unified smallness, a nation of abiding, industrious Yankee farmers and city-state patricians, all Boston Brahmin and Philadelphia brick. Of his youthful libations only his adoration of nature remained. Like Longfellow, he was deeply attached to the mid-century agrarian movement and took sincere pleasure from the symbolic significance of grass and trees, woods and fields. His mentor in these matters was Emerson, who believed the universe was "governed by 'one mind' that revealed itself in man's nature" and in the seasonal cycles of the natural world. Nature—not society or organized religion—provided external evidence of what was within man. American birds and flowers, the day-to-day events of the garden, never failed to arouse and bring out the best in Lowell.

In the autumn of his life Lowell grew less subject to the perturbations of the poetic temperament. The stealing approach of age provided him with the illusion of a philosophy: "I have long been of that opinion which holds that nothing is of much consequence. . . . I shall have to subside ere long into the heavy father parts. My very style belongs to the last century." For a time he persisted in these sentimental reflections, writing to Thomas Bailey Aldrich that "it is better to be a good fellow than a good poet." To Norton he ventured: "It is always my happiest thought that with all my drawbacks of temperament . . . I have never lost a friend. For I would rather be loved than anything else in the world."

In the wake of the Civil War, Lowell spent long periods close to home. He made several brief lecture tours, but seemed most himself when seated in his library at Elmwood, surrounded by his beloved books and all the comforts of Cambridge. His life with Frances Dunlap was in numerous ways extremely satisfying; he referred to her as "the delight of my life"; Annie Fields noted his "chivalrous tender manner toward her."

Early in 1872 Mabel Lowell, by now a tall, graceful young lady in her mid-twenties, returned to Boston from Europe and a memorable visit with Charles Dickens. She was soon to become the wife of Edward Burnett, the son of a successful businessman-farmer from Southboro, Massachusetts. The elder Burnett had invested in a boys' boarding school, which he named St. Mark's, and the first headmaster was the Reverend Robert T. S. Lowell, the poet's brother. As Duberman reports it, James Russell Lowell was "altogether pleased" with his daughter's choice of a marriage partner and rapidly developed "fatherly feelings" toward his son-in-law.

With funds running low, the poet reluctantly sold several acres of Elmwood meadowland. He then took a leave of absence from Harvard and at the beginning of July 1872, in company with Mrs. Lowell, set sail for Europe. They spent the remainder of the summer in England and in the fall crossed the Channel and established themselves in Paris at the Hôtel de Lorraine, 7 rue de Beaune, where they were presently joined by the Nortons and Emersons. The poet returned to England the following spring to receive the degree of Doctor of Law at Oxford, an honor which Cambridge University likewise bestowed upon him.

The summer of 1873 was passed in Switzerland, the following winter in Italy, then back to Paris. By the summer of 1874, they were again at Elmwood, with Lowell teaching part-time at Harvard. The only significant change in his life was the reawakening of his interest in political affairs. Within that realm he considered himself, from roughly 1868 to his death in 1891, as the personification of what John Adams and Jefferson meant by the term "Natural Aristocrat." Lowell's belief in the natural or born aristocrat—an upper-class citizen by virtue of intelligence, learning, clear-sightedness, and general ability, as opposed to outright wealth—manifested itself in a deepening of his conservative tendencies and resided primarily in his assertion that popular government was not necessarily the best type of government; popular government was no better than any other form of government "except as the virtue and wisdom of the people, as individuals, make it so."

Within the Lowell family circle stress had always been placed on the importance of individuality, particularly in the notion that in the intelligent and well-educated individual mind resided the strength and hope of society. Applied to government the doctrine had it that "that form of government is the optimum, which provided the most effectually for a pure selection of the best and wisest men into office." That all men were created free and equal did not mean that they were equally ready to exercise the same functions in the administration of the country; this last must remain a privilege to be obtained only after a long and painful process of self-scrutiny and education. And it was the good fortune of America that all her constitutions—state and federal—were so worded as to give those citizens of proper age and merit the inalienable right to choose their own form and body of government.

That the system was not functioning as it should, suggested Lowell, was both the cause and the result of the country's present plight of widespread corruption. Lowell sincerely believed that the masses, properly advised and indoctrinated, would select the most highly qualified leaders and that these men in turn would eliminate corruption and replace it with a well-oiled, smoothly operating governing machine. As a spokesman for this form of elitism, he wrote: "It is one of the prime weaknesses of a democracy to be satisfied with the second-best; democracy must show its capacity for producing, not a higher average man, but the highest possible types of manhood in all its manifold varieties, or it is a failure."

This frank avowal, insisting on the ability of a few good men to determine the fate of many, put Lowell in league with Wordsworth, who in his later years preached a similar gospel. To both their minds, the poet's duty was to keep alive what was sound in democracy, eradicate what was not, and prevent men from corrupting what remained. This was not by any stretch of the imagination a singular or unique proposition; among the myriad influences and forces that helped shape Lowell's growing faith in a natural aristocracy of virtue and wisdom were Dante, Shakespeare, Burke, Puritanism, Federalism, Darwinism, Carlyle, Holmes, Arnold, and Norton. But Emerson, with his abiding faith in self-sufficiency and individualism, his acknowledgment of "the infinite of the private man," man as his own godhead, was perhaps the strongest single influence.

The evil of the public's condonation of the kinds of Gilded Age crimes perpetrated by "Boss" Tweed and Jim Fisk caused Lowell to lose his early faith in natural goodness. Laying his writing aside, the poet decided, for the first time, to assume a direct, if minor, role in political affairs. The year of the Centennial, 1876, he went as a delegate to the Republican National Convention in Cincinnati. The Republican contest that year was between Ohio Governor Rutherford B. Hayes and Senator James G. Blaine of Maine, considered by many, including the poet, to be a hopeless demagogue, tainted with all manner of buccaneering corruption. Called upon to make a speech on behalf of Hayes, Lowell told the meeting, "I shall not try to captivate your ears or win your applause by any of those appeals to passion and prejudice which are so tempting and so unwise. Politics are the most serious of all human affairs, and I prefer the approval of your understanding to that of your hands and feet."

His appeal succeeded: Hayes emerged victorious and Lowell agreed to serve as a member of the Electoral College. As the campaigns of both parties progressed, the Firesider found himself beginning to side with the Democratic party reformer and nominee, Samuel Tilden. He found Hayes "simple, tender, and sincere," but maintained that the "worst elements" were responsible for the Republican platform, and were busy waving "the bloody shirt" and stirring up old sectional passions, instead of putting their efforts into new issues like civil service or tariff and currency reform. In the end, too full of traditional and lingering doubts of the Democratic party, Lowell supported the Republican nominee.

His partisanship was well rewarded. In the spring of 1877, President Hayes invited the poet to take over the post of United States Minister to Spain. Lowell's long and intimate knowledge of the Spanish language had given him a solid measure of comprehension of Spain's intricate national character and fickle personality. His early training in law, his family background, his ability to read French, German, and Italian, were invaluable tools for the world of diplomacy. Lowell's previous travels through Europe had served to expose him to some of the political complexities he would now encounter firsthand. He was perfectly suited to the job.

Lowell accepted the post, arriving in Madrid with Mrs. Lowell in the middle of an August (1876) heat wave. They were presented at court and feted by local dignitaries. One of Lowell's early contacts was with Manuel Silvela, Spanish Minister for Foreign Affairs and a former university professor; the two scholar-statesmen shared an intense interest in a number of academic disciplines but especially in contemporary European literature. But aside from Silvela, and Lowell's friendship with a Spanish Senator and his wife, Juan and Emilia de Riaño, he did little socializing at first. Lonely, and bewildered over the observance of his diplomatic duties, "José Bighlow," as the Spanish press called him, suffered severe attacks of depression and gout. The same hyperuricemia that caused the gout also caused painful kidney stone attacks. His mental and physical well-being showed improvement only after his first year in Spain, when he began to grow accustomed to the high-living lifestyle of the career diplomat. His daily regimen, as outlined in letters to friends, had an air of aristocratic *gemütlichkeit* about it; in Madrid he lived the life many Brahmin gentlemen and squires chose for themselves in Boston but without the intellectual stimulation that had become so essential to the happiness of this Bostonian courtier:

> This is the course of my day:—Up at 8, from 9 sometimes till 11 my Spanish professor, at 11 breakfast, at 12 to the legation, at 3 home again and a cup of chocolate, then read the paper and write Spanish till a quarter to 7, at 7 dinner, and at 8 drive in an open carriage . . . till 10, to bed at 12 to 1. In cooler weather we drive in the afternoon. I am very well—cheerful and no gout.

Practical, honest, hard-working, he was not used to this life of wasteful leisure and was cheered by his election, as a result of his friendship with Senator de Riaño, to the Spanish Academy; there he could always find somebody with whom to discuss the latest trends in literature and poetry or line up an opponent for a friendly game of chess. But with the exception of the Academy, an occasional concert, and an exhibition now and again at the Prado, Madrid had little to offer the poet in the way of intellectual stimulation. Official functions proved an exercise in tedium. The American preferred to amuse himself by sending humorous dispatches to his political bosses back home, as for instance his memorandum that at a great public celebration he had attended, the prettiest women were those from Andalusia. The most interesting of these dispatches were assembled by Joseph B. Gilder and published in 1899 as *Impressions of Spain.*

Then, late in 1879, Mrs. Lowell fell victim to typhus. As her condition steadily worsened, two doctors, one German and one Spanish, took turns in a continuous vigil. Twice she was thought to be near death, but each time she recuperated and somehow pulled through. When she became at last convalescent, she remained in a semideranged state similar to that suffered by the poet's mother, interspersed with moments of delirium and lucidity.

Lowell, feeling helpless before the vagaries of his wife's illness and deflated by the monotony of Madrid's climate, was himself on the verge of a breakdown. He was saved by the unexpected arrival of a dispatch, dated January 10, 1880, that read: "President Hayes has nominated you to England. He regards it as essential to the public service that you should accept and make your personal arrangements to repair to London as early as may be expected." It was signed "William Evarts, U.S. Secretary of State."

Lowell's appointment to the Court of St. James's, America's highest and most respected diplomatic office, came at a time when he most needed a psychological boost. In England he could move Mrs. Lowell into a more homelike setting, where she would be assured of the most advanced medical assistance available. London, moreover, would provide a more suitable setting for Lowell. In his nostalgic "Cambridge Thirty Years Ago," he compared his boyhood community to a typical British hamlet. Cambridge had been "essentially an English village, quiet, unspeculative, without enterprise, sufficient to itself." Harvard had "in its intellectual atmosphere a repose which recalls that of grand old Oxford." Furthermore, Lowell's conception of an ideal government called for a combination of dignity and patriarchal conscience, with governors who strove to be just and who ruled because they were well suited to rule; this, of course, was also the theory behind British Parliament.

In March Lowell departed for London, stopping briefly in Paris, where he encountered another visitor, Henry James. He was acquainted with James from previous travels abroad and was familiar as well with William James, his colleague at Harvard. Lowell, the embodiment of the genteel tradition in America, was always a favorite topic of conversation between the two brothers. Writing to William, Henry James noted that Lowell looked "old and haggard," yet relieved to get away from the "prolonged vigil" of Mrs. Lowell's sickroom: "He has a most childlike temperament in his way of taking troubles, and relief from them." Henry was convinced that Mrs. Lowell's condition would make her husband's position in London impossible; even without "this impediment" he would have trouble "coping with the big London world"—he was too distracted and impractical; the trying social responsibilities of his position would "bore him to death," and as a result he would flounder.

But James was wrong. Lowell fell absolutely in love with London and Londoners. He blended into the congenial flow of the city as easily as Washington Irving had done a generation before, and found his new position anything but boring.

During the Civil War the poet had been sharply outspoken in response to Great Britain's support of the South. In his essay on "New England Two Centuries Ago," he alluded to "our English cousins (as they are fond of calling themselves when they are afraid we may do them a mischief)"; and "On a Certain Condescension in Foreigners" contains the remark, "Not a Bull of them all but is persuaded he bears Europa upon his back." When Lowell and the English came to know one another, the war was fifteen years over and there was no longer any animosity between them.

The Minister Plenipotentiary was cordially received at his prestigious new post by Prime Minister William Gladstone. At a gala thrown for him by Lord and Lady Ripon he was introduced to Matthew Arnold, who "overwhelmed him with kindness." When he presented his letters to Queen Victoria, she inquired after Mrs. Lowell "with a *human* tone" that deeply touched him. He wrote to Charles Eliot Norton, his replacement at Harvard:

> I like London, and have learned to see as I never saw before the advantages of a great capital. It establishes one set of weights and measures, moral and intellectual, for the whole country. It is, I think, a great

drawback for us that we have as many as we have states. The flow of life in the streets, too—sublimer it seems to me often than the tides of the sea—gives me a kind of stimulus that I find agreeable even if it prompt to nothing. For I am growing old, dear Charles, and haven't the go in me I once had.

If the advancing years slowed him down, they did not stunt his ability to win over an audience. His piquant wit, his gift for informal and formal speech, kept him in constant demand. Attired in dress coat and waistcoat, with knee breeches and silk stockings, pumps, gloves, and top hat, the American Ambassador was a familiar sight at many a private and public dinner table. In England, as in America, his friendships with the truly interesting men and women of his time played a vital part in his life, especially vital now because of the strain on him of his wife's failing health. Lowell went everywhere in London; his name appeared on the guest list of every literary and high societal function. He was so active on the British front that he was accused in the American press of Anglomania, of preferring the company of grandees, of dukes and duchesses, to dining out with fellow countrymen, except in those cases where the visiting American was a personal friend or relation. One American journalist referred to Lowell as "the arch-devil of Anglo-American aristocracy," and another called him an "intellectual anti-American." Lowell insisted that his meetings with men of the station of Disraeli, Lord Granville, Lord Rothschild, Sir John Millais, and the Prince of Wales were of an official nature. His closest companions in England were literary men: Leslie Stephen, Thomas Hughes, Robert Browning, Thomas Hardy, James Anthony Proude. The feeling about Lowell was that he was a captivating but earnest American who read more books and read them with greater care than the clever but comparatively indolent British dilettante "who takes his literary heritage for granted, considering himself and his peers its sole owners and only licensed interpreters."

Of all his associations in London it was his friendship with Sir Leslie and Julia Stephen that afforded him the greatest pleasure. The Stephen household was a textbook example of the respectable, intellectual upper-middle-class Victorian family: the bearded patriarch, the loving mother, and the nicely behaved children, all clothed in the mantle of genteel propriety and bathed in an atmosphere densely packed with words, ideas, and above all, books. Sir Leslie, a free-thinking but austere intellectual, was no ordinary academic slouch; in addition to editing the monumental *Dictionary of National Biography*, he managed to produce fifteen assorted volumes of history, biography, and criticism, and well over a hundred long articles and introductions. He and Lowell were as close as brothers. In Lowell's correspondence with Leslie and Julia he reflected frankly on numerous aspects of life, including his diplomatic career: "There is an endless procession of men I don't know, who become so identical to me after a while that I think they go out one door to come in at the other like an army on the stage." On his diplomatic service in Spain: "Spain appears unchanged for centuries. . . . She goes through all the motions of the modern world with none of the spirit." On aging: "I am losing my memory and my wits by erosion and am turning into a mere digestive apparatus." Lowell felt out of touch with the modern world, but more so with the younger writers of his homeland: "When I read the *Atlantic* now I feel that I belong to a bygone generation. . . . It is astonishing how soon we are forgot." In 1882 Lowell became godfather to Leslie and Julia Stephen's daughter, the future writer and "high priestess of Bloomsbury" Virginia Woolf. Thereafter, in his letters to the family, there is mention of her—questions about her, greetings to be passed on, affectionate flattery.

According to Martin Duberman, Lowell's chief problem in the administration of his London office involved the delicate and difficult "Irish Question." To a large extent he supported Charles Stewart Parnell's parliamentary lead advocating Home Rule. If Ireland was ever to become as "loyal" as Scotland, it had to be recognized that "Ireland was not England and never would be." Lowell's views, asserts Duberman, were thus more openly radical than those of the Gladstone Administration, "which alternated between liberalizing the strict Irish land laws and passing coercive acts designed to insure order." The latest "Coercive Act," the 1881 Protection of Person and Property Bill, declared that anyone remotely suspected of treasonable activity in Ireland could be arrested and detained without bail or trial. Lowell saw the act precisely for what it was, an arbitrary tract "contrary to the spirit and fundamental principles of the British Constitution."

Though he disapproved of the act on moral grounds, there was little he could do to officially oppose it once it was passed into law. To do so would have been to overstep his privilege as American Ambassador to Great Britain. Lowell could properly intervene only in those instances when a United States citizen, having committed no wrongdoing, was detained or arrested, or if it could be demonstrated that the act was being "administered in such a way as to discriminate more harshly against American citizens than against British subjects." The situation was further aggravated by the Fenians, a group of Irish nationals and Irish-Americans engaged in the struggle for Irish independence and in the specific task of trying to liberate those Irish-American citizens imprisoned in British jails under the new act. The Fenians argued that these prisoners were being held illegally, that no charge had been brought against them, and that they should either be tried or released. To do neither was to deny them their constitutional right of habeas corpus.

Lowell, while opposed to unlawful government intervention, found it just as difficult to modulate his "indignation against an organization which resorted to dynamite plots, arson and murder, and whose American members often looked upon themselves as Irishmen who have acquired a right to American protection rather than as Americans who have renounced a claim to Irish nationality." The official position of the U.S. State Department was one of congenial neutrality. There were several inquiries into cases of severe mistreatment by the British of Irish-American citizens, but by and large American officials tended to look upon these suspects as "willing martyrs, men eager to complicate Anglo-American relations." Lowell went a step further. In private conversation with British government officials, the American minister maintained that he "regretted that his Government should have been induced to offer any representations whatever," assuring British leaders that he leaned heavily toward their cause. And yet in public, when interviewed by the press, the Ambassador was much more ambivalent, obviously hedging between two opposing points of view.

It was the old quandary for Lowell, his inability (or unwillingness) to commit, to take a firm stand on a given issue; he supported Home Rule and opposed the oppression of lawful Irish citizens, but could barely bring himself to endorse the practical means necessary to attain the desired ends. While his conduct was approved by his own government and lauded by England's, he was vilified by the Irish, both in Ireland and at home. A mass rally of trade unionists and aldermen was staged in New York; in Boston a public gathering of Irish rebels resulted in hundreds of arrests. At both a feverish cry went up demanding Lowell's resignation and return. A Belfast newspaper denounced the American

Ambassador as a traitor, a "British toady subservient to the cause of imperialism." For months Lowell considered the possibility of resignation but felt that to do so would be an unwillful admission of guilt. He stayed put and weathered the storm.

The storm eventually subsided. By the beginning of his third year in office, all talk of recall had ceased. Now Lowell could resume his round of public appearances and speeches. He gave an important talk at Birmingham, October 6, 1884, entitled "Democracy," in which he proclaimed his "high and reasonable faith in government" by and for the people, "a well-fortified confidence in their good sense and self control." He declared Britain "a monarchy with democratic tendencies" and compared her with the United States, which he viewed as "a democracy with conservative instincts." The presentation led Henry James to reevaluate his friend's qualities as Ambassador; "his career," the novelist wrote, "is in the last analysis a tribute to the dominion of style."

The Birmingham speech was Lowell's last notable accomplishment as Minister to Great Britain. Grover Cleveland had been elected President of the United States to succeed Chester Arthur; the new Administration meant the inevitable changing of the guard. Lowell was prepared to relinquish his position and return to his homeland; he was not prepared, on February 19, 1885, for the sudden death of Frances Lowell. He relayed the sad news a day later in a letter to his daughter:

> Dearest Child,—I can hardly bring myself to write, but I must. You knew long ago that yesterday at 1/2 past 2 our great sorrow came upon us. It was not till Friday the 14th that I dreamed of any other result than recovery. On Thursday Dr. Rupert Reynolds, an eminent specialist, had seen her and spoke with entire confidence of her getting well both in mind and body. But on Friday she began to sink without any apparent reason and continued sinking till all was over. At one time even so late as Wednesday evening I was fool enough to have a gleam of hope—she was so strong and her whole being so pure and wholesome. . . .

He had fooled himself into thinking it would not end this way, that he—older than she—would die first, despite her ongoing illness. "I am more than ever at a loss what to do with myself," he wrote to George Putnam two weeks later. "We had always taken it for granted that she would outlive me—that would have been best. But I cannot live alone in the old home in Cambridge. It would be too dreary." To Mrs. W. K. Clifford, one of his more recent English friends, he said: "In trying to piece together the broken threads of my life again, the brightest naturally catch the eye first. . . . I am getting on as one does—gradually getting my wits together. . . . I have at last found something I can read —Calderon. He has stood me in stead before."

14

THE LOWELL PROBLEM

ON May 1, 1885, Edward J. Phelps was appointed Lowell's successor in London, and by June the poet was back in the States, once more a civilian. The first months of his return were passed at Deerfoot Farm, Southboro, the residence of his daughter and son-in-law. The town, one of those tranquil New England resting places, full of vistas and country lanes, provided a welcome respite after London and the shock of Mrs. Lowell's death. The ancient mariner enjoyed playing "Gramps" to his daughter's five children, reading to them and accompanying them on afternoon outings into the Massachusetts countryside. To Norton he commented: " 'Tis an odd shift in the peep hole of my panorama from London to this Chartreuse. For the present I like it, and find it wholesome. I fancy myself happy sometimes—I am not sure—but then I never was for long."

Although well on in years, the poet remained agile and spry. The winters of 1885 and 1886 were spent at Southboro. Several weeks each year he went to Boston to visit his sister, Mrs. Mary Putnam. Because Mary was herself an occasional author of prose and poetry, she was in a better position than most to offer her younger brother comfort during his late and lonely years. She was able to understand James from a temperamental point of view and could deal with his rapid changes of mood, his anxieties and depressions. He was alarmed that in 1885 Boston elected its first non-Yankee mayor, Alderman Hugh O'Brien, a man of dignity and integrity but nevertheless foreign-born. It was clear to Lowell that the days of the Boston Yankee politicians with their British-derived, New England-worn names were numbered. Phillips, Quincy,

Otis, Eliot, Chapman, Brimmer, Bigelow, Seaver, Lincoln, Wightman, and Pierce would soon give way to Fitzgerald and Curley. What, Lowell wondered, was the world coming to?

To keep himself occupied, the poet undertook several speaking tours of New England and in his capacity as professor emeritus at Harvard, read Dante for a month each semester with a small gathering of graduating seniors. These were his favorite moments. He would lean back in his chair and lecture away, his voice and his presence comprising a seamless whole; in a sense he was Boston's last Renaissance man and his gift was to sing as freely and naturally as he spoke. His presence alone was an inspiration. He might rise occasionally from his chair, thrust his hands deep into the pockets of a baggy sack coat, and pace the front of the room with his heavy laced boots, and stare into space, and discourse of things immemorial, touching every so often on Dante as a window for the light of truth and the ascent of man through the universe. The richness and readiness and aptness of Lowell's power of expression made these hours memorable, and his students carried his lectures about with them as though they were imperishable possessions.

In the summer of 1886 Lowell traveled to England, the first of four return visits in as many years. He found British life so congenial and charming, he confessed to his daughter, that he wondered how Percival Lowle had been able to forsake it in the first place; given his choice he himself might have stayed.

His romantic feelings for England were to some extent based on his immense popularity there—in society, and in the public eye. Petted and flattered like a prince, admired by men and fawned over by women, he elicited in his hosts a warmth that the British rarely lavish upon their own royalty. To these cultivated citizens he was the perfect gentleman and man of the world, dashed by learning, wit, intelligence, manners, success. He was the foreign dignitary par excellence, the exotic scholar and statesman, the cynosure of high society, the darling of the smart set, one of Goethe's Great Oaks. Lowell had once expressed disdain for the powerful conventionalism of the British, the inner falseness of the old landed order, with its etiquette, its manners, its social graces, its pungent afternoon teas; he now took undue pleasure from these same rituals, invoking some of his own: the hunt, the pheasant-shoot, the races. The world of competitive sports kept him within easy eyeshot of the restless wives and daughters of London's rich. That he attained a reputation as a flirtatious, roguish womanizer—rather like the aging Benjamin Franklin in Paris—comes as no surprise; his Brahmin background and rugged appearance—intense blue eyes, blazing white hair and beard—attracted women wherever he went. Yet it was unfortunate that the British made so much of him; his position as near-royalty among the lordly English had the effect of heightening his already exaggerated sense of self.

His own countrymen added weight to this view. For them he was a spokesman of a special group, the Boston aristocrats, "the old Cambridge breed," men (wrote historian V. L. Parrington) of sound culture who could serve God valiantly in the social position in which He had placed them. For better or worse, the opinions of this group mattered; their voices were influential in helping shape public taste, which in turn helped crystallize certain national trends and traditions. But while Brahmin culture was important in rounding out the general configuration of the country's tendencies and inclinations, it hardly represented the "solid realities" of the nation at large. The democracy that these gentlemen sought was closer to the system that had prevailed in Cambridge fifty years before—"a simple patriarchal world, amenable to the rule of the better sort."

During his ambassadorial stint in London, Lowell had shown little or no concern for the liberal teachings of men such as Mill or Arnold or John Morley, and even less for radical thinkers such as William Morris; in America he shared the rigid laissez-faire views of E. L. Godkin, whose refusal to support James G. Blaine as the Republican nominee for President in 1884 led to the establishment of the Mugwump party, a name later applied to any independent voter. Lowell considered himself as fierce a Mugwump as Godkin but with stronger ties to Brahmin Federalism and conservatism. The reaction against the radicalism of his abolitionist past was extreme. "We have got to work back from a democracy to our original institution as a republic again," he wrote to Leslie Stephen. Other activities gave rise to additional expressions of sociological fervor. On November 8, 1886, on the occasion of the two hundred and fiftieth anniversary of the founding of Harvard, Lowell presented his "Harvard Anniversary Address." The speech, later collected in *Democracy and Other Addresses* (1886), reflected on the need for the study of those humanities to which his own life had been given over; he called for educated, upper-class leadership to quell the downward leveling tendency of democracy.

His correspondence contained similar summations. The "Haymarket riot" in Chicago that year, culminating in the bombing death of one policeman and the arrest and execution of seven anarchist workers, elicited a letter from Lowell to Howells calling for the immediate hanging of "those Chicago ruffians." Another letter warned Thomas Hughes against the dangers of suffrage spreading to England, while a third described America's version of democracy, with its underlying mediocrity, as "a Kakistocracy rather, for the benefit of knaves at the cost of fools."

Besides these tart observations, the nativist issued pronouncements directed against "the virus" of labor unions, social legislation, and the shortening of the ten-hour workday. "The Republic will endure," Lowell ventured, "only so long as the ideas of the men who founded it continue dominant." He had serious misgivings about the growing power of the proletariat. To Norton he ventured: "I sometimes feel a little blue over the outlook here, with our penny-paper universal education and our workingmen's parties, with their tremendous lever of suffrage." Earlier he had written to E. L. Godkin about Vice-President Henry Wilson's condonation of an eight-hour workday: "Pray give Henry Wilson a broadside for dipping his flag to that piratical craft of the eight-hour men. . . . I have a thorough contempt for a man who pretends to believe that eight is equal to ten."

Although he took himself seriously as a guide and mentor in matters political, Lowell had never taken the time or trouble to ground himself very thoroughly in the rudiments of the science. He was as cloudy on Karl Marx and Henry George as he had been his entire life on Agassiz versus Darwin; regarding the perplexing dilemma of evolution, Lowell wrote: "I hate it as a savage does writing." Of political literature he was well acquainted only with the writings of Burke, but was otherwise as ignorant of American and English constitutional law and history as any twentieth-century politician.

While politics ranked high on his list of priorities, he managed to keep one hand in the academic till. He was president of the Wordsworth Society and an officer of the newly formed Modern Language Association in New York. He presented another series of lectures at the Lowell Institute. His latest poems—"Credidimus Jovem regnare" and "Fancy or Fact?"—appeared in the *Atlantic*. He contributed an introduction to a two-volume history text, *The World's Progress*, and a preface to a collection of letters by Walter Savage Landor.

Two new Lowell books emerged in 1888, *Political Essays*, a collocation of published articles, which demonstrated the gradual evolvement of the poet's ideology from moderate to liberal to stanch conservative, and *Heartsease and Rue*, a consolidation of recent poems and a gathering of poems excluded from his previous anthology *(Under the Willows and Other Poems)*. An epigram ("Sixty-Eighth Birthday") encapsulated the latest volume's sorrowful tone: "As life runs on, the road grows strange, / With faces new, and near the end / The milestones into headstones change, / 'Neath every one a friend." Human relationships and the existing social makeshifts had dominated his days; now his friends were perishing one by one. In several of these doggedly sincere poems Lowell honors friends, living and dead. These odes, to Agassiz, Holmes, Whittier, Jeffries Wyman, are the pinnacles of a volume otherwise flat and drab.

Following the publication of *Heartsease and Rue*, Lowell published, again in the *Atlantic*, his poem on "Turner's Old Téméraire." Subtitled "Under a Figure Symbolizing the Church," the sequence acclaims Turner's noble canvas and picks up on what was to become a recurrent theme in several of the Firesider's later poems: the role of science in the modern world. In "Téméraire" science is seen as "a black demon, belching fire and steam . . . with wings of smoke and flame," while in "Credidimus Jovem regnare" Lowell asks whether science has found the key that religion has lost; he concludes that it has not. Of scientists in general he maintains: "They tell me that I can't know certain things. I am apt to wonder how *they* can be sure of that, and whether there may not be things which they *can't* know."

There appeared to be no rest for the Brahmin. He spoke before the Reform Club of New York on "The Place of the Independent in Politics," reemphasizing the need for a well-educated voting public. Diverging from the usual, he penned a preface to a reissue of Izaak Walton's *The Compleat Angler; or, The Contemplative Man's Recreation* (1653), a masterpiece on fishing and thought. He fashioned an introduction to a reprint of Milton's "Areopagitica." His most sustained effort, however, went into the preparation of the ten-volume *Writings of James Russell Lowell*, the Riverside edition of his collected works, published in 1890 by Houghton Mifflin. It was the consummation of a lifetime of labor.

Lowell returned to England in the spring of 1888, and in June represented Harvard at the eight hundredth anniversary of the University of Bologna in Italy, which presented the poet with an honorary doctorate.

He received matching degrees during these years from the universities of St. Andrews and Edinburgh. His speeches on these occasions, almost always "off the cuff," were urbane, humorous, entertaining. "At my time in life," he offered, "my memory is gradually becoming one of her own reminiscences." Back home he spent six weeks in Washington, where his son-in-law was a member of Congress. On April 30, 1889, he delivered an address entitled "Our Literature" at the New York centenary of George Washington's presidential inauguration. At the beginning of the summer he sailed for what was to be his final visit to England; that country had become his stepfatherland.

When he returned to America in the fall, it was to reside for a last time at Elmwood, with his daughter and her children as houseguests. His days were running out. Painful attacks of stomach and back cramps appeared to be the result of a cancer. His physician prescribed bed rest and restricted him to a quarter-mile walk every day—"prison rations." His condition grew graver. He informed Howells that having been allowed out of the house, he had gone to nearby Beaver Brook and tried to negotiate it by jumping from stone to stone; he had given up midstream.

His seventieth birthday was celebrated by a special issue of the Boston *Critic* with recollections and reminiscences by contemporaries on both sides of the Atlantic: Prime Minister Gladstone, Presidents Hayes and Harrison, Oliver Wendell Holmes, George Washington Cable, William Story, Whittier, Tennyson, Francis Parkman. A dinner was held in his honor at Boston's Tavern Club, with Charles Eliot Norton doing the honors and Boston's mightiest in attendance. In the summer of 1890 Leslie Stephen visited Elmwood and found his friend deeply immersed in his library, reading Swinburne, Rousseau, Terence, Montaigne, and Boswell. The poet dismissed Rousseau with the comment, "a monstrous liar, but always the first dupe of his own lie." Swinburne suffered the same ills that Lowell had lately discovered in Whitman; his writing was affected, overdramatic, egocentric: "When a man begins to lust after the Muse instead of loving her, he may be sure that it is never the Muse that he embraces." Holmes, paying the author a call, found him resting on the couch; when the visitor inquired after his health, Lowell responded: "Oh, I suppose I'm in pain; I always am more or less, but look here [holding up a book], I've been reading *Rob Roy*. I suppose it may be for the fortieth time, but it is just as good as when I read it first."

Those who dropped by were treated to a running monologue of sorts.

Lowell was still the Harvard lecturer, the Cambridge street-corner philosopher and social lion. When not discoursing on Burke or Dante, his attention wandered to one of several statesmanlike subjects. There was a good amount in the recent development of American life that worried him. He was concerned with the power of the press, which was controlled entirely "by its interests as a business rather than by its sense of duty as a teacher." He despaired over the too-rapid growth of the cities; the alienation of the highly educated from careers in government; the proliferation in higher education of pedantry and specialization as opposed to a wider-reaching, broader cultural base. The swelling ranks of immigrants to the United States alarmed him; he wondered if the country's assimilative powers might not be overtaxed by the vast numbers. For this he had only his own Brahmin flock to blame, the enterprising capitalists responsible for acres of spindles and miles of yarn, whose commercial minds were bent on turning the ambitious daughters of Yankee farmers, and the poverty-stricken Irish immigrants, into efficient revenue producers for the purpose of enriching their own State Street coffers. He looked back longingly to the quiet days "before our individuality had been trampled out of us by the Irish mob." Perched between the older America and the new, the country's very foundations crumbling underfoot, he desperately sought to cling to his antiquated pipe dreams, yearning for orderliness in an age of chaos, peace in an epoch of fury.

He worried about government, high taxes and tariffs, the Knights of Labor and the kind of trade union "coercion" they typified. He insisted there had been a breakdown in civil service legislation and condemned the private sector for its lack of involvement in the actual governing process. He wanted a government free of mediocre manpower and corrupt administrators. In essence, he wanted an old-fashioned Brahmin democracy, a constitutionally administered democracy that worked!

As Lowell's health continued to fail, the velocity of his pitch slowed to a crawl. The malignancy, which had started in the kidneys, had slowly spread through the liver and colon. He knew that he was dying. To Julia Stephen he wrote (October 7, 1890): "I don't bother about Death, but shan't be sorry if he delays as long as he honestly can."

William James came out to Elmwood several times. By letter he reported to his brother that their mutual friend was always "ready to talk and be talked to, alluding to his illness with a sort of apologetic and whimsical plaintiveness that had no querulousness in it, though he coughed incessantly, and the last time . . . was strongly narcotized by opium. . . ." Opium reduced the pain but under its influence Lowell's mind wandered hopelessly. Toward the end, after the cancer had reached his lungs, the manifestations of the disease permeated the entire house; so foul was the stench of the poet's sickroom that visits from outsiders were impossible. As Lowell lay in delirium, it was his daughter who ministered to him and sat with him until the end. Lowell lost consciousness on August 7, and never regained it. He died without pain on August 19, 1891, at the age of seventy-two.

Funeral services were held two days later in the Harvard College chapel. Charles Eliot Norton, Oliver Wendell Holmes and his brother John Holmes, Christopher Cranch, George William Curtis, John Bartlett, Francis Child, and young Abbott Lawrence Lowell, the poet's distant cousin, were among the pallbearers. Following the service, which seemed to draw all of Cambridge, the casket was shouldered and carried from the chapel to Mount Auburn Cemetery, where the body was laid to rest in a family plot "inconspicuous for its plainness, unenclosed by granite curbing or by hedges." On this hot summer day Mount Auburn, with its manicured rosebushes and ivy-smothered stone fences, its sweeping pale-green carpet of grass and tall, straight trees, looked like a painting, some half-classical, half-romantic Arcadia, where Greek temples and laurel bushes stood next to Egyptian monoliths and Roman busts and mausoleums. The Lowell family plot stood like an oasis of stoic simplicity in the midst of all this funereal splendor: small tombstones, plainly engraved and of ordinary stone, marked the separate Lowell graves. "I fancy an honest man easier in his grave," Lowell once said, "with the bare truth told about him on his headstone." His contained only his name and dates.

Several volumes of Lowell's work and correspondence appeared shortly after his death, all but one edited by his literary executor, Charles Eliot Norton: *Latest Literary Essays and Addresses* (1892); *The Old English Dramatists* (1892); *Letters of James Russell Lowell* (2 vols., 1893); *Last Poems of James Russell Lowell* (1895). *New Letters of James Russell Lowell*, edited by M. A. De Wolfe Howe, was not published until 1932. In the years after his death, the reaction of critics to Lowell's lifework varied considerably. Much of his thinking about literature was perpetuated, until the 1920's, by a group of three—Norton, George

Edward Woodberry, and W. C. Brownell—and later by the New Humanists—Irving Babbitt, Paul Elmore More, and Paul Shorey—who worked diligently to resist the "temptations" of modern literary trends. But with the exception of these stalwarts, Lowell's literary stature, which was considerable at his death, has declined steadily.

In *The Romantic Revolution in America* (1927), V. L. Parrington found Lowell an exemplar of Boston Victorianism, of the united dignity and conscience of English liberalism and Cambridge Brahminism, and defined him as "a bookish amateur in letters, loitering over old volumes for the pleasure of finding apt phrases and verbal curiosities." Professor Norman Foerster, in his classic *American Criticism* (1928), suggested that the poet fell short of realizing his ambitions, "partly because his native force was inadequate, and partly because he was sucked into the current of his times." Foerster concluded that Lowell "stood forth among his contemporaries because of his accomplished versatility rather than because of high attainment." Lowell himself had perhaps answered this charge before it was made; in an essay on Carlyle he wrote that "real fame depends rather on the sum of an author's powers than on any brilliancy of special parts."

This statement, although registered in Carlyle's defense, demonstrates an awareness of the critical animosity anticipated by Lowell in conjunction with his own work. He was conscious of his inability to settle comfortably into a single mode of communication or a single style. This "diffuseness," as William Charvat calls it, was to some extent a result of the poet's facility and versatility with words. He could rhyme a letter or lecture almost as easily as he could prose them, and he wrote as naturally as he talked: "He was a brilliant and spontaneous punster; he found it hard to control the fireworks of his wit; and he had his foreign languages at his fingertips." He was versatile and adaptable and just as much at home in prose as in verse. But this facility for tongues, for words, was matched by an inability to write a condensed, tightly constructed essay or poem. He was hopelessly digressive and discursive; he had no gift for unity.

In personal terms, it was possible to blame his lack of sustained focus on his highly impressionistic nature. Lowell never authentically held to anything with convictions that were deep and lasting. He had convictions all right, but he wanted too desperately to be admired by all parties; he was too easily swayed by those close to him. Although he had an uncanny ability to perceive the dualities of existence, he was unable in the end to resolve the myriad conflicts of his age—the claims of head and heart, reason and imagination, aristocracy and democracy, classicism and romanticism, religion and science.

The problem, then, with Lowell, from a critical vantage point, is that as a writer he won a leading place during his own lifetime that was to lapse soon after his demise. Almost every biographer who has ever tackled him acknowledges his weaknesses as a poet and critic. Most attribute this to his many-sided personality and incredible diversity of interests and occupations. Certainly no American writer of Lowell's generation—and few of succeeding generations—made an attempt on such a sweeping scale to consolidate the professions of poet and professor with those of international statesman and national spokesman. In psychogenetic terms he was an amalgam of disparate parts, an artist with a modern sensibility in his personal anguish and bursts of creative inspiration, and an outdated Tory in his draw toward conservative politics. His youth was a quest for moral righteousness; he was a sort of liberal reformer with essentially conservative goals. He wound his life up bemoaning the chaos of the times and the cultural impoverishment of a bourgeois society ruled by avarice and greed. In the span between youth and old age, Lowell's ideals were in constant conflict. He saw the need for a moral standard in literature but lacked the self-reliant individual strength that was needed to combat the traditional claims of upper-class reality. He was competitive with the commanding literary voices of his day but was too willing ultimately to submit to the Gilded Age conventions of popular taste. And yet it is these very aspects of Lowell's life, the contradictions and struggles, the contrasts and travails, that lend it power and substance and make him worth considering and also reading about.

AMY LOWELL
Last of the Barons
1874–1925

PART
III

AMY LOWELL

⤳ 15 ⤳

THE DEBUTANTE

"AMY LOWELL had a genius for everything except the thing she wanted most: permanence as a poet." This stern but accurate assessment, offered at one time by Louis Untermeyer, can as easily be applied to James Russell Lowell, with whom Amy had more in common than mere kinship (her great-grandfather was half brother to the father of James Russell Lowell). The two were from opposite lines of the same family, the elderly James Russell being a product of the venerable, intellectual junior branch, whereas Amy was a member of the wealthier, more elegant senior trunk. At heart both were true Boston aristocrats, clansmen through and through.

Amy's family residence was called Sevenels and was located on the western slope of Heath Street in Brookline, Massachusetts, ten minutes by trolley from Boston Commons and thirty from Harvard Yard. Her father, Augustus Lowell, purchased the property in the fall of 1866, when his father's estate at Roxbury (Bromley Vale) was about to be parceled and sold. The manor in Brookline was named Sevenels because, following Amy's birth in it on February 9, 1874, it sheltered seven Lowells (seven "L's").

Like James Russell Lowell at Elmwood, Amy spent a large part of her life ensconced in the luxury of Sevenels, passing away in the house of her birth, in fact in the same room. In addition, both poets were the youngest members of large families; Amy was the fifth of five offspring, twelve years younger than her next of kin and some fifty-odd years (two generations) removed from James Russell Lowell. During her childhood Amy encountered "the other Lowell" on only a handful of occasions. She remembered their final meeting vividly.

It took place at the end of June 1888 in the Boston domicile of a Lowell in-law. Amy was ushered into the library, where the grand conquistador sat in a large, richly upholstered chair; it was the old and new meeting, she later recalled, "in furious conjunction." Yet their meeting passed without incident. She apparently uttered a few words, while the fastidiously dressed side-whiskered, well-mannered, old gentleman "turned cold eyes down at her." They exchanged the mandatory niceties and Amy departed.

This strained confrontation aside, Amy retained fond memories of her famous poet-cousin and throughout her youth regarded him with the same reverence as the rest of the family, particularly after his triumphant return from the Court of St. James's. Among the treasured books of her childhood was one of his own juvenile possessions, presented to her by the Fireside Poet on her tenth birthday (Walter Ferguson's *My Early Days*, 1827, inscribed "James Russell Lowell from Father, May 3, 1828"). She later noted that among her favorite childhood poems was *The Vision of Sir Launfal*, sections of which she committed to memory. She also acknowledged that the atmosphere created by James Russell Lowell provided her with an "athletic ideal in literary enthusiasms"—whatever that might involve.

Gradually, as she grew older and began to acquire a reputation as an author, she wearied of the constant comparisons with her ancestor; she worried that his reputation as a poet might overshadow and threaten hers, preventing her from emerging as an artist on her own terms. "He was not a real poet at all," she informed one correspondent; to another (J. B. Rethy, of the *International*), she wrote (May 1917):

I am grateful to you for comparing me with James Russell Lowell to the detriment of the latter. This may sound unkind, but if you had had that elderly gentleman held in front of you as a model and a shining goal all your life, you would realize the delight I take in reading such words as yours.

Amy (a compromise of the family name of Amory) was descended from that branch of the family after whom the mill city of Lowell was named, the Higginson-Amory line; her direct ascendants included the Rebel, John Amory Lowell, and Judge John. Through her mother, Kath-

erine Bigelow Lowell, she was descended from the equally awesome
Lawrence family. Described as a plump, mildly handsome woman with
clear blue eyes and regular features, Katherine was an accomplished
musician who played several instruments with enviable passion and
aplomb. She (like James Russell Lowell's mother) had a melodic voice
and liked to sing. Amy inherited her mother's love of music; also her
talkative, urbane, and free-spirited personality. Katherine Lowell was
the daughter of the Honorable Abbott Lawrence, cofounder of Lawrence, Massachusetts, constructed largely with profits derived from
investments in the blue-collar sweatshops of Lowell. Abbott Lawrence,
a driving, forceful, dynamo of a man, was likewise a railroad baron
whose wealth and connections enabled him to get elected to Congress;
his Cotton Whig interests, his friendships with men such as Daniel
Webster, helped him to rise still higher in the political hierarchy; from
1849 to 1852 Abbott Lawrence was American Ambassador to Great
Britain. The Lawrence family, Massachusetts residents since John Lawrence's arrival in the early 1630's, claimed descent from Sir Robert
Lawrence, knighted by Richard Coeur de Lion for his valor at Acre in
1191. Yet for all that plumage and wealth, what is truly noteworthy
about him is that Abbott Lawrence was a self-made man, a boy from the
Massachusetts countryside who rose to distinction through the force of
ambition and power.

Amy's father, Augustus, wealthy beyond dreams, was an archetypical
representative of the Lowell dynasty, his young adulthood a reenactment of all the requisite patrician rituals: Bromley Vale, the Boston
Latin School, Harvard, Porcellian, the Union and Somerset clubs. He
came of age in an environment that celebrated its class-conscious past
but denounced Puritanism for its narrow-minded, hypocritical, cruel,
and superstitious attitudes. One of the chief ingredients of his New
England heritage was good form, the kind of gentlemanly bearing that
precluded both visible emotions and extreme originality. Two of Augustus Lowell's graver concerns were money and kinship. Kinship is what
society (with a capital S) was all about; and money existed for only two
reasons—to be invested wisely or spent constructively.

In their practical-minded way the family had long been interested in
scientific methods and aspects of farming. Members of the clan were
responsible for the promotion of agricultural and horticultural societies,
including Harvard's botanical gardens; the owner of Bromley Vale,
with its long, wooded walks and specially grafted trees, was the inventor

of numerous species of home-grown flowers and plants. This love of the earth was passed on from father to son. For Amy's father it became a way of life, the grounds of Sevenels (Amy informs us) reflecting his passion:

> He covered them with beautiful and exotic flowering shrubs, brought from all parts of the world, and many rare and lovely flowers. The planning of his garden was entirely done by himself. He never allowed anyone else to make any arrangements or decide upon any matter of change or addition. Some idea of his fondness for flowers may be given when I say that he got up at six o'clock every morning and cut his favourites, the roses, with his own hands. I well remember one occasion when he cut a thousand roses in three days.

Two greenhouses supplied the fruit and vegetables for the entire household. A sunken garden was banked on three sides by sloping grass terraces, on the fourth by a raised roadway. There were stables for the horses and cows and acres of uncultivated land, shaded by towering stands of oak, beech, and sycamore. Deer roamed this acreage and through the trees, Sevenels, in its magisterial whiteness, looked like a wedding cake. When he was not working his land, Augustus Lowell exercised more visible forms of patriarchal responsibility: he was the second trustee of the Lowell Institute, a member of the Executive Committee at MIT, treasurer and vice-president of the American Academy of Arts and Sciences, an officer of the Massachusetts Historical Society, board member of the American Association for the Advancement of Science, and honorary director of the Colonial Society of Massachusetts. Among those to profit most during the years of postbellum prosperity when the entire nation was beginning to stabilize its economic position, Augustus Lowell's chief sources of income lay in cotton mills and banks: he happily presided over a phalanx of both, running them as an admiral runs a navy—with a stern hand and a quick mind.

Those who knew him testified that he was steel-willed and unflappable, driving but reticent, a compelling mixture of the dour and the likable. Slight of stature, he possessed dynamic energy coupled with a stubborn streak of Anglo-Saxon persistence. He conducted his everyday affairs with a salting of dry humor and a peppering of eccentricity. He was not of that imperial British school that felt that a well-to-do man need not work, provided he keep occupied with philanthropy, reform politics, or human good works. Rather, he emulated his father, John

Amory Lowell, and his grandfather, the Rebel, in their single-minded, obsessive migrations toward success and achievement. George Santayana unwittingly summed up Augustus Lowell's philosophy in his novel *The Last Puritan*: "Money wasn't a sort of magic spell to cast about you and to make the world dance for your pleasure. Money was a trust, a responsibility. You mustn't think you had it just to save you trouble and fatigue. On the contrary, Money kept you running and working and planning and struggling, until you dropped."

The power of wealth had the same unchallengeable reality as high political office. It gave its possessor the right of sanction as well as veto. Exercising his privilege, Augustus laid down the laws of Sevenels, banning from his house the scientific tracts of Darwin, and the poetry of Shelley, whose atheism he found disturbing. In keeping with these sequestrations he rejected anything that might be construed as issuing from the pen or theories of Thomas Jefferson. Such retrograde blue laws led his son Percival (who later became a devoted Darwinian) to write that his father was advanced in practical, not in theoretical matters: "Widely read as he was, he never seemed to care to theorize. He enjoyed highly the theories of others, when they did not collide with his own."

The carefully appointed rooms of Sevenels, heavy with massive furniture and Oriental rugs, dark with thick draperies drawn against the daylight, reflected Augustus Lowell's serious side. Dinners were served elegantly and punctually on fine silver and fresh napery, with flowers cut routinely from the garden, and everything polished and waxed to perfection. The chores at Sevenels were performed by a large staff of house servants in a smooth, unvarying routine. Dinner-table conversation, even when the family dined alone, was intense and often brilliant.

A stern and in ways intractable figure, Augustus valued mightily the qualities of self-reliance, will, consistency, faithfulness, and integrity, and attempted to instill in his offspring a sense of pride and independence. It may have seemed contradictory considering his unyielding personality, but he wanted his children to think for themselves, to formulate their own ideas and points of view. The result was that, in an era when children were supposed to be seen and not heard, the Lowell young were both visible and highly audible. And though Augustus offered to settle on each of his offspring a life income that would permit the kind of carefree existence he generally disdained, each in turn unhesitatingly chose work.

It was into this environment, then, that Amy was born, late in her mother's life, an event that earned the young one the nickname Miss Postscript. Her brother Percival, nearly nineteen, was a sophomore at Harvard; Lawrence, seventeen, was a freshman; her two sisters, Katherine (named after their mother) and Elizabeth, were respectively sixteen and twelve. The infant was christened Amy Lowell on July 5, 1874, at St. Paul's Church, Brookline. She was raised an Episcopalian, the faith of all the Lawrences, but became an atheist, a believer in the transcendent power of literature and the sacred property of art—the very persuasion her father had tried so implacably to avert.

Sevenels was the palatial setting of Amy's childhood. Thirty acres of sprawling emerald meadow, grove, garden, walks, and walls provided the child with an Edenic wonderland over which to wander. The gardens of flowers bordering the walks, climbing the walls, glimmering in color-coordinated beds, constituted a ready motif to be incorporated into her later verse. She knew these chromatic gardens and flowers like the back of her hand.

Nature enveloped Amy at Sevenels as it did James Russell Lowell at Elmwood; and the bulk of her poetry was underscored by a heavy emphasis on nature and nature's delights. "Sunshine," "Spring Day," and "Lilacs" were among the poems that demonstrated the naturalist's green thumb and firm bucolic grasp. "Lilacs," lilted Amy, "False blue, / White, / Purple, / Colour of lilac, / Your great puffs of flowers / Are everywhere in this my New England." There were numerous samples from the same mold. "In a Garden," a poem on the pleasures of "man-made" nature, was the imagistic work that first brought Amy to Ezra Pound's attention, and which he included in his Imagist anthology:

> . . . Damp smell the ferns in tunnels of stone,
> Where trickle and plash the fountains,
> Marble fountains, yellowed with much water.
>
> Splashing down moss-tarnished steps
> It falls, the water;
> And the air is throbbing with it.
> With its gurgling and running.
> With its leaping, and deep, cool murmur.

She spent three seasons each year in the garden at Sevenels. The fourth, winter, was passed at the family town house, a four-story affair in Boston proper at 171 Commonwealth Avenue. The annual city move provided Amy with another view of the world. Here the other, the junior branches of the clan dwelled amid brick-paved walks and quiet, elm-lined streets, in houses that retained the elegant memories of their colonial heritage: "the polished brass nameplates, knockers, and handles on front doors, transatlantic Chippendale and Adam furniture, darkly polished stairwells delicately tooled, China plate and screens, were reminiscent of Queen Anne's London near the Strand."

Amy clearly preferred the tranquility of Brookline to the noise and confusion of the city. She explored the greenhouses, haunted the stables and carriage house, roamed the paths and trails, mercilessly taunting her poor, benevolent nurse. She frolicked among the shrubbery and flowers, hunted ghosts and Indians in the grove, and listened to invigorating snatches of talk at the elaborate family dinners she was permitted to attend. The lurid details that filled out some of these dinner-table conversations must have proved a stimulating factor in the attentive child's early development.

At age five she was taken to Cambridge by her "educationally-fore-thoughted parents" to see "the great ones of the earth." One of the unforgettable giants present that day was James Russell Lowell's pre-eminent neighbor, the white-bearded author of "The Children's Hour": "Mr. Longfellow carried me round the table in a scrap-basket and the recollection of that ride is quite as vivid as though it were yesterday."

A less momentous event took place a year later: Amy began dancing school. *The* Boston dancing school was Papanti's, operated by Signor Lorenzo Papanti, a toupeed, mustachioed, sprightly old gentleman. It was at his academy, under his discerning eye, that young Boston society mastered the Viennese waltz, the lancers, "the German," and other fancy steps in order to develop charm and poise, prerequisites for entrance into the haut monde.

In the summer of 1882 another rite was enacted; Amy and her sisters accompanied their parents on a tour of Europe, galloping across the Continent "at a fearful rate of speed." They were back home in the fall, and that winter Katherine married Alfred Roosevelt, first cousin to Teddy Roosevelt, the future President. Amy was delighted. She was even more delighted when in the spring of 1883, she was taken out West, an excursion recorded in one of those travel journals that juveniles are sometimes persuaded by their elders to keep. Two other tales that she wrote as a child were included in a small pamphlet *(Dream*

Drops), which Amy's mother published privately and sold to friends to raise funds for charity.

Of paramount importance in the course of the future poet's development was the well-modulated voice of her brother Percival. Her parents were half-a-generation too old to be involved in the process of her growing-up. Her mother had contracted Bright's disease, a malady characterized by bouts of extreme nervousness and heightened blood pressure, and her father, the business tycoon and self-absorbed naturalist, was too busy with his own affairs to give his youngest daughter the attention she craved. It was inevitable therefore that Amy's brother should become an important influence in her life, if only as a symbol of parental dominance and direction.

As a student at Harvard, Percival had performed admirably. Professor James Russell Lowell called him "the brightest young man in Boston," high praise considering the status of its donor. Following his graduation, Percival joined his grandfather John Amory Lowell in the family business, administering the clan's myriad trust funds and cotton mills. Within a half-dozen years he had tasted his fill; determined to travel, he set sail in 1883 for the Far East, arriving in Tokyo and renting a large house that he filled with books and servants. At the behest of a friend, he eventually accepted a diplomatic post with the Korean embassy, punctuating his stay in Tokyo with occasional visits to Korea and the United States.

In Amy's eyes, her distant brother was a folk hero, comparable to the heroes of the storybooks she loved to read: a vision out of the "Little Rollo" series; or perhaps an embodiment of Sir Launfal, the knight in shining armor poised smartly upon the broad back of a white steed. The missives and packages he sent home, full of lengthy descriptions of exotic and wondrous Oriental landscapes, contained pictures and prints, paper fans and fishes, miniature toys and bright bric-a-brac. These items enticed Amy in a way school could not. She was a student in Mrs. Cabot's School, 57 Chestnut Street, Boston. Mrs. Cabot, a Lowell cousin, had founded the school for the purpose of educating her own children and had begun taking in the children of friends and relatives. Mabel Cabot, the daughter of Amy's Brookline neighbor and a student at the same school, observed that Amy was totally indifferent to classroom decorum. Noisy, opinionated, and spoiled, she terrorized the other students and spoke back to her teachers.

The curriculum, which she found tedious, included a smattering of history, geography, French, Italian, and literature. "My family did not consider that it was necessary for girls to learn either Greek or Latin, and I have found this ignorance of the classic languages a great handicap," she later observed. In truth, education for women was only in its infant stage. Amy went to school, but the education she received was limited. What she did learn is best illustrated by examining a year's worth of English themes. The emphasis was on poetry but not on "modern" (nineteenth-century) poetry. She wrote on *Beowulf*, on Gray's life and personal qualities, his "Elegy" and "On the Death of a Favorite Cat"; she wrote about Goldsmith's poetry and about his "Traveller"; she summarized the life of Burns and paraphrased the first stanza of "Cotter's Saturday Night"; she wrote and rewrote a theme on the work of Chaucer; she examined the life of Cowper, created an imitation of Irving's "Rip Van Winkle," and analyzed *The Merchant of Venice*.

In an essay titled "Poetry, Imagination, and Education," published long after her reputation was established, the poet discussed her school days: "We all hate the poetry we learnt in school. Why? Is it because the conditions were such that we never really learnt it at all, the fine inner sense of it and its beauty of expression were both hidden from us?" On her own, she read from the works of Dickens, Thackeray, and Louisa May Alcott. She had always found adventure stories and historical romances exciting, possibly because of the Oriental adventures of Percival, perhaps because her father had read Scott's *Rob Roy* to her as a child—a mirror-image of James Russell Lowell's rereading of the book in old age. Amy had affection for Scott and Cooper, Frederick Marryat, Jules Verne, and R. H. Dana *(Two Years Before the Mast)*. She also developed a fondness for Wordsworth, especially for *The Excursion*, a sequence most highborn young ladies found exceedingly dull.

One of the truly telling documents of Amy's early years was her diary, which she began to keep with the New Year, 1889. In it she recorded an early passion for the theater, a deep interest in history and literature, and a painful, unabiding loneliness: "I feel very much in need of a *very* intimate friend, a friend whom I should love better than any other girl in the world and who would feel so towards me." Later, after summers spent in a succession of luxury resorts—Petersborough, Cotuit, Rye Beach, the Cabots' island off Maine, Newport (with its afternoon *passeggiata* along Ocean Drive)—the focus of her loneliness shifted toward men:

Do you know I was "struck all of a heap" the other day by discovering that I love Paul H.

How long I have loved him I don't know. But I must have loved him for some time.

It is so silly; but when Paul asked Mabel to walk with him I [felt] just like going off alone somewhere and crying. This feeling [was] mixed by a kind of a wish to hit Somebody.

If there was any chance of Paul's ever loving me it would be different and I should not be ready to pound myself for being such a fool as to love him.

But I am ugly, fat, conspicuous, and dull; to say nothing of a very bad temper.

Oh Lord please let it be all right, and let Paul love me, and don't let me be a fool.

The obesity ("I am ugly, fat, conspicuous") was the result of a lifelong glandular condition that she developed at age nine or ten; the physiological effects of her ailment were ultimately far more damaging than the psychological effects. But like any growing child suffering the pangs of self-doubt, Amy allowed her mind to dredge up all the flights and fantasies that adolescence is capable of producing:

I don't think that being all alone, in here, is good for me. In fact I have been building myself castles in the air, and thinking, thinking!

I think that to be married, to a sweet, tender, strong and good man, would be the nearest approach to perfect happiness, of course provided that you love the man. To be his sole, and whole, confident. In short my ideas of what a husband should be are very exalted.

No! I shall be an old maid, nobody could love me, I know. Why, if I were somebody else, I should hate myself.

I am doomed, for how can it be different—? to see the man I love marry somebody else.

While her friends, with their floor-length white skirts and lacing, were preparing to enter the social whirl of wealthy Back Bay, Amy, stout and awkward, was consciously retreating into herself and her own despondency. "I was a fool *as usual!!*" was a typical journal declamation. She saw herself as "a great rough masculine, strong thing"—and despised this aspect of her character. At another point she wrote: "If I were not so self-conscious I would be much better. Everybody thinks I'm a fool (and it's true) and nobody cares a hang about me."

Dancing school provided scant relief. She had progressed to "Friday

Evenings" at Papanti's, for sub-subdebs and Harvard freshmen, but Boston's young men did not exactly rush to her side: "I was left over in 'the German' *as* usual!" She attended a horseback-riding academy, yet found it no easier to make male acquaintances. She was jealous of the freedom accorded her brothers and their friends, whereas the attractiveness of her sisters with their altar societies, card clubs, literary round tables, music circles, and fashionable charities only increased her resentment. In the end she forced herself, probably out of desperation, to enjoy dancing school—at least not to resent it:

> I am in! for the "Saturday Evening" next year. Oh Joy!! I don't know why I'm glad; of course I shall be an awful pill, as I was at the "Friday Evening" last year. I think that I should like parties quite well if only I could dance well and was sure of having a *very* good time. But, of course, I am doomed to be a dreadful pill; doomed to blush very visibly, and waste my sweetness in the vicinity of the wall. But then, you know, I don't care a rap!

In 1891, a year after completing her formal studies, Amy emerged from Papanti's as polished as a gemstone. Boston society beckoned. Miss Lowell managed to play the part of high-society belle with a good deal of panache. For several months she tested the rituals of aristocratic subsistence, attending some sixty dinner parties; she even mastered a few dance steps, which she tried out at the gay, gas-lit Copley Hall assembly balls and at the Somerset, where she made her regal debut.

She joined the Sewing Circle, a cluster of bored debutantes who believed (and had been taught from childhood to believe) that a female's worth derived from purity, piety, domesticity, and service to the community. The ladies of this set, all of fabulously wealthy, America-Firster background, organized philanthropic female voluntary societies and benevolent organizations. For Amy these organizations fostered the notion that there thrived in America a large class of fashionable creatures whose sole contribution to the world was to throng the city promenades in order to display the latest in female finery and frivolities. More than once she was a guest at the elegant, high-ceilinged, white-marble-interior home of Sarah Wyman Whitman, as renowned a fin de siècle conversationalist as her famous male counterpart, Thomas Appleton; Miss Whitman's posh brownstone parties attracted Beacon Hill's best-heeled habitants and choice scattering of nouveaux arrivés. At one of these well-publicized affairs, Amy encountered Mrs. Jack Gardner,

Boston's mysterious First Lady of the horsy set, whose swank afternoon garden parties she also began to attend. But what set Amy apart from her upper-crust contemporaries was her growing dissatisfaction with the polite patois overheard at these repetitive gatherings and the tiresome tirade of grapevine tidbits traded off between cousins and aunts, the same interfamilial trivia Amy had enjoyed hearing as a child but which she now found deleterious. For Amy the search for personal fulfillment and meaning existed in a different realm. She remained individual and insular, refusing to follow the path of what she thought a compromising and self-effacing existence.

The up-and-coming young of Cold Roast Boston had developed their own standards of conversation and style. Wilde's comedies, O. Henry's short stories, the decadence of J. K. Huysmans, Maurice Maeterlinck, Paul Verlaine, and Stéphane Mallarmé were an integral part of the native impulse. Fashionable, too, were the French critic Jules Bois, Aubrey Beardsley and the *Yellow Book* series, Stewart Merrill's *Pastels in Prose*, and Stephen Crane's "underground" hit, *Black Riders*. Henri Murger's myth of Bohemia had recently been revived by several current novelists. And Ibsen, Shaw, Zola, and Kipling—the four horsemen of Nineveh—were as popular as ever.

Literature was only a small aspect of the explosion. Intercollegiate athletics experienced their first flush of popularity (the annual Harvard-Yale boat race was already a tradition). Boston's Louisa Wells, a debutante and a national golf champion, prefigured a minor F. Scott Fitzgerald character in *The Great Gatsby*. Bustles were out, capes and top hats were in; tailored suits for women became the rage, bloomers reappeared. The bicycle did away with the artificial fashions that women had worn for years, although the Kenny & Clark cab kept formal wear stiff and in vogue. At Harvard, students were cultivating that mixture of wit, exquisiteness, and boredom that inspired the epithet "Harvard Indifference."

Amy, from a more conventional, less liberated environment than golfdom's Miss Wells, was familiar with little of this; although her family had close connections with Harvard, she was hardly aware of what passed for the current Cambridge manner. The closest she came to comprehending the Crimson pose occurred while auditing a course in Shakespeare offered by a well-regarded Harvard English professor, Barrett Wendell, at Amy's high school. His lectures, however, struck her as disappointingly stiff and dim: "We learnt everything about the plays

. . . except the things that mattered. Not once . . . were we bidden to notice the poetry. . . . The plays might have been written in the boldest prose for all the eminent professor seemed to care." More to her liking and better suited to her love of action and color were the plays she saw produced at the Boston Museum-Theater, on the same street as Papanti's. These stage dramas, coupled with Amy's discovery of three new novelists—Charlotte Brontë, Anthony Trollope, and Jane Austen —stirred her imagination. But the paramount discovery she made in her young years was the poetry of John Keats.

She came across the work of Keats while perusing a book found in her father's library, Leigh Hunt's lavishly titled *Imagination and Fancy; or, Selections from the English Poets, Illustrative of those first requisites of their art; with markings of the best passages, critical notices of the writers, and an essay in answer to the question 'What is Poetry?'*. Hunt, the English essayist, journalist, and poet who had passed away in 1859 at the age of seventy-four, was far out of fashion when Amy chanced upon him; nevertheless, his critical study served her needs as no book had before. The selections, with Hunt's commentary, ranged from Chaucer to the Romantics, omitting the Gray, Goldsmith, Burns, and Cowper read by Amy in school, but also neglecting Spenser, Marlowe, Jonson, Donne, Milton, Blake, and the *Lyrical Ballads*. For all its omissions, the study "opened a door that might otherwise have remained shut" and "turned" Amy "definitely to verse":

> I did not read it, I devoured it. I read it over and over, and then I turned to the works of the poets referred to, and tried to read them by the light of the new aesthetic perception I had learnt from Hunt.
> So engulfed in this pursuit was I, that I used to inveigle my schoolmates up to my room and read them long stretches of Shelley, and Keats, and Coleridge, and Beaumont and Fletcher. Guided by Hunt I found a new Shakespeare, one of whom I had never dreamed, and so the plays were saved for me, and nothing was left of the professor's lectures except an immense bitterness for the lost time.

The most useful aspect of the study, from Amy's perspective, was the close attention it paid to Keats. Keats, wrote Hunt, reveled in the five senses with greater power of imagination than any poet before him. Keats taught Amy what adolescence had failed to impart—the intractable lessons of emotion, the relative values of the physical and spiritual in matters of love, their purity and oneness. It was from Keats that Amy discovered her own adoration of the moon; the lunar body became an indispensable part of her work, an image that ran consistently "from the first poem in her first volume to the last poems of her last volume."

When James Russell Lowell died, on August 12, 1891, Abbott Lawrence Lowell served as pallbearer at his funeral; Amy Lowell was likewise present that somber day. It is conceivable, even likely, that she was reminded on this memorable occasion of her poet-cousin's early allegiance to Keats and of his fragmentary Keats-inspired poems: "Ianthe," "A Legend of Brittany," "Prometheus," and "Irene." There was a James Russell Lowell sonnet, "To the Spirit of Keats," and the projected Keats biography that came to pass only when Amy saw it to fruition late in her life. Also, there was the Firesider's "lukewarm" essay on Keats, later included in his collected literary works, but originally intended as the introduction to an edition of Keats's *Poems* (Boston, 1854), which demonstrated that Lowell's early enthusiasm for the Englishman had become considerably tempered by critical judgments.

Besides Keats and the other Romantic poets, Miss Lowell derived her greatest pleasure from the stage. She enjoyed the light-vein Hasty Pudding musicals presented twice a year at Harvard. The Globe Theater, which proudly boasted that it was "illuminated by the Edison Incandescant Light," played host in April 1893 to the lithe-figured Eleonora Duse, Italy's premier leading lady. This was Duse's first American tour; in Boston she performed *Camille, Fedora*, and a double bill of *Cavalleria Rusticana* and *La Locandiera*. Miss Lowell attended and, though she had difficulty with the Italian, was greatly moved by the vibrancy of Duse's stage presence. It was not until Duse's tour of 1902, however, that Amy dashed off her inspirational poem for the actress.

In May 1894 the French actor Mounet-Sully came to the new Tremont Theater; Miss Lowell saw him in the title role of Victor Hugo's *Ruy Blas*, and another new world opened its doors to her:

> I came home . . . and demanded of everyone I saw information as to what else Victor Hugo had written. Some one said, *Notre Dame de Paris*, and *Notre Dame* I got out of the library the next day. French, having hitherto been a hated study, I had, of course, acquired as little of as I could and stay in my class. But I wanted to read *Notre Dame*. Many a night did I sit up in bed, reading by the flickering light of two candles, and looking up every word I did not know in the dictionary lest I lose some of the beauty of the descriptions. I believe Victor Hugo woke me up to the meaning of style. I was lifted on the wings of a great poetry; although,

so little had poetry been a thing which I considered, I did not know it was that. . . .

This romantic affection for the stage led Amy to try her own hand at performing. At a younger age she had been offered the role of Tony Lumpkin in a local production of Oliver Goldsmith's *She Stoops to Conquer*, but her mother, unwilling to let her play the role of a man, forced her to withdraw. Later she acted in amateur theatricals, notably several plays produced by the Vincent Club, one of those famed Boston institutions formed to raise funds for the needy. She demonstrated a fair talent in these productions and under different circumstances might well have made a name for herself on the stage.

Amy's mother, a helpless paralytic during her receding years, died in 1895. It was presently decided that Amy Lowell would assume the duties of lady of the manor, organizing her father's domestic setting with the same degree of precision to which he had become accustomed prior to his wife's wasting illness. Before taking charge, however, she was to be sent on a lengthy European sojourn, the purpose of which, aside from its salutary benefits, was that it would enable the twenty-one-year-old to see and experience for herself the manner and ways of the European haut monde.

Accompanied by a girl friend and a chaperone, Amy traveled at a leisurely pace through Italy, Austria, Germany, France, Holland, and England. She was "swept off her feet" by Naples, then again by Venice, which she had seen first as a child. Paris was just as enchanting. The ballet, the opera, the art galleries, even the museums were grander by far than New York's cultural riches. The labyrinth of Left Bank book-stalls yielded untold treasures, stimulating Amy's taste for lavish leather bindings and the costly vice of first editions. London was Amy's last port of call. Her stay there was enhanced by a visit to the Chelsea Studio of James Abbott McNeill Whistler, the American expatriate painter whose birthplace was Lowell, Massachusetts. Looking back on their encounter, Amy could recall two details: a colorful Japanese screen and the farthing, earned in the Whistler-Ruskin libel trial of 1878, that dangled from Whistler's silver watch-chain. Sensing that he was not as prosperous as others claimed, she purchased a small still life from him, which she later mounted on the chimney-breast in the library at Sevenels.

She returned briefly to Boston but soon turned up in Europe again. Rumor had it that while in America she had fallen passionately in love

with a young Harvard graduate, but that her feelings were not reciprocated. The story insisted that the young man had been attracted by
her wealth and not her "beauty"—nor her personality—and that her
vanity was seriously wounded. We can further surmise that she blamed
this disappointment on her unwieldy physical appearance (by age
twenty she weighed some 250 pounds and stood barely five feet tall).
She seemed to feel that further exertions in travel would reduce her
avoirdupois and distract her mind from fears of the future.

Therapy, then, and not escape, was the apparent motive behind her
European return. The realization that she would probably have to face
life alone, that she would remain a "spinster," gnawed at her. The age,
or at least the society in which she lived, demanded that people live
according to the prevailing standards and mores; and marriage, family,
and inheritable property were among the accepted standards of that
world. The dictates of status had it that a woman's sole worth, her whole
reason for being, depended upon her ability to find fulfillment through
a man. Only as a daughter, sister, mother, or wife could a woman's life
attain meaning. The era glorified motherhood and child-rearing, at the
same time as it advised women to temper intellectual pursuits and
reproached women for attempting to further their education. Until the
end of World War I, any female exceeding these demands or failing to
meet them more than halfway, faced the prospect of instant banishment and eternal exile. Woe to the woman with a mind of her own!

Determined to cope with the devolving facts of her development,
Amy began her latest European voyage in London, traveled to Paris for
a week, and on to Hyères; there she was joined by her friend Polly
Cabot for a hastily arranged trip up the Nile. In 1897, expeditions
exploring the Nile basin, while commonplace enough, were nevertheless considered hazardous. The two women sailed from Marseilles to
Alexandria, taking the train to Cairo, where their dahabeah *Chonsu*,
named for the god of the Rising Moon, awaited them. Before embarking, they made a slight detour inland to view the Pyramids and the
Sphinx. Next, according to plan, they ascended the Nile.

Determined to travel in style, they had chartered a Cook's Tour, with
ten sailors, a captain, a steersman, a cook and cook's helper, a waiter and
waiter's helper, and a dragoman (interpreter) aboard: seventeen men
to take a couple of ladies up the river. The dahabeah, only seventy-five
feet from bow to stern, was outfitted with sofas and easy chairs and
Turkish rugs and rubber plants on the upper deck, a small salon and

three staterooms below. Crew and comforts aside, the trip was fraught with excitement. The first incident occurred when Miss Lowell tamed a restless band of North African natives encountered in another boat by threatening them with her fountain pen, holding it aloft like a spear and pointing it in the direction of her adversaries; they were instantly subdued. This episode was immediately followed by another: when the crew of the dahabeah refused to force the boat up a steep stairwell of rapids to the Isle of Philae, the innocent but stout-hearted debutante stepped out and hoisted and hauled it to shore herself. The voyage terminated in Cairo; from there the party sailed on to Naples, drove to Sorrento, viewed the Blue Grotto, visited Pompeii and Paestum, and spent a week in Rome. Among the sights, Miss Lowell visited the Piazza di Spagna and saw the small house where Keats passed away.

Back in Boston she labored for a short time to keep Sevenels in working order for her father. After his death in 1900, she inherited both the mansion and property as well as the overpowering feeling of liberation that came with her recent acquisition of wealth. It was in the position of mistress of the manor that she developed her strange habit of staying awake nights and sleeping days. When she did sleep it was to her third-floor childhood bedchamber that she retired, a room she continued to occupy her entire life.

Among the outward signs of her sudden independence was a budding interest in Brookline's public school system. Presenting herself at the first school-board meeting of the year, she succeeded, single-handedly, in lowering the retirement age of elderly school officials. In so doing she learned that she was a skilled debater, that she could speak well before an audience. If society deemed it unladylike for females to deliver speeches in public, it was certainly not unLowell-like. James Russell Lowell had performed admirably as an orator; the family had produced its share of brilliant churchmen; the oral tradition was in their blood, and Amy was no exception.

Eventually she was elected to the executive committee of the Brookline Education Society, also chairman of its library committee, duties that would normally have fallen into her father's lap had he been alive. In this capacity she delivered a number of addresses, one of which, attacking the school board for forcing students to memorize vast tracts of poetry, prompted a critic to conclude that she clearly evinced her "heritage of 'masculine' Lowell thinking." The passage in her speech that brought about this reaction argued that "Character means Courage, and there is a great difference between the collective courage of a mass of people all thinking the same way, and the courage of one man who cares not at all for public opinion, but goes on his way unswervingly. . . . It is not easy to find men who are willing to think and act at variance with the opinions of their neighbors." It was Amy's repeated use of the "male" gender, her disdain for the masses, and her celebration of the valor of individuality that alarmed her detractor. One of her more caustic remarks that afternoon had it that "The difficulty with American civilization is that it is essentially vulgar in tone, not so much in manner as in essence. The theatres, the newspapers, the popular amusements, all show this. The few people with refined ideas and cultivated tastes can make no impression against the mass of Vulgarism." It was obvious to which camp she assigned herself.

16

"A DOME OF MANY-COLOURED GLASS"

WITH the advent of the new century, the children of Augustus Lowell rapidly elevated themselves into positions of leadership and respectability. Percival Lowell, back from the Far East, turned his attention to astronomy, founding the Lowell Observatory at Flagstaff, Arizona, recording his findings in a series of scientific textbooks and instructional pamphlets. Abbott Lawrence Lowell, his law career behind him, joined Harvard's faculty and started working his way toward the school's presidency. Katherine and Elizabeth, Amy's older sisters, took the more common course for women of their class and social distinction, opting for families of their own and careers as fund raisers and charity organizers. Whereas Katherine Lowell had wed a Roosevelt, her younger sister Elizabeth married the Boston financier William Lowell Putnam and produced a string of impressive progeny, a brood of future lawyers and doctors.

That left Amy, whose "moment of truth" was generated, not so much by her response to the poetry of the written word, as by her reaction to the enchantment of a great actress, Eleonora Duse. Miss Lowell had seen Duse perform during her American tours of 1893 and 1896; now, in October 1902, the Italian diva was again in Boston, this time appearing at the Tremont in a triad of plays by Gabriele d'Annunzio: *La Gioconda*, *La Città Morta*, and *Francesca da Rimini*. Amy attended the opening performance on October 21; the date is important insofar as it marks the inauguration of her career as a poet. That evening she found herself compelled to write a tribute to Duse in seventy-one lines of blank verse. It was her first attempt at poetry; she was twenty-eight:

> When Eleonora Duse came to America on one of her periodical trips . . . I went to see her, as I always went to see everything that was good in the theatre. The effect on me was something tremendous. What really happened was that it revealed me to myself, but I hardly knew that at the time. I just knew that I had to express the sensations that Duse's acting gave me, somehow. I knew nothing whatever about the technique of poetry, I had never heard of *vers libre*, I had never analyzed blank verse—I was as ignorant as anyone could be. I sat down, and with infinite agitation wrote this poem. It has, I think, every cliché and every technical error which a poem can have, but it loosed a bolt in my brain and I found out where my true function lay.

The poem, published years later in a collection of verse by "younger" authors, was as cliché-ridden as Amy had feared. It began:

> For she whom we have come to see tonight
> Is more to be divined and felt than seen,
> And when she comes one yields one's heart perforce,
> As one might yield some noble instrument
> For her to draw its latent music forth.

And ended:

> And as the evening lengthens, bit by bit,
> Little by little, we discern the real.
> 'Tis that which holds us spellbound far, far more
> Than even her most consummate art can do,
> Through all the passion of a simulated grief
> And through the studied anguish learnt by rote
> We feel the throbbing of a human soul,
> A woman's heart that cries to God and fears!

It was an inauspicious start, but it at least set the creative mechanism in motion. Some years later, addressing an audience in New Haven, Connecticut, she wistfully noted that "a poem, like a great actress, conveys a good deal just by how it walks on to the stage, and it is possible to fall in love with a poem, as with an actress, simply by watching it move." Ending her little talk, she remarked that "poetry is the free exercise of the imagination. It is the only thing we have left, the only complete success our species can point to. Only in the sphere of art is humanity able to rise above its failures and inadequacies." And, "if a poet can't face personal problems in his work, and face them frankly, he had better find another profession."

Amy had fallen in love with Duse, and when the actress left Boston, the novice poet followed her to Philadelphia, where a mutual friend was able to introduce them. As Amy entered the actress's hotel suite, she found Duse comfortably reclining in bed, her bountiful hair meticulously parted down the middle and spilling across the actress's silk-covered pillows. Their conversation was brief, Duse's voice "low and intimate," one of the secrets of her attraction, both on and off stage. As Arthur Symons would say: "She talked as if soul to soul." Sara Teasdale, a leading poet of her day (whose relationship with Amy was mutually advantageous rather than warm), described Duse thus: "She looked as though her delicate bones shone through her fair translucent skin, as though a spirit spoke, scarcely a woman, through her lips." Amy left their meeting "almost on air," convinced that in poetry she had found her calling and that by searching her soul she would find a commensurate voice for the inspiration that beckoned.

She was in need of a writer's retreat, a home away from home where her creative seed could blossom, and presently sought out a summer abode at Dublin, New Hampshire, a small but wealthy New England community that housed the MacDowell Artists' Colony and the hillside homes of an intimate cluster of well-respected painters and sculptors. The house that Amy eventually chose, located on sixty acres of heavily wooded land, had formerly belonged to the Crowninshields; Frank Crowninshield, an editor at *Vanity Fair*, who had the annoying habit of grasping one's elbow in conversation, later became a friend of Miss Lowell's. Renting the house the first summer, she found the area very much to her liking and later purchased the property, naming it "Broomley Lacey," after her grandfather's estate, Bromley Vale. At Dublin she found neighborly neighbors with whom to fraternize, a whole contingent of transplanted, well-to-do Bostonians. In this plush but rural setting Amy wrote, she gardened, she puttered, she took long automobile and buggy rides over the winding dirt roads of the surrounding hillsides. She lived a full if not a fulfilling life.

At Sevenels for most of the year, she continued to cultivate her other interests; she made a number of purchases of rare books and manuscripts, expanding her private holdings and donating recent acquisitions to sundry college libraries. Among those institutions that benefited from her generosity were Radcliffe College, Bryn Mawr College, and the Boston Athenaeum, the city's oldest nonaffiliated library, whose holdings included George Washington's large and stately library. Amy's gifts of books to the Athenaeum were made despite a house regulation that at one time prohibited women from belonging to the library, lest they "cause embarrassment to modest men." That bylaw, since lifted, had caused a considerable controversy between affiliates of the Athenaeum.

The Athenaeum suddenly became the focus of another controversy between members of Boston's upper classes; as usual, Amy found herself thrust into the middle of the fray. A group of the library's older stockholders wanted the Athenaeum moved from its long-standing site on Beacon Hill to a plot adjacent to the Public Gardens. Receiving those members of the board who (like herself) opposed the move, Amy outlined a plan to maintain its present location. What was unusual about the meeting was that it took place in Amy's bedroom, the heiress perched atop her bed clad only in an old-fashioned nightshirt, puffing away on a meerschaum; a large golf umbrella shaded her from the sun that streamed in through two open windows. She argued that the location of the library on Beacon Hill had historic associations; to move it would detract from Boston's cultural heritage. She reinforced her contention by writing a long poem about the Athenaeum, which she included in her first volume of verse, and drove her point to conclusion by buying an extra share of Athenaeum stock, thereby raising the power of her vote: the library stayed put.

Amy's deep attachment to books and libraries was closely related to the atmosphere in which she grew up. Deprived of all possibility of any advanced formal education because of her sex (the Lowells were freethinkers, but not *that* free), Amy nevertheless was let loose at a relatively early age to roam at her own discretion through her father's sizable (if slightly selective) library. Her peregrinations led her in several directions at once, and if they did not entirely reduce the resentment she harbored at being denied the schooling offered to her brothers, at least they provided her with an exposure to literature that helped compensate for the deprivation. Amy's early fascination with language expressed itself not only in her voracious reading at home but also in frequent childhood visits to the Athenaeum, the same library she had just gone to such lengths to preserve.

Her next major project entailed remodeling the ground floor at Sevenels; she gave the whole "a curiously weighted and mixed" Boston-Victorian-Adams-Oriental look, combining styles and periods, gathering and mixing designs, wall fixtures, and objets d'art from the farthest corners of Europe and Asia. The central hallway, two stories high, was covered with dark paneling and a set of elaborately carved wooden animal heads. A long teak table near the soaring entranceway supported a matching pair of tall, colorful Chinese vases. A sweeping staircase was carpeted in glowing crimson silk woven to order; a massive grandfather clock presided over the first landing; it had once belonged to John Amory Lowell.

There was a music room as one entered, its walls shimmering with soft yellow satin, its furniture of imported blond wood. A finely polished grand piano dominated the decor. Over the fireplace sat a Monet, the Battersea Bridge in a fog, its colors misty but luminous; five Egyptian watercolors by Joseph Lindon Smith covered the facing wall. Every doorknob in this room (and throughout the house, for that matter) was sterling silver.

The library and the sitting room, formerly two separate rooms, became one—a vast baronial chamber lined high with bookcases, paneled with dark oak, embellished by two massive marble fireplaces and surrounded by heavy carvings of fruit and flowers reminiscent of the work of Grinling Gibbons in the Crane Castle at Ipswich. The floors were covered with Oriental and Persian rugs. Japanese stone carvings and Gothic millefleur tapestries crammed one wall; cabinet photographs and rare daguerreotypes, mounted on purple velvet and framed in richly carved gilt, adorned another. An entire section of false bookcases concealed a safe for Amy's collection of first editions and manuscripts. Close to the velvet-draped twenty-foot-high windows enclosing the front portion of the room stood the table at which the poet sometimes worked; surrounding the table were four great gilded baroque chairs covered with red velvet cushions.

Her taste for wealth and sumptuous living extended to the dining room, which contained painted panels of fruit dating from Amy's childhood. Ornate silverware and priceless antique china ornamented the dining table. Odds and ends were everywhere: music boxes from Lausanne, enameled watches and snuffboxes from Paris, fans and masks from Venice. A sixteenth-century crystal chandelier of elaborate design extended from the center of finely carved ceiling medallions. A dumb-waiter was used to transport food from the coal-burning range in the cellar; imported wines and liqueurs were carried up by hand. Outside, in the formal gardens, Amy installed two huge, white splashing fountains and a number of matching statuettes depicting various unnamed allegories. Two enormous caststone lions, also painted white, stood guard at the main gateway to the estate. While it was easy to be distracted, it was not difficult to enjoy the physical comfort afforded by such surroundings.

Two events took place during these years that were to become part and parcel of the Amy Lowell legend. In the spring of 1908 the stables at Sevenels burned down; half a dozen horses perished in the blaze. Amy chose to replace the horses with a litter of huge, highly pedigreed, rough-haired Old English sheepdogs. Immediately these dogs became very important members of the household. When the pack was complete, they devoured ten pounds of top round and large amounts of ground fresh vegetables daily. They were given free run of the house and property. When guests arrived at the front gate of Sevenels they usually found a servant waiting to escort them to the house, lest they be set upon by the ravenous dogs, as was Maxwell Bodenheim one warm summer evening. The canines were not permitted entrance to the dining room, but after dinner when everyone gathered about the fireplace in the library, the guests were handed bath towels to spread in their laps as protection against the drooling animals. These pets fell victim to food rationing during World War I and were subsequently replaced with a Persian cat, Winky, who appears in several of its mistress's later poems.

The year's second major event was Abbott Lawrence Lowell's ascendancy to the presidency of Harvard. More practical than either his older brother or younger poet sister, he possessed the cold exterior of Augustus Lowell and shared with his father a reputation for being a "hard man." With his brother's removal to Flagstaff, Lawrence assumed an indisputable position of responsibility and leadership in the family circle. His driving energy and hard-nosed personality, his lifelong insistence on the importance of learning, his tenacious ambition, all rubbed off on Amy, for whom he became the perfect father-figure, fitting the same role filled by Percival during the poet's childhood. Although he provided little direct guidance in Amy's life, Lawrence's presence on the scene must have been reassuring. In later years it was Lawrence's suggestion that turned Amy to the composition of *A Critical Fable* in imitation of James Russell Lowell. But being the sister of Harvard's twenty-fourth president had its drawbacks as well. Automatically Amy was catapulted into the lens of the all-seeing public eye; everything she now did took on added dimensions. A month after Lawrence's October 1909 inauguration, she attended a performance of the opera *La Gioconda*, "dressed [as one newspaper reported it] in black satin covered with net pailletted in jet, silver, and gold." Everything she did and said became fit fodder for the dailies. It was stated in one newspaper that she had given up dressing in the outdated and oversized smocks and suits of former days. Her latest costumes were more in keeping with her modish self-image as a poet and artist in extremis, and a powerful member of a socially respected and financially secure Boston Brahmin clan.

Between her appearance in an amateur production at Sevenels of Oscar Wilde's *The Ideal Husband* and her participation on the executive committee of Boston's Toy Theater, Amy was busy writing poetry. After several seasons of plying the trade and with little to show for her efforts, she decided it was time to get her work into print. She was reminded by a notice in a Boston newspaper that her childhood friend Mabel Cabot had married Ellery Sedgwick, the editor of the *Atlantic Monthly*. To Sedgwick Miss Lowell now sent four recently completed sonnets. He surprised her by accepting the lot. One, "Fixed Idea," ran in the issue for August 1910; the others—"A Japanese Wood-Carving," "On Carpaccio's Picture," and "Starling"—appeared in separate issues over the course of the year. A fifth sonnet, "Leisure," was published by *Hampton's Magazine*. This quintet formed the nucleus of Amy's first volume of verse, *A Dome of Many-Coloured Glass*, which came out in October 1912; its publisher was Boston's Houghton Mifflin Company.

The title of her first book, a phrase from Shelley's elegy in memory of Keats, *Adonais*, was reflected in "Fragment," *A Dome's* shortest poem:

What is poetry? Is it a mosaic
    Of coloured stones which curiously are wrought
    Into a pattern? Rather glass that's taught
By patient labour any hue to take

And glowing with a sumptuous splendor, make
   Beauty a thing of awe; where sunbeams caught,
   Transmuted fall in sheafs of rainbows fraught
With storied meaning for religion's sake.

Aside from this entry and one or two others, the collection was of minimal interest; it contained an assortment of sentimental lyrics, jejune moralizing, undistinctive landscapes and still lifes, several tributes to Oriental themes and artifacts, some sonnets, Amy's wordy toast to the Athenaeum, and finally, a farrago of "verses for children." Miss Lowell later wished that the manuscript, save for fewer than a dozen verses, had never been published.

The poems worth considering include "Before the Altar," a lively sequence showing the influence of Keats, and "A Fairy Tale," notable for its autobiographical content. The first contains the lines: ". . . the moon / Swings slow across the sky, / Athwart a waving pine tree, / And soon / Tips all the needles there / With silver sparkles. . . ." The second recalls the unhappiness of the poet in adolescence:

   . . . overshadowing all is still the curse,
   That never shall I be fulfilled by love!
   Along the parching highroad of the world
   No other soul shall bear mine company.
   Always shall I be teased with semblances,
   With cruel impostures, which I trust awhile
   Then dash to pieces, as a careless boy
   Flings a kaleidoscope, which shattering
   Strews all the ground about with coloured sherds . . .

Although Amy had not yet mastered the poetic line, she wrote candidly of what she knew and had seen. Scenes from her childhood appear and reappear: *Dome* is filled with memories of her grandfather's house at Roxbury; of the gardens at Brookline; of a field of blue gentians from a summer spent in the country; of climbing in trees; of watching fish swim in a pond. Occasionally her nature poems wax too poetic, as in a dithyrambic exercise entitled "Song": "Oh! To be a flower / Nodding in the sun, / Bending, then upspringing / As the breezes run; / Holding up / A scent-brimmed cup, / Full of summer's fragrance to the summer sun. . . ."

In many respects the format of the book worked better than its contents. Modeled as closely as possible on the first edition of Keats's

Lamia, it was light in weight and of a size that slipped conveniently into pockets (thus highly portable), with small, distinct type and wide spacing. This aspect of its publication worked so well that all her subsequent volumes of verse followed the same plan of organization, differing only in the color of the binding and the lettering of the label.

Its attractive appearance did not, unfortunately, save it from the critics, who lambasted the book without heed to the familiar family name of its author. The *Minneapolis Journal* assaulted Amy without reserve: "The volume is, on the whole, slightly over the average, and the average is very low. Never do we feel that behind the lines lurks a dynamic personality." Even Louis Untermeyer, later a close friend of Amy's, whose "Memoir" prefaces her *Collected Poems* and with whom she coedited the anthology *A Miscellany of American Poetry* (1922), remained initially unimpressed. In his poetry column for the *Chicago Evening Post* he concluded a review by saying that Miss Lowell's volume "to be brief, in spite of its lifeless classicism, can never rouse one's anger. But, to be briefer still, it cannot rouse one at all." During its first year of life the book sold less than a hundred copies, and this despite a considerable advertising campaign financed almost entirely by Miss Lowell. Amy was disheartened by the final figures but not destroyed; in fact, she was determined to forge ahead.

~ 17 ~

"IMAGISME,"
OR "AMYGISM"

IN 1875 Ralph Waldo Emerson, attempting to capture the literary essence of his epoch, compiled *Parnassus*, a poetry anthology that featured work by a gallimaufry of period favorites: William Cullen Bryant, W. E. Channing, Oliver Wendell Holmes, Longfellow, Whittier, Bret Harte, Thoreau, and James Russell Lowell. Emerson modestly omitted himself, but unwisely left out Poe and Whitman as well. The author of *Leaves of Grass*, preempting his inevitable exclusion, had already blasted his contemporaries in *Democratic Vistas*, written four years earlier: "Do you term that perpetual, pistareen, paste-pot work, American art, American drama, taste, verse? I think I hear, echoed as from some mountain-top afar in the west, the scornful laugh of the Genius of these States."

Although Emerson's anthology helped cap both the Transcendental and Fireside eras, it had little to do with what we now call "modern" poetry. That task was delegated to a former U.S. Assistant Attorney General and Wall Street stockbroker, Edmund Clarence Stedman, the editor of the massive and influential *An American Anthology, 1787–1900* (1900). Stedman, a Connecticut Yankee who conducted simultaneous literary and business careers and who wrote poetry in the style of James Russell Lowell's *The Biglow Papers*, included in his collection selections from Poe, Whitman, and Emily Dickinson—and even a poem by Edwin Arlington Robinson, probably the most serious younger American journeyman of his day.

Stedman's endorsements of Whitman and Dickinson constituted a significant step toward their eventual recognition by a fickle, often misinformed reading public whose tastes favored the pious patriotic doggerel produced in such profundity by the Fireside poets. The inclusion of Whitman and Dickinson in the anthology gave "free verse"— irregularly metered, epigrammatic, impromptu poetry—its first major boost in this country. Here was a "new" kind of poetry, poetry that was contemporary and American in its locality and flavor and open-ended in form. It could be robust and driving, as in the case of Whitman, or quiet and soulful, as in Dickinson. The work of these two literary doyens signaled the start of a developing tradition, a mode of poetic warfare that encapsulated the vitality and imaginative resourcefulness of the age.

In their rampant desire to revolutionize antiquated poetic cadences, Whitman and Dickinson departed dramatically from the romantic conventions of the so-deemed parlor poets—the ornate idioms, Latinisms, and pleonasms that dominated the work of the Victorians. Tennyson calls grass "the herb," a horse a "charger," poetry a "lyre"; Swinburne speaks of "weary wings of love," says "I am fain," writes "terrene" instead of "earthly," and uses "guerdon" in place of "reward." Professor David Perkins in his authoritative two-volume study of American and British poetic developments *(A History of Modern Poetry)* refers to these substitutions as adornments or counterfeit elegances. They "seal the poem off" from the reader, from reality, creating a "false ceiling" that muffles the vital "fury and mire" of human life.

In 1900 literature in America could boast of no less than a baker's dozen of highly acclaimed and accomplished names in the domain of prose: Howells and Twain, Stephen Crane, Ambrose Bierce, Sarah Orne Jewett, Frank Harris, Theodore Dreiser, Henry Adams, John Jay Chapman, William and Henry James, and George Santayana. If the Risorgimento had already taken place in fiction and in literary criticism, it was about to occur in poetry. The times were ripe; all across the land, within a two-decade span, the poets of the future were being born: E. A. Robinson and Edgar Lee Masters in 1869, one in Maine, the other in Kansas; Amy Lowell in 1874 in Brookline, Massachusetts; Robert Frost, a year later, in San Francisco; Carl Sandburg in 1878 in Illinois;

Vachel Lindsay and Wallace Stevens in 1879, the former in Illinois, the latter in Pennsylvania; William Carlos Williams in 1883 in Rutherford, New Jersey; Sara Teasdale in 1884 in St. Louis, Missouri; Ezra Pound in 1885 in Hailey, Idaho; Hilda Doolittle (H. D.) and John Gould Fletcher the next year in Bethlehem, Pennsylvania, and Little Rock, Arkansas, respectively; Robinson Jeffers and Elinor Wylie in 1887, both in Pennsylvania; Marianne Moore the same year in St. Louis; T. S. Eliot in 1888, also in St. Louis; and Conrad Aiken in 1889 in Savannah, Georgia.

The rapid proliferation of poetry in the United States fostered its inevitable backlash, giving rise to an abundance of lesser-quality material and talent. Invariably there are those who look to lost causes and who climb onto bandwagons the instant the wheels give the slightest indication of turning. John Hay's *Pike County Ballads*, for example, although highly touted in its day, was simply a glutinous mixture of slight Western humor and local dialect, comic opera and soapy sentiment pawned off as genuine Western lore. The poems of James Whitcomb Riley and Eugene Field were no better. Riley's *Old Swimmin' Hole* was a conglomeration of lighthearted colloquial verse and uninspired colorations coated with heavy cream. Other names, once much acclaimed, have likewise disappeared into a nimbus of oblivion. Richard Hovey, Bliss Carman, Thomas Bailey Aldrich, William Vaughn Moody, Trumbull Stickney, George Cabot Lodge, John Drinkwater, even Sara Teasdale: how many of these former luminaries can the average undergraduate identify today? One, perhaps two at most? Some of these poets, content with the formal proprieties and moral benedictions of their own generation, resisted the new poetry in order to uphold the old traditions of order and high sophistication. "Making it new" connoted the abolishment of standard rhyme schemes and meter; gone were the sonnet, the ode, the ballad, and in their place the new verse proffered the lyric. The new poetry was tyrannical in its drift, muscular, acerbic, fragmented, colloquial. The new poets described a renewed universe, the post-World War I world of machines, objects, cities, appliances, ennui, godlessness. Here was a poetry, so to speak, that renounced poetry; it wrinkled its nose at poetic diction, mushy drivelings about nature, mysticism, romanticism, and ideology. It called for personal statements uttered in a nervous diction and accompanied by street cries and furtive night whisperings, table thumpings and drumbeats. In a nutshell, the experimentalists believed that what America needed was a kind of verse that would allow its poets to speak more freely. Poetry, even if labored over, must sound spontaneous; the age demanded it.

The problems during these transitional years were twofold. The first had nothing directly to do with lack of will or ambition; missing among poets was a reasonable degree of competence plus the conviction required to implement the revised mode. Too many of our literary doyens were still under the influence of the outmoded forms and flavors of their British (that is, Georgian) counterparts or, in some cases, of Americans who in turn were under the influence of the British. A graver problem was the apparent lack of cohesion among litterateurs in America, especially among poets. The country being large and the poetry-reading public small and dispersed, there was no such thing as a poetic center in America, nothing to compare with London prior to 1914. The last poetry reading and writing nucleus in the States had located in Boston during the reign of the Fireside poets. Despite the resurgence of interest in poets and poetry, it remained essentially an obscure and elitist art form, appreciated by a growing but proportionately minute share of the population.

Consequently this was the literary situation around the country when Amy Lowell published her first volume of verse. Wishing to back the cause of the Muse, she now became involved with an additional aspect of the craft, one which turned her life around. During the summer of 1912, while vacationing in New Hampshire, Miss Lowell received a prospectus from Harriet Monroe, announcing the publication of a new journal, *Poetry: A Magazine of Verse*, to be edited and distributed by Miss Monroe from Chicago. Harriet, the daughter of a well-to-do Midwestern merchandising family, had for some years been art critic for the *Chicago Tribune*. Sensing that something revolutionary and vital was in the making, and determined to become more than one of those faintly comic, meddlesome middlewomen on the fringe of the artistic community, she put her keen fund-raising ability to work on behalf of *Poetry*. An indifferent art critic and a weak poet, she became, through editorial foresight, a central figure in the history of literary modernism in America.

Ezra Pound, T. S. Eliot, William Carlos Williams, Conrad Aiken, and Wallace Stevens were among those to benefit most from the publication of her landmark journal. The whole, new radical turning in poetry that was to catapult it into the present century, found its initial impetus in the monthly magazine. It was because she had read and enjoyed several of Amy's sonnets in the *Atlantic* that Harriet now wrote to her, inviting the poet to contribute both work and funds to the proposed venture, though not necessarily in that order. Miss Lowell responded by enclosing a check for twenty-five dollars and a pledge to submit samples of her verse at a later date, which she did.

The first issue of the journal appeared in September 1912. Listed on the masthead as foreign editor was a name that Amy recognized from other new journals and quarterlies, one Ezra Pound. Pound, like T. S. Eliot and Gertrude Stein, belonged to that generation of cultural expatriates who believed that society, in the sense of "good company," could not be found in the United States. If it existed anywhere, it existed either in the Paris of the *Belle Epoque* or in the London of Swinburne and Yeats. Pound opted for the latter, and in 1908, after several months in Venice, plunged headlong into the bustling tide of London, immediately asserting himself as an authority on the modern idiom. Even Yeats, twenty years Pound's senior, was impressed with this clamorous American export. Pound, he assured Lady Gregory, had come closer to "the right sort of music for poetry" than anyone—"it is more definitely music with strong marked time and yet it is effective speech."

From all appearances young Pound seemed to own a pitch-perfect ear, a truer ear, attested his schoolmate, William Carlos Williams, than anyone save Homer and Shakespeare. Better than any of his contemporaries, Pound understood the cosmography of the written word; he knew where modern poets and their craft had gone astray—and he knew why; he recognized the need for change and made this the central issue in a forceful and drawn-out literary campaign. He wanted, he said, to overhaul the whole face of poetry. He sought tautness and compactness—every word that was not functional, each superfluity, merited elimination. Pound favored a quintessential hardness that had been lost, an edge and sense and brevity such as the classics, "ancient and modern," possessed. Poetry, he declared, should have all the virtues of good prose: "There must be no book words, no periphrases, no inversions . . . objectivity and again objectivity, and espression: no hindside-beforeness, no straddled adjective (as 'addled mosses dank'), no Tennysonianness of speech; nothing—nothing that you couldn't in some circumstance, in the stress of some emotion, actually say." Above all, he had the "precise word" (Flaubert's mot juste) in mind, regardless of its origin, regardless even of the language of its origin, whether foreign or English—a preciseness of expression of which a corresponding exactness of rhythm must be an integral part: "To paint the thing as I see it."

In trying to rid the language of archaisms and similar impediments, Pound was assisted by T. E. Hulme, the British doctrinaire philosopher and poet. Hulme and his followers—Joseph Campbell, Francis Tancred, Edward Storer, and F. S. Flint—formed a group which met regularly at a small restaurant in London's Soho to discuss the latest trends in literature and to propound new and formidable ways of dealing with the old conventional "rubble" which then passed for verse—the moralizing, tendentious whinings of the Victorians and the arid and tiresome laudations of the Georgians, whose ideal it was to write as though the industrial revolution had never taken place. Pound attented the Soho gatherings on and off for a two-year period, 1909–1911, during which time he formulated the basis of the literary thesis he would later apply to his own work.

In attempting to free the language from its flabby, fin de siècle trappings, Hulme, influenced (as was Eliot) by Arthur Symons's *The Symbolist Movement in Literature* (1899), encouraged Pound and the others to study the free verse of French Symbolist poets Baudelaire, Rimbaud, and Verlaine, and to experiment with verse imitations of Japanese tanka and hokku. Pound on his own had discovered the ancient Provençal form; Provençal poetry, as practiced by the troubadours and their jongleurs (musical accompanists), reached its height from the end of the eleventh century to the last decade of the thirteenth and was based on such widespread sources as Hispano-Moresque poetry and music, the May festivals, the Latin verse of the clerics, and the colloquial "dog Latin" songs of the goliards. These sounds helped tune Pound's ear and enabled him to establish a theory of modernization with which he would endeavor to alter the face of twentieth-century poetry.

Five of Hulme's short imagistic poems were preserved for posterity when Pound reprinted them in 1912 as an appendix to his own collection, *Ripostes*. Hulme notwithstanding, the greatest single influence on Pound was probably his friend Ford Madox Ford, the gregarious editor of *The English Review*; Ford, like Hulme, communicated his ideas predominantly through conversation. He rejected the popularly romantic, quasi "cosmic" influence of the Victorians and called for an atomically charged language, "a sort of *pointillisme,*" words shot through with electricity, friction created by ricochet, by the placement of words, one word rubbing up against another. To accomplish this, Ford advocated using "a contemporary spoken or at least speakable language" for literary purposes, the objective being "to register one's own times in terms of one's own time."

Hulme and Ford gave Pound the framework for an idea, a movement or mode of poetry that he called Imagism, or rather *Imagisme*. Some commentators have claimed that the Imagist movement was no more than a collection of personalities, a crowd of pseudo- or para-poets, with a certain predilection "for publicity and self-advertisement rather than any kind of coherence in aesthetic doctrine or poetic practice." Insofar as there was a mode or movement, Pound was not its sole inventor, nor were Hulme, Ford, and Provençal poetry its only inspirational sources. Pound's conceptions were drawn from myriad quarters: Flaubert, Théophile Gautier, Wilde, Henry James, Remy de Gourmont. Other sources included Pater, whose conclusion to *The Renaissance* speaks of finding all value in "impressions, images, sensations." Then there was the young James Joyce jotting down epiphanies in the narrow byways of Dublin (although Pound did not really know of Joyce's work until he was well along). Keats, with his zest for a "certain clarity and intensity" in his verse helped Pound clarify his vision. Also Baudelaire, always concerned with the reinvigoration of language and the discarding of false sentiments, was influential via his formal experimentation and development of a new, a protean consciousness, one that dismissed absolutes, perceived historical impasse, acknowledged doubt as to the underlying coherence of the human enterprise, and preempted Freud's thesis of pervasive psychic division.

Pound did not invent the school of Imagism but he did name it and he formulated a substantial number of its rules, rules whose emphasis was "on concentration and simultaneity and the single timeless moment of revelation that transcends the ordinary flux of existence." He first used the term to describe the objective quality of Hilda Doolittle's early verse, "her ability to get to the nucleus of the word, to present images without representing them." Later called "the perfect Imagist," H. D. turned over to Pound, at his urging, a batch of her best work. Perusing her "Hermes of the Ways," he made several deletions before scribbling "H. D. Imagiste" at the bottom of the page and posting it (October 1912) to Harriet Monroe at *Poetry*:

The hard sand breaks
And the grains of it
Are clear as wine.

Far off over the leagues of it
The Wind,
Playing on the wide shore,
Piles little ridges,
And the great waves
Break over it. . . .

"It is the laconic speech of the Imagistes," read his appended memorandum. "Objective—no slither—direct—no excess of adjectives, etc. No metaphors that won't permit examination.—It's straight talk—straight as the Greek!"

It is questionable whether Miss Monroe knew at this stage exactly what an Imagist was supposed to be, but she introduced the literary sobriquet to her readers with the printing of "H. D. Imagiste's" poems in Vol. I, No. 4 (January 1913). In the same issue, an article by Pound ("Status Rerum") appeared in which he referred to the Imagists as a live literary group in London, but did not mention his connection with them.

He did not, for that matter, publish a formal declaration, an ars poetica, until March 1913. With the appearance in *Poetry* of "A Few Don'ts by an Imagiste," the movement began to define itself. A second article ("Imagisme")—an actual manifesto—signed by F. S. Flint but ghosted by Pound, cited as inspirational lights, in addition to the figures already mentioned, Sappho, Catullus, and Villon, and reduced the school's rules to three:

1. Direct treatment of the "thing," whether subjective or objective.
2. To use absolutely no word that does not contribute to the presentation.
3. As regarding rhythm: to compose in the sequence of the musical phrase, not in the sequence of the metronome.

In addition to listing the movement's tenets, Pound explained what he meant by the term "Image":

An "Image" is that which presents an intellectual and emotional complex in an instant of time. . . . It is the presentation of such a "complex" instantaneously which gives the sense of sudden liberation; that sense of freedom from time limits and space limits; that sense of sudden growth, which we experience in the presence of the greatest works of art. . . .

Behind this explanation and the rules was a scheme designed to eliminate the basic component of traditional English verse, the iambic pentameter, and replace it with a more natural form that would allow the poet greater freedom to develop his own style and method.

The euphoric treatise on Imagism that Pound published in *Poetry* contained the soundest comments on technique Amy Lowell had read since Hunt's *Imagination and Fancy;* H. D.'s poems, published in several issues of the same periodical, led to Amy's amusing announcement, "Why, I, too, am an Imagiste!" The revelation that she was "by divine election" one-quarter of a movement that initially included two American poets (Doolittle and Pound) and a twenty-year-old Englishman (Richard Aldington) came upon her with the force of a cannon blast. And for good reason: the hard sand and great waves, the shining particles of H. D.'s Hellenic poems were a far cry from the standard pulp that was then passing for verse.

Challenged by the commercial indifference that greeted her own book, and stimulated by this unorthodox school, Amy decided to travel to London, locate Pound, and absorb all she could from him. She sailed the summer of 1913, taking with her innumerable trunks and suitcases, and a letter of introduction from Harriet Monroe.

Ensconced like royalty in a five-room penthouse suite atop the Berkeley Hotel, with a view across Piccadilly Square of greater London, Miss Lowell dispatched Harriet Monroe's letter of introduction, and Pound came to dinner. It was served privately: Amy did not enjoy eating in public. Fully aware that she was a member of the wealthy and influential Lowell family of Massachusetts, Pound handled her with kid gloves. He deeply revered the class that she represented. His genuflections before bloated members of that crowd, men and women with money and position, were generally well known. Then, too, Pound was milder in those days and more charming than time and politics would make him. Amy informed Miss Monroe that she found him "a very thin-skinned and sensitive personality opening out like a flower in a sympathetic circle, and I should imagine shutting up like a clam in an alien atmosphere." He thought he could charm her into purchasing a periodical, setting himself up as its editor; she thought she could benefit from his influence in London's combative literary circles, where she would ostensibly be admired as a writer and be able to circulate among intellectual equals. Ultimately they were both disappointed.

At first Pound played along, accepting her poem "In a Garden" for *The New Freewoman,* of which he was advisory editor; later he introduced her to Yeats, Ford, and John Gould Fletcher. Fletcher, a fellow American, shared Amy's enthusiasm for modern French poetry. He called on her and read to her from his self-published volume of poems, *Irradiations.* She was "greatly impressed," especially by his generous use of colors. Fletcher informed her of his plan to write a long poem on a modern city by objectively describing everything the pedestrian sees. He was prepared, he told her, "to risk everything in order to become a modern artist" and was determined "to make and accept every kind of experiment": the consummate artist must arouse "the hatred of the mob." His models included Cézanne, Gauguin, Van Gogh, and Stravinsky; paraphrasing the Irish playwright John Millington Synge, Fletcher announced that "to be human again, we must learn first to be brutal." Having witnessed several Stravinsky concerts, he was convinced that artists everywhere "were turning back to the primitively ugly, knowing that in primitiveness alone lay strength."

Amy was smitten. She and Fletcher met frequently. She wrote Miss Monroe: "Fletcher writes in a style entirely his own, a sort of rhythmical prose, dropping now and then into rhyme, and which he manages so skilfully that it is capable of extraordinary versatility." Her ardor for his verse subsided only when it became clear to her, some time later, that he was not romantically attracted to her. But not before she had financed the American publication in 1915 of Fletcher's *Irradiations.*

While in London, Amy kept herself well occupied, attending the Russian Ballet, just over from Paris, with Nijinsky dancing the principal roles; the performance, with its innovative choreography and executions, filled her with ideas on movement and space. She viewed a Cubist art exhibition at a small gallery in Soho and attended a concert of modernist music, featuring works by Schoenberg and Musil. The fractured surfaces of Cubism and the bold discords and broken, syncopated rhythms of the music helped re-create renewed patterns in her mind. She heard two lectures by Wyndham Lewis, one on Kafka and Klee, the other devoted to Modigliani and Kandinsky. In July she visited Harold Monro's popular Poetry Bookshop in Devonshire Street and bought several rare first editions. She spent an afternoon with Henry James at his home in Rye. James lectured her on the Great Tradition in the arts, the tradition of James Russell Lowell, with whose demise "the muses had fled." This thought gave way to another and James quickly launched into a fierce monologue, confessing his own self-doubts and warning his guest against expatriation: "I have cut myself off from America, where I belonged, and in England I am not really accepted. Don't make my mistake."

Miss Lowell had no such intention. By October she was back at Sevenels. She described her trip in a letter to Miss Monroe: "I have come back to my native land, having had a most interesting summer, and learned many things. Mr. Pound has more than lived up to his kindness when I first arrived." Pound, meanwhile, had spoken of Amy Lowell with a self-absorbed Robert Frost: "When I get through with that girl she'll think she was born in free verse." He wrote to her directly: "I'd like to use your 'In a Garden' in a brief anthology *Des Imagistes* that I am cogitating—unless you've something that you think more appropriate."

Amy concurred with Pound's choice, and *Des Imagistes,* the movement's definitive anthology, appeared as the fifth number of Alfred Kreymborg's periodical *Glebe,* February 1914. The distribution of poems was highly uneven: Pound had six poems; Richard Aldington, ten; H. D., seven; F. S. Flint, five. There were seven other contributors with one poem apiece: Skipwith Cannell, Allen Upward, John Cournos, Ford Madox Ford, William Carlos Williams, James Joyce, and Amy Lowell.

Des Imagistes created quite a stir. New York's Albert and Charles Boni agreed to issue it as a book. It appeared in March 1914, in an edition of five hundred copies, between green cloth covers, and sold for a dollar. It was widely reviewed; Miss Lowell thought, "very ignorantly." The anthology was published in London by Harold Monro's Poetry Bookshop. The English reviewers did not like it; it sold poorly.

Pound, in the interim, had approached Amy in regard to an alternate cause. Late in February, shortly before the anthology's maiden appearance in book format, he wrote to her that *The Egoist* (formerly *The New Freewoman*) was going bankrupt. "Do you want to edit the EGOIST?" his letter began; "Of course there is a string to it." That string was tied to Amy's purse; Pound explained:

> With any sort of business management the thing ought to pay its expenses, or at least to cost so little that it would be worth the fun.

A clever manager could make it a property (perhaps). . . .
If you want that sort of a lark you could at least have a run for your
money.

Amy was intrigued; owning and operating her own journal was in
keeping with the entrepreneurial tradition fostered by James Russell
Lowell, who had launched his career as editor of *The Pioneer*. But what
would she do for a literary staff, she wondered, and how could she
administer a London-based periodical from Boston? Pound had all the
answers: "You can 'run' a paper in Boston and have a staff here." And
who would comprise the staff? "To wit me and Ford and anybody you're
a mind to pay for," he countered. In his next letter he suggested that
Ford, James Joyce, and D. H. Lawrence could help him edit the English
part of it, while Amy and her crowd could edit the American sections.
She wrote back: "I don't know who Joyce is. You say he and Lawrence
are the best among the younger men. I quite agree with you as to
Lawrence, but I never heard of Joyce. What did he write, and who is
he?" Pound told her about Joyce.

She kept busy, writing poems and translating Edmond Rostand's
operetta *Pierrot Qui Pleure et Pierrot Qui Rit*, a trifle about Columbine,
a young lady unable to choose between her two suitors; the two are
identical with the single difference that one only laughs and the other
only cries. *Pierrot* was performed in 1915 before Boston's Women's
Municipal League—of which Amy's sister Katherine was president—
together with Amy's translation of *La Latière de Trianon*, Wekerlin's
light opera with text by Galoppe d'Onquaire. In April 1914 *Poetry*
published eight of her latest poems. But she was dissatisfied on other
grounds. Pound informed her that *The Egoist* had found the necessary
funding without her help. She correctly guessed that she was welcome
at Imagist headquarters only because she was rich, and was determined
to demonstrate—to herself primarily—that she possessed talent in addition to wealth.

In June she again departed for London, this time accompanied by
Ada Dwyer Russell, a recent acquaintance; also Miss Lowell's maid, her
maroon custom-built Pierce Arrow limousine, and a footman and chauf-
feur in matching maroon livery. The London *Standard* made note of
their arrival at the Berkeley Hotel, a few days after the assassination of
the Archduke of Austria. As yet the full significance of Ferdinand's
murder remained uncertain. Amy wasted little time. Her first night in

London she attended the opening of a two-week run of the Russian Ballet, featuring Rimsky-Korsakov's *Coq d'Or* and Stravinsky's *Petroushka* and the *Sacre du Printemps*. At Dorchester she had tea with Mr. and Mrs. Thomas Hardy; like Henry James, they had once been on cordial terms with James Russell Lowell and were content to prattle on about him for hours. Later in the week she entertained D. H. Lawrence and his wife Frieda von Richtofen at the Berkeley. She visited the mud-floored studio of Ezra Pound's young friend, the talented sculptor Henri Gaudier-Brzeska in one of the boarded-in arches of the Putney Railroad Bridge; attended a picnic luncheon with Allen Upward; met Sir Sidney Colvin, the leading British authority on Keats; went to a poetry "squash" at the Poetry Bookshop, where the Georgian versifier Rupert Brooke read his poems, although so inaudibly that Amy could barely make them out.

Finally she visited Pound. To her astonishment his following had changed; there was a new movement afoot and he was, as usual, at its helm. It was called Vorticism, a word of his own invention, and *Blast*, edited by Wyndham Lewis, was its official organ. The aim of *Blast*, No. 1 (June 1914), according to Harriet Monroe's editorial in that August's *Poetry*, was "to blow away, in thick black capitals half an inch high, the Victorian Vampire." In place of romance and sentimentality, *Blast* proposed patterned and power-charged energy—the energy of the "Vortex," as Pound labeled its transmedia electroshock troops: himself, Lewis, Ford, Gaudier-Brzeska, Jacob Epstein, Edward Wadsworth, Arnold Dolmetsch, Rebecca West, and others.

Amy was uncertain what to make of this new movement. It seemed to her something of a burlesque, a takeoff on Marinetti and his similarly oriented (or disoriented) Futurists. It was partly that and partly an extension of Imagism, although its rules were broader in scope than those of Imagism and applicable to all the arts—music, painting, sculpture, as well as poetry. If Imagism was emotion caught in a frame or moment of time, the Vortex was a "radiant node or cluster . . . from which, and through which, and into which, ideas are constantly flowing." Vorticism was not so much a movement as a new sense of form. When describing it, Pound spoke of "new chords, new keys of design, kinesis and stasis," whereas Lewis mumbled something about "rigid reflections of stone and steel," and Epstein talked about "Rock-Drill precision." Amy, her curiosity adequately piqued, decided to find out more about it.

Donning a formal floor-length black gown with matching cape and white opera gloves, high heels, and a large, ornamental fan, she attended a dinner party thrown by the Vorticists at the Dieudonné restaurant, in Ryder Street, St. James's. In the course of the meal, which was otherwise uneventful, she and Ford engaged in a loud ruckus over literary principles and theories. Angry words were exchanged. Still fuming the next day, Miss Lowell decided to outdo the Vorticists by sponsoring a literary evening of her own.

It was held in the same restaurant two nights later. Among her guests were the Pounds, the John Cournos, Fletcher, Flint, Upward, Gaudier-Brzeska, Violet Hunt, and Ford; H. D. and Richard Aldington, recently married, were also present. There were speeches by Gaudier-Brzeska and Upward. The sculptor spoke about the energy of art and the innovations of Vorticism. Upward's talk created some uncomfortable moments for Amy. Cournos had already felt "an undercurrent of hostility among the diners, and if not hostility, then condescension, toward the hostess." Upward chose as his topic Amy's poem for *Des Imagistes*. By the time he got through with the subject of the poem, a bath by moonlight, Amy was the bather, and everyone was doubled up with laughter, save the author, "who sat as straight and stiff as her stoutness would permit, clearly vexed by the performance." She was more vexed when Pound, having briefly left the room, returned holding a small bathtub above his head.

She was disturbed by more than the unsuccessful dinner party. She was dissatisfied with the general handling by Pound of *Des Imagistes*. Spurred on by Fletcher, who had argued with Pound and been excluded from the anthology, she maintained that the best way to help other poets was to reissue the anthology, adding to the list of contributors but this time alloting the same amount of space to each, final selections to be determined by the vote of all. In the days that followed she met independently with various members of the group. The Aldingtons agreed to join with her and Fletcher; Flint and Lawrence soon followed suit. Pound, for his part, wanted nothing to do with the alternative project. Poetry was not "a democratic beer-garden"; he could not trust a committee of poets to uphold the Imagist standards, nor could he waste time quarreling with such a committee. The Lowell forces gained support when Ford Madox Ford came over to their side; Ford expressed the opinion that Pound was being ridiculous, that there was no reason he should dictate all of the group's policies and that a more democratic process might well be adopted.

The altercation continued but was soon disrupted by a more catastrophic event. On July 23 Austria-Hungary issued its forty-eight-hour ultimatum to Serbia; on the twenty-eighth it declared war. In England the price of petrol rose from one to five shillings a can, a strong indication that Britain was about to enter the war. Amy had her limousine crated and shipped home on the next boat. She booked passage for herself and her traveling companion on a ship that sailed the end of August. Her departure from England, however, did not put an end to the bickering with Pound; if anything, their altercations increased in intensity. Pound objected to Miss Lowell's plan for a new Imagist anthology, pointing out that since *he* had coined the term she had no right to use it in her title. Amy maintained that they could use whatever title they wished; after all, they could not very well invent a new literary creed just to satisfy Pound—that would be aesthetic treason! Furthermore, while Pound had created the term *Imagiste,* he had not invented the movement and did not own it.

As a compromise she opted for the title *Some Imagist Poets*—an Americanized spelling of his dubious French version, and "Some" to explain Pound's exclusion from the collection, since he refused to contribute to it. A preface by Richard Aldington explained Pound's exclusion without mentioning him by name. It spoke of "growing literary tendencies which had produced differences of taste and judgment" between "former contributors" and those in the present volume. Amy Lowell wrote a poem, "Astigmatism," dedicated "To Ezra Pound / with Much Friendship and / Admiration and Some Differences / of Opinion." The poem ends with Amy bidding her nemesis adieu: "Peace be with you, Brother. You have / chosen your part."

Amy placed *Some Imagist Poets* with Ferris Greenslet at Houghton Mifflin in Boston. Three volumes appeared over the course of a three-year span, the first in April 1915. Each contained seven to ten poems by the same seven poets: H. D., Aldington, Flint, Fletcher, Ford, Lawrence (whose poetry was anything but imagistic), and Lowell. None of the volumes managed to spark the excitement among journalists and readers that accompanied the American appearance of Pound's anthology. In a published article, Pound contended that under Miss Lowell's proprietorship *"Imagisme"* had evolved into "Amygism"; he dubbed Amy "our hippopoetess" and noted that a new poet, T. S. Eliot, had proprietorship *"Imagisme"* had evolved into "Amygism"; he dubbed Amy "our hippopoetess" and noted that a new poet, T. S. Eliot, had arrived on the scene. Eliot's work owed nothing to Imagism, and yet in its fusion of image, form, and contemporary experience, was precisely the kind of authentically modern poetry that Pound had long been seeking. Henceforth it was Eliot, not H. D. (or Aldington), that Pound was to urge upon the hesitant Harriet Monroe.

18

"SWORD BLADES AND POPPY SEED"

Sword Blades and Poppy Seed, Amy Lowell's second volume of verse, appeared in the autumn of 1914. Although about three-fourths of the manuscript consisted of poems written in meter, the richest samples were those in vers libre, or free verse. The inclusion of even a few free-verse sequences in her latest collection placed its author at the forefront of the American poetic renaissance. This is not to say that her experiments in free verse—or "unrhymed cadence," as she preferred to call it—were wholly successful, or that her theories about the form were extremely original or particularly inductive. While she eventually acquired a moderate skill in verse technique, Amy's real contribution to the revival of poetry was her enthusiasm and salesmanship: she had a keen nose for the scent of the future and a keen sense for the business end of literature. She knew how to package and sell the goods.

In a short preface to her second volume, Amy explained her use of the term "unrhymed cadence." The basis of this species of writing was "organic," that is, a total creative experience, the progression of lines varying with the length of the poet's breath. It was also subject to what Amy called the "effect of the curve," a mysterious term that was somehow related to the "premonition of an appropriate ending in any beginning" and that resulted in a verbal pattern that was "less regular than metrical verse," but which exhibited, more pronouncedly than prose, the occurrence of stresses. The same preface addressed itself to the question of the uses of Imagism in poetry and asked whether or not Imagism could be an effective and popular mode. According to the author, literary schools are formed in reaction to already existent schools and movements predominantly as a means of overthrowing and then supplanting them, one school begetting another much as the Old Testament begat the New. "The present poetic revival," she explained, "has proved . . . that a great many of the younger poets are seeing things their ancestors never saw."

The theory was probably sound though the statement was not. A great many of the younger poets were simply repeating the cliché-ridden, regular verse combinations created by their predecessors. Despite the existence of Whitman and Dickinson and the influence of the Symbolist poets, vers libre enjoyed a rather meager following among Amy's contemporaries. The average eye turned away from unmetered verse because it could not comprehend the genre. Free verse, the saying went, meant that "the poet was taking it easy." Robert Frost often averred that writing free verse was like playing tennis without a net.

In London Amy had seen the future, and it worked! With an eye to the future she labored tenaciously at her craft. Her second book showed considerable technical improvement over the first, although her themes and subject matter remained basically unchanged. People and places constituted one major focus; nature in all its phases represented another. The weather and seasons were described in a profusion of lights, shades, colors. Amy was obsessed with hues, weaving lists of them into the tapestry of her creations. The first ten lines of her poem "The Captured Goddess" illustrate her variegated rainbow thrust:

> Over the housetops,
> Above the rotating chimney pots,
> I have seen a shiver of amethyst,
> And blue and cinnamon have flickered
> A moment,
> At the far end of a dusty street.
>
> Through sheeted rain
> Has come a lustre of crimson,

And I have watched moon beams
Hushed by a film of palest green.

This last, composed in vers libre, was among the volume's highly
regarded lyrics; equally popular were "A Lady" and "The Taxi," both
in free verse. In these poems the poet employs a touch of the dramatic
to lend impact to sharply focused images, utilizing a story-line to
heighten and develop the theme. "The Taxi" is a love poem—

When I go away from you
The world beats dead
Like a slackened drum.
I call out for you against the jutted stars
And shout into the ridges of the wind.
Streets coming fast,
One after the other,
Wedge you away from me,
And the lamps of the city prick my eyes
So that I can no longer see your face.
Why should I leave you,
To wound myself upon the sharp edges of the night . . .

—as is "A Lady":

You are beautiful and faded
Like an old opera tune
Played upon a harpsichord;
Or like the sun-flooded silks
Of an eighteenth-century boudoir.

Another workmanlike sequence, "A London Thoroughfare. 2 A.M.,"
captures nighttime London and the poet's Keatsian attraction to the
moon:

They have watered the street,
It shines in the glare of lamps,
Cold, white lamps,
And lies
Like a slow-moving river,
Barred with silver and black.
Cabs go down it,
One,
And then another,

Between them I hear the shuffling of feet.
Tramps doze on the window-ledges,
Night-walkers pass along the sidewalks.
The city is squalid and sinister,
With the silver-barred street in the midst,
Slow-moving,
A river leading nowhere.

Opposite my window,
The moon cuts,
Clear and round,
Through the plum-coloured night.
She cannot light the city:
It is too bright.
It has white lamps,
And glitters coldly . . .

Here, what is *seen* triggers Amy's imagination. The shine of the lamps, the well-lit wet street, the cabs, the night-walkers, the moon—all are light-giving or light-reflecting objects whose luminescence permeates the dark of night. The juxtaposition of images allows the poet to play one off against the other, to create a tightly bound series of contrasts which in turn is what gives the poem its power and resilience. Although there is nothing profound or ultimately memorable about it, "London Thoroughfare" serves as a fitting sample of Amy's growing poetic talents, her ability to handle new modes of poetic expression.

While the poem's compactness and energy fulfill the requirements of Imagism, the latter is not a strictly imagistic poem. Instead, the poem expands the usual Imagist two-line contrast of images into a two-strophe contrast between the concrete, manmade lights of the first stanza and the purer, natural light of the moon in the second. The result of this extended balancing act is actually closer to Symbolism than Imagism. The Symbolist uses imagery, tone, color, and rhythm to express indirectly the play of his sensibilities and often to intimate a reality betrayed by the sensual world. Whereas the symbol in poetry carries enlarging connotations and emotional power, the image works to define the emotion on a much more specific and limited scale. The more specific the image employed, the more effective is its impact within the scope of the poem.

Amy was convinced that poetry was both a spoken as well as a written craft, best heard not only by the physical but by an interior ear. This theory was fundamentally a contradiction of the largely visual function of Imagism, of the Imagistic moment in poetry, and was based on Amy's conviction that poetry was a total experience, meant to appeal to all the senses. Such was the bulwark of still another form of verse invented by Amy—"polyphonic prose"— of which there were three samples in her second volume—"The Basket," "In a Castle," and "The Forsaken"— and which she defined as

> a metre which I have taken partly from Paul Fort, partly from my inner consciousness. Paul Fort bases his verse upon the alexandrine; I have based mine upon cadence. His is almost always either perfect verse or perfect prose; mine is never either, and I have called it polyphonic because it permits the use of all the methods: cadence, rhyme, alliteration, and assonance, also perhaps true metre . . .

The form was devised as a means of accommodating a variety of meters, rhythms, and techniques, with the advantage of being able to handle them in a more flexible manner than was possible in traditional verse; Amy's purpose was to bring out as many orchestral effects as possible by giving the work multidimensional scope. The outcome was occasionally intriguing, as in "The Basket":

> The inkstand is full of ink, and the paper lies white and unspotted, in the round of light thrown by a candle. Puffs of darkness sweep into the corners, and keep rolling through the room behind his chair. The air is silver and pearl, for the night is liquid with moonlight. . . .
> The golden dome glittered in the orange of the setting sun. On the walls, at intervals, hung altar-cloths and chasubles, and copes, and stoles, and coffin palls. All stiff with rich embroidery, and stitched with so much artistry, they seemed like spun and woven gems, or flower-buds, new-opened on their stems.

The form had been used before; Dryden employed a similar technique in the *St. Cecilia Odes,* which, written as librettos, ran through an infinite combination of meters. And Baudelaire, the consummate innovator, conducted comparable experiments in a number of prose-like poems (as did Rimbaud, Mallarmé, and Valéry).

Of the poems in *Sword Blades and Poppy Seed* not written in polyphonic prose, Amy's alleged favorite was "The Book of Hours of Sister Clotilde," a sequence penned in regular rhymed couplets. In a letter to Ellery Sedgwick (April 2, 1914), Amy described the narrative as "an attempt to portray the consciousness and single-mindedness of a person in the possession of a great idea, and the everlasting and never-to-be-explained miracle of inspiration." Sister Clotilde, illuminating a Book of Hours, is unable to find the right color combination for the Virgin Mary's robe, a theme not entirely remote from Sir Launfal's search for the Holy Grail in James Russell Lowell's *The Vision of Sir Launfal.*

"The Book of Hours of Sister Clotilde" has as setting a convent garden, where Sister Clotilde, working on her painting, sights an iridescent snake. Seizing the adder, she is bitten, and saved from death only by the timely intervention of an aged gardener, who sucks the poison out of the wound. The poem ends on a positive note, the snake's skin providing the nun with the inspirational shade needed to complete her illustration.

The correspondence between the old gardener of "The Book of Hours" and the leper in the poem by James Russell Lowell seems, at first glance, rather striking. The completion of Sister Clotilde's picture and the location by Sir Launfal of the Holy Grail are actions of similar circumstance. While it is highly unlikely that Amy was deliberately restaging her cousin's poem, it comes as no surprise to learn that the two Lowells shared a common literary vision concerning the role of the poet in society. In 1855, discussing "The Function of the Poet," Lowell the Elder ventured that "the Poet is he who can best see and best say what is ideal—what belongs to the world of soul and of beauty." This view of the poet as patriarch, as spokesman for the community-at-large rather than for those who, as individuals, make it up, is precisely the function that Amy envisioned for the versifier—that of fugleman and taskmaster.

Similar to "The Book of Hours of Sister Clotilde" in its use of symbolism is the title poem of *Sword Blades and Poppy Seed.* The narrator of this lengthy set piece, a young man with Faustian characteristics, is accosted by an aged man with "strange eyes flashing through the haze." The two venture to the old man's abode, which houses a "little shop with its various ware / Spread on shelves with nicest care. / Pitchers, and jars, and jugs, and pots, / Pipkins, and mugs, and many lots / Of lacquered canisters, black and gold, / Like those in which Chinese tea is sold. / Chests, and puncheons, kegs, and flasks, / Goblets, chalices, firkins, and casks." These apothecary containers are not the only objects in the room; mounted against a wall are a score of "stabbing, cutting, slashing" weapons of every size and shape. Their purpose is not readily apparent until the old man identifies himself as "Ephraim Bard, Dealer in Words"; the paraphernalia is finally explained by his suggestion that "All books are either dreams or swords, / You can cut, or you can drug with words." Playing on this proposition, the old man offers to sell the younger some poppy seed; these, he claims, have magical powers; they guarantee immortality; they will give the young man the power of seeing, but—"Who buy of me must simply pay / Their whole existence quite away." That price tacitly agreed upon, the visitor departs: "And gently sped upon my way / I stumbled out in the morning hush, / As down the empty street a flush / Ran level the rising sun. / Another day was just begun."

We have here a soundly tuned poem with pleasing counterpoints and rhymes that grow naturally out of the organic whole. The volume itself received high praise from a coterie of critics who saw in it the workings of a creative mind. Josephine Preston Peabody, with her signed review in the *Boston Sunday Herald*, October 11, 1914, was the first; she was followed in quick succession by Ella Wheeler Wilcox in the *Boston American*, Harriet Monroe in *Poetry*, Margaret Anderson in the *Little Review*, Richard Le Gallienne in *The New York Times*, H. L. Mencken in *Smart Set*, and William Dean Howells in *Harper's*. Louis Untermeyer wrote an appreciation for the *Chicago Evening Post*, stating that he found it difficult to believe this book to be by the same author responsible for *A Dome of Many-Coloured Glass*.

Untermeyer's complimentary review elicited a quick response from its intended target. On August 9, 1915, Miss Lowell wrote:

Dear Mr. Untermeyer: I was of course very much pleased with your review of "Sword Blades," particularly as ever since your review of the "Dome" I had regarded you as an implacable enemy. You ask . . . if I am really the author of the two volumes. May I assure you that I certainly am, and not only that, but the "Dome" was clearly the childhood of "Poppy Seed." Still, I have no quarrel with you for liking the second volume best, for it undoubtedly is much better. But I do not think I can quite forgive you your "at least she has the glamour of a great name" in the first review. Do you really consider James Russell Lowell a great name? If so, I must take issue with you, for collateral ancestor though he is, I have no illusions as to the qualities of his work.

The outbursts against her distant cousin were to become increasingly abrasive over the years. The better known she became, the more vituperative were her attacks on James Russell Lowell, as though their respective reputations had to be inversely proportional.

An advertisement for Amy's new volume placed by its publisher, Macmillan, in several newspapers, billed it as "the new Poetry," and Amy as "the foremost member of the 'Imagists'—a group of poets that includes William Butler Yeats, Ezra Pound, Ford Madox Hueffer [Ford]." The announcement, which fell into Pound's hands, revived the breach between the two modernists. A vehement letter from Pound, dated October 19, 1914, arrived at Sevenels, enclosing a copy of the ad:

> In view of the above arrant charlatanism on the part of your publishers, I think you must now admit that I was quite right in refusing to join you in any scheme for turning *Des Imagistes* into an uncritical democracy with you as intermediary between it and the printers. . . .
> I think you had better cease referring to yourself as an Imagiste. . . .
> I don't suppose any one will sue you for libel, it is too expensive. If your publishers "of good standing" tried to advertise cement or soap in this manner they would certainly be sued. However we salute their venality. Blessed are they who have enterprise, for theirs is the magazine public.

A postscript capped the barrage:

> I notice that the canny Macmillan in his ad. refrains from giving a leg up to any of the less well known members of the school who might have received a slight benefit from it.

The note may have pricked her pride, but by this point Amy no longer cared a dot what Pound thought or wrote.

Life at Sevenels had taken a new turn. Miss Lowell had become close friends with Ada Dwyer (Mrs. Harold Russell), her recent traveling companion to England. Ada Dwyer, daughter of James Dwyer, an afflu-ent bookseller, was born in Salt Lake City in 1863 and educated in Boston, where she soon acquired a passion for the legitimate theater. From school plays she graduated to amateur club productions and eventually to the professional stage. She had the ability to perform in a variety of character roles, and by the 1890's had made a name for herself, appearing in such diverse parts as Roxy in *Pudd'nhead Wilson* and Slum Bet in Frances Hodgson Burnett's *Dawn of a Tomorrow.* When her childhood friend Eleanor Robson, herself the daughter of an actress, formed an acting company, Ada joined. For ten years the group flourished, performing both on the road as a small repertory company and, in time, on the more commercial Broadway stage. The company stayed together until 1910, the year that Miss Robson married August Belmont, Jr., a banker and the son of August Belmont, among other things the financier and builder of New York City's subway system. Their marriage spelled an end to Robson's stage ambitions and with it the termination of her performing company. After marriage she addressed herself to philanthropic causes—the Red Cross, higher education for women, the Metropolitan Opera. With the acting company's demise, Ada Dwyer—who had once been married but long since divorced—also prepared to forsake the footlights. It was perfect timing, therefore, that brought her together with Amy Lowell at a ladies' club luncheon in Boston at the same time that Amy's first book of verse was making its debut.

From the outset their personalities seemed ideally matched. They entertained mutual affection for the ballet and the opera; Miss Dwyer had a fondness for reading poetry aloud, and Amy shared Ada's affection for serious drama. Ada was modest, somewhat self-effacing, subdued—traits that complemented Amy's extroverted vigor and nagging need for attention. Ada felt as much at home at a literary cocktail party as she did at a fund-raising dinner party. Her relaxed and gentle nature had the effect of soothing those less at ease: it soothed Amy. Ada was an excellent listener; Amy loved to talk. Ada was well enough informed and secure enough to stand up to Amy; she could provide moral support but also shrewd criticism when needed. Her background in theater enabled her to offer Amy valuable insight into the psychology of an audience and instruction on how best to adapt her work to the medium of the stage. It was her influence that turned Miss Lowell increasingly to the podium as a means of communication. Ada showed her how to incorporate song, chants, shouts, silence, breaks (aposiopesis), stops, starts, and whispers into her act in an effort to push back the boundaries of coherence. Amy learned how to vary her volume, increase her pitch and tempo, shift tone with dramatic suddenness. Ada demonstrated the use of gesture, pace, mime, taught Amy how to cakewalk and how to stamp out the rhythm of her beat. The effect of such instruction in combination with Amy's modernist preoccupation with the phenomenal, "the thing itself," and her natural sense of musical range served her in good stead. Miss Lowell mastered the art of manipulating an audience as readily as a classical musician tuning a delicate instrument.

By winter of 1915, Ada ("Peter" to Amy) was living at Sevenels, having assumed an essential and multiple role in the poet's life. She was both confidante and adviser, as well as traveling companion, amanuensis, nursemaid, and ambassadress of good will, forever soothing the ruffled nerves of those the poet had last jousted with. It was she who "kept house," managed servants, supplies, and accounts, ordered provisions, answered telephones, arranged appointments, rejecting those who were deemed unworthy of Amy's attention. This last was Ada's most useful function. She played the dual role of receptionist and sieve, shielding her friend from the outside world, the known and unknown writers who appeared almost daily for interviews, advice, and other ministrations or favors. No one saw Amy who had not first been screened and thoroughly interrogated by her rectitudinous companion. Within minutes this shrewd woman could determine everything she needed to know about a person, from place of birth, family background, and social connections, to education and immediate intentions. In no uncertain terms, she was "the power behind the throne."

This nearly perfect relationship caused a flock of flying rumors in Boston society and within the family enclave. Amy would later contend that she "owed everything" to Ada. What this presumably meant was that Miss Dwyer had helped liberate the poet from her previous existence while introducing her to a broader, more enjoyable way of life, not necessarily sexual in nature but an emancipated feminism that left her free to write and to write more effectively, to follow her instincts and to mold the patterns of her chosen lifestyle. Amy had broken out of the fragile shell imposed by her aristocratic status and background into an artistic and creative life before meeting Ada, though not with the same measure of self-assurance she demonstrated in her final decade.

Their intimate attachment can hardly be defined by the term "friendship," although there is little of any significance to indicate that it was anything greater than that. Following Amy's death, literary commentators offered a number of conflicting opinions on the intriguing question of the poet's sexual preference. One recent biographical study —*Amy,* by Jean Gould—attempts to draw meaningful parallels between the lives and loves of Amy Lowell and Gertrude Stein, comparing Alice Toklas's devoted attention to Gertrude Stein with Ada Dwyer's affectionate efforts on behalf of Miss Lowell. Expanding this shaky syllogism, Miss Gould concludes that Amy and Ada were indeed passionate lovers, equal partners in what can only be described as a lustful marriage.

Another biographer adopts a slightly different stance, intimating that Amy's sexuality can best be measured by her "masculine appearance" —her short, squat, barrel-chested build—and her compulsive use in verse of a masculine narrator whose voice teems with proclamations of illicit love. Still a third study employs the term "fleshly discomfort" to describe Amy's psychogenic state, her dogmatic, authoritarian, sometimes bigoted (and masculine) self, her biases and beliefs, her refusal to budge from them or suffer opposition to them. The implication is that Amy was everything she ought not to have been—aggressive, outgoing, obstreperous, demanding, conspicuous, in so many words the kind of woman men feared and women loved to hate.

Whether accurate or not, these allegations were only allegations, based substantially on hearsay and Boston's horrified reaction to its poetry-producing den mother. Within the rigid, puritanical society of that tradition-bound town, the bond between Amy and Ada, the very fact that they resided together under one roof, must have "raised eyebrows" and "set tongues clacking." But to suggest that their union was sexual, or at least overtly sexual, seems something of an exaggeration, sheer vagary meant to stir up a storm. The truth of the matter appears to be that in Ada Dwyer, Amy had at last found a companion who understood her completely and whom she could trust absolutely. To reduce their relationship to the simple formula of "husband and wife," with Amy playing the male dominant lead and Ada the role of retiring hausfrau, is to do both a disservice. It seems equally unjust to make assumptions concerning Amy's sex life purely on the basis of her free, spirited, androgynous poetry. Androgyny has for centuries been a popular poetic ploy and is today as common a literary device as free verse. More significant are the conclusions drawn by dissenting critics based on Ada's posthumous destruction of her letters to and from Amy, an act that prohibits literary historians from ever divining their original substance. Whatever else these letters may have revealed, they surely charted a life in which commitment to art takes on a sacred exaltation, an existence yielding powerful visions of spirituality. Amy's letters to Ada were probably among the most honest documents to emerge from the poet's hand, free for once of any posturings of aristocratic superiority, the wretched strategies of expression that obscure the true artist in so many of her public communications. But whether they also contained circumstantial (or even direct) evidence of a liaison, we shall never know. Ada detested speaking about intimate matters—notably about her relationship with Amy. Rather than have it misconstrued, she preferred to erase all memory of those tangled times.

Short of viewing this material, a reasonable and wholly acceptable appraisal of their friendship is provided by Glenn Ruihley in *Amy Lowell Reconsidered: The Thorn of a Rose* (1975). Ada Dwyer, according to Ruihley, deserves credit for giving Amy "a heart" in her poetry, for helping sustain her through the deprivations she felt in her emotional life as well as for the services she rendered as literary factotum and adviser. Amy rewarded her companion by giving unstintingly in every sense—expensive gifts, high salary, generous emotional support. After Amy's death Ada inherited Sevenels and a multimillion-dollar estate in trust. Their relationship, Ruihley maintains, could never replace that lost domain of love—the male companionship, husband, and family that Amy never had—but it did give the poet the support she needed to pursue her career. Ada became the object of Amy's love poetry, a source of artistic inspiration and literary encouragement; in short, Ada helped implant a fuller vision into Amy's developing themes.

Whether Amy and Ada had sex together remains an open-ended and perhaps irrelevant question. Ada, responding angrily to the inevitable gossip, insisted always that they were only friends. In the final analysis we can be sure of only one thing: Amy's bursts of creativity were largely inspired by her beloved companion, for it was only after Ada joined her at Sevenels that the poet came into her own, making her modest—but perceptible—dent in the kingdom of the arts. The name Sevenels cropped up increasingly in Boston's daily newspapers, especially in the ever-popular society columns; the manor became a minor beachhead for artists and performers anxious to make their mark. One small cadre of regulars consisted of musicologists Herman Adler, Carl Engel, and Heinrich Gebhard, and the gifted French soubrette and character actress Lina Abarbanell. Engel, for whom Amy purportedly had romantic feelings, aided her in the production at Sevenels of a series of modern music concerts featuring works by Debussy, Ravel, Fauré, Albeniz, and Franck. Other visitors included poets Sara Teasdale, Josephine Preston Peabody, Robert Frost (whose *North of Boston* Amy vouched for in the *New Republic*), Edwin Arlington Robinson, Yeats, E. E. Cummings. Her guests were almost always involved either in the arts or in academia. John Livingston Lowes, the critic and Harvard professor of English literature, visited frequently in company with his spouse. E. B. Hill and his wife came by on numerous occasions; it was Hill who introduced Amy to French modern music and later set her poem, "Lilacs," to music (it was eventually performed as a choral work by the Boston Symphony). Hill, who also taught in the music department at Harvard, introduced his star pupil Virgil Thomson to Amy. The editors Frederick Marsh and George Brett of Macmillan and their wives were occasional guests. The August Belmonts passed by frequently, as did the exorbitantly wealthy Mr. and Mrs. J. Montgomery Sears. H. D. and Richard Aldington visited whenever in the States, first together and later separately. And so it went. A parade of editors, authors, critics, and professors passed through Amy's portal; the less affluent and more artistic came out of curiosity and sometimes in search of a good meal.

In 1915, the beginning of Miss Lowell's last decade, she embarked on her first transcontinental campaign in support of free verse. The skirmishes took place on the battlefields of Boston, Providence, New York, Philadelphia, Milwaukee, Chicago, St. Louis, and points west, although in many respects the real fighting had already taken place in the Soho restaurants of London, with Ezra Pound and Ford Madox Ford in one trench and the moguls of Fleet Street in the other. Miss Lowell, like Pound, was to become a passionate entrepreneur, a persuasive publicist, a hardworking and plodding promoter of the so-called new poetry.

Amy flung the gauntlet (or the grace note, depending on the critic's point of view) in New York at a meeting of the ultraconservative Poetry Society of America. Following Hamlin Garland's introduction, Miss Lowell read aloud a series of Imagist poems, introducing them with a brief explanation of the philosophy behind Imagism. The dicta she laid down as the basis of the art bristled and provoked the audience to the point where several spectators charged the podium, demanding that Amy step down. Within minutes a mild altercation had escalated into a full-blown fracas. Amy's bold and brash campaign on behalf of modern poetry was underway. The movement's reception as Amy went from town to town was immeasurably enhanced by the Bostonian's magnetic presence. At each train depot she was besieged by hordes of curiosity seekers who surged forward in an effort to catch a glimpse of their new heroine; flanks of special police guarded against the inevitable crush of cranks and crackpots. A gallery of paparazzi with their barrage of fluorescent flashbulbs added to the melee. Amy loved it. She loved the loud, raucous audiences that stormed her lectures, attempting to drown her out with a chorus of jeers and catcalls. She loved the attention and excitement. She loved the publicity, the sensation of being at the center of the storm.

The publicity was not always good. The morning after she appeared before the Contemporary Club on Society Hill in Philadelphia, a local newspaper carried the headline "Tears Punctuate Spots in Vers Libre Debate." Although she denied it, Amy had apparently been shaken by the presence of still another small crew of hecklers and had broken down. She was vulnerable after all. But she bounded back and the next day was again on the road. She had more going for her than any literary sideshow barker of her day. She had obviously done her homework, schooled herself thoroughly in her chosen field. Her presentations were almost always intelligent and composed. She knew her area and was acquainted with her audience. She simplified her task by developing and committing to memory four or five variations on a single theme; these she presented in rotation as the occasion demanded. At the Round Table Club in New York she delivered a talk on "The New Manner in Modern Poetry," incorporating into her lengthy monologue a passing reference or two to her distant kinsman, James Russell Lowell:

> Egoism may be a crime in the world of morals, but in the world of the arts it is perfectly permissible. It makes very good and very interesting poetry. In mentioning it, I am not condemning it, I am only labelling it. It was the manner of the nineties, it is not the manner of today.
>   . . . Bryant, Lowell, Holmes, Longfellow, Whittier . . . were all . . . rather English provincial poets than American poets. Indeed America was, in those days, a province of England in everything except government. America as a nation, with characteristics unlike those of any other nation, had not begun to exist.

She elaborated on the meaning of "modern" and cited those writers who fit her definition, starting with the Irish—Yeats, Synge, James Stephens, Padraic Colum, Joseph Campbell—while slowly wending her way to her own countrymen: Henry James, Robinson, Frost, Josephine Peabody, Pound, and H. D. She included a brace of English poets, Rupert Brooke and Ford Madox Ford, and added two Americans to the list: Edgar Lee Masters, whose *Spoon River Anthology* had recently been published, and Vachel Lindsay, "who cares more to make music than to paint pictures, although some of his pictures are very striking." Masters, in his candid working over of small-town mores, his dark verbal missiles and savage portraitures, and Lindsay, with his exaggerated and theatrical platform reading style, represented respectable models whom Amy could hope to emulate. Both were Midwesterners, and, with Carl Sandburg (their guide in the elementals of free verse), were in the vanguard of the poetic renaissance that put Chicago and the Middle West on the national literary map.

Amy's oral presentation was so forceful and awe-inspiring, so genuine and coercive, that the public soon began accepting her literary judgments as nothing less than gospel. Future Amy Lowell presentations were in their own way equally compelling. Speaking again before the Poetry Society of America, she discussed the parallel difficulties that existed between modern painting and modern poetry, supporting her thesis by reading aloud passages from the correspondence of Vincent Van Gogh, and reciting poems by the Imagist poets F. S. Flint and John Gould Fletcher. To demonstrate the variable tempos that were possible in free verse, she supplemented her discussion by delivering her poem "The Cremona Violin," contrasting it with work by Frost, D. H. Lawrence, Carl Sandburg, and Edgar Lee Masters. To illustrate the effect of polyphonic prose, she recited her early poem "In a Garden" and sections of more recent samples of the genre.

Amy's stage presence was felt wherever she appeared, her magnetic personality drawing overflowing crowds into the largest auditoriums and lyceums. She was indefatigable, tireless, a volcano spewing out a hot, thick, viscous flow of speech, rich and steaming. If she could not become an actress, she could nevertheless play the role of "Amy Lowell, poet" for the sake of reporters, editors, and younger writers, many of whom held her in considerable esteem. Evidence that she was taken seriously in certain quarters was provided by her 1915 election to the chairmanship of the newly founded New England Poetry Club, whose membership included W. S. Braithwaite, Josephine Peabody, Grace Hazard Conkling, Louis Untermeyer, and Conrad Aiken. Aiken, unable to abide Amy's publicity-seeking manner, attended two meetings of the club and then quietly withdrew.

Throughout the war years she kept up a torrid lecture and public-reading pace. From 1915 to 1917 Amy and Ada and an entourage of servants traveled three times by train to Chicago. Each year Harriet

Monroe threw a rousing reception for the poet, introducing her to everyone who was anybody amid Chicago's heralded literary loop. Among others Amy met Sinclair Lewis, who was just beginning to gain national recognition with his short stories in popular mass-market magazines. Her Chicago connection paved a road of access to two other leading authors: Theodore Dreiser and Willa Cather. Highly impressed with Dreiser's work, Amy signed a petition against the suppression of Dreiser's controversial *The Genius* (1915), a long and detailed fictional study of the ruthless type of artistic temperament: "I am very glad indeed to . . . throw what weight I have in the scale of liberty and freedom for the arts to develop themselves as they think fit."

Early in 1915, Harriet Monroe provided Amy with a letter of introduction to Margaret Anderson, coeditor (with Jane Heap) of the *Little Review*, best known in later years for its serial publication of Joyce's *Ulysses*. Miss Anderson's periodical was in many ways more experimental than *Poetry*, which still on occasion catered to the old-fashioned, sentimental rhymers that the Imagists had struggled so valiantly to overthrow. Amy, always interested in the new, took a personal interest in the *Little Review* and offered to support it with a generous monthly stipend. Her proposal to the editor read: "I'll merely direct your poetry department. You can count on me never to dictate." But Miss Anderson, sensing Amy's true intentions, noted that "no clairvoyance was needed to know that Amy Lowell would dictate, uniquely and majestically, any adventure in which she had a part. I should have preferred being in the clutches of a dozen groups." Amy's offer to aid the journal was politely declined.

One of Miss Lowell's select poems for public presentation was "Spring Day," a five-section sequence in polyphonic prose that at first glance appeared to lend itself perfectly to the podium. The first part is entitled "Bath":

Little spots of sunshine lie on the surface of the water and dance, dance, and their reflections wobble deliciously over the ceiling; a stir of my finger sets them whirring, reeling. I move a foot, and the planes of light in the water jar. I lie back and laugh, and let the green-white water, the sun-flawed beryl water, flow over me. The day is almost too bright

to bear, the green water covers me from the too bright day. I will lie here
awhile and play with the water and the sun spots . . .

This selection, although penned as prose, is highly reminiscent of the
night-bath denouement of "In a Garden," that notorious vers libre
sequence which shocked even the London Imagists:

> And I wished for night and you.
> I wanted to see you in the swimming-pool,
> White and shining in the silver-flecked water.
> While the moon rode over the garden,
> High in the arch of night,
> And the scent of the lilacs was heavy with stillness.
>
> Night, and the water, and you in your whiteness, bathing!

Amy Lowell's audience found it impossible to resist a literal interpretation of these poems; they saw the sister of the president of Harvard
cavorting nude with female amorists in bathtubs and swimming pools.
What the Bostonian intended as harmless and playful looked lewd and
lascivious, as though she were flaunting her nude figure and amorous
desires in the faces of her beholders. Amy envisioned these works
mainly as expressions of carefree joy. But because they were evocative
—and because she was controversial—the desired effect was lost. Seeing
this unexpectedly large woman stand upon a stage reciting verse of this
nature, and knowing at the same time that she was a Lowell, was
enough to knock the stuffing out of any self-respecting crowd.

On the other hand, creating a stir was what gave Amy her greatest
satisfaction. She was at heart a ham, a glutton for the spotlight, and like
most egoists would do almost anything to remain stage front and center.
The need to make a kind of technicolor charade of her life was one way
of making up for its essential emptiness. Thus, art and form and style
and the ability to project herself became a matter for Amy of class and
course, a sign of the superior lifestyle, as it had once been for Byron and
Keats. Their verse, oversensual and amative, appealed to their fellow
countrymen, filling the void left by whatever moral and patriotic art
had come out of their individual cultures. In the same way, Amy's life
and personality fascinated as much as her poetry; knowing this, she was
determined to fuse all three.

The consolidation of public and private personalities, the desire to make poetry a more public art form, were concerns that motivated each of the writing Lowells. None of the three was more aware than Amy of the role of the artist-hero as an emblem of social rebellion against the material conventions of the bourgeoisie, or "booboisie," as H. L. Mencken titled the middle class. That she occasionally, in her drive to mobilize the movement, overpowered and offended her contemporaries, goes without saying. "Amy Lowell's talents and temperament," Pound ventured, "will always be political rather than literary or artistic." Amy's bullying, persuasive ways led Eliot to the conclusion that she was a "demon saleswoman." "To argue with her," Carl Sandburg once mused, "is like arguing with a big blue wave."

There are essentially two schools of thought regarding Amy's role in the poetry revolution in this country. As against the Pounds and Eliots, there were those critics who acknowledged her worth and value to the movement, making clear that "Amy Lowell did more than anyone else to win from the general public an understanding reception for the new poetry." Then there were those who maintained that she was peripheral to the movement, that her manning of the barricades and usurpation of power was all exhibition, all show, that she had taken part in the free-verse controversy uninvited and essentially unwanted and never really understood what it was all about. Such allegations were not necessarily without merit. Certainly her campaign had an air of absurdity about it, a kind of idiotic magnificence that even she must have found distasteful at times. And yet at the fore, she was determined to interest the American public in poetry, to inject renewed potency into verse, to demonstrate its potential for experimental forms while casting off the influence of the Aesthetes and Decadents, similarly abjuring the vocabulary and syntax of the Victorians. Basically, she wanted a poetry that utilized the American idiom and that was as American in its sensibility as Whitman's *Leaves of Grass.* She desired a poetry that was penned in the New England vein of Robinson and Frost. She was determined to make verse a popular platform art, using the bold, humorous ploys of Vachel Lindsay, who sang out the names of American hamlets, towns, and cities while reading aloud his poem "The Santa Fe Trail" with its railroad cars rolling westward: "Cars from Concord, Niagara, Boston / Cars from Topeka, Emporia, and Austin. . . ." Miss Lowell wanted a poetry in the style of Pound's "Hugh Selwyn Mauberley" that reflected the influence of the Symbolists, Impressionists, Futurists, Surrealists, Dadaists, and of such modern novelists as Henry James. Amy was wild for the syncopated rhythms of Masters, the singsong chant of James Oppenheim, the fragmented ellipsis of H. D. and Mina Loy, the color symphonies of John Gould Fletcher. She wanted verse that showed the influence of the French poets and painters, that incorporated hokku and polyphonic prose, that moved smoothly and without interruption or seeming transition from line to line and phrase to phrase, a poetry of contrasts that seemed to float free in a timeless void, poetry that recaptured the inveterate virtues of directness and rebelled against the ancient practice of accent-counting and monotonous ticktock rhythms. The "new" poets stressed the notion of "the poetry of unpoetic things," poetry that was written simply and objectively, with "clean edges" and a "sparing use of adjectives." Amy waged the newspaper and lecture-hall battle for free verse and Imagism with vigor and enthusiasm, struggling to convince an often resistent public that verse need neither rhyme nor be romantic in subject or substance. In its own way, Amy's contribution to the cause of modernism was valuable, even precious, particularly in helping poets throw off the yoke of Victorian artificiality and contrivance. As one of our original autodidacts, she alerted the public to some of the nuances of the movement, while showing that poets as diverse as D. H. Lawrence and William Carlos Williams were producing free verse that satisfactorily answered the controversial charge levied by the critics of the movement that the rhythm of free verse did not differ from that of prose. She was just as quick to point out that poets of previous generations had similarly experimented with free verse—the elegiac poets of ancient Greece, the anonymous author of *Beowulf,* Milton (in *Samson Agonistes*), Gray, Blake, Ossian, Novalis, Heine, the French Symbolists, and others. But the free verse of these poets did not always mean nonmetrical verse. *Beowulf,* for instance, is in the Anglo-Saxon stress meter rather than the syllabic-stress meter of most post-Chaucer poetry, whereas the free verse of Fletcher, Pound, Sandburg, H. D., Richard Aldington, and Masters was truly free.

Above all, Amy wanted to create, if not a school, then certainly a breed of poets whose literary center focused on objectivity, "the rendering of outward events rather than impressions and subjective states," a mode that "refused to draw moral generalizations." The single-mindedness with which she pursued her goal, the ballyhoo that accompanied her exaggerated gestures, wiped away any doubt that the cult had become a bandwagon and that poetry was on the move. Roughly, the first phase of the modernist movement lasted from the publication of Pound's *Des Imagistes* in 1914 to the 1922 appearance of Eliot's *Waste Land.*

Miss Lowell's outlandish rituals were the talk of civilized society. In New York or Philadelphia or St. Louis or Chicago she inevitably reserved the largest and most expensive hotel suite in town. Her arrival was well anticipated: mirrors and shiny objects were swathed with folds of black cloth; window shades were drawn; electric clocks were stopped. An extra-wide double bed was set up and reinforced with exactly sixteen plump pillows of down, the same number she kept on her bed at home. She supplied her own handwoven bath towels and silk bed linens, carting along a high-intensity reading lamp for weak eyes, a dozen pairs of reading glasses, and the small, pale Manila cigars that she smoked before, during, and after meals. In private or in company with close friends, she smoked a thicker, darker brand, a stogie that struck outsiders as "a man's cigar" and family members as "outright sacrilege." But smoking helped her blow off steam and tension, and in time her cigars, whether large or small, dark or light, became as much a trademark as the "man-eating" dogs, or the pince-nez perched precariously atop the narrow bridge of her nose. Cigarettes were too brief and untidy, pipes impossible to keep lit. The cigar presented a satisfactory alternative. Yet to proper Bostonians the idea of a female drawing on a stogie proved highly intimidating, a direct threat, one might even say. When America entered World War I, Amy, fearful of an embargo, ordered one last and vast supply of her infamous cigar; a specially constructed humidor served to keep the tobacco fresh and flavorful.

Although she generally opposed the philosophy behind the military, she was as perfervidly patriotic as the rest of Boston. She cheered when Woodrow Wilson delivered his memorable war message to the House of Representatives, castigating Germany for fighting a war against all humankind and beseeching Americans to get behind the war effort. "We will not choose the path of submission," Wilson roared to a chamber crammed with rows of flag-waving senators and congressmen after a German torpedo had ripped through the bow of the *Lusitania* on May 7, 1915, sinking her off the coast of Ireland. Almost everywhere Americans felt the same patriotic urge. In the weeks that ensued, Harvard's Professor Francis Peabody returned his Order of the Prussian Crown to the Kaiser through diplomatic channels in Switzerland. The trustees of Brown University voted to revoke the honorary degree they had conferred on the German ambassador, Count von Bernstorff. The German-born conductor of the Boston Symphony Orchestra, Karl Muck, was suddenly dismissed. Professor Henry van Dyke of Princeton lobbied for American intervention in the war, and was joined by hundreds of politicians and journalists. Boston's twenty-sixth Yankee Division, the pride of New England, in whose ranks the Irish and the Old Yankees had managed to suspend if not submerge their animosities, had been the first of the American Expeditionary Force to be organized, the first to be sent overseas, the first to engage in combat with the German Army.

In England, when the war first broke out, before America's intervention, Amy donated generous funds to a committee organized by Herbert Hoover to aid American citizens stranded abroad. In her own country she joined several fund-raising campaigns to assist war orphans and families of the Allied dead. Once America entered, Amy joined such celebrities as Douglas Fairbanks, Charlie Chaplin, and the opera singer Geraldine Farrar in a series of brief pep talks to persuade the public to buy Liberty Bonds. She also supported the American and British Red Cross, but was less than enthusiastic about spending nineteen months of meatless days and lightless nights, huddled before a portable Simplex oil burner when coal grew scarce.

In spite of the war Amy's paramount concern remained poetry. Inspired by the works of Wilfred Owen and Siegfried Sassoon, she turned out poems about the war, some two dozen, which she let appear in subsequent collections. As a group they are of little interest. "Bombardment," in polyphonic prose, was typical of the lot:

> Slowly, without force, the rain drops into the city. It stops a moment on the carved head of Saint John, then slides on again, slipping and trickling over his stone cloak. It splashes from the lead conduit of a gargoyle, and falls from it in turmoil on the stones in the Cathedral square. Where are the people, and why does the fretted steeple sweep about in the sky? Boom! The sound swings against the rain. Boom, again! After it, only water rushing in the gutters, and the turmoil from the spout of the gargoyle. Silence. Ripples and mutters. Boom!

The poem was written to be read aloud, with a bass drum to beat out the "booms" and a bugle to be blown intermittently to lend authenticity to a composition that essentially failed to capture either the terror or the immediacy of war. It was a well-intended sequence but its treatment of battle was too facile to do the theme justice: it was not well received.

A warmer reception was accorded Miss Lowell's book *Six French Poets: Studies in Contemporary Literature* (1915), essays based on lectures presented before sundry literary clubs and societies on a half-dozen Symbolists: Emile Verhaeren, Albert Semain, Remy de Gourmont, Henri de Régnier, Francis Jammes, and Paul Fort. The study proved surprisingly popular in America, probably because of the rising sympathies among Americans for France in the war. The essays were written in a colloquial and readily comprehensible style, placing the six postdecadent authors in a literary and critical framework that the average reader could easily appreciate.

The book appeared shortly after the death of Remy de Gourmont, whose work Amy had previously discovered through Richard Aldington, one of Gourmont's English translators. She had begun to correspond with the disfigured and reclusive author of such classics as *Les Litanies de la Rose* and *Le Latin Mystique,* sending along samples of her work and receiving in return frequent letters of appreciation and encouragement. When she learned, at the onset of the war, that he was in financial straits, she forwarded an anonymous check for several hundred dollars and tried to arrange for the American publication of a collection of Gourmont's essays on prewar Paris. But Gourmont passed away, lonely and disheartened, before the final arrangements could be made. At the conclusion of her preface to *Six French Poets,* she paid him proper tribute: "By Remy de Gourmont's death, France loses one of the greatest and most sincere artists of his generation." Gourmont, who was certainly among the leaders of the literary avant-garde at the beginning of the century, was to lapse into anonymity after his death—a fate, some claimed, almost worse than death.

❧ 19 ❧

NIGHTLY RITUAL

AMY'S poetry readings and lectures continued unabated. She was a guest reader at the third annual banquet of the Authors' League of America, New York City, of which the honorary president that year (1918) was none other than Winston Churchill. She appeared before the Writers' Equal Suffrage League at the home of a Lowell in-law. She read her poems at the Middlesex Women's Club, Lowell, Massachusetts, and gave a new lecture, "American Poets of Today," before the Roxburghe Club at Masonic Hall, Roxbury. The latter was a reading of modern poets, with an explication of their works; her introductory remarks traced American poetry to its Fireside roots:

> I want to show you this afternoon why the poet of today is as he is, why the work that he is doing differs from that of the great period of American poetry, the period which gave us Lowell, and Longfellow, and Emerson, and Whittier, and Bryant.
>
> Everything has a hand in making a poet. The place he lives in—its climate, soil, and geological formation; the people by whom he is surrounded—their social customs, religious ideas, artistic impulses, warmth or coldness of heart; the books he reads—the breadth or narrowness of their outlook, their insistence upon certain phases of life, the dignity or looseness of their style. An artist feels these influences more keenly than other people by the very fact of being an artist, which presupposes a great sensibility.
>
> Now the great artists I have named were, without exception, New Englanders. They all inherited the English tradition by right of birth, and they were also, by right of birth, puritans at heart, only a few decades [sic] removed from the men who settled this country for reasons of faith.

In many ways there was less change in New England between the times of Cotton Mather and Emerson than has been the case between Emerson's time and our own.

England was the great Protestant country, and the Puritans who came over here were the most extreme example of that Protestantism. Is it any wonder that their descendants should have produced an art which is at once the quintessentialism of the Anglo-Saxon and the Protestant point of view?

She expounded on this theme, stipulating that Puritanism was the proverbial progenitor of New England verse and that the backbone of Puritanism was its moral stance, the distinct "rightness or wrongness" of an action or thought. The interpretation of moral behavior was the business of nineteenth-century American poets; contemporary poets had sundered their ties with the Puritan past. They were freer in the forms of poetry and subjects they could choose, less constrained by the rigid and uncompromising tracts of English Protestantism and Calvinism. Of the poets of the past, few had been able to avoid the limitations imposed upon them by their surroundings; one rara avis was Emily Dickinson, a poet whose essential loneliness and isolation struck deep chords within Amy:

> Strangely enough, there started up in New England a rare (if it had not really existed I should have said an "impossible") anomaly. A true pagan poet shut up in the cage of a narrow provincial Puritanism. But the odd part of this poet was that the cage was not merely the exterior one of family and surroundings, it was the cage of her own soul. I refer, of course, to Emily Dickinson. She was a pagan if ever there was one, but she was also a sincerely religious woman. This led her to address poems to the Deity in so joyous and familiar a strain that her first biographer wrote many pages to explain her seeming irreverence.

Her frankness in speculating about literary affairs and personalities kept Amy at the stormy helm, assuring her of a devout flock of detractors and enemies. Conrad Aiken tore her asunder at every opportunity, especially in articles that appeared in the *New Republic* and the *Boston Transcript*. On January 23, 1916, Joyce Kilmer interviewed poet Josephine Peabody for *The New York Times*: the piece ran under the banner: "Free Verse Hampers Poets and is Undemocratic." Miss Peabody, who once described poetry as "the richest expression of noblest ideals," and who considered herself a friendly rival of Miss Lowell's, claimed

Kilmer had misquoted her as saying that the cult of Imagists wrote worthless poetry and would soon be swept away. The interview, whether true or not, encouraged those seeking documentation to support their antimodernist sympathies.

Another anti-Lowell slur occured on the occasion of the Harvard Commencement of 1915. E. E. Cummings, a magna cum laude Harvard graduate that year, was invited to speak at commencement exercises in Sanders Theatre. He chose to discourse on the subject of "The New Art," bringing into his lecture all form of creative art, from Cubism and Futurism in painting and sculpture to the art of Satie, Schönberg, and Stravinsky in music. To illustrate different phases and different degrees of experimentation in literature, he turned first to the work of Amy Lowell. Introducing her poem, "Grotesque," he noted that "the following offers a clear illustration of development from the normal to the abnormal." The opening lines—"Why do the lilies goggle their tongues at me / When I pluck them"—introduce a poem in which "the lilies are made to express hatred by means of grotesque images." Sanders Theatre shuddered in horror as Cummings read this reversal of the standard Romantic treatment of nature. They shuddered a second time as he meandered through another Amy Lowell poem, "The Letter," composed during one of Ada Dwyer's periodic visits with her family in Salt Lake City, where both her daughter, Lorna, and grandson lived. At one point in the reading of this relatively mild sequence, an elderly woman's voice could be heard above the rest, dismayed that such "lascivious" poetry should even be allowed to be read under Harvard's sacred dome. Abbott Lawrence Lowell, on whose face all eyes were trained, remained as impassive as the Sphinx.

Meanwhile, the *Boston Transcript,* a newspaper that did not truckle to the Brahmins, ran a front-page headline bold enough to rankle the family dead: "Harvard Orator Calls President Lowell's Sister Abnormal." Amy, hypersensitive in her response to any kind of criticism, was absolutely dismayed and threatened to sue unless the newspaper retracted this blatant misrepresentation of Cummings's words. In due course the retraction appeared, though Amy's outrage was never satisfactorily mitigated.

Cummings stayed on at the Harvard Graduate School of Arts and Sciences for another year, earning an M.A. in English literature and organizing the Harvard Poetry Society, which held informal readings now and again. Malcolm Cowley, Robert Hillyer, and S. Foster Damon were among the organization's student members. On February 28, 1916, Amy Lowell addressed the new society on the subject of vers libre, reading aloud for an hour from her most recent work. A small buffet, consisting of beer and pretzels, adorned the large table at which she was to sit following her presentation. The room was filled with Poetry Society members and undergraduates. Finally, the floor was thrown open to them for discussion. John Brooks Wheelwright, a Society poet who was later to refer to Miss Lowell as "Biggest Traveling One-Man Show since Buffalo Bill caught the Midnight Flyer to contact Mark Twain," and who himself had a flair for showmanship, rose to ask a question. It had probably been much considered for its "shock" value.

"Miss Lowell, what do you do when you want to write a poem and haven't anything to write about?"

An immense silence fell over the audience as Miss Lowell peered across the room at the tall, quizzical student. She stared at him for several moments and said nothing.

Attempting to pick up the slack, Cummings now rose and posed his own question. With a quick glance at the centerpiece of beer and pretzels, which nobody had touched, the president of the society asked the esteemed guest what she thought of Gertrude Stein.

"Do *you* like her work?" Miss Lowell replied, with a sly grin.

"Why—yes—."

"*I* don't!"

With that retort—and without further adieu—she swept out of the chamber and into the nighttime street.

In many respects Amy was her own worst enemy. A letter to William Rose Benét (August 30, 1916), literary editor of the *Century,* after several rejections of her poetry by that publication, revealed a trembling indignation:

Look here, William Rose Benét! I want to know just what is the matter between me and *The Century,* because I am beginning to think that something must be. Everybody tells me that you have absolute charge of the poetry, and you accept or reject what you choose. In that case, I can only think that you must have some personal reason for refusing everything which I send. . . .

Do you realize that I have been offering you my best work for the past year, but that it is eleven months since you have taken a poem of mine? You have had the opportunity to publish my best things, and no matter how various they were in kind, they have all come home, one after the other. I offered you my little girl poems, of which you know Mr. Cross of the *Yale Review* thought highly, and one of which was afterwards taken by Mr. Bridges for *Scribner's,* and he thought highly enough of it to hurry it through so that I might have it in my book, and only regretted that lack of time prevented his taking all three. I offered you "Malmaison," which, since its appearance in *The Little Review* a couple of months ago, has earned for me more praise than any poem I ever wrote, except "Patterns." I have given you the opportunity of having some of my New England poems, which have been very much noticed. It makes no difference what I send you, home they all come! and without even a decent reason for their refusal, treating me therefore as if I were a perfectly unknown poet, sending in my first contribution.

A week later, having received an acrimonious response from Benét, she sent him a second letter, this one adopting a half-apologetic, dovish tone:

Look here, William Rose Benét, let's make up! I got mad, and made you mad, but I cannot altogether regret it, for I think it is just as well to know how things are.

I never expected you to take anything because I can "wield a battle-ax." It is not a battle-ax—you must not think it—it is simply that I care so exceedingly much, and that often looks battle-axy. . . .

Amy a battle-ax? Perish the thought. Yet it was she who labeled Sevenels a Storm Center and took pride in her role as a swashbuckling Brahmin impervious to the proprieties of genteel Boston. There was never any shortage of quirky tales concerning her eccentric lifestyle and Napoleonic methods of publicity, her cajoling, enticing, demanding ways with the men and women (mostly men) in positions of power in publishing and the arts.

The legend is somewhat dated by now, but aspects of the saga never lose their flavor. Looking increasingly with age like Holbein's Henry VIII, she ran Sevenels with an iron fist. The day's routine revolved around her needs. She rarely rose before one or two in the afternoon. Bells rang simultaneously in all downstairs rooms, summoning part of the household to her third-floor bedroom and signaling the rest of the staff that the morning silence could now be broken.

Ada, carrying Amy's mail, led the procession of servants up the stairs. She was trailed by the housekeeper, bearing a pitcher of ice water, and Amy's personal maid with the day's wardrobe. The parlor maid brought up packages (usually rare books), and the kitchen maid balanced the breakfast tray. In addition to those in the "procession," her payroll included a cook, a third maid, an aged "houseboy," a butler, the gardener and seven undergardeners, two chauffeurs and a footman, and two secretaries; also a laundress, rarely the same one for more than two weeks, since the ironing was done with considerable difficulty on a huge table with side irons heated on a potbellied stove. A man came weekly to wind the clocks.

During the afternoon Sevenels was a hive of commotion, with its lawnmowers, workmen, telephones all going at once, in preparation for the evening's company. Guests generally arrived at seven and by eight were seated at dinner. It was only then that Amy made her appearance, at once commandeering the conversation, keeping it afloat through the main course and on into dessert. Dinner over with, the party, led by Ada, trailed into the imposing library. There the fire was lit; cigars and cigarettes were offered; coffee and liqueurs were passed. Presently Amy was ensconced in the corner of the sofa to the side of the fireplace, her feet tucked up under her, a Manila cigar in hand. Glasses of water were distributed. And the conversation was resumed.

Good conversation, it has somewhere been noted, is a gift of the Gods; Amy was a master of it. Language was part of breeding, rather like taste in clothes and jewelry, fine wine, or good hands on a horse. But Amy could carry conversation beyond the point of good breeding. She was gregarious, completely unself-conscious, and completely original. She knew how to invest her tales and anecdotes with a wonderfully tart flavor. She relished the quick thrust and parry. She did not disdain the pun. The combination of Brahmin background, poetic sensibility, and cultivated intelligence, made her an irresistible force. She made easy enemies but formed reverent friendships, often with young and upcoming authors and critics such as Cummings, Aldington, Untermeyer, Malcolm Cowley, and Hervey Allen, the future author of the best-selling *Anthony Adverse* series.

Untermeyer, who came to know Amy as well as anyone, recalled meeting her for the first time:

> The shock was only for a moment. I had heard of Hungarian duchesses who smoked cigars imperturbably and, years later, I was to know a Viennese grand dame who cherished a meerschaum pipe. But I was unprepared to watch a Lowell, the sister of Harvard University, knocking the

ash from a colorado claro. (She had a supply of ten thousand.) The appari-
tion seemed the more grotesque because of Miss Lowell's size. . . . To
make the effect still more incongruous, she preferred high-collared
dresses sprinkled with beads and lavishly trimmed with passementerie.
Some glandular defect made the heavy body seem more swollen and the
short frame more stunted than it really was. ("Lord," she would say, "I'm
a walking side show.") Yet the rakish cigar and the abnormal stoutness
were forgotten five minutes after she seated herself. One noticed only
the marvelous neatness, the fine hands and delicate ankles, the small
mobile mouth, the coolly modulated voice, the quick-appraising but not
unkind eyes, the fine features and almost transparent skin. One saw a
woman who was not only intelligent but—there is no other word for it
—pretty.

This was one impression. She struck some observers as haughty, class-
conscious, and high-minded; still others noticed the extraordinary drive
and grinding ambition, like that of an obsessed bombardier. But this was
part of the supersaleswoman guise, the side of her that allowed Amy to
pursue so doggedly the cause of poetry despite its endless setbacks and
defeats. She possessed a sharp eye for the unusual. She liked stories and
fables and believed that a stable, well-defined society was necessary for
the perpetuation of literature. Too much of her own poetry sprang from
the will, not the spirit. Her will was something strong and fierce, as
Carlyle (and Nietzsche) said it must be. And why not? She was both a
Lowell and a Lawrence, a product of two of the wealthiest, most powerful families in America; she was not malicious, nor was she excited by
power for its own sake. But she did like to "run things," if only on a
minor scale, whether dahabeahs on the Nile, dinner parties at Sevenels,
or poetry readings in Back Bay town houses. Possessing the capacity
(and money), she could run things much as she pleased. A female in
turn-of-the-century Boston who liked to write and think needed
strength to stave off the Puritan marionettes—the members of her own
class and clan—whose wrath she was almost certain to incur. What stood
Amy in good stead in these battles was her rationality, her sense of
directness and direction. Civilized taste and behavior were not enough,
so she cultivated an individual vision of the world, in the same way that
she cultivated her speech patterns and stage mannerisms. In her speech
she acquired the vigor of a rough-riding Teddy Roosevelt; his favorite
terms and expressions became hers. She even reflected his Bull Moose
Republican appearance to the world, his semblance of "robust action
and outward glow." She was a Roosevelt in manner but a Lowell in

breeding, a combination of New York ambition and Boston pragmatism, founded on a solid expanse of old American, grande dame persistence.

The nightly gatherings in Miss Lowell's library at Sevenels presented an ideal testing ground for her newest literary ideas and theories. She often droned on about the Georgian poets, referring to them as "caged warblers" and "phonograph poets," accusing them of false emotions and impure motives; they were imitations of imitations, full of bogus profundities and clownish excesses. She was a tyrant when it came to literary taste, rendering pronouncements—mostly invectives—with the rapidity of machine-gun fire. She fulminated against Henry Adams for writing history instead of fiction and faulted Henry James for deserting America. Joyce was vulgar, Dostoevski dull. She rejected Freud as trite, shabby, and fundamentally medieval. Her greatest contempt, however, was reserved for those pettifogging poetry-producing bureaucrats and unctuous, anglophilic critics, the custodians of literary parochialism, who refused to acknowledge the genius of Edgar Lee Masters and Carl Sandburg. She was convinced a conspiracy was underfoot between the critics and writers to exclude the genuinely accomplished from within their ranks.

So while flames blazed in the fireplace, Amy kept up a steady patter of talk, her eyes merry, her voice piping and droning as she ranged from subject to subject. Her conversation had a quality of drama that transfixed listeners. She related marvelous tales about her propaganda efforts on behalf of the movement, her latest struggles behind the scenes, her next game plan to aid this or that deserving author. The last trolley for Boston left Brookline promptly at midnight. By a quarter to twelve the conversation invariably drew to a close, and the guests were ushered to the front door and out in time to catch their ride. With their departure from Sevenels another drama presently ensued.

Now the poet settled down to work in a deep leather armchair before the rekindled fireplace or at a table in a corner of the vast chamber. She wrote through the night, using pencils sharpened to remarkably fine points, discarding them as they became blunt. The floor was her wastebasket; whatever papers were found there in the morning were immediately discarded. Upon retiring, rarely before dawn, she left the finished portion of her manuscript on a table for her secretaries to decipher and type before her next writing session when the previous night's labors would be revised and rewritten. Only the final draft of each poem survived; the rest were shredded and burned.

While some of the poets of the day reacted strongly against the convention of "poeticized" treatment and the flaccid wordiness of Victorian verse, many in their own way perpetuated the practice. Although their subjects were frequently un- or anti-Romantic, their imaginations were not. David Perkins reminds us of Vachel Lindsay's poem on a Chinese laundryman in an American city, typically winging back in time and imagination to a palace in ancient China, where we see the same laundryman in the role of a prince with his lovely and loving princess. In another poem, Lindsay takes a look at crapshooters in a gambling hall and thinks of the Congo River, "cutting through the jungle" amid the primitive "boom" of drums. Writes Perkins: "This mounting of romantic treatment on contemporary material appears [as well] in Robinson, Frost, Sandburg, Masters, and Amy Lowell, even though these poets too were trying to rid poetry of it."

Perkins is correct to count Miss Lowell among those whose intentions were pure but whose poetry was not. A number of the poems in her third collection, *Men, Women and Ghosts* (1916), were sheathed in a mist of passion, while other poems suffered from literary pretentiousness and emotional self-indulgence. In keeping with her previous collection, the present volume combined a variety of poetic modes: rhymed meter, free verse, polyphonic prose. It included the frequently anthologized dramatic monologue, "Patterns," and a block of four dramatic monologues spoken by rural New England dwellers and grouped under the heading "The Overgrown Pasture." A dozen poems, including the raucous "Bombardment," were devoted to military battles, past and present (five, in one section called "War Pictures," were evoked by World War I); four, collectively entitled "Bronze Tablets," presented anecdotal scenes dating back to Napoleon, although Bonaparte himself appears only in passing. Napoleon, like Teddy Roosevelt, represented a heroic persona in Amy's eyes, a forceful, masculine figure of immense intelligence and accomplishment. She admired his genius in warfare and his ability to set in motion currents of revolutionary ideas. To James Oppenheim, editor of the magazine *Seven Arts,* Amy voiced the opinion that with the fall of Napoleon at Waterloo, the cause of free thought, free speech, and individuality vanished from the world.

Considering Amy's interest in the military personality, it is astonishing that her war poems are the fatuous, slipshod exercises they seem to be. "The Hammers," included in the "Bronze Tablets" section of *Men, Women and Ghosts,* begins: "Bang! / Bang! / Tap! / Tap-a-tap! Rap!" and is promptly followed by the nonsensical refrain: "Tap! / Rap! / Squeak! / Tap! Squeak! Tap-a-tap!" The inexplicable taps and squeaks inevitably drum out whatever else this sequence may have to offer.

The quartet of narratives grouped under the title "The Overgrown Pasture" were only slightly stronger in culminating impact. Written in the dialect of the New England farmer, they bear some resemblance to *The Biglow Papers,* or more directly to the work of several of James Russell Lowell's lesser-known imitators, namely Paul Lawrence Dunbar and James Whitcomb Riley, both of whom learned from the Firesider the appeal of rustic speakers using regional dialect. Riley firmly believed—as did Amy—that the public wanted simple statements spoken from the heart, graceful and feeling morsels that were readily comprehensible even by those of limited education.

Another informing angel in these dramatic monologues was Robert Frost, whose work Amy admired as much as the work of any of her contemporaries. Yet she was convinced that her own use of Yankee dialect was at least as convincing as Frost's. Frost, according to his biographer, Lawrence Thompson, disliked the plain country folk of whom he wrote; Amy was accused by her biographer, S. Foster Damon, of condescending to her characters and of bastardizing their speech patterns in her verse, using phonetic word substitutions—"jest" for "just"; "oughter" for "ought to"—instead of authentic Yankee dialect. When Ellery Sedgwick charged her in a review with these same misdemeanors, Amy hit the roof, stubbornly protesting that she had compared her version with the speech in the books of the noted phonetician Alice Brown. In addition to Brown she claimed to have relied upon the wisdom of her grandfather Abbott Lawrence, whose childhood was spent in the New England countryside. And also, she pointed out, "I have been living cheek by jowl with the natives every summer for fifteen years." The latter was a dubious reference to her summertime abode in Dublin, New Hampshire.

In various letters to associates and friends, Amy was always quick to point out those verses in *Men, Women and Ghosts* that she preferred. The selection included "The Cremona Violin," the tale of a neglected housewife engaged in an adulterous love affair because her husband, a devoted concertmaster, showed more interest in his career than in his marriage. That, in any event, was one critic's interpretation of the poem. "My idea," professed Amy, "was not so much that Herr Altgelt's music absorbed him away from his wife, as it was that she was held in subjection to him by this same music." Amy's sympathies were predominantly with the husband; as she explained it, "if a person marries an artist, it is quite clear that they must admit the position of art in the other's life to be paramount; and this does not at all mean that the artist does not give all of himself to the person he loves, but simply that he is dedicated to an ideal which includes the person he loves, and carries him and the object of his love, beyond." That this was a theme close to the poet's heart is suggested by the German name she gives the couple in the poem; "Altgelt" ("old money") is clearly a reference to Lowell family wealth.

Another poem, "1777," a historical sequence that contrasts revolutionary Boston with decadent Venice, enabled the poet to weigh the relative merits of two dynamic republics. The sky-tones and colors of Venice provide the poet with a rich and expansive backdrop:

> Blue-black, the sky over Venice,
> With a pricking of yellow stars.
> There is no moon,
> And the waves push darkly against the prow
> Of the gondola,
> Coming from Malamocco
> And streaming toward Venice.
> It is black under the gondola hood,
> But the yellow of a satin dress
> Glares out like the eye of a watching tiger.

The Boston section of "1777" contains a lengthy description of a garden, presumably the verdant, well-manicured grounds of Sevenels. This acreage inspired another poem in *Men, Women and Ghosts*, entitled "A Roxbury Garden," with its little girls at play "In the yellow sunshine, / Each with a big round hoop." A third sequence, "The Dinner Party," describes what its title suggests—dinner, among guests, at the home of a friend. The poem reveals Miss Lowell's feelings of alienation even from those of her own peerage:

> They sat in a circle with their coffee-cups.
> One dropped in a lump of sugar,
> One stirred with a spoon.
> I saw them as a circle of ghosts

Sipping blackness out of beautiful china,
And mildly protesting against my coarseness
In being alive.

The personal touch can be felt again in "Afternoon Rain in State
Street" and "An Aquarium," both based on Boston adventures actually
experienced by the author and both heavily laden with Amy's by now
exhausted array of tones and colors. "Afternoon Rain" speaks of "Cross-
hatchings of rain against grey walls, / Slant lines of black rain." "Aquarium" begins: "Streaks of grey and yellow iridescence, / Silver shiftings,
/ Rings veering out of rings, / Silver—gold—."

The best-remembered of the offerings in *Men, Women and Ghosts*
is surely "Patterns," with its famous epitaphic last line: "Christ! What
are patterns for?" In the poem a British noblewoman, strolling through
her garden bedecked in Queen Anne finery, receives a letter stating
that the Duke, whom she is about to marry, has been killed at the Battle
of Waterloo. Hiding her tears, the lady completes her walk until, at
poem's climax, the thought of his mutilation "In a pattern called a war"
brings on her final cry of anguish, coupled with her resolve to live the
remainder of her life alone. The poem has frequently been attacked on
the grounds that the highly stylized setting seems inappropriately summarized by an outburst in an idiom too contemporary with our own
feelings to suit its generating episode. According to critics, the temptation is thus to use the exclamation "Christ! What are patterns for?" to
delve psychoanalytically into Amy Lowell's personal life. It is true, for
instance, that Amy often conceived of herself as an American version
of a titled European lady and frequently portrayed herself as one in her
poems. Registering an explicit protest against Puritan inhibitions and
society's repressive conventions, she must have had herself in mind in
these lines from "Patterns":

I walk down the garden paths,
And all the daffodils
Are blowing, and the bright blue squills.
I walk down the patterned garden-paths
In my stiff, brocaded gown.
With my powdered hair and jewelled fan,
I too am a rare
Pattern. As I wander down
The garden paths.

Miss Lowell adopted the tactic of alternating books composed primarily of brief lyrics, such as *Men, Women and Ghosts,* with books of longer narratives. Her next volume of poetry, *Can Grande's Castle* (1918), was named for the refuge where Dante, the Florentine exile, wrote portions of his *Divine Comedy.* The new volume contained only four poems, each penned in polyphonic prose, each depicting a grand and sweeping panorama, the type of setting that best suits this genre.

The book's first narrative, "Sea-Blue and Blood-Red," paints impasto war scenes in Italy, Egypt, England, and at Trafalgar, the drama revolving around Lord Nelson and his mistress, Lady Emma Hamilton. The motif "red" is created by the excessive wartime spilling of blood and by the incandescent bursting of Mt. Vesuvius. "Guns as Keys: And the Great Gate Swings" follows a similar pattern. The poet contrasts Commodore Perry's expedition to force open the ports of Japan to international trade, to the countermeasures adopted by the Japanese to prevent the invasion. In this oratorio Amy measures two alien cultures, the gallant heroism of Japan versus the extroverted self-confidence of America—Eastern stoicism versus Western fortitude. "Hedge Island," the shortest and least workable of these poems, views England before and after its industrial revolution by zeroing in on the English mail and stagecoach system; it investigates the development of contemporary British manners and mannerisms and touches on the interaction between English town and country—overcrowded London as opposed to the sparsely populated, desolate countryside. The last and longest poem, "The Bronze Horses," portrays war scenes witnessed in Rome, Constantinople, and Venice over a span of centuries by the four bronze horses that adorn the façade of St. Mark's Cathedral in Venice. The poem ends with the basic bloodletting theme of "Sea-Blue and Blood-Red"; it reproduces a terrifying Austrian air raid on Venice early in World War I: "The people walk in the brightness of fire. Fire from the Rio della Tanna, from the quarter of Santa Lucia. Bells peal in a fury, fireboats hurry with forced engines along the canals. Water streams jet upon the fire; and, in the golden light, the glittering horses of St. Mark's pace forward, silent, calm, determined in their advance, above the portal of the untouched church."

Although wordiness and confusion obscured these multivoiced prose poems, nothing impaired the prose contained in *Tendencies in Modern American Poetry* (1917), a muster of six essays on six contemporary poets grouped in pairs as literary Evolutionists, Revolutionists, and Imagists. Robinson and Frost, the Evolutionists, represented the inception of the new poetry in their return to realism and natural speech. Masters and Sandburg, the Revolutionists, represented the breakdown of linguistic patterns, an attack on "literary environment," including the liberation of the line from meter. H. D. and Fletcher, the Imagists, represented the realization of the modern point of view, the creation of a contemporary artistic creed, a substantial break with the etymologic past. Amy remained convinced that modernism was the trend of the future, not only in poetry but in all the arts. *Tendencies* attempted to explain the interpenetration of American culture with the modernist sensibility and argued sensibly that modernism was not as dogmatically antisocial and antibourgeois as many tended then to believe. The author presented her ideas with a direct, intimate forthrightness that made clear the differences in the development of these three successive phases of the new poetry.

The half-dozen poets in this study are further illuminated by the inclusion of a fair amount of biographical data, including material on childhood and family. The collection is enhanced by long excerpts of key poems. Its chief deterrent is Miss Lowell's stubborn belligerence, her nagging insistence that she was right and everyone else, no matter what they believed, wrong. Too frequently one gets her dogmatic, sometimes unorthodox views practically shoveled down one's throat. John Gould Fletcher, for one, is described as "a more original poet than Arthur Rimbaud." A few pages further we read that "many excellent books of a past age are neglected [today] because of an overinsistence upon sex." Puritanism is defined as a "virulent poison." *Spoon River,* once highly admired by Amy, is now deemed the "great blot upon Mr. Masters' work."

Amy's most responsive audience was located, as one might suspect, within the confines of her own domain. In Boston and New York, and especially within the circumference of its ladies' circles, she was looked upon as something of a phenomenon. T. S. Eliot, one of Amy's less avid fans, reported in a review of *Tendencies* for *The Egoist* that Miss Lowell's downfall was her pressing need to regard art as another form of politics. "Her own role," he wrote, "is thus Director of Propaganda." Then: "It strikes me as a most unfortunate thing that this all-American propaganda should continue. . . . Literature must be judged by language, not by lace. And standards may come from Paris, or even Rome or Munich, which London as well as Topeka must respect. Provinciality of material may be a virtue; provinciality of point of view is a vice."

Eliot was frankly appalled by the carnival atmosphere, the mystique and aura, that hovered around the new poetry. He concurred with Louis Untermeyer's ultimate estimation that Miss Lowell lacked genuine and lasting talent, attempting to substitute motion and commotion for outright inspiration. To be sure, she was among the first of her profession to incorporate America's love of big business into the realm of the arts, announcing on one occasion that God had made her a businesswoman and she would make herself a poet. "Publicity first," she informed Grace Hazard Conkling. "Poetry will follow."

Eliot was outraged by the American-based Amygists, their persistent need to write coy and clever little ditties in order to procure and hold the kind of audience that was composed principally of native moralists, lady schoolteachers, and miscellaneous middlebrows—the same crowd that formerly embraced James Russell Lowell and his fellow Fireside poets, with their packaged whimsies and homespun philosophy. And yet, there were obvious differences between the two literary schools: the Fireside poets were woodsy, folksy, wholesome, parochial, positive though a bit melancholy; the Amygists used fewer pleasing conceits in their work and were not as melodramatic or garrulous; in addition they managed to achieve a cleaner verbal surface and a purer diction than their predecessors.

Another major difference had to do with each group's respective view of nature. The nineteenth-century poet was more attuned to the great outdoors and more apt to celebrate it, whereas his successor turned to the city and the machine for inspiration. Imagists pointed to nature's recalcitrance and hardness, its refusal to yield Edenic pleasures, its decline and disappearance in the face of proliferating mass industry. In Eliot's eyes the case with regard to Amy Lowell was slightly different; she belonged to a tiny clique of poets (Frost, at his worst, was also a member) who wrote what might best be construed as "false pastoral," poetry that utilized idyllic country settings and simple rural characters for no reason other than to appeal to the masses. True pastoral celebrates the virtues of bucolic existence; but it does not propose that we rest with either simple characters or crude psychology. Instead it uses the idyllic setting to advance complex ideas and sentiments, often implying a serious criticism of the society in which the poet lives. Amy, in her desire to draw the masses, too often produced stiff, provincial lyrics, catering to her own idiosyncracies and minor virtuosities. Even when she is clever, it is the cleverness of a poet holding fast to her limitations.

20

FIGHTING
THE GOOD FIGHT

DURING the summer of 1916, while vacationing in New Hampshire, an accident occurred that had a profound influence on Amy's life. Attempting to hoist the hind wheels of a horse-and-buggy out of a ditch, the poet strained a muscle and incurred what soon became an umbilical hernia. The next year she ruptured the strained muscle by trying to lift a heavy brass bed, and "the ridiculous little hernia" required an operation. Two years later a coughing spell broke open the wound and a second, more difficult operation was performed; the result was a stretched fascia that called for a third operation, then a fourth.

The incessant pain made necessary a daily ritual of pill-swallowing, Epsom salts, hip baths, massages, and Bender bandages. Headaches, arthritis, neuralgia, nausea, sometimes followed by jaundice, were among the side effects; additionally, Amy suffered from high blood pressure and spells of dizziness. Despite these discomforts she was a tireless traveler, touring America on behalf of the cause, fighting for the cause, slaving for it. The impact of the new poetry was explosive, and Amy set off a lot of the dynamite. She trudged from city to city, from town to town, horrifying the pedants, battling the enemy, intermittently blowing fuses and setting forest fires, bowling over audiences with the nonchalance of a ten-ton tank.

Amy's force of will, the secret of her success and failure, was her outstanding "racial" characteristic. This, writes Van Wyck Brooks, was the incrassated Yankee will, the same Puritan resoluteness that motivated Percival Lowle in old age to leave England for the new world, and that drove other forebears to found towns, industries, and universities. Amy was tenacious and stubborn. Her powers of devastation were ineffable. She carried her campaign wherever she went, touching a spark wherever she read. Her voice was not still and frail, but loud and magniloquent. Her bombs burst with all the fury that mass and energy could muster, lighting up the sky and igniting the landscape: "And she whizzed and she whirred, and she rustled and rumbled, and she glistened and sparkled and blazed and blared."

No doubt her externality, both in poetry and style of presentation, reflected her own extroversion. At the same time, her extroversion was no more than a calculated escape from a troubled psyche, an inner self that repudiated repose. Her egotism, though infinitely elastic, was a fragile skin enclosing a gigantic inferiority complex. At any moment the skin might burst. In many respects Amy was never really a poet. The poet in her, suggested Brooks, never struggled through. Amy "seized on the outsides of things" as her only means of effectuality, of survival, and her flair for dramatics achieved the rest.

That she was able to maintain her precarious balance as long as she did, tenaciously warding off her demons while producing furiously lucid artifacts, is a tribute to her other self, the self that was able to transcend emotional chaos and to fashion the ordered, humane vision of her poetry. Amy's achievement, for whatever it was worth, cannot be fully appreciated unless one realizes how the terror and despair that constantly assailed her were overcome in poems which, although fully in touch with human anguish, often succeeded in spite of their dark and forbidding nature. Amy's poems explore those shadowy depths of man's condition with an understanding that in the end affirms our presence, reaffirms our hard-won existence. The final note of so many volumes of her work is not madness or death but simply Amy's exhilaration, her faith.

The good fight, the battle to liberate verse from the shackles of Victorian enslavement, was waged at many levels and on many fronts. New York was the main port of activity. From the St. Regis or the Belmont Hotel, owned by her friends the August Belmonts, the grand panjandrum of free verse plotted her plan of havoc, issuing telephone orders to cowed attendants, receiving and manhandling authors, critics, and editors, unleashing a torrent of pronunciamentos, mandates, and commands. She maneuvered to get what she considered the best men to write the best reviews for the best magazines and newspapers. She treated editors as though they were mailroom clerks. Critics were cajoled and toyed with and usually left her quarters convinced they had been treated to an audience with the Pope. Often, as her biographers have pointed out, there was a touch of bitterness beneath her blandishments. She wrote to her publisher that since he advertised frequently in *The New York Times*, he should force them to be conciliatory in their critical reception of her books. To another publisher she wrote, "I am as bad as Napoleon!" She once admonished Ezra Pound: "You ought to have an impresario—your knowledge of how to 'get yourself over,' as we say in this country, is *nil.*" Of her own public-relations skill, she advised Louis Untermeyer: "I have to be my own impresario. There's no point in having a trumpet—or any brass— if you don't blow it."

To a distant admiring cousin (Carlotta Lowell) she commented (July 18, 1919): "The life of a poet is by no means the dreamy aesthetic one people are led to suppose. A mixture of that of a day-laborer, a travelling salesman, and an itinerant actress, is about what it amounts to." Her wealth did not ease the pain of bad reviews or the long, arduous, lonely stretches of hard work. In Amy's case, it may actually have worked to her disadvantage. Malcolm Cowley thought so: "It is hard to be a true poet when one is rich, blanketed with four per cent debentures and rocked to sleep in a cradle of sound common stocks." Amy touched on the same issue in a letter to the editor of the *New York Tribune* (January 1920): "I started in the world with one of the greatest handicaps that anyone could possibly have. I belonged to the class which is not supposed to be able to produce good creative work."

For years it was an article of faith among American educators and literary savants that no one in Society could ever be a writer of the first water—and particularly not a woman. Edith Wharton helped dispel that notion to some degree, but even *her* reputation had to endure the imposed hardships of gender and social stature. Amy Lowell, although artistically no match for Miss Wharton, felt herself the victim of a similar set of circumstances. In his introduction to her *Collected Poems,* Louis Untermeyer remarked that Miss Lowell was not unaware of a certain ambivalence, a schism that separated the poet in her from the heiress. "I remember," he wrote, "one of the occasions when the implications of her wealth worried her"—

We were attending a performance of Gerhart Hauptmann's *The Weavers*, a drama of class conflict which pictured an uprising in the 1840's. Anticipating Ernst Toller's violent *The Machine-Wreckers*, Hauptmann's play reached its climax as the Silesian workers, starving and desperate, destroy not only the machines, which they hold responsible for their distress, but proceed to smash the home of their employer. Amy Lowell could not help thinking of the industrialized town of Lowell which had been named for her forebears and she, who sometimes referred to herself as "the last of the Barons," flinched. "This is the future," she whispered as the curtain came down on a scene of pillage. "That is what is going to happen to me!"

Money may not have made Amy a better writer, but it did not hinder her either. On the other side, she had considerable difficulty identifying with the lower strata of society. In 1912, when the textile workers of Lawrence and Lowell staged their record-breaking two-month strike, she showed little sympathy for their plight. It was a turbulent struggle that saw the cold-blooded murder of two mill workers by State Police, a calamity that drew the founder of the IWW, Big Bill Haywood, to join ranks with the anarchist leader Carlo Tresca, the anarchist poet Arturo Giovannitti, and Tresca's mistress, the slim youthful firebrand Elizabeth Gurley Flynn, in defense of the mill employees. Amy Lowell spoke out against the predominantly Irish trade unions, which she accused of attempting to undermine and overthrow the democratic system. She courted local political and business bigwigs by throwing a series of lavish dinner parties at Sevenels, intending to gain support for the industrial plutocrats who owned and operated the drab and polyglot company towns.

A second major Massachusetts mill-town strike occurred in 1919, originating with a demand by the mill operatives for a reduction of their six-day nine-hour work week to one of eight hours at the same rate of pay. Tresca and Giovannitti were again on the scene; Ime Kaplan, a Russian alien, assumed command of the rank and file. Violence broke out between picketing laborers and local police. A shot was fired: a worker fell. That night a band of outraged workers firebombed Lawrence's largest textile mill, signaling the start of what would be a seemingly endless war. Amy saw the strike as part of a larger pattern of capitalist disintegration preliminary to the seizure of power by the working class, a logical continuum of the Russian Revolution of 1917.

In political matters of this sort she frequently alternated between complete indifference on the one hand and fiery involvement on the other. For Amy the essential political issue boiled down to whether or not government should control the nation's total resources—its utilities, its energy sources, its money supply. In so many words, should private finance be placed at the disposal of the government to be used as government ordained, or should private enterprise be allowed to rule itself? How could individual wealth be utilized to benefit society as a whole? Would government arrogantly continue its usurpation of private property and resources, or could the state's self-proclaimed supremacy be contained? It was on the basis of these concerns, many of them previously raised by James Russell Lowell, that Amy opposed Prohibition. Although scarcely touched by the ethical or moral issues surrounding alcohol, she did find that the Eighteenth Amendment violated her personal credo regarding the infringement of the basic constitutional rights of the individual in society. Not surprisingly, the violation of individual and class rights aroused her indignation primarily at those moments when her own rights were in jeopardy.

For the first days of the Boston Police Strike of 1919, before the arrival of armed replacements, "the last of the Barons" kept a loaded pistol by her bedside to protect against law-breaking looters and house burglars; newspapers added to her natural fears of violence by running blood-soaked reports of mob rule, street-corner attacks and rapes of helpless older women, store lootings, and indiscriminate beatings of innocent bystanders. At a Boston dinner party thrown by the Untermeyers for the Imagist poet May Sinclair, Amy expressed her feelings regarding the police strike, hurling bricks also at the disruptive strike activities of the nation's mining and steel workers, to say nothing of the entire municipal work force of the city of Seattle, whose members had struck earlier in the year. "Times are changing, we're all of us in danger," she warned those present, her voice taking on an edge of hysteria. She prattled on about "the lawless element" rising up at any moment, about intruders, Wobblies, blackguards, the fall of the upper classes, the breakdown of order; it was people like herself that "they"—the anarchist-loving mobs—were after.

The unlikely fear that her life and fortune were in danger can perhaps be traced to sources surprisingly apolitical in origin. One cause may have been the pressures brought to bear by the ongoing skirmishes of the great poetry war, the petty rivalries and jealousies, the intrigues and backbiting that marked this squalid scenario. The seamy gamesters that opposed the new movement were out for blood; it was Amy's contention that they were mostly out for *her* blood. And why? Because she was a ruthless, power-puffing Tartar, who thought nothing of advancing her own career at the expense of others, and who exploited her personal suffering for the sake of popularity and a morbid, pandering audience. William Carlos Williams had been extremely harsh on James Russell Lowell, referring to him in an essay on Poe as an all-accepting purveyor of "pap," an overly genteel poet of the picturesque. He was just as hard now on Amy Lowell, accusing her—among other capital crimes—of greed. His letters to her seethed with tendentious bitterness:

Oct. 4, 1916

Dear Miss Lowell: Accept my homage—much as I dislike you: "The Cross Roads" is good.

10:30 P.M.
Perhaps I won't like it so much tomorrow. Send me some money for *Others.*

The poem Williams claimed to admire was in polyphonic prose; it appeared originally in *Poetry Review,* and sang rhythmically though not very subtly of death. *Others* was Alfred Kreymborg's literary journal, an experimental publication of the arts that had published Kreymborg, Marianne Moore, Wallace Stevens, Mina Loy, Maxwell Bodenheim, Lola Ridge, and Williams. It was now on the verge of financial collapse, and Williams had appointed himself chief fundraiser. When Miss Lowell refused to contribute to its revival but suggested as an alternative that she and Williams meet, he exploded: "I cannot see the slightest reason why we should meet. I have nothing to talk over with you. . . . To me it is a lamentable stinginess of spirit that permits you to hold your present well-known attitude toward unknown and young American writers."

Miss Lowell, who should probably have let matters subside on their own accord, chose instead to respond to Williams's taunt. "Your letter would be insulting," she barked, "if it were not pathetic." She proceeded to shower her detractor with the names of writers she had aided over the years, financially and otherwise; she mentioned Fletcher, Frost, D. H. Lawrence, Untermeyer, Maxwell Bodenheim, Cummings, and Wallace Stevens. She pointed out that she had been responsible for getting the early Stevens poem "Susannah and the Elders" published in William Stanley Braithwaite's *Magazine Anthology* for 1915: "Possibly you have no opinion of Mr. Braithwaite's taste, but that is an advertisement which is a help with the public at large, and that particular form of notoriety Mr. Stevens owes entirely to me." In the case of Cummings, Miss Lowell had provided him with letters of introduction to the editors of three leading New York magazines—the *Century*, *Scribner's*, and *Craftsman*—in the hope that one would offer the recent Harvard graduate a lucrative staff position. The publication that subsequently hired him was *Collier's*, although Cummings abandoned that post within a matter of months.

Despite strenuous reservations on his part, Williams and Amy Lowell did finally meet; Williams recorded the nonevent in his *Autobiography* (1948): "I saw her once, at a party in her apartment at the Belmont Hotel, pontifical, but rather self-conscious, protecting her privileges as a wealthy woman, of which she was none too sure, and smoking, though not self-consciously, her fat cigars. I had nothing much to say to her."

Several years later, Amy and Ezra Pound had another brief run-in similar to her imbroglio with Williams. Pound, with his zeal in coming to the aid of all those whose work he respected, started what he styled his Bel Esprit project, a plan designed to free T. S. Eliot from his job at Lloyd's Bank of London so that he could devote himself to his poetry. The scheme, involving voluntary contributions by practicing writers, eventually became a nuisance and a source of embarrassment to Eliot, although in the end the publicity he received from it may well have resulted in his being granted the 1922 *Dial* award of two thousand dollars, an amount that allowed him to get some poetry written. When Amy refused to contribute to Bel Esprit, Pound berated her by letter: "Aw shucks! dearie, ain't you the hell-roarer, ain't you the kuss." He wrote to Harriet Monroe that Miss Lowell's poetry was "putrid!" In 1928, in a letter to René Taupin, he summed up Amy and the "Amygists" as a "bunch of goups."

Another small circle of intellectuals added to the Bostonian's travail by perpetrating what became known as "the Spectra Hoax," a plot directed against these same "Amygists." Early in 1917, visiting New York, Miss Lowell was introduced to the poet and critic Witter Bynner. Bynner, a man of modest talents whose name was once as well known as any among the commonality of poetry lovers in America, wrote lyrical and touching poems full of muted pessimism and end-of-the-age sobriety. His poetic models ran the gamut from A. E. Housman to the T'ang poets of China. From the beginning he opposed the rush of new schools and movements such as the Imagists and the various adherents of the new poetry that made the poetry pot boil over. Amid the feverish activities associated with the bubbling cauldron, Bynner referred sarcastically in print to the emancipated champions of vers libre as "verslibertines." On meeting Miss Lowell, he subjected her to a battery of questions concerning "le mouvement," concluding with a query about the so-called "Spectrist School." He had reviewed their recent anthology *Spectra* in *The New Republic,* comparing it favorably with Amy's annual *Some Imagist Poets* and with several of the Futurist texts by Marinetti and friends. In January 1917, *Others* ran a special Spectrist issue, featuring the work of Anne Knish and one Emanuel Morgan, whose Spectrist samples constituted the mainstay of the school. The two poets were not exactly well known. They claimed to have come from Pittsburgh—not then, at least, a major literary port of call. In addition, Mr. Morgan, the word went, had been in Paris for the last twenty years. And Miss Knish was a Bulgarian whose previous poetry had been published in Russian.

Spectra became the talk of the literary community. Newspapers and magazines took note of it; its principles were debated, its authors—mysterious though they seemed to be—were sought out on aesthetic matters, and they were asked to contribute to sundry quarterlies and periodicals. Some big-name writers, including Masters and Williams, rather fancied the work of the Spectrists. Finally, in 1918, in answer to a reporter's question, Bynner conceded that he was Edward Morgan and that Arthur Davison Ficke, a friend and fellow poet, was Miss Knish. Infuriated at being made the butt of their joke, Amy maintained that both Bynner and Ficke were better in *Spectra* than in their own work. Although she continued to correspond with Bynner, she never fully forgave him; to toy with a poet's vanity, especially when that poet was Amy Lowell, was dangerous business.

One conflict quickly led to another. In 1916, Amy found herself inadvertently dragged into the Van Kleek Allison trial, the case of a young man apprehended by Boston Mayor James Curley for distributing birth control literature on the streets of downtown Boston. Bombarded by mail representing both sides of the issue, Amy resisted efforts to be drawn into the altercation. "I believe," she quipped, "that an artist should place art above all other considerations." Regardless of her conviction that art was greater than any artist and should be placed above public affairs on some unofficial hierarchical schedule of disciplines, she voiced a private opinion on the Allison case in a letter to Louis Untermeyer (August 11, 1916):

> As a matter of fact, I think the whole Van Allison business was abominable. The trial was a disgrace, the remarks of the presiding judge were to my mind more objectionable than the theories he was combatting, and they showed a perfect, and I think an intentional, nonunderstanding of the point of view of the radicals. However, I really am in an awkward position, because I agree with neither radicals nor conservatives entirely. If I were heart and soul in sympathy with the methods of these advocates of birth control, it would be simple to come out and say so; but I am not. Their theory, as regards the ignorant proletariat, is open to question, but their methods of action do not seem to be open to question; they seem to me to defeat their own object by pursuing it in a hectic and tasteless manner.
>
> Of course, I believe, like everyone else, that a sane kind of birth control is often necessary, and more often expedient, but I think I also have a distinct feeling that there is too much "prevention," not only of births but of other things in our modern life, and that a certain luxuriance, profusion, waste, and self-sacrifice are necessary to civilization. If I were asked, I should say that we really need large families more than we need birth control. Under these circumstances you will see why it is impossible for me to take sides.

"Luxuriance, profusion, waste, and self-sacrifice": no permutation or combination of nouns better sums up the configuration of Amy's outlook on life. The above letter is self-revealing in still another sense. The author's use of the term "ignorant proletariat" in the first paragraph reflects Miss Lowell's total identification with the higher reaches of Society and her condescending attitude toward the lower, unschooled masses. This preconceived judgment permeated her approach to almost every external problem or demand outside the realm of the arts. It marked her indifference to the women's rights movement, her contempt for those women she felt substituted a theory of living for the burdens and joys of life itself, that is to say, who hid behind a mask of radical conformity as well as the skirts of their feminist allies instead of standing apart as individuals, as beings with voices and opinions of their own. Her letter to the Boston Equal Suffrage Association for Good Government was openly scornful and critical of just such demeanor. As with the Van Kleek Allison incident, it was not *what* the Suffragists stood for that rankled Amy, but the means they used to further their cause. Her brief (October 7, 1918) was penned in response to a circular and letter of solicitation she had received in the wake of the Senate's deferment of a bill granting women the right to vote:

Mesdames: Your letter of October 3rd gives me an opportunity of expressing my opinion, not only upon the letter itself, but upon the actions of the association at this time. I have never been at all active as a Suffragist, but I believe that Equal Suffrage is logical and bound to come about. I do, however, think that the action of the Suffragists of the country at this time is deplorable and can do nothing but hurt their cause.

The first sentence of this letter which reads, "The most amazing insult in all history has been delivered by the United States Senate to the womanhood of America," is childishly silly, and is of the kind which fifty years ago would have been described as being "just like a woman." It seems to me that it is on a par in folly, although not on a par in malice, with the Anti-Suffrage suggestion that the Suffragists are working in the cause of Germany. I am sorry to say that neither of these pronouncements gives one any particular reason to think that women as a whole are yet capable of calm judgment. Perhaps I should say that they do not know the full meaning of language.

The poet went on to say that she repudiated the actions of those Suffragists in Washington who had paraded outside the White House with banners, "making themselves generally obnoxious in a time of great stress to the nation." She reminded "Mesdames" that their British counterparts, "with a knowledge of affairs and a realization of the importance of the present moment far in advance of their American sisters," instantly renounced their demands for Suffrage when the war broke out. The American Suffragist movement suffered both from feeble methods of propaganda and poor timing.

Amy's negative attitude toward feminist politics is surprising only in light of her own "liberated" relationship with Ada Dwyer and her friendship with such enlightened feminists as Winifred Bryher. Bryher, briefly married to the expatriate novelist and small-press impresario Robert McAlmon, made no secret of her sexual preference for women. Following H. D.'s separation from Richard Aldington, she and Miss Bryher, like Amy and Ada, lived together in open and frank violation of the accepted norm. In contrast to the beliefs of these ladies and the convictions of feminists in general, Amy subscribed to the Victorian ideal of a patriarchical society, that being the basis of her primordial family heritage and upbringing.

While strenuously opposed to militant feminism, she was not against the movement in its gentler forms. Encouraged by the Boston blue-stocking Fanny Quincy Howe, Amy donated generously to a circle of female-dominated philanthropies, many of them dedicated to aiding the poor and the underprivileged, a group encompassing both female criminals and prostitutes. Her other primary interest in the rites of the movement resided in higher education for women, a cause she stood up for her entire life. She was more anti-feminist in public than in her private life, donning something of a public mask, a deliberate creation designed to avoid having to reveal herself naked and vulnerable. Her personality struck most acquaintances as a dialectic between absolute skepticism and a terrible need to believe. Heywood Broun, for instance, recalled a meeting between Amy and his wife, Ruth Hale Broun, a loyal supporter of Margaret Sanger and a charter member of the Lucy Stone League. Following Mrs. Broun's attempt to defend the movement, Amy leaned back in a big, overstuffed easy chair, and puffing one of her cigars, remarked: "I have (puff, puff) no patience with the new-fashioned woman (puff, puff) and her so-called rights. I believe (and here she drew deep of the cigar) in the old-fashioned conservative woman and all her limitations." This frolicsome scene, straight out of George Bernard Shaw, raises an interesting point: how was a woman, already in many respects liberated, expected to identify or sympathize with women who were not?

On February 17, 1919, with the Armistice between Germany and the Allies already signed, Amy Lowell wrote to Richard Aldington outlining her latest literary projects: "I have two books on the stocks at present, and I do not know which my publishers will elect to print first. One is a series of war poems called *Phantasms of War,* and the other is a collection of short lyrics which I have been writing at odd moments for the last four years, and which have been printed in magazines and newspapers, but, owing to the scheme of my last two books, have not yet seen the light of day in book form."

Phantasms of War, a proposed expansion of the "War Pictures" section of *Men, Women and Ghosts,* was considered too stagnant a collection for publication and as a result never emerged. The second volume, *Pictures of the Floating World,* appeared in September 1919. Its title was a translation of the Japanese word *ukiyo-e,* a term commonly associated with a form of eighteenth-century Japanese painting that delighted in capturing the passing frivolities, the small pleasures of life. The book consisted of 174 short, free-verse lyrics compiled from some thirty journals and magazines and Amy's three Imagist anthologies. It was her first collection of short poems since *Sword Blades and Poppy Seed,* published a lustrum earlier.

The opening section is a series of fifty-nine "Lacquer Prints," renditions of the Japanese hokku, a fixed lyric form consisting of three short, unrhymed lines of five, seven, and five syllables that are typically epigrammatic or suggestive. By juxtaposing two or three details that coalesce in the reader's mind to form a clear, whole picture, the hokku attempts to rouse the reader's emotion and thereby stimulate spiritual insight. The strict rules governing this poetry are difficult to follow in translation, particularly since Japanese is an unstressed language. The poetic effect of the hokku was imitated by the Imagists; but only a few of them, notably Fletcher and Amy Lowell, ever imitated the actual form. What appealed most to Fletcher and Amy Lowell about hokku was that it was the smallest possible form of poetry—two visual images set side by side, and a flash in the mind interrelated them. Hokku was the tiniest perfect nut form to sharpen one's senses on and practice poetic thoughts with.

The mechanics of the hokku forced Amy to preserve the conciseness of Imagism which her longer poems often lacked. Although she captured the rock-hard and crystal-clear quality of Japanese verse, she lost a good deal of its elliptic impressionism. Miss Lowell's aim, in the majority of her hokku renditions, was simply to record descriptive detail:

CIRCUMSTANCE

Upon the maple leaves
The dew shines red,
But on the lotus blossom
It has the pale transparence of tears.

The choicest selections suggest more than they state and encourage the reader to read between the lines:

OUTSIDE A GATE

On the floor of the empty palanquin
The plum-petals constantly increase.

The poem's plum-petals, biographer S. Foster Damon tells us, suggest that it is spring; the palanquin is the equipage (horse-drawn carriage) of a nobleman; its place near the gate reveals that he is visiting someone; and the accumulation of petals indicates that his visit is a long one. En masse, these details suggest that the nobleman can only be visiting one person: his beloved.

The seven "Chinoiseries" that follow "Lacquer Prints" are longer, less illusory and evanescent; they depend on fewer concentrated images and contain plot as opposed to mere description. Consequently, they are less captivating than the hokku versions. The remainder of the book, the bulk of the volume, departs radically from the Oriental theme suggested by its title. Instead it takes its inspiration from the volume's opening epigraph, a lengthy quotation from Whitman's poem "With Antecedents," which begins: "With antecedents, / With my fathers and mothers and the accumulation of past ages, / With all which, had it not been, I would not now be here, as I am." We are apparently meant to infer from this that Whitman was Amy's antecedent, an appraisal further borne out by the section's Whitmanesque title, "Planes of Personality," itself divided into six subheadings: "Two Speak Together"; "Eyes, and Ears, and Walking"; "As Toward One's Self"; "Plummets to Circumstance"; "As Toward War"; and "As Toward Immortality."

The first plane, "Two Speak Together," is, as its title suggests, partially autobiographical. We may safely assume that the "two" in question in these fifty or so poems are Amy Lowell and Ada Dwyer. The poems themselves are rhapsodies, love songs, sensuous dream-visions in which Amy, the lover of beauty, frankly and provocatively apostrophizes her companion. The section begins with the familiar "Vernal Equinox." Here, the scent of hyacinths stirs the poet's senses; she is "uneasy with the thrusting of green shoots," aware for the first time of her budding emotions. She laments her "lover's" absence: "Why are you not here to overpower me / with your tense and urgent love?" The two women are brought together in another poem, "Madonna of the Evening Flowers," and remain united through "The Garden by Moonlight." The clear bells of "Venus Transiens" are also heard in the present section: "For me, / you stand poised / In the blue and buoyant air, / Cinctured by bright winds, / Treading the sunlight. / And waves which precede you / Ripple and stir / The sands at my feet. . . ."

At least one poem of the fifty—"A Decade"—is overtly and frankly erotic:

When you came, you were like red wine and honey,
And the taste of you burnt my mouth with its sweetness.
Now you are like morning bread,
Smooth and pleasant.
I hardly taste you at all for I know your savour,
But I am completely nourished.

This celebration of woman-love is by far the most sexually explicit of
Amy's poems, though it should probably be read as an intense vagary,
an externalized fulfillment of internalized passion, a pouring out of
heart to the only person in the world the poet could trust. Graphic as
it appears, there is an air of amorous innocence about it. It is, one might
almost venture, *too* graphic to be taken at face value. Taken literally,
it becomes merely a description of lust. Placed within the suggestive
context of Amy's later sonnets to Duse, it retains a Sapphic splendor that
can be interpreted on several planes.

The second of the "Planes of Personality" consists of poems that are
chiefly sensorial and which take up Amy's old but memorable infatuation with Mother Nature. Here we find poems with titles such as "The
Back Bay Fens," "Winter's Turning," and "Trees." It is instructive to
compare Amy's version of "Trees" with Joyce Kilmer's Rotarian period
piece of the same title. Kilmer's "I think that I shall never see / A poem
lovely as a tree" sounds barren and banal beside the fine dandical glitter
of Amy's poem. Kilmer's ditty became a staple of schoolteachers and
Midwestern clubwomen; it symbolized (or was supposed to symbolize)
"the sentimentality and weakmindedness that characterizes middle-
class muddle." It was about poetry, not trees; it talked of God and while
in parts spare, served predominantly as a religious homily. Amy's
"Trees" was not punch-drunk with emotion; it was about trees and the
mystery of a perceiving mind that cannot enter wholly into nature and
yet yearns to:

The branches of the trees lie in layers
Above and behind each other,
And the sun strikes on the outstanding leaves
And turns them white,
And they dance like a spatter of pebbles
Against a green wall . . .

The third plane contains a group of poems reflective of the psychological makeup of the poet and her metaphysical relationship to the world.

The most notable of these is the poem "In a Time of Dearth," which describes, symbolically, a period in which the poet is unable to create. In many respects it is reminiscent of several of T. S. Eliot's early poems, particularly his "Portrait of a Lady." Despite his seeming influence, Amy demonstrated little affection either for Eliot or his work. In *A Critical Fable* (1922), she condemned him for his expatriation and his cold-blooded, methodical intellection, an opinion she shared with Williams, who was convinced that Eliot's *The Waste Land* had set American poetry back some fifty years. In a 1922 letter to *Dial* editor Gilbert Seldes, in whose journal Eliot's groundbreaking poem first appeared, Amy expressed similar sentiments concerning the same poem:

> I have read *The Waste Land* with very great interest. It seems to me that Mr. Eliot is following what Ezra Pound calls the "Sordello form." In spite of interesting passages, I am afraid the poem leaves me rather cool . . . I do not think that Eliot was intended by nature for a poet, and, try as he will, I cannot find his philosophies in verse turn into poems, however I look at them. . . . It is as if he laid a fire with infinite care, but omitted to apply a match to it.

Williams despised the literariness of *The Waste Land,* charging that Eliot had "given the poem back to the academics." In his *Autobiography* he remarked that *The Waste Land* "wiped out our world as if an atom bomb had been dropped upon it. . . . Eliot returned us to the classroom just at the moment when I felt that we were on the point of an escape to matters much closer to the essence of a new art form itself —rooted in the locality which should give it fruit." Amy, although conscious of Eliot's skill, criticized him on the grounds that he seemed, on the surface at least, to possess an unpoetic soul. Most probably she was bitter about a stabbing review Eliot had written for *The Egoist* of her *Tendencies in Modern American Poetry* and held against him his close association with her arch nemesis, Ezra Pound.

Of the remaining poems in "Planes of Personality," only two demand attention. "Appuldurcombe Park" is a tearful ballad about a woman denied physical love by the invalidism of her husband and her subsequent affair with a cousin, later killed at war. The poem's refrain, "I am a woman, sick for passion," struck some readers as Miss Lowell's true confession, a painful, self-analytic revelation based on actual want. The other, "On a Certain Critic," the volume's final poem, is an informal, talky salute to the carefree spirit of the Romantic poets, concentrating on Keats and his passion for the moon; as it progresses, the sequence gradually takes up the question of the critical reception accorded Keats following his early demise. If nothing else, the poem demonstrates that the figure of Keats was still central to Amy's thoughts:

> Well John Keats,
> I know how you felt when you swung out of the inn
> And started up Box Hill after the moon.
> Lord! How she twinkled in and out of the box bushes
> Where they arched over the path.
> How she peeked at you and tempted you,
> And how you longed for the "naked waist" of her
> You had put into your second canto.

In holding to her theory of thematically unified volumes, the poet published her longer poems, eleven of them, in 1921, in a collection called *Legends.* The term applied loosely; the volume was constructed around a group of popular folktales and fables, from which Amy created her own legends, abridging, expanding, collating various drafts and fragments. She drew generously from a wide spectrum for her mythopoeic tales, hoping thereby to create a single interwoven legend that would link the various provenances of her poems: New England, England, Central Europe, China, North America, Yucatán, Peru. "Civilization," she noted in her preface, "is the study of man about himself, his powers, limitations, and endurances; it is the slowly acquired knowledge of how he can best exist in company with his fellows on the planet called Earth."

The eleven poems combine narrative, dramatic, and ratiocinative elements in a lyrically ordered, fast-paced tempo, but they fail to attain the open, emotionally volatile surface that gives poetry life. There are passionate lyric centers, as in "Many Swans," a North American Indian myth based on man's pursuit of the sun; but even in this song emotional coloration is limited to a few fleeting passages, which although poignant, do not succeed in igniting the poem as a whole. The same can be said of "Witch Woman," a legend based on the Yucatán. This flowing, upbeat incantation depicts the agony of a man in love with an evil and avaricious woman, a demon moon-worshiper who personifies death itself. The evil power that she possesses eventually corrupts the moon she adores:

"Witch!
Witch!
Cursed black heart,
Cursed gold heart striped with black;
Thighs and breasts I have loved;
Lips virgin to my thought,
Sweeter to me than red figs;
Lying tongue that I have cherished.
Is my heart wicked?
Are my eyes turned against too bright a sun . . ."

Despite certain continuities, the poem fails to achieve a sense of whole-ness or unification of vision.

The same year another volume misted into print, *Fir-Flower Tablets*, a collection of translations of ancient Chinese verse. The essential diffi-culty here was that Amy read no Chinese and was therefore dependent on the English versions provided her by Florence Wheelock Ayscough, a Sinologist born and raised in China, whose background was Canadian-American. Unable to read the verse in its original, Amy still made grand and sweeping claims for the manuscript: "The great poets of the T'ang Dynasty are without doubt among the finest poets that the world has ever seen."

Once again her motivating force was Ezra Pound. In 1913 Pound crossed paths with an American woman, Mary Fenollosa, whose hus-band Ernest, a disciple of Emerson's, had studied Japanese and Chinese verse and drama in Tokyo. Mrs. Fenollosa turned over to Pound sixteen notebooks, an unedited compilation of her husband's translations of and notes on Chinese poetry and Japanese Noh dramas, and an essay by him on "The Chinese Written Character as a Medium for Poetry."

The Noh dramas were especially exhilarating for Pound because, in his words, "The plays, or eclogues, were made only for the few; for the nobles; for those trained to catch the allusion." Yeats called these spe-cialized dance-dramas with their masked choruses and highly stylized action "an aristocratic form." Fenollosa's Chinese verse translations were exciting in their own way. They reaffirmed for Pound what he already knew but had never considered: the Chinese written character, the ideogram, was actually a picture of a word, hence its visual repre-sentation. The character for "the sun" looked like the sun, a "horse" like a horse. Chinese writing consisted of visual components that were linked and that acted upon one another to form the picture of an idea.

The underlying theory was not far removed from Pound's original conceptualization of Imagism. By uniting or juxtaposing images (or ideograms), a totally new image (or word picture) emerged. It was possible to consolidate disparate images, to form a collage or series of images and consequently a new term of expression, one in which the reader became as much involved as the writer, for he had to help develop the poem's connections; he had to help make the poem cohere.

From this emerged not only Pound's "ideogrammic" (or ideogrammatic) method, a game plan for *The Cantos,* but also *Cathay* (1915), a delicate redaction of seventeen of Fenollosa's transcriptions of Chinese verse, the brunt of them by Rihaku (Li T'ai Po). Amy was determined, she explained, to "knock a hole" in Pound's *Cathay.* She proposed to stun the readers of Harriet Monroe's *Poetry* with renditions of eleven Chinese poems, which would surely set Ezra Pound straight and ward off any of his constituents by demonstrating "for the first time how Chinese poetry really worked."

Miss Monroe was only modestly titillated by the theory of Chinese translation; she found Amy's versions of questionable value. Amy, writes Hugh Kenner in *A Homemade World: The American Modernist Writers* (1975), "took a high hand": " 'It is always well to take a high hand with Harriet,' " Lowell advised a correspondent. She wrote to Harriet that she had conducted an extensive study of the cadence of Chinese verse: "No such study has been made by any other of the *vers libristes* writing in English. Even Ezra has felt and announced his convictions, rather than tabulated, measured and proved." Tabulation, measurement, proof: such titular endorsements constituted insurmountable evidence. Amy's translations appeared in the February 1919 issue of *Poetry,* accompanied by an introduction by Miss Ayscough. The eleven poems reappeared in *Fir-Flower Tablets* together with one hundred additional Lowell-Ayscough transliterations and a sheaf of detailed notes compiled by Amy; the volume included an expanded version of the Ayscough *Poetry* introduction.

Pound read Chinese not much better than Amy, but the freshness, the tang of his imagery and language, the suppleness of his line in *Cathay,* far outclassed the thick-wristed, iron-lung efforts of the two ladies. As in "The Seafarer" and *Homage to Sextus Propertius,* the Pound of *Cathay* sported the mask of the poem's narrator to masterful effect; he could speak in a voice perfectly detached from his own and yet adopt a tone that seemed natural, intimate, conversational. We need only compare his rendition of Li Po's "Separation on the River Kiang" with a small segment of Miss Lowell's translation of "The Terraced Road of the Two-Edged Sword Mountain" by the same author. First Pound:

> Ko-jin goes west from Kō-kaku-ro,
> The smoke-flowers are blurred over the river.
> His lone sail blots the far sky.
> And now I see only the river,
> The long Kiang, reaching heaven.

Then Amy:

> I bid good-bye to my devoted friend—
> Oh-h-h-h-h—now he leaves me.
> When will he come again? Oh-h-h-h-h
> —When will he return to me?

Leave-taking is the subject at the heart of both poems, yet the difference in texture between them speaks for itself. As might be expected, the Ayscough-Lowell anthology was widely attacked by Sinologists, many of whom found it wanting both in tone and accuracy of diction. Arthur Waley, the translator, wrote: "Miss Lowell succeeds best in the reflective and narrative poems. Her renderings of Tu Fu's 'House Unroofed by the Gale' is splendid. In the purely lyrical poems she fails." Since more than half the book consisted of Li Po's predominantly lyrical material, Waley's approval was hardly copious. Amy found a reputable defender in the person of Kenneth Rexroth, who termed it her best overall volume; yet Rexroth's view was clearly in the minority. Hugh Kenner, as strident an Amy Lowell detractor as he is a Pound booster, put it thus: ". . . literature today irrefutably contains Ezra Pound, whereas not even American literature any longer contains Amy Lowell. Pound had genius, Amy had mild talents. . . . Pound had better not be one's mentor, beyond appeal, on questions of scholarly fact. But he believed with purity of heart, in what he was doing; whereas Miss Lowell settled for getting by, with whatever show of expertise would suffice to placate the natives."

Erudite as Kenner tends to sound here, he has completely misjudged Amy. Whatever else she may have been, she was no phony. She believed with purity of soul and vision in what she was doing; she believed with her whole, naive, unknowing, and innocent being in the world of art and in the maxim that insists an artist is justified in subordinating all other values to art. She was by no means a literary giant of Ezra Pound's caliber; she wrote far too much trash. But she was deadly earnest in her endeavor to write. And that, it should even be pointed out, was very probably the core of her problem.

ᵉ⁀ᔐ 21 ᔐ⁀ᵉ

A KEATS SONATA

In the family circle Amy was considered a temperamental, sometimes generous, occasionally extravagant clubwoman, a throwback to the romantically ostentatious social figures that inhabited Fleet Street during the terminal days of the previous century. Although her own family considered her something less than a symbol of civilized taste and intellectual nourishment, they nevertheless acknowledged her driving ambition, her desperate will to establish herself as the heroine of the American literary establishment. Dr. Alice Lowell, of the Cabot-Jackson branch, an internist and retired director of a large New England hospital, recently recalled Amy's commanding presence at the annual Marlborough Street Christmas-day dinner thrown by "Cousin Lawrence"—Abbott Lawrence Lowell:

> They were boiled-shirt affairs, and huge. After a magnificent dinner for Mrs. Lowell's side of the family, the Coolidge, Putnam, and Bundy branches would join the party and we'd all go into the ballroom. There'd be greetings and conversations, and then pretty soon there'd be a hush. The doors would open and in would come Amy, looking perfectly enormous in a vast gold dress cut tent-style. Everybody would scurry to find her a comfortable chair. But Cousin Lawrence who had the wit—he was the life of every Christmas dinner—would pull out one of the large gold ballroom chairs, knowing it was the only chair she could fit onto. Then she'd put her hand into her pocket, take out a leather case, light up one of her fat cigars and chain-smoke for the rest of the party. The grown-ups would "tut-tut," and we children would be aghast. It's one of my clearest memories.

Social life went on in Boston, as in the rest of the world, without any perceptible patterns of change until the end of World War I. At that juncture the whole framework of social existence in America began slowly to collapse. The lives of the supernally rich and powerful, while subject to the alterations imposed by a modern age, changed less overtly than most. Although the members of this class were less concerned with the usual material comforts and the traditional accolades of bountiful wealth, they remained profoundly conscious of their designated place in the social firmament. To the inhibited cousins of the Lowell family, those that preferred standard rhyme schemes and conservative lifestyles to the outré and extremist measures represented by Amy, she must have looked ridiculously overblown. She was on the surface of things a Lowell, a New Englander, and a grand, sometimes snooty, tough-as-nails middle-aged lady. Inwardly she was a molten mass, a spirited, witty, often embittered soldier of fortune, determined to prove the ancient saw wrong that insisted no woman could ever be a major author, especially in an era when no American magazine would publish anything that might offend (as one truthful editor worded it) "a non-existent clergyman in the Mississippi valley."

She was unpredictable in numerous ways, even with respect to her own family. Guy Lowell, an architect and consequently something of a Brahmin outcast in his own right, was one of the few family relations ever to admit publicly to having read her books. Following the publication of *Pictures of the Floating World,* he composed a note of appreciation, singling out "A Bather" (based on a painting by Andreas Dorn) as a poem of rare beauty. Amy's congenial response (August 18, 1917) linked Guy's fate with her own: "Thank you very much for your nice note from Blackstone, Arizona. To think you liked 'The Bather' is a surprise and satisfaction to me. When any of my relations really like my work (brothers and sisters excepted) it is a great satisfaction, for as you say those of us Lowells who are pagans are a little bit out of the brood."

Yet she was less cordial in the case of Mrs. Joseph Lowell, the poetry-writing wife of a distant cousin living in Havana, who made the mistake of sending her a selection of recent poems and a request soliciting a literary critique. Miss Lowell's notice (January 4, 1923) came back like a shot:

> ... I am terribly sorry to be of so little use, but the truth is I have no time to criticize the work of young poets and I have had to make a rule of

refusing those that ask me, as a great many do. I am sure you will understand that it is quite impossible for a busy woman such as I am to devote
time to other people's work, for if I did, there would be little time left
for my own.

Amy wore her insecurities on her sleeve. Her minatory defensiveness
was another manifestation of the half-magnificent, half-ludicrous way
she handled the opposition. Above all she was defensive about being a
Lowell, teetering precariously between the world of high society as
exemplified by Condé Nast's *Vanity Fair* and the world of avant-garde
little magazines typified by such periodicals as the *North American
Review* and Harold Loeb's short-lived, Rome-based *Broom,* both of
which frequently published her work. In actual fact Amy was deeply
rooted to the conventions and social code of her heritage, a code of
behavior that all Lowells were expected to obey and which entailed
going to the right schools, mixing with the right people, and making
one's mark in the world. Becoming a practicing poet was hardly what
one could call conforming to expectations, but if one *had* to become a
poet—and if one *had* to smoke cigars—there were ways and then there
were ways. As Amy aged she found herself gradually adopting most of
the conservative sociopolitical values that ruled the core of the clan.
Horace Gregory, who knew her briefly, attests that neither sentiment
nor logic could sway her in favor of humanitarian causes, at least not
when she was unwilling to let herself be swayed. She was exceedingly
"tough-minded," aware that her name might be used at any time to
advance certain causes in which she did not believe, as was certainly the
case in connection with the women's rights movement. But as conservative as she became in political affairs, she was just the opposite in terms
of her career. While the majority of America's first families behaved like
an aristocracy—forming hundreds of industrial consortiums, devastating thousands of square miles of land, milking millions of impoverished
laborers—Amy backed a poetry movement that at no time in its controversial history boasted more than a few dozen devoted followers. The
making of literature in a world of spreading corruption and technologi-
cal sheen estranged Miss Lowell from her fellow Brahmins as surely as
if she had been imprisoned for life or placed permanently in quaran-
tine.

But in time even her literary affiliations swung sharply to the right.
She severed her ties with the more experimental literary periodicals in

favor of the splashier, slicker pulps, while befriending editors of the mark of John Farrar, Henry Seidel Canby, Robert Bridges, and others in a position to help foster her ambitions. During her mature years, writes Gregory, she revolved mainly in the New York–Boston literary circuit, partaking of its fashions, its splendor, its interests, its opinions, even its quarrels. She was privy to the high and low gossip that circulated freely at dinner parties in the Fifth Avenue mansions of a multitude of New York's upper crust; she attended their social gatherings and became nearly as well known in New York society—among the Belmonts, the Vanderbilts, the Astors, the Huntingtons, the Whitneys, the Fricks, and the Hydes—as she was in Boston society. The fashionable topics of the day included sexual freedom, the woman's vote, Prohibition, left-wing politics, Freud, Marx, the League of Nations. There was a revival of interest in the Shelley and Keats legends, which had somehow become embodied in contemporary America in the work and lives of Elinor Wylie and Edna St. Vincent Millay. It was the cult age, the age of vegetarianism, atheism, nudity, pacifism, and internationalism. Gibson Girls were "in." Goethe was "out." And the Paris-based "lost generation," led by Hemingway and Fitzgerald, was about to find itself.

Through all of this, Amy Lowell remained inimitably, redundantly Amy. Her everyday costume during this period was a blue serge suit, three-quarter-length jacket, stiff net collar, and pince-nez; she looked like an intellectual field marshal, a very imposing field marshal at that. To one set of eyes she looked like Nero in drag. A Boston newspaper reporter captioned her photograph "Amy Lowell from left to right."

The field marshal pose was enhanced by an album of anecdotes. Two in particular stand out. The first involves a talk Amy gave at a Literary Roundtable in Providence, extolling the virtues of her latest published work and reading aloud from the works of fellow poets. After she finished, a man stood up to speak who placed high on the list of Most Tedious Types. In a monotone he droned on and on about a book he had written on refinishing and restoring French antiques. Amy's solution? She simply closed her eyes and dozed off, right there on the dais. Asked to explain her reaction, she later declared, most sensibly, "I'm just too impatient to allow myself to be bored."

The second anecdote is even more typical. While motoring in the countryside near Boston one day, Amy's car broke down. She managed to pull into the nearest garage, where she ordered the Pierce Arrow repaired. When the mechanic, a burly, hardworking local, presented her with the bill, she told him to charge it and started to leave. He objected. After all, he didn't know her and didn't know if her credit was any good. She repeated her formidable surname, but he, with the rock-like Yankee stubbornness of a character out of *The Biglow Papers*, refused to yield. "My brother is president of Harvard," she huffed, suggesting that the mechanic call Harvard to verify her story. Whereupon, she left the garage and walked across the road to a sturdy stone fence. The mechanic called the university, asked to speak to the president, and explained skeptically that "some big, fat dame whose engine broke down wants to charge her bill—claims she's your sister." Abbott Lawrence Lowell, without blinking, asked the mechanic what "the big, fat dame" was doing as they spoke. Well, rejoined the mechanic, "she's across the road sittin' on a stone wall, smokin' a cigar." "In that case," intoned President Lowell, "you may charge the bill."

One of Amy Lowell's lighter poetry projects was her pamphlet, *A Critical Fable*, published in 1922 and modeled after "Cousin James's" *A Fable for Critics*. The turn to humorous verse at this stage made sense. The poet could rationalize the mixed reviews accorded *Fir-Flower Tablets* by telling herself that she had been working outside her true element; she recognized the need for change, the necessity of veering away from confected Confucian landscapes to the familiar topography of Boston and the literary chitchat of the hour. Furthermore, she was a great fan of the kind of lighthearted, teasing parodies Louis Untermeyer often concocted for his syndicated newspaper column.

Untermeyer was partially on her mind when she commenced her latest project, but James Russell Lowell's *Fable for Critics* loomed even brighter on the horizon. She had chosen a worthy model. In its genre his *Fable* was a minor masterpiece, full of imperfections but as artful and shrewd a summation of American literary history up to the middle of the nineteenth century as anyone could hope to find. Previously Amy had shown indifference and contempt for her predecessor's work. This indifference reached its height in 1919, when she failed to attend the ceremony held at Harvard on the occasion of his centenary. By way of explanation she wrote to Elizabeth Cutting, managing editor of the *North American Review:* "With a dreadful modernity I decided that the living were more important than the dead."

Now, with the composition of *A Critical Fable*, Amy again became aware of her ancestor. In varying meter and jestful rhyme, she surveyed the efforts of her poetic contemporaries as James Russell Lowell had surveyed his, not with the same impact of wit and learning, but with a fair measure of energy and boldness. Starting with the six poets of her *Tendencies in Modern American Poetry* (Robinson, Frost, Sandburg, Masters, H. D., and Fletcher), she added to her parody the following: Vachel Lindsay, Conrad Aiken, Grace Hazard Conkling, Hilda Conkling, Alfred Kreymborg, Louis and Jean Untermeyer, Pound, Eliot, William Rose Benét, Maxwell Bodenheim, Edna St. Vincent Millay, and Wallace Stevens. In keeping with James Russell Lowell's *Fable,* she included herself in the poem and published it anonymously.

Although she denied her own part in it and went so far as to accuse others of having perpetrated the hoax, it was obvious to many that she was its architect. At a Boston cocktail party, Conrad Aiken accused her of the poem's authorship. When she denied her role in the project, Aiken told her: "Well, since you didn't write it, I can say what I really think of it. I think it's damn rotten." A year after its publication Amy included the *Fable* in listing her works for the British *Who's Who,* thereby closing the book on the case.

Although an amusing romp, Amy's parody is not as clever as it might have been. If anything, it proves the value of James Russell Lowell's *Fable,* showing his skill as well as the innate difficulty of the form. Amy's version, despite the ease with which some of it is written, suffers from a convoluted format. The shape it assumes—a dialogue between a young bon vivant about Cambridge and an elderly gentleman who turns out to be James Russell Lowell—does not take the reader far. The most commendable aspect of the poem is its author's recognition of Stevens's talent, a discovery she had actually made earlier, and her incisive remarks on the hidden "madness" of the characters in Frost's *North of Boston.* She has also, in her account, given Poe, Whitman, and Emily Dickinson their proper due as the leading American poets of the nineteenth century. But there are plenty of weaknesses, such as the perfunctory way Pound and Eliot are dismissed:

> Where Pound played the fool, Eliot acted the wiseacre;
> Eliot works in his garden, Pound stultifies his acre.
> Eliot's always engaged digging fruit out of dust;
> Pound was born in an orchard, but his trees have the rust.
> Eliot's mind is perpetually fixed and alert;
> Pound goes off anywhere, anyhow, like a squirt.

Pound believes he's a thinker, but he's far too romantic;
Eliot's sure he's a poet when he's only pedantic.
But Eliot has raised pedantry to a pitch,
While Pound has upset romance into a ditch.
Eliot fears to abandon an old masquerade;
Pound's one perfect happiness is to parade. . . .

Miss Lowell's self-portrait seems keener than her multiple portraits of others, demonstrating that she possessed a certain awareness of her public image; the *Fable* cites the prevailing attitude harbored by her sharpest critics:

Conceive, if you can, an electrical storm
Of a swiftness and fury surpassing the norm;
Conceive that this cyclone has caught up the rainbow
And dashed dizzily on with it streaming in tow.
Imagine a sky all split open and scissored
By lightnings, and then you can picture this blizzard.
That is, if you'll also image the clashes
Of tropical thunder, the incessant crashes
Which shiver the hearing and leave it in ashes.
Remember, meanwhile, that the sky is prismatic
And outrageous with colour. The effect is erratic
And jarring to some, but to others ecstatic.

A Critical Fable made Amy a popular figure on the college literary circuit. Columbia University elected her a member of the Phi Beta Kappa Society, while Baylor University, in Waco, Texas, awarded her an honorary doctorate on the occasion of its Diamond (75th) Anniversary. A three-day train ride and a scorching Texas heat wave did not deter the poet from attending the ceremony. In May 1918 the *Harvard Advocate* invited her to read her latest poems at an *Advocate* smoker. Recapitulating the event, she wrote, "I was, as usual, smuggled into an upper chamber and kept quiet with cigars while they heckled me in true undergraduate fashion." Malcolm Cowley, present on the evening of the reading, recalled that Amy, encircled by smoke, "crushed the hecklers as if with bolts from a fat thundercloud." Another reading, presented at Princeton, attracted a standing-room only audience that braved a two-foot snowstorm to hear the poet; as two hefty undergraduates helped carry her to a waiting limousine following the performance, she turned to one and trilled: "Don't drop me, or we'll never get me up."

Amy was fond of the college-aged young. Her appearances before audiences comprised principally of college students enabled her to promulgate, to boom out her views with a minimum of effort. Surveying the literary scene in America she concluded, to begin with, that Louis Untermeyer "as a critic, knows the situation perfectly, but has distinct prejudices in favor of certain types of work. . . . He can never quite escape from his preoccupation with social economics; still . . . he is growing all the time." Conrad Aiken "suffers from a perpetual chip on his shoulder . . . and measures every poet by his own particular theories . . . but it is a biased and therefore unreliable guide." The "old guard" —Robinson, Frost, Masters, Lindsay, and Sandburg—still dominated. What set these poets apart was their distinctive American voice, a collective voice that embodied the farm, the frontier, the big-city street corner, the driving patter of vaudeville, the open-endedness of jazz, the "Homeric" quality of a Sunday evangelist, the steady beat of a brass band, the staccato rhythm of a freight train heading west. When one considered this school, one immediately envisioned Carl Sandburg singing "Go to it, O jazzmen!" or thought of Sandburg's short, imagistic poem on fog or his golden hymn to Chicago: "Here is a tall bold slugger set vivid against the little cities." Or perhaps one imagined Robert Frost penning lyrical, dramatic, and reflective stanzas on running brooks, birch trees, or the hoarfrost of a late autumn New England day. And then there was Vachel Lindsay, the authentic primitive, vocalizing on Abraham Lincoln and on the founding of Springfield, Illinois, while ruminating on the future of the American factory system: "Factory windows are always broken / Somebody's always throwing bricks / Somebody's always heaving cinders / Playing ugly Yahoo tricks."

So much for trend setters. A second rank of poets existed, consisting of Untermeyer, Aiken, Fletcher, H. D., Sara Teasdale, Eunice Tietjens, followed closely by the sisters Grace Hazard Conkling and Hilda Conkling. One might logically inquire of the whereabouts in this two-ring circus of such major figures as Pound, Eliot, Williams, Cummings, Marianne Moore, and Wallace Stevens, none of whom seem to merit inclusion in Amy's pantheon. Indeed, it would be enlightening to hear her defend her individual rankings in the face of recent twentieth-century literary developments. At any rate, she was quick to include herself within the first circle of stars, a poet deserving of recognition on the basis of the verbal extremity of her emotions.

It somehow never occurred to Amy that her literary assessments were the result of personal investments and unobscured prejudices. Verities aside, if one had any intention of being taken seriously after the year 1920, one had better not side with Vachel Lindsay and Edgar Lee Masters as against Eliot, Pound, and Williams in matters of poetic licensure. Lindsay, Masters, et al. were living proof that Pound's notions were straight as the gate; abandoning Imagism/Amygism for Wyndham Lewis and Vorticism had been the right thing to do. Pound knew—Amy didn't—that no literary rebellion can live very long without turning upon itself, without sinking into a bog of mere compliance and/or succumbing to a sort of collective narcissism. Masters's idea of modernism was no more than a lot of stomping around on stage. Sandburg, who could at least write prose, wrote poetry as though presaging Andy Warhol writing advertising jingles. Sandburg's idea of poetry was the etched scene or situation followed by a line or two of grave irony capped by an amplified moral. For those who didn't absorb his meaning first time around, there was always the second stanza. Nothing subliminal in that fresco!

"It was hardly their fault," Irving Howe has said, tallying up the losses: "No fate is harder for a writer than to come late, after a great outburst of innovation, at the point where influence has hardened into subjection." Chronologically, however, they came first. Yet by the time they discovered such a thing as a movement, experimentation had sunk into formula, gestures of defiance into mundane sign language. A good deal of the poetry compounded by Amy's generation of moderns, those who picked it up from Pound, Eliot, Williams, and late Yeats, seems as conventional today as cotton candy. Much of it may have been intelligent, skillful, even wry; but none of it was very interesting.

Never at a loss for words, Amy had stitched together a thesaurus of explanations about the younger poets of her day, her real competition. Almost without exception, according to Amy, they aimed at a relatively minor utterance, espousing a limited vision that resulted in a world view that was too facile, too mundane. Maxwell Bodenheim, for example, was "an intellectual pure and simple with a touch of extraordinary irony" but without the sustaining force that calls new powers into being. William Rose Benét wrote "magazine" poetry that was nevertheless appealing; Stephen Benét's verse was highly imitative. Hervey

Allen, Malcolm Cowley, S. Foster Damon, and John Brooks Wheelwright wrote moving if not always thought-provoking poems.

Inevitably, whenever Amy lectured, the names Elinor Wylie and Edna St. Vincent Millay cropped up. More than any other female poets of their generation, Wylie and Millay captured the hearts and imaginations of the educated young. Millay, the radical darling of New York Bohemia, had risen to fame on the strength of her poem "Renascence," which she composed when only nineteen. An effusion of spiritual and mystical musings, it describes a moment in which the poet finds herself buried and then brought back to life. Before death the poet feels herself crushed beneath the weight of woe and sorrow; when she is reborn, she has only praise and acclaim for God, life, the universe. Amy found Millay "enchantingly able" but denounced her for "attempting nothing beyond the personal, which is the hallmark of a minor poet." Millay, bereft of any discernible philosophy, tended to be repetitious and therefore flat. She maintained her popularity by chronicling her love affairs, of which there were many, and by composing lines that appealed to the new sense of female expression and liberation.

As opposed to the excessively vehement, often overbaked, baroque lyrics of Millay, Elinor Wylie produced work that was equally sensuous though far more reserved and disciplined. Wylie, a novelist and literary editor at *Vanity Fair* as well as a poet, sought to master a "small, clean, polished technique" in her verse; she wanted to produce "brilliant and compact" stanzas as though they were "enamelled snuffboxes." Influenced by Shelley, Elizabeth Barrett Browning, Blake, and Keats, her phrasing alternated between late Georgian and early modernist. It was not until her later poetry, long after abandoning the notion of "enamelled snuffboxes," that she came into her own, partially the result of the guidance of her third husband, the poet and magazine editor William Rose Benét. In "The Eagle and the Mole," which became one of Amy's favorites, this daughter of Washington and Philadelphia society voiced contempt for the "polluted and reeking herd" and praised the heroic "eagle of the rock." Miss Lowell found Wylie's verse erratic and at times artificial, but always cultivated and often challenging. Everything considered, she preferred it to the work of Millay.

Miss Wylie's lifestyle, her marriages and divorces in the first three decades of the century, when divorce was still frowned upon, made her the talk of two continents. To consummate her second marriage she abandoned her family and ran off with a married man who had abandoned his. These tidbits seem not particularly scandalous now, when divorces and extramarital affairs are commonplace, but at the time the reactions of society to this socialite were quite remarkable. She was considered a very spoiled, a very willful, a very difficult and possessive woman, uncaring of consequences, giving vent to her most primitive emotions in an era when discretion and decorum were the standard modes of behavior. Women were horrified by her, men enthralled. Even Amy, who shared some of Wylie's personality traits and was herself a rebel against social tradition, was driven to admonish her on the occasion of her third marriage: "If you marry again, I shall cut you dead —and I warn you all Society will do the same. You will be nobody." With Wylie's untimely death in 1928 at the age of 41, her reputation also died.

A major factor in Amy Lowell's decision to take on her next, her most ambitious project—the long-awaited Keats biography—was her February 1921 delivery of an address at Yale University, honoring Keats on the hundredth anniversary of his death. "I had something very closely approaching an ovation," she advised S. Foster Damon. To Ferris Greenslet she boasted: "It would have amused you if you could have seen the boys at Yale running up to the platform with books for me to sign." Various aspects of the Keats legend appealed to her, dating back to her early reading of Leigh Hunt's study. She had tried to forget, but could not, her early sonnet "To John Keats," with its lamentable opening line: "Great master! Boyish, sympathetic man!" A second sonnet for Keats, "The Poet," was just as lame: "Though faint with weariness he must possess / Some fragment of the sunset's majesty / He spurns life's human friendships to profess / Life's loneliness of dreaming ecstacy."

Her entire writing career had been geared toward the laborious undertaking of a full-length biography. In acquiring first editions, correspondence, manuscripts, and memorabilia, she had concentrated to the exclusion of almost everything on Keats, amassing the largest collection of Keatsiana in private hands, including the entire Rowfant Library Keats collection, purchased in 1905 at great cost, and smaller holdings such as Keats's holograph manuscript of *The Eve of Saint Agnes.* The prize of her collection was her copy of the rare first edition of *Lamia,* inscribed "F. B. from J. K.," Keats's presentation copy to Fanny Brawne. Miss Lowell had been a leading contributor to a committee formed in Hampstead, England, to raise funds for the purchase of Wentworth

Place, the house where Keats wrote his "Ode to a Nightingale." The figure of Keats never lost its glamor for Amy. More upstanding and also more fragile than Shelley, he appealed to her protective instincts. Even at a distance of a hundred years, she felt the need for "some righting of justice," some need to make up for his short and unhappy career. She felt that he had been the hapless victim of indiscriminating rivals and that he had been unnecessarily maligned by critics who never understood him.

The 1,300-page, two-volume biography that she produced was no work of genius, but Miss Lowell made some important discoveries and corrected several lingering misconceptions concerning the poet's life. Her one notable contribution to Keats scholarship was her reevaluation of Keats's relationship with Fanny Brawne, his mistress—previously depicted by biographers as an unfit mate for Keats, incapable by nature of understanding him or of valuing him at his true worth. Amy Lowell became the first biographer to paint Miss Brawne in a favorable, even sympathetic light. Her analysis altered substantially the views of future Keats-Brawne appraisers and provided critics with new evidence for evaluation of his work.

When the manuscript was completed Amy sent it off to Ferris Greenslet, her editor at Houghton Mifflin, who read it and convened with its author to discuss his findings.

She arrived, he reported, nearly two hours late, apologetic and as always completely disarming.

"Well, Ferris, what about it?"

"Amy," he responded, "it's a great book, but you have given the reader the whole process of your research and your thought, not just the results, which are what he wants. I have put faint pencilled brackets about some sentences and paragraphs which would be better out. The more the marble wastes, the more the statue grows."

"Ferris," she countered, "you are a dear good boy, but you don't know a thing about biography, not a *damned* Thing!"

The meeting went on a few minutes more. In the end the publisher was embraced by the biographer, patted on the shoulder and reassured that he was "a good boy," but not a single deletion was made. Amy Lowell would make no concessions where it came to John Keats.

Published on February 10, 1925, the massive hagiography re-created a day-by-day, moment-by-moment account of Keats's ominous comings and goings, his whereabouts and activities, his relationships and writings. The welter of details and reconstruction of daily doings were in one respect breathtaking, in another an ordeal to peruse. But what was most distressing about the project was Amy's pressing need to play custodian to Keats's posthumous reputation. Her desire to protect Keats and restore his tarnished personal image overrode every other consideration in the book.

It can almost be said that Amy plays the role of surrogate parent, endowing Keats with her own aspirations, modeling him after the idealized image of an unborn son. She bestows upon him her own tastes and fancies, a good deal of her limitless energy, her desire for friendly companionship, her moments of loneliness, even her sexual frustrations and fantasies. This two-volume set became the author's "spiritual autobiography," a study that was as much Amy Lowell as it was John Keats.

One critic, Horace Gregory, dubbed Amy Lowell Keats's "maternal patroness," but defended her by pointing out that many of the impulses and traits that she assigned him were not entirely false. Truly, though in ill health a good part of his life, Keats possessed excessive energy, not only in his writings but in his restless wanderings. It is similarly true that he was a social man who enjoyed friendships and the society of congenial and intelligent company, men such as Leigh Hunt and Charles Brown, although he also required solitude as a precondition for his work. The factual details surrounding Keats's love life, particularly his liaison with Fanny Brawne, suggest that the sublimation of emotions stirred by sexual impulses increased his creative energies. He worked harder and with a greater degree of intensity while their relationship was at its height.

Despite its strong points, there is no denying that the book contained instances of serious blunder and misinterpretation. Keats's mother, to cite one example, is described as "a woman of strong passions and appetites, with no particular desire to curb either, but with something redeeming and attractive about her just the same." This comment sounds too much like Amy Lowell describing herself at the beginning of "Appuldercombe Park" as "a woman sick for passion." Of the same order are some of the descriptive passages of Keats as creator:

> I do not suppose that any one not a poet can realize the agony of creating a poem. Every nerve, even every muscle, seems strained to the breaking point. The poem will not be denied, to refuse to write it would

be a greater torture. It tears its way out of the brain, splintering and breaking its passage, and leaves that organ in the state of a jellyfish when the task is done.

This is pure Amy Lowell, histrionic and egotistical. The following passage on Keats as experimentalist is no less rambunctious:

> How hard, how desperately hard, is the way of the experimenter in art! How cruelly do those persons, whose blunt-edged senses cannot keep pace with his alert ones, treat such a man! Keats was, all his life, an experimenter. He knew his English public, but he changed his way not a jot to placate them.

More apropos were Amy's convictions, as registered in behalf of Keats, on the poet's true place in the cosmos. What do poets do? she asked herself. They are not chroniclers, but, rather, they are the dreamers of the race with their authority coming not so much from fidelity to fact, though it is grounded there, as from the quality of their imagination. Poetry, she thought, enriches people, enriches civilization, solidifies culture. It is because of the deep verbal aspiration in us all that poetry appeals. Words are the poet's tool, and depending on how they are used, they can hold the ephemera of our lives together so we can treasure them, and return to them, and pass our reactions on. Poetry is energy: it moves us, it supports us, it sustains us. Poetry addresses itself to the mystery and magic of the world, to runes and spells and riddles and charms, to beatitudes and blessings, to prayers and hexes, to dreams and vagaries. We reach for words and phrases to help unlock the mysteries of the universe. The words of the great poets—poets such as Keats—play upon themselves toward the music of meaning and the memory of the race.

Amy dedicated her magnum opus to Ada Dwyer—"This, and All My Books"—and recalled in a letter to an acquaintance that "James Russell Lowell planned to write a life of Keats and never did so . . . I like to imagine that the task has been deputed to me in his stead." The Keats biography sold commendably—three printings in as many months—but received hostile reviews, especially in the British press. Reviewer upon reviewer accused the author of having penned "a psychological thriller" rather than a critical study or straightforward literary biography. In writing about the English Romantic poet, Miss Lowell had, so to speak, trespassed upon foreign soil. Not only had she invaded British literary turf, she had negated Sidney Colvin's long-established theory of Keats's life which, written in 1887, was still considered the definitive record.

Amy had always suffered extreme anxiety while awaiting the critical reception of her books. Reviews were the bane of her life. They caused her such despair and depression that one must almost wonder why she bothered practicing a profession that left her so open to public censure. During her mature years her rough rhinoceros-tough hide seemed to wither almost visibly; she was battleworn, exhausted, a victim of shell shock. The crowning blow in the case of the Keats book was delivered in a review published in the London *Sunday Times* by Sir Edmund Gosse, one of Colvin's boys. Sir Edmund, as he was known to the press, openly rejected the author's attempt to rehabilitate Fanny Brawne's reputation and summarily swept aside Amy's heterodox thesis regarding Keats's mother. He concluded his lamentation by suggesting that "our ingenuous transatlantic friends are being more and more generally swindled."

Although quick to defend the project, the poet's letters indicate that she was aware of the more controversial aspects of her biography as well as the obsessive nature of her reaction to Keats. "Perhaps it is too much a spiritual confession," she wrote to one literary broker. She denied that the study contained any autobiographical elements, but acknowledged her attempt to consolidate psychology and biography. Of what use was a Keats biography that merely retouched old ground? She was dejected not so much by the reviews themselves, though that too, as by the personal tone adopted by the critics. She felt that she was being persecuted, as she always had been, simply because she was a Lowell, a Boston Brahmin who happened also to be an author and a woman. She attempted to rationalize these fierce attacks by assuring herself that Keats had been victimized by similar currents. But for once she found it exceedingly difficult to master the disappointment that inevitably followed the publication of her works. The dejection and lassitude that swept over her like a cloud refused to drift away. Her days were characterized by a great emptiness, a great loneliness, as though she had lost something that she had never quite possessed.

From beginning to end the Keats biography proved an unhalting jinx. The morning that the advance copies of the book arrived at Sevenels, Amy's sister Katherine fell (or jumped) to her death from a fifth-story suite at the Hotel Vendome in New York. "Katie died like a captain on his quarter deck, serving her beloved Municipal League," Amy wrote to "Bibi" (Carl Engel). This was the second tragedy of the year. On Easter Monday, April 21, 1924, while on an American theater tour, Eleonora Duse suffered a fatal heart attack. Shortly before her death she paid a first and last visit to Sevenels. Amy recorded the occasion in a poem, "To Eleonora Duse, 1923," which contained lines considered too intimate to publish at the time:

> The sight of you is piercing as a cry,
> Your loveliness betrays my eyes to tears, . . .
> I am no hero worshiper,
> Yet for your sake I long to babble prayers
> And overdo myself in services.
> Is this not love?

The same poem presaged Duse's end:

> Dead to the sting of anguish,
> The misery that you ache no more
> Is aching so preponderant and huge
> You walk within it as an atmosphere
> And breathe its bitterness like some gaunt poison
> Easing you into numbness
> Even of its slow insidious advance.

Miss Lowell presaged her own death in her nostalgic "Penumbra," included in "Two Speak Together" in the volume *Pictures of the Floating World*. The poem envisions a time when Amy, deceased, will be succeeded at Sevenels by her friend Ada. "What will it be like for you then?" the poet asks:

> You will see my narrow table
> At which I have written so many hours.
> My dogs will push their noses into your hand,
> And ask—ask—
> Clinging to you with puzzled eyes. . . .

Fate, in the form of the mammoth Keats project, had dealt its creator an unkind blow; Amy's ill health and strenuous labors for several years in preparing the manuscript had sapped her remaining strength. Although she had formed new alliances with writers, among them V.

Sackville-West, John Masefield, Siegfried Sassoon, and Archibald Mac-Leish, she rarely entertained at Sevenels anymore. Both by choice and necessity, contact with the outside world was restricted to the domain of letter writing; her correspondence was enormous but she became too weary to keep up with it, and it too soon lapsed.

Frequent hospitalizations and ongoing medical treatment for the chronic hernia had taken their toll. During her final years, while completing the Keats manuscript, she was forced to rely on the potentially lethal combination of alcohol and morphine to ease the intense postoperative abdominal pain. Toward the end she changed doctors every other week, convinced that somewhere there existed a physician who would save her life. But in her case medicine would only disappoint, providing false hope and no promises. When blood vessels burst in both eyes, Amy found herself totally incapacitated. Somehow she forced herself to complete the Keats opus.

She was a stalwart soul. On April 4, 1925, she attended a gala affair thrown in her honor by the literary "400" of Boston in the grand ballroom of the Hotel Somerset. The sponsors of the affair were John Singer Sargent, Ellery Sedgwick, William James, Mark A. DeWolfe Howe, and Charles Martin Loeffler. John Livingston Howes, dean of Harvard's Graduate School of Arts and Sciences, and chairman of the English Department, was toastmaster; the distinguished speakers included Henry Seidel Canby, Elinor Wylie, Grace Hazard Conkling, Hervey Allen, John Farrar (editor of the *Bookman*), Irita Van Doren (managing editor of *Books*), and Glenn Frank (editor of the *Century*). Frank, speaking out of turn to catch the midnight train for New York, nominated Amy for President of the United States. After the laudations and after supper, while the coffee was being served, Amy opened her cigar case, withdrew a cigar, and proceeded to light up. To tumultuous applause she rose and read "Lilacs" and "A Tulip Garden" in her best style, acquired she noted from a family of orators. It was a glamorous evening, a fitting last hurrah.

During her last days she experienced a final surge of energy. She formulated plans for a summer reading tour of select schools and universities in Great Britain with stopovers at Oxford, Cambridge, Eton, and Edinburgh; she was anxious to make the journey if only to console herself over the desultory press accorded the Keats biography in England. She also had in mind a coast-to-coast lecture tour across the

United States to take place upon her return. What promised to be an active and rewarding year for the poet ended before it began. A week after the Somerset fête, a day before she was to leave for New York to lecture prior to sailing for England, a piercing pain shot through her. Complete rest was ordered, and her lecture and sailing were canceled. On May 2, she wrote Ferris Greenslet what was to be her last letter, enclosing a list of corrections for a proposed new edition of *Keats*. "I have two nurses now," she sighed, "and I am no good at all for anything. The sooner we get through these corrections the better."

An operation was decided upon for the thirteenth of May. On the morning of the twelfth she complained of head pains. Later in the day she suddenly found her right hand numb. Looking in a mirror she saw the right side of her face drop. She had suffered a stroke. For long minutes she lay stretched across her bed, barely able to breathe, unable to move, her hand grasped tightly by Ada Dwyer. Ada had summoned both an ambulance and Amy's personal physician, though neither would arrive in time. Amy began to perspire profusely as Ada swaddled her securely in blankets, like a newborn baby. Amy's pulse had dropped to a faint, irregular flicker; her breathing was shallow, labored. Momentarily her pulse failed, her breathing stopped: she expired with "Pete" (Ada) by her side. There were those in Boston who would later opine, with grim and callous morbidity, that she had been done in by John Keats. To which they would then invariably add that at fifty, stubborn and comfortless, she was still in her literary prime.

She wanted no formal funeral or gathering, and no religious service. At her behest her body was cremated and the ashes strewn inside the family plot at Mount Auburn Cemetery. Her collection of rare books and manuscripts, including the capacious Keats material, went to Harvard. A portrait of the poet as a debutante was placed inside Lowell House by Abbott Lawrence Lowell after its construction. Three volumes of Miss Lowell's verse were published posthumously: *What's O'Clock* (1925), *East Wind* (1926), *Ballads for Sale* (1927). In 1930, *Poetry and Poets*, a selection of Amy's prose writings, appeared. *The Collected Poems*, containing some 650 titles, was published in 1955, a compilation of eleven volumes composed over a twelve-year span.

What's O'Clock, a collection of short lyrics, was awarded the Pulitzer Prize for poetry—ironically, a year after Miss Lowell's death and four years after Edna St. Vincent Millay became the first woman to win the same prize. *What's O'Clock,* whose central theme is the reciprocation and completion of love, was the last volume Amy had prepared for publication; it contains several of her best known and most mature poems: "Lilacs," "Purple Grackles," "Meeting-House Hill," "Nuit Blanche," "In Excelsis," and a half-dozen worshipful sonnets for Eleonora Duse. "Lilacs" and "Purple Grackles" are samples of literary naturalism, odes to the beauty and divinity of flowers and birds, poems laced with reflective descriptions of small moments amid the grand outdoors. The next two are compositions of a vaguer, more subjective nature. In "Meeting-House Hill" a church spire is imagistically transposed into the mast of a ship afloat in a blue sea of a sky, the poet imagining herself transported back in time. In "Nuit Blanche" the poet uses Keats's favorite symbol—"A red moon leers beyond the lily-tank. / A drunken moon ogling a sycamore, / Running long fingers down its shining flank . . ."—to depict the passing of a mood: "Music, you are pitiless to-night. / And I so old, so cold, so languorously white."

"In Excelsis," written for Ada Dwyer, arises out of the poet's sense of incompletion, her search for totality and sexual fulfillment. It is endowed with the Sapphic touch that pervaded much of the verse being written in Paris at this time by the pagan cultists: Renée Vivien, Colette, and Nathalie Barney; as such it is highly imitative and in ways extremely artificial:

> I drink your lips,
> I eat the whiteness of your hands and feet.
> My mouth is open,
> As a new jar I am empty and open.
> Like white water are you who fill the cup of my mouth,
> Like a brook of water thronged with lilies . . .

Several other poems in the same collection follow a similar pattern. "Which, Being Interpreted, Is As May Be, or Otherwise," is, according to Jean Gould, a symbolic and provocative sequence that deals with the autobiographical theme of deviate love; it substantiates the fashionable tenet that it is not who or what one loves but the emotion itself that counts. "The Sisters" looks at the subject of female poets ("a queer lot"), while "Fool o' the Moon" deifies both the lunar surface and the naked female form, pointing indirectly to Amy's sexual awakening and rejuvenation in middle life. "The Green Parakeet" is an understated, ironic, figurative study of guilty love, the death of purity, the ruination of nature. It, and a block of Amy's other later lyrics, gave rise to further speculation among critics concerning the subject's latent and emerging homosexuality, a doctrine that members of the Lowell family perpetually detested and currently deny.

But it is just such poetry that has led to a latter-day resurgence of interest in Amy Lowell, particularly among American and British feminists. A new generation of poets and critics has reinterpreted her work. By this crowd Amy is considered if not the literary equal of Emily Dickinson, H. D., or Marianne Moore, then at least their coequal in spirit. Among her contributions to poetry they cite the perfecting, in her purest work, of the technique of free verse; her almost unrivaled command among American poets of the vocabulary of sensuous impressions; the wide range of the themes to which she has given poetical expression; and the clarity and restrained beauty of many of her shorter poems. In a letter to this biographer the poet and critic Adrienne Rich summed up what is probably not a singular view: "Of the Lowells you're writing on, Amy is by far the most interesting. I hope you can get *her* right."

Amy's second posthumous collection, *East Wind*, featured a total of thirteen longish narratives, among them "The Doll" and "The Day That was That Day," poems that continued Amy's informal competition with Robert Frost for laurels as recorder of native New England dialect. On the whole, the volume is only of peripheral interest. It was not until her third title, *Ballads for Sale*, a selection of descriptive lyrics and brief tributes to persons and places, that the poet expressed a new sentiment —self-distrust and doubt. Such are the circumstances that surround a poem such as "On Looking at a Copy of Alice Meynell's Poems, Given Me, Years Ago, by a Friend":

> How strange that tumult, looking back.
> The ink is pale, the letters fade.
> The verses seem to be well made,
> But I have lived the almanac.
>
> And you are dead these drifted years,
> How many I forget. And she
> Who wrote the book, her tragedy
> Long since dried up its scalding tears.

Another sequence in the same volume, "Still Life: Moonlight Striking Upon a Chess-Board," strikes the same chord and like other of her late poems is a return to a more regular form of verse, a retreat beyond the experimental:

I might have been a poet, but where is the adventure to explode me into
    flame.
Cousin Moon, our kinship is curiously demonstrated,
For I, too, am a bright, cold corpse
Perpetually circling above a living world.

These lines serve as a last, perhaps fitting epitaph for Amy Lowell, although D. H. Lawrence furnished an equally evocative memorial in a letter addressed to the poet: "How much nicer, finer, bigger you are, intrinsically, than your poetry." In the final analysis, she left behind a legacy of personality. She stood out—emphatically, powerfully; she was an individual, a strong independent, her own person, in no wise an echo. Wealthy, cultivated, aloof, imperious, formidable: a string of adjectives readily attach themselves to her name. Like Edith Wharton, she grew up in a world of country estates and well-kept town houses in an age that was as chromed as it was gilded. As a woman, Amy was expected to know enough to perform the tiresome rites and chores of domesticity and to be a perfect hostess; to be self-educated and well-read was tantamount to being pushy, a cardinal sin for a woman in the narrow Puritan orb of early twentieth-century Boston society.

The tragedy of Amy Lowell's life is that while she managed to free herself from the cellblock of her own confining Brahmin prison, she never fully escaped it. This is most evident in her work; although she possessed a surface feeling for the new and experimental, Amy's true poetic affinities belonged to the nineteenth century, the century of her birth. She was an acknowledged leader of the group in America and England that called itself the Imagists; yet at the center of her radicalism beat the heart of a conservative. Her vivid and striking personality, her intellectual drive and independence and her passion for life permitted her a conspicuous and in some respects a unique place on the front lines of the American literary crusades. But in truth she never truly abandoned the conventional verse forms of the Victorians, and for some years before her death was affiliated with no literary school or movement whatever.

Hers was a roisterous personality, but the rectitudinous family from which she hailed was too great a part of her. By the last years of her life it was impossible to separate the legendary and the real Amy Lowell. She passed away an isolated patrician, antagonistic toward radicals, suspicious of liberals, scornful of "the ignorant proletariat." Durable and determined, a believer in personal imperialism and attracted to the prototypical "Superman" *figura,* she became a silent but ardent supporter of Mussolini, whose March on Rome in late October 1922 announced the arrival in Europe of Fascism. Amy Lowell feared for the future of her clan and shared with her brother Abbott Lawrence Lowell the gnawing presentiment that theirs—the tenth generation—could well be the last of a dynasty doomed to extinction. Amy's ethos and style, like that of her old American WASP aristocratic family, can best be described by such ideological Nietzschean tropes as "Heroic Materialism," "Heroic Vitalism," "Will to Power." By the end of her life her imperial and reactionary opinions and beliefs mirrored those of her cousin James Russell Lowell, during the later stages of his life. The mysterious enchantment that marked some of her best work had been undercut by a set of standards which, like Rudyard Kipling's political visions, strike one as repugnant and simplistic. That she is currently being touted by feminists as an early and leading Imagist does not vitiate her later right-wing bearings. In retrospect, nobody seems to have characterized her with greater accuracy than the outspoken Vachel Lindsay; given her aura and personality and her descent from a line of public-spirited lawyers and wealthy men of affairs, it sometimes seems a pity, he remarked, that she was so determined to become a poet. She would have been happier as the Senator from Massachusetts.

ROBERT LOWELL
Noble Savage
1917–1977

PART
IV

ROBERT LOWELL

ಊೂಌ 22 ೱೲೲ

"CALIGULA"

DISCUSSING Robert Lowell's *Life Studies* in 1959, Elizabeth Bishop offered a statement that was to serve as a synopsis of a major portion of Lowell's work, early and late. "Somehow or other," Miss Bishop wrote, "in the middle of our worst century so far, we have produced a magnificent poet, a poet whose burning and cutting as acid verse defines the age we live in." Lowell's oracular and penitential voice, the transcendent spirit and ursine power of his presence, designated him as someone for other poets to watch. Even those poets and critics who found his nightmarish world too rectilinear and the complexity of his personal creed too numbing succumbed to the magic and strength of his words. When Robert Lowell died on September 12, 1977, at age sixty, it was generally (though not unanimously) agreed that literature had lost the most distinguished poet of the postwar era, the finest American poet since T. S. Eliot, and that in effect, an office of accomplishment had fallen vacant, an office that would not soon again be filled.

To gaze into the kaleidoscope containing bits and pieces of Robert Lowell's life, to study the jagged shapes and crystalline forms of his evolution, is to glimpse reflections not just of a man and his mind, but of an age, a literary era. By early middle age, Lowell had already attained a reputation as a belletristic poet of keen perception and unusual sensibility, a creator whose work affirmed the enduring traditional values in poetry, and whose public and historic personalities tied him inexorably to the events and lives of his own generation.

Remembering the poet, the Irish bard Seamus Heaney linked his

death to that emblematic medieval phrase, "the fall of the princes."
"Just as in that older dispensation the order and coherence of things
were ratified in the person of the prince," stipulated Heaney, "so in the
person and poetry of Robert Lowell the scope and efficacy of the artistic
endeavor seemed exemplified and affirmed." Obituaries tend to bring
out the most laborious side of the would-be praise singer; Lowell's
poetry was not the infallible church or heavenly order that Heaney
ordained it to be. But Lowell's life, it seems (despite obvious exorbi-
tances), did have a representative value for many people, a value far
beyond any the poet himself attached to it. In many respects he was
both apart from and part of the age of his existence, scion of a capitalist
Puritan clan ruled by arrogance, pride, vanity, and accomplishment—
the principles of dominance—and yet by birth a Bostonian, a New
Englander, above all an American. Beneath these categorizations was
a man unwilling to reconcile himself to anyone or anything, least of all
to himself.

That he knew how to proclaim New England in his verse without
praising it was a talent that neither James Russell nor Amy Lowell
possessed in great measure. More than just the burning verse and intensity of emotion was the suffering lifestyle, Robert Lowell's vivid connections with every living tempest that Massachusetts Puritanism tended
to deny. This stoical rage provided the popular base of his reputation.
His gestures of defiance, of anger, of pain, coupled with his determination to live his art, bore witness to the poet's condition of being present
in our time. Lowell's voice, at its loudest, clearest, most naked, spoke
for an entire generation, confirming the poet's position as the crown
prince of the self-styled Confessional School of poetry. Correctly assay-
ing the main source of his personal popularity, Lowell wrote: "It may
be that some people have turned to my poems because of the very
things that are wrong with me; I mean the difficulty I have with ordinary living, the impracticability, the myopia."

Lowell's inability to find equanimity of disposition, his insatiable need
to dramatize his troubled interior in poem after poem soon became part
of the poet's legacy, almost as if his interior emotions were a reliable
measurement of the world's ills, a weathervane to the universe's unbearable turbidity. James Russell Lowell during the days of the New
England Renaissance established himself along similar though less elevated lines; his followers regarded him as a romantic individualist, who
valued personal freedom and artistic creation, whose ideal was a Good

Society in which individuals might flourish. The company that he kept, though it shifted now and again, was substantially liberal/left. But in a true sense, his party was the Poets' Party; he had more in common with Longfellow, Bryant, and Holmes than with the idealogues of any bona fide political congregation. The younger Lowell differed from the older primarily in the emotional quality of his attachments to the outside world. His entire life was one debilitating, headlong response to public events, falling into them further and faster than his literary forebear and reacting to events with a more intense state of mind. Never at peace with himself, Robert Lowell risked more of himself than James Russell Lowell because he invested more, both on a personal and on a professional level. He was willing, suggested the critic Denis Donoghue in *The Hudson Review*, to take upon himself, in his work, "the trouble his readers felt and were afraid or unable to acknowledge." The danger of this approach, as expressed by the same critic, was that the relationship between Lowell's mind and experience was, in that sense, topical, "and it is possible that with time and the change of circumstance his poems will lose the urgency that they forced upon their first readers."

There is no way to predict what fate awaits Lowell's literary reputation in the years to come. It is impossible to say how much fury will remain in the poet's words once the full impact of their occasions no longer exists. Lowell, though troubled by this consideration, was never so beset by it that it crippled him, as it did others of his generation. "It's a waste of time," he insisted, "to dream of immortality." He did dream of it, as most writers do, but not as often or despairingly as most. He was absorbed with another, more immediate (and interesting) question, namely that of his patrician, class-conscious ancestry, including his two poetry-writing predecessors.

Although neither James Russell Lowell nor Amy served as a direct influence on his work, both were important to him as a means of measuring his relationship to the dynastic family of his birth. Lowell was asked at a late-1960's meeting of the Modern Language Association in Chicago how he felt about the two poets:

> . . . Well, they were considered by my immediate family almost as disreputable as I was when I began writing. They were no support that way, except of course that's the best support. They're both creditable writers that I naturally didn't imitate, I think, and . . . well, I remember something. Let's name-drop. I was in Cambridge with T. S. Eliot about fifteen

years ago, I think, and sort of stuck in traffic—we were going somewhere, and talked about this and that of no importance—when he suddenly turned to me and said, "Don't you loathe being compared to your relatives?" I didn't know what to say to him (just as I don't know what to say to you) and I paused, and he said, "I do." He had a fine voice that deepened, and he said, "I've been reading Poe's book reviews lately, and he reviewed two of my relatives, and he wiped the floor with them." I looked with admiration. And he paused and said (and the traffic was going back and forth and we weren't advancing), "And I was delighted!" No, I think James Russell Lowell in his *Biglow Papers* about the Mexican War and the Civil War was a minor great poet, really, and a really . . . not very interesting poet the rest of the time. And Amy I can't get at all but I admire her character and admire her poetry in a way; but I don't get it really and I wish she hadn't disliked Ezra Pound so much.

He registered a variety of views in a number of voices. A caustic but humorous comment of Ezra Pound's about Amy is recorded in "Joy," one of the titles in Lowell's *Notebook 1967–68:* " 'Amy Lowell is / no skeleton to hide in a closet.' " Another sequence in the same volume, the conversational poem "T. S. Eliot," emerged from the same anecdote Lowell related at the MLA: "Caught between the two streams of traffic, in the gloom / of Memorial Hall and Harvard's war-dead. . . . And he: / 'Don't you loathe to be compared with your relatives? / I do. I've just found two of mine reviewed by Poe. / He wiped the floor with them . . . and I was *delighted. . . .' "*

In a revealing conversation with Ian Hamilton, reprinted in *The Review* (Summer 1971), Lowell touched on several of the same familial tangents:

I never knew I was a Lowell till I was twenty. The ancestors known to my family were James Russell Lowell, a poet pedestalled for oblivion, and no asset to his grand-nephew among the rich athletes at boarding school. Another, my great-grandfather, James Russell's brother, had been headmaster of my boarding school, and left a memory of scholarly aloofness. He wrote an ironic Trollopian *roman à clef* about the school [*Antony Brade, A Story of a School*]. There was Amy Lowell, big and a scandal, as if Mae West were a cousin. And there were rich Lowells, but none as rich as classmates' grandfathers in New York. Of course, we were flesh and blood, but I am talking down rumours of our grandeur. My immediate family, if you have an English equivalent, would be the Duke of Something's sixth cousins. We gave no feeling of swagger. Later I felt a blood kinship with James Russell's savage vernacular anti-Mexican War and . . . Civil War *Biglow Papers*—they were not for the Thirties. Was

Amy a rebel artist or an entrepreneur? Ours was an old family. It stood
—just. Its last eminence was Lawrence, Amy's brother, and president of
Harvard for millennia, a grand *fin de siècle* president, a species long dead
in America. He was cultured in the culture of 1900—very deaf, very
sprightly, in his eighties. He was unique in our family for being able to
read certain kinds of good poetry. I used to spend evenings with him, and
go home to college at four in the morning.

In an earlier (1961) *Paris Review* interview conducted by Frederick
Seidel, the poet reaffirmed his family's view of his writing ancestors: "To
my family, James Russell Lowell was the ambassador to England, not a
writer. Amy seemed a bit peculiar to them. When I began writing I
think it would have been unimaginable to take either Amy or James
Russell Lowell as models." Later, in a letter to the present author,
Lowell expressed further thoughts on his patrician lineage, suggesting
that he didn't like being coupled with Amy and James Russell Lowell,
though he appreciated and respected them. He said he would acknowledge his indebtedness to the James of the Civil War *Biglow Papers*. The
only mystery here is Lowell's identification with the second and not the
first series of the *Papers*.

Robert Traill Spence Lowell IV, an eleventh-generation member of
the clan, shared with his poetic forebears a rebellious, grudging attitude
toward the sea-wracked Puritan tradition the family had come to represent. The triad possessed an energetic, curious inventiveness. They
were conservative by birthright, individualistic, formal, and ceremonious. But they were also excruciatingly honest, educated, urbane, sensitive, and uncompromisingly dedicated to the cause of serious literature.
That Robert Lowell identified more readily with great-granduncle
James Russell Lowell than with Cousin Amy may be due, in part, to
their common heritage: both were members of the distinguished but
highly eccentric Russell-Spence line, the intellectual junior branch of
the family oak, the segment of the tribe that was considered alienated
from the rest—a kind of dislocated gentry. Robert was the great-grandson and (like his father and grandfather) a namesake of the headmaster
of St. Mark's School, which he later attended. In "91 Revere Street," the
prose section of his full-throated *Life Studies,* Lowell points out the
proximity of his childhood Revere Street residence on Beacon Hill to
great-great-grandfather Charles Lowell's West Church, "praised in an
old family folder as 'a haven' from . . . religious orthodoxy."

"91 Revere Street," with its similarities in style and tempo to Henry

James's autobiographical *A Small Boy and Others* and to Henry Adams's *The Education of Henry Adams*, is an unmitigated exploration of Lowell's upbringing. If Adams and James in their memoirs are a trifle too willing to portray the gilded façade of life in nineteenth-century Boston, Lowell is not. His is no ordinary family sketch to be filed away in the capacious storage bins of Harvard's Houghton Library, locked up in the barren void of a time capsule to be unearthed years hence. The evasive rhetorical devices that distort the surface of that minor literary tradition or subgenre known in publishing circles as the "character study," are reversed in "Revere Street," the family sketch enriched by a poignant and ironic prose style that crackles with spite. Lowell focuses on the family's moral, spiritual, and financial decline, its disgraces, failures, skeletons-in-closets, psychoses and neuroses. Here we have the grit and glitter of aristocratic existence in America, an aspect of the Brahmin graph more or less neglected by both Adams and James.

Born in Boston on March 1, 1917, into a family whose roots were inextricably twined with New England's, Lowell was at first unwilling to acknowledge the historical importance of his ancient heritage, preferring instead to emphasize the fading traditions of 1920's Boston—cultural, religious, sociological. The poet's father was Commander Robert T. S. Lowell (Annapolis, 1906)—a distant cousin of Aaron Burr—portrayed in his son's violent record as a dim, weak, fumbling man. A career Naval officer, whose assignments necessitated the family's living in Philadelphia and Washington, D.C., Lowell finally vacated his position with the military for a series of stable, but disappointing civilian posts, each bringing in less money than the one before, ending as a brokerage-house customers' man in Boston. The "real commander was mother," wrote a newsmagazine reporter, referring to Charlotte Winslow Lowell, a onetime high school prom queen born in Raleigh, North Carolina, in 1894. Lowell's father was ineffectual, a disbeliever in the Church, devoid of real character or charm. After he left the Navy, he could never reconcile himself to civilian life, on one occasion painting his name in large block letters on a garbage can, followed by the military designation "U.S.N."

Lowell's mother, like her son, was temperamental and highly opinionated. She had a penchant for heroic figures in history and was a fond reader of historical biographies. More than once she referred to her husband as a "weakling," whose sole interests were "steam, radio, and 'the fellows.' " It was she who nagged him into retiring from the Navy (in 1927, when their son was ten), simultaneously (by threat of divorce) badgering him out of the deeds of his house and property:

> Mother had violently set her heart on the resignation. She was hysterical even in her calm, but like a patient and forbearing strategist, she tried to pretend her neutrality. One night she said with murderous coolness, "Bobby and I are leaving for Papà's." This was an ultimatum to force Father to sign a deed placing the Revere Street house in Mother's name.

Lowell's hard, flat vision of the realities of his parents' decimated lives is reflected not only in the prose but in the poems of *Life Studies.* "Commander Lowell" charts the Commander's downward course from the Navy to employment at the Cambridge branch of Lever Brothers:

> "Anchors aweigh," Daddy boomed in his bathtub,
> "Anchors aweigh,"
> when Lever Brothers offered to pay
> him double what the Navy paid.

When his father left the Navy for Lever Brothers, the future poet nagged for his dress sword with gold braid, and cringed because Mrs. Lowell, new caps on all her teeth, "was born anew at forty." His father bought a new car (as he did whenever he switched jobs), while Mrs. Lowell continued to drag to bed alone, read Menninger, and grew more and more distant. As for the Commander—

> He was soon fired. Year after year
> he still hummed "Anchors aweigh" in the tub—
>
> . . .
>
> Father's last employer
> was Scudder, Stevens and Clark, Investment Advisors,
> himself his only client.

After losing his job at Scudder, Stevens and Clark, he went into permanent retirement.

The poet's ancestors on his mother's side, the Winslows, were as patrician and hierarchical as the Lowells, if not more so. Like the Lowells, they were early New England colonists, dating back to the *Mayflower* journeyman Edward Winslow (1595–1655), the Pilgrim father responsible for the colonists' first treaty with the Massasoit and Wampanoag Indians. Edward Winslow was three times the governor of

Plymouth (1633, 1636, and 1644), and built at Marshfield the first block-house, a structure of heavy timbers used for military defense, with sides loopholed and pierced for gunfire. *The Dictionary of American Biography* credits him as "the first man to achieve political success in England after receiving his training in government affairs in America."

Mary Chilton, later married to the early settler John Winslow, was the first female to step foot off the *Mayflower*. Other notable Winslows, some of whom were buried in the venerable King's Chapel Burial Ground, included the son of Edward Winslow, Edward II, "a mighty Indian killer" and a twice-elected governor of Plymouth Colony. His son, Edward III, was a high sheriff and a noted silversmith, whose fine silverwork is among the silver most valued by American collectors today. Also a ferocious Indian-killer was Josiah Winslow, commander-in-chief of the colonial forces in the brutal King Philip's War. Lowell's mother was related to the New Hampshire frontiersman John Stark, a Revolutionary War brigadier general, who in 1759 founded the New Hampshire township of Starkstown, later renamed Dunbarton; Lowell once portrayed him as "not quite stubborn but very determined," and claimed to have inherited these very qualities.

Ninety-one Revere Street, the house where Robert Lowell lived from age seven to ten (his summers were spent at Barnstable, on Cape Cod), stood midway between the rich of "Beacon Hill British" and the poor of the local North End Italians. This section of the Hill had been re-cently reacquired by Yankee families "from the vanguards of the lace-curtain Irish," who having made their wealth in wool or construction or politics had built mansions in suburban Dorchester and Brookline. (Even the Joseph Kennedys lived there before moving to New York because Boston WASP society was closed to them.) The steep, narrow gaslit streets and alleys of Beacon Hill, lined with closely set red and brown brick houses interspersed with Bulfinch mansions, remained a symbol of wealth, privilege, and Yankeedom. During the 1920's this was still the Brahmin residential and political bastion, from which they could look down on the Democratic rabble from the Republican safety of the State Legislature, enacting various "reforms" directed to block the progress of the Irish. The permanent migration of the old rich to the "horsier" suburbs of the North Shore had only just begun.

The middle-class pocket of the Hill occupied by 91 Revere Street proved an embarrassment to Charlotte Lowell. "We are barely perched on the outer rim of the hub of decency," she upbraided her husband. She felt uneasy about the possibility of being associated with anything other than pure Brahmin stock and in this spirit never stopped trying to convince her book-club friends that her branch of the family was wealthier than it was: "She did not have the self-assurance for wide human experience and needed to feel liked, admired, surrounded by the approved and familiar." In Mrs. Lowell's hypercritical eyes, the four-story residence became a symbol of her husband's failure, "his inability to realize himself as a man, either professionally or in his family life."

Lowell's father was a Harvard and MIT man but only of the special-student variety, having attended both schools as a postgraduate while an ensign in the Navy. Annapolis, according to his son, had been his Waterloo: "By the time he graduated from Annapolis, he had reached, perhaps, his final mental possibilities. He was deep—not with profundity, but with the dumb depth of one who trusted in statistics and was dubious of personal experience." Moreover, "he was a mumbler. His opinions were almost morbidly hesitant, but he considered himself a matter-of-fact man of science and had an unspoiled faith in the superior efficiency of northern nations."

The poet's childhood was an ongoing battle with his parents; he had built up a considerable aversion toward them, rebelling against the values they and their society represented. Throughout his growing up, the boy was a pawn, a go-between in the perpetual battle that raged between them. Constantly his mother would take him into her confidence as a means of winning him over; always he was forced to choose between his parents and to act as chief mediator in their senseless altercations, not only to the detriment of his own well-being but to theirs. That they never separated or divorced was a testimonial to their sadomasochism; they depended on one another's misery and instability as fodder for the reenactment of those fantasies that each so desperately needed to survive.

At one juncture in "91 Revere Street," Lowell analyzes his parents in popular, but ostensibly apt Freudian terms. His father was fatherless (born in New York two months after his own father's death); his mother had been "overfathered" by a domineering and autochthonous patriarch, an example of the type of man she gradually came to admire. One cringes before Lowell's continued description of the Commander, his impotent optimism, mock heroism and idealism, his inability ever to enjoy his leisure. "He never," Lowell writes, "even hid his head in the sand." By the same token, Charlotte Lowell "hated the Navy, hated naval society, naval pay, and the trip-hammer rote of settling and unsettling a house every other year when Father was transferred to a new station or ship." The emotional crucifixion Lowell suffered as a child was as crippling as Cousin Amy's childhood crucifixion, and like her he became a winningly skeptical dynast; unlike her, he wrote of these years with almost terrifying control: "All day I used to look forward to the nights when my bedroom walls would once again vibrate, when I would awake with rapture to the rhythm of my parents arguing, arguing one another to exhaustion. . . . My parents' confidences and quarrels stopped each night at ten or eleven o'clock, when my father would hang up his tuxedo, put on his commander's uniform, and take a trolley back to the naval yard at Charlestown."

The anguish of Lowell's youth manifested itself in sundry ways. M. L. Rosenthal, in *The New Poetry* (1967), reminds us that the child was always either doing unpleasant things or experiencing them—"cheating another little boy, being cruel to one who had been his friend, bloodying others' noses, rejoicing in the disgrace of a charming little girl who proved incontinent in the classroom and then, in his 'excitement and guilt,' sitting in the sopping chair left empty when she fled." The setting of this event was Boston's exclusive Brimmer School: "When I entered Brimmer I was eight and a half. I was distracted in my studies, assented to whatever I was told, picked my nose whenever no one was watching, and worried our third-grade teacher by organizing creepy little gangs of boys at recess." Lowell the child was no different from most; he was girl-shy, thick-witted, narcissistic, thuggish, and less rather than more bookish than his peers.

Robert Lowell at Brimmer was not wholly remote from James Russell Lowell at Miss Dana's school for girls: "Boys were a sideline at my Brimmer School. The eight superior grades were for girls only. . . . The school's tone . . . was a blend of the feminine and the military, a bulky reality governed in turn by stridency, smartness, and steadiness." Brimmer's atmosphere mirrored the priggish, life-negating atmosphere of 91 Revere Street; both were female-dominated and stringent, the cause of tension and turmoil on the part of young Lowell. To be a boy at

Brimmer was to be "small, denied, and weak"; to be a man in Charlotte Lowell's home entailed similar risks.

Lowell senior's avenues of egress are noted in "Terminal Days at Beverly Farms":

> Each morning at eight-thirty,
> inattentive and beaming,
>
> . . .
>
> Father stole off with the *Chevie*
> to loaf in the Maritime Museum at Salem.
> He called the curator
> "the commander of the Swiss Navy."

Lowell junior's routes of escape were internal. He suffered myopia, migraines, and asthma—the latter was cured not by a physician but by a chiropractor. The boy loved playing in the attic with toy soldiers and spent months memorizing the names and dates of some two hundred real life French generals. He shared Amy Lowell's lifelong fascination with Napoleon, reading every Bonaparte biography he could lay hands on. In "Revere Street" he admits to an ardent infatuation with the military personality; their uniforms and exploits were the bedrock of the youthful poet's pent-up imagination.

That he keened on toy soldiers, did not like baseball or school, and was curiously accident-prone can be deduced from his letters at this time, one of which the eleven-year-old sent to his grandfather, Arthur Winslow. That letter, dated April 28, 1928, indicated a strong attraction for the sport of marbles. Probably young Lowell liked their colors and smooth texture. The letter went on to say that though he was the pitcher on the beginner's squad, he didn't enjoy baseball. He already had a black eye and minor cuts. He went horseback riding and collected 450 toy soldiers. The letter ended by reporting that he ranked nineteenth out of twenty-seven in his class.

By this point the Lowells had moved to a more fashionable residence at 170 Marlborough Street in Boston proper, a four-story town house with bay windows, skylight, front yard, rosebushes, wrought-iron fence, and a small courtyard separating it from the town house next door. It was hardly ideal, but it was at least a step closer than 91 Revere Street to Charlotte Lowell's effete vision of a Brahmin nirvana.

Robert Lowell had likewise stepped up in the world. At age thirteen he was removed from Brimmer and enrolled at St. Mark's, the lordly prep school in Southboro, Massachusetts, where Greek, Latin, philosophy, and manliness were the major courses of instruction. The boarding school is described in considerable detail by Geoffrey Wolff in his biographical study of another St. Mark's product, Harry Crosby (*Black Sun: The Brief Transit and Violent Eclipse of Harry Crosby*, 1976). St. Mark's, during the days of Lowell's attendance, was apparently heavily grounded by rules; the outwardly rebellious student immediately found himself confined by regulations that prohibited smoking, alcohol, drugs, dating, cardplaying, gambling, sex, music (with the exception of classical music), and cars. The milieu was highminded, correct, superior, competitive, indifferent. The average student at St. Mark's was the beneficiary of inherited wealth, carefully attired, disposed toward cruelty, coldness, and arbitrariness. Hair had to be worn short and ties and jackets were required in class and at all school functions. The school catalogue, even as late as 1930, warned parents that "boxes and packages of all kinds are forbidden without the express consent of the Headmaster. Whenever it is necessary that a body should go home in term time, the reason must always be stated in advance; but leave of absence will not be granted except under extraordinary circumstances. Important letters and telegrams should be addressed to the Headmaster."

If there were any benefits to the prep school regime, it was simply that the prospective graduate was exposed to a microcosmic simulation of a Darwinian universe in which "standing up on one's own two feet" was at a premium. Survival was everything in this harsh, cold Siberia of a Massachusetts prep school. Having survived, the survivor could think of himself as an individualist, as someone special. It was a rite of passage, an initiation into the competitive byways of State Street or Fifth Avenue. One came out of prep school as hardened as a West Point cadet and as ascetic as a monk in a monastery.

At St. Mark's, Lowell picked up the nickname "Cal," after the despotic Roman Emperor Caligula, "because he was so uncouth and imperious," according to a *Time* magazine cover story (June 2, 1967), which featured a portrait of the poet as Emperor Caligula by Lowell's friend, the Australian painter Sidney Nolan. The name, which actually means "soldiers' boots" *(caligae),* appealed to Lowell's baser instincts. Aware of its connotation, he continued its use, celebrating it in a poem in *For the Union Dead;* reduced from fifty-one to fourteen lines, the poem reappeared in *Notebook 1967–68:*

> My namesake, Little Boots, Caligula
> you disappoint me. Tell me what you saw—
> . . . your body hairy, badly made,
> head hairless, smoother than your marble head
>
> . . .
>
> my namesake, not the last Caligula.

His namesake is further described as having hollow eyes, hollow temples, red cheeks (that seemed touched with rouge), spindly legs, clammy hands (hands that no other hands wanted to touch), a balding head, thin neck. In other words, he saw himself at this stage as a strange-looking, gangly-limbed fellow with an extremely nasty disposition. A classmate of his has said that Lowell seemed out of place at St. Mark's, but would have seemed out of place anywhere.

In *Notebook 1967–68,* "Caligula" follows "Night Sweat," another partial portrait of the artist as a young man, in which he says of himself: "always inside me is the child who died / always inside me is his will to die—." The child who "died" was an awkward, insecure, cheerless youth, lazy in his studies but enthused by American history and English literature; upon entering St. Mark's he began reading commentaries on the *Iliad* and the *Divine Comedy.* But his grades, even in his favorite disciplines, floundered. During the first term of his second year there he received a grade of 60 in English, 61 in Latin, 64 in French, 78 in math, 80 in history. More often than not his name appeared at or near the bottom of the class list.

His roommate at school, the future painter Francis Parker, recalled Lowell's precocious philosophy: "The point was that you could put yourself into heaven or hell by your own choice. You could make your own destiny. That became Cal's text." To test the text, he donned padded helmet and shoulder pads and threw his "powerful but ill-coordinated body into the game of football." He passed the test by earning his varsity letter as second-string offensive tackle. "It was more will power than love of the game," insinuated Parker. "It was his own way of exercising the moral imperative."

Influenced by Parker, Lowell had taken to reading histories of art, "looking at reproductions, tracing the Last Supper on tracing paper, studying dynamic symmetry, learning about Cézanne, and so on." The study was not too remote from poetry. And from there he began. He began by reading Elizabeth Drew and Louis Untermeyer on modern poetry. Both were conventional but informative on free verse, which struck Lowell as an easy form, simple to re-create. Clumsy on the football field, he proved more agile with words and even illustrated several of his early poems. Had Parker not already made enormous headway in this domain, it is feasible that Lowell could well have become another Klee, rather than his age's Cicero.

There was an additional factor concerning Lowell's budding interest in poetry. St. Mark's had on its faculty the young poet Richard Eberhart, a graduate of Dartmouth and Cambridge, whose work was beginning to break into print and with whom Lowell was able to establish an easy rapport. Eberhart was intellectual, gregarious, and stimulating. Lowell found him a mite pretentious but on the whole impressive: "He'd smoke honey-scented tobacco, and read Baudelaire and Shakespeare and Hopkins—it made the thing living—and he'd read his own poems." Eberhart saw himself as a "relativist," though others saw him as a charismatic, for he regarded poems as inspired, stipulating that "when the poem is ready to be born, it will be born." Thus, in this otherwise parched, puritanical, athletically oriented finishing school for rich boys destined to attend Harvard and become bankers, lawyers, or directors of industry, Lowell had found someone who cared. It was the only saving grace during "six uncomfortable years" among students he considered "neither efficient nor humane nor cultured." The ultimate hardships of a strict disciplinary academy in harsh New England winters were accentuated by Lowell's personality. Bored by most of the things that interested other boys, he was never overly popular at St. Mark's and found himself the butt of the usual schoolboy run of taunts, threats, and bad practical jokes. The school taught him to dislike and distrust the sons of the Brahmin rich.

He was a junior, a fifth-former, by the time he wrote his maiden poem, a lengthy, draining, blank-verse epic on the Crusades, a pastiche culled from Joseph Michaud's *History of the Crusades;* a poem that followed directly on its heels, "Madonna," became his first published work, appearing in *The Vindex*, the school's literary periodical. It showed little in the way of talent, its subject matter easily outclassing its form: "Her hands were made divine; / But the Virgin's face was silvery bright / Like the holy light! Which from God's throne / Is said to shine. . . ."

Summarizing these years, Eberhart recalled that Lowell's writing was shabby at first, but that he enjoyed the young chap, believing "his extravagances of nature" to be a sign of artistic promise. Eberhart expressed a more personal view of Lowell at St. Mark's in a verse play called *The Mad Musician,* in which the student rails against the prep school as "that washed old school where none was free" and against his parents: "my father I loathe, my mother I cannot endure." Full of anguish and anger, Eberhart's Lowell hates and berates himself most of all.

Eberhart's encouragement was important for the neophyte; it helped him cope with the bitterness he felt toward his parents and his past. He was able to transcend the spare, bleak setting of that oppressive social and familial swirl that one associates with white, Anglo-Saxon, New England upper-class stratagems, a world of grace, cultivation, and—always—money. During his final year at St. Mark's, Lowell brought Eberhart a bound manuscript of some sixty poems—the first fruits of his extended labors—shyly placing it on teacher's desk one day after class. Lowell's writing had improved; Eberhart reported that the manuscript revealed the fledgling poet influenced by Latin models, with true strokes of imagination showing through: "The poems demonstrated his mind was heavy and that it was essentially religious." In fact, it was a "heavier" mind than Eberhart had cause or reason to believe. One of Lowell's lyrics sang blithely of "bright angels dropping from the sky," an obscure allusion to a poem by his ancestor, the Reverend Robert T. S. Lowell, first headmaster of St. Mark's, one of whose inspirational odes sang of an "angel's symphony . . . out of highest heaven dropping."

It is Steven Gould Axelrod, in his illuminating *Robert Lowell: Life and Art* (1978), who draws our attention to this little known fact. Axelrod also informs the reader that during the summer before entering Harvard, Lowell read Wordsworth's *The Prelude* and Amy Lowell's biography of Keats, and was moved by "the picture both give of the young poet forming into a genius, their energy, their rapid growth and above all their neverending determination to succeed." In a letter to Eberhart, he wrote: "I have come to realize more and more the spiritual side of being a poet. It is difficult to express what I wish to say, but what I mean is the actuality of living the life, of breathing the same air as

Shakespeare, and of coordinating all this with the actualities of the world."

The transition from St. Mark's to Harvard was not easy. From the outset Lowell had serious misgivings about attending his hometown school. He expected that it would be a comedown, he confided to Arthur Winslow, after a sixth-form year at a boarding school, to find himself in a position of no importance among his college classmates. Anonymity was not Lowell's idea of fun, but he matriculated at Harvard in 1935 and soon found himself beset by further doubts. He was particularly perturbed by the pedantry of the university's English department, whose faculty he once described as "outworn and backward-looking." He remained isolated at first, restricting himself to his dormitory room, its bare green walls covered with prints by Leonardo da Vinci and Rembrandt; he listened to Beethoven on the phonograph and read "soiled metrical treatises . . . full of glorious things: rising rhythm, falling rhythm, feet with Greek names." Influenced by his readings he rolled out Spenserian stanzas on Job and Jonah surrounded by recently seen Nantucket scenery: "Everything I did was grand, ungrammatical and had a timeless, hackneyed quality." There were no poets of note in Harvard's English department, but Robert Frost that year gave the Norton lectures, which Lowell attended and found of substantial interest. Perhaps hoping that Frost could be a spiritual guide and artistic mentor, Lowell went to see him at his temporary Cambridge residence on Fayerweather Street and brought along a draft of his much reworked Crusades epic. Frost, reading the first page, looked up and said: "It goes on rather a bit, doesn't it?" He meant that Lowell had no compression. Then, with a sly grin, Frost read aloud William Collins's short poem "How Sleep the Brave" and remarked, "That's not a great poem, but it's not too long." Besides giving him his first lesson in compression and narrative, Frost instructed Lowell in the dynamics of contrast. He read to his visitor from Keats's "Hyperion," pausing at the point in the poem where the Naiad presses a cold finger to her lips. "There," said Frost, "the poem comes alive. Keats's true voice jolts through." Lowell began to see the poem in a new light, no longer as the "big Miltonic imitation" he had once thought it. Although their meeting was fruitful for Lowell in terms of instruction, he noted that Frost was too preoccupied with his latest work to take an active interest in the work of others. Lowell became disenchanted and depressed with his own recent effusions, describing them to a classmate as diffuse and monotonous and not written in a very believable voice. The student was still searching for the right pitch and tone with which to capture his flow of impressions.

"A leader must first learn to follow" was the unwritten motto at Harvard. Lowell "chafed" at Harvard, especially at the conventionality of its approach to the humanities, its lack of interest in the arts and stifling indifference to anything that could be construed as "modern." Harvard repudiated as tainted and worthless everything written after the Civil War. There were only a few exceptions to this confining rule, and modern poetry was not one of them. Determined to make the best of a bad situation, Lowell submitted samples of his work to *The Harvard Advocate*, the undergraduate literary magazine in whose pages had first appeared the work of T. S. Eliot, Wallace Stevens, E. E. Cummings, among others. Eliot later told Donald Hall of *The Paris Review* that the *Advocate* of his own day provided literary types with an arena for competitive and often vicious brawling: "Everyone threw his poems into a basket, and then they held a round robin to see who could say the most sarcastic things about the other man's work." Lowell, as heir-apparent to Boston's literary throne, already had two strikes against him. Having handed in his work, he was summoned by the *Advocate*'s editors to their offices with several other candidates to help tack a carpet and paint some walls, a hazing process that usually preceded initiation into the *Advocate*'s ranks. In Lowell's case, however, the editors were merely flexing their muscles. When he had finished his assigned task, the *Advocate*'s chief editor informed him that his poems had been rejected and that he needn't return.

The rejection was magnified in Lowell's mind by virtue of his family background, the fact that two "name" poets had already emerged from within the tribe. His pride was badly pricked. Several weeks later he informed his family that he was about to quit college and elope to Europe with a girl friend, five years his senior. His parents were outraged. Prodded by his wife, the Commander composed a letter to the girl's father, which she promptly intercepted and presented to her beau. Robert brooded over it, then "punctiliously" handed it to his father and knocked him to the ground. That fight and the arguments that ensued over Anne Dick between father and son provided enough material to fill a half-dozen poems. The "Charles River" sequence in *Notebook 1967–68* (rewritten as "Anne Dick I. 1936" in *History*) relates one side of the story:

My father's letter to your father, saying
. . .
you'd been going to my college rooms alone—
I can still almost crackle that slight note in my hand.
. . .
Then punctiliously handing the letter to my father,
I knocked him down. . . .

The poem recounts the boy's anger on seeing his father's "tersely and much too stiffly" worded letter to Mr. Dick; he envisions Anne's outraged father, the poet brooding "in fire and a dark quiet" on the abandoned steps of the Harvard Fieldhouse, trying to calm himself by reciting "Lycidas," then perpetrating his act of violence, watching his father sprawl to the carpet, Mrs. Lowell calling from the top of the stairs. There was "no cover . . . no retreat."

Time's version had it that "father and son quarreled. The violence that churned in Lowell's poetry burst out, and he knocked his father to the floor." As Commander Lowell saw it, the crazed boy would have to be packed off to an insane asylum, "but family friends convinced him that his poet son needed not so much the company of keepers as that of other poets."

The physical violence, the actual act of knocking his father down, became symbolic in his mind, playing repeatedly through his future verse: "I struck my father; later my apology / hardly scratched the surface of his invisible / coronary . . . never to be effaced." This too was from *Notebook;* in "Rebellion," from *Lord Weary's Castle,* he wrote:

> There was rebellion, father, when the mock
> French windows slammed and you hove backward, rammed
> Into your heirlooms, screens, a glass-cased clock,
> The highboy quaking to its toes. You damned
> My arm that cast your home upon your head
> And broke the chimney flintlock on your skull . . .

Despite its poetic reenactment, Lowell's "primal crime" was never entirely exorcised. It pursued him, comments Philip Cooper in his critical biography of Lowell (*The Autobiographical Myth of Robert Lowell,* 1970), "like original sin, down the years, into 'Middle Age' in *For the Union Dead.*" That poem laments the passing of the poet's youth and recalls his own father at his age:

"CALIGULA"

At forty-five,
what next, what next?
At every corner,
I meet my Father,
my age, still alive. . . .

The poem begs his father's forgiveness, acknowledging that he had sinned by knocking his father down, but reminding his father that he too had been injured—metaphysically, one must presume—and had been willing to forgive and forget.

It is possible to attach various shades of meaning to Lowell's attack on his father and its significance in his poetry. Symbolically, one might think of it as a later-generation Lowell rejecting the vacuity, spiritual hollowness, and pretensions of his ancestry, deriding Lowelldom and everything that the rich, upwardly mobile (and desperately declining) clan stood for and came to represent: businesses, banks, mill towns, society balls—the mordant proprieties of Brahmin wealth, the class-bound symbols of a universal order. While Lowell could admire the advantages of inherited class privilege and distinguish between class power and polemic, he felt grossly offended by most aspects of commercialism and embarrassed by the excruciating rites of high WASP gentility, with its aristocratic trappings and special advantages, its incivility, despair, and moral disarray. The moral chain of being was located for Lowell in the gap between this class's philanthropic charade and the lack of any true communal or family stability.

The Anne Dick affair reached its harrowing climax during March of 1937 and was as brutal as Lowell's poems make it out to be. Not just one, but a flurry of malicious, compromising epistles from Lowell's parents preceded the fisticuffs between father and son. A note from Lowell's mother to Anne Dick revealed her stone coldness toward the girl, her bitter reaction to a letter Anne had sent her requesting permission to announce "Bobby's" engagement to her. Mrs. Lowell stressed that she and her husband would not condone the marriage until Cal was self-supporting. The letter from Commander Lowell to Evans Dick that first upset the applecart demanded that Anne not be permitted to visit Bobby's rooms at college unchaperoned. In contrast to the Lowells, Anne's parents exercised the utmost forbearance in the delicate situation. Responding to the Commander's opprobrious brief, Joan Dick, Anne's mother, indicated that while she was unhappy about their behavior, she did not question their love.

Complications gave rise to further complications. In response to her son's claim that a Harvard education was deleterious and of no value, Charlotte Lowell took the position that they would render Robert financial assistance only so long as he observed their standards of conduct and treated his elders with respect. They would be of assistance when they felt that what he was doing was right, but he could expect no help if it were otherwise. Her intentions were clear: if he dropped out of Harvard, if he married and absconded with his bride to Europe, he had better be prepared to foot his own bill. Few parents breathe who have not, at one time or another, issued similar ultimatums.

It was during this crucial period that the sophomore encountered Ford Madox Ford at a Boston cocktail party. Ford, the ancient mariner who had once feuded with Amy Lowell, knew everyone in literary New York, Boston, London, and Paris, from Pound and Eliot to Yeats and Dylan Thomas. He was likewise closely acquainted with a number of the Southern Fugitive poets and critics, including John Crowe Ransom, Robert Penn Warren, Cleanth Brooks, Laura Riding Jackson, Austin Warren, Donald Davidson, and Allen Tate, mainliners of a regional poetic upsurge, a self-made neoclassical movement with ties to the traditional and restrained base that for years dictated British literary currents. The Old South, its dream of a glorious borderland of leisure shattered by the invasion of Northern commercial interests, now gave birth to a new culture of fictionists, the first wave consisting of Faulkner, Katherine Anne Porter, and Erskine Caldwell. It was on the basis of this triad's rise to fame, and on the strength of their writings about the South, that the poets and critics of this region gained recognition.

From 1922 to 1925 they published nineteen issues of a magazine called *The Fugitive,* a periodical built on a combination of enthusiasm, very little money, and noble if naïve intentions. Its contributors met regularly to read each other their latest poems and indulge in literary discussion. It was ironic that the American region which had been the most willfully self-contained was also the last to make itself felt in the national literature. Having launched their careers with a fierce social passion, the Fugitives gained a following among the literary young as models for pure or formalistic criticism.

One of the root purposes of any regional literary movement is to depict the life and times of the region it represents. As the Transcendental Movement opened the New England mind fully to nineteenth-century literary discourse, paving the way for the spirit of place as exalted by the Fireside poets, so the Agrarians opened the Southern mind fully to the discourse of the twentieth century. In so doing, it substantiated the modern realm of letters in the South and pointed the way for the Southern literary renaissance. The authority of orthodox religion is what gave impetus to the New England movement of 1820 to 1860. Other regional literary movements emerged out of the "old Southwest," where folk humor reached its apotheosis in Mark Twain, and in the Midwest, where the revolt against the village signified a giant step toward a new-found freedom of expression, a dialect that blended formal prose with native speech, the heritage from England with the improvisations of the American provinces.

The Fugitives did not come into their own until the publication of their influential 1930 symposium, "I'll Take My Stand," which called for a stable, religious, Southern society, while opposing the commercial and industrial values of the North, including the city, the machine, modern science, labor unions, centralized government. The Fugitives were all for a way of life exemplified by dignity, courtesy, culture, leisure, a style of existence that "grew unbrokenly out of the antebellum past"; a world of high literary tastes based on the loftiest, most aristocratic models and that catered predominantly to poets and critics. The kind of poetry that drew them was ironic, elegant, courtly, difficult, elusive, and severe. Poetry, they polemicized, must be formal, programmatic, dispassionate, never personal or romantic, never psychological or erotic. As a rule they were fond of "strategies," props, ceremony, and historical pageantry. They wanted their verse to be symbolic, violent, orderly, lyrical, enigmatic—a comfortless exploration of the human condition.

The Fugitives were quick to point out that since the Depression American literature had been in a state of rueful decay and collapse. The right books were not being read (or writ); the world of poetry and prose had been displaced by the dreary cosmos of journalese; contemporary taste was of ashcan worth; literary criticism had failed. Here was a chorus of new voices, a sort of hermeneutic mafia of the critical circuit, intent on reversing these crippling trends. For years their home base had been Vanderbilt University in Nashville, Tennessee. When Lowell learned from Ford that he was about to spend the summer at "Benfolly," Allen Tate and his wife Caroline Gordon's rundown mansion at Clarksville, an hour outside Nashville, he decided to abandon his European plans in favor of a trip to the Deep South. Tate, with his penchant for exclusiveness, was one of the pillars of this clique, a poet-critic who thrived on the rarefied air of classic literature and felt that the sacerdotal function of the teacher-critic was to *dictate* taste. He further believed that the *Summa Theologica* of the religion of literature was reducible, in the present century, to the poetic possibilities of T. S. Eliot, Mallarmé, and Baudelaire; Flaubert led the way in prose.

Lowell had heard of Tate but was unfamiliar with his work. After hastily devouring what poems he could find, he set out, reaching Benfolly a few days later, his head bursting with "Miltonic ambitions," his suitcase "heavy with bad poetry." In a vignette titled "Visiting the Tates," published in the *Sewanee Review* in 1959, Lowell described that eventful day in April 1937 when he burst into the lives of his startled hosts: "I was brought to earth by my bumper mashing the Tates' frail agrarian mail box post. Getting out to disguise the damage, I turned my back on their peeling, pillared house. I had crashed the civilization of the South."

He had received two speeding summonses along the way and arrived in a mood "close to desperation." "Like a torn cat," Lowell observed, "I was taken in when I needed help, and in a sense I have never left."

His arrival on the scene was unannounced. The Tates knew the name Lowell but nothing of its young, poetry-writing heir. Ford had not yet appeared, and the Tates had their hands full with other houseguests. The story, well known by now, is that Lowell, "ardent and eccentric" and brimming with "youthful callousness," went to a nearby Sears, Roebuck and invested in an olive green umbrella tent that he proceeded to rig up on the Benfolly lawn. Tate was too polite to tell him that he was imposing on them. Lowell took his meals in the house, and slept in his tent. He stayed four months.

Partly from Ford, partly from Tate, the poet discovered that he was "Northern, disembodied, a Platonist, a Puritan, and an abolitionist." He was also told that his forebears had been idealistic New Englanders full of magisterial enthusiasm, a clan which through three centuries of heroism and tragedy had been reduced to "moral decadence and depravity." Lowell found Tate sympathetic and gentle, sensitive to his needs, learned and willing to share his knowledge with anyone who cared to listen. Here was the poetic father Frost could never be, the surrogate patriarch the Commander never wanted to be. At one point Lowell even addressed the older poet, almost twenty years his senior, as "Father Tate," a moniker that caused the Fugitive extreme embarrassment. Tate, nevertheless, saw in Lowell a younger version of himself, an "autocratic, extravagant, generous" young man able to respond well to instruction.

As Lowell has said, the amount of work done at Benfolly that summer was enormous. Typewriters were set up in every corner. Tate worked day and night on his novel *The Fathers,* the story of aristocrats in Virginia at the time of the Civil War; Ford, at times growing impatient with Lowell, rapidly dictated *The March of Literature* to him; Caroline Gordon pounded away at a collection of short stories. Lowell was reading Edith Sitwell's essays on formal structure, while writing "grimly unromantic" poetry of his own. After two months of listening to Tate's abrasive discourses on the "secondary and minor" efforts of a cordon of free-verse cognoscenti, including Carl Sandburg and William Carlos Williams (whose work Lowell had begun to read at Harvard), the young poet became converted to Tate's brand of formalism, a style that combined impersonality and personal experience in what can only be construed as a basically paradoxical bond. Lowell's reading of Williams had encouraged him to experiment, if only briefly, with modes of free verse and concentrated patterns of construction. Now the challenge was to depersonalize experience, to convert it from chaotic shapelessness into order and knowledge, to transform language from scattered stuttering into killing eloquence. Tate insisted that a good poem was nothing more than "a piece of craftsmanship, an intelligible or *cognitive* object," the product of tensions, and that "strong verse can bear the closest literal examination of every phrase, and is its own safeguard against our irony." In his bid to revitalize the formal and classic mechanisms of bygone literary epochs, Tate represented the heroic master rebelling against the prevailing powers of free verse, a model of rebellion against the sort of modernist sensibility Lowell himself would be fighting for the next ten years.

The summer passed quickly. Indoors, "life was Olympian and somehow crackling; outdoors, Uncle Andrew, the calf, sagged against the tent sides." There were cows, horses, chickens, children, parents, and a herd of visiting poets and critics. There was always something up and someone about. Ford found the rich Southern fare prepared by the Tates' cook too rich for his thinning blood, whereas Lowell could never get enough of it. Overall it was a hot, muggy, noisy summer, and there was a decided lack of privacy in the house. Ford claimed that living with the Tates was "like living with intellectual desperados in the Sargasso Sea." Lowell described the lifestyle as "stately yet bohemian, leisurely yet dedicated."

In the middle of July, Lowell accompanied Ford, Janice Biala, Tate, and Caroline Gordon by automobile to Olivet College in Michigan to attend a summer writers' conference. Lowell met Theodore Roethke there, and as Roethke later testified, never lost an opportunity to recite his latest poems. Ford had been offered a part-time lectureship at Olivet and after settling his private business affairs, he joined his companions on a junket to a second writers' conference at the University of Colorado in Boulder. It was there that Lowell, through Ford, met his future bride, Jean Stafford. Inspired by the snowcapped peaks of the neighboring Rockies, Lowell decided once and for all to transfer out of Harvard and into a school that would better accommodate his interest in literature. Because John Crowe Ransom was a member of its English faculty, his first choice was Vanderbilt University. But when Ransom, formerly Tate's mentor, was dropped by Vanderbilt and his contract subsequently picked up by Kenyon College in Gambier, Ohio, Lowell followed suit.

He attempted to convince his father, with whom he had made a tentative but shaky peace, that Ransom was unquestionably one of the great men in the country in his field and that the advantages of studying under him were inestimable in terms of dollars and cents. Instead of terminating the letter on this dour but practical note, Lowell began to excoriate his father for trying to elicit information about him behind his back from both Ford and Abbott Lawrence Lowell, of all people.

In a letter to his father he complained of his father's attitude. He accused his father of being unreceptive and of rebuffing him. He wondered why the Commander had been so secretive about consulting with Ford and Abbott Lawrence Lowell about his problems. He also complained that his father's letters lacked affection and that the responsibility for maintaining their relationship had been entirely his.

The peevish and acrimonious tone of the letter sounded more like a father scolding his wayward son, than a son his wayward father. It was clear from the letter that Lowell had not the slightest intention of returning to Harvard, now or later, and although it might have seemed impious to his elders for a member of the family to reject that hallowed grove of academe, they made no further attempt to press the issue. "They'd rather," charged the poet, "have had me a genial social Harvard student, but at least I'd be working hard this way. It seemed to them a queer but orderly step." They were encouraged in their thinking by a new family acquaintance, Dr. Merrill Moore, a Boston psychiatrist and sonnet writer. Moore, originally from Tennessee and a member of the Fugitives, had seen the troubled youth as a patient on several scattered occasions before advising the Lowells that their son could do worse than to study poetry and literature under the sage guidance of John Crowe Ransom.

Lowell arrived in the small but attractive and genteel town of Gambier dressed in a soiled and crumpled white suit, carrying a duffel bag filled with books and dirty laundry. He was in need of a haircut and a shave and looked as ungainly and uncoordinated as a newborn calf, his long legs stumbling over one another, his elbows flying out in all directions. He had poor posture, and whenever he sat in a chair he appeared always on the verge of tumbling out. Yet there was something extremely fine, attractive, even moving about him, an energy, a love of literature, an enthusiasm that was immediately contagious. With his quick and inquiring if undisciplined mind, he wasted no time in making himself known. "He did more than come under our official attention," Ransom reminisced, "he passed beneath the lintel of my door, and lived for a year in our house. . . . Lowell was not the man, as he is not now the man, that one could hold off very long at an official distance. His animal spirits were high, his personality was spontaneous, so that he was a little bit overpowering. We had Randall Jarrell in our house too, an M.A. graduate; and if a few others came sometimes, our tone became that of a hilarious party, and Lowell was the life of it."

Jarrell, a student of Ransom's at Vanderbilt, had followed him to Kenyon. He and Lowell shared a book-cluttered room in Ransom's house. His second year at Kenyon Lowell moved, with Peter Taylor (another of Ransom's charges at Vanderbilt), into a long, gabled third-story room in Douglass House, one of Kenyon's dormitory cottages. He and Taylor, a budding short-story writer, shared a single oak desk, piled high with books. Books lay everywhere in the room—on the floor, under the beds, over the furniture. John Thompson, a future critic and English professor, began a friendship with Lowell at Kenyon and remembered him curled up in bed with a book, surrounded by a wall of books, his clothing scattered and piled into heaps. Less cranky and morbid than he had been at Harvard, he was still the restless and untamed beast. Years later he recalled himself at the small Episcopal college as "loud-humored, dirty and frayed—I needed to be encouraged to comb my hair, tie my shoes and say goodbye when leaving a house." Taylor thought him "the most slovenly and ragged-looking of us all," a book-starved legionnaire whose favorite topics of conversation were writing and himself.

Taylor modeled a character named Jim Prewitt in one of his early short stories, "1939," after his roommate. Based on a real event, the tale recounts an altercation between the two students on the train back to college from a holiday outing in New York. Lowell reciprocated by capturing Taylor in "To Peter Taylor on the Feast of the Epiphany" *(Lord Weary's Castle),* and in "For Peter Taylor" *(Notebook 1967–68).* Taylor, Lowell, and Jarrell were inseparable at Kenyon. Jarrell, a gradu-ate instructor, was highly opinionated but full of insights, willing and able to instruct those in need. He possessed a phenomenal ability to communicate ideas, to bring forth hidden sensitivity in people. He was a teacher not only of literature but of emotions. He taught people about themselves. Those who studied with him learned about the mechanics of feeling. Whether they went on to become writers or not, they emerged from their relationship with him vastly enriched, their per-ceptions greatly expanded.

Lowell's comradeship with Jarrell endured a lifetime, Jarrell becom-ing Lowell's literary conscience, reading and editing most of his manu-scripts and always providing a sympathetic ear. Jarrell was a born teacher, whose dedication was such that he would have gladly paid for the privilege. In a way he did pay. His expectations were too grand, his standards too high for an imperfect, anti-intellectual, uncaring world. Even more than Lowell and Tate, he lamented the passing of heroism and cultural grace. In 1967, two years after Jarrell's suicide, Lowell—with Taylor and Robert Penn Warren—edited an anthology *(Randall Jarrell, 1914–1965)* containing essays by Hannah Arendt, Cleanth Brooks, Alfred Kazin, and others who had known and admired him.

Ransom, a generation older than both Lowell and Jarrell, was more an intellectual guide than a direct influence on Lowell's poetry. There was a bit of James Russell Lowell in Ransom: he was exceedingly well read, a conversationalist of incomparable finesse, an academic but not a dry academician. He and Jarrell quibbled incessantly over metaphys-ics, poetry, history—all in good faith and fun. Jarrell remained unmoved by Fugitive sophistry; a fierce opponent of all strictly ordered intellec-tual movements, he was instrumental in eventually helping to break its stranglehold over Lowell. Jarrell, as Lowell wrote to Richard Eberhart, was a devout modern—"a complete abstraction who believes in Shelley, machines, 'ambiguities,' and intelligence tests." A psychology major, he was thoroughly schooled in Marx, Auden, Freud, Empson, Kafka, "the ideologies and news of the day." Ransom, the holder of a graduate degree from Oxford, was expert in the more refined world of Greek, Latin, Aristotle, and England. The dialectically opposed views of both men played a corresponding role in Lowell's eclectic frame of reference, the essential difference being Ransom's failure to make a substantial impression in terms of his poetry. Ransom's verse—elegant, trivial, ironic, deft—was stylistically remote from the emotional core of Lowell's weightier literary nexus. Lowell perceived early that his own work bristled with power where Ransom's merely purred, that his was the more forceful, less graceful of the two, and that the twain could never meet.

Yet it was Ransom's influence that encouraged Lowell to major in the classics at Kenyon. The student was fascinated, finding the Greeks "wild yet sophisticated," the Romans "terribly frank" and "corrosive in their attacks on the Establishment." He took courses in the classics, and in languages, literature, and philosophy, auditing a seminar in the poetry of Pope and Dryden, reading Elizabethan plays, devouring the nineteenth century (British and American), attending as well a course in the novel. He performed extremely well in his written work, but the considerable burden of his course work and the exacting formal demands of the New Criticism of Ransom and Tate took their inevitable toll on his latest freshet of verse. He published prose and poems in *Hika*, Kenyon's student-run literary magazine, which (with Robie Macauley) he coedited during his senior year. When not reading or teaching himself to write, he could be found on the athletic fields—playing tennis with Jarrell or trying out for the varsity football team. He shocked his friends by entering and winning a statewide debating contest, held each year in Cleveland.

In retrospect, his transfer out of the insular, self-satisfied atmosphere that pervaded Harvard, his departure from the murky infidelities and sheltered affluence of Boston, into the calm and restorative environment of Gambier and Kenyon, proved a wise choice. He graduated fully decorated: summa cum laude, Phi Beta Kappa, class valedictorian—or as he thought of himself, a perfect undergraduate, half felon, half scholar. On closer examination one discovers that with the exception of his tight literary circle, Lowell was dissatisfied with the student body at Kenyon, finding his classmates interested only in athletics, beer, dating, and future careers. In an essay for *Hika,* he reveals a sense of alienation from the school; the average Kenyon student, according to the article, found his studies only "a matter of intermittent interest" and considered his college degree as possessing "commercial value" and nothing else. Steven Axelrod makes the point that Lowell's tone here resembles that of Tate's Agrarian manifestos, a curiously elitist yet radical voice, snobbish, aristocratic, defensive.

More exaggerated was Lowell's valedictory address, titled "From Parnassus to Pittsburgh," in which he described Kenyon as an "Episcopal Valhalla" with compulsory classes, wherein "Incongruous learning, a rotation of polite daisy-picking and brutal cramming, is the precious, or at worst, purple pabulum of transcendental moonshine." He next turned his attention to the town: "Green with sweltering summer and breathless with a solemn, valetudinary fragrance, Gambier advertises the sociable splendors of a landscape where students drink beer and skim books." The "ignorance and irresponsibility" of a Kenyon education, he assured his fellow graduates, "are auguries of the opulence of your fathers." Lowell noted that it was not what one learned in the classroom, so much as "the conversations that mattered." This was certainly true in his own case, given the companionship afforded by the likes of Ransom and Jarrell.

Lowell's commentary on Kenyon reveals a pent-up and perhaps misdirected rage at what, to his mind, was the misappropriation of educational facilities. The failure of institutions in America became a central theme in the poet's oeuvre, ranging from the failure of the family unit to the rampant failure of the national government. For Lowell, Kenyon had attained the status of a poor man's Harvard, replete with Harvard shabbiness and indifference, the only real difference being the presence at Kenyon of a stimulating and artistic mind or two.

Lowell graduated not only a Phi Bete but a husband and a member of the Roman Catholic Church. He had begun his conversion during his last months at Kenyon. On April 2, 1940, he married California-born Jean Stafford (also a Catholic convert), daughter of John Stafford, a farmer and unsuccessful writer of Western stories under the nom de plume Jack Wonder or, occasionally, Ben Delight (before Jean's birth he wrote under his own name and he published his best known novel, *When Cattle Kingdoms Fall*). Allen Tate, who was fond of Jean, gave her away at the marriage ceremony. Two years older than Lowell, she was highly motivated, romantic, intense, introspective, a scrupulous craftsman—qualities that helped her become a top-flight author of fiction. She was awarded a master's degree from the University of Colorado at Boulder (where Lowell first met her), the same year (1936) that she was granted the baccalaureate. Wanting to break out of the mold of the provincial life she felt around her, she spent a year studying at the University of Heidelberg in Germany. She had gone there a political naif; Hitler meant nothing to her. She came away, she claimed, repelled by the German state. Yet when Lowell saw her again she looked like an Austrian farm girl, wearing white dirndl, pigtails, a white flower in her sunny hair; underarm she carried a mint copy of Christopher Isherwood's *Goodbye to Berlin,* which Lowell promptly commandeered and read. And so with his wife (to whom he would later dedicate *Lord Weary's Castle*), his bachelor's degree, and his Roman Catholic conversion, the poet at last stood outside the menacing shadows of Lowelldom and Beacon Hill, a whole-cloth Brahmin exile about to embark on the grand adventure.

~23~

"FIRE-BREATHING CATHOLIC C.O."

As THOUGH looking ahead to Robert Lowell's dilemma (while presumably delineating her own), Amy Lowell served up a tidbit in her *Critical Fable* that fairly crackled with irony:

> No one likes to be bound
> In a sort of perpetual family pound
> Tied by *esprit de corps* to the wheels of the dead . . .

These lines can be seen as an attempt on Amy's part to disassociate herself from her vain and preeminent ancestor James Russell Lowell, her bid to be recognized as a poet in her own right and not simply as a poet by coincidence of birth. The same words might as easily have been spoken by Robert Lowell, who shared with Amy, according to the British critic J. F. Crick, "her spinsterish refusal to conform"—not, obviously, in terms of marriage but in the choice of a career and life-style and in the attempt to break away from the darkness of a Puritanism stained by habits of guile, self-denial, taciturnity, and penitence. Clearly, Robert Lowell's nonconformist attitudes and concerns differed from those of Amy Lowell. His early life, Crick tells us, "is the old story of social position without the means to live up to it; 'cut down, we flourish,' the family motto of the Winslows and of the Kavanaughs of a Lowell poem, has a [wry] ring about it." The jockeying for social status, the garden party parlor-dream mentality, the tedious nature of benefits and philanthropies, held little or no interest for him; Robert Lowell would deal with the traditional claims of his heritage on an individual basis: through poetry—"and he would write New England's epitaph" rather than draw a Norman Rockwell day-glo caricature.

Knowing what he wanted to do had its advantages. Now he had only to set his temperament to the task, stop living like a writer and start writing. He was increasingly convinced that he should live conventionally, at least in appearance, he informed Merrill Moore in 1939. The poet should make his impact through his work not by flamboyant behavior. At the end of his letter to Moore he appended an emotional coda concerning the rapidly deteriorating political situation in Europe. He felt that artists and thinkers had an obligation to stand up for the Jews. His interest in politics, however timorous or stunted, would rise sharply over the next few years, peaking at the height of World War II, then receding dramatically until the mordant and destructive 1960's.

For the moment it was his financial predicament that remained uppermost on his list of priorities. At first he and Jean Stafford lived on expedients, and on what she could accrue from an assortment of teaching jobs. Lowell's parents contributed funds here and there in the form of birthday and Christmas presents. Although generous, the Lowells could not condone their son's wanderlust, his unwillingness to buckle down and prepare for a "proper profession." His mother felt, and expressed, the usual concern which, however elegantly phrased, comes down at last to a proper way of life for an absent son—proper diet and hygiene, proper social conduct and behavior, proper calling or profession. She was indefatigable in her pursuit of propriety, weighting her letters with witless remarks about "this Lowell" or "that Winslow" succeeding at such-and-such an enterprise or profession. The letters never ceased; they flowed like the Danube, continuing to arrive long after the poet's explosive retort of April 22, 1940, stipulating that he resented his mother's comments about his lack of direction and pointing out that what might be suitable for her might not be appropriate for him. He declared that he had not changed his direction for six years and could scarcely be banished for respecting the intelligence and heritage that had been the mark of his family.

To be sure, Lowell was not standing still but was slowly making headway in the world. John Crowe Ransom, who was now editing the newly founded *Kenyon Review*, accepted a pair of Lowell's poems for the first issue, published Winter 1939. Ransom followed this favor up by helping his former student procure a summer (1940) teaching post at Kenyon, also introducing him to the critic I. A. Richards. Richards, then at the summit of his career, convinced Lowell for the sake of his poetry to attain a working knowledge of mathematics and the sciences and to broaden his familiarity with his own country's history. Realizing that Richards spoke from a position of authority, the poet wrote to Abbott Lawrence Lowell, exploring the prospect of a Junior Fellowship in the Society of Fellows at Harvard. It was Abbott Lawrence Lowell who had founded this ambitious program for students seeking an interdisciplinary graduate program.

He began his letter to his Cousin Lawrence by saying that he was commencing a life devoted to poetry and a search for knowledge. In moving terms the poet pointed out that he not only had to learn about all of the arts and sciences, he had to preserve his spirituality, for poetry was both spirit and flesh. He was opposed to traditional graduate programs but was interested in the Society of Fellows program because he would be paid and would not have to write a thesis. In addition, a Fellowship would offer a wider choice of disciplines.

Lawrence's response was not encouraging. He seemed to feel that Lowell's presence in Boston would revive old family feuds. For one thing, it had gotten around the family circle that Lowell had not just knocked his father to the ground, but that he had knocked his father from the top of the stairs to the bottom, that he was black and blue, hospitalized for days, and had suffered a minor concussion.

While Lawrence found his relation's general plan of studies quite excellent, he pointed out that the Society of Fellows accepted only six or seven candidates a year who had already demonstrated standards of scholarship, which Lowell had not yet met. He advised Lowell to apply to some other large university where he could find the type of program and the kind of faculty that suited him.

Whatever the intimations of Lawrence's brief, Lowell was set on augmenting his undergraduate training with graduate courses in history and science. In September 1941, Lowell enrolled in a graduate program at Louisiana State University in Baton Rouge, where he was able to audit whatever courses suited his needs, including a seminar in contemporary poetry taught by Robert Penn Warren. Jean Stafford supported her husband that year by assisting Warren and Cleanth Brooks on the staff of the *Southern Review*, a well-endowed literary quarterly deeply entrenched in the doctrines of the Fugitive movement and in the elementals of New Criticism. Brooks and Warren, both graduates of Vanderbilt and both holders of Rhodes Scholarships to Oxford University, believed in the arena of discourse, in the existence of an unspoken literary order, and in the the timeless struggle between history and tradition, a conflict they attempted to explore in greater depth in their influential joint text, *Understanding Poetry* (1939), a mainstay of the Southern Agrarian school and a foundation stone of the New Criticism.

Lowell, as demonstrated by his correspondence at this point, felt uneasy about the prospect of being able to continue in the arts; he possessed neither the necessary financial resources nor an adequate background in theology to suit his discriminating literary needs. He portrayed himself in humid and muggy Baton Rouge as a transplanted urbanite, at base a good old Boston boy, at heart a lower-case catholic convert trying to cope with his upper-case Roman Catholic guilt. Catholicism had become for Lowell a significant emblem of his identity, and one he would make ample use of in his verse. Here was a ready retreat from urban manipulation and consumption, from the supposedly pristine Yankee ethos, from Protestant phlegm and the lethargic laissez-faire attitude of the industrial Northeast.

In a semi-autobiographical Stafford short story, "An Influx of Poets," published in *The New Yorker* late in 1978, shortly before her death, Lowell's first wife bitterly recorded what she considered the character called Theron's [Lowell's] "strange and unusual" behavior during their respite in Louisiana. Confession, daily mass at seven in the morning, benediction in the late afternoon, rosaries, communion, fasts, a remarriage ceremony in the Catholic church were all part of the daily ritual. Giving himself over completely to the seraphim and saints, Lowell mounted black-and-white photographs of Bellini's "St. Francis Receiving the Stigmata" and Holbein's "Thomas More" over their living room couch. From Dauber & Pine in New York, the poet ordered a leather-bound set of Cardinal Newman's works, which he perused while his wife read John of the Cross and Teresa of Avila's "Interior Castle." Although she underwent baptism at age eighteen, Stafford was no longer a believer: "I [Cora Savage] did not believe in any of it—not in the Real Presence, not in the Immaculate Conception, not in God." During mass she occupied herself by composing lists—lists of books she had read, lists of books she wanted to read, lists of birds, and lists of lists.

Lowell termed his wife's religious doubt "the dark night of the spirit" and maintained that hers was a temporary affliction. "But it isn't *doubt,*" she retorted, "it's positive repudiation!"

Lowell, at one time immersed in the rhythms of Gerard Manley Hopkins the poet, was explosively ignited by Gerard Manley Hopkins the Jesuit. A Christian poet, a convert to Roman Catholicism who became a Jesuit priest, Hopkins held Lowell's interest for the sheer physical sensuousness and emotional immediacy of his verse, as well as his austere strivings for religious purity. His exploration of rhythm and stress effects anticipated by a century many of the verbal patterns of contemporary poetry. But it was his absorbing love of God and abnegation of worldly love that enabled his work to blossom, and it was this aspect of the Jesuit's life that attracted Lowell. Before departing Baton Rouge, in order to authenticate his religious conversion, he submitted to the rites of baptism. He told friends that the act had both purified and freed him.

By 1940 the Tates had moved to Monteagle, not far from the University of the South at Sewanee. Tate's literary stock had skyrocketed, and his new home there had become a mecca for every literary pilgrim south of the Mason-Dixon line. Tate had clearly established himself as Eliot's devoted follower, writing poetry rich in allusion, symbol, and imagery, and essays that gave intensity and meaning to the work of forebears and contemporaries. "When I was twenty," Lowell told an interviewer, "Allen Tate, Eliot, Blackmur, Empson, and Winters, and all those people were very much news. You waited for their essays, and when a good critical essay came out it had the excitement of a new imaginative work." Through these critics, as well as Ransom and Jarrell, Lowell found himself taken up with the poetry of Emily Dickinson, Hart Crane, Wallace Stevens, Yeats, Dylan Thomas, Robert Bridges, Karl Shapiro, and Louis MacNeice, and such earlier poets as Donne, Herbert, Milton, Herrick, Shakespeare, Marvell, Crashaw, Jonson, Carew, Raleigh, Marlowe, and Samuel Daniel. He entered his favorite verses by these writers into a notebook, the better to get the feel of their use of phrase and line. Tate's house became everything for Lowell his own home in Boston had never been—a repository, a sanctuary of books and learning, an example of what James Russell Lowell called "the realms of gold." Although Lowell had trepidations about returning to Tennessee and immersing himself still further in the dated mannerisms of the Old South, he was happy to be back among friends. Sympathetic to the plight of Lowell's literary anxieties, Tate attempted as before to instruct the poet, guiding him through the rigid humanities, picking up where Ransom had left off at Kenyon. His success was duly recorded:

> Tate and Ransom, poets and critics, were Southerners and the line they took was that Southerners looked at the whole thing, and not just at intellect like a Yankee. If Ransom writes a poem about a man and a woman, the man is Calvinist and the woman a Southerner who knows flowers, the flesh, beauty and children. One might say that Catholicism notices things, the particular, while Calvinism studies the attenuate ideal. I have been too deep in that dogfight ever to get out.

The "dogfight" spelled out here by Lowell for the benefit of Ian Hamilton had its controversial, nonliterary side. The Southern Agrarians were conservative in their poetics and reactionary in their politics; they were opposed to the fashionable "Trotskyite" radicalism that was associated with Northeastern urbanity during the 1930's, the combative insularity and self-consciously fragmented modernism of the *Partisan Review* crowd, a freshet of faces that drew energy from Eastern European Marxist factionalism and introspective aggressiveness from Freud and his followers. The Southerners despised the literary and artistic currents that ruled "radical" factions such as the John Reed Club, the W.P.A. Writers Project, the *New Masses,* and the daily gatherings of Socialist intellectuals and Greenwich Village bohemians at Stewart's Cafeteria on Sheridan Square. The Nashville Fugitives deplored the fact that these sects were composed not only of liberals, which was bad enough, but of Communists, which was worse. The Agrarians felt that the prevailing cultural and literary divisions of the North had developed, not out of a tradition of rationalism or a belief in the principle of moral and intellectual authority, but as a result of the subordination of individual thought and rights to social demands and needs. It is astonishing therefore to discover in the prose writings of the Agrarians denunciations of "capitalism" almost indistinguishable in ferocity from those of their liberal adversaries. If Philip Rahv and Dwight MacDonald belligerently decried the philistinism of the public and the mendacity of the government, Tate and Ransom were equally critical. The natural arrogance that dominated the writings of the South's cultural elite can be found in sufficient measure in the flailing jottings of the fervid New York crowd. As time passed it became apparent that the two factions were not nearly as far apart as they at first appeared. *Partisan Review* eventually opened its pages to the New Critics and a tentative peace was reached.

Alan Williamson, in *Pity the Monsters: The Political Vision of Robert Lowell* (1974), attacks Tate's generation of writers for their "ivory-tower and apolitical (or theoretically reactionary) stances," a theme seized upon and expanded by Louis Simpson in *A Revolution in Taste* (1978). Simpson points to the separation of art and politics in the New Criticism as a dangerous, antihumanitarian position, made more precarious by the tenure of the times and the rapid ascension of the Fascist regime. Williamson and Simpson here are following the initiative of Van Wyck Brooks and Archibald MacLeish, both of whom attacked Tate and his circle for their political biases, labeling them "The Irresponsibles." Williamson blamed Tate and his fellow Fugitives for their indifference to the tragic events of 1939–1945, characterized principally by Tate's espousal that the war was the result of America's failure at statesmanship and that "the real victor in any war is war itself."

Tate's convictions, rife with isolationist and protofascist innuendo, are further defined by the title of his 1936 volume, *Reactionary Essays on Poetry and Ideas,* and by his World War II poem, "Pro-Consuls of the Air," in which he attacks American airmen for their bombing raids and subsequent destruction of the traditional values of Europe: "Dive, and exterminate / The Lama, late / Survival of old pain / Go kill the dying swan." Tate, adhering to the doctrines of New Criticism, insisted that literature must not be used for political purposes, pointing to the "universality" (as opposed to the "expediency") of art. Tate's claims notwithstanding, his convictions were blatantly political; as Simpson points out, Tate never hesitated to express his contempt for modern democracy, uncovering "Reds" and "Commies" wherever he looked. Convinced that he and his friends constituted the hub of an exclusive club, he opted for the kind of aristocracy that had existed in the antebellum South, a totem-pole society consisting of masters and drones. Simpson goes so far as to compare Tate to Ezra Pound, whose raucous chants on behalf of Mussolini made him a pro-Axis radio celebrity during World War II. Tate wasn't quite as extreme as Pound, but didn't lag far behind.

Tate's heterodox sentiments were bound to have their cumulative effect on Lowell. During the late 1930's and early 1940's he worked on a long poem called "Great Britain's Trial," which was weighted down by rhetoric and conventional right-wing, monolithic propaganda, seemingly modeled after Byron's "The Vision of Judgement" and not too

remote from James Russell Lowell's early *Class Poem,* at least in antilib-
eral swag. Robert Lowell's unpublished epic, writes Steven Axelrod,
"lifelessly lampoons Great Britain for its conventionality, materialism,
and anti-German foreign policy." In the poem, John Bull stands trial
with his codefendant Custom, his "ox-eyed queen." Other prominent
"personages" in the poem include Mammon and Armageddon, "along
with Satan who is a character witness for John Bull's defense." "The
callow turbulence of youth," to borrow a phrase once uttered by Lowell, is more in evidence in this epic than either craft or elegance.

It was not idle speculation, then, that sent the Boston poet scurrying
into the Southern Agrarian antiwar camp, but long hours of informed
discussion with a corps of highly articulate and intelligent Dixiecratic
writers, men such as Tate who saw man as fallen and government as an
instrument to protect man from his own base nature, from his own
egocentric sins. It was the rediscovery of fallen man, the nature of his
fall, and the failure of government to uplift and sanctify man that
provided the fabric for so much Fugitive writing. Lowell saw in their
ideology and in Roman Catholicism a way of rejecting the restricted
political views and narrow intellection of his native New England. Alan
Williamson, although unable to draw any hard or fast conclusions, picks
up on this point: "Lowell's conversion itself seems a radical gesture in
the Bostonian context, involving *déclassement* and the repudiation of
his ancestors' most cherished beliefs." The same motives that attracted
Lowell to the Agrarian/Fugitive movement, attracted him to Roman
Catholicism—the desire to rebel openly against his roots. What better
way to rebel than to align oneself with so alien a literary base as that
of the Southern Fugitives or so distant and orthodox a nuptial as his
marriage to Catholicism? Young and anxious to prove himself, he per-
severed in both directions.

Years later, conversing with Ian Hamilton, Lowell was able to rationalize his visitation into the rituals of the Roman Catholic church:

> I am not a Catholic, and yet I was. It came from despair and exuber-
> ance, the exuberance of learning a religion, and despair at my circum-
> stances, a student's problem—I was just married and couldn't get a job.
> I was too tense to converse, a creature of spiritual severity. Christianity
> was a welcome. I kept following more and more for a number of years,
> though now it seems unbelievable. When I meet knowing Catholics, I go
> along with them and feel I have somewhat their geography. I don't
> believe, but I am sort of a gospeller, I like to read Christ's own words.

Conversion to Roman Catholicism was a gradual affair that reached fruition for Lowell in Baton Rouge, but was inspired in part by his college readings: Hawthorne, Melville, English seventeenth-century preachers, Calvin himself, Gilson and others, some of them Roman Catholics. "Catholics and Calvinists," Lowell stated, "are rather alike compared to us in our sublunary, secular sprawl. From zealous, atheist Calvinist to a believing Catholic is no great leap." But the leap from nonbelieving Protestant New Englander to the Church of Rome was great enough and could not have been negotiated without the influence of the separatist Southern Agrarians.

It was from the Fugitives that Lowell learned to despise the mediocre tastes and abject emptiness of middle-class, bourgeois society. Lowell perceived in the formal rites of Roman Catholicism a viable means of flight, a way to leave the sterility and material strivings of Boston behind and symbolically transport himself to the city of Rome, a journey he managed to make vicariously by regularly attending mass. Besides the aesthetic attraction of Catholic formalism, there was the question alluded to earlier, of his rebellion against his dark, oppressive Puritan origins. Lowell felt constrained by the straitjacket of his heritage, the strict, complacent community of his upbringing, where class consciousness and racial prejudice reigned as imperiously as ever. In Boston, money did not talk—it screamed!

From the beginning Lowell was avidly aware of his self-image and of the impression that his image made on the outside world. He was extremely wary, for instance, of the title "American aristocrat," a descriptive tag that was silently pronounced whenever his name appeared in print. He once inquired of the present author whether the word aristocracy was not a red flag. It made no difference that he had used the term himself in a letter to his mother devised to defend his exploratory trek into the field of literature. If critics and reviewers insisted on associating him with the patrician class in America, he wanted it made clear that he was without their affectations, that he did not share their visions, that he possessed only a fraction of their material wealth. That fraction, of course, represented a rather tidy sum that allowed him more leisure and fewer responsibilities than most men. But it was not until 1954, with the death of his mother, that Lowell inherited the major portion of his legacy.

Lowell's religious conversion was in many respects foreshadowed by the conversion of T. S. Eliot. In 1926 Eliot converted to Anglicanism because it had something of the authoritarian and grandfatherly aura of the New England Unitarian church of his childhood and because of its ageless tradition and structured principles. In rejecting his American experience, Eliot concluded that "the virtuous man" must subordinate his selfish desires to the good of church and community, in order to accept a new order based on royalism, classicism, and Anglo-Catholicism. But Eliot, at the time of his conversion, was living in England and therefore found it unnecessary to transport himself all the way to Rome for his religion. Lowell, to escape the onus of his Puritan forebears, had all the reason in the world to make the long spiritual pilgrimage.

Allen Tate, still prodding Lowell, introduced him to the work of Jonathan Edwards, the graybeard Calvinist divine, encouraging him to write a critical biography of the early plutocrat. Although it never materialized, Lowell's exposure to Edwards reinforced his Catholic and classical aspirations; Edwards became the motivation for several expository poems, including the complex and doomsaying "Mr. Edwards and the Spider" and "Jonathan Edwards in Western Massachusetts." Edwards was also the triggering device behind Lowell's fond recollection of this period in the pages of *The Paris Review:*

> I was going to do a biography of Jonathan Edwards and Tate was going to write a novel, and our wives were going to write novels. Well, the wives just went humming away. "I've just finished three pages," they'd say at the end of the day; and their books mounted up. But ours never did. . . . We were in a little study together separated by a screen. I was heaping up books on Jonathan Edwards and taking notes, and getting more and more dumb on the subject, looking at old leather-bound volumes on freedom of the will and so on, and feeling less and less a calling. And there we stuck.

It was a "heady" period, a time, Lowell later ventured, "when the lid was being blown . . . when a power came into the arts which we perhaps haven't had since." The quartet in question labored diligently on their respective manuscripts. Caroline Gordon worked at her novel *The Woman on the Porch,* while Stafford churned out pages of the novel that became *Boston Adventure;* both were published in 1944. Tate toiled at a sequel (never completed) to *The Fathers,* and Lowell did his best to advance the Edwards biography. Finding themselves stymied, Tate and Lowell gathered their forces to edit jointly an anthology of sixteenth- and seventeenth-century poetry. The two found the verbally dense, complex, ambitious material of that period extremely bracing. Eventually, however, they abandoned the anthology, returning instead to their own work, Lowell producing some of the verses that would appear in his first two volumes, or at least the first drafts of those poems.

Camped midway between the poetic theories of Tate and Ransom and greatly influenced by the metaphysical practitioners, Lowell's poems became difficult, ironic, and ambiguous, substituting polemics and intellection for lyricism. Tate, leaning toward a Roman Catholic course (he converted from Protestantism to Roman Catholicism in 1950) and blasting the slipshod efforts of most of his contemporaries, influenced his admirer's early poems more than anyone, serving both as model and inspiration. Randall Jarrell would note that the "Allen effects" were everywhere in the early Lowell, the style, the theme, and the idea of "high discipline," the language containing "the heavy armor of the past." Lowell admired Tate because he was "the compleat book-man"—essayist, poet, translator, teacher, editor—and because he dressed his poems within the strict confines of traditional meters and forms, "the more demanding the better."

Behind Tate, of course, was Ransom, whose lamentations on the death of manners and good society found their most effective form of communication in the essays of *The New Criticism* (1941), a volume that sounds the call for a "self-consciously Aristotelian, ceremonious, and politically orthodox intellectual culture." Ransom's ideals, literary and otherwise, recalled the modificatory theories of I. A. Richards, William Empson, Yvor Winters, Cleanth Brooks, R. P. Blackmur, Kenneth Burke, and T. S. Eliot. Eliot's was the genuine voice, the strongest force behind the new critical method. His tremendous prestige as a poet gave such credulity to his critical opinions that the appearance of his collection of essays, *The Sacred Wood* (1920), with its first reference to the doctrine of impersonality, initiated a fresh trend in modern literary aesthetics. The trend stressed the importance of irony and paradox, while insisting that poetry be increasingly formal, elegant, and metaphysical. The emphasis was on the use of poetic tension and the employment of glimmering, sonorous meters that both pleased and educated the ear: "To write in meters but to make the meters look hard and make them hard to write." The poets most deeply influenced by Eliot, besides the Fugitives, were the members of the Middle Generation, those born in the first and second decades of the century. This group included Richard Eberhart, Randall Jarrell, Howard Nemerov, Theodore

Roethke, Delmore Schwartz, Karl Shapiro, Richard Wilbur, and of course, Robert Lowell.

As an interpretive tool the New Criticism called for the textual and not the contextual analysis of a poem. The job of the critic was to "explicate" the text, applying a rigorously empirical analysis of the relationship between words and ideas. The same rule held for other forms of writing: fiction, drama, the essay. The New Critics enjoined their followers to concentrate on the poem itself (the text), not on the poem's history and not on the history of the poem's maker. The reader ought to be interested neither in the poet's life nor his intentions (the intentional fallacy), not even in the work's effect upon the reader's emotions (the affective fallacy). The idea was to look at the work of art as if it had been created in a vacuum, as if, to give one example, the date when the work of art was produced was irrelevant to its understanding. The intelligence of the New Criticism attempted to isolate the words, phrases, and lines of a given work, to divorce these elements from the world that created them. By focusing on the isolated literary object, the reader would presumably be able to see the poem in its purest form, without the distraction of materials extraneous to a fuller comprehension of what the poem meant and how it worked.

By 1942 the Lowells, still leading their nomadic, carefree existence, had moved from the green hills of Tennessee to the hard pavement of New York City. At first they occupied a succession of small, modest apartments, including a cramped railroad flat at 131 Third Avenue under the El. They settled finally into one floor of a renovated brownstone at 12 Gansevoort Street in Greenwich Village. The poet had taken a position as an editorial assistant with the Catholic publishing firm of Sheed & Ward, founded in London in 1026 by the late Maisie Ward and Frank Sheed, that indomitable duo of Roman Catholic intellectuals. Brought to America in 1933, Sheed & Ward was considered the most avant-garde, often iconoclastic religious publishing house in this country, perhaps in the world.

Like many another writer, Lowell found the cosmopolitan world of New York exhilarating; it added the mayhem, the danger, the heat of living close to the edge, to the mostly theoretical schoolroom teachings that he had previously absorbed from Ransom and Tate. Traffic, skyscrapers, the cold texture of steel, the odor of ozone replaced the gentle, loafing pace of Boston's wealthy reaches and the polite gentility of agrarian Tennessee to which Lowell had been exposed during his years in the South. The sights and sounds of the poet's childhood expeditions to Walden Pond, Hyannis Port, Mattapoisett, and Provincetown could presently admix with the dizzying pattern of city streets, the splashy monad of metropolitan images. He became a walking pilgrim, prowling the city streets at all hours of the day and night, sensing the excitement of a blistering new setting. He was as much a foreigner amid this boiling sea of strangers as James Russell Lowell had been during his brief, youthful sojourn in New York. "The unforgiveable landscape" that was Manhattan would burrow deep into Robert Lowell's subconscious: "Now the midwinter grind / is on me, New York drills through my nerves, / as I walk / the chewed-up streets." The experience would lend dimension and substance, a new way of looking at things, to other, more remote sites. "The Public Garden" of his Boston youth would be recalled with the violent imagery that one normally associates with an urban poet such as Allen Ginsberg; Lowell saw it as "Burnished, burned-out, still burning as the year / . . . / The city and its cruising cars surround / the Public Garden. All's alive. . . ."

His poetry and position in publishing consumed him. Gradually other currents began to ripple the surface of his awareness: for one thing, there was a war on. Gasoline rations had been established and plans were underway for the government rationing of certain foodstuffs. Lowell, nervously conscious of the transitoriness of his present lifestyle, reflected on the question of the draft in a letter to his maternal grandmother, Mary Devereaux Winslow, stating that the coming war draft had a leveling effect on him. Nobody, whether conventional or not, had a clear future. Lowell felt that he was a prime prospect for the draft. But he was not opposed, and was willing to go in the event of war.

Acutely aware of the distinguished war record compiled by members of the family in previous wars, Lowell wasted no time in attempting to enlist, first in the Navy and then the Army; poor eyesight disqualified him from both. In time, with Tate's vociferations still reverberating in his ear, Lowell came out against the war, against the intervention of the American government on the side of the Allied command. His own evaluation of the war was that it was a horror and that only a Southerner could recognize the true terrors of being ruthlessly overpowered. In August 1943, when the draft finally called, the only response it elicited from Lowell was a letter addressed to President Franklin D. Roosevelt in which he outlined his refusal to report, and a three-page "Declaration of Responsibility" explaining his stance in greater depth. As the press saw it, Lowell wrote not as a dissident citizen to the all-powerful President of the United States but haughtily, as a Boston Lowell to a Hudson Valley Roosevelt:

Dear Mr. President:

I very much regret that I must refuse the opportunity you offer me in your communication of August 6, 1943, for service in the Armed Forces.

I am enclosing with this letter a copy of the declaration which, in accordance with the military regulations, I am presenting on September 7 to Federal District Attorney in New York, Mr. Matthias F. Correa. Of this declaration I am sending copies also to my parents, to a select number of friends and relatives, to the heads of the Washington press bureaus, and to a few responsible citizens who, no more than yourself, can be suspected of subversive activities.

You will understand how painful such a decision is for an American whose family traditions, like your own, have always found their fulfillment in maintaining, through responsible participation in both the civil and the military services, our country's freedom and honor.

> I have the honor, Sir, to inscribe
> myself, with sincerest loyalty and
> respect, your fellow-citizen,
>
> Robert Traill Spence Lowell, Jr.

The thousand-word Declaration of Responsibility that followed maintained that though members of his family had served in all of America's wars since the signing of the Declaration of Independence, "modern wars had proved subversive to the democracies, and history had shown them to be the iron gates to totalitarian slavery." When Pearl Harbor was attacked, Lowell imagined that his country was in intense peril and come what might, unprecedented sacrifices were necessary for national survival. He attempted to enlist, he said, but today

America's adversaries are being rolled back on all fronts and the crisis of the war is past. But there are no indications of peace. In June we heard rumors of the staggering civilian casualties that had resulted from the mining of the Ruhr Dams. Three weeks ago we read of the razing of Hamburg, where 200,000 noncombatants are reported dead, after an almost apocalyptic series of all-out air-raids. This, in a world still nominally Christian, is *news*. And now the Quebec Conference confirms our

growing suspicions that the bombings of the Dams and of Hamburg
. . . marked the inauguration of a new long-term strategy, endorsed and
co-ordinated by our Chief Executive. . . . By demanding unconditional
surrender we reveal our complete confidence in the outcome, and de-
clare that we are prepared to wage a war without quarter or principles,
to the permanent destruction of Germany and Japan. . . . If this program
is carried out, it will demonstrate to the world our Machievellian contempt for the laws of justice and charity between nations; it will destroy
any possibility of European or Asiatic national autonomy; it will leave
China and Europe, the two natural power centers of the future, to the
mercy of the USSR, a totalitarian tyranny committed to world revolution
and total global domination through propaganda and violence.

In closing his argument, Lowell wrote: "With the greatest reluctance,
with every wish that I may be proved to be in error, and after long
deliberation on my responsibilities to myself, my country, and my
ancestors who played responsible parts in its making, I have come to the
conclusion that I cannot honorably participate in a war whose prosecu-
tion, so far as I can judge, constitutes a betrayal of my country."

A carbon of this letter was dispatched by its author to Local Draft
Board 17, 412 Sixth Avenue in Manhattan, and they in turn sent it to
Assistant U.S. Attorney K. B. Friedman. It was Friedman who informed
Lowell of the penalties attached to the federal crime of draft evasion.
Lowell responded by stipulating once more that he had not the slightest
intention of reporting for induction into the U.S. Army.

For better or worse and with all that it entailed, he had taken a stand.
Under the headline "To Act on Draft Evader," *The New York Times* of
September 9, 1943, filed a report documenting the case in its entirety.
A day later the *Boston Post* conducted an interview with Charlotte
Lowell at her rented summer cottage in Manchester-by-the-sea: "Char-
acterizing her son's recent actions as 'poetic temperament' in refusing
service in the armed forces, Mrs. Robert Traill Spence Lowell, 20 Har-
bor Street, Manchester-by-the-sea, and also of Marlborough Street in
Boston, reaffirmed her faith in Robert T. S. Lowell, Jr., and added that,
'Everyone should have convictions and be respected for them.' "

In the final analysis, Lowell's decision to oppose induction during
World War II proved an embarrassment both to his parents and to the
Lowell family as a whole. Although the Brahmins were generally considered conservative, they were far from reactionary, and Lowell's declaration of intention to Roosevelt, while claiming conscientious objec-

tion, contained some of the same rhetoric adopted by our most extreme right-wing America Firsters. Individual members of the Lowell tribe claimed that their native son had failed to carry on the high tradition of his heritage, a charge levied against him by the press as well.

In dealing with members of his family, Lowell maintained a strong and forthright front, taking the full burden of responsibility for his actions. In writing to his Grandmother Winslow, he revealed that he had received counsel from two Catholic ministers and had carefully considered all possible alternatives before making his decision.

Lowell apologized to his grandmother for having caused her so much pain. He assured her that his two priests—the one in New York, the other his baptismal minister in Louisiana—had advised him to follow his conscience and trust in God. He had prayed and had tried unsuccessfully to persuade himself that he was mistaken.

To his mother he wrote that he would not ask for her moral support. He asked only that she not blame Jean Stafford for what were substantially his own ideas of how not to fight the war. He asked his mother not to be too concerned about what would happen to him.

Although Lowell seemed perfectly at ease with his proclaimed position, there was the larger philosophical question—so far as one can philosophize about war—of ultimate right versus ultimate wrong, the relative weights of empirical versus "democratic" conduct. At the very least, Lowell appears to have grossly, though not intentionally, misread the military situation as it existed in 1943. By September of that year, when he issued his controversial declaration, the United States had by no means stabilized its position on any major war front, save North Africa. Lowell's assertion that "the crisis of the war was past" and that America was rolling back her adversaries "on all fronts" was simply not the case. The truth is that the Allies were unable to gain a secure foothold either in Europe or in the Pacific until the early months of 1944. And at that point Josef Goebbels, Germany's astute propaganda minister, used the Allied demand of unconditional surrender for Germany in order to whip the German people into a state of all-out resistance so that for several months the two major forces were more or less deadlocked in a strategic stalemate. To the end, Hitler's warlords entertained notions of, if not a military victory, at least a political compromise. As late as 1945, Goebbels threatened terrible vengeance on the Axis "traitors" who welcomed the Americans with white flags, while planning his Werewolf underground to aid officers determined to resist

the Allied occupation. The Allies remained obdurate in their uncondi-
tional-surrender policies, at the same time that Goebbels advocated the
use of poison gas and renunciation of the Geneva Treaty in regard to
prisoners of war (he wanted to execute all Allied prisoners, provoking
the Allies to kill German P.O.W.'s in retaliation, thus deterring German
troops from surrendering). Given these historical facts and considering
the horrendous and appalling circumstances surrounding the Holocaust, one might well wish to delve deeper into the process of Lowell's
reasoning. Why, we must ask, was Lowell so concerned with the "national unity" of Germany or Japan when it was clearly the preservation
of the Jewish race that should have taken moral precedence? Why was
Lowell preoccupied with Russian expansionism at a moment in history
when the National Socialists were threatening to cannibalize the world?

There are no ready or easy answers. Certainly up to the time of Pearl
Harbor there were few indications of vacillation on the poet's part. He
wrote one poem entitled "Prayer for the Jews," and in his first volume
of verse included a poem ("Cistercians in Germany") highly critical of
the Nazi regime:

> Here corpse and soul go bare. The Leader's headpiece
> Capers to his imagination's tumblings;
> The Party barks at its unsteady fledglings
> To goose-step in red-tape, and microphones
> Sow the four winds with babble.

If the Nazis are portrayed as brutal heathens in this poem, Lowell
nevertheless believed that the war was largely economic in origin,
beneficial both to German and American financiers, bankers, and munitions manufacturers. He agreed wholeheartedly with Ezra Pound that
there was a drastic need for monetary reform in America, if for no other
reason than to break the financial bear hug of the power-hungry indus-
trialists. While an avid reader of the secular works of St. Augustine, St.
Bernard, St. Bonaventure, and St. John of the Cross, Lowell also followed closely several America-Firster publications, among them *The
Catholic Worker.* Like his friends at the *Worker,* Lowell believed that
somewhere along the line the American Constitution had been sub-
verted and America's ideals shattered; he insisted that after 1942 the
war was no longer constitutional and that American legislators had the
mental set and moral courage of cockroaches.

Sounding like a modern-day Henry James, Lowell called his homeland "this massive and mannerless democracy," a description supported in part by his more recent study of the writings of Christopher Dawson, Jean de Ménasce, Etienne Gilson, Wyndham Lewis, Eliot, Pound, and Tate, all of whom were right-wing adherents and part of a Christian revivalist movement. In addition to their conservative, religious, and political beliefs, the majority of these writing celebrities were both socially alienated from and bitter toward the moneyed ways of the democratic nations. Influenced by his reading, Lowell attacked money interests in several poems, citing Protestantism as a corrupting influence and capitalism as the ruination of religion. By cleaving art and politics, Lowell was in open violation of the New Critical tenet that prohibited such associations. So assiduously did the prospect of America's ruination vex Lowell that he made it the central theme in his first volumes of verse.

In subsequent collections he took the theme a step further, placing the blame for democracy's downfall on members of the tribe, particularly on the Winslows, whom he accused of aiding the war effort for reasons of personal gain, fiscal and otherwise. One of his central targets was Grandfather Winslow, whom he greatly admired on a personal level, but whose sole contribution to the world had been to make a fortune mining gold, before losing the bulk of it in Boston real estate, while purchasing yachts, homes, jewelry, and other personal possessions for his wife.

Lowell was equally perturbed by what he called "America's tendency toward violence in times of panic." He asserted that continued warfare with Germany could right none of that country's wrongs, nor bring back to life the soulful dead. It could only destroy what little honor and few lives remained. He violently opposed the idea of "total bombing," the all-out offensive launched by the Allies against Germany, because it made no distinction between military and civilian objectives in its rampant destruction. In an idealistic sense he opposed all warfare, placing Hitler and Churchill on roughly the same plane, condemning each for his murderous ways. One can only conclude that the war must have disturbed Lowell to such an extent that he was willing to make the most outrageous statements, allowing himself to rationalize the most vile pretensions.

In a symposium with Hannah Arendt and others in the Winter 1962 issue of *Partisan Review*, Lowell declared that "Every man belongs to his nation and to the world. He can only, as things are, belong to the world by belonging to his own nation. Yet the sovereign nations, despite their feverish last minute existence, are really obsolete. They imperil the lives they were created to protect." J. F. Crick has likened Lowell's position here to Arthur Miller's during the rage of McCarthyism, when the playwright expressed a similar point of view in opposition to the House Un-American Activities Committee. The comparison rapidly breaks down, however, when one recognizes that Miller's was a confirmed and total commitment to a set of standards that in retrospect seemed both reasonable and humane, whereas the known quantities surrounding the Second World War now make Lowell's convictions look increasingly foolish.

The apt counterpart in the case of Lowell is not Arthur Miller but Ezra Pound or perhaps Robert Frost, who spurned Louis Untermeyer's plea to lend his influential pen to the American war drive on the grounds that the war was an example of "British inadequacy and American irrationality." Frost, who wrote advertisements for himself his entire life, unabashedly announced that he was "nobody's propagandist." Later, following a partial shift of mood, he accompanied William Faulkner on a brief USIA reading tour "to help cheer the boys."

Lowell's statements in the *Partisan Review* are helpful as a guide to his sympathies at the time of his trial. "No nation," he declaimed, "should possess, use, or retaliate with its bombs. I believe we should rather die than drop our own bombs." The sentiment thus expressed sounds fine on paper, less practical when one considers that Germany too possessed, used, and retaliated with bombs. Lowell's response, while infused with elements of Gandhi's nonviolent philosophy, addresses itself only in the most indirect way to the political situation as it existed then and not at all to the exigencies of the military. The inflection of Lowell's discernments becomes more complex when we take into account additional information, such as the lines in his early poem, "Christ for Sale," in which anti-Semitism clearly emerges for the first time:

> In Greenwich Village, Christ the Drunkard brews
> Gall, or spiked bone-vat, siphons his bilged blood
> Into weak brain-pans and unseasons wood:
> His auctioneers are four hog-fatted Jews.

Few critics have taken up the question of Lowell's peculiar wartime sentiments. Jerome Mazzaro, author of *The Poetic Themes of Robert*

Lowell (1965), is among the few to single him out for his untimely strategies:

> For anyone emotionally engaged in fighting a war and to whom Hitler is pictured as the Devil incarnate, [Lowell's] sentiments . . . seem vindictive and nearly traitorous. To ask for fellowship and peace and to attack war and capitalism in the midst of such a struggle for existence seem to place superhuman demands upon one's fellowman.

John McCormick, whose interview with Lowell ("Falling Asleep Over Grillparzer") appeared in *Poetry* in 1953, has taken the position that Lowell was sentenced as a felon because at his trial, a decade earlier, "he offered in defense not religious convictions or standard pacifistic volutions but arguments against the Allied, and specifically American, demand for unconstitutional surrender, and against saturation bombing." An examination of the transcript of the trial bears this contention out.

Lowell's nonconformist ways, his developing despair and horror of warfare, found their familial corollary in James Russell Lowell's reaction to warfare, particularly as expressed in both series of *The Biglow Papers* and in other poems, tracts, essays, and papers. James Russell Lowell limited the scope of his antimilitaristic fervor to the written page but was active early in his career in behalf of certain radical causes. Robert Lowell may not have been directly influenced by his ancestor's distaste for war, but there is something to be said for each man's willed affectlessness in conflicts where the basic moral issues seemed so clear-cut. World War II, in Europe at any rate, was a struggle against blatant evil, knowingly plotted and routinely executed. The unspeakable acts perpetrated by the Nazis made it abundantly clear that this was not just another local squabble over territorial rights. One reason for the war was the Weimar's policy of conscious genocide, the ultimate crime against humanity, a crime insupportable by the moral standard of any age. World War II was no Vietnam, no undeclared war fought unconstitutionally behind the closed doors of the Pentagon. Robert Lowell's active opposition to America's ongoing participation in World War II was ultimately more extreme than James Russell Lowell's tragic shift of faith during the Civil War, itself a moral struggle in its secondary issue of slavery. While it is easier to understand the earlier poet's distaste for the blood-soaked and one-sided war in Mexico as depicted in the first series of *The Biglow Papers*, it is difficult to comprehend his basic objection to a war that had more to do with racism and oppression than with anything else. The difference between the two Lowells is that James Russell Lowell in analyzing the Civil War described its folly and futility, but did not disparage the moral fabric of those who participated. One senses that the old poet, if called upon, would gladly have fought on the side of justice.

Robert Lowell was granted a last opportunity to recant his position. He refused, and on October 1, 1943, an indictment was issued against him by a Federal grand jury. On October 12, he pleaded guilty in Federal Court in New York to violation of the Selective Service Act. Several days later he was sentenced as a felon by a trial judge who, in rejecting the young man's plea of conscientious objection, tossed Lowell's family name into his face: "You are one of a distinguished family, and this will mar your family traditions." In sentencing the poet to a year and a day, the judge showed unexpected leniency; the standard sentence for draft evasion during World War II was three years. In the end, Lowell served only five-and-a-half months, working the remainder of his sentence off mopping floors at a Catholic hospital in Connecticut: "It was filthier work than jail, but I was free and with my wife."

The sentence was evenly divided between Manhattan's former West Street Jail and the Federal Corrections Center at Danbury, Connecticut, where his companions were "mostly well-heeled gentlemen from the New York black markets, fallen, momentarily, from grace." West Street, as recalled in "Memories of West Street and Lepke" *(Life Studies)*, with its murderers, rapists, German Bund loyalists, hardened criminals, was an entirely different story. Rough, tough, and overcrowded, it was run in a very strict manner by officials who had little understanding for the human condition. For an hour each day, however, Lowell and his fellow convicts were taken to an exercise yard on the roof of West Street. The enclosure reminded him of his "school soccer court." In the distance, between sooty clothesline entanglements and bleaching khaki tenements, he could make out the Hudson River. Looking back from his present perspective, he wrote:

> These are the tranquilized *Fifties,*
> and I am forty. Ought I to regret my seedtime?
> I was a fire-breathing Catholic C.O.,
> and made my manic statement,
> telling off the state and president. . . .

One detects in Lowell's tone (*"manic* statement"; *telling off* the state and president") slight intimations of guilt, as though he had come to regret his wartime statements after all. Yet this is not the case, for as Lowell eventually admitted (to Ian Hamilton), he had nothing to repent or regret. In fact, jail had come as an almost welcome respite; it was boring but not unbearable:

> Jail was monotonous and weak on incident. I queued for hours for ciga-
> rettes and chocolate bars, and did slow make-work like wheeling wheel-
> barrows of cinders. I found life lulling. I slept amongst eighty men, a foot
> apart, and grew congenial with other idealist felons, who took home-
> made stands. I was thankful to find jail gentler than boarding school or
> college—an adult fraternity. I read—*Erewhon* and *The Way of all Flesh*
> . . . and God knows what . . . two thousand pages of Proust. I left jail
> educated—not as they wished *re*-educated.

In the same interview, Lowell said: "I refused to report to the Army, and sent a rather silly bombastic statement to President Roosevelt. I still stand on it."

So Lowell, always prepared to choose sides, had sided with Roosevelt's adversaries. The experience of a half-year behind bars surrounded by felons helped transport him out of John Foster Dulles's "tranquilized *Fifties"* into the politically dissonant Sixties. In time he came to look upon his incarceration as a process he was forced to endure in order to step up to the next rung of life's experiential ladder. ("I left jail educated —not as they wished *re*-educated.") In one sense he was a victim of happenstance just as Murder Incorporated's Czar Lepke (nee Lou Buchalter), a fellow prisoner at West Street soon to be electrocuted, was a victim of happenstance; by poem's termination, Lepke, with his Catholic rituals and patriotic zeal, becomes the poet's alter ego, a counter-persona against whom Lowell would measure his own disillusionment and failing mental health: "Flabby, bald, lobotomized, / he drifted in a sheepish calm, / where no agonizing reappraisal / jarred his concentration of the electric chair— / hanging like an oasis in his air / of lost connections." On another occasion he offered the following reappraisal of Lepke: "He was a mild soul—looked like an art critic I knew but less dangerous. Lepke was evil only as a negative reality." The art critic was presumably Clement Greenberg.

Another poem, "In the Cage," a sequence similarly reflective of the poet's prison experience (from *Lord Weary's Castle*), endeavors to contrast the prisoners ("Lifers") to canaries who "beat their bars and scream." The setting here is one of deprivation and desolation—mud, darkness, isolation, hopelessness, death: "It is night, / and it is vanity, and age / Blackens the heart of Adam. Fear, / the yellow chirper, beaks its cage." It is not clear in these lines whether Lowell means to suggest vanity as a possible motive for his wartime position. Ezra Pound, long a literary paradigm for Lowell, in the *Pisan Cantos* blames Vanity for baiting and drawing him further down the political path than he ought to have ventured, convincing him that he was Mencius and Confucius combined, a poet whose responsibility it was to issue mandates to his fellow countrymen on how to live and what to think. (Eliot had a passing flirtation with Charles Maurras and his royalist Action Française, but it was nothing compared to the noisy anti-Semitism and revolutionary rant spewed forth by Pound in the course of his elaborate defense of Fascism.)

At the core of Pound's prescription for "a house of good stone" was the unnerving drive of an American populist, the old-time rural zealot convinced that commercialism and liberal democratic capitalism were responsible for much of the social and economic injustice in the world. Lowell's mind-set was similar to Pound's. His moral indignation, always pressing hard on his sensitive and vulnerable conscience, found solace in the Agrarian movement's nostalgic bid for a more honorable and essentially monastic lifestyle. Less voluble and strident than Pound, Lowell nonetheless shared the older poet's contempt for America's wartime President. But while Lowell was by birth an aristocratic guardian of a culture he wanted badly to influence, Pound was an outsider to that culture, an exile whom the aristocrats had always ignored. Pound's problems were not Lowell's, and vice versa. Nor was discreet anti-Semitism in the hands of a few self-selected Southern nabobs the same thing as Pound's plundering tirades against Jewish bankers and moneylenders, "the hype of kikedom."

Although reluctant to admit it, Lowell was affected by his incarceration in a manner that seemed to have long- rather than short-term significance. Within a year of his release, he spent several weeks as a patient at McLean's, the private sanatorium in Belmont, outside Boston, where the mother of James Russell Lowell passed her last years. The hospital, with its elegant country-club ambiance, was filled with Boston Brahmins and wealthy New England men of letters. The strain of his prison term, while not dangerous in and of itself, no doubt exacerbated whatever potential for psychological debilitation already existed. Lowell's manic-depressive illness (which he jokingly attributed to "Spence negligence") became a recurrent problem resulting in periodic terms of institutionalization and incessant and often dangerous experimentation with medication and other modalities of therapy: megavitamins, hydrotherapy, wet sheets, hypnosis, insulin therapy, electroshock therapy, psychotherapy, and psychoanalysis. In the course of narcosis, which he was forced to endure for much of his adult life, he was administered enormous doses of such drugs as lithium, thorazine, and sodium amytal. Withdrawal from some of these medications often caused irritability, anxiety, tremors, even seizures. In later years, when Lowell tended to drink too much, the medication problem became even more acute.

Although he rarely mentioned it in public, he underwent several sessions of electroshock therapy, the first of these during his post-prison incarceration in McLean's. Sylvia Plath, in her haunting novel *The Bell Jar,* provides a graphic description of what it must have been like:

> Dr. G. fitted two metal plates on either side of my head. He buckled them into place with a strap that dented my forehead and gave me a wire to bite. I shut my eyes. There was a brief silence like an indrawn breath. Then something bent down and took hold of me like the end of the world. Whee-ee-ee-ee-ee, it shrilled through the air crackling with blue light and with each flash a great jolt drubbed me till I thought my bones would break and the sap fly out of me like a split plant.

Symbolically, one can probably attach manifold meanings to the bolts that crackled at Lowell's temple, reading into his poetry a caravan of related themes, none necessarily accurate. Is there any relationship, for example, between these sessions and his tendency to see in the advances of science and technology only the catastrophes and destruction they can cause? Is there a correlation between electroshock therapy and the central role that Lowell's body assumes in his work, or the excessive wounding and pain that are inflicted upon the body by the poet's psyche? The flesh in Lowell's later work is dangerously vulnerable to outside threats and forces seeking to invade and destroy it. Is this phenomenon also related to his early treatments? Who is to say what meaning the subconscious places upon certain aspects of the real? Pain cannot be precisely duplicated by the nervous system, but it can be recalled: cells have a memory. Surely when the poet describes the lobotomized criminal Lepke strapped into the electric chair, his mind "hanging like an oasis in his air of lost connections," he is registering his own reactions to "the great blue jolt."

Psychotherapy and psychoanalysis, both of which Lowell endured, encouraged him to acknowledge some of the warring forces within— the tensions between himself and his family, between himself and his country, between himself and his work. His mother, an avid believer in psychiatry and psychoanalysis, felt confident that in the charmed hands of a trained analyst, her son would discover the root cause of his unhappiness and that thenceforth his attacks would be permanently allayed. For several years Mrs. Lowell worked as receptionist and researcher for Merrill Moore in Boston and through him met a number of renowned psychologists and psychiatrists, who probably reinforced her conviction that her son could only benefit from therapy.

By his own admission, Lowell's approach to psychotherapy was that of the schooled intellectual. Exceedingly suspicious of the profession, he tended to look down on anyone who practiced it, and was convinced that most practitioners knew not a thing about the workings of the human mind. He tolerated Merrill Moore's advice only because of Moore's connections with the Southern Fugitives. Despite an inability to identify, Lowell was ever on the lookout for a new therapist and continued to seek help in this area for years, concurrently reading with extreme care Freud's *The Interpretation of Dreams* and other of the physician's classics; in addition he familiarized himself with Adler, Pfister, Ferenczi, Rank, and Wittels. And while he recognized Freud as the greatest of these, he soaked himself in Freud's coworkers and rivals and followers, the best of whom, he believed, had made valuable contributions to the understanding of man and his consciousness. Lowell was not, in any real sense of the term, a doctrinaire Freudian, but maintained the same degree of skepticism toward aspects of Freud's thought that he reserved for most of the therapists he conferred with in treatment. His appreciation of Freud was limited primarily to the scientific terminology of the discipline and an interest in the genius and "magic" of the man; the discipline itself, with its questionable Oedipal propositions and nominalistic probes into sexual identity, left him cold:

> I get a funny thing from psychoanalysis. I mean Freud is the man who moves me most, and his case histories, and the book on dreams, read almost like a late Russian novel to me—with a scientific rather than a novelist's mind. They have a sort of marvelous old-order quality to them,

though he is the father of the new order, almost the opposite of what psychoanalysis has been since. All that human sort of colour and sadness, that long German-Austrian . . . culture that Freud had, seems something in the past; but it was still real to him. There is something rather beautiful and sad and intricate about Freud that seems to have gone out of psychoanalysis; it's become a way of looking at things.

Leaving Freud behind for a moment, it should be noted that manic-depressive illness—alternating cycles of boundless elation and acute depression—is an area of relative mystery to the medical community, although recent findings have linked it increasingly to what can best be described as a set of biological clocks in the human body that fail to keep proper time. These biological clocks—thermostats might be a better term—regulate a variety of physiological functions: the rise and fall of body temperature, the production of important hormones and other substances that determine such basic urges as sleep and hunger. Every human being has ups and downs of mood, but depression or elation severe enough to be classed as illness is far more profound. The simplest daily tasks become impossible in the patient's mind. In the depressive stage, patients have been known to commit suicide. In Lowell's case, the depressive state was characterized by a slowing down of both mental and physical activity. He tended to complain of great misfortunes and believed himself guilty of many wrongs, while bemoaning the fact that nothing could be done about the situation. He was dejected, maintaining that he had disgraced himself and his family and that he was a hopeless failure in life. He could do little more than sit around or remain a prisoner in bed. He insisted that he was not fit to live, wished that he were dead, and sometimes asked those around him to take his life. So unable is the depressive to act that his simplest needs must be taken care of by others. In its more acute stages, the withdrawal of the patient is almost complete. If spoken to, he will not respond. The least movement requires tremendous exertion of will. When he does talk, it comes out in a mumble and is almost always self-deprecating. He sees himself as a sinner who is responsible for the unhappiness of many others. There are expressions of unreality, occasional hallucinations and delusions. Only in the most extreme state does the patient become totally unresponsive and stuporous. Otherwise there is little loss of intelligence, no deterioration of mental powers; in fact there is usually much insight but little desire to communicate, so that the heightened awareness does the patient little good.

The manic state, which usually precedes depression, is most consistently marked by overexcitement, overactivity, an uncontrollable flight of ideas. The manic personality simply cannot sit still. Superficially, the picture is one of a self-confident individual who is having a glorious time, flitting from one form of activity to another. The patient's reactions are speeded up to an unusual degree and if it were not for his easy distractability he might be capable of accomplishing a great amount of work. His attention, however, is difficult to catch and almost impossible to hold for any considerable length of time, since he responds actively to each new stimulus that presents itself. His conversation may appear incoherent because of the endless rush of ideas which follows each new stimulus, but he is generally in contact with reality. He is inclined to show off, especially before strangers, and does not hesitate to butt into the affairs of others. He frequently clowns around or acts outrageously for those around him and is likely to address pointed remarks to anyone who appears in his vicinity. He is witty in his rejoinders, with quick answers for every question and situation, and in a group tends to monopolize the conversation, always insisting on being the center of attraction. In hospital, he is up and down the corridors, looking into each room and talking with everyone, from nurses to fellow patients. In its more acute form, the illness affects the patient in such a way that he becomes excessively dogmatic and intolerant of criticism. He is under the impression that he can do almost anything, that he can do everything better than anyone else, and that his knowledge is unlimited. The patient may become disoriented in acute mania, and there may be considerable clouding of consciousness with transitory hallucinations of the wish-fulfillment type. Ecstasy often turns to irritability, impatience, anger, even violent anger, the patient breaking furniture, pounding walls and floors, attacking bystanders. At his most extreme, the subject must be forcibly restrained.

Researchers have been able to determine that many symptoms of manic-depressive illness, previously thought to be random events, are actually biological rhythms, albeit abnormal ones. Those who suffer from the disease have been found to have biological rhythms that drift away from the normal twenty-four-hour cycle dictated by terrestrial day and night. The same drifting has been observed in normal persons who have been isolated for long periods in closed environments such as caves, where the steadying signals of sunlight and darkness and other environmental clues are not present. Thus when a patient goes through a manic stage and is unable to sleep for many hours, his sleep cycle has simply been rearranged by improper bodily impulses. Scientists have isolated the hormone melatonin, a chemical created by the pineal gland and known to be intimately involved in the regulation of biological clocks, and have determined that production of the hormone is much greater in manic-depressive patients than in normal individuals.

What circumstances might produce this condition in humans is presently unknown, a target of future research. Experiments in which rats are kept for long periods in environments of abnormal light and other unusual conditions suggest that this kind of derangement can be induced artificially. One can assume, therefore, that the enforced conditions and prolonged artificial lighting of a penal institution might conceivably have a similar effect on a person already prone to the disorder. If this is the case, Lowell's World War II imprisonment could easily have played a catalytic role in helping set off his manic-depressive condition.

Future generations of dissertation writers may wish to traffic through the poet's collected works for traces of time imagery and symbolism in connection with his cyclical ailment. A strong case can probably be constructed in support of the thesis that mental illness determined the flow and outcome of many of Lowell's poems. Certainly we can see in a number of his sequences, particularly those in *Life Studies,* the effect on the poet of the Freudian case study, the tendency to examine up close the psychological characteristics of his subjects, the zoomed-in portrait of the over-life-size character. Metaphor, which plays an astonishingly large part in psychoanalysis, plays an even larger role in poetry. Freud imparted the universal lesson that new words, like good poetry, can extend and increase our understanding or sense of an experience. Freudian methodology also imparted the lesson of detachment as a necessary precondition for any kind of in-depth personality probe, the sort that we find scattered throughout Lowell's oeuvre.

The Freudian view of man as a being largely determined by unconscious needs and desires strengthened the poet's belief that poetry, very much like the dream, was a "release of emotion and energy." In opposition to Freud (or as an extension of Freudian thought), Lowell sensed that poetry was a cerebral reaction to internal stimuli and that only at certain moments were subconscious forces released, molding and choosing and coloring, lending the poem a glitter and sheen, a technicolor vividness that was closer to the vividness of a dream than the vividness of life. At these instances, usually after many rewritings of the poem, the subconscious took over the poet's self-willed cerebral reactions; the poetic process, at its highest creative level, "involved the release of a series of verbal discharges which proceeded in associated chains which, stored in the unconscious, were self-generating once they were set in motion by a stimulus." It was for this reason that the emotional impact of the finished poetic product usually exceeded the stimulus from which the poem originated, the theory being that the poet's subconscious charged the poem with emotions and meanings of which he was barely aware.

The manic highs and desultory lows of Lowell's mental condition came upon him in spurts, suddenly, without warning: "Mania is extremity for one's friends, depression for one's self. Both are chemical. In depression one wakes, is happy for about two minutes, probably less, and then fades into dread of the day. Nothing will happen, but you know twelve hours will pass before you are back in bed and sheltering your consciousness in dreams, or nothing. It isn't dangerous; it's not an accomplishment. I don't think it a visitation of the angels but dust in the blood." Depression, despite what people say, was no boon to creation: "Depression's no gift from the Muse. At worst, I do nothing. But often I've written, and wrote one whole book—*For the Union Dead*—about witheredness. It wasn't acute depression, and I felt quite able to work for hours, write and rewrite. Most of the best poems, the most personal, are gathered crumbs. I had better moods, but the book is lemony, soured and dry, the drouth I had touched with my own hands. That too may be poetry—on sufferance."

"Dust in the blood" and "Spence negligence": these tropes meant little to Charlotte Lowell. In a brief to Merrill Moore she registered her own analysis of her son's condition. Her feeling, based on her reading of psychiatric tracts, was that Bobby's emotional problem stemmed from an insufficiently developed ego, which left him unable to manage the libido when he was excited. In defense of her theory she quoted Jung's statement that "A man must stand firmly on his ego function. He must fulfill his duty toward life completely. Anything that he neglects in this respect descends into the unconscious and reinforces its position." She wrote that her son's lack of a sense of responsibility, and the need to protect his own egocentricity, was a constant threat to him. She wondered how such an attitude could result in any mental stability. She added that writing poetry was no excuse for his unacceptable behavior.

Although to say so is to grossly oversimplify matters, Mrs. Lowell's commentary is a classic illustration of a mother's boldfaced attempt to belittle, even to emasculate her son, as she had earlier and under altered circumstances belittled and emasculated her husband. Here we have the model for the nagging, pushing, matriarchical figure of *Life Studies,* the woman who wrote to Jung about her son, read books on psychiatry, discussed her husband's failings in front of others, and expatiated on the decline of the family fortunes to her only child.

Small wonder, as one critic phrased it, that "the dominant women in Lowell's poetry seem monster-Clytemnestra-projections" of this behemoth of a woman. She truly believed that her son could modify his behavioral pattern at will, turn his feelings on and off as readily as one regulates a water faucet. Her hardened attitude led Lowell to suspect that she lacked respect both for him and his profession, that she neither understood his career nor cared at all about it. As time passed it seemed to him that her sole concern was that he succeed, regardless of the price, regardless of the cost. In a sad way, this reflected his own response as well.

Lowell's repeated respites in mental hospitals, his perpetual struggle to stay sane, provided the smarmy substance for any number of syntactic jottings on the subject of insanity. His three-month stay during 1954 at McLean's became the focus of a triad of poems in *Life Studies:* "Waking in the Blue," "Home after Three Months Away," and "Man and Wife." In "Waking in the Blue," we learn that McLean's "seems to collect people of old stock . . . thoroughbred mental cases," among them Stanley, a man now sunk in his sixties, once a Harvard all-American fullback ("if such were possible!"), who still sports the build of a boy in his twenties and is consumed by the welfare of his body; and "Bobbie," Porcellian '29, a replica of Louis XVI, "redolent and roly-poly as a sperm whale." Both are the pathetic relics of a New England no longer extant, a Boston alive only in photographs. Only at McLean's, a place where the psychotic rich are pampered instead of given serious psychotherapy, will one find an atmosphere that re-creates the aristocratic glitter of Harvard thirty years earlier. The very grandeur that Harvard attempts to produce in its graduates is fit fare, Lowell seems to be saying, only for the unreality of a looney bin.

Placing himself within the context of this unreality, a voyeur but at the same instance "one of them," Lowell concludes the poem on a further irony:

> We are all old-timers,
> each of us holds a locked razor.

Although open-ended, this unrhymed couplet suggests that only suicide (or death) can deliver these mummified wrecks from the futility of their lost lives.

The prisoners of West Street and the patients at McLean's, though from markedly different social backgrounds, begin to merge in Lowell's verse, as they undoubtedly merged in his mind. As the poet tells it, Czar Lepke was as devout an aristocrat, with his cell full of contraband—"things forbidden the common man: a portable radio, a dresser, two toy American flags"—as Stanley and "Bobbie" on their ward in Bowditch Hall (a name that reeks as much of Harvard as it does of McLean's). The lunatic and criminal each stand outside the pale of conventionality. To this brotherhood, Lowell attaches still another category: the religious. Orthodox Catholic symbols pulse through all the prison and asylum poems. Lowell has marshaled a Trinitarian gathering of ego-damaged exiles: "The lunatic, the lover and the poet / are of imagination all compact." "Lowell's poetry, his lunacy, his felony, and his Catholicism all conspired," writes Philip Cooper, "in his revolt against the heritage of the Puritan Fathers. But he is a puritan, a father, a patriot and WASP citizen, descendent of the *Mayflower,* at the same time that he contrives his revolt." Lowell was a mutinous member of that caste which from the outset had supplied the leading men and women of the community: the divines, the scholars, the judges, the commanding officers —"in short, the shepherds of the common herd."

~~S~~ 24 ~~Q~~

BLACK MUD

IT WAS impossible to write poetry in America in the 1940's or '50's and avoid the influence of T. S. Eliot; the authority that Eliot commanded in the literary and academic marketplaces of that period was unsurpassed. Lowell was no exception in his idolatry of a literary reputation that inspired an almost religious following. "Eliot," he wrote, "made an achievement unparalleled in our time: his work all hangs together and his greatest poems are long ones. Not since Pope, perhaps, has anyone written so well at such consistent length." While Eliot's poetry did not directly influence his own, Lowell was inadvertently influenced by Eliot's poetics. In his 1921 essay "The Metaphysical Poets," Eliot wrote: "The poets of the seventeenth century, the successors of the dramatists of the sixteenth, possessed a mechanism of sensibility which could devour any kind of experience. . . . Those who object to the 'artificiality' of Milton or Dryden sometimes tell us to 'look into our hearts and write.' But that is not looking deep enough; Racine or Donne looked into a good deal more than the heart. One must look into the cerebral cortex, the nervous system, and the digestive tracts."

In a 1944 essay on Gerard Manley Hopkins published in the *Kenyon Review,* Lowell said much the same thing about Hopkins that Eliot had said about Racine and Donne, insinuating that Hopkins too had searched his innards and incorporated his visceral findings in the best of his work: "Hopkins was able to use most of his interests and experiences in his poetry. . . . If we compare him with his peers in the 18th and 19th Centuries, we see that he was able to do this rather more than others." Lowell shared Eliot's conviction of the necessity for total commitment to the craft of poetry, a secular, almost holistic devotion to it. Eliot and Hopkins, both of whom Lowell came to appreciate through the offices of Tate and the Agrarian Fugitives, were important models for Lowell at the beginning of his professional career. The strong and orthodox faith that permeated their poetry took form as the central metaphor in his own slim first book, *Land of Unlikeness*, hand printed in 1944 by Harry Duncan's Cummington Press, Cummington, Massachusetts, in an unpaginated edition of 250, with an introduction by Allen Tate and a wood engraving by Gustav Wolf of a cross and gargoyle intersecting. The title page contained a legend from St. Bernard, which translated read: "As the soul becomes unlike God, / So also it becomes unlike itself." The grotesque image of cross and gargoyle coupled with the epigraph depict a nightmarish inferno, a land (America) whose inhabitants have lost their likeness to God and whose sole tie to reality is the eternal struggle that transpires in any harshly materialistic society. Fittingly, Lowell had corrected the proofs in prison.

True to its form, the volume records the quest of a modern Christian for religious salvation in a world of chaos and doom. Lowell's World War II wasteland is composed of a grid of settings, an essentially native landscape with a shelled-out, postwar Europe hovering in the background. Churches, graveyards, and crucifixes join hands with Christ, the Virgin Mary, and the Holy Ghost in a colorful, littered mosaic of complex stanzas and tortured lines. Merging poetry with religion and equating both with culture, the poet utilizes a hard, strained iambic measure, in three-foot, four-foot, and five-foot lengths, straying from the standard beat in order to avoid monotony and to achieve heightened poetic effects. Lowell engages a number of the techniques he would repeat and refine in his later work: alliteration, contrast, repetition, parallelism, ideogrammatic transitions.

The book opens with "The Park Street Cemetery" and closes with "Leviathan," a despairing Miltonic revision of the Cain and Abel legend, whereby Cain's descendants, atoning for his sins, are tortured by the evils of a modern-day metropolis. The graveyard setting of the first poem, with its roll call of "the stern surnames: Adams, / Otis, Hancock, Mather, Revere," announces what would become a permanent theme in Lowell's work: the bespotted heritage of Boston's Puritan past, with its hierarchical order of villains and heroes, makers of war and peace. Related concerns emerge piecemeal: salvation and damnation, poverty and wealth, good and evil. These were the focal points around which the ambitious young poet would weave his first collected strands of published verse. And always, peeking over his shoulders—Amy on one side, James Russell Lowell on the other—are the relentless members of his own patrician clan.

With his extreme sense of society, the poet perceived himself as the inheritor of a *Mayflower*-rotted "poor bred-out stock," a clan of patriarchs whose collective guilt he must now in some way share. The fast-vanishing past, therefore, is always part of the poet's present. Lowell's vision of the historical process—like Spengler's, Toynbee's, or Ortega y Gasset's—resides in the notion that history is an active force, a living organism, forever fluid and capable of renewed change. Ezra Pound in *The Cantos*, Eliot in *The Waste Land* and *Four Quartets*, and Joyce in *Ulysses* had navigated the same waters. Already in *The Spirit of Romance*, his 1910 study of Provençal poetry, Pound expressed a view of time that is basic to a good deal of Eliot and Joyce and later to Lowell: "It is dawn at Jerusalem while midnight hovers above the Pillars of Hercules. All ages are contemporaneous."

In Lowell's verse, Boston's past and present are treated as tangential and contemporaneous dimensions, the one illuminating the other. In "The Park Street Cemetery" the rainbow reveries of the Pilgrim ("The stocks and Paradises of the Puritan Dracos / New World eschatologies / That fascinated like a Walpurgis Nacht") are contrasted with today's Boston, a diminished city where Easter throngs crowd the Commons and "strangers hold the golden Statehouse dome." The city where Puritan and patriot, Yankee aristocrat and proud immigrant came to settle, is here portrayed as having been swept into total decay. But even colonial Boston, with its narrow streets and narrow minds, did not broaden into anything but a brutal vista in Lowell's eyes. Nor is Boston the only locus of ruin. Salem and Concord, with their rich heritage, are likewise the sites of rampant commercial and moral decay. At Salem, "sea-sick spindrift drifts or skips / To the canvas flapping on the seaward panes" and "sewage sickens the rebellious seas"; Concord, in Lowell's eschatological record, is left only with its "ruined bridge and Walden's fished-out perch." Lowell's vision of Concord segues back to Emerson's less ironic version of "the ruined bridge" in "Concord Hymn," that uplifting hymnal to the tiny wooden bridge where Major Buttrick's Concord Minutemen tangled with militant redcoats, sending the country over the Revolutionary brink. The reference to "Walden's fished-out perch" connotes not just present-day stultification but brings Thoreau to mind. Thoreau works here in a subliminal, associative sense to return the reader to Emerson and his heroic ode. The reader may also denote echoes of several James Russell Lowell poems, such as "Lines Suggested by the Graves of Two English Soldiers on Concord Battleground" and "Ode Read at the One Hundredth Anniversary of the Fight at Concord Bridge," which themselves segue back to Emerson's "Concord Hymn." Their common point of departure is what accounts for the partial similarity between the poems of the two history-bound Lowells.

But it is Roman Catholicism, not history or literature, that supplied Robert Lowell with the symbols and terminology for the majority of these poems, especially the ones emphatically about war. "Christmas Eve in the Time of War: A Capitalist Meditates by a Civil War Monument" reappeared in his next volume *(Lord Weary's Castle),* somewhat altered and retitled as "Christmas Eve Under Hooker's Statue." In the first version a wealthy profiteer "bawls for Santa Claus and Hamilton / To break the price-controller's stranglehold," before experiencing a religious revelation that enables him to recognize that his own material gains were the result of youthful greed and venality. The second version emphasizes the same conflict between faith and peace on the one hand and materialism and war on the other. The main difference between them is that in the later rendition Herman Melville, and not an apocalyptic Christ, is the spokesman for God: " 'All wars are boyish,' Herman Melville said; / But we are old, our fields are running wild: / Till Christ again turn wanderer and child."

More puissant than either version, although similarly endowed with religious symbolism, is "The Bomber," a poem ironically addressed to an American airman:

> O godly bomber, and most
> A god when cascading tons
> Baptized the infidel Huns
> For the Holy Ghost,
> Did you know the name of flight
> When you blasted the bloody sweat
> And made the noonday night:
> When God and Satan met
> And Christ gave up the ghost?

Allen Tate, in his introduction to *Land of Unlikeness,* probably had just such a poem in mind when he suggested that Lowell's style, his symbolic language, though bold and powerful, had the effect of being willed; Donne-inspired puns and Blakelike shifts of tone, combined with strained religious symbolism, overload the poem and the volume's circuits. Not by coincidence, Tate's criticisms can as easily be applied to his own work, with its patented air of formality, heightened syntax, regular meter, stylistic dislocation, linkage of abstractions with the concrete. Stylistically, Tate emulated Donne and Dickinson, while Lowell imitated Tate. "The Bomber," for instance, is very nearly a rewrite of Tate's "Ode to Our Young Pro-Consuls of the Air." Among other similarities, both poems derive their inspiration and perspective from a characteristic politics of orthodox conservatism. That Tate was able to recognize these failings in Lowell's output but not in his own is most peculiar indeed.

To his parents, Lowell wrote that the poems in *Land of Unlikeness* were prayers for the historic freedom and dignity to remain Christians in a Christian society. As religious poetry goes, these premature efforts while well intentioned were riddled with an overabundance of argument and ornamentation, though not enough air and light to be as readable as they otherwise might have been. What the collection amply demonstrated was that Lowell's poetry possessed the energy that only imagination can supply; he had still to master the rudiments of Gresham's poetic law of diminishing returns, which states that the more sounds and images you crowd into a poem, the less spark they generate. Or as Auden said, the poet's job is to find out the images "that hurt and connect."

R. P. Blackmur, reviewing *Land of Unlikeness* for the *Kenyon Review,* was in accord with Tate's analysis: "Lowell is distraught about religion; he does not seem to have decided whether his Roman Catholic belief is the form of a force or the sentiment of a form. . . . What is thought of as Boston in him fights with what is thought of as Catholic; and the fight produces not a tension but a gritting." For the record it should also be noted that Blackmur criticized Tate for depending too heavily in his verse on the idea that an objective body of religion and a political body of myth are prerequisite to the construction of a complete culture. In his desire to imitate the T. S. Eliot of *The Waste Land,* Tate (according to Blackmur) was guilty of the same militant willfulness and strident arbitrariness that turn up in the early Lowell. Both poets churned out selections that too often read as though they had been written, and written again, and then written some more. The result was

a poetry that was overly solemn and serious, crammed with a sometimes laborious theology and enough deadly metaphors to fill the stuffed
owl's mouth for generations to come.

In compiling his next volume of verse, *Lord Weary's Castle* (1946),
the poet was able to recognize some of the earlier collection's faults. He
included approximately one-half of the poems, greatly revised, from the
first collection: "I took out several that were paraphrases of early Christian poems, and I rejected one rather dry abstraction, then whatever
seemed to me to have a messy violence. All the poems have religious
imagery, I think, but the ones I took were more concrete. That's what
the book was moving toward: less symbolic imagery."

The second collection, although slightly toned down, was a further
exploration, via complex stanzaic patterns and rhyme schemes, of
Boston, World War II, and the religious concerns of modern man.
The strained figures of speech and exaggerated melodrama of the
first book had been reduced, but the poetry remained dense with
images and allusions, frequently of a Catholic origin. The reader's
problem then had not essentially changed: those who did not share
the poet's faith were forced to exercise a suspension of disbelief in
reading the new book; as in the previous volume, there was a kind
of stilted robustness to the versifier's religiosity that too often failed
to convince.

The title for Lowell's second volume comes from an old ballad:

> It's Lambkin was a mason good
> As ever built wi' stane:
> He built Lord Wearie's castle
> But payment gat he nane. . . .

"Lambkin," as Lowell spells it, suggests both lamb and Cain, contrasting
symbols: "the murderous Cain and the merciful Lamb of God." The
Lord Weary of the title can be regarded as a veritable *Jedermann,* an
Everyman; his castle, described in "The Exile's Return," the volume's
opening poem, stands for the ravaged structures and "torn-up tile-
stones" of occupied Germany. Man's task, as the poet would have it, is
to reconstruct this symbolic castle, and by reconstructing it provide
shelter for a society "unhouseled" by war.

Extending our perceptions, we can see the Exile of "The Exile's

Return" either as a German refugee (perhaps a German Jewish refugee) returning to his battered homeland following World War II or, in literary terms, as Lowell himself reentering the world following his wartime incarceration in a federal prison. It is significant that for the purpose of the poem Lowell has borrowed phrases and ideas freely from Thomas Mann's novella, *Tonio Kröger*; Kröger, preempting Lowell, stands uncomfortably between two worlds, the world of the merchant and the world of the artisan. In the poem, as in Mann's novella, the dispossessed Exile lumbers "down the narrow gabled street," past his "gray, sorry and ancestral house." This sequence suggests a return not only to bombed-out Germany, but to 91 Revere Street, a metaphorical return to the scene of the primal crime, where a boy (reenacting Cain's attack on Abel) knocked his father to the ground.

The various motifs that course through the book are bound together by a single pervasive theme, which according to Randall Jarrell was that "Betrayal and bloodshed everywhere mark the human predicament with the brand of Cain." Ever the questing pilgrim, Lowell sought a mocking, ironic, aggressive, visionary poetry, a poetry resonant with prophetic significance and full of fiery denunciations. Everything is bleak, dark, oblique, depressing. Yet the strongest of these soulful carpings are charged with electricity.

Although he later renounced it as a lesser poem, "Colloquy in Black Rock" strikes this reader as illuminating, engaging, volatile. The sequence came to Lowell all of a piece, "Wordsworthian-wise—walking," following his release from prison but while he was still on parole, mopping up black mud in a Catholic hospital in Black Rock, Connecticut, reporting once a week to his parole officer, while reading Toynbee on his days off. The cycles and spheres of Toynbee's moving picture of history influenced the poet's nontransitional mode, his tendency to glide back and forth in his verse between history, religion, and current events without the slightest break in flow. The craftsmanship and power of language signal the coming of a major voice:

> Black Mud, a name to conjure with: O mud
> For watermelons gutted to the crust,
> Mud for the mole-tide harbor, mud for the mouse,
> Mud for the armored Diesel fishing tubs that thud
> A year and a day to wind and tide; the dust
> Is on this skipping heart that shakes my house . . .

Just as powerful is "The Dead in Europe," with its familiar opening lines: "After the planes unloaded, we fell down / Buried together, unmarried men and women." An ode to the victims of war bombings, the poem was written during those decisive days when Lowell was particularly perturbed by the problem of whether or not to become a conscientious objector. Here again Lowell's use of imagery is of a highly graphic and suggestive order, the Catholic mode underlying everything. In the poem, the dead ask the intercession of Mother Mary on the day of Resurrection, expressing their symbolic fear of damnation unless they are buried, as Catholics should be, in blessed ground: "O Mother, snatch our bodies from the fire: / Our sacred earth in our day was our curse." The poem ends on a personal note, the poet expressing the fear that man has permanently renounced God.

Throughout the most interesting parts of the book, historical and religious themes intertwine in equal proportion, while autobiographical fragments also occasionally enhance the flow. In both "The Drunken Fisherman" (Lowell's first popularly recognized poem) and in "As a Plane Tree by the Water," Lowell marches to the martial music of rebellion against the crush of his Puritan, New England, capitalist heritage. "The Drunken Fisherman" is all allegory, with its mining out of such powerful rhymed couplets as: "Is there no way to cast my hook / Out of this dynamited brook." "As a Plane Tree by the Water" is much more a direct indictment of the past, without the allegorical trappings:

> Darkness has called to darkness, and disgrace
> Elbows about our windows in this planned
> Babel of Boston where our money talks
> And multiplies the darkness of a land
> Of preparation where the Virgin walks . . .

"Children of Light," a ten-line sequence, attacks the turmoil of the Puritan fathers in a poetry of epistemological thrusts, utilizing language that stretches the outer reaches of our shared assumptions. The short poem epitomizes Lowell's preoccupation with the failure and death of the Puritan tradition. The decisive break with tradition finds dramatic expression in the juxtaposition of past and present, wherein the crime of Cain is magnified many times by the crimes of the Puritans against the Indians and italicized by the horrific events of World War II:

And here the pivoting searchlights probe to shock
The riotous glass houses built on rock,
And candles gutter in a hall of mirrors,
And light is where the ancient blood of Cain
Is burning, burning the unburied grain.

Other poems, though outwardly more gentle, often seem less compelling. "Mary Winslow" was written for Lowell's long-lost *Mayflower* relation: ". . . our Copley ancestress, / Grandiloquent, square-jowled and worldly-wise, / A Cleopatra in her housewife's dress." "In Memory of Arthur Winslow" is a four-part dirge for the poet's grandfather, the once-wealthy mining engineer and mine owner, a stalwart Bostonian, member-in-good-standing of the Union Yacht Club. But the relationship between the child Lowell and his grandfather is plumbed in greater depth in "91 Revere Street," where we learn of the boy's strong attachment to the old man, their trips together to the Stark-Winslow family burial ground in Dunbarton, New Hampshire, to rake the autumn leaves from the plots and gravestones. Arthur Winslow was that pillar of strength for Lowell that his weak and impotent father had never been: "A ray of hope in the far future was my white-haired Grandfather Winslow, whose unchecked commands and demands were always upsetting people for their own good—he was all I could ever want to be: the bad boy, the problem child, the commodore of his household." Other sections of *Life Studies* sing of Grandfather Winslow in a similarly laudatory voice. In "My Last Afternoon with Uncle Devereux Winslow," his grandfather's summer house is described thus: "Like my Grandfather, the décor / was manly, comfortable, / overbearing, disproportioned." The same poem opens with Lowell snubbing his parents in favor of his grandfather: " 'I won't go with you, I want to stay with Grandpa!' / That's how I threw cold water / on my Mother and Father's / watery martini pipe dreams at Sunday dinner."

"In Memory of Arthur Winslow" is an emotional etiology, a brief Kaddish for the poet's grandfather, whose body was interred in that same small country cemetery in Dunbarton; the cemetery is featured in several of Lowell's poems, particularly in one named for the site, which begins: "My grandfather found / his grandchild's fogbound solitudes / sweeter than human society." "In Memory of Arthur Winslow" re-creates his grandfather's death by cancer, in Phillips House, a private hospital in Boston, where Lowell himself was admitted years later, ill with pulmonary edema, water on the lungs, an episode captured in "Phillips' House Revisited" (*Day by Day,* 1977). Cancer, in the Winslow poem, is symbolized by its zodiac sign: "Your people set you up in Phillips' House / To settle off your wrestling with the crab— / The claws drop flesh upon your yachting blouse." The awful specter of cancer is a central Lowell metaphor in a number of poems, including "Half a Century Gone" *(Notebook),* where the poet ponders "the intimations of my family cancer, / With us no husband could sit out the marriage; / those shadowy patriarchs, once gamed like children, / they lacked staying power, not will to live. . . ."

Another of Lowell's somber symbols is the figure of Charon, ferryman of the dead, who appears in the Arthur Winslow elegy to bear the old man's body away—"and crush the crab." In the end it is Christ the Savior who bears his grandfather's weightless body upon a trumpeting black swan up the River Charles to the Acheron and beyond. In "Mary Winslow," Charon, "the Lubber, clambers from his wherry" to stop Mary's "hideous baby-squawks and yells." Her death and deliverance are measured by the tolling bells of King's Chapel Tower that cry " 'Come, / Come home . . . / Come, Mary Winslow, come; I bell thee home.' " In both poems the Charles serves as the River Styx, the channel Charon crosses to claim the bodies of the dead.

A third Winslow, the poet's cousin Warren, is honored in "The Quaker Graveyard in Nantucket," easily *Lord Weary's* finest moment. The sequence, penned originally in seven sections, interweaves strands of biblical and classical imagery with ecology, geography, and New England marine biology to depict in dispassionate and sprawling terms the essential paradox of Christian faith at the same time that it explores the more tangible theme of the death at sea of Warren Winslow. It is apparent by now that all the water imagery in *Lord Weary's Castle* ("the deep where the high tide / Mutters to its hurt self, Mutters and ebbs") and the use of water as a governing image in other volumes make Lowell one of the chief aquatic poets of his day. Astrologers in search of due cause will point out that Lowell was a Pisces, which he acknowledged in "To Allen Tate I" *(Notebook 1967–68):* "my month Pisces." The ruling planet of the sign of Pisces is Neptune and the symbol is the Fishes: water was Lowell's natural astrological habitat.

Factual account has it that the young sailor Warren Winslow perished aboard the USS *Turner* on January 3, 1944, the victim of a massive, self-inflicted explosion in the engine room. The *Turner* sank, not in the

North Atlantic as the poem indicated, but while anchored at the entrance to New York harbor, about two miles south of Rockaway Point. The disaster, reported in the next day's *New York Times,* provided the poet with the basic material for his work. He prefaced "The Quaker Graveyard" with a biblical epigraph: "Let man have dominion over the fishes of the sea and the fowls of the air and the beasts and the whole earth and every creeping creature that moveth upon the earth." The sequence, as the epigraph portends, is not merely the portrait of a dead kinsman; in its broadest terms the poem's reviling of war and Puritan roots and the slaughter of innocent whales by the "peace-loving" Quakers of Nantucket suggests life's futility and the senselessness of death. This is no political poem but an attack on an immoral social order, a furious rant in the face of impending disaster, a painful examination of the paradox of religious grace.

The poem's length and complexity add to its three-dimensionality and mythic potentiality; it echoes the deaths by water of Edward King and John Keats. In attempting to resolve the unnecessary death of a young man, it bears a distinct resemblance to Milton's "Lycidas." The command of medium, the sense of rhythm, the technical virtuosity and compact imagery, are on a par with early Eliot, specifically *The Waste Land.* Lowell's intricate tapestry of biblical and classical references and New England history contains all the power and objectivity of the Pound-edited Eliot epic.

There is an additional point of comparison between early Eliot and early Lowell. Eliot's first published volume, *Prufrock and Other Observations,* was dedicated to Jean Verdenal, a French medical student whom Eliot had befriended in Paris during 1910–1911. Verdenal, an assistant medical officer in World War I, was killed in 1915 while dressing a wounded soldier on the field of battle. His death, which occurred during the Battle of the Dardanelles, saddened Eliot immensely. Adapting the incident to fit his literary needs, Eliot made death by drowning ("Death by Water") a major motif in *The Waste Land.* Verdenal is very likely Phlebas, the Phoenician sailor whose drowning is recalled in the recurring line "Those are pearls that were his eyes." Water images and sounds are scattered throughout Eliot's long blank-verse sequence.

Lowell plunges into Eliot's wake. "The Quaker Graveyard at Nantucket" begins with a twelve-line adaptation of "The Shipwreck," the introductory chapter of Thoreau's *Cape Cod.* It then proceeds to Ahab's relentless chase of the great white whale in *Moby-Dick.* This metaphysical pursuit underscores the first five sections of the poem; it relates to the harsh descriptions of man's violence and greed as seen in the figures of the New England whalemen who, in the "mad scramble of their lives" for the riches of the sea, provide a meaningful base of comparison to the youthful innocence of Warren Winslow. Winslow, a Harvard graduate of about Lowell's age, represented, in the poet's view, a close ally whose untimely death mirrored all the wasted lives lost in wars.

As in *The Waste Land,* the events surrounding Warren Winslow's death have been transmogrified by the poet to accommodate his every literary need. In the first section, presumably narrated by a member of the crew of a battleship in the North Atlantic, the corpse of a dead sailor is fished out of the choppy sea. Weighted down by sandbags, the body, its open, staring eyes now sealed, is given a proper sea-burial replete with two-gun salute. Parts II, III, IV, and V take place at a Quaker graveyard in Nantucket; the speaker is the poet, addressing his drowned cousin; his elegy for a kinsman dead at sea wonderfully mingles the terror and grandeur of the Atlantic with a lament for a lost tradition and heritage characterized by the separation of man from his Maker. The speaker berates the Ahabs of this world who destroy everything that man lives by, including God. The brutal description of the white whale's violent capture and mutilation in Section V signifies the extent of man's corruption and evil. The whale's penetration by the harpoon is purposefully sexual, the wound pulsing with the whale's fluids:

> The fat flukes arch and whack about its ears,
> The death-lance churns into the sanctuary, tears
> The gun-blue swingle, heaving like a flail,
> And hacks the coiling life out: it works and drags
> And rips the sperm-whale's midriff into rags,
> Gobbets of blubber spill to wind and weather,
> Sailor, and gulls go round the stoven timers
> Where the morning stars sing out together
> And thunder shakes the white surf and dismembers
> The red flag hammered in the masthead . . .

"Thunder shakes the white surf" marks the poem's shuttering climax and transports the reader to the postcoital calm of Section VI. This "little tranquil island in all the fury" is characterized by an old shrine at Walsingham, England, where the speaker, a pilgrim, sees a statue of the Virgin; her "expressionless" face "expresses God." Structurally, this penultimate segment helps bridge the gap between the cataclysmic opening portions capped by Section V and the peaceful tones of the poem's denouement, with its depiction of the Quaker graveyard in Nantucket, where "the empty winds are creaking and the oak / Splatters and splatters on the cenotaph."

The added significance of the "Our Lady of Walsingham" sixth section is that it helps elevate the poem from a moral to a mystical level. While the ugly slaughter of the whale echoes the harpooning of a whale in Chapter LXI of *Moby-Dick,* there are obvious biblical references as well, suggesting the crucifixion of Christ and the coming of Judgment Day (apocalypse). The Walsingham interlude is necessary as a means of tying together the religious symbols found in the earlier sections of the poem and the metaphysical conceits of the final episode. Based substantially on E. I. Watkin's description of the same statue in *Catholic Art and Culture,* published by Sheed & Ward in 1944, the Walsingham section sets up the poem's final resolution, whereby Lowell resigns himself to Warren Winslow's terrible fate, and thereby to the terrible fate of all humankind.

25

"BETWEEN THE PORCH AND THE ALTAR"

THE LATE 1940's represented an active period for Robert Lowell, a period of transition, enhanced by the stunning reception accorded *Lord Weary's Castle*. The volume was awarded the 1947 Pulitzer Prize for Poetry in addition to the coveted American Academy of Arts and Letters Prize, and helped Lowell win a Guggenheim Fellowship—an astounding sweep for so young a poet. Yet what was perhaps most satisfying for him was the acclaim he received from critics and writers of his own generation, from Louise Bogan and Paul Engle to Delmore Schwartz and Howard Moss. Randall Jarrell, with his marvelous intelligence of poetry and sympathy for literature, immediately saw Lowell as the poet of a generation; Jarrell lived and died for literary excellence and when he recognized it in the work of others his public praise knew no limitation:

> I know of no poetry since Auden's [he wrote in *The Nation*] that is better than Robert Lowell's. Everybody who reads poetry will read it sooner or later. . . . *Lord Weary's Castle* makes me feel like a rain-maker who predicts rain, and gets a flood which drowns everyone in the country. A few of these poems, I believe, will be read as long as men remember English.

Jarrell's reference to "predicting rain and producing a flood" constituted a flurry of well-deserved self-congratulation; he had spotted

Lowell's talents from the first and had never backed off. With the publication of *Lord Weary,* he began to look more and more like a soothsayer. Other poets, of more immense reputation, offered similar words of laudation. George Santayana, living in Rome, found in *Lord Weary* "the barrenness of Puritanism and the lure of antiquity." William Carlos Williams wrote Lowell that the famous Boston family of his birth had finally produced a poet of note. Williams, opting always for a straightforward literary style, had not expected to find Lowell to his liking and was pleasantly surprised:

> . . . I have been reading *Lord Weary's Castle;* it's interesting to me that you have found a way to mention local place names without that jumping out of context which so often occurs to make a work false sounding. It's very hard to treat of American things and name them specifically without a sense of bathos, of bad sentimental overlap resulting. . . . Look at Thoreau. Something happens, something happened even to Henry Adams, even to Henry James when the United States was mentioned. It is very difficult and somewhat obscure what happens—but you have got by nicely I think. Maybe it's because you anchored your data in ground common to Europe and to Christianity. . . .

T. S. Eliot considered Lowell "up to form"—reserved, but for Eliot, generous praise. John Berryman ventured that the world had before it "a talent whose ceiling is invisible," while Peter Viereck exclaimed that "the great American poet of the 1950s" had arrived. Donald Hall, a half-generation younger, said that "it took us some years to scratch out, in our own poems, the sounds of *Lord Weary's Castle.*" Only Leslie Fiedler, in *The New Leader,* expressed reservations, not so much for the poetry as the theology behind it. It was generally agreed that of the 43 poems in *Lord Weary* (ten of them from *Land of Unlikeness*) almost all demonstrated the poet's ability to zero in on concrete particulars in an intense and animated manner. Lowell's imagery worked. His "still breaking sea" rose up as if to engulf everyone who cared for poetry. It was an aggressive volume, full of plosives and hammering energy, a masculine voice such as one finds in the strongest rhythms that emanate from Ezra Pound. Tate's magic had swept over Lowell, and out of Tate's influence had evolved something quite unexpected: a new voice, without the vision of grace that we find in Dante and in parts of Tate. No grace at all, just the burning spirits of Hell, and the faint hope that Christ really did die for our sins after all.

New doors opened for Lowell. Nominated by the Fellows in American Letters and approved by the Librarian of Congress, Luther Evans, the thirty-year-old Bostonian assumed the position of Consultant in Poetry at the Library of Congress, Washington, D.C. During his year-long term (1947–1948) he laid the foundation for an archive of recordings by America's leading contemporary poets, to be made available at low cost to educational institutions, libraries, and interested individuals. Among the poets drafted by Lowell for the collection were Eliot, Williams, Auden, Warren, Cummings, Wallace Stevens, Robinson Jeffers, Carl Sandburg, and Marianne Moore.

The rewards may have been evident, but the strain of having come so far so fast began to tell. For one thing, Lowell's marriage to Jean Stafford had been limping along now for a number of years. At the termination of Lowell's parole in Connecticut the couple moved to a four-room apartment on Kirkland Street in Cambridge, Massachusetts. Living so close to home apparently wore on Lowell. He argued incessantly with his parents and with his wife. Stafford, it seemed to him, shared many of his mother's worst features, particularly the stubbornness and the grating will. His drinking and his demands on her became increasingly unbearable. One day he was ready to join a mission house in Dorchester, the next day they were packing their suitcases for an extended stay on an uninhabited island in the South Pacific.

They settled instead for a simple farmhouse, an attached barn, and a tree-shaded lawn at Damariscotta Mills on the coast of southern Maine. Jean Stafford had purchased the house and property with monies received from the sale of *Boston Adventure*. While she supervised carpenters, plasterers, plumbers, and electricians in their attempt to renovate the house, her husband dawdled in Cambridge or spent time at a Trappist retreat in New Jersey. The Maine house was a cozy affair with red velvet draperies, Swiss-organdie glass curtains, a mossy wall-to-wall carpet in the living room. Its charm evaded Lowell, who closeted himself away in a small study and worked on his poetry, producing a substantial number of the antiwar poems contained in *Lord Weary's Castle*.

A fierce winter with two feet of snow at a time and only an antique oil-burning stove and two small electric heaters (one used primarily to keep the pipes from freezing over) made life in Maine difficult. If Lowell's poem, "The Old Flame" (its title borrowed from a passage in Virgil's *Aeneid*), is any indication, life in Maine must have been extremely difficult: "How quivering and fierce we were / There snow-bound together / Simmering like wasps / in our tent of books! / Poor ghost, old love, speak / with your old voice / Of flaming insight / That kept us awake all night. In one bed and apart."

At first they were happy in Maine, a part of the country that was new to them, and which they explored together with excitement, sharing its throbbing sights and sounds. The house itself gave pleasure. It was old and derelict but its lines and doors and window lights were beautiful, and the couple was pleased with it all. In the blue evenings they read at their ease, hearing no sound but that of night birds—loons by a neighboring lake and owls in the tops of trees—and in the afternoons they took long walks into the wooded surroundings or they rowed on the lake or ran errands together—prepared meals and washed dishes, tended the fires, and shopped for supplies and staples in the general store of the village.

Gradually the magic of the moment dissolved into irresoluble conflict. As the shorter days of winter came and went, Lowell spent more time alone behind the closed doors of his study and less in company with his mate. The arrival on the scene of itinerant house guests—Peter Taylor, Frank Parker, Randall Jarrell—temporarily alleviated the tedium of his days, driving the couple even farther apart. "It was the first summer after the war," Jean Stafford reminisced, "when people once again had gasoline and could go where they liked, and all those poets came to our house in Maine and stayed for weeks at a stretch, bringing wives or mistresses with whom they quarrelled, and complaining so vividly about the wives and mistresses they'd left, or had been left by, that the discards were real presences, swelling the ranks, stretching the house, *my* house. . . ."

These overextended visits obviously annoyed Stafford, who would much have preferred to be alone with her husband. "At night, after supper," she complained, "they'd read from their own works until four o'clock in the morning, drinking Cuba Libres. They never listened to one another; they were preoccupied with waiting for their turn. And I'd have to stay up and clear out the living room after they went suddenly to bed—sodden but not too far gone to lose their conceit. And then all day I'd cook and wash the dishes and chop the ice and weed the garden and type my husband's poems and quarrel with them."

Stafford's indictment of her husband's decorum in those days was justifiably harsh. He had adopted an attitude of accepting as little responsibility for his share of the relationship as humanly possible. But one hand cannot clap alone; by staying around for too long, Stafford only made herself an accessory to the crime. She aided and abetted Lowell in his violation of her rights. She placed herself in a compromising position, accepting his abuse without the least resistance. When she was not cleaning or cooking or fussing about the house, she became his typist—and if he "changed an 'a' to a 'the' the whole poem had to be typed over again."

To ward off apathy and loneliness, Stafford turned out fiction at a reasonably comfortable pace. *Boston Adventure* (1944), a novel about the proud and futile decadence of Boston society, crept steadily up the best-sellers chart, netting the author a tidy income for several seasons; it was followed by *The Mountain Lion* in 1947. Stafford's prose explored such popular literary themes as cultural dissolution, self-alienation, family disintegration, childhood, the lesions of isolation and loneliness, the quests for love and self-justification. Thematically, these probes resembled his, at least those probes that he made after *Lord Weary's Castle*. Yet their relationship was gradually growing apart, and there seemed no conceivable way of healing the wounds. Separated at the end of August 1946, they were granted a Virgin Islands divorce two years later.

In his study of Lowell, Philip Cooper reminds us of a *New Yorker* short story by Stafford, "A Country Love Story," with its impressions of life with her "difficult" husband, and her creation of an "imaginary" lover. The fiction provided fragments of the imagery for Lowell's "The Old Flame," with its hint of the poet's second wife, Elizabeth Hardwick. A double link occurs in the poem in the lines, "No one saw your ghostly / imaginary lover / stare through the window. / and tighten / the scarf at his throat." Jean Stafford's imaginary lover had been mysteriously preempted by Elizabeth Hardwick; the title of Hardwick's first novel, published in 1945, was *The Ghostly Lover*, an autobiographical story about a young Kentucky girl anxious to escape a family that she had outgrown but that enforced her allegiance by appealing to her sense of guilt.

The schism between Lowell and Stafford manifested itself in his refusal to spend time with her and was aggrandized by her inability to win over his family. Her visitations with her husband to the Boston residence of the Lowells were marred by long stretches of silence and anger on the part of everyone concerned. Convinced that their son had married beneath his social class, the Lowells never treated her as a member of the family and on several occasions attempted to embarrass and belittle her.

Another probable factor in the dissolution of their relationship was the critical and fiscal success that greeted Stafford's first novel, which came at a time when Lowell was still struggling to establish the first traces of his own literary reputation. It was Stafford who supported them during these difficult and lean years. Her breadwinning capabilities, her willingness to bankroll her husband, must have become a major psychological threat in his mind, reinforcing his view of himself as a disinherited scion of the last aristocratic clan in America.

Inspired by the improbability of making a financial killing on the basis of his poetry, Lowell tried his hand at penning a novel, composing several hundred pages of not very convincing melodrama over a three-month period before aborting the project and returning to his chosen craft. Resuming his lonely vigil, he reopened the breach between husband and wife. Hardly a day passed that they did not bicker over one thing or another; they might dispute a question of fact, argue a matter of taste, catch each other out in an inaccuracy. Every quarrel ended with Lowell's declaration that he had nothing to say to his bewildered spouse, followed by his inevitable retreat behind the locked door of his study, which was by now located in a finished room in the barn.

Their daily jousting, which in time increased markedly in timbre, was underscored and reinforced by the distilled and voluminous taste of aged whiskey, followed by chasers of beer or milk. Both parties attempted to relieve their anxieties and frustrations by drowning themselves in alcohol. The drinking only led to more blatant hostilities. They argued bitterly over who drank more. She claimed he did. He claimed he had learned to drink "at home in the drawing room," so that he knew *how* to drink. "You don't drink well, dear. Not well at all," was a favorite refrain that he threw at her whenever other words failed him. And he was right: she didn't drink well. After one particularly brutal bout of arguing and drinking, Stafford—at the end of her tether—ground out a lit cigarette on the back of her left hand. Beyond pain and unable to break her drinking habit, she hid away in sleep, oftentimes sleeping for hours in the daytime, suffering what she later claimed were religious hallucinations and somatic disturbances. Then, no longer able to sleep or hold down her food, she suffered nervous tremors and migraine headaches that forced her, temporarily, to abandon her art. A late-summer trip out West to visit her sister terminated instead in the locked ward of a mental hospital in downtown Detroit, with steel bars on the windows and screaming madmen roaming the corridors. Released from the institution, she traveled aimlessly from Chicago to Denver and back, emerging several weeks later in a gruesome little room facing a dank, dark courtyard in a seedy hotel in New York's West Village. A year later she no longer remembered the name of the hotel or where in Greenwich Village it was located.

During this period she came into contact with almost no one; she drank heavily, added antidepressants to her daily regimen, and cried for hours on end. Even when her doctor prescribed sleeping pills, they rarely worked, because the habit of sleep was broken so completely that she was helpless to form it again. Afternoons she would go downstairs to the hotel bar and sit there until it closed at three in the morning and then she would return to her room and drink applejack, waiting for the morning to dawn, contemplating insanity and suicide. She stopped washing herself or her clothes, wore dark glasses indoors and out, and began to spend more and more time in bed. By early 1947 she had committed herself, at the instigation of her psychiatrist, into Payne Whitney Clinic on Sixty-Eighth Street and First Avenue. For the next year she found herself a virtual prisoner on the same ward her husband would occupy at a somewhat later date. Her illness was diagnosed as conversion hysteria, also known as conversion reaction, characterized by episodes of disorientation accompanied by periods of deep depression and anxiety, even panic. Amnesia, paralysis, constant fatigue, and mutism, which are also symptomatic of the illness, occurred only in mild form. She went through several hysterical twilight states in which she was confused and distressed, an experience having an unreal and dreamlike quality for her. For months she was unable to bring herself to speak above a whisper. This bodily symptom represented a converted form of energy, thus giving the ailment its name.

One cause of her psychological collapse can be traced to the duress she experienced as a result of her husband's affair with Gertrude Buckman, an editor and occasional critic whose reviews and articles appeared periodically in *The New York Times Book Review, Partisan Review, The New Republic,* and *The Nation,* and whose difficult marriage in 1939 for six years to Delmore Schwartz paralleled Lowell's precarious betrothal to Jean Stafford. Short, dark, emotional, but also pretty and curvacious, Miss Buckman had serious aspirations as a classical musician. Outwardly, at least, she struck Stafford as a strange choice of companion for her status-conscious, Boston Brahmin husband: "She was not the kind of woman he liked; she was flirtatious, competitive, argumentatively political." She was also Jewish. Lowell, writes Stafford, "was, by heritage and by instinct, anti-Semitic, and soon after we met [Delmore Schwartz], he dumbfounded me by saying, 'I would never have a Jew as a close friend.' And they never had been close—not in the way he was close with friends from boarding-school and college days."

The affair that Lowell began with Buckman while she was staying with the couple at their Maine homestead turned messy predominantly because it took place directly under Stafford's nose. And because it transpired in her own backyard, Lowell's wife misapprehended the intensity of the affair. True, Lowell was attracted to Buckman. Her natural assertiveness and sense of independence, her warmth and patience appealed to him, but only at a point in his life when he had little intention of becoming permanently involved with any other woman, least of all Buckman. He admired her sense of self, her native strength and cosmopolitan sophistication, her ability to commingle comfortably with any combination of people from any walk of life. She was also an intense and interested listener, and this ability in tandem with his own overt desire to confess were the main ingredients in their short-lived but intense attachment, the first of many such extramarital arrangements for the poet. In effect, he was taken with her because she was taken with him.

In addition he was bored with his wife, whose "nesting and neatening compunctions" he looked on as comparable in manner to the "plebeian, anti-intellectual, lace-curtain Irish." Her pride of house was the sin of pride. But pride was all she had left: "Dishonored, I would ascend refreshed, putting aside the ruin of this marriage shattered so ignominiously by *the other woman,* by that most unseemly of disgraces, above all by something not my fault, giving me the uncontested right to hate him."

Lowell's farewell to his wife was delivered with unfeeling alacrity: "I don't want a wife," he had said, "I want a playmate." Before closing the Maine house for the summer (hence for good), Lowell had drowned the family cat and her litter of kittens, placing them in a gunnysack and weighting it with stones, then rowing out on the lake and dropping them among the perch and pickerel. Both literally and figuratively their marriage was dead.

Following their separation, Stafford's letters to him bristled with indignation and pain, enunciating the intensity of her suffering; spilling her deepest feelings into these confidential letters, she complained of being misunderstood and mistreated by Lowell. It is not clear if the letters helped alleviate the anxieties that haunted her, although they did illustrate and illuminate the pervasive suffering to which she was subject. In brief they insisted that, for some time Lowell had loved another and that his guilt made him hateful and cruel. Nevertheless, she would wait for him, because she loved him and wanted to be married to him—at least, she would always have the hope that he would return.

Stafford, unable to resign herself to the failure of her marriage (though able to admit that she herself had committed indiscretions), maintained that they had never really tried marriage. The conditions, she said, had never been right. Now they were presumably perfect: She had stopped drinking, the Church was no longer of such importance to him, and he was now successful.

Lowell had indeed gained position, but neither the Pulitzer Prize nor his poetry chair at the Library of Congress brought peace of mind. And although he had finally renounced the cause of Catholicism, even Stafford was amazed by the suddenness and arbitrariness of his religious renunciation.

In another series of somewhat strange and ambivalent letters, Stafford intimated that she was daily seized with the terror of losing her mind and with the desire to take her own life. She was distressed beyond words, deflated beyond reason. Her equilibrium had been destroyed, her strength sapped, her ego deflated. Her days were spent alone in a darkened room, her mind filled with cement, her body a useless instrument of pain. She received almost no visitors. On the other hand, she wanted no visitors. She was ashamed of her collapse and her dismal condition, humiliated by her husband's lack of interest in her welfare, his failure to respond to her cries. From the start Lowell had been too much the intellectual for her, she too old for him. Pondering the future, Stafford wondered if she could ever again face life, concluding that all friendships were now over for her. Even her editor, Robert Giroux (then at Harcourt, Brace & World), who was also Lowell's editor (first at Harcourt and later at Farrar, Straus & Giroux), would no longer want to know her. She was leaving the hospital destitute and friendless, which, she suggested, was more difficult for a woman. Any woman who had spent a year in a mental hospital was branded for life; and any woman whose husband had deserted her for another woman was considered socially undesirable, a human outcast.

Lowell's ineffectual response to his wife's grievances only fueled her mounting fury. She raged against the childishness of his conduct toward her, treating her either as his mother or his enemy. His treatment of her was insulting. In response to a Lowell letter accusing her of abusing his friends, Stafford snapped that she had abused only the intruder who had invaded her home.

In time, partially through psychotherapy, Stafford's anger began to subside and she developed a theory that helped explain the complexity of her relationship with her former husband. Her reasoning, at best a bit of warmed-over Freud, indicated that Lowell's resemblance to Stafford's father and Stafford's resemblance to Lowell's mother were more than mere coincidence. She argued that there was the guilt of not having loved their parents, and, if it was not guilt, it was the need for revenge for what their parents had done to them.

Stafford developed her psychiatric explanation in a seven-thousand-word brief to Lowell, maintaining that both parties were to blame for behavior that was at best extremely self-destructive, at worst criminal. She admitted that she had added to their difficulties by robbing her husband of any sense of emotional and financial responsibility. But he had allowed it to happen. Stafford charged that Lowell had transformed her into the image of his mother until, out of her own distress, she adopted this resemblance; and the same thing happened to Lowell in relation to Stafford's father, so it was as if Lowell's mother, Stafford's father, Cal, and Jean all lived under one roof.

Lowell was numb with guilt, entirely closed off, shocked awake by his sudden literary renown, and yet he was unable to respond to his wife's shattering recriminations and lamentations. The divorce proceedings ground ever forward while both parties haggled heedlessly over money. She accused him of offering her too small a settlement and of making his offer in bad faith. He would act this way with no one else, she wrote. Although he offered to pay his wife the ridiculously small figure of $1000, it must be remembered that he was far from wealthy at this point in his career, and that even this paltry sum represented a considerable amount for him.

When Stafford's mother developed terminal cancer, Jean implored Lowell to delay their divorce. She suffered immensely under the twin burdens of her mother's illness and the ceaseless torture germinated by her own broken life. For Lowell that was also a testy period—a period of subdued confusion, a period of uncertainty and of radical readjustment and revision.

Alfred Kazin in his autobiographical *New York Jew* (1978) recalls meeting Lowell at Yaddo in the winter of 1948, a year after the final resolution of the poet's divorce. Yaddo, the writers', artists', and composers' colony in Saratoga Springs, not far from the famed racetrack, was a mixture of primeval forest and genteel tradition. There were perhaps a dozen people in residence that winter, and they lived and worked in a huge gray stone Victorian mansion or in the farmhouses and studios scattered about the five-hundred-acre estate. The main house contained a complete old-fashioned library with pink-shaded lamps and crimson rugs and photographs and portraits of Mr. and Mrs. Spencer Trask, the wealthy stockbroker and his wife who, in 1926, bequeathed their sprawling estate and a million-dollar portfolio for the benefit of the arts. There was nothing to do all day but to write, paint, or compose, after working to walk in the pine-scented woods or stroll into town to buy the newspaper and cigarettes. Yaddo was an ideal refuge for those seeking solitude. Katherine Anne Porter had labored there for years over *Ship of Fools;* Theodore Roethke, Elizabeth Bishop, John Cheever, and many others had made it their temporary home. Evenings during the summer months the guests played tennis on the courts and croquet on the vast, carefully manicured lawn or passed the night at the racetrack losing their shirts. Sunday morning brunch was sometimes served among the statuary in the Italian rose garden.

Flannery O'Connor, the gifted Southern short-story writer, a devout Catholic, was present at Yaddo when Kazin and Lowell were there. Both she and Kazin were struck by Lowell; he was "handsome, magnetic, rich, wild with excitement about his powers, wild over the many tributes to him from the critics for *Lord Weary's Castle.*" In addition he was a Lowell: "he was in a state of grandeur not negotiable with lesser beings." Placing him in company with Milton, Hardy, and Eliot, O'Connor seemed to be attending Lowell with nothing less than rapture. Kazin, however, was soon struck by another quality—the poet's political ardor. Lowell reminded Kazin of Evelyn Waugh rampaging against the wartime alliance between the Allies and Russia. Like Waugh, Lowell had worried more about Soviet power and cold-war politics than about the war. Now, with the fatal spread of the McCarthyite epidemic, he showed signs of returning to that deadly and deadening political languor. It was a gloomy time for Kazin, having to listen to Lowell "at his most blissfully high orating against Communist influence at Yaddo and boasting of the veneration in which he was held by those other illiberal great men Ezra Pound and George Santayana." It was Lowell's contention that Yaddo's trusted director of many years, Elizabeth Ames, a proper widow from Minneapolis, was not just a "party line" sympathizer but was deviously plotting the overthrow of the American government. He went to the F.B.I. about it. Next he had the Yaddo trustees convened, confided to them the great things Santayana and Pound had said about him, and demanded that the director be dismissed.

The director was not dismissed, but the investigation that ensued caused considerable turmoil among the colony's members and followers. Eleanor Clark, the future wife of Robert Penn Warren, and Kazin rounded up support for Ames from many writers, composers, and artists who had worked at Yaddo over the years. Many refused to support the director because they had families, jobs, "could not take the risk." According to Kazin, "the lesser poets were not only the biggest cowards, but impossible to shut up in their boring, whining self defense. They were concerned with Lowell's power to affect their reputations even when they had no reputation."

With the passage of time, Lowell became increasingly concerned with anti-Communist causes. Following the Yaddo blowup, in Spring 1949, he, Elizabeth Hardwick, Dwight Macdonald, and Mary McCarthy "infiltrated" the once-famous Waldorf Conference, of which Lillian Hellman was a prominent sponsor. In the name of unity, a gathering was organized by "the Cultural and Scientific Conference for World Peace," a group dominated by Communists and their friends, effectively a last stand for the fellow-traveling intellectuals in this country. They blamed the United States for the developing Cold War with Russia.

McCarthy, Macdonald, and Lowell—anti-Stalinist, independent radicals out for blood—began firing questions from the floor at the composer Shostakovich, who was one of the Russian delegates and who looked as if he wanted to be anywhere but where he was. The threesome next took on the Russian cultural commissar Alexander Fedayev, bombarding him with questions concerning the fate of Russian writers persecuted by the regime. Pursuing his own line of interrogation, Lowell asked about the sufferings of conscientious objectors in the Soviet

Union. The sole objective of the intrusive triad was to splinter the meeting beyond repair, a goal they nearly attained.

Flannery O'Connor (who died in 1964 at age thirty-nine of lupus erythematosus) found Lowell the politician less endearing than Lowell the Yaddo sage. In 1950 she joined Lowell, Hardwick, and McCarthy for a late dinner. The conversation soon turned to politics and there it remained for the rest of the evening. O'Connor, living with her mother on a dairy farm outside Milledgeville, Georgia, felt outclassed by her sophisticated companions and added little to the conversation. Recalling the experience several years later, she told a friend: "Having me there was like having a dog present who had been trained to say a few words but overcome with inadequacy had forgotten them."

Jean Stafford's mercurial fluctuations of mood did not entirely cease with her release from Payne Whitney Clinic. She remained tense and shy, often veering from cool gales of laughter to torrid waves of tears, bewildering herself and others by her rapid swings of temperament. But she remained in therapy and was able to return to her writing, twice remarrying, the first time to then *Life* magazine editor Oliver Jensen and finally, quite contentedly, to the late *New Yorker* author A. J. Liebling. Reconciling their differences, Lowell and Stafford eventually became friends. They were far better friends after their divorce than they had been before.

Elizabeth Hardwick, Lowell's second wife, was born in 1916 in Lexington, Kentucky, into a large family of nine children. Lexington, a town of racetracks and Main Street segregated movie houses and five-and-dime stores, was to imprint itself on her memory as a blotch of trees and flowers, peaceful old houses with walled gardens, some Gothic revival and white columns, flat, triumphant farms on the outskirts of town, the whole washed in a harsh, hard light and bathed in scent of dogwood and lilac, whiskey and fried bacon. Hardwick attended the University of Kentucky in Lexington, where she discovered *Partisan Review,* identifying with the political and cultural scenery contained in its pages. "I'm afraid my aim was—if it doesn't sound too ridiculous—my aim was to be a New York Jewish intellectual." It does sound somewhat peculiar, but she nevertheless informed an interviewer, years later, that she wanted to be Jewish "because of their tradition of rational skepticism; and also a certain deracination appeals to me—and their openness to European culture . . . the questioning of the arrangements of society, sometimes called radicalism."

She took an M.A. in English literature at Columbia University in New York, living in the student rooming houses that surrounded the campus, later moving to a shabby hotel in midtown Manhattan and visiting the small, forbidden jazz clubs of Harlem. She was soon writing personal and literary criticism for *Partisan Review,* prose bits that were personal, unpejorative, unpretentious, semi-political, anti-academic. She identified with *Partisan's* causes, signed its petitions, found in its cosmopolitan and revolutionary stance an affiliation that helped shape her driving intellect. In the words of William Phillips, a founding editor, the Marxist-oriented journal strove "to represent a new and dissident generation in American letters," a vitalized breed of dedicated intellectuals, energetic, argumentative, restless. Amid this group Hardwick and Lowell ultimately stood politically to the right of center and intellectually to the left.

When *Partisan Review* began publication early in 1934, first as a pro-Communist organ of the John Reed Club and later (following the Moscow trials) as a pro-Trotskyite, antisocialist journal without official political ties, its essential aim was to reconcile the modernist spirit, which was often conservative and antihistorical, with a political consciousness that emphasized the liberal and historical dimensions of art. The "new" *Partisan Review,* having outgrown the youthful radicalism of the thirties, was becoming more and more conservative, to the point where its editors were not only more critical of all socialism but also less critical of the status quo. Anti-Stalinism first turned into anti-Communism and then into antiradicalism. If the *New Masses,* the official cultural organ of the Communist party, converted all literary questions into political ones, then the *Partisan Review* transformed politics into literature. Intent on maintaining an open, undogmatic intellectual and political position, *Partisan's* main thrust was literary—the publication of the best and most advanced writing around. Its iconoclasm induced it to attack almost everything—philosophy, books, art, theater, cinema. "You could attack them in all honesty," Mary McCarthy said. "Nobody else did it. We on *Partisan Review* were the only ones, as I recall, who were attacking right and left from an independent position." *Partisan* saw its task as that of opposing both the crackpot politics on the right and the lies of the Communist left; they were, in turn, subjected to pressures from both sides: from the left for having abandoned their radical heritage, from the right for not being anti-Communist enough.

But their true enemy was anything that was not founded on an intellectual stance; they opposed commercialism, ambition, and fame, though most of them were themselves ambitious and would soon attain financial success. Among the first contributors were André Gide, Edmund Wilson, Henry James, Meyer Schapiro, Max Brod, Leon Trotsky, Clement Greenberg, Harold Rosenberg, John Dewey, Auden, Dos Passos, Delmore Schwartz, Lionel Trilling, and Mary McCarthy.

Even within the confines of this crowd, the Lowells stood out as a brilliant and arresting couple. Miss Hardwick was tall, handsome, with cynical steel blue eyes and a charming Southern drawl; convinced of her own worth, she emitted an aura of poise and repose that made her appear menacing, reflective, self-confident. She and Lowell were married in Massachusetts on July 28, 1949. Lowell's account of their early days together in "Man and Wife" refers to a series of mental breakdowns he suffered at about this time, beginning with his collapse—following a trip to Chicago—inside a terminal at what was then Idlewild Airport, when "powerful and sweating," he fell to the ground:

> All night I've held your hand,
> as if you had
> a fourth time faced the kingdom of the mad—
> its hackneyed speech, its homicidal eye—
> and dragged me home alive . . .
> . . .
> you were in your twenties, and I,
> . . .
> outdrank the Rahvs in the heat
> of Greenwich Village, fainting at your feet—

The private reference to the "Rahvs" is to the late and opinionated critic Philip Rahv and his then-wife Nathalie, both heavy drinkers; Rahv, like Phillips, was a founding father of the *Partisan Review.* In the same poem Lowell recalls himself as having been "too boiled and shy and poker-faced" to make a pass at Miss Hardwick, who frightened him at first with the "shrill verve" of her "invective," a quality that she demonstrated in even greater measure when he began indulging in romantic flings outside their marriage.

Lowell's airport crisis led directly to the psychiatric ward of Bellevue Hospital, thence to the more exclusive bedlam of the Payne Whitney Clinic, the same hollow, whitewashed ward occupied earlier by Jean Stafford. "Elation" was the mysterious cause he gave for his incarcera-

BETWEEN THE PORCH AND THE ALTAR"

tion. Whole days were consumed with diatribes on the horrors of childhood, supplemented by lengthy perorations on the tensions that divided his immediate family and the Lowell clan as a whole. He informed a fellow patient on the ward that he had turned to Catholicism
because it represented a "higher court" than the religion of his forebears, the parochial WASPishness of Boston's main-line upper crust.

Lowell's moods changed with the weather. He frequently suffered
severe tension headaches, dark depressions, thundering rages, colds,
coughs, hives, insomnia, aphasia, nausea. These sporadic ruptures occurred without warning and lasted for days at a stretch. The center was
not holding and the outer edges were wasting away. At his worst he
alternated between durations of icy anger and spans of sullen silence
when he could not be reached. Superficially serene on the surface, his
insides might be churning in despair. Even shock therapy could not
shake him loose.

Nor could the letters he received from home. His father depressed
him further by opposing his plans to remarry on the grounds that
Lowell had only recently been released from hospital and was in no
position to take care of himself, let alone look after and provide for a
wife. The Commander's tone mellowed slightly after the marriage became official and there was nothing left to do. The poet always believed
that behind his father's negative feelings lingered the dour disapproval
of his mother, whose approbation of her son's vocation had always been
tempered by reserve.

It was for this reason that he concealed his internment at Payne
Whitney from them. Informed of his illness by Hardwick, Lowell senior
wrote to his son that he had nothing to fear, that psychiatry could be
useful but that most people went into it only because someone else
wanted them to, and of course the results would always be disappointing. Cal's response was brutally honest; he had not written because he
was ashamed and puzzled.

During much of 1949 Lowell was involved in another controversy. As
one of the elected Fellows in American Letters of the Library of Congress, he was instrumental in the decision to award Ezra Pound the first
Bollingen Prize in poetry for the provocative *Pisan Cantos.* Anticipating a storm of protest, the interminable debate over the age-old question of a man's art versus his political beliefs, the committee—whose
membership included Aiken, Auden, Tate, Eliot, and Katherine Anne
Porter—issued a cautionary statement:

· 371 ·

The Fellows are aware that objections may be made to awarding a prize to a man situated as is Mr. Pound. . . . But to permit other considerations than that of poetry achievement to sway the decision would destroy the significance of the award and would in principle deny the validity of that objective perception of value on which civilized society must rest.

Declared insane by a panel of examining psychiatrists, Pound had not stood trial for treason during World War II, but was placed instead in a locked ward for the criminally insane at St. Elizabeths Hospital, Washington, D.C., where he remained from 1945 to 1958, an exile in his own land. Allen Tate, at the time living in New York and not feeling particularly sympathetic toward Pound—although he was all for giving Pound his prize—warned Lowell that at St. Elizabeths the elder statesman was interested only in gathering about him disciples who could "give him the illusion of influence." Lowell, hopeful that Pound wanted more— or at least willing to cast himself in the role of devoted disciple— became a frequent visitor at St. Elizabeths, especially during his own stay in Washington. One of his self-appointed tasks was to bring Pound whatever books he needed from the Library of Congress. One afternoon he brought along an armload of books and a friend, John Berryman: "I remember nothing [wrote Lowell] except a surely misplaced image of John sitting on the floor hugging his knees, and asking with shining cheeks for Pound to sing an aria from his opera *Villon.* He saw nothing nutty about Pound, or maybe it was the opposite." Pound, the discoverer of Hemingway, Frost, Joyce, and Eliot, saw in Lowell a literary torchbearer for the younger, postwar generation. In 1950, when Lowell's retrospective *Poems 1939–1949* appeared, Pound bestowed the same high praise upon it he had earlier bestowed upon *Lord Weary's Castle.* Inevitably Pound began giving the younger poet directives, instructing him on what to read and how to write, as Tate feared he would. But it was Williams, not Tate, who instructed Pound "to lay off Lowell"—"he don't need either you or me to further him in his career. In fact our presence would only hamper him in what he has to do. Leave him alone." In March 1958, about the time he was released from St. Elizabeths, Pound wrote to Lowell: "Our job: to build light as the wheat surging upward / From serenitas to hilaritas." Lowell was thus anointed.

During the spring term of 1950, Lowell and Hardwick were stationed in Iowa City, the poet teaching creative writing and literature in the experimental Writers' Workshop at the University of Iowa, a program directed by the late poet Paul Engle. Regarding the art of instruction, Lowell informed his elders that there were many traps and bewilderments facing the beginner; he further advised them that he had committed himself to a year of therapy with a highly recommended local psychiatrist, who agreed that he was well out of his worst problems and that while he still had a way to go, he was coming along.

Robie Macauley, Lowell's classmate at Kenyon, was on the faculty at Iowa that year. Otherwise the Lowells kept mostly to themselves. Allen Tate, who helped procure the job at Iowa, came twice to visit. Tate was likewise instrumental in securing the poet a summer post at the Kenyon College School of Letters, founded in 1948 by Lionel Trilling, F. O. Matthiessen, and John Crowe Ransom. During the summer of 1950, when he taught there, Lowell was joined on the faculty by Delmore Schwartz, William Empson, Kenneth Burke, Tate, L. C. Knight, and several other literary notables. That August the Lowells visited his parents at their recently purchased summer retreat on Grove Street in Beverly Farms, thirty minutes outside Boston. Lowell's father had been reduced to a state of semi-invalidism by a nearly fatal coronary the year before. The sight of the old man shuffling about to the background strain of Charlotte Lowell's shrill, grating voice turned the poet to stone. He found it difficult to sleep at night, and could be heard anxiously prowling the floor of his room or wandering through the darkened house silent as a ghost, composing poems in his mind's eye and wishing himself far away. When Lowell left for Iowa later that summer he sensed that he would never see his father again.

His father died on August 30, 1950. Charlotte Lowell placed their residence at 170 Marlborough Street on sale and moved into a smaller town house a few blocks away on the same street. While her husband was still alive she treated him with barely veiled animosity and disdain, addressing him in a voice tinged with sarcasm; after his death, she spent much of her own remaining life mourning him, talking about him as though he had been the passionate core of her existence. Lowell despised the hypocrisy of his mother's outlandish statements and for the first time was able to admit just how much he disliked her. Candid admission of his schismatic love-hate relationship with her had a purgative effect that released a flood of extreme reactions. For several months he behaved irrationally, drinking, arguing, brawling, brooding. His equilibrium was restored only when it was decided that he and Elizabeth would re-create a long-standing family tradition: they would travel abroad.

They were to spend the next three years in Europe, the first year almost exclusively in Italy, principally in Florence, Venice, and Rome. In Florence they rented a one-bedroom apartment on the Lungarno Vespucci, number 2. "We passed the winter of 1950 in Florence and used to go out to see Bernard Berenson, as so many had gone before and would go afterward," mused Elizabeth Hardwick in an essay ("Living in Italy: Reflections on Bernard Berenson"), describing their visits to I Tatti, Berenson's spacious villa in Settignano, outside Florence, which struck some as a museum, others as a mausoleum. Berenson, the formidable art collector and authority on Renaissance painting, entertained the Lowells with tales ranging from his childhood in a Lithuanian *shtetl* to memories of Mrs. Jack Gardner's Boston mansion and celebrated drawing-room gatherings. The couple also met Dylan Thomas, that often-outrageous Welshman, whose popular concept of passionate, externally oriented poetry would influence Lowell's taste for years to come. Responding to a complaint of theirs about America, Thomas chimed: "You needn't live in that bloody country, America! You could go somewhere else, you know."

They traveled to Rome, where they visited the aging George Santayana, confined now to the Convent of the Blue Nuns on Via San Stephano Rotundo. Santayana, ardently drawn to *Lord Weary's Castle,* was cheered by Lowell's visit, noting his impressions in a letter to John Hall Wheelock:

> I am, and have been for some years, particularly interested in Robert Lowell's mind and work. He is now in Italy, and spent a week or more in Rome in the autumn, when I saw him almost every day. I think that he is a good deal like Rimbaud, or like what Rimbaud might have become if he had remained devoted to his poetic genius. There are dark and troubled depths in them both, with the same gift for lurid and mysterious images: but Lowell has had more tragic experiences and a more realistic background. . . . Although he is not a person about whose future we can be entirely confident, it may well turn out to be brilliant.

In their day, both James Russell and Amy Lowell had been seduced by Italy, comforted by the peaceful surroundings, relaxed by the landscape and weather. Robert Lowell experienced the same tide of release, his senses projecting for miles, the effect of a temperate climate and a soothing ambiance. He recorded his attraction to the country, his fundamental inclination toward the people, in letters home to William Carlos Williams, adding to these impressions his current reactions to the latest volumes of *Paterson*, which he perused as they appeared and became available.

Lowell had greeted the first book of *Paterson*, published in 1947, with a positive endorsement in the *Sewanee Review*, curiously remarking that Williams "has much in common with Catholic, aristocratic and Agrarian writers." Williams, it is clear, had nothing in common with the Southern Agrarians. He was liberal, antiorthodox, antitraditional, practically transcendental in his thinking. Tate, in his allegiance to Eliot, dismissed Williams as a mere "byline to modern poetry." Lowell, beginning to turn away from the Tate camp, was even more enthusiastic about book two of *Paterson*, comparing it favorably (in *The Nation*) with the best writing of Eliot, Stevens, and Auden, drawing a parallel between *Paterson's* first two books and Whitman's *Leaves of Grass*. "*Paterson*," declared Lowell, "is an attempt to write *the* American Poem. It depends on the American myth, a myth that is seldom absent from our literature. . . . [the myth] is assumed by Emerson, Whitman, and Hart Crane; by Henry Adams and Henry James. For good or for evil, America is something immense, crass, and human. We must unavoidably place ourselves in our geography, history, civilization, institutions, and future."

After the appearance of this review, Lowell and Williams began what in time became a tight friendship, Williams gradually supplanting Tate as surrogate father, a literary totem the Bostonian could hope to emulate. They saw one another only occasionally but corresponded regularly. Williams, recuperating from a mild stroke, was elated over Lowell's letters from Europe and delighted to hear that his continuing epic had found so receptive an ear. He was less pleased to read between the lines that Lowell, like Pound and Eliot before him, could seriously consider the possibility of remaining permanently abroad. The idea that still another fine young American poet should be lost to his homeland unsettled Williams no end:

> I hope you are having a profitable experience in Europe. I know that
> you are, you must be profiting, it can't be otherwise. I envy you your
> opportunity, it is another Odyssey from which, not like some earlier
> American writers, I hope to see you return to your Penelope (America)

much enriched in your mind and ready to join your fellows here in pushing forward the craft. You can bring great riches to us or you can ignore us; it's your choice. But I wouldn't be myself if I didn't say that I look forward to your return. I think you are keeping your original frame of reference and not junking it. That, at least, is how I look at you and what I crave from you. Come back enriched in experience but come back; do not allow yourself to be coaxed away from us.

Following their years in Italy, the Lowells, after brief visits to Istanbul and Athens and layovers in London and Paris, wound up in Amsterdam. Riding the coal-driven European trains reminded the poet of "the conspicuous waste of [his] grandparents on their grand tours," those stolid "Victorian sages" who had breezed "on their trust funds through the world." He was amazed to discover in Amsterdam a city that had all the earmarks of cultivated nineteenth-century Boston: waterways, churches, baroque red- and yellow-brick houses, narrow, winding cobblestone streets reminiscent of Back Bay. They rented an unfashionable but cozy apartment on the Nicolaas Witsenkade, a busy, bourgeois avenue within sight of the Rijksmuseum, a block of houses with stone steps lined up one next to another. It was a decent but somewhat forlorn street with autumnal tile decorations on the façades of houses, the rooms cramped and stuffy with their dark paneling. A round lamp with a shade of old tasseled silk was suspended above the round dining table. A squat, round, shiny black stove failed to keep out the winter cold. Instead, the Lowells were warmed by the small-town friendliness of the local Dutch citizens. Also, there was much to occupy them: museums, theater, concerts, the opera, the ballet, walks along the inky waters of the Amstel. They took a train to Haarlem to view the old almshouse captured on canvas by Frans Hals. They visited Antwerp and Ghent. They drank gin too much and argued. But these were sweet days. Lowell advised Randall Jarrell that they read continuously, enumerating some of the books: twenty volumes of the Nuremberg trials; psychiatric studies on Russian prisoners of war; Hannah Arendt on totalitarianism; Clarendon; Macaulay's *History of England;* North's *Plutarch;* Motley's *Rise of the Dutch Republic;* Fromentin on the old Dutch painters; Ovid; Yeats; Valéry; Larbaud's *A. O. Barnabooth, His Diary.* They read Laforgue, Mayakovsky, Colette, and anything Lowell could find by the American historian Charles Francis Adams. He shared with Amy and James Russell Lowell a fascination for history and historical tracts; history was a constant, an element of steadfastness in a universe of tumultuous flux. He felt saturated with miscellaneous knowledge, his letter to Jarrell continued. By way of closing the brief, he wrote that Europe was much more lovable than America.

In the spring of 1952, Charlotte Lowell turned up in Europe, joining her "children" in Amsterdam, accompanying them on several side trips to Italy and France. Lowell's nightly anxiety attacks returned, but this time he was philosophical about them. He had resigned himself to the chilling fact that his mother brought out the worst in him, that he had an infantile and childish relationship with her, that his identity tended to merge with hers, and that in no way would or could she ever change. She would never be able to deal with him on any terms other than her own, yet he was determined to be with her from time to time without losing control, without needlessly angering himself. A letter to a Winslow cousin described their difficult travels together, and a later letter to the same stateside in-law betrayed a touch of homesickness.

Lowell's perceptions of the Continent varied with the locale and season. At times he seemed anxious to return home, mindful of his place as a stranger in a strange land. At other points he expressed complete satisfaction with the trip, noting that he felt and talked "like a guidebook . . . full of gaps, irreverance and amnesia." He basked in wonderment; everything was "overwhelmingly astonishing . . . so much that is harmonious, unbelievably wonderful, odd, unforeseen, varied . . . all one's European history to learn over. . . . It's like going to school again. . . . One feels so ignorant, so conscious that one won't have forever, that it's hard to stop."

From Holland, after the departure of Charlotte Lowell, the couple journeyed to Germany and Austria. They found Austria's capital less charming than expected. Writing to her mother-in-law, Elizabeth Hardwick described Vienna as pleasant, though rather deserted and forlorn. It probably had always been that way, she suggested. Parts of the city were enchanting but other parts were shabby and isolated. But at least the weather was pleasant and they were in fine spirits. Their pensione, the Vera, reminded Hardwick of the Old South, everything dilapidated and falling apart. Afternoons were passed sightseeing or at the Berlitz studying German; evenings were reserved for concerts or the opera.

During the summer of 1952, he taught a course in Contemporary American and British Poetry at the Salzburg Summer Seminary, an international symposium held annually in the Tyrolean Alps. John

McCormick, a student in the seminar, reported that Lowell preferred lecturing extemporaneously without benefit of notes: "Lowell's method ... is to circle in upon his man like a dog upon a bird; he came to Hart Crane by way of Tate, Emerson, Dante, and Virgil. All were relevant. ... The method is personal, it brooks no questions or resistance and it is highly effective, even though, in the diction of the social-relations people, on the authoritarian side."

He lectured in a singsong Boston nasal twang with a slight Southern intonation, pointing and poking as he spoke, stabbing his large hands at the chilled mountain air. He was singularly immersed in writing, acutely aware of the cultural climate and the prevailing weather conditions. When asked to comment on current storm patterns in his own country, he unleashed a monologue of considerable verve. Lowell's manner was always formally courteous, but his judgments were uncompromising, his language to the point, his tone sardonic, sometimes softening into incisive humor. The foremost poets among his own generation were Elizabeth Bishop and Randall Jarrell; Frost and Eliot were the leaders of the older generation: certainly no one had written religious verse to compare with the *Four Quartets*. Williams, Ransom, Tate, Pound, Crane, Marianne Moore, and Stevens would be read as long as Catullus and Tibullus were read. Of recent authors of fiction he admired "the holy trinity"—Fitzgerald, Hemingway, Faulkner . . . Faulkner towered. Katherine Anne Porter stood out in her perfection. He didn't care for Dos Passos or know much about him. At the moment he was reading a selection of authors: Dostoevski, Lord Acton, Goethe, Kafka. But he was not and could never be what one would call "a professional reader of fiction."

Although fiction was not his métier, Lowell remained the only Anglo-American poet in years (save Auden) able to write descriptive verse with the best of the novelists. He demonstrated this ability in 1951 with the publication of *The Mills of the Kavanaughs,* a volume written for the most part during 1948 and 1949, dedicated to his mother and in memory of his father. The collection combined psychological, naturalistic, and clinical images and perspectives, avoiding the phantasmagoric and strict religious symbols of his two previous volumes.

That he was diverging from religious symbolism came as no surprise to the critics, many of whom pointed out that "Between the Porch and the Altar" *(Lord Weary's Castle)* had spelled out the approaching disunion. That poem's narrator "thinks the past / is settled. It is honest to hold fast / Merely to what one sees with one's own eyes," which is a clear renunciation of the metaphysical in favor of the physical: what one sees, not what one wants to see. The poem's title, from the Ash Wednesday epistle of the Book of Joel, was the title also of a Jean Stafford short story. Both poem and story reach for the autobiographical, the experience of self as opposed to the restrictive voice of "otherness." But only in the most oblique sense do the two works overlap. Personal experience comes into play on several occasions in *Lord Weary*, as in the following lines from "After the Surprising Conversions"—

> A gentleman
> Of more than common understanding, strict
> In morals, pious in behavior, kicked
> Against our goad. A man of some renown,
> An useful, honored person in the town,
> He came of melancholy parents, prone
> To secret spells, for years they kept alone.

Despite such periodic divertissements it was not until *The Mills of the Kavanaughs* that the poet began seriously to surrender his affiliation with the Catholic Church, turning for inspiration to the rites and rituals of Western civilization and the crisis of personal behavior instead of the sobering ordinances of Christianity.

Following the publication of *Lord Weary's Castle*, Lowell became acutely aware of the pressing need to find a new poetic voice, a language less mannered though still infused with reverberations of the academic—Lowell was too much the scholar, although a defrocked one, to give it up entirely. He wrote to Jarrell that he was stuck between reluctance to repeat and the fear of the untried. He was moving in the direction of the kind of poetry that in the coming decades would become clearly and uniquely his own, that stark, confessional line with the infallible rhythms and sure feel for words.

The Mills of the Kavanaughs reflects the increasing influence on Lowell of the stronger narrative poets of the past, among them Chaucer, Milton, Browning, Hardy, E. A. Robinson. Instead of the metaphysical poets and such difficult modern poets as Hart Crane, one detects in the new volume a leaning toward the elements of prose: plot, theme, character, sequence. Lowell has said that he was consciously aware of incorporating techniques picked up from his reading of Henry James, Tolstoi, Chekhov, and Faulkner. The influence of Frost is also evident, for Lowell has reined his tendency toward generalization and accusation, while loading up on dramatic irony, conversational flow, an attempt at vivid characterization. New themes crop up here: the driving motives of distorted and blocked love, mental exacerbation, insanity, jealousy, symbolic and actual homicide and suicide. For the first time, Lowell comes to grips with the dual nature of good and evil, the imperfect but de facto conditions of a world governed by chaos and imperfection. To some degree he attempts to create a compressed line, eliminating as much of the early obscurity as possible, his purpose being to develop a style and technique that will bring the poetry closer to the coordinates of the modernist era.

Psychological and sexual images connect line to line, poem to poem. Latent incest, for instance, lies at the core of "Her Dead Brother," a poem narrated by the sister of the deceased, who recalls the unspeakable acts of "that August twenty-third, / When Mother motored with the maids to Stowe, / And the pale summer shades were drawn—so low / No one could see us; no, nor catch your hissing word." The poem represents a response in part to Jean Stafford's second novel, *The Mountain Lion,* a story of two children, brother and sister, and their years of bitterness between childhood and adolescence. Stafford, like Lowell, is able to create an intense atmosphere with a few striking phrases. Both her novel and his poem contain intimations of childhood mortality and comment on the contrasting courses of youth and aging, innocence and experience. Stafford's tale re-creates the accidental death of a girl at the hands of her brother, whereas Lowell reverses the sequence of events by killing off the brother and sparing the sister. In real life, Jean Stafford lost a brother in World War II, an event that lends Lowell's poem the power of personal credence and the infamy of a cruel private joke.

Dedicating her 1948 novel "To Cal," Stafford became incensed that he should publish his poem, with its obvious play on her story, in *The Nation,* where it appeared a week before her own publication date. Insofar as both works of art shared the common theme of latent incest, she accused Lowell in a letter of perpetrating an act so dishonorable that it was almost insane. Because she was still a patient at Payne Whitney, Stafford was particularly vulnerable at this time, unable to cope with the realities of commercial publishing, or the inconsistencies of Lowell.

More macabre is another poem, "Thanksgiving's Over," whose tangent points touch on adultery, madness, and suicide. The scene is succinctly set at the fore in language befitting a play: "Thanksgiving night, 1942: a room on Third Avenue. Michael dreams of his wife, a German-American Catholic, who leapt from a window before she died in a sanatorium. . . ." Lowell here is not announcing the death of faith per se, only his own loss of faith in the supernatural as reflected by the attempted suicidal plunge and institutionalization of a practicing Catholic. That he still believed in the moral teachings and rituals of the church was amply demonstrated by "Mother Marie Therese," the portrayal of a nun drowned at sea, a litany full of direct religious imagery and symbolism. In its grand sweep and technical control of language the poem bears a certain resemblance to Hopkins's *The Wreck of the Deutschland;* the two poems are most alike in terms of subject matter. And yet beneath the surface of Lowell's religious orthodoxy there lurked a solid expanse of skepticism. Nowhere is this more in evidence than in "Falling Asleep Over the *Aeneid,*" the poetic saga of an old man who, neglecting to go to church services one Sunday morning, falls asleep while reading Virgil and dreams that he is Aeneas at the funeral of Pallas, an Italian prince. His reverie is interrupted by the musical peal of church bells; suddenly the old fellow remembers that he has not missed church in years; but having drawn a strange set of instructions from the *Aeneid,* he resumes his musings, refusing to rouse himself for the habitual Sunday morning service.

The Mills of the Kavanaughs in all contains five long poems, one very long narrative poem of some six hundred lines, and a translation of Franz Werfel's short "The Fat Man in the Mirror," a sequence that teems with self-hatred. The longest narrative, the book's title sequence, utilizes the same symbolic gestures of incest, madness, and the death of God that we find elsewhere. Dealing with the decline of a wealthy and powerful Maine family, "The Mills of the Kavanaughs" is told from the point of view of Anne, a poor girl from a family of thirteen children, who is first adopted by the Kavanaughs and then married to the youngest son, Harry, in the hope that she will help revive the Catholic bloodline and bring life to it. Joining the Navy prior to Pearl Harbor, her husband returns from the war on the verge of a nervous breakdown; he attempts and fails to suffocate his wife in bed one night because she speaks aloud, while asleep, to a man in a dream; Harry fears that she has committed adultery. Shortly thereafter, greatly distraught, he takes his own life. Anne, left alone in the Kavanaugh garden near her husband's grave amid Grecian statuary, reflects on the Kavanaugh myth, their heritage of success and failure, sometimes addressing her dead husband, sometimes not. The poem is bereft of religious symbolism; instead, Ovid's mythological account of Persephone in *Metamorphosis*, V, is brought into play by the poet's use of a four-part organization in imitation of Persephone's circle of seasons. Spring (stanzas 1–7) dates Anne's meeting with Harry; summer (8–15) recalls their courtship; autumn (16–22) reflects the course of their marriage; and winter (23–38) is the season of his manic depression and collapse. Recalling her husband's suicide, Anne asks herself, "Is it well?" Her affirmative reply reaffirms Lowell's final departure from the Roman Catholic Church: "Yes, very well. He died outside the church / Like Harry Tudor." The same myth was further debunked in "Beyond the Alps," the first number in his next major opus *(Life Studies):* "Much against my will I left the City of God where it belongs." And in "Jonathan Edwards in Massachusetts" *(For the Union Dead)* he wrote: "Hope lives in doubt / Faith in trying to do without / Faith."

Insofar as they are a well-propertied, old family of decaying means, the Kavanaughs and their mills resemble the Lowells and the Winslows. The poet imbues the Kavanaughs with the Winslow family motto: "Cut down we flourish." We are told that the Kavanaughs were once powerful Indian fighters, a historical trait that finds its corollary in both New England families. Harry Kavanaugh's military failure and final deterioration are reminiscent of Lowell's father. A huge snowplow, the couple's fierce bedroom fight, Harry's mental collapse are themes that come from Lowell's life. Anne's widowhood bears a resemblance to the real-life situation of Charlotte Lowell. The protagonist's position as an outsider to the clan also corresponds to Lowell's perception of his own role as aristocracy's fabulist, a would-be intruder with his nose pressed against the ancient manor's glass walls. Conversely, Lowell's high-born status gave him access to corridors and secret staircases that more ambitious reporters have been forbidden to tread. In the final analysis, nobody was better equipped to anatomize the downfall of the landed gentry than their own native son.

"Now that the young lion has returned to his den and gone forth into the jungles, I know you feel a great sense of relief and I do too," wrote

Merrill Moore to Charlotte Lowell in January 1953, shortly after the couple's return from Europe. Their last months abroad were spent at the Pensione California on the Via Aurora in Rome, a small guesthouse on the Pincian Hill, just off the Via Veneto, between the Villa Borghese and the Piazza di Spagna. Their living quarters consisted of two tiny rooms in a part of Rome that reminded him so much of Boston that he thought he and Elizabeth were in danger of becoming Victorian spinsters, alien and fearful.

During the latter part of his stay, while visiting Munich, Lowell suffered a mild recurrence of the manic-depressive illness that was now an integral part of the overall pattern of his life. He spent several days in a hospital in Munich, recuperating for an additional ten days at an expensive Swiss mountain sanatorium. Thanks to Elizabeth Hardwick's alertness the attack never went much beyond a state of nervous excitement—in a period of three weeks Lowell went through the progressive stages of exuberance, confusion, and depression, then quickly recovered and suffered no further setbacks.

In the last days of their stay in Europe, Lowell went to Monte Carlo, where he indulged in a brief but extravagant gambling spree, managing to lose a fair share in the process. He went to Assisi to see Lady Berkeley, born Mary Emlen Lowell, the eldest sister of Ralph Lowell, at her palatial home. Her friendships with the cream of European cultural society—Berenson, Menuhin, Picasso—made her a novelty in Lowell's mind, a rebel among members of the Boston clan. Lowell found her chatter about Europe's intellectual elite scintillating but was less impressed with her brash and pretentious manner.

Back in the States, the poet presented a series of lectures on contemporary American poetry at Oberlin College in Ohio before embarking on a trip to Kenyon to see the Taylors and Ransom. During February 1953, with nothing better looming on the horizon, the poet resumed his teaching career at the University of Iowa, joining John Berryman on the faculty. His letters at this time indicate that Boston, not teaching, was on his mind. He felt increasingly that he had been born a part of Boston itself—both the contemporary and old Boston—and that only a sort of unthinking rebellion had made him leave it. Now he felt sufficiently mature to be at least outwardly conventional.

Perhaps he felt guilty for having deserted his mother. Charlotte, clearly vexed by her son's refusal to return to Massachusetts, had to be consoled by Merrill Moore, who attempted (with grave difficulty) to convince her that "Bobby" was better off away from home:

> ... I don't know a better place to be sane than Iowa. It's even better than Boston. If he wanted to come back here he could and someday probably will. . . .
>
> At the moment he needs someone like Elizabeth and I'm not sure but that all men throughout their whole lives do to some extent. It is not everyone who, early in life, develops a very strong character and a very strong inborn sense of direction. It is, in fact, unusual but all people follow their own laws. I have a deep feeling Bobby is following his. . . .

Frozen in Anglo-Protestant propriety, Lowell's mother was ultimately unable to reconcile herself to her son's literary commitment; hounding him to the end of her days in the name of New England respectability, she was never able to shake his indomitable faith in his chosen profession.

In rustic, unassuming Iowa City the Lowells resided in a fourth-story walk-up apartment on Burlington Street. His classes, as reported by a student writer in *Mademoiselle,* consisted of "Five Poets in Translation" (Rimbaud, Baudelaire, Valéry, Rilke, Horace), during the spring term, and a "Greek Poetry Workshop" in Homer and Pindar, the following fall. Reading the poets in the original and loosely translating them, he proceeded to commentary: "Lowell would describe a phrase in terms of another phrase, another poet, a group of people, a feeling, a myth, a novel, a philosophy, a country. . . . He would compare and contrast, describe." This summation matched perfectly McCormick's description of Lowell circling "in upon his man like a dog upon a bird."

Between semesters, in the summer of 1953, John Crowe Ransom arranged a teaching job for his former student at Indiana University in Bloomington. By this time the Lowells had wearied of the Middle West, and as if to document this fact, Elizabeth Hardwick wrote to Merrill Moore that they were living in an area of high humidity, which, with the rising heat, made life impossible. They had both tired of being there. The country had become overwhelming and, for a visitor, was debilitating. Perhaps a settler could bear it better than a wandering scholar in one furnished room after another.

Their restless, wandering existence continued for the remainder of the year. During August they again joined Ransom and the Peter

Taylors in Gambier, Ohio, which by some mystery of geography was at least cooler than Indiana. Lowell struck the Taylors as highly excitable and disoriented, not exactly agitated but far more anxious than usual. He talked incessantly in their presence, his conversation rambling here and there without direction. It seemed to them that he had no desire to return that fall to Iowa. Come September, however, he and Hardwick were back in Iowa City, Lowell as usual teaching his few courses in the creative writing program. A mild fall turned into a bitter winter, a series of snowstorms burying the wheat belt. On February 14, 1954, Lowell received a telephone call from Italy. His mother, while vacationing in Rapallo, a quiet resort town on the Italian Riviera, not far from Genoa, had suffered a cerebral hemorrhage. Lowell flew to New York and from New York to Genoa, arriving in Rapallo a few hours after his mother's death. One of her last afternoons, he was told, had been spent over tea with Bernard Berenson at I Tatti in rhapsodic discussion of art and literature. Berenson had spoken highly of her son.

The death of Lowell's parents, his father in 1950 and his mother four years later, was taken up by the poet in his memory-laden volume, *Life Studies*. "Terminal Days at Beverly Farms" records his father's two coronaries and final year:

> Father and Mother moved to Beverly Farms
> to be a two minute walk from the station,
> half an hour by train from the Boston doctors.
> They had no sea view,
> but sky-blue tracks of the commuters' railroad shone
> like a double-barrelled shotgun
>
> . . .

The air of pathos surrounding these lines perpetuates the chronicle of his father's mediocre naval career and even more undistinguished business career through to the bitter end. In "For Sale" we see the Beverly Farms cottage left vacant after the Commander's death:

> Empty, open, intimate,
> its town-house furniture
> had an on tiptoe air
> of waiting for the mover
> on the heels of the undertaker.

The same poem provides a sympathetic cameo of Lowell's mother, a sensitive depiction of helplessness compared to the hardened figure painted in other poems: "Ready, afraid / of living alone till eighty, / Mother mooned in a window, / as if she had stayed on a train / one stop past her destination."

She reaches her destination in "Sailing Home from Rapallo," a re-staging of the poet's arrival in Italy to escort his mother's body back to the Stark and Winslow family cemetery at Dunbarton, under the White Mountains, where his father already lay buried, "the only 'un-historic' soul to come here / . . . beneath his recent / unweathered pink-veined slice of marble." The Commander was as much a misfit in death as he had been in life: "Even the Latin of his Lowell motto: / *Occasionem cognosce,* / seemed too businesslike and pushing here. . . ."

"Sailing Home" begins with a three-line threnody for his mother in what is this poem's only suspended moment of compassion:

> Your nurse could only speak Italian,
> but after twenty minutes I could imagine your final week,
> and tears ran down my cheeks. . . .

The next two stanzas present the bright but clashing colors of the Italian Mediterranean, the coastline "breaking into fiery flower," as though in homage to Charlotte Lowell, who travels "first class in the hold." The Risorgimento black-and-gold casket that transports her reminds her son of Napoleon's casket in the Hôtel des Invalides: only in death does she achieve the grandeur she had aspired to her whole life. Later, she is denied even this touch of passing grace. Her final resting place at Dunbarton is a study in ugliness in contrast to the warm and sunny Italian coastline. Surrounded by its fence of iron spear-hafts, the tiny country cemetery is "dour and dark against the blinding snowdrifts." In the subzero weather, "the graveyard's soil was changing to stone— / so many of its deaths had been midwinter." The burning cold illumi-nates "the hewn inscriptions of Mother's relatives: / twenty or thirty Winslows and Starks. / Frost had given their names a diamond edge." The representation of the permanent oblivion of the family name is given further body in the poem's final stanza, a four-line passage of hokku-like vividness:

> In the grandiloquent lettering on Mother's coffin,
> Lowell had been misspelled *LOVEL*.
> The corpse
> was wrapped like *panetone* in Italian tinfoil.

Panetone is Italian hot bread, wrapped in tinfoil to retain its heat; the tinfoil that encases his mother's corpse insulates it from the hot Mediterranean sun. The final indignity, the misspelling of the family name, in "grandiloquent lettering" no less, underlines the depth of the family's fall, its collapse into inglorious anonymity.

~⚬§ 26 §⚬~

BACK TO ROOTS

THE unexpected death of Lowell's mother, just when she was beginning to recover from her husband's recent demise, precipitated a delayed reaction on Lowell's part. By June of 1954 he had been remanded to the Payne Whitney Psychiatric Clinic, where he remained for the duration of the summer, "self-enclosed, unable to function, depressed," attempting to reach some finite understanding of his shattered relationship with his mother. Ten years of psychotherapy had not been enough to work the relationship through. The bond that should have afforded him the greatest comfort and happiness provided little more than heartache and rue.

Following his release from Payne Whitney, he and Hardwick remained temporarily in New York. As a guest lecturer at the University of Cincinnati during January 1954, Lowell proved exceedingly popular with the student body. He now contemplated an offer to teach there full time, ultimately declining in order to relocate to Boston instead. With money inherited from his family, he purchased a large, lovely, Back Bay town house at 239 Marlborough Street, not far from the main branch of the Boston Public Library. "The idea," suggested a friend, "was to test his heritage. It was their first attempt to be the Boston Lowells." In keeping with this new image the couple threw expansive dinner parties. Edmund Wilson and Philip Rahv were regular visitors, as were Williams, Eberhart, Richard Wilbur, Berryman, I. A. Richards, and W. D. Snodgrass, a promising poetic talent Lowell had first known at Iowa. It was obvious that the Brahmin was drawn to successful writers.

"Like him," read a newsmagazine, "they were reproductive; they had stayed the course."

A letter to David McDowell, an editor at Random House, captured Lowell's new lifestyle, testifying that they had bought a house in Boston and intended to stay put in the same block where he had grown up. He was becoming conventional and, indeed, was considering voting Republican, if he regained his citizenship, in local elections. (His voting privileges, suspended because of his criminal conviction, were eventually restored, though he assuredly never voted Republican.)

After the hardship of Iowa City, Boston seemed the height of sophistication. According to Elizabeth Hardwick's short, quasi novel, *Sleepless Nights* (1979), the handsome Lowell home was stocked with flowered curtains made to order, rugs cut to size, built-in bookshelves, wood-burning fireplaces, pine chests, oak tables, old china, silverware, plants, mahogany desks, photographs, English wallpaper, Venetian mirrors, decorated vases, fading black and pale green marble mantels, hibiscus blooming in the windows: objects of permanence. On the second floor of the four-story habitat were two grand parlors crammed with valuable antique furniture. A maid prepared meals. Lowell, feeling his oats, washed his vodka down with quarts of cold milk and sometimes late at night pranced about the den in time to his wife's jazz records. Such rituals of domesticity, wrote Hardwick, were somehow reminiscent of the trials of the poet's youth. His parents, says Hardwick, were overly fond of fine bed linens, silk undergarments, soft cushions, and electrical kitchen equipment. His father played a passable game of tennis and was a member of a nearby country club. His mother was a health faddist and a boastful anti-Semite. Lowell's parents insisted on dressing formally for supper and demanded their son do the same. Lowell recalled those dismal days and noted that even in Grandfather Winslow's eyes he had been a failure. He couldn't shoot a gun, ride a horse, sail a boat. So what good was he?

Conjecture was the meat of tedium. The strain of ease and boredom encouraged Lowell's mind to wander. When it was not putting him to sleep, Boston simply vexed him. Its crassness became an unremitting source of conversation in the Marlborough Street household and readily wound its way into the writings of both Lowells. Hardwick in an essay titled "Boston: The Lost Ideal" (included in *A View of My Own,* 1962), charged that the old things of the city "are too heavy and plush," while

the new "either hasn't been born or is appallingly shabby and poor."
Boston had changed: the patriotic Sons of Liberty had multiplied and
divided into an anonymous mass; the Liberty Tree had been displaced
by a red light district; Cambridge proper was overrun by pizza parlors
and chintzy, glass-and-chrome boutiques. Even Beacon Hill had gone
downhill; the walled-in gardens, the old trees, the mews, the drawing
rooms of Louisburg Square, the coach houses, the cobblestone streets,
were still noble but essentially empty, bereft of all cultural impact.

From where Robert Lowell and Elizabeth Hardwick stood, Boston
was "defective, out-of-date, vain, and lazy." It was a legend, but only
a legend: "The tedium of its largely fraudulent posture of traditionalism, the disillusionment of the Boston present as a cultural force make
quick minds hesitate to embrace a region too deeply compromised."
The Boston that the Lowells watched tumble down about them—with
its collapsible religious and social institutions, its crotchety and anemic
intellectual adherents, its high-minded biases and class-weary prejudices—was depicted by the poet in *Life Studies* as a kind of death
march. Surrounded by magnolia trees, brass bannisters, French chande-
liers, servants, Lowell, in his makeshift castle, was simply reliving the
living death of his ancestors.

Not just Boston but the entire Eastern seaboard was falling prey to
the wasteful wages of the age. A two-day car trip to Newport revealed
an Atlantis on the precipice of decay. Lowell's faith resided not in the
cities but in the remote regions of America's hinterland, the probable
result of his early days in the Agrarian South. In the fall of 1956 he and
a friend were hydroplaned to Lake Chamberlain in Maine, not far from
Moosehead, the state's largest, most popular lake and James Russell
Lowell's old stomping ground. Drawn by reports of excellent autumn
trout and black bass fishing and the presence of a crackerjack local
fishing guide, the pair waded in and cast their lines. Lowell found the
region invigorating and refreshing; a cold and dense forest where wild
life contrasted with noisy modern conveniences and the ubiquitous
fisherman. The trip reminded the poet of James Russell Lowell's *Moosehead Journal*.

Aside from his sympathetic reaction to James Russell Lowell, the
poet's need to disassociate himself from the traditions of his New England past was such that he had earlier denied Ferris Greenslet permission to include his name in the family history, *The Lowells and Their*

Seven Worlds. This self-consciousness in connection with his heritage did not, in any case, prevent him from creating his own familial dynasty. His wife's pregnancy at age forty elicited a sharp outburst of male pride on his part. He reminded Harriet Winslow in a letter how he used to feel about little children and he reflected on their faces, smiles, and moods.

A daughter named Harriet was born January 4, 1957. The event helped dissolve a block that had mysteriously interrupted the author's creative flow. He was writing again, he gleefully informed Randall Jarrell, for the first time in four years and was loosening up the meter. He wanted to do away with the extremely disciplined techniques that marked his former volumes. He didn't want to just continue working at the old machine, Lowell said, attempting to explain the long silence between *The Mills of the Kavanaughs* and *Life Studies*.

The critical reception accorded his previous volume had been decidedly mixed and may have shaken Lowell's confidence. In 1947, after the startling success of *Lord Weary's Castle*, *Life* magazine introduced Lowell as an "amiable young man" who had "already reached the stature of a major literary figure." Auden, Marianne Moore, and William Empson, on separate public occasions, read from his work, touting him for his extravagant talent. In keeping with his penchant for collecting literary awards, Lowell won *Poetry*'s esteemed Harriet Monroe Prize in 1951 for *The Mills of the Kavanaughs;* but prize or no prize, he was aware of the book's shortcomings. Randall Jarrell, although much taken with "Mother Marie Therese" and "Falling Asleep Over the *Aeneid*," was on the whole a good deal more sparing of praise than he had been for the earlier, dogma-ridden poems. Of the title poem, Lowell himself claimed that he was not simply out to tell a story; he was writing "an obscure, rather Elizabethan, dramatic and melodramatic poem," its plot drawn both from myth and real life. Jarrell thought this confection an implausible exercise in rhetoric, with characters that failed to come alive except as manifestations of Lowell's own personality, a sequence overburdened by meaningless details, and told in antiquated, worn-out rhyme. Amy Lowell's critics had drawn a similar bead on her many rather unconvincing narrative poems. But where she resisted such correctives, Robert Lowell gave into them, writing to Williams: "I've been wondering if my characters and plot aren't a bit trifling and cumbersome." Lowell had failed to find an appropriate or plausible voice to put into the mouths of his cast, particularly into the mouth of his chief narrator. The result, wrote Louise Bogan in *The New Yorker,* was "a dark mid-point" that "must in some way be transcended."

Any future verse had to break away from the past. To repeat himself would be to fall into mannerisms, to risk being a one-volume poet. As early as 1948, Lowell realized that in order to emerge as the leading poet of the postwar generation he would have to bring his work out of its medieval trance, into the modern age, and perhaps beyond. "How few modern poems," he grumbled in a 1948 essay, "have the distinction of good conversation. . . . Literary people as a rule have less of their own to say and consequently use words with less subtlety and precision than a Maine farmer." He recognized the problem but saw no ready solution. Williams, in "The Poem as a Field of Action" (1948), commented that poetry must be written in such a way as to "let our feelings through." What was required was not only a personal style but a form to accommodate it.

Williams, with his warmhearted and avuncular demeanor, helped Lowell emerge from his rootless rut, affirm a new faith in clarity and complex thoughts clearly expressed. Williams addressed himself to Lowell's literary prejudices, gradually forcing him to force himself into a revolutionary style of writing that was at once personal, vibrant, and free of constraining strictures such as meter and rhyme. It was not easy. At first Lowell resisted, insisting that Williams's open forms were beyond him, that he was as uncomfortable without meter and rhyme as Williams was with them. From Williams (and also from Pound, Ford, Delmore Schwartz, Elizabeth Bishop, and Allen Ginsberg), Lowell learned that he could dispense with rhyme and meter but still manage the resonant form he so stubbornly demanded. He did it by reading Williams, studying Williams, internalizing Williams. But he did not, could never, imitate Williams. Their styles were at heart too alien, their indoctrinations too dissimilar. Rather, he gained from Williams the notion that in a poem, "form is meaning," which implies that form is only "an arrangement of the words for the effect, not *the* arrangement, fixed and unalterable."

In 1956, Lowell attended a poetry reading that Williams gave at Wellesley College. The Rutherford poet read his recent work, ending with the Coda to "Asphodel." Lowell, who was seated in an aisle of the crowded college auditorium, was visibly moved by Williams's presentation. In his essay "William Carlos Williams," Lowell recalled the occasion: "It could have been no more crowded in the wide-galleried hall and I had to sit in the aisle. The poet appeared, one whole side partly paralyzed, his voice just audible, and here and there a word misread. No one stirred. In the silence he read his great poem 'Of Asphodel, That Greeny Flower,' a triumph of simple confession."

When Lowell came upon a style that he thought compatible with his needs he adopted it, dissolving the creative block that had stymied him since *Lord Weary's Castle*. But the process was slow in coming and slow in developing once it was found. Once developed, the new style allowed him to pump out poems with renewed vigor. On September 30, 1957, he wrote to Williams: "I've been writing poems like a house afire, i.e. for me that means five in six weeks, fifty versions of each. I've been experimenting with mixing loose and free meters with strict. . . . I feel more and more technically indebted to you." Several months later he sent Williams fifteen of his latest poems, including "Skunk Hour," and an epistle: "At forty I've written my first unmeasured verse. . . . I've only tried it in a few of these poems, those that are most personal. It's great to have no hurdle of rhyme and scansion between yourself and what you want to say most forcibly." Williams was overwhelmed by these "terrible wonderful poems" and said as much: "You have opened a new field. You needed that break, rhyme could not contain you any longer, you have too much to say for that." Lowell's gratitude poured forth: "I feel more love for you than for any man of your age." And again: "I'll go down to my grave in time thanking God that I met Williams. . . . Ah, we are brothers."

Copies of his new work also began to flood Randall Jarrell's home. On October 24, 1957, Lowell wrote Jarrell that he had completed seven or eight lengthy and personal poems since August. He was reading Catullus, Pasternak, Wordsworth, Baudelaire, Rimbaud, and Keats's *Letters*, which were Amy Lowell's favorites. There were references to other texts. He was charmed by Robert Graves. Dostoevski was the strongest of the novelist *maudits*. The French poets from Baudelaire to Apollinaire had given poetry a new lease on life and inspired what was best in modern American poetry. Lowell thought Rilke gentle and Germanic, Karl Shapiro like Donne with something racy and Jewish added to Auden's wit. He was impressed, too, with the work of Philip Larkin, in England, and Snodgrass, in the States. Larkin, five years younger than Lowell, was associated after World War II with the movement capitalized as "The Movement," the poetic equivalent of "The Angry Young Men" in the theater.

If Williams was Lowell's prodigal father, Snodgrass was his prodigal son. Snodgrass had endured many of the same personal hardships as Lowell: divorce, disillusionment with the academy, mental illness. As a graduate student at Iowa in 1953–1954 he came to know Lowell and began attending the poet's seminars. Snodgrass, on his own, was working out of a tradition similar to the later Lowell of *Life Studies,* writing poems of a personal nature based on his child, his divorce, life in Iowa City, all handled in expert little stanzas. They lacked the grandness of Lowell's panorama, were more polished, less lively and universal. As though depicting his own literary technique, Lowell observed: "Snodgrass's experience wouldn't be so interesting and valid if it weren't for the whimsy, the music, the balance, everything revised and placed and pondered. All that gives light to those poems on agonizing subjects comes from the craft."

From 1955 to 1960, between guest appearances at Bennington, Vassar, and other Ivy-establishment institutions, Lowell taught creative writing and literature courses at Boston University: "I teach like a painter, almost no preparation but very hard at work in class. In that way it's very exciting for me, like going fishing." His bait had a powerful lure. Among his students were Anne Sexton, George Starbuck, Sylvia Plath, and future literary critic, Helen Vendler.

The poetry-writing seminar met weekly in a dismal institutional room the shape of a shoebox. "It was a bleak spot," recalled Sexton, "as if it had been forgotten for years, like the spinning room in Sleeping Beauty's castle." As she remembered him, Lowell was formal, endearing, Bostonian, witty, slightly awkward; he possessed a distinctive reading voice: "It seems to me that people remember the voice of the teacher they loved long after they have forgotten what he said. At least, I have noticed this among poets and their teachers. Mr. Lowell's reverence for John Crowe Ransom's voice was something I couldn't understand until today as I find myself remembering Lowell's voice and the way *he* would read a poem."

As crucial as anything actually imparted in class was the mere fact of Lowell's presence; his suffering, his openness, his soulfulness made him an exceedingly popular figure among the young. His verse, seared with fiery desperation, fueled by rage and self-laceration, had immense appeal in the tight-lipped cold-war world ruled by Khrushchev and Eisenhower, a domain whose literary boundaries were still safeguarded by the doctrinaire New Critics, the Intentional Fallacy, and the "whole elaborate iron dogma by which poetry was separated utterly from the man who made it."

The example of Robert Lowell's 1959 *Life Studies* helped shape the contours of contemporary verse and break the backs of all those who subscribed to the dictates of the New Criticism. The volume reversed the previously irreversible ordinance demanding poetry's exclusion of personal emotions and feelings in addition to anything that hinted at autobiography or family history. Lowell was not the only defector to write finis to the movement that had fed and nourished his early literary imagination; Robert Penn Warren, in his later poetry and fiction and criticism, demonstrated similar disdain for the New Critics. But Lowell was far more popular than Warren among the poets of the younger generation. Striking in appearance, born to aristocracy, younger than most of his celebrated associates, Lowell was at war with society, often at odds with himself—twin stances that insured his popularity and influence. To his admirers he represented the wounded, self-sacrificial poet-warrior. He legitimized suffering, made self-destruction fashionable, and was cheered on in his self-destructiveness by those around him. The public's favorable response to Lowell's suffering is perhaps best exemplified by Donald Hall's brief comment in his 1978 memoir, *Remembering Poets:* "The human being who confronts darkness and defeats it is the most admired human being."

It is commonly assumed that the artist must censor nothing; if he is to succeed in "feeling" his art he must allow himself to experience pain. He must endure tears and misery; he must suffer without anesthetic, without the buffer of pipe dream or the escape hatch of fantasy. A raft of examples supports the notion that suffering is pandemic to poets. Dylan Thomas annihilated himself with drink; alcohol was a precondition for much of Thomas's work. Robert Frost looked into his desert places, faced his desire to enter the oblivion of the snowy woods, but disdainfully drove on, deftly enduring. T. S. Eliot courted disaster at every step of the voyage, marrying a virtual death-muse (Vivienne Haigh Haigh-Wood), but ultimately prevailed by inventing his famed doctrine of impersonality, cloaking himself in verse and stubbornly pushing ahead. Building partially on stones laid by Thomas, Frost, and

Eliot, Lowell began the wave of personalism and intimate revelation that became known as confessionalism and that charted the wounded but articulate intellectual's painful trek across the underbelly of the national frontier. His poems were his heroic effort to come to terms with the harsh incongruities of his childhood and of his difficult struggles with his parents, the will imposing shards of experience upon the poet's sensibility. The influence of *Life Studies* was such that it touched the very life chords of Lowell's followers. A. Alvarez discusses the ramifications of Lowell's influence on Sylvia Plath in the course of his piercing study of suicide, *The Savage God* (1971):

> Though Sylvia had attended Lowell's classes at Boston University . . . she never picked up his peculiarly contagious style. Instead of style, she took from him a freedom. She told a British Council interviewer: "I've been very excited by what I feel is the new breakthrough that came with, say, Robert Lowell's *Life Studies.* This intense breakthrough into very serious, very personal emotional experience . . . has been partly taboo. Robert Lowell's poems about his experiences in a mental hospital, for example, interest me very much. These peculiar private and taboo subjects I feel have been explored in recent American poetry." Lowell provided her with an example of the quality she most admired outside poetry and had herself in profusion: courage.

Plath's initial encounter with Lowell took place in June 1958, at Northampton, Massachusetts, where she was then living with poet-husband Ted Hughes in a floor-through attic apartment; she was teaching at Smith College, her husband at the University of Massachusetts in nearby Amherst. Sylvia described their meeting with Lowell in a letter to her brother Warren Plath, published after her death:

> We met the mad and very nice poet Robert Lowell (the only one, 40-ish, whom we both admire, who comes from the Boston Lowells and is periodically carted off as a manic depressive) when he came to give a reading at the University of Massachusetts. He is quiet, soft-spoken, and we liked him very much. I drove him around Northampton, looking for relics of his ancestors, and to the Historical Society and the graveyard. We hope to see him in Boston when we move down. . . .

Lowell's visit to Northampton provided the sound track for his poem "Jonathan Edwards in Western Massachusetts" from *For the Union*

Dead, in which he recalls his journey: "On my pilgrimage to Northampton, / I found no relic, / except the round slice of an oak / you are said to have planted."

If Lowell prospered from his visit, Plath also gained. She derived from her future mentor what Alvarez calls "a vast sense of release," the force and fortitude to examine human individuality, her own individuality, the interrelationship of sex, the psyche, the nervous system as channels for the realization of an antisocial and subversive flow of impersonality. But the frenetic force, the fire, the masterfully improvised fatalism of her form, were strictly her own. Although she has been appointed headmistress of a contemporary school, her work was individual, singular, sensual, strong; there was little of the quailing or whining that the feminist school which appointed her so often projects. She stood head and shoulders above her poetry-producing soul mates.

The difference between the fantasies of Plath and those of her colleagues is that they are falling; she is diving. At first Lowell was unable to guess her inner torment; she bore it with grace and hid it behind the cheerful aspect of pink cheeks and a tailored pageboy hairdo. To Lowell she seemed a "distinguished, delicate, complicated person in whom there was no intimation of what would come later." He characterized her early poetics as "controlled and modest," and was "startled by the burst of talent she later displayed." Few could guess the seriousness of her endeavor, the grim reality of her steely resolve. The marvelous talent that he later discerned led him to write a preface to the American edition of Plath's *Ariel,* wherein he noted that "In these poems, written in the last months of her life and often rushed out at the rate of two or three a day, Sylvia Plath becomes herself, becomes something imaginary, newly, wildly and subtly created—hardly a person at all, or a woman, not another 'poetess,' but one of those super-real, hypnotic, great classical heroines." Lowell placed Plath in the select company of Emily Dickinson, Marianne Moore, and Elizabeth Bishop—by common consent America's most esteemed female poets. That Plath killed herself in 1963, in England, at the age of thirty meant that we had only a moderate body of her work to consider. The sense of loss was therefore all the keener.

No less tragic was the life of Anne Sexton. In a memoir, "The Barfly Ought to Sing," Sexton recalled that after their seminar meetings, she, Plath, and Starbuck would go to a local Boston bar, where they would sit for hours and argue the meaning of life: "Often, very often, Sylvia and I would talk at length about our first suicides. . . . We talked death with burned-up intensity, both of us drawn to it like moths to an electric light bulb. Sucking on it!" Talk of psychoanalysis and suicide stimulated all three, "as if death made each of us a little more real at the moment."

Sexton's poetry aggrandized the themes of madness and anguish, though in a far less subtle and effective manner than we find in the passionate work of Plath. One might call Sexton a "poor-woman's" Plath, a poet of far more accessible range and fewer gifts. She carried her readers with her through marriage to a middle-aged Boston business executive, children, futile assignations with strangers, affairs with intimates, isolation, depression, death. Her work has been termed the world's longest suicide note; "Sextonics" made its way into the feminist lexicon, a synonym for "hysterics." The conventions of society—security, comfort, domesticity—drained her, drove her mad. If she tattooed her poetry liberally with violent images, it was because the violence of the written word helped stem the tide of her turmoil. But poetry was no panacea: Anne Sexton took her own life in 1974.

Art-induced death was nothing new. And madness? That affliction was the common property of all artists. Rimbaud had a split personality, Verlaine was a psychopath, Van Gogh killed himself, as did Mayakovsky, Modigliani, Hart Crane, Jack London, Hemingway, Paul Celan, and Virginia Woolf. Alcoholism killed F. Scott Fitzgerald, Brendan Behan, Jack Kerouac, Delmore Schwartz, and Dylan Thomas. And Christopher Smart, Hölderlin, Nijinsky, Antonin Artaud, and Ezra Pound spent years in lunatic asylums.

Lowell survived, but barely. His suffering—the music of mortality—as depicted in his confessional poetry was partially expiated by his desire to understand the root causes of his pain. The label "confessional poetry" is misleading in that it is more from the analyst's couch than the church confessional that the confessional writers derive their style. The confessional poets are concerned primarily with their own psychic turmoil; they possess a passion for tracking their past experiences and present thought patterns for a clue to their own inner conflicts. The self-defining confessional genre, with its persistent assertions of identity and its emphasis on a central mythology of the self, had a tradition that could be loosely traced through such previous self-mythologizers as St. Augustine, Rousseau, Whitman, Yeats, Proust, Wordsworth, and Byron. None of these poets, however, was quite as demanding in his self-examination and self-dramatization as Lowell.

That most lyrics are expressive of intimate personal feelings does not in itself make them confessional. The term has come to be associated with private experience extraordinarily harsh, mean, or ugly —and stemming from or at least related to the harrowing experience of public life in our time. Confessional poetry, unlike lyric verse, involves a form of exorcism. When the Elizabethan odist Samuel Daniel writes a poem that declares, "Love is a sickness full of woes," it is not with an eye toward exorcising his despair; nor does Poe have exorcism in mind in his lament, "From childhood's hour I have not been / As others were— . . ." Confessional poetry is usually associated with a poet's private mental aberration or with extreme societal disaffection. Babette Deutsch, in her *Poetry Handbook,* provides the example of Robert Lowell's "Waking Early Sunday Morning," from *Near the Ocean,* in which he sees above the fog the white spire and the white flagpole sticking out "like old white china doorknobs, sad / slight useless things to calm the mad." We can cite any of dozens of Sylvia Plath's or Anne Sexton's poems. Portions of John Berryman's many-voiced *Dream Songs* with, as Deutsch says, "their black humor, and the naked pathos of their colloquial avowels," fall into the same category. Poets such as Ted Hughes, Stanley Kunitz, Denise Levertov, Donald Finkle, even Leroi Jones and Allen Ginsberg have been placed within the confessional camp, although none was as extreme as Lowell or Berryman. When Berryman chimes, "I'm scared by only one thing which is me," we have no reason to doubt him. The appeal of the new school was particularly strong for women poets, whose previous careers had often been relegated to silence or neglect or both. Those who followed the lead provided by Lowell included Adrienne Rich, Diane Wakoski, Muriel Rukcyser, Gwendolyn Brooks, Erica Jong, and Margaret Atwood. Many of these poets expressed a certain fascination with madness and suicide, while their predecessors —Lowell, Ginsberg, Berryman, Plath, and Sexton—went to extremes to detail their stays in mental institutions, their attempts (often futile) to rehabilitate themselves.

The intensely personal and painfully private world of *Life Studies* bespeaks Lowell's suffering during the period since his previous volume. A dozen years had elapsed since his Pulitzer Prize for *Lord Weary's Castle,* eight years since the publication of *The Mills of the Kavanaughs.* Chronologically he had reached the turning point; a man

approaching middle age, already in his early forties, yet young enough
to dwell in the elegiac manner upon his own antiquity, he reflected on
his evolving life:

> I have a nine months' daughter,
> young enough to be my granddaughter. . . .

His daughter's infancy accentuated his own aging:

> Our noses rub,
> each of us pats a stringy lock of hair—
> they tell me nothing's gone.
> Though I am forty-one,
> not forty now, the time I put away
> was child's play.

A touch of confusion surrounds the concluding line—the time the poet
"put away" was anything but child's play. Randall Jarrell has amply
testified to the difficulty of Lowell's life: "He was struggling with two
dynamos, one leading him to some kind of creative work, the other
tearing him apart." Jarrell remarked that the "incredible tensions"
manifested by Lowell's relationship to his parents would have totally
annihilated most men: "I don't see how he survived that family. He has
written about it, but the reality is worse than he has written." He wrote
about it in *Life Studies,* examining the psychopathology of his family
life with its sinister shifts in sex roles, infantile regression, libidinal
politics, tribal mores, transmuting the whole into something dark and
glowing.

Dark and glowing as well are Lowell's descriptions of mental illness.
Acting as a leitmotif, they expand outward in such a way that Lowell's
personal crisis is felt at the same time as a symbolic embodiment of
national and cultural crisis. M. L. Rosenthal, originator of the term
"confessional poet," notes that the "myth" that Lowell creates is of an
America "whose history and present predicament are embodied in
those of his own family and epitomized in his own psychological experience." Despite his stouthearted search for positive values, the poet
repeatedly comes up against a resistant force of personal distemper and
antagonism. "Man and Wife" uses loud and clashing colors to reflect the
poet's alienation from the world around him, a technique mildly similar
to Amy Lowell's utilization of colors as symbol and image:

> Tamed by *Miltown,* we lie on Mother's bed;
> the rising sun in war paint dyes us red;
> in broad daylight her gilded bed-posts shine,
>
> . . .
>
> At last the trees are green on Marlborough Street,
> blossoms on our magnolia ignite
> the morning with their murderous five days' white.

Not even heavy sedation with Miltown can relieve the poet's inner pain, nor dull his perception of the schism between himself and his wife. The incongruity of dulled emotion and heightened terror is reflected and measured by the glare of colors and lights. The trajectory of mood inspired by "war paint dyes," "gilded bed-posts," and a "murderous five days' white" subsides somewhat as the poem progresses toward conclusion. As Hardwick and Lowell lie in bed, her talk rekindles memories of his initial infatuation with her, when her tirades were still "loving"—

> Sleepless, you hold
> your pillow to your hollows like a child,
> your old-fashioned tirade—
> loving, rapid, merciless—
> breaks like the Atlantic Ocean on my head.

The next *Life Studies* poem, " 'To Speak of Woe That Is in Marriage,' " is told from Elizabeth Hardwick's perspective. A sonnet, it is introduced by an epigraph from Schopenhauer: "It is the future generation that presses into being by means of these exuberant feelings and super-sensible soap bubbles of ours." The sexually effervescent tinge of this introductory fragment quickly hardens into rancor, as the speaker tries to imagine their future together:

> "My hopped up husband drops his home disputes,
> and hits the streets to cruise for prostitutes,
> free-lancing out along the razor's edge.
> This screwball might kill his wife, then take the pledge.
> Oh the monotonous meanness of his lust. . . . ."

It is evident that the stateliness and formality of technique are more relaxed in the poems of *Life Studies* than in any of Lowell's previous tomes. The iambs march along less precisely, and the rhyme, when it exists, is casual. There is the mellowness that comes with age, a looking-back à la Proust, sometimes in amusement, frequently with bittersweet remembrance, often at one or another forebear. All that remains of the former maker of Alexandrian complexities is the unspeakable craft and skill, as toward the beginning of "Grandparents," wherein he writes of the Winslows as being "altogether otherworldly now." He portrays them in his "throw-away and shaggy span" of youth going for their ritual Friday afternoon drive, stopping at the pharmacist and at the five-and-dime in Brockton, when merchandise at Woolworth's still sold for a nickel or a dime:

> . . . Grandpa still waves his stick
> . . .
> Grandmother, like a Mohammedan, still wears her thick
> lavender mourning and touring veil;
> the Pierce Arrow clears its throat in a horse-stall.
> Then the dry road dust rises to whiten
> the fatigued elm leaves—
> the nineteenth century, tired of children, is gone.

Hemingway's phenomenalistic use of imagery comes to mind in this and in several other poems of *Life Studies*. "Dry road dust" rising "to whiten the fatigued elm leaves" contains the bouquet of the opening of *A Farewell to Arms:*

> . . . In the bed of the river there were pebbles and boulders, dry and white in the sun, and the water was clear and swiftly moving and blue in the channels. Troops went by the house and down the road and the dust they raised powdered the leaves of the trees.

Hemingway's talent for setting a scene quickly, his feel for the texture and touch of atmosphere, were techniques he adopted in part from Pound and Gertrude Stein; Lowell mastered the same technique through his appreciation of Williams and his reading of the poet Elizabeth Bishop, whose ability to depict character and landscape through expert use of detail surpassed anything Lowell had seen in poetry before. A reading tour to the West Coast in the spring of 1957 also helped him break away from the ossified, closefisted language and dandified ironies of his earlier work:

> . . . I had been giving readings on the West Coast, often reading six days a week and sometimes twice in a single day. I was in San Fran-

cisco, the era and setting of Allen Ginsberg, and all about very modest poets were waking up prophets. I became sorely aware of how
few poems I had written, and that these few had been finished at the
latest three or four years earlier. Their style seemed distant, symbol-
ridden and willfully difficult. I began to paraphrase my Latin quotations, and to add extra syllables to a line to make it clearer and more
colloquial. . . . I am no convert to the "beats." . . . What influenced
me more than San Francisco and reading aloud was that for some
time I had been writing prose. I felt that the best style for poetry was
none of the many poetic styles in English, but something like the
prose of Chekhov or Flaubert.

His trip took him from Seattle along the winding coastline to San
Francisco and Los Angeles. He gave readings at colleges along the way.
He found the West Coast a welcome relief from the congestion of the
East. San Francisco exuded charm. He wrote home to Harriet Winslow
that he had to admit San Francisco was glorious.

The Beat Poets and literary Hipsters of North Beach, with their free,
Freudian, colloquial sounds, a compelling admixture of the poems of
Charles Olson, Dylan Thomas, Williams, Pound, Crane, and Whitman,
inspired Lowell to reexamine his own literary style. From Olson the
Beats derived what D. H. Lawrence, in his own day, called the idea of
a "poetry of the present," which meant nothing more or less than verse
emanating strictly from the poet's experience, arising out of the confusion and excitement of the poet's life. It was not a particularly new or
revolutionary idea. Even Dante, one of Allen Tate's favorite poets,
drew on his personal experience as raw material. Tate, who purportedly
disliked literary criticism that looked beyond the page, said of another
poet, his friend Hart Crane, "Out of the desperate conditions of his
private life, Crane created the great poetic achievement of his generation." It was impossible to write, in fact, *without* drawing material and
a mode of perception from the life lived. The art came not from the act
of gleaning from life but from the methodology of transforming a given
stream of gleanings. The alteration or distortion of experience for aesthetic and other impossible-to-divine reasons was what separated the
men from the boys.

Olson's projectivist theories, based partially on a fleeting knowledge
of science, called for open-endedness but objected to "the lyrical inter-
ference of the individual as ego," on the grounds that "a man is himself
an object." Certainly Dylan Thomas would not agree with this; nor the

Romantics (though Eliot, Auden, and the late Wallace Stevens might). The Beats were too self-involved to buy the line. They were all for open-endedness but otherwise leaned toward the bardic tradition as exemplified by Dylan Thomas. Poetry was an extension of the self; one need know nothing beyond the self, provided one had a voice. Thomas had as melodic a voice as ever there sang. His reading tours of America in the early 1950's at once relegated Auden to a shelf and brought out every minor, sour-voiced warbler for miles. Thomas simply sang out his poems in the manner of the bard, a variation on the prophetic tradition of Whitman, a further variation on Ginsberg's concurrent Jeremiah mode. To this potpourri the Beats added the random impromptu notes associated with jazz, just to keep the confection local. If there was a method to this madness it was simply that feelings, phrases, and images led to attendant feelings, phrases, and images, thereby projecting the poem forward in space. What Dylan Thomas put back into poetry was passion, and it was this ingredient more than any other that motivated the antiacademic, anti-intellectual Beats. Theirs was a legitimate movement, albeit a minor one. Ginsberg was a minor poet with a major influence.

To the Beats Lowell was a charismatic rogue—shrewd, somewhat sentimental, theatrical, monolithic, insightful. But his poems, those from *Lord Weary's Castle* and *The Mills of the Kavanaughs,* were too constrained, unfree, unfeeling. The poet's association with his new friends, with Ginsberg, Lawrence Ferlinghetti, Kenneth Rexroth, Gary Snyder, made Lowell aware of the inadequacies of his own style: "I felt my old poems hid what they were really about, and at times offered a stiff, humorless and even impenetrable surface. . . . They seemed like prehistoric monsters dragged down into the bog and death by their ponderous armor. I was reciting what I no longer felt."

The poet's latest associations, besides introducing him to a new lifestyle, offered the opportunity to rethink his old poetics, to apply the freer, fresher, more direct mode that he heard recited in San Francisco's cafés and coffeehouses and that came to him via his reading of the exploratory and original work of Williams and Bishop, specifically Williams's "bare objective language" and the exquisite craftsmanship of Bishop. Through his talks and recitation of poems, Lowell mastered the principal poetic devices that he would use for the first time in *Life Studies.* By adding transitional phrases and translating into English foreign phrases, he was able to make his art more accessible, his voice

and vision more individual. He wanted to employ a plain, straightforward style in his writing, nothing that plastered difficulties and mannerisms on what he was trying to say or that interfered with the honesty
of sentiment he was after, and nothing that would overshadow the style
of "91 Revere Street," the volume's longish prose section.

Although it made for easier reading, this looser, less formal style was no
easier to write. One problem was that, though autobiographical, the
poems were not always veracious. As with Ginsberg's *Kaddish* or Plath's
Ariel, the poet was opting for a rough sketch of his own life, not necessarily the life as lived. Subsequently, there was a good deal of tinkering with
fact. Details were omitted; the poet might want to emphasize this and
not that. Factual events were in constant flux, but to reduce the flow of
experience to poetry was to break up that flux, to pick and choose, to
place experience in a sort of hierarchical time tunnel where one event
superseded and became more relevant than another. To wit: the poet
was forced to invent facts, change dates, fabricate events, yet arrive at a
point where the poem rang true. Lowell compared this version of
confessional poetry to a form of historical documentation: "You want the
reader to say, this is true. In something like Macaulay's *History of
England* you think you're really getting William III. That's as good as a
good plot in a novel. And so there was always that standard of truth
which you wouldn't ordinarily have in poetry—the reader was to believe
he was getting the *real* Robert Lowell."

To attribute the artistic merit of *Life Studies* to pure confession—
Lowell's ability to write off the top of his head or from the depth of his
gut—is to say nothing at all about the convexity of the literary process.
Although critical commentators have attributed the composition of his
poems to isolated bursts of unconscious creativity, such an explanation
overlooks completely the poet's recourse to the tools of self-editorial
genius so confidently displayed in volume after volume. In truth, Lowell (like Auden) was a tireless reviser and rewriter of lines, forever
juggling, excising, moving things about. To alter was for Lowell a creative act. Repeatedly he took over passages from earlier poems, rewrote
them, and placed them within new contexts. Phrases, lines, even whole
pieces were constantly being polished to remove the tarnish. The garbage was frequently culled and burned. Hart Crane, a prodigious re-
worker of scraps, constructed *The Bridge* out of a maze of razor-edge
possibilities, finally creating a long lyric poem that had too many un-
heightened private moments to work well as a cultural epic of public

proportion. *Leaves of Grass* comprises all the poems Whitman ever wrote rewritten a thousand times. And it has been said of Emily Dickinson that her evanescent, vaporous poems are nothing if not a fragmented epic, a bolus of fascicles reprocessed and congealed into solid mass. So there was a tradition for Lowell's nervous habit, his notion that all his reworked poems were in a sense one poem and that sections of poems sometimes belonged in other poems—or, if prime, by themselves.

Lowell's literary progression, from the monastic and ambiguous but rich tone of *Land of Unlikeness* and *Lord Weary's Castle* to the detailed but understated content of *Life Studies*, resulted in as brave and revolutionary a volume as *The Waste Land* or *The Pisan Cantos*. Its only viable competition on the American scene were Allen Ginsberg's *Howl*, published three years earlier, and Snodgrass's *Heart's Needle,* which appeared the same month as the Lowell. But *Howl,* because Ginsberg was considered an underground poet, did not receive its rightful due until the more progressive and political 1960's. And the Snodgrass, though it was awarded a Pulitzer Prize, was far less full in scope and erudition and failed therefore to create the excitement of *Life Studies.*

Life Studies caught the public's eye partially because its author was already known and partially because of the close attention it paid to the always stimulating subject of insanity. Probing the recesses of the author's mind, the volume recited the rattling daymares of a man trapped in the psychic gloom of a miasmic universe, where "Crows maunder on the petrified fairway / Absence! My heart grows tense / as though a harpoon were sparring for the kill. / (This is the house for the 'mentally ill')." In this and in other poems the poet confesses more about himself than the average reader really needs or wants to know. But the craftsmanship is as keen as a cutting edge. There is an up-and-doing here, a striving, even a frenzy mingling with frustration, despair, fear. Taken as a single poem these fragments are a record of "the process"—they capture the essence and quality of life "alive."

This is not to say that the volume was universally appreciated. Joseph Bennett, in *The Hudson Review,* found the book to be "a collection of lazily recollected and somewhat snobbish memoirs, principally of the poet's own wealthy and aristocratic family . . . it is more suited as an appendix to some snobbish society magazine, to *Town and Country* or *Harper's Bazaar,* rather than a purposeful work." One could have hoped for a more purposeful attack. Bennett seems to have missed not only the boat here but the dock to boot. The fact that Lowell's mainline family was wealthy, aristocratic, and snobbish is the very point of Lowell's portrait. In a manner as direct and immediate as his early poetry was literary and allusive, the poet skirts back and forth between memories of childhood and family and reminiscences of more recent times, tracing his heritage from the days of his Great Aunt Sarah through the first months of his infant daughter's life. By way of a swirl of juxtaposed details, the poet conveys an unsparing but artistically shaped picture of the death of the Lowell-Winslow dynasty and the ensuing smothering of their dreams.

The irony of the volume's title becomes apparent as one begins to connect the still life portraits that make up the book. The total effect of reading through the poems is not unakin to viewing a series of light and dark Rembrandt portraits in Amsterdam's Rijksmuseum: details begin to coalesce after the fact that one is barely aware of during the actual viewing process. *Life Studies* is not a study of life at all but of death, of ruination, of past glory spent. Each of the Lowells and Winslows that the poet portrays exists in a false Garden of Eden, a world of pipe dreams and broken promises, no more real or viable than the pipe dreams that keep alive a clutch of beaten alcoholics in Eugene O'Neill's *The Iceman Cometh.* For Lowell's elders the shattered dream consisted of the social gaiety of "Fontainebleau, Mattapoisett, and Puget Sound," a round of Brahmin sights and sounds to which they aspired but which they failed to attain. Lowell's father, once the youngest ensign in his class at Annapolis and the captain of a gunboat on the Yangtze River, spends his years of retirement at Salem's Maritime Museum with his "calc" and "trig" books, his clipper ship statistics, and his ivory slide rule. After the Commander's death, Lowell discovers in his naval blue-and-white bedroom a blue kimono, Chinese sandals with blue plush straps, a clear glass bed-lamp covered with a white doily shade, and volume two of Lafcadio Hearn's *Glimpses of Unfamiliar Japan,* bearing the flyleaf inscription "To Robbie from Mother." For Lowell's Winslow grandmother the dream dissolved in her treasured Edwardian "rose garden." His grandfather surrounds himself with photographs, mementoes, false bravado, and memories of better days. Great Aunt Sarah early renounced her dream of becoming a concert pianist. Uncle Devereux's parting desire was a trip around the world.

The bonding of diminished dreams, the careful attention to details and language, is no less intense in the prose section "91 Revere Street," with its zany cast of characters and salient sense of alienation. Central to the cast and to his feeling of alienation is the poet's nineteenth-century ancestor, Major Mordecai Myers: "Mordecai Myers was my Grandmother Lowell's grandfather. His life was tame and honorable. He was a leisured squire and merchant, a member of the state legislature, a mayor of Schenectady, a 'president' of Kinderhook Village." We soon learn that Major Myers fought in the War of 1812, after gaining military experience and rank in a New York militia regiment organized by Colonel (later, President) Martin Van Buren. Despite his war record he "sponsored an enlightened law exempting Quakers from military service in New York State," a deed that Lowell, the conscientious objector, could well admire. Just as important for Lowell was the fact that Mordecai Myers was a Jew, a German Jew to be precise—"no downright Yankee." A Jew fighting for just social causes was a man with whom Lowell, the Brahmin outcast, could hope to identify: "Great-great-Grandfather Mordecai! Poor sheepdog in wolf's clothing! In the anarchy of my adolescent war on my parents, I tried to make him a true wolf, the wandering Jew! *Homo lupus nomini!*"

Whatever the intent, his final words imply ultimate disappointment, an inability on Lowell's part to link himself with this remote and exotic ancestor. Lowell's quandary remained more or less unresolved from the days of his youth. The question was still, with whom could he hope to identify or bind himself? *Life Studies,* which endeavors with greater perspicacity than any of his previous volumes to tackle this problem, examines the social and psychological lives of four consecutive generations of vestigial New England aristocrats. Chronologically, the progression of poetry and prose transports the reader from Lowell's childhood through his adolescence and young adulthood into the present tense of parenthood and middle age. We not only observe him growing older but witness his reaction to his environment at every consecutive stage of development. Although the volume's title alludes specifically to the fourth and last section of the book (divided into two parts), it can be said to represent the volume as a whole. One life obviously under scrutiny is Lowell's.

As a child he clearly identified with Grandfather Winslow, whom we see as an aristocrat spanning three eras—Victorian, Edwardian, and Georgian—secure in his upper-class, old-wealth status, confident in the knowledge that there is a raison d'être to the Darwinian order of mankind and a reason for his being at the top. Arthur Winslow belonged to a generation of men who not only believed in the survival of the fittest but "felt that the world they inhabited was exactly as they had created it, and, indeed, that it was inherently a good world." The old man regarded himself as necessary to his age, the padrone of his family, protector of a rapidly fading way of life. Unlike his son-in-law, the Commander, he was not "lost/in the mob of ruling-class Boston," but stood at its helm. It made no difference to Arthur Winslow that twentieth-century Boston was no longer what it once had been. In his imagination he lived in the past; he not only lived there, he reigned.

Robert Lowell's parents are characterized by a considerably altered set of standards from those used to identify his grandfather. Because they inhabited a universe of their own making, the elder Winslows lived false but not totally barren lives. Lowell respected them in ways he did not respect his parents. Personal and social lassitude discolored the very substance and fabric of Mr. and Mrs. Lowell's paltry existence. Lowell talks freely about the alienation the Commander introduced into his son's life by his passing involvement with the Navy and its counterpart, the sense of continuity his mother introduced into their home on the downward side of Beacon Hill through her use of heavy traditional furnishings, silverware, drapes—all the essentials of plush living, despite the abode's less than glamorous location. Although grievously unsuited for one another, both Lowells were traumatically formal and remote, Charlotte dreading any kind of lapse from the protocol of class, the Commander shirking all parental and social responsibility. Agonizing over the difficulty of his relationship with them, their son nevertheless broke with each and every one of their values, discrediting and deconstructing them whenever the opportunity presented itself. In keeping with the pattern established by his aggressive ancestor, Amy Lowell, Robert seldom had a good word to say about any members of the clan, not even for his literary predecessors. Not surprisingly, his rebellion exacted its toll; remorse, guilt, and a fair sampling of psychologically induced ailments were his lifelong enemies.

The prose of "91 Revere Street" is a poet's prose, recognizably so in its intensity of expression and musicality of rhythm. For all its grittiness, it remains eminently readable, with not a trace of sentimentality or self-pity. Nowhere is he more effective or affecting than when describing his relationship with his family. Of his father, Lowell laments: "In his forties, Father's soul went underground; as a civilian he kept his high sense of form, his humor, his accuracy, but this accuracy was henceforth unimportant, recreational hors de combat. His debunking grew myopic; his shyness grew evasive; he argued with a fumbling languor. In the twenty-two years Father lived after he resigned from the Navy, he never again deserted Boston and never became Bostonian."

The poet's mother is portrayed as a woman who has lost faith both in herself and her age. She is a totem pole of disguises, one moment resembling the most elegant of grandes dames and the next, standing "rigid and faltering, as if she feared being crushed by her own massively intimidating offensive." Her lack of faith in the future of American nobility is accentuated by a comparison in "91 Revere Street" between herself and the Napoleonic figure of Amy Lowell. The speaker in this case is William Harkness, a cigar-smoking, Annapolis classmate and close friend of Lowell's father, a "regular" at Sunday night dinners at Revere Street:

> Harkness went in for tiresome, tasteless harangues against Amy Lowell, which he seemed to believe necessary for the enjoyment of his after-dinner cigar. He would point a stinking baby stogie at Mother. " 'Ave a peteeto cigareeto, Charlotte," he would crow. "Puff on this wacking black cheroot, and you'll be a match for any reeking señorita *femme fatale* in the spiggotty republics, where blindness from Bob's bathtub hooch is still unknown. When you go up in smoke, Charlotte, remember the *Maine.* Remember Amy Lowell, that cigar-chawing, guffawing, senseless and meterless, multimillionheiress, heavyweight mascot on a floating fortress. Damn the *Patterns!* Full speed ahead on a cigareeto!"

Charlotte Lowell's response to the attack was characteristic: "Whenever Amy Lowell was mentioned Mother bridled. Not distinguishing, not caring whether her relative were praised or criticized, she would say, 'Amy had the courage of her convictions. She worked like a horse.' Mother would conclude, . . . 'Amy did insist on doing everything the *hard* way. I think, perhaps that her brother, the President of Harvard, did more for *other* people.' "

The confrontation between Harkness and Mrs. Lowell gave rise to the poet's longest, most complete statement concerning Amy Lowell:

> Amy Lowell was never a welcome subject in our household. Of course, no one spoke disrespectfully of Miss Lowell. She had been so pluck, so *formidable, so beautifully and unblushingly immense,* as Henry James might have said. And yet, though irreproachably decent herself appar-

ently, like Mae West she seemed to provoke indecorum in others. There was an anecdote which I was too young to understand: it was about Amy's getting migraine headaches from being kept awake by the exercises of honeymooners in an adjacent New York hotel room. Amy's relatives would have liked to have honored her as a *personage,* a personage a little *outrée* perhaps, but perfectly within the natural order, like Amy's girlhood idol, the Duse. Or at least she might have been unambiguously tragic, short-lived, and a classic, like her last idol, John Keats. My parents piously made out a case for Miss Lowell's *Life of Keats,* which had killed its author and was so much more manly and intelligible than her poetry. Her poetry! But was *poetry* what one could call Amy's loud, bossy, unladylike *chinoiserie*—her free verse! For those that could understand it, her matter was, no doubt, blameless. . . .

If decline and fall, "the dissipation of the old aristocracy based upon birth, wealth, family, institutional affiliation, and social bearing," were the guts of the matter in *Life Studies,* it was clear that in the poet's mind Amy Lowell stood outside the pale; she was part of his grandfather's world, otherworldly now, and apart from the crumbling, rundown cosmos of his parents' generation. She, in her turn, shared his grandfather's illusion that the inherited status of the highly pedigreed Brahmin was worth something, that the family name was a commodity one simply passed down from generation to generation like a family heirloom, that one inherited status without having to earn or work for it.

If Robert Lowell found it difficult to identify with Amy Lowell, the remainder of *Life Studies* clearly demonstrates that he found it just as impossible to identify with the so-called "common man," the *Volk,* that great homogeneous mass depicted in "Sailing Home from Rapallo" as look-alike ship passengers "tanning on the Mediterranean in deckchairs" or as the "slaves of habit" of "A Mad Negro Soldier Confined at Munich." Following a tradition established by James Russell Lowell and continued by Amy, the last of the writing triad demonstrated little true affection or understanding for the more unfortunate members of society —the lame, the poor, the dumb, the obscure. His imagination had room only for great men and cataclysmic events. The little man, the run-of-the-mill, was of no consequence to Lowell. When he did write about the masses it was usually with a tinge of disdain. In the ever popular "Skunk Hour," for instance, the throngs appear in the form of predatory skunks "that search in the moonlight for a bite to eat." Lowell, vacationing in Maine, watches them march on their soles up Main Street:

a mother skunk with her column of kittens swills the garbage pail.
She jabs her wedge-head in a cup
of sour cream, drops her ostrich tail,
and will not scare.

Summer skunks in search of nourishment and unafraid of the pretensions of class privilege also mirror the greedy materialism of the fallen aristocracy, and therein to some degree remind Lowell of himself, of his own plight. Skunks in search of food or sustenance are equated in the poem with Lowell's Whitmanesque search for fulfillment. Lowell's "ill" spirit, the collapse of the current social structure, the wreckage of civilization all conspire to set the scene in this littered landscape. In existential terms, the poet is alienated from his environment and must plunge to the very depths of his soul to redeem himself and his art. Explaining his passage through the secular dark night of the soul, Lowell noted in an essay "On Skunk Hour" (1964) that "my night is not gracious, but secular, puritan, and agnostical. An Existentialist night. Somewhere in my mind was a passage from Sartre or Camus about reaching some point of final darkness where the one free act is suicide. Out of this comes the march and affirmation, an ambiguous one, of my skunks in the last two stanzas." Like his skunks Lowell pushes on, undaunted.

The question arises, Why employ skunks to symbolize isolation, ruin, psychological distress? Aside from the sequence's similarity to "The Dark Night," a sixteenth-century mystical poem by St. John of the Cross, and to part three of Eliot's "East Coker," Lowell has said that he based the march of his skunks on Elizabeth Bishop's "The Armadillo." Bishop's armadillo escapes the scene of a fire, "head down, tail down." He is as much a survivor as Lowell's stubborn family of skunks or Marianne Moore's "armored animals." Lowell's skunks, swilling the garbage pail for nourishment, in a way reflect Lowell and his generation of poets exhausting the annals of the literary past, searching for some refreshing mode of expression, a means of reinventing their present lives. Yet this may be reading more into the poem than Lowell meant to implant. He has said that "the skunks are both quixotic and barbarously absurd, hence the tone of amusement and defiance." The inference here is that these skunks are only skunks, no more than that and no less.

If one is inclined to make something of these skunks, and it seems one must, the overwhelming temptation is to say that their strong will to survive reflects the poet's extreme desire to live. If the poem affirms Lowell's determination to struggle on, the volume as a whole is a looking back, a sifting through the shards of memory, a search for Lowell's "lost self," for the key that will presumably unlock his present self. Lowell's backward glance is no Wordsworthian ode to innocent immortality or splendor in the grass, adrift with pastoral images and English ecstasies, the romantic moth flittering back and forth between then and now. Nor is it a "poem of manners," a salute to Trollope, Thackeray, James, or Wharton and their "lavender" excursions into the stiff and formal lives of the rich and powerful. Rather the poet is diving into the depths of his own submerged past, through the murky waters of despair and past protruding reefs of anguish.

Amid an extraordinary tribal closeness among members of the Lowell dynasty, the cream of the in-group elite, a clan that took seriously the illusion of the survival of hierarchies and royalty, Lowell stood miles and ages apart. He looked on the family, with its demurely understated style and quiet elegance, as part of the establishment that ran whatever was worth running: corporations, banks, law firms, Ivy League colleges, the Junior Leagues. These public-minded autocrats were also the power connection that ran the CIA, the State Department, and the local election board. They, in their turn, regarded Lowell with suspicion and probably a grain of fear. They feared him because he had opted for a career not as a lawyer, a banker, or a businessman, but as a writer, a thinker, an individual. He did not feel that unconventionality was degrading; respectability was degrading. He portrayed the moneyed old-family WASP with "background" as an object of disdain, derision, pity, a "ghost" that needed to be laid to rest. He did not reveal the clan so much as betray it.

Oppressed by his failure to absorb the ideal into his life, Robert Lowell, in keeping with his own predilection, enacted all the ironies of his dilemma, connecting and disconnecting ties between past and present, surveying the wreckage of a society from which he remained an exile for much of his life. The images with which he depicts the family are often grotesque, overbearing, disproportioned, as in "My Last Afternoon with Uncle Devereux," set at *Char-de-sa*, Arthur Winslow's Massachusetts farm with its "diamond-pointed, athirst and Norman alley of poplars" and its "scary stand of virgin pine." This is perhaps as close as Lowell will ever come to Elmwood or Sevenels, country estates that reflect the rising expectations of the social registrites who once inhabited them, those handsome, sports-loving, card-playing, smartly dressed, unintellectual, yet simple, affectionate, easily homesick denizens, with their spent dreams and their scorn of the lower classes.

As one rummages through "My Last Afternoon"—originally construed as prose—the impression derived is one of ruined wealth and wasted grandeur. A clock ticks off time, connecting three generations. The poet sits on a stone porch, "looking through screens as black-grained as drifting coal," one hand cooled by a pile of black earth, the other warmed by a pile of lime. Snapshots of grandfather's *Liberty Bell* silver mine out West and of his school at Stuttgart am Neckar (he attended high school in Germany) sit side-by-side with nuggets of fools' gold, while a porch floor of octagonal red tiles, "sweaty with secret dank," lies underfoot. The poet recalls a puppy (named "Cinder") that died, "paralyzed from gobbling toads." Surface glitter is highlighted by ponds that shine like "sapphires" and the remembered image of a small boy (Lowell) dressed in clothing from Rogers Peet's. Everything is of a different age; nothing retains the grace of splendor it once possessed. Extending the symbolic image of himself as a well-dressed child, Lowell's reflection becomes distorted in the bottom of a basin until it resembles "a stuffed toucan with a bibulous, multicolored beak," another aspect of the fat man in the mirror. *Life Studies* examines Lowell's life from many angles, the poet's eye operating on several planes at once, as though adhering to Freud's reasonable suggestion that the subconscious has no tenses. Mirrors, binoculars, magnifying glasses, water surfaces, glass, screens, constitute the seeing-eye tools of the poet's memory. Out of bits and pieces the reader is encouraged to splice together the various fragments that make up the protagonist's life. The volume ebbs and flows from lightness to darkness and back again to lightness, beginning and ending on an affirmative, life-giving note. This nearly circular configuration became the blueprint for all of Lowell's volumes from *Life Studies* forward.

One dimension of his life consists of a rejection of life's trappings. In *Life Studies* the poet abnegates both poles of the social spectrum—upper class and lowest—in the same manner he had earlier dispensed with one carefully rehearsed pose after another, ultimately renouncing an entire panoply of poses: childhood's dream of privilege; Boston Pilgrim; Southern Agrarian; Roman Catholic; "manic" pacifist. The latter was characterized by the writer David Berman as having been "more rebellious than pacific." It led to New York's West Street Jail, where Lowell encountered the genuine article, the "real" pacifists: Jehovah's Witnesses on the one hand, Abramowitz on the other:

Strolling, I yammered metaphysics with Abramowitz,
a jaundice-yellow ("It's really tan")
and fly-weight pacifist,
so vegetarian,
he wore rope shoes and preferred fallen fruit.

Abramowitz is contrasted in the same poem with Bioff and Brown, a pair of Hollywood pimps, whom he tried to convert to his own peculiar vegetarian diet. As opposed to tiny Abramowitz, Bioff and Brown are described as hairy, swarthy, muscular fellows, dressed in chocolate double-breasted suits, with fast tempers. On one occasion they apparently "blew their tops" and beat Abramowitz "black and blue," hardly a true pacifist's just desert.

Lowell's final *Life Studies* pose was not a pose at all, but "dust in the blood," insanity. There was nothing about it to reject, it was simply there—on again, off again: "My mind's not right. / . . . I hear / my ill-spirit sob in each blood cell, / as if my hand were at its throat . . . / I myself am hell." Identity and life-meaning for Lowell resided not in the old-line Brahmin retreads he encountered at McLean's, with their splintered dreams and ruined ambitions; it resided in the desperate act of art: the professed poet must keep writing, "scrivening to the end against his fate," to quote Edwin Arlington Robinson. Writing is the justification and purpose of life. To be conscious of this, suggests Lowell, is to place oneself in the select company of men as noble as Ford, Santayana, Delmore Schwartz, and Hart Crane, "those who have sought and found in intelligent suffering the truths that neither the common man nor the degenerate aristocrat is able to face or find."

Four poems in *Life Studies* are given over to these men. Of the four, Lowell's favorite was the one for Ford, which begins: "The lobbed ball plops, then dribbles to the cup. . . . / (a birdie Fordie!) But it nearly killed the ministers." Speculating on the effect of the poem, the poet later wrote: "Something planned and grand, and something helter skelter and unexpected seemed to come together in this poem. I thought for a long time I would never catch the tone of the man; now I think I have perhaps."

The ode "To Delmore Schwartz," probably the most candid of the lot, recalls the brief period during 1946 when Lowell and Jean Stafford lived in Cambridge, not far from Schwartz. Lowell's account of Schwartz in his rundown Ellery Street house captures that poet at a time when he was an English instructor at Harvard and an associate editor of *Partisan Review,* having joined the staff in 1944. The poem underlines Lowell's identification with his companion by insisting that both were societal outcasts. "We couldn't even keep the furnace lit," wails Lowell, thereby testifying to the dilapidated state of Schwartz's residence and their shared inability to perform even the most mundane of tasks. There is talk in the same ode of their "universal *Angst*"; they were drunk on anxiety, ambition, and gin, and these were unusually difficult times: "We drank and eyed / the chicken-hearted shadows of the world." Toward the end of the poem Lowell quotes Schwartz paraphrasing a line from Wordsworth's "Resolution and Independence": *"We poets in our youth begin in sadness; thereof in the end come despondency and sadness."* These words were particularly significant in the case of Schwartz, whose early promise—born out of a manic need to turn experience into art—was never fully realized in the works and years to come. The mysterious allusion in this poem to Schwartz's "stuffed duck," whose "bill was a black whistle, and its brow . . . high and thinner than a baby's thumb," was eventually clarified by Schwartz in a letter to Lowell (April 12, 1959): "The stuffed duck belonged to Bill Van Keuren and he shot it—I've never shot anything but pool." The same letter made note of the openness and honesty of *Life Studies,* "that peculiar honesty which Eliot speaks of in Blake and which he says other human beings often find unpleasant." Lowell's ability to be so open and subjective gave his writing a new quality of intensity, "an intensity so moving that it is heartbreaking."

A subsequent Lowell sequence, "In Dreams Begin Responsibilities" (a sonnet from *History* whose title is the same as Schwartz's first book of poems), restates several of the old themes, while engraving Schwartz toward the end of his life at his bedraggled worst:

> . . . Delmore—your name—Schwartz,
>
> . . .
> scanning wide-eyed the windowless room of wisdom,
> your notes on Joyce and porno magazines—
> the stoplights blinking code for you alone
> casing the bars with the eye of a Mongol horseman.

James Atlas, in his biography of Delmore Schwartz (*Delmore Schwartz: The Life of an American Poet,* 1977), points out that Schwartz, who was poor and Jewish and therefore insecure about being on the faculty at Harvard, "was envious of Lowell's Brahmin background." His envy increased after Lowell took him to dinner at his parents' Back Bay house on Marlborough Street. Schwartz, "intimidated by the servants, heirlooms, and a certain reserve on the part of the Lowells," was piqued by the Commander's jeering insistence that his son "talked like a Jew." The inference was clear enough. Schwartz likewise resented Lowell's constant chatter on the subject of his "Jewish forebear" Mordecai Myers, a large portrait of whom in a military uniform adorned a wall in his parents' drawing room and whose presence in *Life Studies,* as we have already seen, was prominent. "Things," writes Atlas, "were never the same after that evening. Delmore baited Lowell mercilessly, made fun of his parents' home, and tried to destroy his marriage [to Jean Stafford] by circulating malicious rumors."

The crowning blow for Schwartz came with the discovery that his former wife Gertrude Buckman, for whom he still had deep feelings, was involved with Lowell. On one memorable occasion, during a heated dispute over literary affairs, a fist fight broke out between Lowell and Schwartz, and Jean Stafford had to intervene. Their relationship flagged, but the two poets never completely lost their mutual respect. Each recognized the other's unholy penchant for self-destruction, the desperation and compulsive drive for fame and glory. In 1959, with Schwartz practically coming apart at the seams, Lowell sent his comrade-in-arms money and tried to encourage him by complimenting his latest work. Several years after Schwartz's bitter death in a shabby mid-Manhattan hotel, Lowell informed an interviewer that though they had often quarreled, he had "never met anyone who had somehow so much seeped" into him. He presumably had in mind Schwartz's unending faith in ideas, his dedication to the power and craft of words, his rigorous battle against the Fugitive view that poems must be metrical and contain stringent moral instructions.

❦ 27 ❧

NEW YORK, NEW YORK

IN *Life Studies,* Lowell, borrowing a phrase from Henry James, apologizes for taking up "a whole house on 'Boston's hardly passionate Marlborough Street,' where even the man scavenging filth in the back-alley trash cans"—another rendition of Lowell's "common man"—"has two children, a beach wagon, a helpmate, and is a 'young Republican.' " Claustrophobic Boston, with its narrow geography and suffocating family pressures, clearly provided the impetus for *Life Studies*—as it had earlier provided the background for *Lord Weary's Castle*—enabling the poet to perceive a livid connection between West Street's Czar Lepke and those "victorian figures of bravado ossified young" inside McLean's. But the staleness of the city had worn cardboard thin, draining both Lowells with its vast emptiness and hollow astringencies.

Having spent an evening in New York with the Rahvs and the editor Jason Epstein, Lowell presently wrote to Epstein (December 19, 1959) that they had enjoyed their visit and were again homesick for the city and the civilized mind. On more than one occasion Lowell wrote Jarrell that he was tired of Boston and bored with all of its residents except the eccentrics. Elizabeth Hardwick shared her husband's sentiments exactly; describing the offspring of the town's rich in her essay on "Boston," she even managed to echo his words: "They are often descendants of intellectual Boston, odd-ball grandsons, charming and sensitive, puzzlingly complicated, living on a 'small income.' These unhappy men carry on their conscience the weight of unpublished novels, half-finished paintings, impossible historical projects, old-fashioned poems, unproduced plays. . . ."

Marlborough Street's electrically operated imitation gas lamps and tidy colonial architecture no longer held their magic sway over the poet. He was tired of the gray- and brown- and white-stone houses with their large bay windows, iron gates, and wide front steps. The sights and sounds of Boston brought back memories of his powerful but constraining heritage. Here was located 91 Revere Street, unchanged since Lowell's childhood, still "a flat red brick surface unvaried by the slightest suggestion of purple panes, delicate bay, or triangular window-cornice—a sheer wall formed by the seamless conjunction of four inseparable facades, all of the same commercial and purgatorial design." Not far from his Marlborough Street town house was Boston's Public Garden, from which he had been expelled during his fifth-grade school year for bullying other children. That garden, whose swanboats he recalled in *Lord Weary's Castle* ("Grandfather Winslow, look, the swanboats coast / That island in the Public Gardens. . . ."), was soon to become the symbolic site of lust and illicit love in his translation of Racine's *Phaedra*. Not far from the Public Garden, inside historic King's Chapel, were located further relics of the poet's Puritan past; a bust relief of John Lowell ("The Rebel," 1796–1840) adorned one wall; the Lowell coat of arms and the family motto adorned another; outside, in the old chapel graveyard, lay the graves of John and Mary Winslow, colonial ancestors of Lowell on his mother's side, among the Indian fighters described by the poet in "At the Indian Killer's Grave." Facing the Common, on Beacon Street, was a monument celebrating the founding of Boston, a bas-relief of Indians and Puritans and a plaque bearing an excerpt from Governor John Winthrop's famous sermon, "A model of Christian Charity," delivered aboard the *Arabella* in the spring of 1630: "For wee must consider that wee shall be as a citty upon a hill, the eies of all people are upon us, soe that if wee shall deale falsely [with our god] in this worke wee have undertaken . . . wee shall be made a story and a byword through the world." It read, wrote Lowell, as if worded to describe his own clan's exaggerated view of itself.

During the summer of 1958, Lowell, the one-time Harvard dropout, returned to teach a seminar in the Harvard summer school. The idea of eventually teaching full-time at Harvard probably appealed to his aristocratic sense of himself, though assuredly not to his sense of place. Determined to sever their ties with Boston, the Lowells made their permanent break in 1960. One reason for their wanting to leave was

Lowell's continual struggle with manic-depressive illness. The pressures brought to bear upon the couple by their residence in Boston could only have aggravated the condition. "I am tired," the poet would write in a later poem. "Everyone's tired of my turmoil." The three-month "black-out" that landed him in McLean's during his composition of *Life Studies,* a duration covered in "Three Months Away," had become a chronic condition whose intermittent cessations left him feeling "frizzled, stale and small." "My mania has broken" was a common refrain that appeared in letters to friends, but that somehow failed to convince. During 1958 he spent March, April, and a good part of May at McLean's, and in 1959 passed August through October there; in between he was an outpatient at the psychiatric unit of Massachusetts General Hospital, which owned and operated McLean's. There were occasional moments of comic relief. Lowell was once "free associating" at length on Goethe for the benefit of a psychiatrist at Massachusetts General. "Is he a family connection?" the befuddled doctor inquired. But such moments were rare, and Lowell's annual hospital sojourn soon became the talk of cultivated Boston, an example for intellectuals of what becomes of our leading bards. Allen Ginsberg, half of whose friends had been institutionalized at one time or another, sent Lowell a seriocomic letter, dated April 5, 1959, summing up the outsider's common point of view:

> Someone told me . . . that when you went mad it was because you went Manic—and I suddenly had a . . . picture in my head of you sitting stooped, gloomy, in chair, talking low, about tradition, and bursting out in maniac laughter running down street, shouting gay haikus, doing something extraordinarily sane in fact, and being clapped into bughouse for that burst of Mad Butterfly—I mean, do you really go mad . . . or do you become insupportable in *that* gloomed-up, hoked-up, evil MEAN suppressive atmosphere. I mean Harvard and its Minds which as far as I have been able to see are not only ill educated poetically (no Soul, and they don't even read Mayakovski mostly) but also creepy-mannered. That audience. You call that Civilization?

The Lowells finally moved from Boston to New York, living first at 154 Riverside Drive, later in a cooperative duplex apartment at 15 West Sixty-seventh Street, off Central Park West on the same block as the Hotel des Artistes. The block was lined with trees and charming old apartment houses of moderate size constructed shortly after the turn of the century for the accommodation of artists who wanted to live and paint in the same quarters. Large French windows let in a stream of bright sunlight. Opposite their house stood a stable, a handsome brick edifice painted a muddy yellow, looking like an Italian villa. In his *Notebook* poem "Half a Century Gone," Lowell depicts his apartment building as "the last gasp of true Nineteenth-Century Capitalist Gothic," a reference to its aging elegance and well-maintained appearance.

During his first year in New York, Lowell showered friends with letters full of praise for the city. He wrote to Randall Jarrell that he found talk and companionship in New York, particularly in small groups, more to his liking than what Boston had to offer. He communicated the same impression to Stanley Kunitz: "Our move from Boston to New York gave me a tremendous push. Boston is all history and recollection: New York is ahead of one. Sympathetic spirits are a rarity elsewhere. Here there is a whole community of the arts, an endlessly stimulating fellowship . . . at times too stimulating. No one is too great for New York, and yet I grant there is something frightening about it." At other times Lowell characterized New York as a town "with no past . . . no landmarks" and as a place where one "has a great sheer feeling of utter freedom. And then when one thinks back a little bit, it seems all confused and naked." The shock of transplanting themselves was eased a bit by their immediate assimilation into New York's cultural establishment. Robert Lowell, like his poetry-writing ancestors, was a socially conscious being who took great pleasure in rubbing elbows and minds with his fellow sufferers in the arts. *Life Studies* was made the recipient of the 1959 National Book Award for poetry, the Longview Foundation Award, and the Guiness Poetry Award, which Lowell shared with Auden and Edith Sitwell. Thus he was more than an ordinary foot soldier joining the elite ranks of New York's intellectual infantry; his growing international reputation established him as a grandee among his peers, placing him squarely on the literary front line with immediate access to the centers of power.

He attended the World Series with Marianne Moore and George Plimpton, drank at the White Horse Tavern on Hudson Street with John Berryman and Auden, partied with Truman Capote and Katherine Graham at a masked ball held in the Plaza Hotel, a gala billed in somewhat grand terms as "The Party of the Century." He rubbed shoulders with the Kennedys, supporting John F. Kennedy during the 1960 presidential campaign, later becoming a friend of Mrs. Kennedy. More than once he was a dinner guest at Jacqueline Kennedy's duplex apartment on Fifth Avenue, following the assassination of the President. It was a time when American intellectuals seemed to be trying to secede from the human race, and Lowell was at the head of the parade. He was popular with the inner sanctum at the *Partisan Review* and was often seen in company with William Barrett, Mary McCarthy (who was a close friend of Elizabeth Hardwick), F. W. Dupee, and Dwight MacDonald. He played host to a constant stream of young writers and critics who flocked to New York to see him. On November 4, 1960, he introduced T. S. Eliot to a large audience at the Poetry Center of the Ninety-second Street YM-YWHA, then remained seated on stage at Eliot's behest while the elder poet recited his latest writings; it constituted Eliot's acknowledgment of Lowell's poetic talents. Lowell himself lectured and read his work at the Library of Congress and on the campuses of numerous colleges: Columbia, Yale, Princeton, William and Mary, the University of Pennsylvania, Bard, and elsewhere. During his first year in New York he was one of eleven writers awarded a $7,500 fellowship by the Ford Foundation for a year in "close working relationship with a theater or opera company in the United States or the United Kingdom." He worked with the New York City Opera Company and the Metropolitan Opera Association, attending rehearsals at the Met with the poet William Meredith, a fellow opera buff; together they worked briefly on an opera score that was eventually discarded.

As a member of the "inner circle," the intellectual aristocracy, Lowell served on any number of advisory commissions and committees on the arts. In this capacity he became involved in several fiery disputes, the most notable of which took place during February 1962 in connection with the Helen Burlin Memorial Award, a prize presented annually by the Ninety-second Street "Y" to help encourage promising young poets. The award committee that year, consisting of Lowell, Stanley Kunitz, and Louise Bogan, selected as its first choice a manuscript belonging to Frederick Seidel, entitled *Final Solutions*. The incendiary nature of Seidel's writing and the suggestive manner with which he tackled subjects as controversial as sex and violence set the stage for a confrontation between the award committee and the Board of Directors of the "Y." Louise Bogan annotated the general state of affairs in a letter to a friend:

The YMHA jury for the H. Burlin award went through some strange gyrations yesterday afternoon. The result is as you see. —This Seidel guy is, according to Cal Lowell, about 23; Harvard; v. sophisticated; married to the granddaughter of Learned Hand. The MS . . . is v. shocking indeed; an orgy that outdoes Suetonius is described in *one* longish poem. Also, a great deal of Sade (so S. Kunitz said). Slime, excreta, pederasty, etc. —It is, however, a *fiercely* projected set of inner experiences; and certainly not dirt for dirt's sake, as in the case of the Beats. There will be a scandal, I should imagine.

The board's objection to Seidel's work centered, as one might expect, on his use of the controversial title "Final Solutions." Yet the charge that this phrase suggested racial violence was countered by the total absence in the poetry itself of all racial slurs and allusions. Consequently, it appeared as though Seidel was the one being discriminated against and that the "Y" was the party doing the discriminating. Lowell, outraged by the turn of events, wasted little time in publicly denouncing the organization for its blatant censorship tactics and obvious infringement of the controversial First Amendment. One by one the members of the tripartite poetry committee resigned. Their collective statement to the board pointed to censorship as the bane of all democratic nations, the very foundation upon which Fascist societies are built and sustained.

Now that he was a New Yorker, the poet's afternoons were spent with his daughter Harriet in Central Park. They took long walks together, often visiting the Central Park Zoo at Sixty-fourth Street. "When I was young," he ventured, "I read the complete Thornton Burgess out of love for animals and then won a nature cup for catching snakes and butterflies." His relationship with Harriet was charted in a later volume of poems, *For Lizzie and Harriet*; Harriet made her first appearance in *Life Studies* ("When / we dress her in her sky-blue corduroy, / she changes to a boy, / and floats my shaving brush / and washcloth in the flush . . ."), and appeared again in *Near the Ocean* ("Blue-ribboned, blue-jeaned, named for you, / our daughter cartwheels in the blue— / may your proportion strengthen her / to live through the millennial year / Two Thousand. . . ."). The latter poem, "Fourth of July in Maine," was dedicated to Harriet Winslow, his maiden cousin from Washington, D.C. who wrote experimental, nihilistic poetry that she refused to submit for publication; Lowell dedicated his translation of *Phaedra* to her and in his poem "Soft Wood" admitted: "[she] was more to me than my mother."

Notebook 1967–68 was dedicated to his daughter: "For HARRIET / Even before you could speak, / without knowing, I loved you; / and for LIZZIE." Lowell was to tell an interviewer from *Life:* "Advising, as Sartre has, that fathers and their own children can't get on together is rot. To say that's a reason not to have children is to say, 'Don't go out for a walk, because if you do your feet might get hurt.' I am quite optimistic about getting along with my daughter." To Cousin Harriet he wrote that he did not support the premise that said all children under five were unspeakable terrors; nor did he believe that children from five onward were automatically engaged in an eternal struggle with their parents.

He was an arduous laborer, reserving mornings and evenings for his writing. He was producing poems, translations of poems, and short plays. It was evident that Lowell had once and for all freed himself from the conservative influence of the Fugitives. Not unexpectedly, Allen Tate objected to the confessional mode of *Life Studies,* finding the poems morbid, far too personal, highly disorganized. He thought that these miscellanies of Lowell's private affairs read like bloodless sketches, such as a writer might make as an outline for his own life story, and consequently were of interest to no one but the person who had recorded them. Although others would later voice similar objections, for now Tate remained the sole dissenter. More and more in his verse Lowell was falling under the influence of Elizabeth Bishop. Her bold language and seamless construction aided him in his quest for new forms, his rejection of formalism and attraction to unscanned and ir-regularly rhymed poetry. As Lowell admitted to Stanley Kunitz, he saw Bishop as a bridge between Tate's formalism and Williams's colloquial and informal art. Older than Lowell by six years, she had already demonstrated in her first volume of verse—*North and South* (1946)—the elegant line and formidable control of a seasoned veteran. Lowell reviewed the book favorably a year after publication, thereby gaining the friendship and trust of its author. Several of Lowell's poems, among them "Water" *(For the Union Dead),* hint that the two enjoyed a brief but failed romance following Lowell's divorce from Stafford and before his marriage to Hardwick. Their friendship, however, endured; in 1959, Lowell went to visit Bishop at her adopted home in Rio de Janeiro, Brazil. Three years later, after a week's layover in Trinidad, Lowell (accompanied by Elizabeth Hardwick) returned to Brazil and from there flew to Buenos Aires to spend time with Bishop. This trip led to a new spate of poems by Lowell, including "Buenos Aires" and "Dropping South: Brazil." In these he blames the dictatorial regimes of Brazil and Argentina for their lamentable right-wing policies. There was an irony at work here: the 1962 junket had been arranged and paid for by the Congress of Cultural Freedom, which happened to be a CIA-funded organization; when Lowell learned of the connection between the Congress and the Central Intelligence Agency, he was horrified and proceeded to deride his own "gullibility and shallowness" for not realizing sooner. Essentially, his relationship with Bishop was instrumental in helping him to perceive literary characters in terms of landscape, while encouraging him to eliminate verbosity. He dedicated "Skunk Hour" to her, and *Imitations* as well.

Imitations, published in 1961, was a collection of Drydenesque translations or adaptations, a mode with which he experimented for the first time in several *Lord Weary* poems, such as "The Shako," based on a poem by Rilke. But with the exception of a few isolated instances, translation was a relatively untried art form for the poet. A need to change, to pass through still another phase, helps explain the raison d'être behind his latest project.

One reason for being interested in these translations, aside from the pleasure of the poems themselves, is that we are presented in *Imitations* with a statement and exemplification of Lowell's aesthetic. The poet takes a distinctly holistic attitude toward his verse, he conceives of translation (and, by virtue of his craft, the writing of original poetry) as the construction of a spiritual gestalt. He neither translates nor writes "words," but attempts to render a certain world, a mode of sensibility. Lowell's introduction to *Imitations* details the cause: "This book is partly self-sufficient and separate from its sources, and should be first read as a sequence, one voice running through many personalities, contrasts and repetitions. . . . Boris Pasternak has said that the usual reliable translator gets the literal meaning but misses the tone, and that in poetry tone is of course everything. I have been reckless with literal meaning, and labored hard to get the tone. . . . I have tried to write alive English and to do what my authors might have done if they were writing their poems now and in America."

What we have in these "imitations" of sixty-six "important" poems by eighteen poets (from Homer to Pasternak) in five languages (Greek,

German, French, Italian, Russian), is not the classroom English that poets of the past employed in translations, but something akin to a colloquial American dialect, the vernacular that our ears have been trained to recognize. In broader terms the methodology of "imitation" is not translation as we know it but rather transubstantiation, an attempt to re-create in another idiom the essential effect of the original poem. Ezra Pound had always advocated a method of translation that managed to capture the emotion of the original poet. In the preface to his translations of Cavalcanti (1910), Pound wrote that he had "tried to bring over the qualities of Guido's rhythm, not line for line, but to embody in the whole of my English some trace of the power which implies the man." Pound's school of translation, psychological and intuitive rather than objective and textual, suited Lowell's needs, helped him break away still further from the dictums of the New Criticism, which defined poetry as a language bereft of emotion and which concerned itself with the analysis of concrete textual modules in an exegetical manner that proceeded word by word, line for line.

Like most innovative techniques, Lowell's worked well only part of the time; he seemed acutely aware of its manifest peculiarities:

> My licenses have been many. My first two Sappho poems are really new poems based on hers. Villon has been somewhat stripped; Hebel is taken out of dialect; Hugo's "Gautier" is cut in half. Mallarmé has been unclotted. . . . The same has been done with Ungaretti and some of the more obscure Rimbaud. About a third of "The Drunken Boat" has been left out. Two stanzas have been added to Rilke's "Roman sarcophagus," and one to his "Pigeons." "Pigeons" and Valéry's "Helen" are more idiomatic and informal in my English. Some lines from Villon's "Little Testament" have been shifted to introduce his "Great Testament." And so forth! I have dropped lines, moved lines, moved stanzas, changed images and altered meter and intent.

Many critics, including George Steiner, found the imitation a fine form for Lowell to adopt; it allowed him to say things in the voice of another poet that he was unable to get out under his own power. But critics such as John Simon and Louis Simpson took exception with the genre, insisting that Lowell had done more than just take liberties and licenses with texts. He had repeatedly used his method of translation as an occasion for projecting and imposing a mood of his own as opposed to drawing out a mood implicit in the original poem. And while he

announced his intentions—"one voice running through many personalities"—there was no reason to suppose that this method of poetic
interpretation was better than any other.

The main defect was the monotony of the form. Regardless of the
poet Lowell was "imitating," the voice heard was always his; it was
therefore broken here and there by shocking and vigorous flashes that
roiled and hissed with originality and beauty. Yet the adroitness of
Lowell's versions varied markedly from poet to poet and poem to
poem. His fragmented renditions of Homer and Sappho were drasti-
cally off-key. Lowell's Villon was a charred skeleton, the randy-roman-
tic, often naughty original meek as a lamb. Hebel and Heine were
devoured by Lowell's personal style; their tendency toward quietness,
their curious and highly effective use of scholarly and at times pedantic
diction, sound nothing like Lowell's translations. Nor was Leopardi
done justice. Lowell's talky, almost tabloid style was ultimately best
suited to the "moderns": Montale, Baudelaire, Rimbaud, Mallarmé,
Valéry. And yet Lowell's updatings of these poets are not always facile;
they require the originals to complete them. Of all his choices, Lowell
is probably most comfortable, in style and personality, with the work of
Baudelaire; "The Swan," "Voyage to Cythera," and "To the Reader"
are masterly translations, Lowell's versions more powerful than those
of the original artist. So winning were they that in 1968 they were
issued as a separate volume: *The Voyage, and Other Versions of Poems
by Baudelaire.*

A bigger question mark surrounds Lowell's versions of Pasternak.
From reading other translations of the Russian's poetry, Lowell had
come to feel that here was an important poet, one of the most important
poets of the century. But Lowell knew no Russian. He had tried to
improve on the translations of Pasternak by intermediaries and had
been helped by exact prose versions provided by Russian readers. The
difficulties inherent in such a method are multiple. Simply stated, when
one translates not from the original but from a prose crib of the original,
all sense of meter and rhythm is inevitably lost; the sound and shape of
words in the original remain out of reach. All that is left is the "sense,"
the literal "meaning" of the original. What Lowell was translating
therefore was not the poem but the prose crib of a poem. It was no
longer imitation, simply the shadow of an imitation, the same obstacle
that confronted Amy Lowell in her attempt to render Chinese verse
from Florence Ayscough's English cribs in her *Fir-Flower Tablets.*

Imitations was equivocally reviewed, praised for its inventive use of diction, criticized for its digression from the original text and monotony of voice. Most critics seemed confused by the form and the poet's intentions: was *Imitations* translation or was it original composition? Could it be both? A. Alvarez, in *The Observer,* decided it was *not* a book of translations: "It is a magnificent collection of new poems by Robert Lowell, based on the work of 18 European poets. . . . It is a work of the first importance both as a piece of literature in its own right and as a new development in that constantly expanding imaginative universe in which Lowell orbits." Edmund Wilson, in *The New Yorker,* agreed that the poems, full of personal statement, were variations on themes provided by these other poets but that the volume was really an original sequence "by Robert Lowell of Boston." It had, in general, it seemed to him, been stupidly received: "It is absurd to complain, for example, that Lowell has not followed Baudelaire literally when he has made a point of explaining in his foreword that he has taken every possible liberty—has changed the order of stanzas, invented stanzas of his own, and contributed his own new images. He has also in many cases transmuted the whole tone and color of the poem which he has taken as a point of departure." Very well, one can argue, but then why imitate at all? Why not write wholly original poems? Nor does Wilson's statement address itself to the problem of unevenness, the quality of these imitations (exclusive of their existence as translations) ranging from highly unsatisfactory to startlingly adept.

Successful or not, Lowell's volume appealed to sensibilities as diverse as those belonging to Williams and Tate. Williams termed the poems, "the real thing." Tate found the manuscript highly skilled and crafted. As though making amends for his negative reaction to *Life Studies,* Tate remarked that he believed the poet was making the art of translation an original art: "The best of these versions are yours quite as much as theirs." His single suggestion was that Lowell adopt another title for the book. "Imitations" understated the draftsman's achievement; he recommended using the title "Versions: A Book of Free Translation." T. S. Eliot, under whose auspices the British edition was published by Faber and Faber, opted for the original title to "keep clear of pedantic literalists." Eliot's endorsement helped the volume gain both a Harriet Monroe Prize and the 1962 Bollingen Prize in Translation, an honor that Lowell shared with Richard Lattimore for his rendition of *The Frogs,* by Aristophanes.

The year of *Imitations* also saw the publication of Lowell's translation of Racine's *Phaedra,* undertaken at the suggestion of theater critic Eric Bentley. The play premiered at Wesleyan University in Middletown, Connecticut, with the actress and ballerina Vera Zorina performing the lead role; it appeared in book form in tandem with Jacques Barzun's *Figaro,* a translation of the Beaumarchais comedy *Figaro's Marriage.* Barzun, the formidable Columbia University scholar, critic, and editor, was married to a Lowell, the concert violinist Mariana Lowell, a member of the music faculty at Bennington College. Born in Boston, Mariana, the sister of Dr. Alice Lowell, the New England hospital administrator, attended the Longy School of Music in Cambridge and, later, in Paris, she studied with Nadia Boulanger. She also pursued her music studies under the instruction of Nauwinck at the Paris Conservatoire. Alice and Mariana Lowell, of the Cabot-Jackson branch, were evidently Lowell women with minds of their own. As for Barzun and Robert Lowell, they had known each other since adolescence and frequently encountered one another on social occasions and at literary functions.

Barzun's translation was more conventional and flat than Lowell's, who chose to sacrifice linguistic accuracy for the sake of tonality and pitch. He created a jazzed-up version of *Phaedra,* stoking the rhymed couplets with fire and ice, imbuing it with a flavor of its own:

THESEUS

You'll find fitting companions. Look for friends
who honor everything that most offends.
Pimps and jackals who praise adultery
and incest will protect your purity!

HIPPOLYTUS

Adultery! Is it your privilege
to fling this word in my teeth? I've reached the edge
of madness . . . No I'll say no more. Compare
my breeding with Phaedra's. Think and beware . . .
She had a mother . . . No, I must not speak.

Although entertaining, Lowell's deliberate raciness usually leads him astray. As often as not, his idiom is too severe, his inflection overly brittle. Phaedra's description of Theseus—"Volage adorateur de mille

objets divers"—is reconstructed as "lascivious eulogist of any belle."
"Belle," notes Louis Simpson in an early review of the play for *The
Hudson Review,* conjures up Gibson girls, dance-hall matrons—even
worse. At another point, Hippolytus complains that "the gods have
made me creep," where "crawl" is what the translator means. Describing Aricia, princess of the royal blood of Athens, Hippolytus uses the
redundant phrase "unwooed and childless." The "muck and jelly" of
Phaedra's second-act speech is laden with anachronisms.

The story behind the play comes from Greek myth via the *Hippolytus* of Euripides. Hippolytus is the illegitimate son of Theseus,
slayer of the Minotaur, and Hippolyte, single-breasted queen of the
Amazons. Hippolytus lives in the home of Theseus and Theseus's youthful bride, Phaedra. An outdoorsman and adventurer, Hippolytus neglects the service of Aphrodite, goddess of love. Enraged, she places a
spell on Phaedra, who falls passionately in love with her stepson, Hippolytus. She is rejected by him, and in revenge tells Theseus that his son
has made advances on her virtue. Theseus invokes his father, the sea
god Poseidon, to destroy Hippolytus, meanwhile banishing his son from
Troezen. As Hippolytus drives along the seashore, Poseidon sends a sea
monster to attack his horses. Flung from the chariot, Hippolytus is
killed.

As Euripides developed it, the tragedy was nature's rebuke to pride,
a chain reaction triggered by Hippolytus's denial of the goddess of love.
In Racine's version the focus is on the scorned woman, the furor caused
by her unrequited love, the power of her drive for revenge. Lowell's
Phaedra writhes on the brink of agony:

> Oh Gods of wrath,
> how far I've travelled on my dangerous path!
> I go to meet my husband; at his side
> will stand Hippolytus. How shall I hide
> my thick adulterous passion for this youth,
> who has rejected me, and knows the truth?

The play rises and falls on the strength of Phaedra's imminent collapse,
and Lowell's daring, sometimes brazen use of language. At times the
poet simply takes possession of the original dialogue and dominates it;
at other times the dialogue dominates him. As a dramatic presentation,
Phaedra is hopelessly unbalanced.

In 1964 Lowell completed another theater project, three one-act plays, bearing the collective title *The Old Glory*. The first two, *Endecott and the Red Cross* and *My Kinsman, Major Molineux*, are based on short stories by Hawthorne; the third, *Benito Cereno*, is drawn from Melville's novella by the same title. *My Kinsman* and *Benito* were the inaugural productions in 1964 at the off-Broadway American Place Theater; *Endecott* was not presented there until 1968; and the three plays had to wait until 1976 to be produced as a trilogy.

Jonathan Miller—a British physician as well as a writer and director, who first came to public attention as coauthor and performer in that zany revue, *Beyond the Fringe*—staged the original round of these Lowell productions. Because they were based on the works of Hawthorne and Melville and because a Pulitzer Prize–winning poet was responsible for them, they were considered the season's highbrow hit, not in the classical vein of Euripides, Goethe, or Schiller, but something approximating the astringent appeal of Eliot's *The Cocktail Party* or Fry's *Venus Observed*.

In adapting these early American tales to the stage, Lowell aspired to the creation of the same horrific, menacing, yet luminous image of the American Dream that he had developed in his verse, his lines exploding in the reader's face with the violence not of personal intimidation but of all our sordid American wounds—especially Lowell's. He seemed to retain dazzling connections with every latent tempest so long embedded in the New England soul, an entire historical repertoire of jibes and japes. Alfred Kazin has recently stated that Lowell's great intuition was to write poetry as history and theater as history because after all, "any Lowell seems to himself a significant piece of history." Kazin's intimation that even his plays were of a highly personal order matched the view registered by Jonathan Miller, who suggested that *The Old Glory*, in order to work on stage, had to be performed as a kind of surreal, living dream, something akin to an opera without words. But, in fact, even this device could not save the neck of Lowell's rather futile productions.

In *Endecott and the Red Cross* a benevolent Puritan Governor of Salem in the 1630's is sent to the settlement of Merrymount to investigate reports of collusion between colonists and the local Indian tribe. The leader of Merrymount, the Oxford-trained Englishman Thomas Morton, lives with the daughter of a neighboring chief and conducts a thriving fur trade with the Indians, bartering liquor and firearms for the valuable hides. Selling the Indians firearms and teaching them how to use them struck at the very existence of colonists already wary of Indians. But what truly disturbs the Puritans is that Merrymount, with its annual Maypole dance, is an enclave of rapture as Morton and his companions invite "the Indian women for their consorts, dancing and frisking togither," indulging in "ye beastly practises of ye madd Bacchinalians." A friend of Ben Jonson and doubtless a devoted customer of London's rollicking Mermaid Tavern, Morton saw no reason to forgo the gay life just because his neighbors were sobersided. Initially, John Endecott, the Puritan Governor of Salem, is reluctant to take action against the Merrymount revelers. But then a clerical emissary from England arrives to announce that King Charles intends to revoke the charter of Massachusetts Colony and place it under the jurisdiction of the Archbishop of Canterbury unless immediate measures are taken against Merrymount. Delivering a flaming polemic against the King, Endecott rips down the red-crossed flag of England and tramples it underfoot. At the same time, despising himself for it, he orders Merrymount burned to the ground and the Indians massacred. The play, which draws breath from a pair of Hawthorne's *Twice-Told Tales—Endecott and the Red Cross* and *The Maypole at Merry Mount—*registers the unmistakable message that in the wholesale slaughter of the American Indian was born a legacy of violence that has remained a central symbol for the American way of life.

In *My Kinsman, Major Molineux—*based on a Hawthorne short story by the same title—Robin, a young rustic from Deerfield, arrives in Boston with his younger brother on the eve of the American Revolution. He hopes for a career from his rich uncle, an agent of the King in charge of the redcoats in Boston. The atmosphere is ghoulish, eerie, with strange characters drifting in and out. A ferryman resembling Charon—no stranger to readers of Lowell's poetry—warns the brothers of impending but undefined danger. A parson, a prostitute, and a wealthy citizen, all full of obscure speeches and menacing gestures, confront the brothers as they wander down a succession of crooked and narrow streets; "Everyone answers me in riddles," complains Robin, adding that "we're learning how to live." What they presumably learn in the midst of these public tirades and demonstrations is the impossibility of innocence. When they finally locate their kinsman, he has been tarred and feathered by a hell-bent lynch mob; tortured and beaten, he still chants allegiances to the throne. The mob demands his head.

"Whatever we do is our own affair, the breath of freedom's in the air," sings a voice. The boys watch their kinsman die. The country's gain is ultimately their loss; nothing is got for naught.

Lowell's romance with Hawthorne, incidentally, predated *The Old Glory*. In 1963 he wrote an introduction to a new edition of *Pegasus, the Winged Horse. A Greek Myth retold by Nathaniel Hawthorne,* a children's book with drawings by Herschel Levit. Hawthorne, with his strict attention to the self as seen within the context of the historical moment, appealed to Robert Lowell, just as he had once appealed to James Russell Lowell. The latter had contemplated writing a short biography of Hawthorne; when *The House of the Seven Gables* appeared in 1851, the earlier Lowell wrote that "it was the most valuable contribution yet made to New England history," the literary historian's task being "to reconcile the present with the past." Steven Gould Axelrod observantly notes that Robert Lowell, a hundred years later, made almost the same remark about the same book; writing to Williams in 1958, he said that *The House of the Seven Gables* "has enough economic history to set the Commonwealth of Massachusetts back on its toes." Unfortunately, neither *Endecott,* nor *My Kinsman* do Hawthorne a great deal of justice.

Benito Cereno, the last of *The Old Glory*'s three plays, though written first, is by far the most persuasive of the lot. The year in this Melville adaptation is 1800. The place is the Caribbean. An American ship, the *President Adams,* has encountered a Spanish slave trader off Trinidad. On boarding her, the American captain finds a strange scene: the Spanish vessel's captain, Benito Cereno, is dying; the crew has been cut in half by disease; a number of slaves also appear to be missing. We soon discover that an uprising has occurred, that the boat is under the command of slaves (whose leader is called Babu), and that members of the crew were tortured and killed in the mutiny. The production, full of violence and contemporary political significance, enacts the retaking by the Americans of the ship. In terms of drama, the final moments of *Benito Cereno* represent *The Old Glory*'s finest moments, probably its only moments.

Lowell had not yet come to grips with the finer points of dramaturgy. Viewed as a whole, the production revealed a fledgling but as yet unfulfilled talent. The one-act play, the demands of stagecraft, the problems of dialogue eluded the poet. A graver obstacle was his inability to comprehend the physical nature of the stage. What works on the written page or in the body of a poem is not necessarily the stuff of the theater. If Lowell was aware of those elements that enliven a dramatic production—not only action and conflict, but variations in tone and voice, movement, pathos, wit, timing, and so forth—he demonstrated little or no ability to incorporate them coherently.

Clive Barnes, reviewing the trilogy for *The New York Times* during its 1976 engagement, was less than enthusiastic:

> Lowell knows as little about the theater as a churchmouse at a bacchanalia, and his writing is too often dead and deadly. He takes a symbol for a truth and a metaphor for a ride. In the theater, truth is nothing, but significance is all. Mr. Lowell can tell the truth about America in 101 puny ways, each one more pretentious than the last. He deplores America—he deplores our puritanism, our pusillanimity and our racism. All these attitudes are perfectly reasonable, even, it might be thought, laudable, but Mr. Lowell is such a tiresome, and obvious, bore in expressing them.

Barnes's criticism is harsh but accurate. Incredibly, *The Old Glory*, as produced at the American Place Theater, was the winner of no less than five Obie Awards for the 1964–1965 season, including Best Play. One can only surmise that, while the judges' hearts were in the right place, their ears and eyes were not. As a whole, the trilogy is a tired, static, dreary night in the theater. What little humor the plays emote is bunched up all in one or two places. The dialogue is forced, bereft of life; the gestures are empty. This is poetaster stuff, soporific and gray, with a certain unappealing intellectual pomposity. "Hurrah for the Republic! / Down with Major Molineux!" shouts the crowd in *My Kinsman*. Captain Delano, the American captain in *Benito Cereno*, at one point shouts: "God save America from Americans!" It is all very trite, very affected and windy, without the eloquence or subtlety of the poetry.

The Lowells of page and stage are closer and the stagecraft less forced in his 1967 version of Aeschylus's *Prometheus Bound*, originally penned for the British director Peter Brook. In composing his version Lowell worked from an English prose translation, "one of the dullest I could find. Seldom was there any temptation to steal a whole phrase." Lowell's *Prometheus* was first staged at the Yale School of Drama on May 9, 1967, in a production directed by Jonathan Miller and featuring British actor Kenneth Haigh, best known for his portrayal of Jimmy

Porter, the first of the angry young men in John Osborne's *Look Back in Anger*. Lowell was writer-in-residence at the Yale School of Drama in 1967, driving twice weekly from New York to New Haven to teach his courses. He, his wife, and his daughter, attending the opening night's performance, bore witness to a lively Haigh as an angry, ageless Prometheus, more unbound than bound, the scene set, remarkably, in the dungeon of a seventeenth-century castle, symbolic chains dangling from an unseen ceiling. As usual, Lowell had taken liberties with his text. Half his lines are not in the original and the other half are so altered as to bear almost no resemblance to the Aeschylus version.

Lowell's Prometheus is far less the stoic than his Greek counterpart and, as one might suspect, far more loquacious. His talk consists largely of a self-questioning skepticism with long bursts of existential commentary on the nature of God and man. Lowell's title character is a humanist, a political radical, a complainer, full of contempt for the minor gods who, with the unctuousness of minor political functionaries, make themselves at home under the despotism of Zeus. For Zeus, Prometheus has only implacable loathing. The play created by Lowell is not too remote in kind from James Russell Lowell's radicalized "Prometheus," his long, early poem written in defense of abolitionism: "Yes, I am that Prometheus who brought down / The light to man, which thou, in selfish fear, / Hadst to thyself usurped,—his by sole right, / For man hath right to all save Tyranny." It would not be too farfetched to suggest that there was a touch of Prometheus in both poets.

28

POLITICO

LOWELL worked in a large, pleasant, whitewashed studio three flights above the family apartment, a private and solitary room lined with bookshelves, the space overflowing with books, papers, journals, stray newspaper and magazine pages—the sort of organized disarray one might sooner expect of a struggling college student than one of America's leading poets. Against one wall sat a portrait of Ezra Pound; also bearded, over a desk, James Russell Lowell stared down from a yellow, cracked photograph dusty with age. A dining-cum-writing table stood against a wall; on it sat a desk lamp and a well-worn portable typewriter, used by Lowell primarily for correspondence. The room contained several upholstered armchairs, a desk chair, a standing lamp, and a narrow bed. Lying in bed, Lowell orchestrated his lines, patched them together, chain-smoking his way through a clutter of words. He described the process: "I lie on a bed staring, crossing out, writing in, crossing out what was written in, again and again, through days and weeks. Heavenly hours of absorption and idleness . . . intuition, intelligence, pursuing my ear that knows not what it says. In time, the fragmentary and scattered limbs become . . . something living . . . a person."

Ernest Hemingway, convinced that an uncomfortable position kept the dendrites flowing, wrote standing up, leaning against a lectern mounted atop a desk for support. Thomas Wolfe, tall as a door, did likewise but used the top of a refrigerator so as not to stoop. Lowell, like Balzac and Edith Wharton, preferred toiling in comfort; all three wore bed clothing and wrote in prone position. Lowell sometimes rose, sauntered to the window, and peered out at the spreading vista that was New York. Rattling water pipes and a whistling winter radiator were the sole distractions.

He once declared that he could find the inspiration for a poem anywhere—in a short-story theme, a paragraph from a novel, a passage from a play, a musical movement, a fleeting image that might materialize from out of thin air. He subscribed to the theory that said a poem, by its very nature, could never be finished or made perfect; imperfection and open-endedness in literature are as American as Robert Frost and Carl Sandburg. The internecine struggle that consumed the artist took place in trying to gloss over the poem's pitch toward perfection and in shaping the jigsaw cut of its imperfection: "In a way a poem is never finished. It simply reaches a point where it isn't worth any more alteration, where any further tampering is liable to do more harm than good."

While Lowell wrestled with his muse in the refuge of his study, Elizabeth Hardwick battled hers in their duplex apartment below. She wrote essays and fiction, using as work space the large antique dining-room table or the coffee table in the library–living room, a chamber of grand proportions with its twenty-foot ceiling and overhanging railed balcony. Many of the furnishings—high-backed chairs, oak wall panel, fading red pine chest, fumed oak blanket chest, marble mantelpiece, red velvet sofa—were from Lowell's parents' house in Boston. The décor was dominated by an "unauthenticated Burne-Jones" hanging above the fireplace; tall buckets of spears stood in each corner; a basket of gaily colored peacock feathers (given to Lowell by Flannery O'Connor) also stood in a corner; richly toned Persian rugs and runners covered finely finished wooden floors. As one visitor saw it, there was an air of dream-vanished Victorian immortality to this stylishly appointed space. Far up on the fortress-thick north wall a sizable, arching skylight stared down. Twin walls rose in tiers of books, twenty shelves high and fifteen feet wide. Each wall was bounded by angled traveling ladders attached to brass ceiling rods. The books were worn, cracked, ancient, leatherbound, and arranged in sets.

There was more: sepia-toned Civil War photographs against a distant wall; a reddish Pre-Raphaelite painting of two nudes; a smooth white-marble bust of a boy-man crowned with russet perched atop a white pedestal. Another patch of wall was covered with black-and-white Sidney Nolan line drawings and miniature family portraits of Lowells and Winslows; there were antique woodcuts and colorful wall hangings. Studies of Pasternak as a young man were mounted near blowups of Robert Lowell at various stages of his career. A knotted, brown, wooden chandelier, old as the *Mayflower,* was suspended from the ceiling. The walls of the stairwell leading upstairs contained a gallery of stills of Lowell's literary confederates: Eliot, Pound, Williams, Frost, Ransom, Edmund Wilson, Allen Tate, among others. This was a reminder for the poet of what he liked to consider his true and natural heritage; this was aristocracy.

Lord Lowell's quarters represented an artist's studio and residence such as few poets in America possess. (Of his contemporaries, only the poet James Merrill, an heir of the Merrill Lynch, Pierce, Fenner & Smith fortune could claim equal or superior wealth.) If this was some-one's idea of rebellion, a revolt against the silver spoon and velvet-lined channel, it was insurrection of a very special brand. At the core of the poet's rebelliousness was his dislike for the wealth of the idle rich—the Boston rich to be precise—and the spiritual suffocation that went with it. Yet Lowell's living room, with its Wagnerian vastness and splendor, bore a distinct resemblance to Amy Lowell's royal chamber at Sevenels. Moreover, Robert Lowell had entered a social quadrille of no uncertain luxury: summers in Maine, weekends in the Hamptons, dinner parties and informal outings with friends. The difference between Robert Low-ell and others of his social milieu was that the poet preferred partying with fellow literati—bluebloods of the mind, not of the pocketbook.

Their summers, since 1957, had been spent in Maine, the family piling their Spanish housekeeper, records, Harriet's pets (a Persian cat, two guinea pigs, a pair of gerbils) into a station wagon and pushing off for the tiny but wealthy coastline community of Castine, where they maintained an old white colonial frame house on the Common, a gift from Harriet Winslow, who also bequeathed Lowell a generous annual subsidy; the property was not too far from the house he had once occupied with Jean Stafford. A barn, fronting Oakum Bay, was fur-nished to serve as Lowell's workroom. A fair portion of *Life Studies* and of *For the Union Dead* were composed there.

The best recollection of Lowell's eleven summers in Castine can be found in Philip Booth's memoir, "Summers in Castine," published in *Salmagundi* on the occasion of Lowell's sixtieth (and last) birthday.

Booth, also a local summer resident, recalls Lowell's unorthodox tennis style: "His legs never get him to the right place on the court at the right moment, but he compensates by attacking the ball with all the immense strength of his upper body." He was a poor but eager sailor, good swimmer, unlucky but avid fisherman. Athletics aside, he was an exhaustively gifted raconteur, a superb dinner-table conversationalist, a wonderful and entertaining and gracious host, a marvelous friend. With his far-ranging knowledge and dancing imagination, he could turn the dinner table into center court at Wimbledon: "As if in total relief from writing, or from shop talk," writes Booth, "Cal tries every shot in the book: dropshot, lob, slam. There are a few long rallies; it is almost impossible to drive Cal back to some conversational baseline. But dinnerparties, supperparties, are stunning games of intelligence at play, every exchange ending and never ending in strokes of quick victory or happy collapse." Lowell possessed the same gift for gab, the same wit and deadly charm demonstrated by James Russell and Amy Lowell before him. And like these literary connoisseurs he was a prodigious and wonderful letter writer; there is an intentional degree of difficulty about his letters—as there was about his early poetry—that is mysteriously appealing.

His summer guests—William Meredith, I. A. Richards, John Berryman, Robert Silvers, Elizabeth Bishop, Mary McCarthy, W. S. Merwin—marveled at his conversational finesse. The humor that was lacking in *The Old Glory* poured forth in great volume over dinner and drinks. Poetry, politics, women, history: he turned from one to the other with barely a pause. Names as diverse as Philip of Macedonia, Thomas Mann, Aristophanes, Shakespeare, and Edward Kennedy rolled off his tongue in rollicking tales of Chaucerian versatility. Or he could chatter for hours about Eliot, Stevens, Horace, Tate, Empson, Ovid, and dozens of others whose works he skillfully and in a wonderfully poetic prose style dissected in the pages of *The Kenyon Review* and *The Sewanee Review*. His days in Castine passed with almost tedious repetition: breakfast, post office, newspaper, barn for work, late lunch, rest, tennis, more work. At night they often entertained or visited with friends. And on weekends there were clam bakes, afternoon hikes, sailing parties, picnics, cocktail parties, summer stock. Frigid ocean temperatures made swimming difficult; the Lowells would occasionally visit a nearby lake. As much as his ancestors, Robert Lowell had a strong affinity for people, a broad stripe of curiosity about their foibles and fancies; he never wearied of hearing their humorous tales of woe.

From a literary standpoint the big push in Lowell's career was to go on from *Life Studies,* to push ahead. To Randall Jarrell he admitted (May 11, 1964) that in his own work he too often detected a monotony and a tameness that he loathed. He felt exhausted, he informed M. L. Rosenthal, and realized that the next creative effort would have to be totally different—in style and substance. As the guest of honor at the Boston Festival of the Arts, held in the Public Gardens on June 5, 1960, Lowell informed an audience of four thousand, including Eleanor Roosevelt, that the artist's work and existence were inseparable and that the composition of *Life Studies* had therefore meant having to relive his "sordid past." Noting that Boston was "a rapidly emerging center of highways and parking places," the rebellious scion of the famed proper-Bostonian family began reading from "For the Union Dead," his last completed poem. Drawing waves of applause, he began to tell those gathered about his childhood, about how he had once been ejected from the Public Gardens for misbehavior—"but tonight partly makes up for it." He spoke of his Boston childhood in terms of the terror he had felt coming of age within the embrace of "a public family." Then he spoke of the difficulty he was experiencing in regard to his work. Since *Life Studies* his output of poetry had dropped markedly. A few months earlier, accepting the 1960 National Book Award, he said: "When I finished *Life Studies,* I was left hanging on a question mark. I am still hanging there. I don't know whether it is a death-rope or a lifeline."

Similar entries of despair found their way into other Lowell releases. To Allen Tate and Tate's new wife Isabella Gardner, Lowell defined his present state as "one of those dread empty vacation periods between bursts of writing." Another letter, this one to Isabella on the occasion of her first volume of verse, presaged the conclusion of "Eye and Tooth," a forthcoming Lowell poem: "Writing's hell, isn't it? I tire of my turmoil, and feel everyone else has, and long for a Horatian calm."

One result of his inner conflict was Lowell's 1964 *For the Union Dead,* a progression of poems that recorded the struggle to become a great poet. Reading through it, one cannot help but feel that to exercise imperial sway is an exercise so ruinously difficult that it obsesses the poet's whole outlook. Lowell's latest volume captured the desolating, but also the heartening and compassionate sense of the pressures of creativity, the sheer madness of attempting "to make art." As in *Life Studies,* the poet's "self" is at the heart of the issue, the literal self being poetry's central symbol, confessionalism being about oneself, unashamedly. But there were discernible differences between this and Lowell's previous collection of original poems. If *Life Studies* was passionately, pointedly, even embarrassingly personal, *For the Union Dead* was a step back into the world, away from the direct, strident statements about his own feelings, away from the abject negativism with which he regarded every living soul. He was more interested these days in such sociological tropes as politics and morality, the individual in society, mass culture and intellectual poverty. His perspective on life itself was milder, less caustic, more direct. Having investigated the existence of his own psyche, he was determined now to go a step beyond, to flee personal experience in favor of the cosmos. Dedicating the volume to his friend the playwright William Alfred, the poet for the first time had endearing words for his father, his ancestors, even for that total tyrant, Caligula, a manifestation of his "other" self.

Lowell's confidences produce the impression that he was slowly digging out from under the oppressive weight of his ancestry. The sterility and deadness that howl through the museumlike landscape of *Life Studies,* take on a tone of tolerance, understanding, and randomness in *For the Union Dead.* He was no longer rooted to the past, stranded in a Sahara of mordant statuary and architecture; if his present landscape was crushed and crumbling, he nevertheless had freedom to roam, to explore. His earlier rebellion had been familial; his present rebellion was social. For the first time he had created a form large enough to swim in, while simultaneously embracing Williams's radical dictum, "To write down that which happens at that time." In *For the Union Dead* the craftsman creates a personal rendition of Yeats's global village, an instrument of portrayal that regards the world of public lies as well as those the poet must tell himself in order to survive. The bomb, the city, commercialism, a hostile social climate are the grim realities of our universal struggle; as such these entities become the objects of Lowell's piercing outward gaze. For once public and private worlds merge, the health of one determining the welfare of the other.

The poems in *For the Union Dead* assume the added dimension of public responsibility, a public conscience and voice. Such a poem is

"Law," whose basic thematic struggle resides in the distinction Lowell draws between two bodies of law: one for civic man, another for the imagination—

> Under one law,
> or two,
> to lie unsleeping,
> still sleeping on the battlefield . . .

For those in society who make and implement legislation, Lowell has utter disdain. "July in Washington" expounds on "The Elect, the elected . . . they come here bright as dimes, / and die dishevelled and soft." "Tenth Muse" reflects on the divine origins of our present system of jurisprudence; the poet tells us that the concrete tracts of Moses are engraved on stones "we cannot bear or break," suggesting that the Ten Commandments no longer suffice, given the complexities of the modern age. "I like to imagine it must have been simpler in the days of Lot," the poet ventures, playing on the name of that lofty Old Testament figure.

When civic law fails, the public space that it occupies is threatened or extinguished and it is up to literature to take over as the repository of values. The embalmment of the ordered past becomes the duty of every poet. One method employed by Lowell in carrying out his share is the use of deft wit and wry, savage humor, a mode first experienced in *Life Studies* and carried forward over the remainder of his canon. "I suppose even God was born / too late to trust the old religion," he quips at one point in the present volume. At another juncture he compares his childhood self to a quasi Peeping Tom, wringing humor out of still air: "No ease for the boy at the keyhole / his telescope, / when the women's white bodies flashed / in the bathroom. Young, my eyes began to fail."

At other times he is as earnest as a cardinal, painting the landscape in thick coats of black paint. "The Mouth of the Hudson," ostensibly the mouth to hell, is a one-sided view of New York at its purgatorial worst. "The Public Garden" is Boston in late fall, dead leaves rolled into balls, the moon like chalk, everything dead or dying. Darkly depressing "Florence" portrays that ancient city, a reminder that the classic themes and structures—beauty, art, civilization—are gained at no small cost to humankind:

> Oh Florence, Florence, patroness
> of the lovely tyrannicides!
> Where the tower of the Old Palace
> pierces the sky
> like a hypodermic needle,
>
> . . .
>
> Greek demi-gods of the Cross,
> rise sword in hand
> above the unshaven,
> formless decapitation
> of the monsters, tubs of guts,
> mortifying chunks for the pack.

A common Lowell ploy is employed here, the postromantic ardor of the line "Oh Florence, Florence" countered by the harshness implicit in such gritty verbalisms as "tyrannicides," "hypodermic needle," and "tubs of guts." The poem is honed and sharpened by the careful balancing and juxtaposition of the old and new, the world of peaceful antiquity and the sinister reality of twentieth-century bloodlust; the tower of the Old Palace does not simply rise, it *pierces* the sky as though in sexual violation of time and space.

Although the poems in *For the Union Dead* are generally accessible, some nevertheless contain instances of opaque and untouchable privacy; those verses that on the surface appear explicit, often merely tickle the mind's fancy with references that elude the uninitiated reader, as for instance the opening stanza of "Eye and Tooth"—

> My whole eye was sunset red,
> the old cut cornea throbbed,
> I saw things darkly,
> as through an unwashed goldfish globe.

—which is simply the refraction of Lowell's unsuccessful attempt to wear contact lenses instead of glasses. The poem plays heavily on the "eye/I" pun, suggesting more meanings than it actually imparts, looking to St. Paul for his "through a glass darkly" image and keeping Tiresias in mind as the mythological character who went blind after seeing something (the future) he shouldn't have. Another poem, "The Flaw," elaborates on the same image, the hairline cut on the cornea of Lowell's eye: "Some mote, some eye-flaw, wobbles in the heat, / hair-thin, hair-dark, the fragment of a hair."

Physical deterioration, the result of creeping middle age, and physical annihilation, the result of uncontrollable conditions in the world, are related themes that crop up repeatedly. The scratched cornea of "The Flaw" leads, in the same poem, to a vision of sudden destruction—"In a flash, I see us whiten into skeletons"—that points to the potential dangers of atomic warfare, while looking back to a line in "My Last Afternoon with Uncle Devereux." Of his uncle, who had been stricken by Hodgkin's disease, Lowell wrote: "Come winter, Uncle Devereux would blend to the one color." Devereux's fate is universalized in *For the Union Dead*'s "Fall 1961," where the obsessional and mechanical ticking of a grandfather clock (an image suggesting the purposeful passage of present time and the passing of another age) is measured against Lowell's omnipresent fear of extinction by atomic bomb: "All autumn, the chafe and jar / of nuclear war." The rhythm of the grandfather clock's ticking is likewise measured against the "back and forth, back and forth" swinging pattern of an oriole's nest: "my one point of rest." The same poem, itself an indictment of an age wherein mechanical time replaces organic time, contains a stunning and apocalyptic image of anguished spiders: "We are like a lot of wild / spiders crying together, / but without tears."

"Fall 1961" is a public poem, filled with private allusions. Written during the Berlin crisis of 1961, it reflects the tension Lowell experiences when East German troops seal off the border between East and West Berlin, giving rise to a resumption of nuclear testing by the United States and Russia. If, during World War II, Lowell seemed to be self-absorbed, his eyes closed to certain convenient facts, his present disposition was one of wide-eyed anxiety. He tossed and turned in a bed of revulsion, his lyricism no longer edged with the phantasmagoric imagery of *The Old Glory* but with outright streaks of fear. He was a man obsessed.

Death's skull and crossbones permeate the entire volume. In "Myopia: a Night" Lowell hears "the lonely metal breathe / and gurgle like the sick." In "Night Sweat" the poet remarks: "I've felt the creeping damp / float over my pajamas' wilted white . . . / Sweet salt embalms me and my head is wet." "Alfred Corning Clark" recounts the suicide at age forty-five of a former prep school classmate, a fellow Brahmin with whom Lowell clearly identified: "I was befogged, / and you were too bored / . . . / You are dear to me, Alfred; / our reluctant souls united. . . ." "Middle age" concretizes the poet's fear of dying prematurely, Lowell being the same age as Clark: "At forty-five, / what next, what next?" "The Drinker" describes a man killing time with a drink, while time and drink kill him. Harriet Winslow slowly succumbs in "Soft Wood," the victim of a crippling terminal disease.

In "Hawthorne," written for a Centenary Edition of Hawthorne's selected works, we witness the resurrection and sudden aging of James Russell Lowell and his Fireside companions: "Look at the faces— / Longfellow, Lowell, Holmes and Whittier! / Study the grizzled silver of their beards." By contrast to this group, Hawthorne is remembered as having a "blond mustache" and a "golden General Custer scalp": he sports a "hard survivor's smile . . . touched with fire." Lowell imbues Hawthorne with some of the same qualities that he applied to his quartet of craftsmen in *Life Studies*, his attempt to isolate the creative personality.

James Russell Lowell is again invoked, albeit indirectly, in the new volume's title sequence, a poem that looks back a century both to the ode for the Union dead recited by the earlier Lowell at Harvard in 1865 and the ode ("Memoriae Positum R.G.S.") that he wrote to honor Colonel Robert Gould Shaw. Allen Tate's 1928 classic, "Ode to the Confederate Dead," with its ragged wealth of visual and auditory imagery, is recalled as well. The poems of all three authors—James Russell Lowell, Allen Tate, Robert Lowell—are marked by what the "Ode Recited at the Harvard Commemoration" calls "the passion of an angry grief." Comparing the poems of the two Lowells, we note obvious differences in form and content, similarities in social philosophy and political consciousness. Each man's respective slant, encompassing both the terrors of responsibility and the terrors of alienation, makes an unavoidable statement concerning their high regard for "the stalwart soul." If this gives way to what seems like self-contradiction on the part of Robert Lowell—loathing for war, admiration for the war hero—it can perhaps be more easily grasped in terms of an explanation Lowell later gave to Stanley Kunitz: "One side of me is conventional, concerned with causes, agitated about peace and justice and equality. My other side is deeply conservative, wanting to get at the roots of things, wanting to slow down the whole modern progress of mechanization and dehumanization, knowing that liberalism can be a form of death too." Presumably what Lowell meant to infer was that he was a conservative not by virtue of political affiliation but rather by dint of his basically rigid view of history, a respect for the past, an admiration for rebellion and heroism growing out of the orthodox notion that in history he could find the faith that he craved but was unable to locate in any organized form of religion.

In the final analysis, it was art—not history—that became Lowell's personal cause, a means of uniting his divided self and of dealing squarely with death, with guilt, with weakness and self-deception. Heroism in its most trenchant guise—in the form of the man of power and principles—fascinated the poet. He identified more readily with the military men in his family than with his literary ancestry. In all fairness to Lowell, it must be said that he responded not to the thick-witted, unthinking soldier who dropped bombs on the unwitting inno-cent, the possessed bombardier or Pentagon general who felt no pain; instead he responded to and admired the stoicism of the suffering man, the man who felt and sensed all—the terribleness and agony of death, the irony of life, the senselessness of history. He admired the man who stuck to his guns, who fought on with grace and bearing and honor in the face of almost certain defeat. In all three Lowell poets a deep strain of conservatism vied with a streak of liberal humanitarianism and avant-garde poetic sensibility; in none of the three were these warring forces ever satisfactorily resolved.

Robert Lowell's "For the Union Dead" is a reprint, with minor varia-tions, of "Colonel Shaw and his Massachusetts 54th," which first ap-peared as the last poem in *Life Studies,* where it provided the poet with one more heroic figure whose valor in leading one of the first black regiments during the Civil War he could balance against his own ex-periences and thoughts. In James Russell Lowell's "Memoriae Positum" we come across this unrhymed couplet: "Our wall of circumstance / Cleared at a bound, he flashes o'er the fight." Robert Lowell altered these lines to fit his own needs: "He is out of bounds now. He rejoiced in man's lovely, / peculiar power to choose life and die." Lowell's imagi-nation was engaged not only by Shaw's burial in a large, common plot with his men, but by the construction of a bas-relief of the Colonel's troops by the sculptor Augustus Saint-Gaudens opposite the Massachu-setts Statehouse at the entrance to the Boston Common. The monu-ment, bearing a Latin inscription which translated reads, "They gave up everything to serve the Republic," was dedicated in 1897 by William James, with additional addresses and readings by Thomas Bailey Al-drich, Booker T. Washington, and Oliver Wendell Holmes, Jr. With four lines from "Memoriae Positum" engraved upon the relief's base, the monument consists of a determined-looking Shaw mounted atop his horse surrounded by a flank of foot soldiers and above them, waving them forward, a floating female spirit. Shaw and large numbers of his men were killed after having scaled an outside wall of the enemy fortress. Although the Confederate commander of Fort Wagner denied his Union counterpart an officer's burial, efforts were later initiated in the North to bring the body home. Shaw's father refused on the grounds that "a soldier's most appropriate burial place is on the field where he has fallen." Shaw's last ride formed the basis for poems not only by both Lowells, but by Paul Laurence Dunbar, William Vaughan Moody, Emerson, and John Berryman, among others. Not coincidentally, Elizabeth Hardwick was concomitantly preparing an edition of William James's letters, including one to his brother Henry describing his oration on the occasion of the dedication of the Saint-Gaudens statue. This material may well have been the lure that first drew Lowell's attention to the project.

His composition of the original version of "For the Union Dead" took place during a period when the Common was under construction to make room for an underground parking garage and at a time when the civil rights issue was constantly in the news; because of the construction the bas-relief had been bound and propped up. The poem opens by establishing a basis of comparison between Boston's aristocratic past and the tawdriness and dilapidation of her present state:

> The old South Boston Aquarium stands
> in a Sahara of snow now. Its broken windows are boarded.
> The bronze weathervane cod has lost half its scales.
> The airy tanks are dry.

The poet reflects on a visit he paid to the Aquarium as a child, his nose crawling like a snail on the glass, his hand tingling "to burst the bubbles" that drifted up from the noses of the "cowed, compliant" fish. But the Aquarium that Lowell cherished as a youth had fallen into the same miserable state of decay as the uprooted Common: "One morning last March, / I pressed against the new barbed and galvanized / fence on the Boston Common. / Behind their cage, yellow dinosaur steamshovels were grunting / as they cropped up tons of mush and grass / to gouge their underworld garage." The Common, with its barbed and galvanized wire, half-constructed underground parking emporium, and grunting steamshovels, looked to the poet like a bombed-out war zone; it drew Lowell's attention to the Saint-Gaudens relief of Shaw. Distressed by the typically aggressive military figure in American history, Lowell placed Shaw on a higher pedestal; Shaw's energies were not simply devoted to the service of destruction; his self-sacrifice helped preserve and restore the Republic. Seen in this supernatural light, he becomes a version of the Japanese kamikaze, a divine essence and highest rank of stoic.

The uprooting of the Boston Common, the development of a parking lot, the destruction of nature and automatization of the twentieth-century metropolis, all conspired to make Shaw, his heroism, and the bronze figures of his men appear increasingly remote: "the stone statues of the abstract Union Soldiers/grow slimmer and younger each year." The Aquarium's fate and the fate of those ideals that Shaw and his black Union soldiers embodied are tragically linked. In a hundred small New England towns, the flags that "quilt the graveyards" of the Union Army dead are frayed and tattered. This vision of loss and damnation points the reader toward the poem's denouement, a fleeting glimpse of the Aquarium's demise, a picture of entropy and corrosion as tropical fish metamorphose into sharks and sharks turn into cars:

> The Aquarium is gone. Everywhere,
> giant finned cars nose forward like fish;
> a savage servility
> slides by on grease.

If James Russell Lowell served "For the Union Dead" as a model of historical reference, it was Amy Lowell who inadvertently supplied many of its most effective images. Her "Afternoon Rain in State Street" and "An Aquarium"—both from *Men, Women and Ghosts*—contain phrases and flavors startlingly similar to phrases and flavors contained in "For the Union Dead." "Afternoon Rain" cites State as a *"greasy, shiny"* street, while "An Aquarium" describes a "Grey-green opaqueness sliding down"; together these two add up to "a savage servility" sliding "by on grease." Amy's "Aquarium" also speaks of "nosing the bubbles" and refers to "Metallic blue fish, / With fins wide and yellow and swaying." This becomes "giant finned cars nose forward like fish" in the later Lowell. The convergence of Amy and Robert Lowell's work here has to be more than mere coincidence.

"For the Union Dead" is essentially a poem of contrasts, one salient set comprised of Colonel Shaw's old-fashioned idealism versus the turgescence and spread of urban blight. For all its retrospection and historicity this is distinctly a poem of the late 1950's, depicting an era of material overabundance and commercial dross, a theme commonly associated with the work of the Beats—Lawrence Ferlinghetti, Gregory Corso, Allen Ginsberg. Unlike the Beats, Lowell's work "moves the reader without trying to," depending for effect on subtlety and cleverness as opposed to dogmatism and demagoguery. Nor does Lowell embarrass the reader with a superfluity of emotional statements, a quality that underlies the work of so many confessional artists. The best of Lowell's iterations are understated, the poet a central presence but his work reaching out beyond the narrow confines of personal declamation.

Extended in contemporary directions, the poem addresses itself also to the failed premise of civil rights, the country's inability to set right the causes of disunion that took place with the Civil War, and the failure of the intervening years to effect change in that domain. This explains the significance of the lines, "Their monument sticks like a fishbone / in the city's throat," as well as the reference to the news coverage accorded the sobering reality of schoolroom segregation: "When I crouch to my television set, / the drained faces of Negro school-children rise like balloons." The balloons transport us back to the bubbles that once drifted from the fish in the now deserted aquarium, and these in turn relate to the bubble of idealism that Colonel Shaw continues to ride: "Colonel Shaw / is riding on his bubble, / he waits / for the blessèd break." Hiroshima "boiling over" (sacrilegiously represented in Boston by a commercial photograph for Mosler Safes) also suggests bubbles, the result of the giant mushroom cloud from an atomic blast that makes a furnace of the city. Lowell toys with these and other images, tying the poem together into tight and resilient verbal knots. Using excerpts from the dedication speech of William James, the poet invests the present sequence with a power that bonds national history with personal experience to the distinct literary advantage of both. The difference between this poem and James Russell Lowell's "Memoriae Positum" is that the latter, attempting to justify Shaw's death (and the author's survival), looks hopefully to the future, radiating an aura of renewed faith in the country's pending rebirth. Conversely, Robert Lowell sees the failure of the past reflected in every aspect of contemporary Boston, Shaw's ideals as dead as the victims of Hiroshima, moral bankruptcy infiltrating every nook and cranny of American society. A century after the promise expressed by the James Russell Lowell poem, the Firesider receives his answer in the poem and person of Robert Lowell.

By and large the fifties represented a decade of sterility and futility in America, a period dominated by intellectual malaise, dimmed hopes, disillusionment, and dishonesty in the arts, particularly in literature. There were notable exceptions—Hannah Arendt, Edmund Wilson, Samuel Beckett, Saul Bellow, Norman Mailer, Henry Miller, Bernard Malamud, Vladimir Nabokov, and Ralph Ellison produced works of considerable merit. One can cite John Berryman's *Homage to Mistress Bradstreet* and the verse of William Carlos Williams as examples of ongoing fervor in poetry. Lowell, aware of these isolated instances, was nevertheless alarmed by the general morass of ennui in the arts. At the time that *For the Union Dead* appeared, Lowell told A. Alvarez that it was "a miserable time, more than others, with the world liable to blow up. We're in some transition domestically: I mean in one's family and everything else. . . . It's a very confused moment." Lowell's bleak Manichean vision of spiritual and cultural starvation found poetic expression in "Inauguration Day: January 1953" (the date of Eisenhower's presidential inauguration):

> Ice, ice. Our wheels no longer move.
> Look, the fixed stars, all just alike
> 　　　. . .
> and the Republic summons Ike,
> the mausoleum in her heart.

Anomie in the fifties gave way to activity in the sixties, a decade that rebelled against and overthrew the politically repressive age of Joseph McCarthy. In many respects the 1960's was an era when for the first time since the Depression, American writers found themselves worrying about the political relevance of their art. If "The Auden Generation" made a sincere and concerted effort to come to grips with the monumental political and social issues of the 1930's, the intellectuals of the sixties raised similar questions, with particular emphasis on the one question, "What is the private, creative self to do when public events demand effective moral action?" What is the moral imperative?

There was no single or simple answer. Every man or woman, each concerned artist, had to make up his or her own mind. Lowell's political convictions had been developing for nearly twenty years, since the day of his monumental decision against serving in World War II. His correspondence during the period of his incarceration, though perused by prison censors, demonstrated his evolving frame of reference. From West Street he informed Randall Jarrell that he was for the first time reading Vanzetti's letters to Sacco's son: "Their cause is mine—I'm sure the pro-Russian traitors are secretly supported by *certain* rich men—those who have sold us (The poor—who's worse paid than the poet—even carpenters get more and work less) for a 'pair of shoes'—when I get out I'm going to do everything in my power to get the Sacco case re-opened, so that those responsible are imprisoned and *electrocuted.*" There was profound irony in this statement, for it was Abbott Lawrence Lowell, the chairman of the three-man Sacco-Vanzetti gubernatorial review commission, who had played such an instrumental role in their conviction and execution.

The need for a renewal of political subscription was driven home to Lowell shortly after his 1960 arrival on the New York literary scene. He taught for a semester at the New School for Social Research, attended political rallies, parades, lectures, conferences, befriending a whole new contingent of highly educated and privileged liberals, a group whose integrity of conviction seemed to change almost with the weather. Lowell's lack of faith in any steadfast political persuasion was the one unifying and dogmatic stance that he consistently espoused, although he clearly believed that the American liberal came closer to an effective morality than the American reactionary or moderate. The virtues of liberalism were perhaps limited, but it was through the liberal cause and through humanism that the poet attempted to define the world according to Lowell. It was also through this cause that he came into contact with those who shared his vision. Via Jarrell, for example, he met Hannah Arendt and her husband, the philosopher Heinrich Bluecher, at whose Upper West Side apartment in New York he was a frequent guest.

Lowell's political conscience was elevated another notch by an invitation he received at this time, along with fifteen other American poets, to attend President John F. Kennedy's inauguration on January 20, 1961; it was the day that Robert Frost, an aging figure in the Washington sun, read his memorable "The Gift Outright" to the gathered throngs. Kennedy, eager to court the intellectual set, several months later invited Lowell to a White House dinner party in honor of André Malraux, an event the poet recalled for an *Encounter* interview with A. Alvarez:

> I was invited to the White House for Malraux's dinner there. Kennedy made a rather graceful joke that "the White House was becoming almost a café for intellectuals. . . ." Then we all drank a great deal at the White House, and had to sort of be told not to take our champagne into the concert, and to put our cigarettes out like children—though nicely, it wasn't peremptory. Then the next morning you read that the Seventh Fleet had been sent somewhere in Asia and you had a funny feeling of how unimportant the artist really was: that this was sort of window dressing and that the real government was somewhere else, and that something much closer to the Pentagon was really ruling the country. And maybe this is how it must be.

The possibility that this was the case, that the President was an ordinary cog in an immense political machine, did not totally discolor Lowell's perception of him. The assassination of the President brought to mind the heroic gestures of Colonel Shaw and Beau Sabreur; here was one more example of Lowell's esteemed stoic, a mortal struggling to see and reach and touch all:

> Kennedy represents a side of America that is appealing to the artist in retrospect, a certain heroism. You feel in certain terms he really was a martyr in his death; that he was reckless, went further than the office called for, and perhaps that he was fated to be killed. That's an image one could treasure, and it stirs one.

Lowell's firmest commitment to liberal politics came about late in May 1965, when he was invited by President Lyndon Johnson to participate in an all-day White House arts festival, to be attended by some four hundred writers, artists, critics, and art patrons—representatives from every branch of the art world. Accepting the invitation to read his poetry, Lowell soon experienced a change of heart. His telegram to Johnson rescinding his acceptance constituted the latest of a growing series of proclamations of discontent on the part of intellectuals in response to U.S. foreign policy in Vietnam and the Dominican Republic. Only a few weeks before, Lewis Mumford had issued an angry antiwar statement before an audience at the American Academy of Arts and Letters. Lowell's denunciatory statement (dated June 3, 1965) arrived simultaneously at the White House and at the offices of *The New York Times*, which published it in its entirety under the headline "Robert Lowell Rebuffs Johnson As Protest Over Foreign Policy." Lowell's statement read:

Dear President Johnson:

When I was telephoned last week and asked to read at the White House Festival of the Arts on June fourteenth, I am afraid I accepted somewhat rapidly and greedily. I thought of such an occasion as purely artistic flourish, even though every serious artist knows that he cannot enjoy public celebration without making subtle public commitments. After a week's wondering, I have decided that I am conscience-bound to refuse your courteous invitation. I do so now in a public letter because my acceptance has been announced in the newspaper, and because of the strangeness of the Administration's recent actions.

Although I am very enthusiastic about most of your domestic legislation and intentions, I nevertheless can only follow our present foreign policy with the greatest dismay and distrust. What we will do and what we ought to do as a sovereign nation facing other sovereign nations seem now to hang in the balance between the better and the worse possibilities. We are in danger of imperceptibly becoming an explosive and suddenly chauvinistic nation, and may even be drifting on our way to the last nuclear rain. I know it is hard for the responsible man to act; it is also painful for the private and irresolute man to dare criticism. At this anguished, delicate, and perhaps determining moment, I feel I am serving you and our country best by not taking part in the White House Festival of the Arts.

Respectfully yours,

Robert Lowell

At the White House the telegram was turned over to the festival's organizer, Dr. Eric Goldman, professor of history at Princeton University and President Johnson's chief cultural adviser. It was not the only document of refusal to arrive; others who declined included writers Edmund Wilson (who sent one of his typically brusque missives) and E. B. White; professor of drama Robert Brustein; the photographer Paul Strand; Jack Levine, the painter; and Alexander Calder, the sculptor. Lowell's, however, was the only communication that was delivered at the same time to *The New York Times.*

That fact infuriated the President and his aides. According to Goldman, "the roar in the Oval Office could be heard all the way into the East Wing." Within hours the White House issued a statement condemning Lowell. Arthur Schlesinger and other Administration foils denounced Lowell as a traitor. One of Lowell's staunchest detractors was McGeorge Bundy, the President's chief foreign policy adviser, against whom Lowell had also spoken to the press, stipulating that "when your private experience converges on the nation's experience you feel you have to do something." McGeorge Bundy was Lowell's cousin, a Boston Brahmin, therefore a natural enemy: the poet could not escape the conclusion that American history and Lowelldom were in some way wed.

These were dangerous and exasperating days what with America's bombing raids on Communist targets and the increasing numbers of American troops that were being sent to Vietnam to fight an undeclared war. Lowell felt the "heavy burden" of his position to be a kind of calling, a responsibility that placed him in league with Senator William Fulbright and other critics of the war. Lowell took part in teach-ins and peace demonstrations and told the press that he was disturbed most by the thought that a technologically advanced country such as America could wantonly destroy Vietnam and their civilization, just as it had once destroyed the civilization of the American Indian. American ambition, power, and idealism could induce the government to inflict untold damage upon the rest of the world. "I have never gotten over the horrors of American bombing," he announced. "For me anti-Stalinism led logically—oh, perhaps not so logically—to my being against our suppression of the Vietnamese."

Lowell's tactics, particularly his telegram to the White House, found favor among fellow liberals. Both Murray Kempton and Dwight Macdonald wrote lengthy articles in praise of Lowell. Eric Goldman, however, was outraged that Lowell should use the White House invitation for his own publicity and as a public political forum—the injection of irrelevant grand issues in high-sounding language, the play to the newspapers—without any real provocation. By telephone he urged Lowell to withdraw his telegram to the *Times* and to let it simply be said that he had discovered he could not attend for personal reasons. Goldman maintained that Lowell's basic assumption was wrong. President Johnson was sponsoring the event not as an ideological or policy test but as an attempt to broaden appreciation of the arts and to make the arts a more integral part of American living. In fact those invited to the

festival represented not only every race, creed, and geographical region, but every form of political persuasion, from far right to extreme
left. Acceptance implied neither approval nor disapproval of the President's policies.

Moreover, Goldman argued, he believed that Lowell's letter would
have an important effect which was contrary to the poet's own wishes.
Lowell wanted, Goldman was sure, to broaden appreciation of the arts
in the United States and also to maintain a forum whereby ideas might
be interchanged between Presidents and men like himself. Toward
these ends it was helpful to have Presidents and intellectuals and artists
get together. It was more than helpful to have Presidents of the United
States—particularly a President who was known to have no great personal taste for the arts—celebrate them from the nation's first house.

Lowell replied that he had carefully considered the matter before
sending the telegram, that he had conferred with a number of friends,
some of whom even argued in the White House's behalf, but that he
could not escape the feeling that his presence would express, to some
degree, support of the President's Dominican and Vietnamese inter-
ventions, and he found these acts so morally reprehensible that he could
not attend. He apologized to Goldman for having accepted thought-
lessly and for the position in which he had placed President Johnson and
the White House. But the decision was made, and in good conscience
he could see no alternative.

Goldman did not raise the issue of the impropriety of releasing a
telegram to the press before it was received by the addressee, in this
case the President of the United States. But Lowell's self-righteous
attitude and his need for some sort of public platform disturbed him.
It disturbed him equally that the newspapers continued to play up the
story. Robert Silvers, a close friend of Lowell's and a coeditor of *The
New York Review of Books,* used Lowell's letter to good advantage,
informing the press that Lyndon Johnson had "contrived the festival to
present a false front to the world that writers and artists are backing the
Vietnam War," and was "trying to use" Lowell for this purpose. There
was a "moral duty to attack the festival" and those writers, such as Saul
Bellow, who agreed to participate in it; there were also "the plain
politics of the situation," making certain that Lowell's withdrawal be
felt on all fronts, particularly by those writers and intellectuals who still
supported Johnson.

To reinforce this point, Silvers, aided by Stanley Kunitz, drafted their own telegram to President Johnson stating support for "Lowell in his decision not to participate in the White House Festival of the Arts. . . .": "We would like you to know that others of us share Lowell's dismay at recent American foreign policy decisions. We hope that people in this and other countries will not conclude that a White House arts program testifies to approval of Administration policy by members of the artistic community." The statement, which similarly appeared in the *Times,* was signed by some of the leading constituents of the intellectual community; besides Silvers and Kunitz, the names belonged to: Hannah Arendt, John Berryman, Alan Dugan, Jules Feiffer, Philip Guston, Lillian Hellman, Alfred Kazin, Dwight Macdonald, Mary McCarthy, Bernard Malamud, Larry Rivers, Philip Roth, Mark Rothko, Louis Simpson, W. D. Snodgrass, William Styron, Peter Taylor, Edgar Varese, and Robert Penn Warren. Of these only Macdonald, Rivers, and Rothko had actually been invited to attend the festival.

The festival itself, held on June 14, was colored by a subtle but readily discernible undercurrent of dissent. The President, in addressing the guests, alluded to the ferment when he said, "Your art is not a political weapon. Yet much of what you do is profoundly political." A reference to dissent was made at the outset of the morning's first program of prose and poetry readings, when Mark Van Doren, introducing the readers —Catherine Drinker Bowen, Saul Bellow, Phyllis McGinley, and John Hersey—expressed regret over the absence of Robert Lowell. Van Doren observed that "Mr. Lowell may or may not have been correct" in his actions, and added that he himself did not "commit any of the writers here present to agreement or disagreement." He went on: "I have been troubled as to whether I should speak of it at all; I do so now, after several previous attempts, merely as honoring the scruples of a fine poet, who, in his own terms, was 'conscience-bound' to stay away."

At the morning session, John Hersey read from *Hiroshima,* a form of protest that further embarrassed the President. Dwight Macdonald, present despite having signed the protest, circulated a petition in support of Lowell. Phyllis McGinley, an author of light verse, added a new couplet to an old poem in the course of her reading: "And while the pot of culture's bubblesome, / Praise poets even when they're troublesome." Saul Bellow informed a newspaper reporter that while he did not support the war, he had attended the festival out of respect for the office of the President. Ralph Ellison, author of *The Invisible Man,* was almost alone among invited artists in claiming to support the war.

Johnson later typified Lowell and all other dissenting intellectuals as "fools, traitors, and sonsofbitches."

Lowell's involvement with the Johnson Administration did not end there. Near the outset of "Waking Early Sunday Morning"—Lowell's next major poem—the President is parodied as a "top-heavy Goliath in full armor" and further in the same sequence as a constipated, ineffectual, bearlike creature, seen swimming nude in the poet's ubiquitous ocean,

> girdled by his establishment
> this Sunday morning, free to chaff
> his own thoughts with his bear-cuffed staff,
> swimming nude, unbuttoned, sick
> of his ghost-written rhetoric!

The grossness of Johnson's figure is matched only by the poet's degrading portraits of Caesar, Mussolini, Stalin, and other morally depraved dictators in his volume *History*.

The presidency, although of a different age, forged its way into Lowell's prose as well. In 1965, he contributed a brief essay on Abraham Lincoln to an anthology on the Gettysburg Address, published by the University of Illinois Press, in which he wrote that "Lincoln was the last President of the United States who could genuinely use words." A sonnet for Lincoln in *History* demonstrated further faith in the Commander-in-Chief: "You, our one genius in politics"—while raising a somewhat disconcerting question: "Your war was a continuation of politics— / is politics the discontinuation of murder?"

Combining political fervor with intellectual commitment, Lowell became involved in the 1963 founding of *The New York Review of Books*. The idea for the periodical was conceived one night during that year's 114-day New York newspaper strike, when the Lowells were having dinner with Jason and Barbara Epstein, who lived on the same street as the Lowells. The first issue was pasted together on the dining-room table of the Lowell apartment. Barbara Epstein, a former staff-member of the *Partisan Review,* and Robert Silvers, an editor of *Harper's Magazine* and *The Paris Review,* jointly shared the title of "editors," although Jason Epstein made many of the early editorial decisions. Elizabeth Hardwick was given the title "advisory editor" and later became the *Review*'s theater critic (the same position held earlier by her friend

Mary McCarthy at *Partisan*). Robert Lowell, on the six-man board of directors, remained a silent editorial voice, but was plainly visible as "official" obituary writer and poet-in-residence.

From the beginning the list of contributors read like the Hall of Fame of twentieth-century belles-lettres: Edmund Wilson, Isaiah Berlin, Erik Erikson, Lewis Mumford, W. H. Auden, Alfred Kazin, Mary McCarthy, Hannah Arendt, Susan Sontag. In many respects, despite occasional flare-ups over editorial policy, *The New York Review of Books* was the most scholarly, intelligent, and politically sophisticated periodical around, rivaling *The Times Literary Supplement* in London for top honors in sound intellectual book coverage and social commentary, picking up the slack left by the fast-sinking *Partisan Review.* That the *NYRB* created its proportionate share of enemies and angry critics goes without saying. Norman Podhoretz lost no opportunity to attack the *Review* in the pages of his own *Commentary,* lambasting its *"trahisons* ... against the defining values of the intellectual life."* Tom Wolfe called it "the chief theoretical organ of radical chic," thereby coining a new phrase. Irving Howe in the pages of *Dissent* wrote that the *Review* was "a link between campus 'leftism' and East Side stylishness, the worlds of Tom Hayden and George Plimpton." Even *Esquire* had a go at it, remarking that "from among the *New York Review*'s authors the next Stalin and his speechwriters will emerge."

Envisioning itself as the guardian of Ivy League culture, *The New York Review* made a practice of keeping watch over the trends and wrinkles, the opinions and social mores of the Eastern liberal intelligentsia. It was perhaps inevitable therefore that "radical chic" should indeed become more than a Tom Wolfe catchphrase, more than a passing euphemism for the political orientation of the *Review*'s editors, contributors, and critics. Thus while Francine du Plessix Gray covered the Black Panther rally in New Haven for the *Review,* Leslie Fiedler reported on his pot bust in Buffalo, and Elizabeth Hardwick dashed off a participant's account of the 1965 Selma march led by Martin Luther King. Peace marches in Washington and fund-raising extravaganzas thrown by Leonard Bernstein and Andy Warhol became the order of the day. The crowd surrounding the *Review* participated in "Poets for Peace" readings at Town Hall, attended civil rights rallies, signed letters to the editors of boundless newspapers and magazines in support of a plethora of causes. An emotional letter by Lowell on the Vietnam War appeared in the pages of *The New York Review* of February 29,

1968. Attentive readers of Lowell recognized the plea as a duplication of a speech by the title character in *Endecott and the Red Cross,* with the single difference being the substitution of the Vietnamese for the American Indians:

> We should have a national day of mourning, or better our own day of mourning, for the people we have sent into misery, desperation—that we have sent out of life; for our own soldiers, for the pro-American Vietnamese, and for the anti-American Vietnamese, those who have fought with unequaled ferocity, and probably hopeless courage, because they preferred annihilation to the despair of an American conquest.

This invocation was followed three years later by another in the same publication, this time in reaction to the mass murder of Vietnamese peasants by Lieutenant Calley and other American soldiers in an open ditch at My Lai: "No stumbling on the downward plunge from Hiroshima. . . . In a century perhaps no one will widen an eye at massacre, and only scattered corpses express a last histrionic concern for death."

On October 21, 1967, Lowell participated in the now historic march on the Pentagon, an event described at length in Norman Mailer's *The Armies of the Night,* and in a pair of poems by Lowell subtitled "The March," from *Notebook 1967–68:* "The remorseless, amplified harangues for peace— / lovely to lock arms, to march absurdly locked." Mailer, Lowell, Ginsberg, Linus Pauling, Noam Chomsky, the Reverend William Sloan Coffin, Dr. Benjamin Spock, Paul Goodman, Denise Levertov, Susan Sontag, Dwight Macdonald, and a hundred thousand others glided down the public thoroughfare of the nation's capital, the Heart of Darkness, like so many shining knights on a midnight mercy mission. Nobody seemed to mind that the occasion reeked not only of the sweet essence of *cannabis sativa* but of the more pungent odor of radical chic: this was a day to remember!

Norman Mailer, Lowell's fellow spokesman for the age, compared the event to some mystical advance by the ghosts of the Union Dead upon the Bastille on Liberation Day. In the course of the march he discovered that in Lowell lurked the grandeur of the American aristocrat, the noble savage, though Lowell in his poem on the march characterized himself as "cowardly" with "foolhardy heart." A trifle miffed by Lowell's past reference to him as "America's finest journalist" (as opposed to novelist), Mailer circumscribed his subject, made a modern highbrow icon of him. Reading it, one is struck by the feeling that the better the portrait, the worse Mailer's deed: "Lowell's shoulders had a slump, his modest stomach was pushed forward a hint, his chin was dropped to his chest as he stood at the microphone, pondering for a moment. One did not achieve the languid grandeur of that slouch in one generation—the grandsons of the first sons had best go through the best troughs in the best eating clubs at Harvard before anyone in the family could try for such elegant note." Lowell—tall, gray, lean but broad shouldered, with a soft, reluctant reading voice—was everything Mailer claimed he was, and more.

In the early evening of the day before the march, Lowell spoke briefly before demonstrators about Section 12 of the National Selective Service Act, pertaining to those "who knowingly counsel, aid, or abet another to refuse or evade registration or service in the armed forces." "I was asked earlier today," Lowell began in his fine stammering voice, "why I was not turning in my draft card, and I did not tell the reporter who inquired that it was a stupid question, although I was tempted to. I thought he should have known that I am now too old to have a draft card, but that it makes no difference. When some of us pledge ourselves to counsel and aid and abet any young men who wish to turn in their cards, why then you may be certain we are aware of the possible consequences and do not try to hide behind the technicality of whether we literally have a draft card or not. So I'm now saying to the gentlemen of the press that unlike the authorities who are running this country, we are not searching for tricks; we try to think of ourselves as serious men, if the press, that is, can comprehend such an effort, and we will protest this war by every means available to our conscience, and therefore not try to avoid whatever may arise in the way of retribution."

It was said softly, Mailer reported, on a current of intense indignation and Lowell had never looked more dignified nor more admirable. Each word seemed to come on a separate journey from the poet's mind to his throat, along a winding route or through an exorbitant gate. Each word cost him much—Lowell's fine grace was in the value he attached to words. "He seemed to emit a horror," wrote Mailer, "at the possibility of squandering them or leaving them abused, and political speeches had never seemed more difficult for him, and on the consequence, more necessary for statement."

At a second gathering that night Lowell delivered his poem "Waking Early Sunday Morning." He sounded, reported *The New York Times,* "as though he were reading with a hot potato in his mouth." His inspiration for the poem had been Marvell, the public poet of the seventeenth century and author of one of the best-known political poems in the language, "An Horatian Ode on Cromwell's Return to Ireland." "Waking Early Sunday Morning" is the twentieth-century equivalent of Marvell's ode, and a grim response to Wallace Stevens's hedonistic "Sunday Morning," a poem that had intrigued Lowell since his student days at Kenyon College. The Stevens poem, acclaimed by the New Critics, was a marvel of verbal elegance, an unironic elegy for the Christian ideal of god, the poem's final perspective being an exploration of the dark contingency of self. Lowell's daring rejoinder, written in loosely rhymed couplets (thus a return to the more formal air of *Lord Weary*), weaves back and forth between public and private commentary, between the bedroom and the podium. The work satirizes the war-heavy state, berates a god no longer interested in human affairs and a people not able to break free of constricting binds, and looks into the inner recesses of the poet's mind. There are several profound silences, a seriousness more intent than one usually associates with his global poems, with a thin edge of nervous humor that threatens to break the poem into ragged ends. The poem at once debunks and reaffirms, strikes out at the Machiavellians of society, defends the moral act, is both skeptical and humanistic, simultaneously sensuous and austere. The sequence terminates on a classic note of resignation and finiteness, with a sonorous yet realistic plea for the preservation of Spaceship Earth:

> peace to our children when they fall
> in small war on the heels of small
> war—until the end of time
> to police the earth, a ghost
> orbiting forever lost
> in our monotonous sublime.

The poem brought those gathered this night on the Pentagon steps to their feet, the applause building into a sweeping ovation. Mailer was moved. If Lowell was an aristocrat with an inborn air of superiority, he was also that rare combination of great strength and weakness. His customary stance was the mournful hunch. His was a figure of dejection, the soulful cavalier; but beneath the affectations of weariness, the literary logrollermanship, the neutralsmanship, was the man—fine, good, honorable, dedicated. Mailer took in the poet's despondent gaze, the wide-open, blue-green eyes through thick black-rimmed spectacles sliding down the nose, bulking forehead, long gray hair feathered and falling, elongated face, thin lips, jutting, muscular jaw: radiating darkness of soul but also quiet strength, his noble visage belonged to another age. To quote Mailer: "Robert Lowell gave off at times the unwilling haunted saintliness of a man who was repaying the moral debts of ten generations of ancestors. So his guilt must have been a tyrant of a chemical in his blood always ready to obliterate the best of his moods."

The Washington march terminated in expected fashion: draft-card burnings, tear gas, Mace, head busts, a random score of arrests. A grim but tender-eyed Lowell was arrested with the others and herded into a cell: "All night we slept to the sawing of immense / machines constructing: saws in circles slicing / white crescents, shafts and blocks, as if the scheming intellectuals had rebuilt Tyre and Sidon *ab ovo.*" Back in New York the poet resumed the struggle: "The world is very much under my skin and really seems like a murderous nightmare when one looks outward. . . . I am sick of nations armed to the teeth." He lost no opportunity to castigate the government's role in Vietnam. At Manhattan's Town Hall he introduced Soviet poet Andrei Voznesensky to an audience of fifteen hundred writers, students, teachers, book editors, Soviet Russians, and Russian émigrés. Voznesensky and Yevgeny Yevtushenko had led the post-Stalin poetry charts in the Soviet Union and were popular attractions whenever they toured the U.S. They did not so much recite their poetry as perform it. Voznesensky exploded his verse on stage, his voice deep, reverential, moving, the audience shaken by the drama, thrilled by the virtuoso performer. Dressed in a light brown suit with a bright yellow silk shirt open at the throat, his legs spread, one hand on a hip and the other beating the air, he drove home poem after poem in his native, singsong Russian.

Lowell, leaving no opportunity unchallenged, used the Russian poet's reading engagement, the finale of a four-week American tour, to comment on certain political issues. "This is indiscreet," he remarked after praising Voznesensky's work, "but both our countries, I think, have really terrible governments. But we do the best we can with them, and they'd better do the best they can with each other or the world will cease to be here." Voznesensky, dutifully avoiding mention of either the Soviet or U.S. governments during his tour, turned away when asked by reporters to comment on Lowell's remarks, his face showing no reaction.

Similar remarks on Lowell's part had been advanced shortly before during his introduction of Yevtushenko to a large audience at the Poetry Center of the Ninety-second Street "Y." The American poet described the Russian as a "world-wide cultural and political figure, one who had stood up for a number of causes, among them the right of poets to talk about politics." Then, referring to his own political activities, he offered in a fillip of irony the thought that "if you're Jane Austen, you can ignore Napoleonic wars if you want to." "The undercurrent of Lowell's brief introduction," wrote an on-the-scene journalist, "seemed more than just hands-across-the-border protocol. There was an edge to his words, as of hanging lightning; and the diffidence of delivery, the way he clasped and unclasped his hands, the steps he took (as if in pain) away and toward the microphone, all added to a taut portrait in motion of a middle-aged poet doing battle with himself—and in a way for the audience looking on—to find that means by which art and conscience merge and must stand." To test the water, Lowell made a small joke of what Yevtushenko had told him, that we must find a way "to get rid of the two black cats that stand in our paths," meaning their respective governments. He ended his introduction with what seemed an invocation: "I have a sense of a classical moment, of someone Greek standing in the wing, preferably a lady, telling us that the hour is one of danger. . . ." He hesitated, pursed his mouth, put away the few scratch notes he held, notes that he hardly referred to in the course of his talk; he then introduced Yevtushenko, whose method of declamation, of "styling" poetry as an acted-out experience combined the stage tactics of Mayakovsky with those of Dylan Thomas.

Lowell's preoccupation with radical politics found a new cause in the April-May 1968 student uprising and sit-in on the Morningside Heights campus of Columbia University. Lowell commemorated the student strike in a medley of *Notebook* poems called "May." His involvement in the student rebellion culminated in a biting exchange of letters in *Commentary* with Diana Trilling, wife of Lionel Trilling; an essay of Mrs. Trilling ("On the Steps of Low Library"), attacking the SDS, appeared in the same publication. Playing on the title of the opening to Mailer's *Armies of the Night* ("The Steps of the Pentagon"), the essayist debunked Lowell's overtolerance of youth at the same time that she lambasted the half-baked experiments and ideas that she saw demonstrated by radical students at Columbia. Her article drew a clear distinction between the various political factions of the day and drew attention to the splintering effect on liberalism precipitated by the countercultural and antiwar movements. Lowell's letter of response sharpened the dilemma further, pointing to Mrs. Trilling's lack of sympathy for the innocence and idealism of the young, those who were trying to escape from the system without getting caught in the rigid ideologies that had once ruled. To her mind the student body at Columbia was ignorant, petulant, and self-indulgent, the mainstay of a pop culture that managed to be both alienated and modish, whereas the Trillings considered themselves part of a class structure devoted to order, rationality, and tradition.

Lowell decried her obsessive need to categorize, to pit Old Left and New Left against one another. "I want to explain to her, finally I hope, that I have never been New Left, Old Left, or Liberal," he ventured. "I wish to turn the clock back with every breath I draw, but I hope I have the courage to occasionally cry out against those who wrongly rule us, and wrongly lecture us." Lowell's indictment of the Trillings was based primarily on their increasing admiration and defense of middle-class values, their refusal to speak out against the Vietnam War or in favor of other liberal causes. Lowell actually saw the young of the sixties as a multitude brought up to believe that the nation was a wonderfully moral place. When they discovered after such atrocities as Vietnam and the Bay of Pigs, that it was something quite different, they locked arms and joined ranks with a spontaneity that had not been witnessed in this country since the American Revolution. But unlike the colonists who beat back the British, the youth of the sixties had no overall game plan, no program, not even a Declaration of Independence to guide them. And yet it was this very naïveté and openness that attracted Lowell to them in the first place. He admired the movement because it arose out of moral indignation and grew despite its amorphousness and lack of precise definition.

Conversely, it was this very shapelessness that alarmed the Trillings. Mrs. Trilling accused Lowell of being a trendist, a publicity hound, an "old man" trying to cling to some mysterious notion of youth. It was the usual story: the redaction of a sensitive issue to the tiresome, frustrating nod of intellectual debate, the great and near-great scrabbling over one another, battling one another, each calling attention to the other's faults and to his or her own unassailable virtues.

The same spring, while campaigning in behalf of Eugene McCarthy as Democratic nominee for President, Lowell was awarded an honorary doctorate by Yale University, providing him still another excuse to sound off about the war and other public tragedies. He had met McCarthy in 1967 and was soon accompanying the candidate on the primary trail, speaking up for him before primaries in California, Indiana, and Oregon, acting the part of personal adviser and intellectual companion whenever McCarthy "wanted to get away from the hail and brimstone of the campaign, and talk and relax and talk seriously." McCarthy, the great white liberal hope, became in his desperate role a heroic figure in Lowell's eyes. Lowell took his stand on "Why I'm for McCarthy" in *The New Republic* (April 12, 1968):

> I feel no competence or longing to take on the burden of a political logician or polemicist. Of the announced or seriously offered Democratic or Republican candidates, only Senators Kennedy and McCarthy seem morally or intellectually allowable. Of these McCarthy is preferable, first for his negative qualities: lack of excessive charisma, driving ambition, machinelike drive, and the too great wish to be President. But I am for him most for what he possesses, his variable, tolerant and courageous mind, lungs that breathe the air. When the race against President Johnson was hopeless and intractable, he alone hoped, entered and won.

Sundry members of McCarthy's staff have attested to the inefficiency with which the campaign was run; there seems also to have been much resentment on the staff's part directed against Lowell. An important staff member termed Lowell "McCarthy's astrologer," one of a "circle of sycophants and friends" that included journalists Shana Alexander and Mary McGrory. Arthur Herzog, the popular novelist, recalled an occasion when Lowell discussed poetry with McCarthy "while speech writers, press aides, and others waited impatiently in the hall." Richard Stout, in his book *People,* observed that during one important briefing, "Lowell broke in with: 'You know, Senator, this reminds me of the situation that existed between King James I and the Archbishop of Canterbury in 1604.' Spasms of chuckling ensued, and the briefing went down the drain." Another campaign aide, Andreas Teuber, held Lowell personally responsible for McCarthy's poor showing in his televised debate against Robert Kennedy, his chief opponent for the Democratic nomination. Lowell apparently joined McCarthy for the limousine ride to the television studio where the debate was held. En route they composed "a twentieth-century version of 'Ode to St. Cecilia's Day' in the back seat." By the time McCarthy arrived at the studio, he was totally distracted and unprepared.

Steven Gould Axelrod, in his study of Lowell, comments on several encounters that the poet had with Robert Kennedy during this crucial campaign period. When they first met, at Jacqueline Kennedy's urging, Lowell "tried to read portions of *The Education of Henry Adams* aloud to Kennedy." In the middle of the reading, Kennedy suddenly rose and excused himself. Lowell followed him right to the door of the bathroom, still reading. Bobby shut the door and said, "If you don't mind." Lowell responded, "If you were Louis XIV, you wouldn't mind," a reference to the French monarch who thought nothing of relieving himself in public. On a second occasion Lowell met Kennedy alone, ostensibly to urge more cooperation between the two candidates. Kennedy insisted that McCarthy withdraw from the race immediately. Lowell responded, "These are just debater's arguments. You mustn't talk to me this way." Kennedy: "Well, I guess we have nothing more to say." Lowell: "I wish I could think up some joke that would cheer you, but it won't do any good." Commenting on their meeting, Lowell later informed McCarthy that he felt like Rudolph Hess parachuting into Scotland.

In public Lowell had mostly negative things to say about Kennedy, characterizing him as "shy, calculating, and rude, tarnished with former power and thirsting to return to that power." But this, suggests Axelrod, was merely campaign invective. Lowell admitted that Kennedy "is a lot better than he seems to a lot of people." As an occasional poet, McCarthy was the sentimental favorite with Lowell; the two shared a "temperamental affinity." But Lowell was aware of McCarthy's shortcomings, his inability to lead. "Who will swear you wouldn't / have done good to the country," he writes in "For Eugene McCarthy" *(Notebook).* McCarthy was too naive, too soft for the job: "Picking a quarrel / with you is like picking the petals of the daisies." "R.F.K.," also included in *Notebook,* and penned after the assassination, lauds Kennedy as one of Plutarch's men, "made by hand"—

> Doom was woven in your nerves, your shirt,
> woven in the great clan; they too were loyal,
> and you too were loyal to them, to death.
> . . . Untouched
> alone in my Plutarchan bubble, I miss
> you. . . .

Lowell had given Jacqueline Kennedy a Plutarch, which Robert Kennedy, the poet later discovered, borrowed and read. Lowell, always fascinated by poets like Wyatt, Raleigh, and Edmund Burke, who were also statesmen and showed a double inspiration, tended to place Kennedy in the same category. He saw in Kennedy that class of American hero of whom epic poems are sometimes written—another Robert Gould Shaw, another Charles Russell Lowell. Conscious of his nobility, Kennedy was also extremely aware of the danger of pride and fate.

All of Lowell's achievers, his seekers, his artists, his warriors, and the malevolent forces that try to control and destroy them, are to be found within the sheepmeadow of his *Notebook* landscape. His figures are real and they are illusions at the same time. They become at once themselves but also the machinery for creating myths. Events become the stuff of myth as well. The 1968 Chicago Democratic convention, with its lunatic-asylum street scenes and political upheaval, fueled the section of *Notebook 1967–68* that Lowell styled "The Races"; youth (including Black Power groups, Weathermen, hippies, dippies, and Yippies), love, violence, war, pacifism, the Chicago Police Department, and Lowell's presence as witness are the synchronic conceits that hold this particular myth together. "After five nights of Chicago," bleats his poem "After the Convention," "I am so tired and hard, clichés are wisdom, / the clichés of paranoia."

29

LOVE AND FAME

LOWELL'S poetry kept pace with his correspondence; both were strewn with notations on the ills of aging and infirmity. "Can I suppose I am finished with wax flowers / and have earned my grass on the minor slopes of Parnassus?" he inquired in "Reading Myself" *(Notebook)*. From his fortieth year, Lowell had expressed apprehension over the trauma of growing old. A letter to Cousin Harriet (April 1957) remarked that the author had noticed thinning spots on his head, but that his old classmates, whose heads he carefully surveyed, were having the same problem.

The effects of illness and aging were slowly but surely claiming Lowell's confreres. Toward the end of 1964, after several years of severe depression, Randall Jarrell suffered a complete breakdown, landing in the psychiatric ward of a private hospital. Lowell, familiar with the symptoms of the illness, advised Jarrell that the worst part of it was the groveling low-as-dirt purgatorial feeling with which one emerged from the bout; this sensation, however, was only temporary: Jarrell could expect a full and rapid recovery. But Jarrell's illness was more severe than anyone realized. A year after his release from the hospital, Randall Jarrell committed suicide. Lowell penned an obituary for *The New York Review of Books* that he later read aloud to students and faculty at the annual Founder's Day ceremony at Kenyon College, adding to his text several minutes of extemporaneous talk. He recalled the arguments over Shakespeare's sonnets years earlier between Jarrell and Ransom. He remembered his own literary discussions with Jarrell over 15-cent chocolate milkshakes in the Kenyon College canteen. Nobody had been more immersed than Jarrell in classic literature and poetry. Along with Auden, Randall Jarrell had provided the literary world with some of the shrewdest poetic criticism of the century. Randall's *Poetry and the Age* would live as long as language lived.

The Age of Anxiety and its direct aftermath, full of broken promises and shattered illusions, claimed additional lives: Theodore Roethke, who once accused Lowell face-to-face of owning "a tin ear," died in 1963; Delmore Schwartz in 1966; John Berryman in 1972. Roethke, institutionalized almost as frequently as Lowell, knew of what he spoke when he wrote:

> What's madness but nobility of soul
> At odds with circumstance? The day's on fire!
> I know the purity of pure despair,
> My shadow pinned against a sweating wall.
> That place among the rocks—is it a cave,
> Or winding path? The edge is what I have.

No other poet wrote with greater sorrow than Roethke—or with greater joy. Lowell wrote with greater depth, addressing himself to a wider spectrum of themes. But Roethke, as even the picayune Yvor Winters has attested, was the master of literary form, more attuned to form than any poet since Rilke. Following Roethke's alcohol-induced death, Allen Tate lavished Lowell with one of his rare compliments stating that among the writers of his day, Roethke, older than Lowell by ten years, was the only peer that he had when it came to the quality of their writing, although they were totally opposite in other respects.

John Berryman, himself too often a guest on locked alcoholic wards, had turned in his poetry from the outgoing, public, historical world of *Homage to Mistress Bradstreet* to the private woefulness of *The Dream Songs,* a year-to-year cyclical record of his drinking bouts, love affairs, literary misadventures, and depressions—a chronicle that slowly developed into a poetic exploration of a father's suicide, the loss of love, the deaths of friends, the devilish godliness of drink, the poet's own projected suicide. He had penned his own epitaph, as it were, full of self-recrimination, violence, hilarity, guilt, and expiation.

By the time he took his life—leaping from a swaying suspension bridge in Minneapolis onto the frozen Mississippi—Berryman had come to grips with his own mortality. Killed by "the giant killer," Berryman was a driven man, his life colored by authoritativeness, cockiness, the pangs of success, the pressure of reaching the top and of remaining there. Success, that dazzling "bitch-goddess," that unattainable bluest patch of sky, exacted from its pursuers more than they could give, more than they could afford to give. Drink was the great solvent, the great catalyst, the inspiration for all great ideas, the problem solver, the equalizer. It made poor men rich and rich men poor, made fools of poets and poets of fools. The drive for success, the uphill struggle toward fame, drove Berryman to the bottle. The pressures of "making it" hung heavy over an entire generation. Berryman, Jarrell, Roethke, Schwartz, were all bitten by it. In "Dream Song 153" Berryman sings of his dead driven friends, including the not nearly deceased Lowell:

> I'm cross with god who has wrecked this generation.
> First he seized Ted, then Richard, Randall, and now Delmore.
> In between he gorged on Sylvia Plath.
> That was a first rate haul. He left alive
> fools I could number like a kitchen knife
> but Lowell he did not touch.

If Berryman harbored one peculiar habit it was his overbearing need to lionize his associates, particularly those whose imaginative works he admired. Delmore Schwartz in the 1940's, Saul Bellow and Robert Lowell in the late 1950's and early 1960's, became the anointed recipients of his devotional trumpet bleatings. "You are only the best poet around," he wrote to Lowell upon reading *Life Studies.* Lowell's pressing desire for admiration and respect was partially satisfied by Berryman and partially by Elizabeth Bishop, whose letters to him were saturated with benevolent words for his latest works. On one occasion she wrote that the power and drive of his poems were such that she dared not read him while working on something of her own, lest she be unwittingly influenced. Surprisingly, Wallace Stevens said much the same thing, though not to Lowell's face. Lowell drew sustenance from the compliments lavished upon him by his fellow poets, but for some reason found Berryman's vociferous laudings harder to swallow than most. "Thrustingly vehement in liking" was the phrase he offered to describe Berryman's obsequious tendency. But in "For John Berryman," a poem written at a later date, Lowell showed himself to be "thrustingly vehement" in his own right, and a bit of a self-immolating egoist as well: "John [he wrote], we used the language as if we made it." To which one is tempted to reply: Yes, and that's precisely the problem.

The best minds of that promising and accomplished generation had indeed been destroyed by madness. Lowell endured, but at enormous cost—personal and otherwise. "I have nothing," he told an audience that had trudged through snow and ice to hear him recite his verse. "I'm afraid I haven't written anything. I'm drained." He was more than drained: he was barely alive. True, since 1963 he had been teaching three days a week at Harvard, though he was sometimes forced to remind himself of that fact. He was commuting between New York and Boston, not enjoying either one. Elizabeth Hardwick, meanwhile, was teaching part-time at Barnard College. And Harriet was a student at the Dalton School, a progressive grade school and high school on Manhattan's Upper East Side. Her Dalton teachers described her as a bright, serious, retiring student. Extremely shy as a child, her parents were forced to organize social functions—parties, picnics, and the like—to help her make friends. In 1975 she enrolled at Barnard College. Her Dalton years were duly recorded in a bevy of her father's poems, as were his travels during this hectic period—to Jerusalem, Cairo (where he guest-taught at the University of Cairo for part of a semester), Mexico, England, Venezuela, Brazil, and Argentina (where he still paid regular calls on Elizabeth Bishop).

There was a sameness to Lowell's days in New York that began to weary him. He slept late, lunched out, often with what his old friends called "his girl of the moment," one of whom—a beautiful young poetess less than half his age—said, "His depressions generally disappear with his second drink and reappear with his fifth. From that moment on, it's all downhill." His luncheons, at Quo Vadis or 21 or The Palm Court at the Plaza, were sometimes followed by a futile hour or two at a gym. Evenings he might read, have dinner with his family or a friend, attend a party—usually only fine and fancy ones—where he proceeded to drink himself into an even deeper stupor. The "quick scanning eyes" with which he had once trolled rooms full of partygoers were now bleary and bloodshot. The dynastic, artistic voice became husky and hoarse.

Gradually, as he became more famous and visible, he became less inspired, less and less himself, alternately splashing eloquences and insults into the faces of wide-eyed young followers. He could be a breezy reed talking down a classroom full of literary auditors or a flash torrid in female pursuit. His luncheons soon assumed new forms. Sprinted affairs and tumblers of scotch and bourbon kept him young while he quickly aged. Public displays of rage, once in an Argentinian nightclub, once in a Boston restaurant, a third time in the lobby of a posh London hotel, made the New York gossip columnists sit up and take notice. Wherever he went during these difficult days, Lowell left a trail of ruin and chaos, engaging in imbroglios, insulting colleagues, playing the inebriated fool and insulted lover. He tried punishing himself by washing his face in lye, and periodically fell prey to bouts of depression and hysteria. During these manic episodes he confused himself with Christ, St. Paul, and Hitler—"especially Hitler, whose dark spirit rose violently to possess him," remarked Stanley Kunitz. A second Kunitz recollection re-creates a visit he paid to Lowell at McLean's Hospital: "He read 'Lycidas' aloud to me, in his improved version, firmly convinced that he was the author of the original."

Even when not under the influence of alcohol or his own madness, the Jewish question remained something of a conundrum for him. On the one hand he signed a 750-word appeal calling on writers in the Soviet Union to use their influence in restoring Jewish cultural institutions and facilities; on the other hand he refused to sign a public appeal for American support of Israel at the height of the Middle East crisis in June 1967. "I thought," he advised the press, "we should have guaranteed the boundaries of Israel and, if necessary, helped to defend them. I did not think the United States should have forcibly opened the Gulf of Aqaba. President Johnson's handling of the affair turned out to be both correct and humane. However, this war should have never happened; for this, Russia and America, the suppliers of weapons, are heavily to blame."

He was more tenacious about such affairs during those manic highs, when the sotto voce charge on his part had it that Jewishness was other than an American literary theme, that it lay at the very core of the arts, that Semites controlled the arts in all its amber shades. These parochial intimations reached hurricane proportion under the spell of alcohol, a state that saw him become less good company and more a spectacle. The shrill voice of that anguished persona produced sounds that only he could recognize. This was no moral blot on his character, rather the result of excessive indulgence in his hyper self. Himself again, he would proudly point to his own fractional Jewish heritage and to those Jews he called friends. Subsequent volumes contained poems of gentle Jewish lore; several touch on the harrowing experience of the Holocaust. "Deutschland über Alles" *(Notebook 1967–68)* depicts Hitler as a mad dog: "his eyes were glowing coals, the world turned dark." A painful saga of impasse, it realistically portrays the horror inside the House of Carnage.

Lowell's friends tolerated his strange, sometimes brutish, behavior only because they recognized his instability and admired his skill, the grinding labor that went into his work. "I have never known anyone so singularly immersed in writing as was Cal," said Stanley Kunitz. Lowell seemed to take a certain grim pleasure from his growing reputation as an enfant terrible, a spoiled (but hard-working) soul from a privileged and historical background. He insulted his friends by letter and in person and thought nothing of taking up with women and then dropping them without a word. His closest friends rarely questioned his behavior, while others were justifiably perplexed. If he was the personification of "clear-eyed ego" (as he boasted in one of his poems), he was also a wretched, brawling conniver, a self-absorbed literary politician of the meanest, most ordinary sort. At literary gatherings he relished playing the game of rating the opposition, particularly when the opposition was present. He had them all precisely ranked and rated— all below him—and with "high-keyed zest and malice" thought nothing of reeling them off. Fame and titles attracted him with the same demon draw they had once exercised upon James Russell Lowell. Of writers of his own generation, only Norman Mailer (and perhaps Gore Vidal) played the game so violently.

"Amid the complex, dull horrors of the 1960's poetry is a loophole. It's a second chance of some sort: things that the age turns thumbs down on you can get out in poetry." Such is the cathartic experience of writing poetry that it enabled Lowell, as he here testified, to chart an inner course in which commitment to art took precedence over everything, from his now failing second marriage to the escalation of the country's political dilemma. He had filled his time with other projects but after *For the Union Dead* never completely stopped writing poems. *Near the Ocean,* published in 1967, covered no new ground; it merely retouched a canvas fairly streaked with the colors of previous tomes. It did not advance Lowell's literary reputation so much as consolidate it.

A small, in-between book, *Near the Ocean* is divided into two nearly equal halves. The first half consists of seven strictly measured original poems, scenic ruminations set partially in Maine, partially in New York, poems to persons, and a sixteen-line elegy for Theodore Roethke that pays homage to Roethke's apostrophes to nature. The volume's second half consists of translations from Juvenal and Horace, from the Brunetto Latini canto of Dante's *Inferno,* and from the Spaniards Quevedo and Gongora, dealing with the theme of the ruins of time, the struggle between transience and permanence. The two halves complement each other, reflecting Lowell's disillusionment with contemporary America. Overall, the volume attempts to draw a comparison between the corruption of power and government in ancient Rome and the corruption of power in atomic-age America. The Roman propensity for greed and lust, as reflected in Lowell's imitations, has presumably washed over the American soil. Between Rome and America lies the ocean of the title. America is near the ocean in the sense that it is as close to being drowned and destroyed as its ancient predecessor. In Juvenal's Rome "each shadow hides a knife or spear"; Quevedo in "The Ruins of Time," entertains his own vision of the collapse of civilization: "I saw the musty shingles of my house, / raw wood and fixed once, now a wash of moss / eroded by the ruin of the age / turning all fair and green things into waste."

These versions do not stray as far from their originals as the poet's previous translations. At the same time the titles of the seven new poems express a certain neutrality that the poems themselves do not convey. The book's first original sequence, "Waking Early Sunday Morning," with its fruitless and sterile God ("Each day, He shines through darker glass"), is not just an antiwar poem but also a sequence of harsh self-scrutiny, reflecting different levels of the poet's irony: "Dim confession, coy revelation, / liftings, listless self-imitation, / whole days when I could hardly speak, / came pluming home unshaven, weak / and willing to read anyone / things done before and better done." Written in the formal mode of rhymed iambic tetrameter (like some of Robert Frost's descriptive poems, in addition to Marvell's), "Waking Early Sunday Morning" contrasts the poet's own freedom to feel and think with the global unfreedom of a world blanketed by bombs and napalm. Fascinated by the symbolic value of the salmon—a fish that mysteriously returns to the waters of its birth to spawn its own young and then to die—the poet begins his work with a stanza that describes the ichthyological process: "O to break loose, like the chinook / salmon jumping and falling back, / nosing up to the impossible / stone and bone-crushing waterfall. . . ." Constraint and freedom in their varied forms are a major theme in both poem and volume.

The title sequence, dedicated to Elizabeth Hardwick, is an inordinately complex contemplation of the human condition; rife with grandiose connections, the poem borrows themes and treatments from a variety of sources—mythical, intellectual, personal. The critic Jonathan Raban recommends reading it as a sequence of discontinuous scenes, "each one an enactment of Man's relations with Woman." There are suggestions in the poem of Lowell's first marriage, expanding into his exhausted second marriage, the drama played out against a decimated New England backdrop. The work is likewise an in-depth examination of political currents, the individual in society buried beneath the weight and power wielded by the government, corporations, and the military. The despoiled universe is matched by the poet's doomed marriage, itself paralleled by the tenuous relations that exist between the Arab countries and Israel: "Lost in the Near Eastern dreck, / the tyrant and tyrannicide / lie like the bridegroom and the bride." A psychological unification of sexual and political cycles, "Near the Ocean" is a doomsaying poem patched together out of private allusions and public concerns, the ocean a symbol of the permanence that endures long after man's final demise. Calling this reverie his private "Dover Beach," Lowell closes it on a note that soars:

> Sleep, sleep. The ocean, grinding stones,
> can only speak the present tense;
> nothing will age, nothing will last,
> or take corruption from the past.
>
> Monster loved for what you are,
> till time, that buries us, lay bare.

"Fourth of July in Maine" was occasioned by an Independence Day parade down the main street of Castine, still the site of Lowell's summers. The holiday provided the poet with an excuse to examine the state of the Union, the fate of American history, that "dark design / spun by God and Cotton Mather." Although light in timbre, the poem espies darkness and destruction wherever it peers; running-down gardens and propped-up barns mirror the country's self-ruination. No golden age here, only a dying past and a troubled future.

"Central Park," influenced in part by Williams's *Paterson* segment "Sunday in the Park," is just as gloomy. No pastoral or peaceful ode to life in the city, this poem is a purposeful and frenetic study of civic corruption and urban violence. Written at a time when Lowell was in psychoanalysis and in the habit of walking daily across the park to see his East Side therapist, the poem is appropriately introspective, with glimpses of sexual impoverishment and spiritual deadness; it crackles loudest when describing the plight of modern man trapped in a mechanistic and figurative jungle. Central Park—a paradise by day, an inferno by night—serves nicely as Lowell's jungle purgatory, a place peopled after dark by perverts and killers. The poem deals with two distinct strains, the depraved and lawless versus the authoritarian and rich—in Lowell's eyes the more dangerous of the two: "Then night, the night—the jungle hour, / the rich in his slit-windowed tower . . . / Old Pharaohs starving in your foxholes, / with painted banquets on the walls, / fists knotted in your captives' hair, / tyrants with little food to spare." Juvenal's frightening description of a shadowy Rome ("each shadow hides a knife or spear") is resurrected at the end of "Central Park," the poet's intimation being that authority and the law are more threatening than the criminal element they are supposed to deter:

> We beg delinquents for our life.
> Behind each bush, perhaps, a knife;
> each landscaped crag, each flowering shrub,
> hides a policeman with a club.

Notebook 1967–68, published in 1969, was a bulky package of 274 sonnets composed principally over that two-year span. "I lean heavily to the rational," the author explained in a prose note, "but am devoted to surrealism." The rationalism is based on his repeated use of the conventional fourteen-line standard; his surrealism—Lowell's term for it—finds its origin in his decision to shuck rhyme and meter, both of which he had used through most of *Near the Ocean.* Berryman's *Dream Songs* played by the same rules regarding free verse; but while Berryman's "I" was frequently disguised by the comic voices of Henry and Mr. Bones, Lowell's was a candid "I," a personal "I." Berryman's poetic voice was more playful and less formal than Lowell's. Both poets conceived of their respective works as voluminous poem-novels. "The poems in my book," remarked Lowell, "are written as one poem, jagged in pattern, but not a conglomeration or sequence of related material. It is not a chronicle or almanac; many events turn up, many others of equal or greater reality do not. This is not my diary, my confession, not a puritan's too literal pornographic honesty, glad to share private embarrassment, and triumph." (Berryman was just as anxious to prove that Henry's voice in *Dream Songs* was not his—Berryman's—voice. Henry was an imaginary character—"not the poet, not me.")

Lowell's negations aside, the individual sonnets often take fuel from private obsessions. And while the events that chart the volume's topography remain well known—Vietnam, the black riots in Newark, the Pentagon march, the assassinations of the Kennedys and Martin Luther King, the 1968 Republican and Democratic conventions, the Russian occupation of Czechoslovakia—the privacies attached to these occurrences help round out this immense tale of the tribe. It is true, on the other hand, that the confessional material as such is more controlled and formalistic than in former volumes. F. W. Dupee called it *"poisie à clef,"* arguing that its measured control made it Lowell's strongest volume to date; Robert Penn Warren thought the poems strongly defined, making them forceful statements, with Lowell's imprint clearly upon them. It was as though Lowell had found new sources for his expression that he had never used before, or had never used with this particular voice. There was a distinct originality in the way that these carefully wrought poems touched experience and then eluded it, weaving back and forth from darkness to brightness, somehow enlightening the fount of their inspiration. The reader of Lowell, in this instance, finds that they are not simply the reflection of a slice of life, but rather poems that have somehow been self-generated and then reproduced of themselves in a seemingly unending pattern. In Lowell's own words, *Notebook* was "a hybrid poem, largely invention and largely record." *Life Studies* reproduced the poet's past as through a camera lens or on a canvas, while *Notebook* was a record, a slide show of his present life, the day-to-day events dictating much of the volume's movement. Seen from a slightly different angle, Lowell is a storyteller weaving tales out of the mythos of the zeitgeist, distilling nectar, sweet and sour, from the blooming profusion of life. The resultant mini chapters cohere into a single, effusive epic, similar in certain respects to other modernistic sagas, not only *Dream Songs,* but Williams's *Paterson,*

Olson's *Maximus Poems,* Pound's *Cantos,* and Stevens's *Notes Toward a Supreme Fiction,* a vibrant collocation of tentatively arranged meditations.

That was more or less the idea, the creation of a poem that unfolds gradually, the record of a large and compelling mind enduring the vulgarity and muddle of the late 1960's, and also a logbook of people, places, things, events, happenings, and meanings; there are no continuing characters as such (save the author), and sonnets are organized under simple titles or rubrics: "The Muse," "Symbols," "Names," "Writers." Their cumulative effect is ideogrammatic, the illumination fusing into a total picture. All in all, however, the picture formed remains out of focus, the volume failing to cohere as manifestly as it probably should. Reading it is akin to flipping through a book of meditations; the sonnets reflect shifting beams of light, permeating the water, coloring objects on the bottom with light and dark shades. There are moments of intense illumination, moments when a clear pattern begins to emerge. *Notebook 1967–68,* in considerable measure, has a richness and color in its language and imagery that has reminded readers of Elizabethan writings. One must look to Yeats to find a poet capable of producing so solid a poetic underpinning—not the Yeats of the big setpieces but the Yeats, for instance, of *The Wild Swans at Coole,* where there is a sense that the basic experience must have inspired the poetry, rather than vice versa. Too often in poetry the language is merely framed or shaped to accommodate a poet's theme. In the stronger works of the best poets the entire atmosphere breathes, the poem lifting off the page in veritable flight, a poetry more of the spirit than the intellect.

Yet for all their élan and eloquence, the sonnets too often seem artificial, injected with false excitements, the poet a main character but somehow not at the core of his work. The sonnets spin off on meaningless tangents, the images so extreme and arch and sensational that they fail to convince. The Self that holds *Life Studies* and *For the Union Dead* together is so scattered here as to seem practically abstract. The focal center that gave substance to previous works and through which the poet was able to view and reshape the world is noticeably absent. There is nothing to hold the magnitude of released energy together. Having taught us how to read his poems, how to interpret the apocalyptic structure and epistemology of a new sensibility, Lowell is off and running again, creating still another new concept of reality, a teleology suffused with skepticism and doubt. One must wonder about the decision to compose poems in the form of the sonnet, while abjuring the sonnet's essential properties—meter and rhyme. To write an unrhymed sonnet seems a meaningless and arbitrary exercise, meant to startle rather than inform, an imitation of Berryman's more sensible regular form (three stanzas of six lines each) in *Dream Songs.*

Lowell's attempt to wed convention to innovation, formality to colloquy, centers on three major themes: autobiography, history, and realpolitik. While the Lowell of the Left focuses modishly on Che Guevara, Martin Luther King, Robert Kennedy, Norman Mailer, Stalin, and Eugene McCarthy, the right eye glints outward to Agamemnon, Sir Thomas More, Napoleon, Nixon, King David, and Attila the Hun. Like characters that come and go in a novel these and dozens of other personages keep the flow of action at a peak. In one sense they constitute the story's center; at its outer edge are the loose strands of numerous subthemes and events waiting to be tied: insanity, hostility, fame, the New York intellectual, art, Harvard, Boston, family, alcoholism, and suicide; but there is also much about the Puritans, Federalists, and Transcendentalists—groups and subjects that link the poet ineffably to the American past. One might remark that Lowell attempts to cover too much ground; the results are mixed.

The anguish of mental illness as documented in some dozen poems is a subject that has cropped up before in Lowell, but nowhere as emphatically as here. The hospital experience, as described by other confessional poets, is usually airbrushed in shades of white, symbolizing both purity and death. Thus, for Sylvia Plath, the white light in "Fever 103°" is "hygienic as heaven," the hospital sheet is a "snowfield." Mental illness was never so inviolate, so virginal, for Lowell; at choice moments he is able to inject a fillip of humor. Humor softens the glare of his despair. His mental plight, coupled with an ironic wit, lends his most downcast poems a life-affirming quality that other extremist poets lack. "Mania" recalls a love affair the poet had in 1958 while undergoing treatment in hospital. "Hydrotherapy" explores some of the less therapeutic results of water therapy and applies the symbol of the mode to the world-at-large. "The Doctor" and "Another Doctor" deal with the problems of patient-physician relations on one level, the shortcomings of orthodox analysis on another. "In Sickness," the most explicit treatment of mental illness in the volume, summarizes Lowell's experiences with the disease:

Sometimes my mind is a rocked and dangerous bell,
I climb the spiral steps to my own music;

. . .

the cure: rest, exercise, fresh air and meals,

. . .

In sickness, the mind and body make a marriage.

Father, mother, grandparents, aunts, and uncles inhabit Lowell's literary extravaganza. Aunt Sarah ("who once jilted an Astor") makes an appearance, as does Beau Sabreur. The poet's wife and daughter fade in and out. *"Das ewig Weibliche"* ("The Eternal Feminine"), a title expropriated from the final, famous words of Goethe's *Faust,* tackles the question of the female's role in marriage; James Russell Lowell published a poem by the same title in *Heartsease and Rue* in memory of his second wife, Frances Dunlap Lowell.

Where *Life Studies* was all recollection, *Notebook 1967–68* is mostly the present moment colored by historical anecdote. Both volumes capitalize on aspects of the confessional voice—not in the sense of sensational self-gossip but as a method by which the poet transforms "the untidy stuff of life into the formal perfection of art." Confessionalism allows the poet to confide a personal faith or conviction, to subject his entire life to artistic interpretation. The source of the creative act becomes the poet's daily peregrinations, the process of creativity existing in the poet's ability to combine two or more habitually incompatible ideas, images, representations, or what have you. The inherent conflict in such a system, in one reader's words, is comparable to "a stone being thrown uphill against the downward rush of habit." Because the confessional material in *Notebook 1967–68* is handled in a more controlled and formal manner, one would expect it to reflect a more complete, less haphazard look. It may be that the speed with which Lowell rushed out these sonnets—four or five daily over a period of months—prevented them from coming out looking more polished. Things he saw or felt or read were "drift in the whirlpool." His haste left an unpleasant aftertaste in Lowell's mouth. He sensed that the looseness and jagged finish of the collection detracted from its appeal, and by 1970 had revised and rearranged the poems to form a new edition, which dropped the dates from its title. The preface to *Notebook* apologized to the reader for asking him to buy the book a second time: "I couldn't stop writing, and have handled my published book as if it were a manuscript." To this he added, "about a hundred of the old poems have been changed, some noticeably. More than ninety new poems have been added." The brunt of the sonnets that he reworked were not noticeably improved. The additions to the collection only added to its fragmented and disjointed appearance. What had worked better as a kaleidoscopic two-year scrapbook had grown into a shapeless, unwieldy mass. The original organic quality of *Notebook 1967–68* had vanished and in its place was an amorphous manuscript in drastic need of revision.

There were some questionable locutions in *Notebook*. In several instances, such as "Night Sweat," Lowell simply extracted the poem from a previous volume, cut it to sonnet length, and tossed it into the fray. In at least one case he showed himself to be unsympathetic toward a friend, namely Allen Tate. In 1966 Tate married his third wife, Helen Heiny. Twin sons were born to the couple in 1967, but one of them died in an accident in infancy. Lowell described the accident in graphic detail in "For Michael Tate":

> gagging on your plastic telephone,
> while the one night sitter drew water for your bath,
> unable to hear your groans. . . .

In a companion poem, "Letter from Allen Tate," Lowell quoted some of Tate's reactions: " 'As you must guess, / We're too jittery to travel after Michael's death.' " The poem concluded on a note of admiration: "How sweet your life in retirement! What better than loving / a young wife and boy; without curses writing, / 'I shall not live long enough to see him through.' " But the damage had already been done; Tate was so upset by the poems that he broke with Lowell over them, mending their friendship only after a duration of several years.

Notebook attempts to examine historical mass cruelty and social injustice in terms of the torment of the individual soul and psyche, but those poems in the volume that deal with personal suffering are curiously devoid of emotion. The work is drained of feeling, as if past works had wrung him dry. "Obit" is a vision of his own death, but he says "I am learning to live in history." In former volumes Lowell had risked all, pushing into new and unexplored territory, the mind poking at the limits of the intolerable, the poet pursuing his demons of grief, rage, hostility, and death. His preoccupation was with the painful, the hideous, with the cruelty and tragedy of life. An extremist, Lowell had measured real losses, suffering for them, becoming the embodiment of

Stephen Spender's hypothesis that the literature of despair is the "dead end where individual vision goes on repeating the same lesson of emptiness derived from every experience." Yet for once Lowell is too detached from his suffering, the body no longer able to absorb the excessive wounding inflicted by the soul.

A disgruntled Lowell returned to the drawing board, again sorting and rearranging, this time emerging with two separate volumes out of the one, *History* and *For Lizzie and Harriet,* both issued on the same day as his latest new volume, *The Dolphin,* in 1973. He had tried to sort out those sonnets too personal to fit into his diorama of world history. *History* struggled under the same burden as *Notebook,* reading now like an overcrowded Boot Hill of obituaries, with its four hundred sonnets covering an impossibly wide spectrum of historical names, including Beethoven, Thoreau, Margaret Fuller, Sappho, Harpo Marx, Elisabeth Schwartzkopf, Winston Churchill, and Franz Schubert (Lowell's favorite composer). One name had little or nothing to do with another. And there were too many names, an oversupply of faces, facts, and feats. Sublime tiles of color and glitter obfuscate the mosaic, until it becomes impossible to distinguish one tile from another. Eventually all blend together into a single, homogenized mess.

The grandiloquent, all-encompassing title of the volume indicates that Lowell was not quite certain what to do with these poems, how to group them, or where they would lead. With nothing less than rampant confusion in the face of an ordered world, he attempts to reduce all of human history to the two-dimensional surface of the printed page. Centering the sheaf between two nicely crafted but otherwise fatuous sequences—"History" and "End of the Year"—Lowell reiterates his enduring faith in the same volume he had twice before abandoned:

> About 80 of the poems in *History* are new, the rest are taken from my last published poem, *Notebook,* begun six years ago. All the poems have been changed, some heavily. I have plotted. My old title, *Notebook,* was more accurate than I wished, i.e. the composition was jumbled. I hope this jumble or jungle is cleared—that I have cut the waste marble from the figure.

Lowell had plotted all right but to little or no avail. Piling poem on poem, ply on ply, he raced down the corridors and footpaths of the demotic age as though at each turn in the road and behind every clump

of shrubbery the secret of the universe—terrible, demonic, inevitable
—waited to be discovered. The prevailing assumption on Lowell's part
that poetry has something to tell us about our experience, our history,
and that history in turn tells us who we are and where we are going,
is true only to a limited extent. Poetry is no more or less infallible a
Baedeker to the universe than any other science or branch of learning.

Lowell's oversimplified division of historical subjects into the two
classifications of hero and villain raises a question as to whether or not
he is truly justified in his endeavor to interface the dual disciplines of
history and poetics within the confining scope of a single setting. In
doing so he stalks the grand terrain previously traversed by many of the
great humanist visionaries—Aristotle, Aquinas, Erasmus, Voltaire, and
Hegel—all of whom addressed both philosophical and political issues
without the least sense of exceeding their competence. With the advent
of the present century, however, these separate, relatively shallow
streams of knowledge had broadened considerably; modern man could
obviously no longer cross and combine disciplines with the same degree
of ease as the learned sages of the past. Gentle streams of knowledge
had grown into choppy and treacherous seas, full of fast currents and
awash with unnavigable rips and tides. Ezra Pound had tried to ride the
rips in *The Cantos,* a mammoth poem into which he attempted to toss
chunks of bait and lure from an entire repertoire of disciplines. The
impossibility of the task ought to have warned Lowell off. Despite the
refining fire of his own literary prowess, Lowell could no more walk on
water than Pound. *History* was doomed to sink, not so much by dint of
execution as by error of conception.

The "Robert Lowell problem," if we can call it that, was indigenous
to his poetry-bound ancestors as well: the problem of an opinionated,
amateur historian inhabiting the same skin as the worthy, sometimes
extraordinary poet. In intellectual terms, the discrepancy stems, possibly, from these poets' underestimation of the difficulty of historical
knowledge, which for them always lacked the rigor of literary analysis.
The faulty thesis has it that every thinker has a right to a political
opinion. Turning their attention to the actual record of human achievement, the three Lowells in their work tend to see events and personages only in shades of black or white. Without the disciplined training
and inductive power of reasoning of the true historian, they rip their
way through the complex fabric of human behavior with the single
intent of demonstrating its stupidity and mendaciousness. Distorting

the historical record to suit their individual needs, they automatically conclude that all rulers are inherently wicked; all revolutionaries are by nature blessed.

The discrepancy is further enhanced by the Brahmin world view that feeds on the natural opposition between the Few and the Many (hoi polloi). For the Lowell trinity, as for the Greek philosopher Heraclitus, the Few were the good, the intelligent, the independent; the Many were the barbaric, the ignorant, and the easily swayed. Heraclitus, of course, implied that one could choose to belong to one or the other, whereas the Lowells knew that hazard, conditioning, genes, and environment determined one's fate. The complex tension in the human condition that existed between these two major groups was based on fear, not arrogance. The Few were afraid of being overthrown, the Many of being underfed. The axiom that claimed the rich have power, while the poor have time, was never more apropos. It is hardly conducive to a firm understanding of the historical process to believe, as did the Lowells, that the Few are by nature better or more important than the less fortunate Many. Yet it was common for the triad to speak out against the glamorization of the inarticulate hero. The common man was the bane of civilization, not its crowning glory; the man on the street needed education, not adulation. In full accord with this weltanschauung, Robert Lowell was not a fellow to celebrate the masses. His strongest suit by far was the individual voice, the regal perspective. That voice was his gift to the world of poetry, his footnote to the history of literature.

For Lizzie and Harriet contained the ingredients for a richer heritage than Lowell's volatile *History.* Consisting of sixty-seven poems "for" and about his wife and child, the latest volume is what remained from *Notebook* after *History*'s extraction. Was it a going-away present? Lowell and Hardwick were divorced in 1972. *For the Union Dead*'s "The Neo-Classical Urn" and "New York 1972: Fragment" (with its reference to "the termites digging in the underpinning") contained further intimations of impending marital doom. The termination of twenty-plus years of love and marriage became the new book's main thrust. "We never see him now at dinner, / then you quarrel, and he goes upstairs": Harriet's sorrowful tone recalls her father's flight from the nest. Their daughter tolerates her "unwise" parents, while Lizzie patiently waits, impatiently completes essays on the subjugation of women. *Seduction and Betrayal: Women and Literature,* published in 1974, was a collection of *New York Review* pieces on female vulnerability, women's relations to men, their work, their independent lives.

The poems in *For Lizzie and Harriet,* although "about" his family, are really "about" Robert Lowell—his insecurities, feelings of guilt, fantasies, emotions, disappointments. Remorse and self-recriminations were primarily the result of his infidelities, the pressures of maintaining a public image, the inability to confront the stunning failure of his marriage. He summed up the accumulation of twenty years of frustration with one sweep of the pen: *"Pace, pace.* All day our words / were rusty fishhooks—wormwood . . . Dear Heart's-Ease, / we rest from all discussion, drinking, smoking, / pills for high blood, three pairs of glasses— soaking / in the sweat of our hard-earned supremacy." Tender moments inevitably follow these tendentious bitternesses: "Lizzie, I wake to the hollow of loneliness, / I would cry out *Love, Love,* if I had words: / *we are all here for such a short time, / we might as well be good to one another."*

Their twentieth wedding anniversary provided the impetus for a disrespectful and wry litany on the death of marriage: "This week is our first this summer to go unfretted; / we smell as green as the weeds that bruise the flower— / a house eats up the wood that made it." There is talk of an "almighty God casting weak husbands adrift in the hands of a wife." A dream wafts through the poet's mind: "O when will I sleep out the storm, dear love, / and see at the end of the walk your dress glow / burnt-amber, as if you had absorbed the sun?" Suffering is diminished by a touch of humor: "Old campaigner, we could surrender something, / not talking for a victory but survival; / quarrels seldom come from the first cause, / some small passage in our cups at dinner / rouses the Dr. Johnson in a wife." There is the memory of passion: "You quiver on my finger like a small / minnow swimming in a crystal ball, / flittering radiance on my flittering finger . . ."; fatherly advice to his daughter: "Don't hate your parents, or your children will hire / unknown men to bury you at your own cost . . ."; and the final, sinking realization of marriage's demise: "Our love will not come back on fortune's wheel / . . . / After loving you so much, can I forget you for eternity, and have no other choice?"

"Voi ch'entrate, and your life is in your hands": Lowell, living out the nightly terror of insomnia, found himself slouching down the midnight streets of Times Square, bright as a neon day, steering his way past

enclaves of drug pushers, pimps, prostitutes, addicts, alcoholics, derelicts, the garbage of society. He was immune to the grimness of these streets. Purple lights, bars, burlesque houses, pawnshops, one-night stand hotels paved his way. In this world of lost connections, the silently probing poet struggled toward a form of being that remained essentially out of reach. Frigidly detached, he meandered through this stodgy limbo like a character out of Beckett—out of life but not quite into death, "without the courage to end or the strength to go on."

Early in 1970, Lowell journeyed to England on vacation, he informed Ian Hamilton, from his Furies. The Furies that he tried to elude included, in addition to Cambodia and Vietnam, his rapidly sinking marriage and the artistic failure of his *Notebook/History* venture. "It's an American theme," he told a *New York Times* interviewer, "the discovery, the pioneer going into the wilderness. After a while the wilderness changes into the Europe of Henry James and Eliot—a freehold almost barbaric in its newness." In virgin, verdant England, he hoped to renew himself, to make his life over and reenergize his work.

Shortly after arriving he settled into a brownstone on Redcliffe Square in the Earl's Court section of London. The mid-Victorian houses of the neighborhood were not too alien from those he had known in Boston, although perhaps more depressing. He described them as "aboriginal," "sour," "condemned by age, rebuilt by desolation." But it was good to find oneself in a new environment with the potential for revitalization all around. That spring, Lowell served as Visiting Fellow at All Souls College, Oxford University, which in 1966 rejected his bid for its prestigious Poetry Chair in favor of Edmund Blunden, British pastoralist, a disappointment partially mitigated by Lowell's receipt that year of the Sarah Hale Award for distinguished contribution to New England literature. Now, in 1970, less British in personal style than Auden or Eliot and less American than Williams or Cummings, Lowell showed himself to be an electrifying lecturer. His sessions on contemporary American poetry and New England literary history were better attended than any others at the university.

He was as comfortable among the British as James Russell Lowell once had been. From the fall semester of 1970 through 1972 he served as professor of English literature at Essex University, replacing Donald Davie, whose transfer to an American university created the faculty vacancy. It was during this period that Lowell's Dominican Republic divorce from Hardwick came through, enabling the poet to marry a third time. His new bride, a former companion of Robert Silvers of *The New York Review of Books*, was born (1931) Lady Caroline Blackwood, daughter of the Fourth Marquis of Dufferin and Ava, the Baron Basil Sheridan Blackwood, an eccentric nobleman remembered for his lavish dinner parties. Caroline's mother was a Guinness, a family grounded in British royal society, a dynasty of enormous wealth. Lady Caroline, married previously to the abstract artist Lucien Freud, was the mother of three girls by her first husband. Like Lowell's two former wives, she too was a writer, having published *For All That I Found There*, a gathering of "socially ironic" stories and reportage. Several novels soon followed, including *The Stepdaughter*, a short epistolary work about a woman abandoned by her husband, which was awarded Britain's David Higham Prize for the best first novel of 1976; *Great Granny Webster*, published in the United States after Lowell's death, was another sharp-edged cameo of an isolated woman, a fiction alive with a macabre sense of humor and an introspective feel for character.

Lowell had been briefly acquainted with Lady Caroline in 1966, during a visit she paid to the United States. He encountered her again soon after arriving in London four years later. If there is such a thing as an explosion of emotion, Lowell experienced it. The couple set up housekeeping almost immediately, first at his Redcliffe Square residence and then at Milgate, the ancient Blackwood estate at Kent. When interviewed by the British press about his stay in England, he responded: "I'm not here in protest against conditions in America, though here there's more leisure, less intensity, fierceness. After ten years of living on the front lines, in New York, I'm rather glad to dull the glare."

Kent, a quiet oasis an hour outside London, is probably the least spoiled of all the city's many surrounding "villages." It was here, in the spacious old house, that Caroline gave birth in August 1971, while Lowell was still legally married to Hardwick, to the poet's second child, a son, Robert Sheridan Lowell. The new arrival was proudly heralded in Lowell's subsequent volume of verse, *The Dolphin*, published in 1973. *The Dolphin* shared that year's Pulitzer Prize for Poetry with Allen Ginsberg's *The Fall of America*.

The volume, containing 103 new poems, "For Caroline," is an affectionate and sustained record of "the poet's change from one life and marriage in America to a new life on new terms with a new family in England." To this description, offered by the book's publisher, Lowell added his own; he informed Christopher Ricks that it was "the story of changing marriages, not a malice or sensation, far from it, but necessarily, according to my peculiar talent, very personal." A number of critics held that "invasion of privacy" more accurately characterized the book's slant.

The dolphin, "part fish, part mermaid, part woman," is clearly the elegant and irrepressible Caroline, "all muscle, youth, intention," a "rough slitherer" in her "grotto of haphazard," constantly renewing herself, yet always steadfast, always there when needed: "When I was troubled in mind, you made for my body / caught in its hangman's-knot of sinking lines." The sonnets in this volume, unlike those in *Notebook 1967–68,* celebrate a life of promise, hope, joy, growth: "It's enough to wake without old fears, / and watch the needle-fire of the first light / bombarding off your eyelids harmlessly. By ten the bedroom is sultry. You have double-breathed; / we are many, our bed smells of hay." Often the sonnets are lyrical, vibrant, graceful. Domesticity has been partially restored; Lowell's weariness has dissolved.

The dolphin, a symbol of ambiguity in Yeats's "Byzantium," retains a multifaceted complexity in Lowell's version. In the dual roles of Eros and muse she alternates between moments of grace and beauty; as temptress and tease she is swift and dangerous. More than once she is described as "blindingly" beautiful. As *The Dolphin* proceeds she becomes less real and more symbolic—a study in shimmering duality, delineated in one poem ("Mermaid") as having "Alice-in-Wonderland straight gold hair," and being "fair-featured, curve and bone." At times she is also grotesque with "bulge eyes bigger than your man's closed fist, / slick with humiliation when dismissed." She can be "bright as the morning star or a blonde starlet," and vengeful as a "baby killer-whale." The metaphors frequently flow as fast as a river. Lowell informs us he has been "searching the rough black ocean" for her for years. At another juncture he calls her a "conjunction of tail and grace," a Rabelaisian play on the colloquial function of the word "tail." She is half human, half goddess or mermaid, a combination of all-consuming love and all-consuming art. Her duality spirits him on; she becomes a symbol of rebirth, of metamorphosis and self-transcendence.

Aside from its usefulness as a record of Lowell's neurological setbacks during his years in England, *The Dolphin* charts the poet's chronological progress during the same period. His "Book of Life," as sequential as any Jamesian novel of self-discovery, starts at Redcliffe Square and trails Lowell closely through a battery of changes. His

affair with Lady Caroline, while physically satisfying, is at first emotionally estranging. The "story" takes on new shades of meaning when
Caroline leaves Lowell to take her vacation in Scotland. The poet, left
to his own devices, suffers during her absence. His feeling of abandon-
ment gives rise to other psychologically draining emotions; he feels
his "old infection" coming on. During July and August of 1970 he is
hospitalized. Physically removed from his muse, he endures moments
of grave self-doubt, during which he dismisses his work as largely val-
ueless. Caroline visits him in hospital; he does not recognize her.
Elizabeth Hardwick writes and visits, her presence causing further
confusion. Slowly, recalling his old love for Lizzie and his new surge
of feeling for Caroline, the poet recovers his health. Released from
hospital, he joins Caroline at Milgate, teaching part-time at Essex, la-
boring full-time at his poetry.

Lizzie continues to reveal herself as an understandably fragile
woman of uncommon decency in a series of anguished letters to her
husband, sections of which he transplanted without modification or
permission into his poetry, no doubt convinced that in light of the
earlier Jean Stafford letters (following his first divorce) such material
represents the universal female condition, woman's perpetual plight on
this "bitch of an earth." His efforts succeeded in making enemies of
former friends. "A cruel invasion of her privacy, morally and estheti-
cally objectionable," scolded Stanley Kunitz; Adrienne Rich was similarly outraged, while Marjorie Perloff attacked the volume in *The New
Republic,* suggesting that "Lowell no longer quite succeeds in transforming his life into art, and his revelations, sometimes embarrassingly
personal, sometimes boring, should indeed have remained 'sealed like
private letters.'" All agreed that the poet's single strategy seemed to
be to want to contrast a woman's tearful defeat with her man's new-
found but rocky happiness, weighing the reality of the real world of loss
against the gain reaped by the necessarily counterfeit world of invention or art.

"In the Mail" cements fragments of one such epistle: "'I love you,
Darling, there's a black void, / as black as night without your hand.'"
In "Hospital II" we hear Hardwick's wracked voice again: "'That new
creature, / when I hear her name, I have to laugh, / You left two houses
and two thousand books, / a workbarn by the ocean, and two slaves / to
kneel and wait upon you hand and foot.'" Marjorie Perloff may have
been correct in her assertion that the material in *The Dolphin* was

"embarrassingly personal." But she was mistaken on another count: the volume is not boring—it is anything but boring!

There is a kind of morbid fascination that one derives from watching *The Dolphin*'s soap-operatic plot slowly unfold, the poet torn between the two women in his life, between "the dismay of my old world" and the mystery of "the blank new." For a time Lowell spends weekends alone in London, while Caroline and her children remain behind at Milgate. By himself, he again feels a profound sense of loss and begins to long for his family in the States. "My family," reads one poem, "why are we so far?" Lizzie's response comes with the impact of a sledgehammer: " *'Don't you dare mail us the love your life denies.'* " Then comes change, Lowell's sudden realization, an awakening. The poet and his "new bride" experience a resurgence of emotion, climaxing in sexual and spiritual ecstasy:

> I am waiting like an angler with practice and courage;
> the time to cast is now, and the mouth open,
> the huge smile, head and shoulders of the dolphin—
> I am swallowed up alive . . . I am.

The birth of their son reinforces their bond. Lowell comments on his season of regeneration with a new wife, new child, three new step-daughters: "After fifty so much joy has come. / I hardly want to hide my nakedness— / the shine and stiffness of a new suit, a feeling, / not wholly happy, of having been reborn." In December 1972 he returns to New York to spend the holidays with Lizzie and Harriet. The vacation provides the impetus for poetic and personal vacillation: "Even the licence of my mind rebels / and can find no lodging for my two lives"; "One man, two women, the common novel plot." The poet examines his "stormy life blown towards evening," finds himself awakening at night in tears, lamenting that "love wasn't what went wrong." He visits Boston, whose ambiance rekindles the memory of his ruined youth and ravaged parentage: "My mother and father dying young and sixty / with the nervous system of a child of six." In "Alimony" he rails: "I'm somewhere, nowhere; four Boston houses I grew from, / slashbrick expressionist New England fall; / I walk, run, gay with frost."

His stay in old and familiar surroundings elicits a rainbow of moods, days that range in temper from bad to better. In New York he presents a poetry reading for the students and faculty at the Dalton School,

inscribing his daughter's yearbook: "You must be strong through solitude, said Fate, for the present this thought alone must be your shelter."
New York, like Boston, pricks his nerves, transports him back in time
"through the thirty years / to the New York of Jean Stafford, Pearl
Harbor, the Church." He calls on Jean Stafford at her home in East
Hampton, Long Island, and imagines himself "almost obscenely, com-
plaisantly on the phone with / my three wives, as if three-dimensional
space were my breath." New York serves as a reminder that old friends
are no longer extant: "Most of my old friends are mostly dead, / entitled
to grow infirm and lap the cream." Disheartened, agitated, distraught,
he boards the next plane for London. The poet imagines his return to
Caroline, conscious that the moment of erotic transcendence in which
she became his savior-dolphin is over for him. All that remains of the
story is a thirteen-line prologue, "Fishnet," which lays out some of the
manuscript's important themes and ideas, and an epilogue, "Dolphin,"
whose fifteen lines give the volume its title and a sense of completion:

> I have sat and listened to too many
> words of the collaborating muse,
> and plotted perhaps too freely with my life,
>
> . . .
>
> to ask compassion . . .
> my eyes have seen what my hand did.

Two imperfect but autonomous sonnets are thus conjoined to form a
new meditation, an artwork as integrated as Lowell's life and imagination. In *History* Lowell allowed many of his personages to speak in their
own recorded words, a form of "imitation" that may help explain his use
of Hardwick's letters in *The Dolphin.* The sonnets of this volume somehow seem less contrived than those of *History,* perhaps because the
subject matter of *The Dolphin*—frailty, rebirth, and desire—is more
unified, more of a piece, and better suited to the habitually romantic
genre with which one traditionally associates the sonnet. If there is a
single overriding message in *Dolphin,* anything even modestly approaching a moral lesson, it is probably contained in the line, "Change
I earth or sky I am the same."

Although it reaped him his second Pulitzer, *The Dolphin* received
less than glowing notice from the critics. One group of literary assayers,
no longer enthused by the confessional mode, found the individual

poems invigorating but the volume as a whole lacking in culminating impact. They charged that interest was artificially aroused by the inclusion of biographical material and sustained by stream of consciousness, the use of ellipses, metastases, proselike fragments, constant shifts in tone. The rebellious British versifier Geoffrey Grigson went further, calling Lowell's work "worthless . . . hiccupping . . . verbal non-coherence and verbal insensitivity." Harold Bloom, the heralded Yale critic, rejected confessional verse as "self-defeating . . . from Coleridge down to Lowell and his disciples." John Ashbery objected to the "brilliance" of the writing, complaining that Lowell lacquered each of his poems and hung them in a museum. There was too much still life in Lowell's poetry to suit Ashbery and not enough of the action painting that hung in the Whitney Museum or the Museum of Modern Art. Ashbery's mentor, the late Frank O'Hara, objected for much the same reason, observing that Lowell's "confessional manner" lets him "get away with things that are plain bad but you're supposed to be interested because he's supposed to be so upset." Robert Bly was of the opinion that Lowell hadn't had a new idea in years, that he was surrounded by false flatterers such as Jason Epstein, Stephen Marcus, and A. Alvarez ("perfect examples of the alienated establishment intellectual"), and that he was counterfeiting emotions in his poems—emotions he did not possess. Bly insisted that Lowell had been drawn away from himself, away from his own center, and that American readers were incapable of discerning bad from good.

Lowell's return from America to England precipitated what was to be a difficult period in his life. Despite his second Pulitzer, his disposition had taken a downward plunge. For several months he teetered precariously between days of buttery happiness and moments of grand slippage. Lowered good humor and an ominous rise of irritable enthusiasm announced the beginning of decline. The noble savage felt himself alienated from his environment, separated from family and friends. He lost all appetite for food, all ability to concentrate on work. Anxiety and the cold sweat of sleeplessness made him appear gray and weary, old before his time. A steady diet of liquids, cigarettes, and antidepressants depressed him further. During one manic bout he plunged an arm up to the elbow through a plate-glass window. In London he tolerated his twentieth hospital stay in as many years. Visitors were greeted by a voice that rasped in fits and starts, the speaker's craggy visage contorted and twisted with rage. He was obsessed by suspicions of conspiracy betwen American government officials against the poor. Lowell's medical report was as dour as his prognostication of the age. Medics diagnosed him as suffering "acute psychomotor retardation"—Delmore Schwartz's and John Berryman's ailment—attributing it to excessive alcoholism and an overdose of drugs. A poem he composed in hospital noted the aftereffects of sedation: "Minutes last a day; days, a month." In his roller-coaster madness, Lowell identified with a "scatological" Hamlet standing beneath a "clotted London sky," and in another poem from *Dolphin* commented, "I come on walking off stage backwards."

He was little cheered by the first Copernicus Prize, presented to him in 1973 jointly by the Copernicus Society and the Academy of American Poets, of which he was an honorary chancellor. The medal, which carried with it a $10,000 emolument, was given to Lowell for his enduring work, "for having kept alive the best values of American literature." In May 1977 the American Academy and Institute of Arts and Letters, to which he had belonged since 1947, honored him with the National Medal for Literature; it too carried an award of $10,000.

Generously laden with honors, awards, and admirers, the poet now spent one semester of every two in the United States, teaching literature courses at Harvard, living in Leverett House, where he conducted informal "at homes" for the benefit of students and local Boston writers. But by and large, "Mister Lowell," as he was known to his students, had become hardened to the levities of the classroom; more and more he saw himself withdrawing into a private world of seclusion. He taught these poetry classes, according to one pupil, by going "word by word, then line by line, through each poem until there wasn't an inch of verbiage flapping on the page." Exegesis came easier than the free-floating lecture; to many an observant eye he seemed to be teaching by rote, as though only the motions mattered any more.

Otherwise Lowell continued to fulfill his main purpose, that of an active poet. His readings, few and far between, were considered *events* when they did take place. Introduced by his friend and former student, the poet Frank Bidart, he read on December 8, 1976 at the Poetry Center of the Ninety-second Street YM-YWHA. Released a week earlier from a mental institution in England, the poet looked tired and gaunt; his voice and hands trembled in unison; he spoke with a noticeable tremor but recited his poems with energy and passion, interrupting himself from time to time to offer a droll or humorous aside. Of "Skunk Hour," he exclaimed: "That's my most popular poem and I'm rather sick of it." During the reading, taped for distribution by Caedmon Records, he spoke in passing of the craft of writing, the art of transforming reality into verse: "Memory is the mother of the muses, but obviously a poem has to be more than just memory. . . . You have to do something with it."

He seemed in slightly better health some ten weeks later during a reading he gave with Allen Ginsberg at Greenwich Village's St. Mark's Church, that mini–Roman Forum of the oral literary tradition, the site of his marriage to Elizabeth Hardwick. They made an odd couple, Ginsberg and Lowell, contrasts in physical shape and poetic form— "Bearded Paterson-East Side guru and tense ruddy history-ridden New England Brahmin," intoned Sidney Bernard in *The New York Times Book Review*. Ginsberg, chanting and stroking his lines, delivered "rolling thunder" perceptions on Australia, comic relief on Einstein, cosmic dialogues on death between himself and his ailing father. Lowell, moving tentatively, reciting in the "pained, totemesque whisper" that had become his trademark, read for the first time his Homeric version of "Ulysses and Circe," a reverie of seagoing softness, a poem finely tuned and turned. At one point in the reading Lowell commented on a notice in *The New York Times* that spoke of Ginsberg and himself as representing "opposite ends of the spectrum." He remarked that they were not really so different as the *Times* would have it; if anything, they were simply opposite ends of William Carlos Williams—the suggestive comment elicited loud laughter on the part of the audience.

Lowell's last public reading was given, as fate would have it, at Sanders Theater, Harvard University, during May 1977. As absentminded as a professor, in addition to being color-blind, the poet wore one brown sock and one blue sock and again brought down the house.

"Ulysses and Circe" and "Domesday Book," also a recent poem, appeared together in the special 1977 issue of *Salmagundi,* marking Lowell's sixtieth birthday. "Domesday," with its exploration of Cromwellian politics and investigation of class taxation, is thematically a throwback to the poems of *History.* Additional innovations turned up in *The New York Review of Books, Ploughshares, London Magazine, The New Republic, Shenandoah,* and *American Poetry Review.* When *Newsweek* requested a poem for its Bicentennial week issue, Lowell complied by turning out an appropriate wit-twister on Nixon and Watergate titled "George III," drawing the inevitable comparison between the twin "monarchs" of England and America.

The Bicentennial afforded Lowell an opportunity to visit the Soviet Union on a reading tour arranged by the State Department. Accompanied by Voznesensky, he visited Boris Pasternak's grave in the tiny cemetery on the outskirts of Peredelkino, "the community in the woods." They passed the small lake where Lara, the heroine of *Doctor Zhivago,* once lived. They then saw Pasternak's long-neglected house, half hidden behind an apple orchard in midsummer bloom. The nearby cemetery sat huddled against the side of a grassy knoll. A tall, otherwise ordinary stone marked Pasternak's grave, the poet's face carved into the stone's smooth surface, his signature running along the base. Physically, Lowell reminded Voznesensky of Pasternak; both men carried their heads slightly askew like violinists, but without the violin. A month after Lowell's death, Voznesensky, remembering their pilgrimage, visited Lowell's gravesite at Dunbarton, placing upon the mound four branches broken from a rowanberry tree that grows near the grave of Pasternak. The scarlet berries, prolific in winter, are a motif in *Zhivago.* They are a symbol of Russia; because of their winter brilliance they supposedly represent life in death.

The same year (1976) saw the publication in England and the United States of Lowell's *Selected Poems;* a slightly revised edition of the same volume appeared a year later. About two hundred poems—many of them rewritten and rearranged—had been drawn from each of his volumes of verse (excluding *Land of Unlikeness* but up to and including *The Dolphin*). Second and third thoughts on poetic intensities in many cases forced him back to the original: "MUCH MAKESHIFT—From my last three books, I have chosen possible sequences, rather than atomizing favorite poems out of context." His later sequences—"half fictions" —had been sifted with a fine-tooth comb; substantial cuts helped tighten "The Mills of the Kavanaughs," "Thanksgiving's Over," and four of the five poems he reprinted from *Near the Ocean.* But the 1977 *Selected Poems* restored the selections from *Near the Ocean* to their original length, while cutting and altering other sequences. The future editor of the variorum edition of Lowell's poems will undoubtedly have his work cut out for him.

The most appealing detail of the new compendium was the emergence of a fresh sequence, a section titled "Nineteen Thirties," two dozen poems from *Notebook* held together by a common theme and time scheme. The anthology—"My verse autobiography"—provides an excellent perspective on Lowell's complete works, enabling the reader to trace his metric growth from the rolling thud-meters of the early volumes and the chatty prose style of *Life Studies* to the Marvellian eight-line, four-foot stanzas of *Near the Ocean* and the unrhymed mock-sonnets and free verse of his later books—a line of development that at times veered toward Tolstoian narrative and at other times toward economic compression ("something highly rhythmical and perhaps wrenched into a small space"). A cover-to-cover perusal reveals the meandering path of the poet's spiritual excursion "from Roman Catholicism to general Christian piety to a kind of agnostic existentialism"; scanning his own poetic daybook, Lowell felt he had produced something approximating a Wordsworthian mosaic—dark and light spots of time arranged to relate a story of unfolding, often discontinuous perceptual growth, a life:

> Looking over my *Selected Poems*, about thirty years of writing, my impression is that the thread that strings it together is my autobiography, it is a small-scale *Prelude*, written in many different styles and with digressions, yet a continuing story . . .

There was to be a final collection, *Day by Day*, an appropriately titled gathering of poems published in September 1977, containing "Ulysses and Circe," "Domesday Book," and other recent journal and magazine jottings. These plainspoken, diary-extracted inkblottings, in following a pattern established by his later volumes, turn for inspiration to the poet's youth and adolescence, with scattered recollections of friends (named and anonymous), ex-wives, parents and revenants, the pain of being an "unwanted child," life with his own children, scenes of trout fishing, meditations on nature. Further autobiographical revelations describe the hardships of aging, alcoholism, insomnia, mental illness, and death. In sum the volume is an intimate, day-by-day chronicle of Lowell's inner life rendered in shades that make it readily accessible to the average reader. The obligatory breakdown and recovery scenes, leavened with generous helpings of humor, appear in poems called "In the Ward," "Visitors," and "Notice." The poet is forever falling apart: "My detachment must be paid for, / tomorrow will be worse than today." Mental illness is here equated with punishment; Lowell's crime, if it can be called that, was to be "an unwanted child." If *The Dolphin* was partially about the slow agony of rebirth, the painful task of reordering the psyche, the present collection returns again to the subject

of alienation, the poet burdened by his solitude within society. Concern
with his own mind is an occupational hazard for Lowell; nowhere is he
more consumed by that subject than in *Day by Day*.

Bringing his phantoms out into the open, Lowell confronts them yet
again; but creativity is not a catharsis for his emotional burdens; art does
not cleanse the psyche; there is no therapeutic dispelling of demons
through poetry. Confessionalism intensifies the experience, brings the
confessor face to face with his darkest self, unlocks the vault of pain but
does not balance the books. Where previous volumes examined at
greater length the psychic unrest experienced by modern man and its
relation to art, *Day by Day* simply acknowledges the might of psychic
undercurrents, the stark and chaotic strivings of our unconscious needs.
There is an air of tranquility, a finality to this collection. Nothing now
is unrelated to death. The odor of death pervades the poet's thinking
and he, himself, becomes death, pouring forth the onus of an impending
end into his art. It is as if he has at last come to accept the existential
truth: "Man's being is an existence toward death and the certitude of
dying overshadows all his life."

Suicide is fleetingly considered but ultimately rejected: "You only
come in the tormenting hallucinations of the night, / when my sleeping,
prophetic mind / experiences things / that have not happened yet,"
Lowell writes. Happier hours stir an occasional song: "joy to idle
through Boston, / my head full of young Henry Adams / and his unnoticed white silk armband, / worn for a day to free the slaves." Nevertheless, the darker moments prevail.

Between the transparent lines of the volume can be detected traces
of another secret, the weight of a third dying marriage. Short, luminous,
Horatian phrases depict the attrition of Lowell's relationship with Caroline Blackwood, the poet looking ahead with foreboding to a beclouded
future. Describing himself in one poem as "groping and monomania-
cal," Lowell reconstructs the scenario behind this book: the poet's life
in Kent, his hospitalizations in England, Caroline Blackwood's illness,
their brief respite in Boston, their separation, a temporary reconcilia-
tion, a further rupture, an altercation and parting in Ireland, Lowell's
solo flight to America, his lingering relationship with Elizabeth Hardwick, furtive gestures toward new conquests.

His breakdowns appear to be increasing in frequency. At one hospital
the psychiatrists label him "A model guest," comically remarking that
they would " 'welcome Robert back any time / the place suits him.' "

Caroline, he insists, no longer loves him, misinterpreting his illness for desertion. In a pivotal poem called "Unwanted," he equates his present marital estrangement with the experience of being an estranged, unloved, unwanted child. The psychic wound incurred as a result of the childhood trauma has been reopened, and by early 1977 Lowell is back in New York and in Castine, Maine, with Elizabeth Hardwick, a relationship with insurmountable hazards of its own.

If he must renounce love, the poet will not renounce art. At the end of *Day by Day,* he takes up the subject by announcing his decision to surrender for good the failed epic style of *Notebook* in favor of a loosely structured and more sincere style, one tinctured by invention and imagination: "Those blessèd structures, plot and rhyme— / why are they no help to me now / I want to make / something imagined, not recalled?" The struggle to see and feel and express has worn the poet down. "I am too weak to remember," he observes in one poem; in another he wearily observes that "Age is the bilge / we cannot shake from the mop." The burden of Lowell's pained withdrawal tells on every page of *Day by Day.* The raw chamber music of the confessional voice, a measuring of time, love, despair, the continuum of daily retribution reverberates to the bitter end, "until the wrist watch is taken from the wrist." Lowell wrote the volume knowing it would be his last.

The critical barrage that had been levied against his other recent works continued to haunt him. Denis Donoghue, in *The Hudson Review,* pointed out that Lowell was guilty of covering the same ground he had covered before: "The themes are the old congenital ones, brought up to date: loss, end, suicide, the way we were in Baton Rouge, Peter Taylor, 'Red' Warren, the good old days, dreams, Jean Stafford, Elizabeth Hardwick, rural England, 'my unhealthy generation,' Caroline, Sheridan Lowell, turtles, ants, a dolphin. Nothing wrong with these, as themes. But Lowell can do little or nothing with them; or nothing beyond what he has already done." The gist of Donoghue's caveat is unclear. Does he mean to imply that Lowell ought not to have written a quasi-sequel to *The Dolphin,* or simply that he should not have reemployed symbols used before in other volumes? Although he fails to elucidate, Donoghue presumably intended to suggest that for the poet to write so much out of himself depleted his sense of the world and decreased his sensitivity to fresh experience. Despite the excitement of having a superabundance of personal crises in one's life, we can become too predictable to ourselves. Lowell may have overused himself and his personal problems in earlier volumes, leaving too little in reserve for the books by which he wanted to be remembered.

This excess of fluency, the addiction to jotting down personal poems as though they were mere journal entries, induced one annoyed critic to characterize Lowell's method as "an act of spiritual masturbation conducted in public." The old ideal in poetry has it that the poem is something *made,* an entity unto itself that should transcend human feelings and not just report them. A poem does what it is supposed to when it helps the reader understand his own feelings. Lowell, suggests fellow poet Donald Hall in *The Georgia Review,* has fallen prey to an ease of utterance that had become the bane of most modern writers. It was Hall's contention that *Day by Day* was "as slack and meretricious as *Notebook* and *History.* . . . The great poet died thirteen years earlier with the publication of *For the Union Dead.*" Hall's alarming outcry is two-pronged. He first of all sees *Day by Day* as "semi-indulgent self imitation," the collection failing essentially to transform experience into art. Few examples are provided, but one can reasonably assume that Hall has in mind such samples as Lowell's limpid lines for Merrill Moore ("When I was in college, he said, 'You know / you were an unwanted child?' ") or those for Carl Jung ("That year Carl Jung said to mother in Zurich / 'If your son is as you have described him, / he is already an incurable schizophrenic.' "

Hall's second reservation involves Lowell's craftsmanship. *Day by Day,* he asserts, "is filled with cliché, the sort of cinderblock that publicity releases are built with." Hall's contention that Lowell's first grave missteps had been made in *Notebook 1967–68* stemmed from his feeling that the book was filled with nothing but "diffuse and self-serving gossip, slovenly clichés assembled with a zeal like Roget's." What particularly upset Hall was Lowell's failure to capture the great and trailblazing realization of inner experience against the lurid backdrop of the revolutionary sixties. The intellectual questions raised by *Notebook* are nowhere resolved. How does one reconcile the differences between the excesses of the sixties—the intoxication with power that was central to the concerns of the Presidency, the sexual explosion, the impetus of radical politics, the triumph of big business and labor unions, and of course Vietnam—with the turmoil of Lowell's inner life, the tragedy and triumph of Lowell's heritage? Instead of dealing directly with this dichotomy, *Notebook* takes the easy way out, dousing all with a weary narcissism, a celebration of self that fails for the most part to dramatize

Lowell's mind on paper. And why does Lowell submit to these weaknesses? Because, argues Hall, he surrounded himself with maggots and pilot fish, toadies who applauded everything he produced, lackies dazzled by his celebrity, groupies who exalted his every sentiment. He was like the wine baron of one of his last poems, crowded in by foolish admirers and groveling sycophants.

Hall's grumblings, on the whole tainted by exaggeration, nevertheless convey some modicum of truth. The pith of his argument is that if Lowell received any astute criticism during his last years it came neither from the media, which almost always lauded his work, nor from friends, who were too busy feuding among themselves to be of use to anyone else. Lowell's own sad but gifted generation of poets, the Berrymans, Roethkes, and Schwartzes, who might have been able to provide sound advice, were either already dead or in the process of dying. But even assuming he had found someone to offer guidance, it seems unlikely that Lowell would have listened. He ignored those friends who had criticized his extrapolation of passages from Elizabeth Hardwick's correspondence in *The Dolphin,* the public exploitation of a woman's private lamentations, offering the lame excuse that he had usurped them only to sharpen his self-criticism, embellish his guilt, which had been a minor but visible theme in the book.

Hall's other charge, that the Bostonian no longer possessed the gifts that had previously enabled him to transform his life into art, also has some basis in fact. There is little question that the craftsmanship and creative energy of earlier days had been diminished. Overproduction—his need to hammer out seven books of poetry over the last nine years—prevented him from gaining the distance he needed from his work. He penned such an enormous array of poems out of his life that he was no longer able to distinguish one poem from another. Repetition, lack of focus and range, represented the price exacted by his urgency to produce. For all the suffering and distress behind his distractions, different feelings and emotions tended to sound too much alike, lending the poems a varnished finish rather than the brittle edge one usually associates with confessional poetry.

It may be that in his latest efforts he simply ran out of things to say; instead of standing mute, he wasted himself on listless ironies and implications. The sheer strength of intellect and learning that yoke other volumes together are exhausted by the time of *Day by Day.* There is also the tendency on his part to sum up the universe on every page, to offer random observations of sweeping implication that in fact only rarely apply. On another plane, he was a scrupulously honest poet, whose tautological inquiries were most readable when they explored the familiar territory of psychological duress, home, family, modesty, immodesty, fame, honor, love. A faint sense of shame at being wealthy and coming from a distinguished, aristocratic clan permeates almost the entire body of his private and public deliberations. Likewise, there are the pride and self-assurance, the incontestable and coy charm that come with being a Lowell: these gracious qualities are everywhere to be found.

What is perhaps most chilling about *Day by Day* is its morbid sense of an impending end, its prophetic references to the poet's imminent death. Even when he writes of the fertility of nature, it is never without allusion to the temporality of man. Mournful expressions of death and premature aging hover throughout, at times gliding by almost unnoticed: "Now that I am three parts iced-over . . . I ask for a natural death"; "Being old in good times is worse / than being young in the worst"; "It's an illusion death or technique / can wring the truth from us like water"; "I see myself change in my changed friends— / may I live longer, yet break no records"; "less than ever I expect to be alive / six months from now."

He died shortly after the book's publication. On September 12, 1977, having arrived by plane from Ireland, Robert Lowell suffered a massive coronary in the back seat of a New York City taxicab that was taking him from Kennedy Airport to Elizabeth Hardwick's West Side Manhattan apartment. Without a word he had slumped over, and when they reached his destination, the driver could not rouse him. The cab raced on to Roosevelt Hospital, half a mile away. "His body was still warm," testified an attending paramedic; but his heart and breathing had stopped.

Although even *The New York Times* failed to carry the full story, it is typical of the celebrity grapevine that others soon "knew" the intimate details of the poet's recent past. He had spent his last two weeks in Dublin with his six-year-old son, and his estranged wife and her daughter Ivana. Caroline Blackwood would later report that when he left them in Ireland, he looked tired and out of sorts, not at all himself. But then he had not been "himself" for many months.

Not long after his death, on January 19, 1978, the National Book Critics Circle awarded its 1977 prize for poetry to *Day by Day*. The concerted efforts of Elizabeth Hardwick, a member of NBCC's board of directors, were instrumental in gaining Lowell the prize. Presenting the award at the Time-Life auditorium in New York, Richard Locke, an editor of *The New York Times Book Review,* read several selections from the prize collection. Robert Giroux, chairman of the board and Lowell's longtime editor at Farrar, Straus & Giroux, accepted the award on behalf of the late poet. He concluded an elegant acceptance speech by reading "Epilogue" *(Day by Day)* with its beautiful ending lines: "We are poor passing facts, / warned by that to give / each figure in the photograph / his living name."

January 1979 marked the posthumous publication of Lowell's translation of the *Oresteia* of Aeschylus, whose *Prometheus Bound* had first gained his attention. The origin of Lowell's efforts to render the Greek trilogy, comments Frank Bidart in a brief introduction, dated to the early 1960's, when New York's Lincoln Center Repertory Theater considered producing an earlier Lowell version of *Agamemnon,* the first and best of these three plays. Although plans for the project fell through, they were briefly revived a decade later by producer Joseph Papp, who found Lowell's *Agamemnon* "naturalistic, simple, not flowery." Encouraged by Papp's intervention, Lowell not only revised the *Agamemnon* but set to work translating the remaining brace of plays. While Lowell was in London working on the trilogy, Papp showed the Bostonian's *Agamemnon* to his director Andrei Serban, who decided it was not right for him.

After an interval, Lowell called Papp to say that the trilogy was ready, and Papp had to tell him that they had changed their minds and decided to go instead with Edith Hamilton's translation of *Agamemnon.* Lowell was terribly disappointed and hurt. He felt it was a rejection and was mortally wounded. And Papp was utterly dismayed, because he very much respected Lowell as a poet and as a man of principle. Compounding the problem at the time was a feeling Papp had that, when he spoke to Lowell, both in London and New York, the poet was low in spirits and ill. Papp's sole consolation was that his connection with the translation of the *Oresteia* was beneficial, since it was the expectation of its production that encouraged Lowell to complete the work.

Several details of the story were appended by Bidart, most notably in the final (and weakest) play of the trilogy, which the poet for lack of time and patience was unable to revise, although he came back to it briefly in December 1976–January 1977. The basic plot-line of the trilogy, steeped in bloodlust, deals with the succession of crimes and their retribution in the House of Atreus. The series had started, before the action of *Agamemnon* began, when Atreus denied his brother Thyestes his rightful line of ascent to the throne of Argos, precipitating a flood of misadventures that in the keynote drama sees Thyestes's son Aegisthus and Agamemnon's wife, Clytemnestra, murder Agamemnon and seize the throne. In the next play, *Choephoroe (The Libation Bearers)*, Orestes avenges his father Agamemnon's murder by assassinating Clytemnestra (his mother) and Aegisthus. The final play, *Eumenides (The Furies)*, finds Orestes on trial, the Olympian deities sitting in moral judgment of his crime, the very crime that they ordained—a not unheard-of contemporary plot. That he is ultimately acquitted comes as no surprise.

Lowell, who repeatedly expressed aversion to the canonical decree of "an eye for an eye," may well have been drawn to the trilogy because it so purposefully explores the manifestation of retribution and revenge. In this work Aeschylus implies that the ambiguities and contradictions of myth provide human beings with an appropriate paradigm for the rehabilitation of a polymorphic world. Lowell's interpretation, supplanting religiosity with philosophy, is both good and bad—good because it purports to teach us something about the human condition; bad because it teaches us not enough. The effectiveness of Lowell's rendition of the original decreases with each succeeding play.

The revival of the classics is partially the result of their contemporary relevance. Contemporaneity is what the *Oresteia* boasts in greatest profusion, telling us more about ourselves today than any presidential address or congressional investigation. War, politics, murder, moral decay, revenge, domestic intrigue bind act to act, play to play. In the central character of Orestes we have the ageless example of the tragic hero caught between conflicting sanctions; ordered by Apollo to avenge the murder of a monarch, he must either murder his mother or betray the Gods. He can evade neither the choice nor its consequence. The structure of almost all Greek tragedy is geared toward a development in which the lonely protagonist, like the compulsive gambler, must sooner or later lose. In describing the syndrome one might look, suggests drama critic Jan Kott, at the metaphor of the mousetrap. You have a house with a basement, and in the basement there is a mouse. Regardless of what happens, in the end the mouse has got to get caught. He has a choice, but the environment, the general pattern, the general mechanism, all work in such a way that there can be only one solution.

The main difference between this rather simplistic metaphor and ancient Greek tragedy is that in the latter no one knows precisely who set up the mousetrap which eventually traps the poor mouse.

The metaphor has wider-reaching implications when applied directly to Lowell's life. Because he conceived of himself as an aristocrat-turned-rebel, Lowell came to believe that he was somehow destined to wander ceaselessly over a topography littered with proverbial mousetraps; he saw himself as an individual liable to reprisals on every front, a man (much like James Russell Lowell or Abbott Lawrence Lowell) considered radical by reactionaries and reactionary by radicals. The resultant self-image further explains his attraction to the Aeschylus trilogy. In *History*, in fact, he included five poems identifying his own family with the House of Atreus. He himself appeared as Orestes, torn between conflicting loyalties to military father and frustrated, angry mother. In the end in real life he rejected both.

For the major part the rich and subtle poetry of the Aeschylus drama is an ideal medium for Lowell's highly trained eye. Recurrent images and verbal patterns test his feel for language, while the swiftness and drama of the action, the moral implications and psychological innuendo of the plot, add to the sweep and scope of the work. In a prefatory note to the volume, Lowell spells out his modest proposal "to trim, cut, and be direct enough to satisfy my own mind." More haphazard is his desire to satisfy as well "the simple ears of a theater audience." If Lowell underestimates the sophistication of potential playgoers, so also did Robert Browning, whose quirky Victorian version of the same trilogy fell far short of the mark. T. S. Eliot, failing to find suitable English equivalents, aborted his own translation of the identical project. In Lowell's presentation, despite drastic reductions, there remain too many long lyric exchanges between characters, especially in *The Libation Bearers*. These lengthy perorations, consisting predominantly of prayers and invocations, prove lame in translation. It can probably be argued, however, that they are necessary from a histrionic point of view insofar as they help prepare the audience for the heinous enactment of matricide, the trilogy's fulcrum and turning point.

Another dilemma, one that Lowell gives no indication of having resolved, relates to the Greek chorus. The function of the chorus has always been a cause for concern among the modern producers of the ancient Greek. If one can imagine for an instant the great actors such as Scofield or Olivier playing the lead role and at the same time having a nonverbal or quasi nonverbal, yet deeply involved chorus, you have roughly the dramatic clash between the two media—the nonverbal chorus and the verbal action on stage—much as it was in the Greek drama of the day. This necessary division, the division of chorus and characters, is one that can be activated only by applying some of the newer stage technology to the old form, the technology developed by some of the more innovative directors, a Grotowski or Brook for instance. Whether or not Lowell's adaptation lends itself to the application of parallel techniques is something that can be determined only at such time as the tragedy is produced.

These built-in weaknesses aside, Lowell's modification of the *Oresteia* is low-key and eloquent. There is little of the flash or glitter here of a Shakespeare or Marlowe, few memorable soliloquies or orations, but that is not Lowell's intention. His language is somber, for the most part, and constructed with compressed solidarity. There is a deliberate retreat from the fireworks of his earlier lapidary efforts. There is power and passion, but it is subdued and therefore all the more sinister. As in his volume *Imitations,* the versifier has tried to write alive English and to do what Aeschylus might have done had he written these dramas now and in America. In his delirium, following his devastating act of revenge, Lowell's Orestes sounds as au courant as a postfight Muhammad Ali: "I feel my heart pounding like a boxer's / weighted fist on my ribs. Always / the beat is rising, as if I led the singers / in the dance of anger through Argos to their deaths." This is a strange, anachronistic vernacular for ears more accustomed to the slow perambulation of what today passes for conventional Greek tragedy. And while this method of rendition—psychological and intuitive rather than objective and textual—may alarm the pedants, it probably lends itself more readily to the modern stage.

What is more problematic is Lowell's continuing practice of translating not from the original but from the work of another translator. At the fore he informs us, "I do not want to cry down my translation of Aeschylus, but I have written from other translations, and not from the Greek. One in particular, Richmond Lattimore's has had my admiration for years. It is so elaborately exact." That, of course, speaks well for Lattimore, less well for Lowell. It is one thing to translate for mood and not accuracy of text; it is something else again to improve the translation of Aeschylus by an intermediary. Yeats's translation of the Oedipus plays for the Abbey stage were also versions, the new creations pieced together from existing English translations rather than the Greek. But Yeats had never depended so tenaciously on a single version, whereas Lowell has made Lattimore his sole guiding light, placing his faith all in Lattimore's scholarly but unpoetic corner. What he has produced, then, is not a translation of the Aeschylus so much as a rendition of Lattimore. The result is a translation that again has little in common with its intended original.

In addition to the disappointment of the rejection of his *Oresteia* by Papp, Lowell experienced further setbacks. Leonard Bernstein, an admirer of Lowell's work, asked him to write three texts for songs to be incorporated into the composer's new choral work *Kaddish.* Finding the poet's efforts too obscure, Bernstein was forced to reject them, though they are now slated to appear in a forthcoming edition of Lowell's complete poems. To be included as well are two poems he completed in the weeks before his death for Caroline Blackwood and Elizabeth Hardwick; these are, respectively, "Summer Tides," published in *New Review,* and the as yet unpublished "Loneliness."

Other projects in the offing include a collection of Lowell's essays tentatively titled *A Moment in American Poetry,* featuring eighteen previously uncollected themes on writers such as Wallace Stevens, Frost, Williams, and Ransom; also to be included is an unpublished essay on New England writers, revised during his last summer. A precisionist of the senses, Lowell's prose is clean, tender, guiltless; at times it soars like Shelley's skylark. The same beating of wings can be heard in his correspondence; a sizable bundle of his letters is purportedly slated for publication in the near future.

Less than a year before his death, recovering from a severe breakdown from a respiratory ailment caused by congestive heart failure, Lowell addressed a letter to Caroline Blackwood in which he contemplated a tentative end, suggesting that, while death was inevitable, it might be without suffering and an anticlimax, bereft of grandeur.

In a letter to poet Seamus Heaney, posted from Ireland a few days before the end, Lowell forgot about death long enough to describe a day spent in Dublin playing with his young son: "I spent until about two with Sheridan. We had a merry amiable time, except that he (wisely) preferred people to swans and a rubber tire swing to people."

Fogbound, tired, worn haggard, it was an effort for Lowell to do much of anything at this stage in the campaign. Mrs. Ian Fleming (widow of James Bond's creator), and a friend of Caroline Blackwood, would later testify that the poet was usually so weak with fatigue he could barely bring himself to answer his correspondence. But he did manage short notes here and there, mostly to close friends, occasionally to strangers. He took pains to scrawl a few lines to the present author in response to a query about his heritage. Dated September 7, the letter arrived the day after his death. It said that the Family Lowell had waged war against the world's ills by means of charity and education. Amy Lowell's extravagances were accompanied by the belief that she was nourishing the economy; JRL realized at an early age that the Brahmin lifestyle was ending, but this knowledge did not prevent him from attempting to live like one.

A *New York Times* memoir by Stanley Kunitz, published shortly after Lowell's death, reminds us that both his parents died at sixty, his mother of a cerebral hemorrhage, his father of a heart attack. Warned by physicians that his own heart was dangerously enlarged and that he drank and smoked excessively, Lowell had said that he wished to die as insects do in mid-autumn: "Instantly." An unpublished fragment located among his papers conveyed the same sobering prospect:

> Christ,
> may I die at night
> with a semblance of my senses
> like the full moon that fails.

A second fragment, this one published, touched a similar tangent:

> I ask for a natural death,
> no teeth on the ground
> no blood about the place . . .
> it's not death I fear,
> but unspecified, unlimited pain.

The funeral, on September 16, at Boston's Church of the Advent on Brimmer Street in Beacon Hill, near Lowell's boyhood home, attracted an army of literary eminences: Saul Bellow, William Styron, Elizabeth Bishop, Richard Wilbur, William Alfred, Susan Sontag, and others. Boston Brahmin relatives, old friends, and young admirers had gathered to pay their last respects to one of the stalwarts of twentieth-century literature. Caroline Blackwood had flown over from Ireland with Sheridan and her three daughters. Elizabeth Hardwick and Harriet Lowell were also in attendance. All were distraught with grief.

The service, in the form of an Episcopalian solemn requiem mass, was a ceremony (noted a newspaper reporter) "as bound by tradition as Lowell's poetry was not. Indeed, the only variation came in the words of Robert Lowell, a reading of 'Where the Rainbow Ends,' the last poem in *Lord Weary's Castle*"; it was read from the high pulpit by Peter Taylor, in a tone befitting the occasion:

> I saw the sky descending, black and white,
> Not blue, on Boston where the winters wore
> The skulls to jack-o'-lanterns on the slates . . .

The mass was conducted by the Reverend G. Harris Collingwood, rector of the church where Lowell had been a sometime congregant in the years following his renunciation of Roman Catholicism. "Robert Lowell knew intimately and painfully those dark chaotic forces forever threatening the firmament," Mr. Collingwood preached in his homily.

Ten friends of the poet served as pallbearers, accompanying the plain wooden coffin down the aisle at the start of the ceremony and carrying it to the silent, autumnal street after the short but reverent service. Others were Blair Clark, former editor of *The Nation,* and a classmate at St. Mark's; Frank Bidart; Frank Parker; John Thompson; the poet and translator Robert Fitzgerald; and Robert Giroux. The same group, and a corps of assorted figures as familiar as Norman Mailer, Eugene McCarthy, Joseph Brodsky, Robert Silvers, Helen Vendler—125 in all —gathered several evenings later at the American Place Theater in New York to conduct an informal hour of poetic tribute and personal remembrance.

The most resounding remembrance was sounded almost twenty months after the fact by Elizabeth Hardwick in an interview in *The New York Times Book Review.* She recalled an in-joke that her husband had cracked on several occasions that reflected his weariness with her *"Partisan Review* soul." "I am going to put you," he had told her, "in a crate with a glass of water and a copy of *Partisan Review,* take the crate to the railroad station and put a big sign on it saying: 'One Way.' " In the same interview she noted: "As for Robert Lowell himself, he was the most extraordinary person I have ever known, like no one else— unplaceable, unaccountable."

Sterben ohne zu Vergehen ist Ewigkeit. Robert Lowell's body was laid to rest in the small, hideaway family burial ground at Dunbarton, New Hampshire, near the graves of his forebears—the second Lowell to be

buried among the Puritan Starks and Winslows. The cemetery covers
an acre of overgrown underbrush. An adjacent road separates a placid
country lane from a stand of New England woods: birch, pine, maple,
elm. In the distance the eye discerns a plowed field with reddish soil.
The deep tones of autumn, the first edgings of orange and yellow and
brown slowly drain the green out of the year. Pine needles from swaying red and green pines blanket the earth. A light rain mists the air,
glazing trees, slanting softly upon the crooked crosses and headstones
of Dunbarton. The rain covers the countryside, coats the barren thorns,
the rolling hills and flat meadowlands, the humped mounds of Dunbarton's scattered and desolate dead.

AFTERWORD

ROBERT LOWELL'S staying power as poet laureate is best illustrated by his inclusion in two consecutive editions of the formidable *Oxford Book of American Verse,* an anthology issued at durations of twenty-five years. The 1950 version, edited by F. O. Matthiessen, featured eight selections from Lowell's Pulitzer Prize-winning *Lord Weary's Castle.* In the subsequent, the 1976 issue, compiled by Richard Ellmann, the elder statesman of personal and confessional verse was again represented—this time by some nineteen selections drawn from a scree of assorted texts, including three of eight sequences from the original Matthiessen collocation. The significance of Lowell's appearance at age thirty-three and again at age fifty-nine, besides demonstrating his literary longevity reveals an undiminished ability to ignite the collective imagination of a new generation of readers with at least a smattering of the same material that fired up the old. There are those, for that matter, who still consider *Lord Weary's Castle* to be the culmination of the poet's finest hours, a Churchillian flood of blood, sweat, and tears.

In his introduction to the 1950 Oxford anthology, Matthiessen speculated that "Amy Lowell, had she lived long enough to know him, might have found Robert Lowell an exception to her earlier appraisal that 'I'm the only member of my family who is worth a damn.' " "Cal was convinced," maintained his friend John Berryman, "that nobody in his family was worth a damn, including himself." Born into a world of privilege and celebrity that is today, for the contemporary reader, the equivalent of Versailles, Lowell retreated from his station in high society to a contiguous station in the upper reaches of the cultural elite.

Making Lowelldom his private domain, he violated the clan's unspoken taboo against a career in the arts to create a poetry of shock and sorrow.

Most alarming for the endogamous New England tribe was the celerity with which Lowell allowed the outside world to scrutinize the inner folds of his private life. Like it or not, Robert Lowell was a Brahmin, and Brahmins were expected to take their privacy to heart as if it were a sacred trust. Lowell's artistic endeavors, his serious and dedicated existence as a poet, had the net effect of detaching him from the conventional values of his social peers. That he remained, geographically and spiritually, close to the world in which he was born while harboring ambitions it neither understood nor tolerated was the source of the central conflict in his life. Between his public persona—his life as a literary figurehead—and his private life of emotions and feelings there remained a vast open space, and it was this space that he attempted to explore in his poetry.

His terrible conflict gave him his style, his literary style, his lifestyle. Trying to absolve the pain of his life with the grace of an enduring poem, the poet produced volumes. To put it another way, he turned his troubles into poems, created art out of the confusion of his life. As a man living his life, Lowell was rarely at peace with himself; as a poet writing it, he was *never* at peace. The troubles of mundane, everyday experience became the troubles in his verse. The same force that drives a spectator to the scene of a grisly accident brought Lowell readers in droves. We enjoy watching the bloodcurdling spectacle of the kill, provided we ourselves are not on the bill of fare. Lowell, in his poetry, in his life, was our sacrificial lamb.

Of the talented Lowell triumvirate, he alone so earnestly confronted the myth of his illustrious heritage, slowly and painfully coming to terms with himself and his past. History has shown that literary reputations come and go, ebb and flow in incomprehensible biorhythmic cycles. Lowell was the last of his generation of poets to perish. At his death he was recognized by most critics as the epoch's major talent. Berryman has always been admired for his fine, though less expansive gift, while Delmore Schwartz and Randall Jarrell have settled into a lower, but respectable niche among the minor laureates. Theodore Roethke, a modern nature poet of punishing dignity, remains an enigma, not yet placed and possibly impossible to place within the realm of his contemporaries. Lowell himself remains something of a puzzle, eliciting schismatic responses from readers and critics alike.

There are those who claim that confessional poetry is a false mode and that Lowell's reputation was ill-deserved, that he was the benefactor of literary cronyism, whereby the poet was protected and sanctified by friends in high places. But there are also those who swear by Lowell's literary talents, who extol as unique his emotional immediacy and startling originality. Still others criticize these qualities, pointing to his need for self-exposure and his elitist tendencies as his outstanding flaws.

Whatever the extent of his final journey up the steep slopes of Mt. Parnassus, it is clear that the later Lowell has climbed higher than either of his family predecessors. James Russell and Amy Lowell are today both considered anthology poets, representatives of a given time and place. James Russell Lowell, carefully groomed for the role of Boston Gauleiter in the arts, was at best only a period poet, a creator who gave to poetry the finest parts of his mind and spirit but whose relevance was dated and therefore limited. A personal poet, he discovered in love, in nature, in friendship, even in death, many of the themes that underscored his most perdurable work. Amy Lowell, on the other hand, was a shooting star, a literary nova that blazed across a summer sky and faded. Novas that fade quickly without a trace sometimes reappear years later in the telescopes of literary astronomers only to vanish, never to be heard from or seen again.

For his part, Robert Lowell's struggle was toward a poetry of extremes, a poetry in which the protagonist tells us openly, without a trace of self-pity or embarrassment, not just what it means to be a twentieth-century Lowell but what it means to possess an unsettled mind and what it feels like to exist on the periphery of the accepted social order, a vagabond "walking in the light of his inner heroism." The fortitude with which he bore this vagabondage brings to mind a phrase from *Day by Day*—"the age burns in me"—that serves to remind us that he dominated his age with the same authority exhibited by Eliot and Auden during their respective reigns.

In *History* he summarized his oeuvre as "this open book . . . my open grave." He was never afraid to reveal his inner secret self; nor did he hesitate to place himself at the center of his drama. His willingness to put himself on the line was in one respect admirable, in another respect dangerous. If parts of *Lord Weary's Castle, Life Studies, For the Union Dead,* and *Near the Ocean* are immortal, parts of other volumes are as perishable as human flesh. In *Dolphin,* for example, he endeavored to reveal the contradictions inherent in his love life by portraying a threesome overcome by the need to persevere, even in the face of impossible circumstances. Elizabeth Hardwick—erratically kind, harshly demanding, pathetic in her loneliness, and ridiculous in her anger—is pitted against the sophisticated, robust, self-reliant Lady Caroline. Between the two extremes stands Lowell, a figure whose desperation matches Hardwick's, though it is disciplined by the presence of reawakened purpose, his new life in England, his marriage to Caroline Blackwood.

It would be nice to report that Lowell's last poems are the culmination of his life's labor, masterpieces of range, intensity, sensibility, that they give the saga the ending it requires, some Stevensian ideal of a poet's last poems being an affair of the whole being, the justification of it all, the moment when a whole life and whole poetic oeuvre become suddenly transparent. That sort of end game holds for some poets (Williams, Yeats, Shakespeare) but not for others. Several of Lowell's closing notes seem almost prophetic. "I will leave earth," he writes in *Day by Day*, "with my shoes tied, / as if the walk / could cut bare feet." But with few exceptions Lowell's diary vignettes tend to sound as hollow-cheeked as a tuba. The material of *The Dolphin* appears stretched far beyond its functional or useful limits. The events of his personal life during the period described skid by like the Orient Express. The reader unfamiliar with Lowell's parents, relatives, wives, and children can comprehend the volume on a superficial level only, never fully understanding what the poet is trying to say—or, not to say. In general, the last poems are slack and confused, their language flaccid, their tone self-serving. The ending trails off: with a whimper, not with a bang.

A year before his death, in a letter to Frank Bidart, Lowell summed up the experience of his past, fleshing out a final scenario: "I think in the end, there is no end, the thread frays rather than is cut, or if it is cut suddenly, it usually frays before being cut. No perfected end, but a lot of meat and drink along the way." Looking back, one must probably conclude that Robert Lowell's early greatness was his aristocracy of achievement. Of no other poet does Jean Cocteau's bon mot seem so appropriate, that the artist is a kind of prison from which the works of art escape. At its best, art does not redeem; it just is.

NOTES

WHEN and where possible the author has attempted to incorporate the source for a quotation or letter directly into the text of the manuscript. Otherwise, source material is indicated by the use of an identifying catch phrase and by the citation of page numbers. Of the countless volumes of biography and criticism available on the Lowells—as a family and individually—the following titles proved invaluable for the purposes of the present study: Ferris Greenslet, *The Lowells and Their Seven Worlds* (Boston, 1946); Edward Weeks, *The Lowells and Their Institute* (Boston, 1966); Martin Duberman, *James Russell Lowell* (Boston, 1966); Ferris Greenslet, *James Russell Lowell: His Life and Work* (Boston, 1905); Charles Eliot Norton, ed., *Letters of James Russell Lowell*, 2 vols. (New York, 1894); Horace E. Scudder, *James Russell Lowell: A Biography*, 2 vols., (Cambridge, 1901); S. Foster Damon, *Amy Lowell* (Boston, 1905); Horace Gregory, *Amy Lowell* (New York, 1958); Steven Gould Axelrod, *Robert Lowell: Life and Art* (Princeton, 1978); Philip Cooper, *The Autobiographical Myth of Robert Lowell* (Chapel Hill, 1979); *Robert Lowell's Poems: A Selection,* edited and with an introduction and notes by Jonathan Raban (London, 1974); Michael London and Robert Boyers, eds., *Robert Lowell: A Portrait of the Artist in His Time* (Saratoga Springs, 1979); Hugh B. Staples, *Robert Lowell: The First Twenty Years* (London, 1962). The sources for poems and fragments of poems in this volume are the standard published editions: *The Writings of James Russell Lowell,* 11 vols. (Boston, 1890) and *The Complete Poetical Works of Amy Lowell* (Boston, 1955). Robert Lowell's *Land of Unlikeness* was published in 1944 by The Cummington Press; *Lord Weary's Castle* (1946) and *The Mills of the Kavanaughs* (1951) were published by Harcourt, Brace & World. Robert Lowell's subsequent works appeared in the United States under the imprint of Farrar, Straus & Giroux. It should be further noted that the Lowell family archives, including the correspondence and manuscripts of the three family poets, are housed at The Houghton Library, Harvard University, Cambridge, Mass.

Page   *Preface*
ix   The familiar scrap: see Patricia Linden, "The Lowells Are Boston," *Town and Country,* April 1976.
ix   one can fairly hear: *Ibid.*
ix   The term "Aristocracy": see Cleveland Amory, *Who Killed Society?* (New York, 1960), p. 59.
ix   Its original connotation. . . . practically its equivalent.: *Ibid.,* 59–60.

Chapter 1: Heirs and Forebears

3   "A Brahmin's Self-Laughter" was not published during JRL's lifetime. It appeared for the first time in *Manuscripts,* Summer 1963.

3   "lampoon the absurdities": Martin Duberman, *James Russell Lowell* (Boston, 1966), p. 5.

4   Fleets of merchant ships: Ferris Greenslet, *The Lowells and Their Seven Worlds* (Boston, 1946), p. 6.

5   sixteen in all: *Ibid.,* 9–10.

6   "Percival Lowle, Gent": *Ibid.,* 14.

Chapter 2: Reverend John

8   family name: The precise documentation concerning the change in spelling is difficult to trace. Probably Percival Lowle began spelling his name Lowell as insurance against having to pay taxes to the mother country.

8   salt fish . . . and rum: Greenslet, *The Lowells,* p. 26.

8   ". . . commanding looking person": *Ibid.,* 27.

9   ". . . fierce orthodoxy of the Mathers": *Ibid.,* 28.

9   Sewall, Wolcott, Hancock, and Winslow: *Ibid.*

10   The New England parson: Samuel Eliot Morison, *Three Centuries of Harvard, 1636–1936* (Cambridge, 1936), p. 67.

10   "lush but fearsome jungles . . .": *Ibid.*

10   "West of Worcester . . .": Van Wyck Brooks, *The Flowering of New England* (New York, 1936), p. 33.

Chapter 3: The Old Judge

16   210 man-years: Greenslet, *The Lowells,* p. 76.

Chapter 4: Mill and Mansion

17   I have met . . .: June 14, 1782, see Cushing Papers, Library of Congress, Washington, D.C. Fragment quoted in L. Anson, "The Lowells of Massachusetts," *The Vancouver Review,* fall 1944, p. 19.

20   under one roof: John Coolidge, *Mill and Mansion* (New York: 1942), p. 12.

20   first family money: Linden, "The Lowells," p. 24.

21   unmarried young women of the farms: Coolidge, *Mill and Mansion,* p. 12.

21   ". . . debase them socially": *Ibid.,* p. 14.

23   ". . . a shining example": Benita Eisler, ed., *The Lowell Offering: Writings by New England Mill Women* (Philadelphia, 1977), p. 15.

Chapter 5: The Lowell Institute

27   indistinguishable comforts of Christianity: Duberman, *James Russell Lowell,* p. 9.

28   Let me, my son: Greenslet, *The Lowells,* p. 219.

29   "Lowell, Higginson, Amory, Cabot, and Jackson . . .": *Ibid.,* 220–221.

30   a safety clause . . . in his stead: Edward Weeks, *The Lowells and Their Institute* (Boston, 1966), p. 13.

31   *streng verboten:* Linden, "The Lowells," p. 24.

Chapter 6: War and Peace

34   great planters of the Old South: Greenslet, *The Lowells,* p. 264.

35   His corpse was defiled and heaved: Steven Gould Axelrod, "Colonel Shaw in American Poetry: 'For the Union Dead' and its Precursors," *American Quarterly,* October 1972, p. 524.

35   ". . . the disparities and inhumanities of war": *Ibid.,* 528.

page
36   "peers of our realm": Gore Vidal, ed., *Great American Families* (New York, 1977), p. 7.

36   *gaudium certaminis:* Greenslet, *The Lowells,* p. 324.

37   "Hospitable, comfortable . . .": *Ibid.,* 332.

Chapter 7: Modern Times

39   C. F. Briggs writes: *Ibid.,* 239.

40   "as racy a Yankee": Horace E. Scudder, *James Russell Lowell: A Biography* (Boston, 1901), pp. 13–14.

43   "yet very British and tweedy": Stephen Birmingham, *The Late John Marquand* (Philadelphia and New York, 1972), pp. 29–30.

46   Immigration Restriction League: Roberta Straus Feuerlicht, *Justice Crucified: The Story of Sacco and Vanzetti* (New York, 1977), p. 382.

46   "The suspicion grows . . .": *Ibid.,* 381.

46   "criminal cases. . . . an executioner": Israel Shenker, "Lowell's Papers on Sacco and Vanzetti Are Released," *The New York Times,* Feb. 1, 1978, p. A10.

47   "To tell the truth . . .": *Ibid.*

48   the circle is pulled together: Linden, "The Lowells," p. 24.

49   meetings were held sub rosa: *Ibid.*

51   "There are five . . . around the corner": Linden, "The Lowells," p. 69.

51   powerful tribal dowager: *Ibid.,* 76.

Chapter 8: Youth and Poetry

55   One could approach the Village . . . well-rested souls: Richmond Croom Beatty, *James Russell Lowell* (Vanderbilt, 1942), p. 2.

55   Traveling the rising countryside: The opening paragraph of this section, including its keynote sentence, is in fact JRL's description. See his account "Cambridge Thirty Years Ago" in the *Collected Works.*

56   "the garret": Henry W. L. Dana, "Lowell at Elmwood," Cambridge Historical Society *Publications,* I, XXIII–XXV.

56   All the students here were girls: Duberman, *James Russell Lowell,* p. 15

57   "animal spirits": *Ibid.,* 22.

58   In May 1837 . . . "specially want": Leon Howard, *Victorian Knight-Errant* (Berkeley, 1954), p. 1.

59   "damning everyone": *Ibid.,* 16

60   It was with considerable reluctance . . . "the written word": Ferris Greenslet, *James Russell Lowell: His Life and Work* (Boston, 1905), p. 28.

62   enlightened, well-read women: Hope Jillson Vernon, ed., *The Poems of Maria Lowell with Unpublished Letters and a Biography* (Providence, 1936), p. 12.

64   "a general inquest into abuses": *Ibid.,* 10–11.

66   the foremost literateurs: Duberman, *James Russell Lowell,* p. 46.

68   ". . . in general enlightenment": *Ibid.,* 49.

Chapter 9: The Humanitarian

72   "My grandmother," Lowell ventured: Scudder, *James Russell Lowell,* p. 11.

72   Family historian Ferris Greenslet: Greenslet, *James Russell Lowell,* p. 9.

74   Briggs took a rather dim view . . . contributions to the magazine.: *Ibid.,* 64–67.

74   small room, third-floor rear: Duberman, *James Russell Lowell,* p. 69.

75   "posed too great a danger": *Ibid.,* 74.

76   The articles were published anonymously: *Ibid.,* 410, *n.* 26.

76   "I must say . . .": See Charles Eliot Norton, ed., *Letters of James Russell Lowell,* 2 vols. (New York, 1894).

83   a full tableau of responses: see Duberman, *James Russell Lowell,* pp. 100–101.

page

88 "If we could know . . .": Beatty, *James Russell Lowell*, pp. 85–86.
88 "common sense and canniness . . .": Greenslet, *The Lowells and Their Seven Worlds*, p. 255.

Chapter 10: Fireside Poet

91 "accurately describes a group . . .": William Charvat, "Henry Wadsworth Longfellow and James Russell Lowell," in *Major Writers of America* (New York, 1962), I, 793.
91 The word "Fireside" . . .: *Ibid.*, 794–795.
92 "Their view of life,": *Ibid.*
92 There were additional factors . . .: *Ibid.*
93 their images and metaphors . . .: *Ibid.*
93 For the first time . . .: *Ibid.*
93 Another consideration . . .: *Ibid.*
95 . . . poetic freedom and spiritual gain.: *Ibid.*, 799.
97 . . . altogether tasteless affair.: Duberman, *James Russell Lowell*, p. 125.
98 . . . acquainted with his own family.: *Ibid.*, 127.
98 "I am tired of broken promises": see Vernon, ed., *The Poems of Maria Lowell*.
98 "I cannot bear to write it,": Oct. 6, 1853, *Letters of James Russell Lowell*, I, 203.
98 "I have the most beautiful dreams": Scudder, *James Russell Lowell*, p. 358.
100 "But still bad as I am . . .": Vernon, ed., *The Poems of Maria Lowell.*

Chapter 11: Harvard Redux

101 "I know perfectly well . . .": Duberman, *James Russell Lowell*, p. 137.
102 M.L. anima beata!: *Ibid.*, 138.
102 On many days: *Ibid.*
103 "for the injuries received . . .": *Ibid.*, 133.
105 "I confess frankly . . .": see Greenslet, *James Russell Lowell*, pp. 123–124.
106 "It is little to say . . .": *Ibid.*
107 the "human friendliness": Barrett Wendell, "Mr. Lowell as a Teacher," *Scribner's Magazine*, May 1891.
107 He had a worldly air: Charles W. Norton, "James Russell Lowell as a Professor," *The Harvard Graduates Magazine*, June 1919.
108 "a publisher has gone mad . . .": Duberman, *James Russell Lowell*, p. 163.
108 From the beginning: for information on JRL's involvement with *The Atlantic Monthly*, see Duberman, *James Russell Lowell*, pp. 163–165.
109 Lowell refused to reprint . . .: *Ibid.*, 165.
109 More serious was the charge . . .: *Ibid.*, 168.
110 Thoreau was a flag . . .: *Ibid.*, 170.
111 It became a mouthpiece: Greenslet, *James Russell Lowell*, pp. 138–139.
111 The reaction to Lowell's wedding . . .: see Duberman, *James Russell Lowell*, p. 156.
113 not what literary historians . . .: *Ibid.*, 188.
114 James Russell Lowell declared he had "never seen . . .": *Ibid.*, 190.

Chapter 12: The Blue and the Gray

118 "in never moving too far . . .": *Ibid.*, 216.
119 Birdofredum Sawin was still Birdofredum Sawin: Beatty, *James Russell Lowell*, p. 166.
120 There is possibly a slight lessening . . . true ring of artistry: Scudder, *James Russell Lowell*, II, 36.
120 "careful tracing of many . . .": *Ibid.*, II, 102–103.

page
120 to be fitted out: Duberman, *James Russell Lowell*, p. 209.
124 ". . . a return to national purpose.": Donald Stauffer, *A Short History of American Poetry* (New York, 1974), p. 187.
125 closed-in, claustrophobic feeling: *Ibid.*
125 in a poetic diction reminiscent: Examples of JRL's prose style in this section derived largely from Greenslet, *James Russell Lowell*, p. 289.
126 in his essay on Dante, he writes: *Ibid.*
126 Thus two diametrically opposed: *Ibid.*
127 helped delay the general acceptance: Charvat, *Major Writers*, I, 801.
128 ". . . each individual had his accepted place": *Ibid.*
128 "literature which celebrates the ego . . .": *Ibid.*
128 "melancholy liver-complaint . . .": H.H. Clark and N. Foerster, *James Russell Lowell, Representative Selections with Introduction, Bibliography, and Notes* (New York, 1947), p. xv.

Chapter 13: The Plenipotentiary

129 "intractable and unreliable": Duberman, *James Russell Lowell*, p. 229.
129 "were first restored . . .": *Ibid.*
130 "hallmark of advanced opinion . . .": *Ibid.*
130 "who had espoused the cause . . .": Kenneth S. Lynn, *William Dean Howells: An American Life* (New York, 1970), p. 145.
131 In tracing the history of the Jews: Material in this section derived largely from John Higham, "Anti-Semitism in the Gilded Age," *Mississippi Valley Historical Review*, March 1957, and Edmund Wilson, "Notes on Gentile Pro-Semitism: New England's 'Good Jews,'" *Commentary*, October 1956.
132 "for a return to a monolithic faith . . .": Stauffer, *A Short History of American Poetry*, p. 188.
132 "an age that lectures . . .": *Ibid.*
133 provided external evidence: see Quentin Anderson, "Legend with Buttons," *The New York Times Book Review*, March 19, 1978, pp. 12, 42.
134 "altogether pleased": Duberman, *James Russell Lowell*, p. 242.
136 tariff and currency reform: *Ibid.*, 279.
139 "He has a most childlike temperament . . .": *Ibid.*, 300.
140 "who takes his literary heritage . . .": T.S. Matthews, *Great Tom, Notes Towards the Definition of T.S. Eliot* (New York, 1974), p. 60.
141 Lowell's chief problem . . .: see Duberman, *James Russell Lowell*, p. 321.
142 "administered in such a way . . .": *Ibid.*, 322.
142 "indignation against an organization . . .": *Ibid.*, 325.
142 "willing martyrs . . .": *Ibid.*, 324.
143 "high and reasonable faith . . .": Clark and Foerster, *James Russell Lowell, Representative Selections*, p. 497.
143 Dearest Child: M. A. DeWolfe Howe, ed., *New Letters of James Russell Lowell* (New York, 1932), p. 280.

Chapter 14: The Lowell Problem

146 Lowell had once expressed disdain: Will David Howe and Norman Foerster, *Selected Literary Essays from James Russell Lowell* (Boston, 1914), p. xvi.
147 "the old Cambridge breed": V.L. Parrington, *The Romantic Revolution in America* (New York, 1927), II, 451.
147 For better or worse: *Ibid.*, 462.
150 "Oh, I suppose I'm in pain . . .": Duberman, *James Russell Lowell*, p. 369.
151 growth of the cities . . .: *Ibid.*, 358.
152 "inconspicuous for its plainness . . .": *Ibid.*, 371.

page
152   "I fancy an honest man . . .": *Ibid.*
153   He could rhyme a letter: Charvat, *Major Writers,* I, 801.
153   "He was a brilliant and spontaneous punster . . .": *Ibid.*

AUTHOR'S NOTE: Unless otherwise noted, the letters of James Russell Lowell in this section are contained in Charles Eliot Norton, ed., *Letters of James Russell Lowell,* 2 vols. (New York, 1894).

Chapter 15: The Debutante

158   committed to memory: S. Foster Damon, *Amy Lowell* (Boston, 1935), p. 86.
158   I am grateful . . .: *Ibid.*
160   He covered them . . .: *Ibid.,* 29–30.
163   "the polished brass . . .": Horace Gregory, *Amy Lowell: Portrait of the Poet in Her Time* (New York, 1958), p. 7.
163   "Mr. Longfellow carried . . .": Damon, *Amy Lowell,* pp. 42–43.
165   emphasis was on poetry . . . *The Merchant of Venice:* Damon, *Amy Lowell,* p. 87.
165   her diary: see Damon, Chap. 5, "girlhood to womanhood," pp. 84–120.
168   Wilde's comedies . . . as popular as ever: *Ibid.,* 102–103.
168   "Harvard Indifference": *Ibid.,* 103–104.
169   I did not read it, I devoured it: Damon, *Amy Lowell,* p. 98.
170   When James Russell Lowell died . . . critical judgments: see H. H. Clark and N. Foerster, *James Russell Lowell, Representative Selections with Introduction, Bibliography, and Notes* (New York, 1947), p. 467.
170   The Globe Theater . . . poem for the actress: Damon, *Amy Lowell,* p. 111.
170   I came home . . .: *Ibid.,* 112–113.

Chapter 16: "A Dome of Many-Coloured Glass"

176   When Eleonora Duse . . .: Damon, *Amy Lowell* p. 148.
179   "a curiously weighted and mixed": Gregory, *Amy Lowell,* p. 51.
182   Aside from this entry . . . had never been published: F. Cudsworth Flint, *Amy Lowell* (St. Paul, 1969), pp. 9–10.
182   the format of the book . . . lettering of the label: Damon, *Amy Lowell,* p. 186.

Chapter 17: "Imagisme," or "Amygism"

185   David Perkins: David Perkins, *A History of Modern Poetry: From the 1890s to High Modernist Mode* (Cambridge, Mass., and London, 1976), p. 233.
185   E. A. Robinson . . . Savannah, Ga.: Damon, *Amy Lowell,* pp. 174–175.
186   Some of these poets. . . . the age demanded it.: Thomas Lask, "Poetry in Retrospect," *The New York Times,* July 23, 1977, p. 17.
190   "for publicity and self-advertisement . . . poetic practice.": Bernard Bergonzi, "Little by Little," *The New Review,* Feb. 15, 1979, pp. 67–68.
190   Also Baudelaire . . . psychic division.: Irving Howe, "Witness to a Radical Turning," *New York Times Book Review,* Nov. 19, 1978, p. 54.
190   "on concentration . . . flux of existence.": *Ibid.*
190   Hilda Doolittles's early verse: Hugh Kenner, *The Pound Era* (Berkeley and Los Angeles, 1971), p. 174.
191   The hard sand breaks: Hilda Doolittle, from *Collected Poems of H. D.,* Copyright 1925, 1953 by Norman Holmes Pearson.
191   It is questionable. . . . connection with them.: Kenner, *The Pound Era,* p. 174.
191   He did not. . . . rules to three: A. Alvarez, "The Wretched Poet Who Lived in the House of Bedlam," *Saturday Review,* July 18, 1970, p. 27.
193   "were turning back . . . lay strength.": Perkins, *A History of Modern Poetry,* p. 341.

page
194   "I have cut myself . . .": Damon, *Amy Lowell*, p. 212.
197   "who sat as straight . . .": Charles Norman, *Ezra Pound* (New York, 1960), p. 151.

Chapter 18: "Sword Blades and Poppy Seed"

200   "effect of the curve": Flint, *Amy Lowell*, p. 18.
201   The average eye: Hugh Kenner, *A Homemade World: The American Modernist Writers* (New York, 1975), p. 9.
204   a metre which I have taken . . .: Amy Lowell, preface to *Sword Blades and Poppy Seed* (New York: 1914).
209   "kept house": Gregory, *Amy Lowell*, p. 73.
217   "Amy Lowell did more": see Jean Gould's approving feminist study of Amy Lowell, *Amy: The World of Amy Lowell and the Imagist Movement* (New York, 1975).
218   *Beowolf* . . . was truly free.: see Perkins, *A History of Modern Poetry*, pp. 310–314.
218   "the rendering of outward events . . .": *Ibid.*, 327.

Chapter 19: Nightly Ritual

222   I want to show you. . . . point of view?: Damon, *Amy Lowell*, pp. 328–329.
223   Strangely enough: *Ibid.*, 331.
224   Another anti-Lowell slur. . . . impassive as the Sphinx.: *Ibid.*, 312.
224   Cummings stayed on. . . . "*I* don't!": see Charles Norman, *E. E. Cummings: The Magic Maker* (New York, 1958), pp. 47–48.
227   Amy made her appearance: Damon, *Amy Lowell*, p. 265.
227   The shock was only: Louis Untermeyer, *From Another World* (New York, 1939), pp. 101–102.
228   she did like to "run things": Gregory, *Amy Lowell*, pp. 45–46.
228   rough-riding Teddy Roosevelt: *Ibid.*
229   The floor was her wastebasket: Damon, *Amy Lowell*, pp. 268–269.
230   "This mounting of . . . rid poetry of it.": Perkins, *A History of Modern Poetry*, p. 302.
233   The poem has frequently: Flint, *Amy Lowell*, p. 29.
234   *Tendencies in Modern American Poetry:* Damon, *Amy Lowell*, p. 427.

Chapter 20: Fighting the Good Fight

239   "And she whizzed . . .": Van Wyck Brooks, *New England: Indian Summer, 1865–1915* (New York, 1940), pp. 33–34.
239   Amy "seized on the outsides . . .": *Ibid.*, 538.
243   Dear Miss Lowell: *The Selected Letters of William Carlos Williams*, edited, with an introduction by John C. Thirwall (New York, 1957), p. 36.
243   "I cannot see": October 12, 1916, *Ibid.*, 37.
245   *Spectra* became the talk . . . dangerous business.: Thomas Lask, "Shades of Spectra Past," *The New York Times*, May 26, 1978, p. C-20.
250   S. Foster Damon: Damon, *Amy Lowell*, p. 506.
251   Rotarian period piece . . . a religious homily.: Guy Davenport, "Yes, 'Trees' is popular with Rotarians . . . ," *The New York Times*, Feb. 28, 1978, p. 21.
252   *Autobiography:* William Carlos Williams, *Autobiography* (New York, 1948), pp. 174–175.
254   "The plays, or eclogues . . .": Ezra Pound & Ernest Fenellosa, *The Classic Noh Theatre of Japan* (New York, 1959), p. 4.
255   "for the first time . . .": Kenner, *A Homemade World*, p. 10.
255   "take a high hand": *Ibid.*
256   "Separation on the River Kiang": Ezra Pound, *Personae* (New York, 1971), p. 137.
256   ". . . literature today, irrefutably . . .: Kenner, *A Homemade World*, p. 10.

Chapter 21: A Keats Sonata

258 They were boiled-shirt affairs: Linden, "The Lowells," p. 125.

259 "a non-existent clergyman . . .": Gore Vidal, "Of Writers and Class: In Praise of Edith Wharton," *The Atlantic Monthly,* Feb. 1978, p. 67.

266 Irving Howe has said: Howe, "Witness to a Radical Turning," p. 55.

269 she arrived, he reported: Greenslet, *The Lowells,* p. 390.

274 On April 4, 1925: see Damon, *Amy Lowell,* p. 696, and Greenslet, *The Lowells,* p. 391.

275 done in by John Keats.: Louis Untermeyer, *From Another World,* p. 99.

276 according to Jean Gould: Jean Gould, *Amy,* p. 347.

277 "Of the Lowells you're writing on . . .": Adrienne Rich to author, Feb. 7, 1977.

AUTHOR'S NOTE: All references to and excerpts from Ezra Pound's letters to Amy Lowell are from *The Letters of Ezra Pound, 1907–1941,* edited by D. D. Paige (New York, 1950). Amy Lowell's correspondence is housed at The Houghton Library, Harvard University, Cambridge, Mass.

Chapter 22: "Caligula"

283 "Somehow or other": "The Second Chance," *Time,* June 2, 1967.

283 Seamus Heaney: Seamus Heaney, "On Robert Lowell," *The New York Review of Books,* Feb. 9, 1978, p. 37.

285 "their first readers.": Denis Donoghue, "Lowell at the End," *The Hudson Review,* spring 1978, pp. 196–201.

285 they were considered by my immediate family: Philip Cooper, *The Autobiographical Myth of Robert Lowell* (Chapel Hill, 1970), pp. 15–16.

286 related at the MLA: *Ibid.,* 16.

287 he didn't like . . .: Robert Lowell to author, Oct. 18, 1975.

288 It was she who nagged: *Time,* June 2, 1967.

289 Mother had violently: Robert Lowell, "91 Revere Street," *Life Studies* (New York, 1959).

291 "She did not have the self-assurance . . ." and other quotations on pages 291–293 are from "91 Revere Street."

291 "his inability to realize . . .": M. L. Rosenthal, *The New Poets: American & British Poetry Since World War II* (New York: 1967), p. 37.

292 *The New Poetry: Ibid.*

293 That letter, dated April 28: Robert Lowell letter.

294 The school catalogue: Geoffrey Wolff, *Black Sun: The Brief Transit and Violent Eclipse of Harry Crosby* (New York, 1976), p. 23.

295 the future painter Francis Parker: Parker, who was Lowell's roommate during their senior year at St. Mark's, writes (*The Harvard Advocate,* Nov. 1979) of their common experience as counselors in the summer between their junior and senior years, at Brantwood Camp, a two-week summer program sponsored by St. Mark's for underprivileged children: "Moody, solitary, antisocial, Cal nonetheless wanted to prove that he could be a good counselor. Community life; songs; hikes; competition for the cleanest hut [Lowell's did not win]; best record for knot-tying and campfire building—to all these tasks Cal brought an unnatural fervor." Although he disliked St. Mark's and despised regimentation, Lowell wanted to prove to himself that "he could do whatever he chose to do." At the end of the camp term, Lowell told Parker that somehow it had been worth the effort, though he admitted he would never want to do it again.

295 insinuated Parker: *Time,* June 2, 1967.

297 Eberhart recalled: *Ibid.*

297 "The poems demonstrated . . .": *Ibid.*

297 In a letter to Eberhart: Steven G. Axelrod, *Robert Lowell: Life and Art* (Princeton, 1978), p. 170.

298 to Arthur Winslow: Robert Lowell letter, March 18, 1935.

page
298 He remained isolated: *Time*, June 2, 1967.
299 Lowell "chafed": *Ibid.*
299 Donald Hall: Donald Hall, *Remembering Poets: Reminiscences & Opinions* (New York, 1978), p. 84.
300 Philip Cooper: Cooper, *The Autobiographical Myth*, p. 20.
301 The Anne Dick affair: All paraphrased references to letters in this section are from Robert Lowell's correspondence.
303 "grew unbrokenly . . .": Martin Green, *Re-Appraisals: Some Commonsense Readings in American Literature* (London, 1963), pp. 17–18.
304 "close to desperation": Frederick Seidel, "An Interview With Robert Lowell," *The Paris Review*, winter–spring 1961.
304 The story, well known by now: *Ibid.*
304 "Northern, disembodied . . .": *Ibid.*
305 Tate insisted that a good poem: John Crowe Ransom, "A Look Backwards and a Note of Hope," *Harvard Advocate*, November 1961.
305 Indoors, "life was Olympian . . .": see Arthur Mizener, *The Saddest Story: A Biography of Ford Madox Ford* (New York, 1971), pp. 402, 439–441.
306 "like living with intellectual desperados . . .": *Time*, June 2, 1967.
306 In a letter to his father: Robert Lowell letter.
306 "genial social Harvard student": Seidel, "An Interview With Robert Lowell," *The Paris Review.*
307 Ransom reminisced: John Crowe Ransom, "A Look Backward and a Note of Hope," *Harvard Advocate*, Nov. 1961, pp. 22–28.
307 John Thompson: "Robert Lowell, 1917–1977," *The New York Review of Books*, Oct. 27, 1977, p. 14.
308 Taylor modeled a character named Jim Prewitt: Cooper, *The Autobiographical Myth*, p. 22.
309 "a complete abstraction . . .": Axelrod, *Robert Lowell*, p. 30.
310 "Incongruous learning . . .": *Ibid.*, 29.
310 "ignorance and irresponsibility": *Ibid.*

Chapter 23: "Fire breathing Catholic C. O."

312 the family motto: J. F. Crick, *Robert Lowell* (Edinburgh, 1974), p. 6.
313 ". . . New England's epitaph": *Time*, June 2, 1967.
313 He was increasingly convinced . . .: Robert Lowell letter.
313 he resented his mother's comments . . .: Robert Lowell letter, April 22, 1940.
314 He began his letter . . .: Robert Lowell letter, Feb. 18, 1940.
314 Lawrence's response: Lawrence Lowell letter, Feb. 21, 1940.
315 He portrayed himself in humid and muggy . . .: Berg Collection, New York Public Library.
316 "the dark night of the spirit": Jean Stafford short story, "An Influx of Poets," *The New Yorker*, Nov. 6, 1978, pp. 43–60.
316 He told friends that the act: *Ibid.*
316 "When I was twenty": Seidel, "An Interview with Robert Lowell," *The Paris Review.*
317 Tate and Ransom, poets and critics: Ian Hamilton, "A Conversation with Robert Lowell," *The Review*, summer 1971, pp. 26–27.
318 as Simpson points out: Louis Simpson, *A Revolution in Taste* (New York, 1978), p. 134.
319 writes Steven Axelrod: Axelrod, *Robert Lowell*, p. 33.
319 I am not a Catholic: Hamilton, "A Conversation with Robert Lowell," pp. 26–27.
320 He once inquired: Robert Lowell to author, Oct. 18, 1975.
321 I was going to do a biography of Jonathan Edwards: Seidel, "An Interview with Robert Lowell," *The Paris Review.*
321 power came into the arts: *Time*, June 2, 1967.
323 still leading their nomadic, carefree existence: *Ibid.*

page
324 the coming war draft had a leveling effect: Robert Lowell letter.
324 His own evaluation: Robert Lowell letter.
325 As the press saw it: *Time,* June 2, 1967.
325 Dear Mr. President: *Ibid.*
325 America's adversaries are being rolled back: "To Act on Draft Evader," *The New York Times,* Sept. 9, 1973.
327 apologized to his grandmother: Robert Lowell letter.
327 To his mother: Robert Lowell letter.
330 Frost, who wrote advertisements: John McCormick, "Falling Asleep Over Grill-parzer: An Interview with Robert Lowell," *Poetry,* LXXXXI (1953), p. 271.
330 "Christ for Sale": Robert Lowell, *Land of Unlikeness,* Cummington Press, Cummington, Mass., 1944.
332 racism and oppression: see Eliot Fremont-Smith, "Modesty, False and Otherwise," *Village Voice,* May 7, 1979, p. 99.
332 "It was filthier work . . .": A. Alvarez, "A Talk with Robert Lowell," *Encounter,* Feb. 1965, p. 40.
332 "mostly well-heeled gentlemen . . .": Hamilton, "A Conversation with Robert Lowell," pp. 26–27.
333 Jail was monotonous: *Ibid.*
333 "I left jail educated . . .": *Ibid.*
333 "He was a mild soul . . .": "Memories of West Street and Lepke," *Life Studies.*
335 *The Bell Jar:* Sylvia Plath, *The Bell Jar* (London, 1963), p. 151.
336 "hanging like an oasis . . .": "Memories of West Street and Lepke," *Life Studies.*
336 I get a funny thing: McCormick, "Falling Asleep Over Grillparzer."
339 "involved the release of . . .": Claudia C. Morrison, *Freud and the Critics* (Chapel Hill, 1968), p. 145.
340 the poet's subconscious charged the poem: *Ibid.,* 145.
340 "Mania is extremity . . .": Alvarez, "A Talk with Robert Lowell."
340 Bobby's emotional problem: Jan. 12, 1953, Merrill Moore Papers, Library of Congress, Washington, D.C.
341 the nagging, pushing, matriarchical figure: Crick, *Robert Lowell,* p. 6.
341 "the dominant women . . .": *Ibid.*
342 "things forbidden the common man . . .": "Memories of West Street and Lepke," *Life Studies.*
342 But he is a puritan, a father: Cooper, *The Autobiographical Myth,* p. 25.
342 ". . . the shepherds of the common herd.": *Ibid.*

Chapter 24: Black Mud

346 common point of departure: Axelrod, *Robert Lowell,* p. 67.
346 The second version: Stephen Stepanchev, *American Poetry Since 1945* (New York, 1967), p. 19.
347 To his parents: Robert Lowell letter.
348 "I took out several . . .": Seidel, "An Interview with Robert Lowell," *The Paris Review.*
351 "A ray of hope . . .": Lowell, "91 Revere Street," *Life Studies,* 1959.
354 "little tranquil island . . .": Robert Fass, "Lowell's Graveyard," *Salmagundi,* spring 1977, p. 70.

Chapter 25: "Between the Porch and the Altar"

357 . . . I have been reading: *The Selected Letters of William Carlos Williams,* pp. 261–262.
358 made life in Maine difficult: *Time,* June 2, 1967.
359 "It was the first summer": Jean Stafford short story, "An Influx of Poets," *The New Yorker,* Nov. 6, 1978, pp. 43–60.

NOTES

359   "At night, after supper": *Ibid.*

360   an 'a' to a 'the': *Ibid.*

361   "You don't drink well, dear . . .": *Ibid.*

363   "was, by heritage and by instinct": *Ibid.*

363   "nesting and neatening compunctions": *Ibid.*

363   "I want a playmate": *Ibid.*

363   ". . . among the perch and pickerel.": *Ibid.*

364   In brief they insisted: All paraphrased references to letters in this section are from Jean Stafford's correspondence.

366   Alfred Kazin in his . . .: see Alfred Kazin, *New York Jew* (New York, 1978), pp. 203–204.

366   struck by another quality: *Ibid.*, 204.

367   "party line" sympathizer: *Ibid.*, 203.

367   "could not take the risk.": *Ibid.*

367   "the lesser poets . . .": *Ibid.*

368   "Having me there . . .": Sally Fitzgerald, ed., *The Letters of Flannery O'Connor: The Habit of Being* (New York, 1978).

368   a blotch of trees: see Elizabeth Hardwick, *Sleepless Nights* (New York, 1979).

368   "I'm afraid my aim . . .": Richard Locke, "Conversation on a Book," *The New York Times Book Review*, April 29, 1979, p. 61.

369   We on *Partisan Review:* see William Phillips, "On *Partisan Review,*" pp. 130–143, in *TriQuarterly 43* ("The Little Magazine in America: A Modern Documentary History"), fall 1978.

369   *Partisan* saw its task: *Ibid.*

371   because someone else wanted them to . . .: Robert Lowell letter.

371   he had not written . . .: Robert Lowell letter.

372   "Our job . . .": March 13, 1958, Ezra Pound archives, Beinecke Library, Yale University.

373   Lowell informed his elders . . .: Robert Lowell letter, March 10, 1950.

373   the Kenyon College School of Letters: James Atlas, *Delmore Schwartz: The Life of an American Poet* (New York, 1977), p. 289.

374   "We passed the winter of 1950 . . .": Elizabeth Hardwick, *A View of My Own: Essays in Literature and Society* (New York, 1962), p. 204.

374   I am, and have been: Jan. 30, 1951, Daniel Cory, ed., *The Letters of George Santayana* (New York, 1955), pp. 406–407.

375   I hope you are having a profitable experience: *The Selected Letters of William Carlos Williams*, pp. 302–303.

376   "the conspicuous waste . . .": *Lord Weary's Castle.*

376   They rented an unfashionable: Hardwick, *Sleepless Nights*, pp. 97–103.

377   He felt saturated . . .: Robert Lowell to Randall Jarrell, Feb. 24, 1952, Berg Collection, New York Public Library.

377   to a Winslow cousin: Robert Lowell letter to Harriet Winslow, Dec. 30, 1952.

377   "like a guide-book . . .": Robert Lowell to Randall Jarrell, Oct. 6, 1952, Berg Collection, New York Public Library.

377   Writing to her mother-in-law . . .: Elizabeth Hardwick to Charlotte Lowell, June 23, 1952, Merrill Moore Papers, Library of Congress.

378   "a professional reader of fiction.": McCormick, "Falling Asleep Over Grillparzer," p. 271.

379   He wrote to Jarrell: Berg Collection, New York Public Library.

380   accused Lowell in a letter: Jean Stafford letter.

382   poet's use of a four-part organization: Jay Martin, *Robert Lowell* (Minneapolis, 1970), p. 21.

382   "Now that the young lion . . .": Merrill Moore Papers, Library of Congress.

383   two tiny rooms: Robert Lowell letter to Charlotte Lowell, Oct. 19, 1952.

383   He felt increasingly: Robert Lowell letter to Harriet Winslow.

page
384   . . . I don't know a better place: Jan. 21, 1953, Merrill Moore Papers, Library of Congress.

384   in an area of high humidity: n.d., *Ibid.*

Chapter 26: Back to Roots

389   "Like him," read a newsmagazine: *Time,* June 2, 1967.

389   they had bought a house: Robert Lowell correspondence, Manuscript Collection, Columbia University.

389   His parents, says Hardwick: Hardwick, *Sleepless Nights,* pp. 107–108.

390   "The tedium of its largely fraudulent posture . . .": "Boston: The Lost Ideal," *A View of My Own.*

390   Lowell found the region . . .: Robert Lowell letter to Harriet Winslow, Sept. 17, 1956.

390   *The Lowells and Their Seven Worlds:* Although Lowell discouraged Greenslet from including him in the family history, it is clear that he perused or at least glanced at it. Christopher Ricks in an observant piece on Lowell, "For Robert Lowell" (*The Harvard Advocate,* Nov. 1979), pp. 17–18, testifies to having seen the volume on the poet's bookshelves. Ricks also points out that sections of the Greenslet were adapted and transposed to fit Lowell's needs. Several of Lowell's ancestral poems, including "Colonel Charles Russell Lowell 1835–64," use Greenslet both for theme and language; "Revenants" does likewise.

391   he reflected on their faces: Robert Lowell letter, Sept, 17, 1956.

391   He wanted to do away . . .: Robert Lowell to Randall Jarrell, Berg Collection, New York Public Library.

391   "an obscure, rather Elizabethan . . .": Axelrod, *Robert Lowell,* p. 88.

392   "an arrangement of the words . . .": *Ibid.,* p. 91.

393   In his essay "William Carlos Williams": *Ibid.,* pp. 84–92.

393   On September 30, 1957: *Ibid.*

393   "At forty I've written . . .": *Ibid.*

393   "I feel more love . . .": *Ibid.*

393   On October 24, 1957: Robert Lowell to Randall Jarrell, Berg Collection, New York Public Library.

394   "Snodgrass's experience . . .": Seidel, "An Interview with Robert Lowell," *The Paris Review.*

394   "It was a bleak spot": Anne Sexton "Classroom at Boston University," *Harvard Advocate,* Nov. 1961, p. 13.

394   "It seems to me that people . . .": *Ibid.*

395   "whole elaborate iron dogma . . .": A. Alvarez, *The Savage God: A Study of Suicide* (New York, 1972), p. 23.

396   We met the mad and very nice poet: Sylvia Plath, *Letters Home,* selected and edited with commentary by Aurelia Schober Plath (New York, 1975), p. 396.

397   To Lowell she seemed "a distinguished . . .": Robert Lowell, Introduction to Sylvia Plath's *Ariel* (New York, 1961).

399   *Poetry Handbook:* Babette Deutsch, *Poetry Handbook: A Dictionary of Terms* (New York, 1969), pp. 35–36.

399   When Berryman chimes: *Ibid.*

400   "I don't see how he survived . . .": *Time,* June 2, 1967.

400   M.L. Rosenthal: Rosenthal, *The New Poets,* pp. 15, 61.

402   *A Farewell to Arms:* Ernest Hemingway, *A Farewell to Arms* (New York, 1929), p. 30.

402   . . . I had been giving readings: Robert Lowell, in the symposium "On Robert Lowell's 'Skunk Hour'," in Anthony Ostroff, ed., *The Contemporary Poet as Artist and Critic: Eight Symposia* (Boston, 1964), pp. 108–109.

403   He wrote home to: Robert Lowell letter, Apr. 10, 1957.

page

404 "I felt my old poems hid . . .": Robert Lowell in the symposium "On Robert Lowell's 'Skunk Hour,' " *The Contemporary Poet as Artist and Critic,* pp. 108–109.

405 "You want the reader to say . . .": Seidel, "An Interview with Robert Lowell," *The Paris Review.*

408 Poor sheepdog: Robert Lowell, "91 Revere Street," *Life Studies.*

409 ". . . a good world.": David Berman, "Robert Lowell and the Aristocratic Tradition," *Harvard Advocate,* Nov. 1961, p. 18.

410 ". . . and never became Bostonian.": Robert Lowell, "91 Revere Street," *Life Studies.*

410 "rigid and faltering . . .": *Ibid.*

410 Harkness went in: *Ibid.*

410 "Whenever Amy Lowell was mentioned . . .": *Ibid.*

410 Amy Lowell was never: *Ibid.*

411 "the dissipation of the old . . .": Berman, "Robert Lowell," pp. 18–19.

414 entire panoply of poses: *Ibid.*

415 "those who have sought . . .": *Ibid.*

415 "Something planned and grand . . .": Paul Engle and Joseph Langland, eds., *Poet's Choice* (New York, 1962), p. 164.

416 born out of a manic need: for further information on Lowell and Schwartz, see Atlas, *Delmore Schwartz.*

417 "never met anyone . . .": Seidel, "An Interview with Robert Lowell," *The Paris Review.*

Chapter 27: New York, New York

418 they had enjoyed their visit: Dec. 19, 1959, Robert Lowell correspondence, Manuscript Collection, Low Library, Columbia University.

418 "he was tired of Boston: Feb. 15, 1959, Berg Collection, New York Public Library.

418 "They are often descendants . . .": Hardwick, "Boston," *A View of My Own.*

419 "a flat red brick surface . . .": Robert Lowell, "91 Revere Street," *Life Studies.*

419 During the summer of 1958: see Richard J. Fein, "Looking for Robert Lowell in Boston," *The Literary Review,* spring 1978, pp. 285–303.

420 Someone told me . . .: Ginsberg letter to Lowell.

421 Opposite their house stood: see Hardwick, *Sleepless Nights,* pp. 71, 87–88, 148–149.

421 "Our move from Boston . . .": Stanley Kunitz, "A Conversation with Robert Lowell," *A Kind of Order, A Kind of Folly* (Boston, 1975), p. 154. This article appeared first in *The New York Times Book Review,* Oct. 4, 1964.

423 The YMHA jury: Ruth Limmer, ed., *What the Woman Lived: Selected Letters* of Louise Bogan (New York, 1973), p. 339.

424 He thought that these miscellanies: Robert Lowell letter, Dec. 3, 1957.

427 What Lowell was translating therefore: see D.S. Carne-Ross, "Conversation with Robert Lowell," *Delos,* I (1968), pp. 165–175.

431 "any Lowell seems to himself . . .": Alfred Kazin, "Books," *Esquire,* Jan. 1977, pp. 20–22.

434 If Lowell was aware of those elements: John Simon, "Strange Devices on the Banner," *Bookweek,* Feb. 20, 1968.

Chapter 28: Politico

436 "I lie on a bed staring . . .": Robert Lowell, "After Enjoying Six or Seven Essays on Me," *Salmagundi,* spring 1977, p. 112.

437 "In a way a poem . . .": Kunitz, "A Conversation with Robert Lowell," *The New York Times Book Review,* Oct. 4, 1964.

NOTES

472   washing his face in lye: conversation with Patricia Cristol, May 21, 1977.

472   confused himself with Christ: Stanley Kunitz, "The Sense of a Life," *The New York Times Book Review*, Oct. 16, 1977, pp. 34, 36.

472   "He read 'Lycidas' aloud . . .": *Ibid.*

473   "I have never known . . .": *Ibid.*

473   "high-keyed zest and malice": *Ibid.*

473   "Amid the complex, dull horrors . . .": Seidel, "An Interview with Robert Lowell," *The Paris Review.*

475   "each one an enactment . . .": *Robert Lowell's Poems: A Selection,* edited and with an introduction and notes by Jonathan Raban (London, 1974), p. 178.

477   "The poems in my book . . .": Preface to *Notebook 1967–68.*

480   "the untidy stuff . . .": Raban, ed., *Robert Lowell's Poems,* p. 180.

482   About 80 of the poems: introductory note to *History* (New York, 1973).

488   "the story of changing marriages . . .": Christopher Ricks, "The Poet Robert Lowell," *Listener,* June 21, 1973, pp. 830–831.

492   Robert Bly was of the opinion: Louis Simpson, *A Revolution in Taste* (New York, 1978), pp. 155–156.

493   Leverett House: In fact the time and location of Lowell's "at homes" changed from semester to semester. For several semesters in the late 1960's they were held at Quincy House. Among the better known poets who attended were Jean Valentine, Helen Chasin, Richard Tillinghast, Courtenay Graham, and Grey Gowrie.

493   by going "word by word . . .": Terry Kennedy, "Robert Lowell, 1917–1977: Auras of the Prodigal," *NewsArt,* Oct. 15, 1977, pp. 57, 60.

496   "something highly rhythmical . . .": Thomas Parkinson, "Introduction: Robert Lowell and the Uses of Modern Poetry in the Universal," *Robert Lowell* (Englewood Cliffs, 1968), p. 8.

496   Looking over my *Selected Poems:* Robert Lowell, "After Enjoying Six or Seven Essays on Me," p. 113.

497   "Man's being . . .": Jean Paul Sartre, *Essays in Existentialism* (New York, 1965), p. 26.

498   "The themes are the old . . .": Donoghue, "Lowell at the End," pp. 196–201.

499   "as slack and meretricious . . .": Donald Hall, "Robert Lowell and the Literary Industry," *The Georgia Review,* spring 1978, pp. 7–12.

500   already dead or in the process: *Ibid.*

501   "His body was still warm": Interview with Neils Foran, Roosevelt Hospital, Oct. 19, 1977.

501   Caroline Blackwood would later report: Reported to the author (September 1979) by Steven Aronson, a personal friend of the late Ralph Lowell.

502   "naturalistic, simple, not flowery.": see Thomas Lask, "Book Ends," *The New York Times Book Review,* July 23, 1978, p. 35.

503   drama critic Jan Kott: C. David Heymann, "An Interview with Jan Kott," *Drama & Theatre,* spring 1971, pp. 139–140.

506   *Kaddish:* The three poems that Lowell wrote for Bernstein's third symphony, *Kaddish,* were first published in *Ploughshares,* vol. 5, no. 2 (1979). Their appearance substantiates Bernstein's rejection of the poems and subsequent decision to write his own. The three Lowell efforts, none longer than thirty lines, while an ambitious undertaking and fluid in their psalm-like solidarity, fail to excite. They are ambiguous to the point of opaqueness. What can Lowell possibly have in mind, for example, when he writes "we know that by creating we create"?

506   unpublished essay on New England writers: The essay, "New England and Further," is long and for the most part uneven. The concluding section of the essay, subtitled "Epics," appeared in *The New York Review of Books,* Feb. 21, 1980. According to a brief introductory note supplied by Frank Bidart, Lowell intended to spend the first two months of the fall school term of 1977 polishing the essay

(he had contracted to teach again at Harvard, beginning the month of his death). He spent part of the summer working on the essay in Castine, Maine, almost without books, writing quickly to complete a draft. The "Epics" section looks at works by Homer, Milton, Dante, Vergil, and Melville.

506 a letter to Caroline Blackwood: quoted in Seamus Heaney, "On Robert Lowell," *The New York Review of Books,* Feb. 9, 1978, pp. 37–38.

506 "I spent until about . . .": *Ibid.*

507 Dated September 7: Robert Lowell to author, Sept. 7, 1977.

507 A *New York Times* memoir: Stanley Kunitz, "The Sense of a Life," pp. 34,36.

507 Christ,/ may I die at night: *Ibid.*

508 "as bound by tradition . . .": *The New York Times,* Sept. 17, 1977, p. 1.

508 Frank Bidart: On March 1, 1977, during Lowell's last semester as lecturer at Harvard, Bidart threw a birthday party for him at his home in Cambridge. Robert Fitzgerald, who was present on the occasion, recalls (*The Harvard Advocate,* Nov. 1979) an amusing discussion on dentistry that ensued between the late Elizabeth Bishop (who was also teaching that semester at Harvard) and Lowell: "They amused each other with fictitious accounts of what their common dentist said about the dental plights of each." Fitzgerald ends his tribute to Lowell on a touching note: "I wish I could look ahead to another such birthday party." It was of course to be Lowell's last.

508 in an interview: Locke, "Conversation," p. 62.

Afterword

510 F. O. Matthiessen: In 1947 Matthiessen authored *The James Family,* notable as a group biography of another of America's most distinguished intellectual families, that of the clergyman Henry James (1811–82). It is composed in large part of selections from his formal and informal writings and those of his children, the novelist Henry James (1843–1916), the philosopher William James (1842–1910), and the journal-keeper Alice James (1848–92). Now available in paperback, this is a fascinating study of a single generation of family writers and thinkers, as opposed to the Lowells who represented three separate generations.

510 a Churchillian flood: Axelrod, *Robert Lowell,* p. 14.

513 some Stevensian ideal . . .: Steven Gould Axelrod to author, Feb. 4, 1979.

513 Looking back: Lowell's most unsparing line about his own loss of powers is contained in *Near the Ocean:* "fierce, tireless mind, running downhill. . . ."

INDEX

INDEX

Amory family, 20
Amory, Rebecca, 18, 28
Amsterdam, 376–77
Amy, 209
Amy Lowell Reconsidered: The Thorn of a Rose, 211
Anderson, Margaret, 206, 215
Androgyny, 210
Annals of the Lowell Observatory, 41
Annapolis, 291
Anthony Adverse, 227
Anti-Gallican, Or the Lover of his Own Country, 18
Anti-Semitism, 130–31, 330, 363. *See also* Jews
A. O. Barnabooth, His Diary, 376
Apollinaire, Guillaume, 393
Appledore, 104
Appleton, Nathan and William, 20
Appleton, Samuel, 25
Appleton, Thomas, 167
Aquinas, Thomas, 483
Arabella, 419
Arcturus, 65
Arendt, Hannah, 329, 376, 450
  and the *New York Review of Books,* 458
  and Randall Jarrell, 308
  and Robert Lowell, 451
  and the White House Festival of the Arts, 456
Ariel, 397, 405
Aristophanes, 428, 439
Aristotle, 483
Armies of the Night, 459, 463
Armour family, 38
Arnold, Matthew, 98, 136, 139, 147
Artaud, Antonin, 398
Arthur, Chester, 143
Ashbery, John, 492
Astor family, 38, 261
Atlantic Club, 113
Atlantic Monthly, 122, 127, 181
  Amy Lowell and the, 188
  James Russell and the, 107–11, 117, 119, 141, 148–49
Atlas, James, 416–17
Atwood, Margaret, 399
Auden, W. H., 309, 356, 358, 370, 378
  and the Beat poets, 404
  and the Bollingen prize, 371
  and the Guiness Poetry Award, 421
  and the *New York Review of Books,* 458
  personal style of, 486
  and Robert Lowell, 375, 391, 393, 421
  techniques of, 405
Austen, Jane, 169, 463
Author's League of America, 222

Autobiographical Myth of Robert Lowell, The, 300
Axelrod, Steven Gould, 297, 310, 319, 433, 466
Ayscough, Florence Wheelock, 254–55, 427

Babbitt, Irving, 153
Bacon, Francis, 57, 127
Bagley, Sarah G., 23
Balfour, David, 72
Ballads for Sale, 275, 277
Balzac, Honoré de, 436
Bancroft, Mrs. George, 62
Band of Brothers and Sisters (The Band), 62–64, 68, 83
Bard College, 422
"Barfly Ought to Sing, The," 397
Barnes, Clive, 434
Barney, Nathalie, 276
Barrett, William, 422
Bartlett, John, 152
Barzun, Jacques, 429
Baudelaire, Charles, 159, 384, 393
  Allen Tate and, 304
  Imagism and, 190
  poetic innovations by, 204
  Richard Eberhart and, 296
  Robert Lowell's translation of, 427–28
Bay of Pigs, 464
Baylor University, 264
Beardsley, Aubrey, 168
Beat Poets, 405–6, 423, 449
Beaumont, Francis, 169
Beckett, Samuel, 450, 486
Beethoven, Ludwig van, 298, 482
Behan, Brendan, 398
Bel Esprit project, 244
Belle Epoque, 188
Bellevue Hospital, 370
Bellini, 315
Bell Jar, The, 335
Bellow, Saul, 453, 507
  and John Berryman, 470
  and the White House Festival of the Arts, 455–56
Belmont, August, Jr., 208, 212, 239
Belmont family, 261
Belmont Hotel, 239
Benét, Stephen Vincent, 266
Benét, William Rose, 225–26, 266
  and *A Critical Fable,* 263
  and Elinor Wylie, 267
Benfolly, 303–6
Benito Cereno, 431, 433–34
Bennet, Joseph, 406
Bennington College, 394, 429

INDEX

INDEX